PERSONALITY DISORDERS
DIAGNOSIS AND MANAGEMENT
(Revised for DSM III)
Second Edition

PERSONALITY DISORDERS
DIAGNOSIS AND MANAGEMENT
(Revised for DSM III)
Second Edition

John R. Lion, M.D.
Professor of Psychiatry
Department of Psychiatry
Institute of Psychiatry and Human Behavior
University of Maryland School of Medicine
Baltimore, Maryland

with 33 contributors

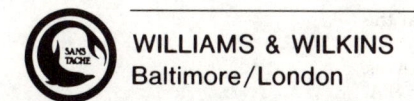

WILLIAMS & WILKINS
Baltimore/London

Copyright ©, 1981
Williams & Wilkins
428 East Preston Street
Baltimore, MD 21202, U.S.A.

All rights reserved. This book is protected by copyright. No part of this book may be reproduced in any form or by any means, including photocopying, or utilized by any information storage and retrieval system without written permission from the copyright owner.

Made in the United States of America

First Edition, 1974
Reprinted, 1975

Library of Congress Cataloging in Publication Data

Lion, John R
   Personality disorders.

Includes index.
1. Personality, Disorders of. 2. Psychotherapy. I. Title.
RC554.L55 1981   616.85'82   80-25797
ISBN 0-683-05044-3

Composed and printed at the
Waverly Press, Inc.
Mt. Royal and Guilford Aves.
Baltimore, MD 21202, U.S.A.

Preface to the Second Edition

This revision follows the 1980 American Psychiatric Association Diagnostic and Statistical Manual of Mental Disorders (DSM III). New chapters describe the Schizotypal, Narcissistic, and Avoidant entities while other writers discuss redefinition of Schizoid, Histrionic, and Dependent personalities. There is an individual chapter on the Passive-Aggressive personality and an expanded chapter on the Antisocial personality, reflecting the extensive data available for the diagnosis of this disorder. The Histrionic personality replaces the Hysterical personality; the simple switch in adjective belies new conceptualizations of the disorder. Thus, major revisions have been made in this chapter as well as in the chapter on Borderline personalities. The chapter on Compulsive and Paranoid personalities is reprinted almost unchanged, reflecting the stability of these entities.

Readers will miss the Explosive, Cyclothymic, and Inadequate and Asthenic personalities, and their fates are discussed in the introductory chapter of this edition. The World Health Organization's Ninth Edition Revision of the International Classification of Diseases (ICD-9) went to press before DSM III was complete so that there is not perfect congruence between personality disorders as found in both references. For example, an "Affective" personality still appears in ICD-9; this is the old DSM II "Cyclothymic" personality.

DSM III allows the diagnosis of an Organic Personality disorder to now be made under the Organic Mental Disorder section. A chapter on this subject is reprinted with some changes. Within the Affective Disorder section of DSM III are the entities of Dysthymic Disorder and Atypical Depression; a chapter on the subject of Depressive and Sadomasochistic personalities is also reprinted here from the first edition.

The first edition of this volume also had chapters on drug dependency and sexual deviancy. The former has been thoroughly revised under the heading of Addictive Personalities, even though there is no formal term in DSM III. The latter chapter is reprinted with minor changes.

A new chapter on the topic of personality disorders of adolescence is included. This reflects clinical interest in the developmental issues of personality formation. A chapter on the subject of aging and personality is also newly included.

Treatment of the personality disorder has always been a subject of concern to the practitioner. Chapters on the subjects of private practice, behavior therapy, and hospitalization have undergone major revisions, and a new chapter on the subject of family therapy has been added. A critical review of pharmacologic treatment has also been updated.

I have grouped together those personality disorders which offer the most difficulty from the point of differential diagnosis whereas DSM III clusters together personalities on the basis of general clinical appearance (i.e., "eccentric," "dramatic," "fearful"). This matter is discussed within the first chapter. My aim in producing this book was to present the clinician with a practical reference text.

I remain grateful to Ruth Silvano for her diligence and advice in the preparation of manuscript material. I also thank Beth Dawson, who skillfully attended to the completion of chapters and other editorial matters.

John R. Lion, M.D.

Preface to the First Edition

This book is designed to fill a void in the literature regarding personality disorders and their clinical care. As a teacher and therapist I have become aware of deficits in both psychiatric training and treatment of this very large group of patients about whom much less has been studied than neurotic and psychotic disorders. This book is written from clinicians' vantage points, and most of the chapters reflect an interest in diagnosis and treatment of patients with disturbances of character pathology. A few theoretical chapters are nonetheless included for the sake of completeness.

I have urged adherence to the 1968 American Psychiatric Association Diagnostic and Statistical Manual of Mental Disorders (DSM II) in describing the various types of personality disturbances. I have grouped together in single chapters those personality disorders which I have felt to be dynamically or descriptively similar. For example, Obsessive-Compulsive and Paranoid Personalities are discussed in one chapter, while another chapter describes the more labile and often aggressive personalities of the Antisocial, Passive-Aggressive, and Explosive types. A separate chapter discusses the withdrawn and more stable Schizoid, Asthenic, and Inadequate types of disorders. Cyclothymic and Hysterical Personalities are also grouped together as examples of more emotionally labile types.

Implicit in the definition of personality disorders is their more valid applicability to adults whose formations are complete; thus I have only briefly discussed personality disorders in children within a larger chapter on the diagnosis and treatment of personality disorders. Here, also, I have discussed personality problems of aging of personality, and some statistical considerations and therapeutic issues.

Sexual deviations and alcoholic and addictive personalities are described in separate chapters as belonging to the group of "Nonpsychotic Mental Disorders" which are classified along with the Personality Disorders in DSM II.

Added are several chapters on other types of personality disturbances which I believe to be commonplace in psychiatric practice. These chapters describe Depressive and Masochistic Personalities, Borderline Personalities (actually classified under the Schizophrenias in DSM II), and Organic

Personality Disorders. The words "personality" and "character" are interchangeably used throughout the text. Historically, character is the term used by early psychoanalytic workers while personality is more a concept used by nonclinicians who have worked on psychological, sociological, and cultural theories of human development. DSM I used the terms "trait" and "pattern" to describe the characteristics of patients; these terms have since been dropped in favor of the more global word "personality."

I hope that this book serves to draw attention to further clinical research and treatment so necessary in the case of this ubiquitous class of psychiatric disorders.

I thank Dr. Russell Monroe of the Institute of Psychiatry and Human Behavior, University of Maryland School of Medicine, for encouragement and time to assemble this book. Dr. Carlos Azcarate of this department gave his expert advice on bibliographic matters, and Dr. Morton Kramer of the Biometry Branch of NIMH kindly provided some statistical data. Mr. James Gallagher, Associate Editor-in-Chief of Williams & Wilkins, gave valuable advice in the preparation of this volume. Ms. Patricia Lovell dutifully and cheerfully typed and proofed manuscripts. My wife Jill continually encouraged me to work on the book, edited the text, and provided valuable suggestions for revisions.

John R. Lion, M.D.

Contributors

Albert, Joel, M.D.
Clinical Assistant Professor
Department of Psychiatry
Yale University School of Medicine
New Haven, Connecticut

Bach-y-Rita, George, M.D.
Clinical Assistant Professor
  of Psychiatry
University of California
School of Medicine
San Francisco, California

Blumer, Dietrich, M.D.
Chairman
Department of Psychiatry
Henry Ford Hospital
Detroit, Michigan

Carney, Francis, Ph.D.
Supervising Psychologist
State of Maryland
Patuxent Institution
Jessup, Maryland

Covi, Lino, M.D.
Associate Professor of Psychiatry
Director
Outpatient Clinical Research Unit
Phipps Clinic
Baltimore, Maryland

Gallahorn, George E., M.D.
Clinical Associate Professor
Department of Psychiatry
Institute of Psychiatry &
  Human Behavior
University of Maryland
  School of Medicine
Baltimore, Maryland

Gross, Herbert S., M.D.
Professor of Psychiatry
Associate Director
Institute of Psychiatry &
  Human Behavior
University of Maryland
  School of Medicine
Baltimore, Maryland

Harbin, Henry T., M.D.
Associate Professor of Psychiatry
University of Maryland
  School of Medicine
Director
Psychiatric Education & Training
Mental Hygiene Administration
Department of Health
  and Mental Hygiene
State of Maryland
Baltimore, Maryland

Hedlund, Douglas A., M.D.
Psychiatric Consultant
Abbott-Northwestern Hospital
Minneapolis, Minnesota

Kemp, Katharine, M.D.
Clinical Assistant Professor
  of Psychiatry
Department of Psychiatry
Institute of Psychiatry &
  Human Behavior
University of Maryland
  School of Medicine
Baltimore, Maryland

Leaff, Louis A., M.D.
Associate Professor of Psychiatry
Director, Residency Training in
  Psychiatry

The Medical College of Pennsylvania
Department of Psychiatry
Philadelphia, Pennsylvania

Liebman, Mayer, M.D.
Director of Adult Admissions
Sheppard-Enoch Pratt Hospital
Baltimore, Maryland

Lipman, Ronald S., Ph.D.
Chief of Clinical Study Section
Branch of Psychopharmacology
  Research
NIMH
Rockville, Maryland

Lion, John R., M.D.
Professor of Psychiatry
Department of Psychiatry
Institute of Psychiatry &
  Human Behavior
University of Maryland
  School of Medicine
Baltimore, Maryland

Lucas, Mary Jane, R.N.
Assistant Director
Sexual Behaviors Consultation Unit
Instructor in Psychiatry
Department of Psychiatry
Johns Hopkins University
  School of Medicine
Baltimore, Maryland

Malinow, Kenneth L., M.D.
Clinical Assistant Professor
Department of Psychiatry
Institute of Psychiatry &
  Human Behavior
University of Maryland
  School of Medicine
Baltimore, Maryland

Marohn, Richard C., M.D.
Director of Adolescent &
  Forensic Services
Illinois State Psychiatric Institute
Associate Professor of Psychiatry
University of Illinois
  School of Medicine

Attending Psychiatrist
Michael Reese Hospital
Chicago, Illinois

McDaniel, Ellen, M.D.
Associate Professor
Director
Adult Ambulatory Service
Institute of Psychiatry &
  Human Behavior
University of Maryland
  School of Medicine
Baltimore, Maryland

Meyer, Jon K., M.D.
Associate Professor of Psychiatry &
  Surgery
Director, Sexual Behavior
  Consultation Unit
Department of Psychiatry
Johns Hopkins University
  School of Medicine
Johns Hopkins Hospital
Baltimore, Maryland

Millon, Theodore, Ph.D.
Professor and Director
Graduate Clinical Training Program
Department of Psychology
University of Miami
Coral Gables, Florida

Monroe, Russell R., M.D.
Professor & Chairman
Department of Psychiatry
Institute of Psychiatry &
  Human Behavior
University of Maryland
  School of Medicine
Baltimore, Maryland

Parks, Susan L., B.A.
Research Associate
Department of Psychiatry
Institute of Psychiatry &
  Human Behavior
University of Maryland
  School of Medicine
Baltimore, Maryland

CONTRIBUTORS

Penna, Manoel, M.D.
Clinical Associate Professor
  of Psychiatry
Department of Psychiatry
Institute of Psychiatry and
  Human Behavior
University of Maryland
  School of Medicine
Baltimore, Maryland

Phillips, Jay A., M.D.
Clinical Assistant Professor
Institute of Psychiatry &
  Human Behavior
University of Maryland
  School of Medicine
Baltimore, Maryland

Rappeport, Jonas R., M.D.
Chief Medical Officer
Medical Service of the Supreme Bench
  of Baltimore
Baltimore, Maryland

Reid, William H., M.D., M.P.H.
Associate Professor of Psychiatry
Clinical Research Coordinator
Nebraska Psychiatric Institute
The University of Nebraska
  Medical Center
Omaha, Nebraska

Schmidt, Chester, Jr., M.D.
Chief, Department of Psychiatry
Baltimore City Hospitals
Baltimore, Maryland
  Associate Professor of Psychiatry
  Johns Hopkins University
    School of Medicine
  Baltimore, Maryland

Siever, Larry J., M.D.
Clinical Neuropharmacology Branch
NIMH
NIH Clinical Center
Bethesda, Maryland

Solomon, Kenneth, M.D.
Assistant Professor of Psychiatry
Institute of Psychiatry &
  Human Behavior
University of Maryland
  School of Medicine
Baltimore, Maryland

Strange, Robert, E., M.D.
Director
Northern Virginia Mental
  Health Institute
Falls Church, Virginia

Tupin, Joe P., M.D.
Professor & Chairman
Department of Psychiatry
University of California
  School of Medicine at Davis
Sacramento Medical Center
Sacramento, California

Weintraub, Walter, M.D.
Professor & Associate Chairman
Director of Graduate Training
Department of Psychiatry
Institute of Psychiatry &
  Human Behavior
University of Maryland
  School of Medicine
Baltimore, Maryland

Wurmser, Leon, M.D.
Professor of Psychiatry
Director
Alcohol and Drug Abuse Program
University of Maryland
Baltimore, Maryland

Contents

Preface to the Second Edition v
Preface to the First Edition vii
Contributors ix

1. A COMPARISON BETWEEN DSM III AND DSM II PERSONALITY DISORDERS. *John R. Lion, M.D.* 1
2. CLASSIFICATION OF PERSONALITY DISORDERS. *Manoel W. Penna, M.D.* 10
3. SCHIZOID AND SCHIZOTYPAL PERSONALITY DISORDERS. *Larry J. Siever, M.D.* 32
4. NARCISSISTIC PERSONALITY. *Jay A. Phillips, M.D.* 65
5. BORDERLINE PERSONALITY DISORDERS. *George E. Gallahorn, M.D.* 74
6. HISTRIONIC PERSONALITY. *Joe P. Tupin, M.D.* 85
7. DEPENDENT PERSONALITY. *Kenneth L. Malinow, M.D.* ... 97
8. THE AVOIDANT PERSONALITY. *Theodore Millon, Ph.D.* ... 103
9. PASSIVE-AGGRESSIVE PERSONALITY. *Kenneth L. Malinow, M.D.* 121
10. THE ANTISOCIAL PERSONALITY AND RELATED SYMPTOMS. *William H. Reid, M.D., M.P.H.* 133
11. COMPULSIVE AND PARANOID PERSONALITIES. *Walter Weintraub, M.D.* 163
12. ORGANIC PERSONALITY DISORDERS. *Dietrich Blumer, M.D.* 182
13. DEPRESSIVE AND SADOMASOCHISTIC PERSONALITIES. *Herbert S. Gross, M.D.* 204
14. ADDICTIVE PERSONALITIES. *Leon Wurmser, M.D.* 221
15. PARAPHILIAS AND PERSONALITY DISORDERS. *Chester W. Schmidt, Jr., M.D., Jon K. Meyer, M.D., and Jane Lucas, R.N.* 269

16. PERSONALITY DISORDERS AND ADOLESCENCE.
    Richard C. Marohn, M.D. 296
17. PERSONALITY DISORDERS AND THE ELDERLY.
    Kenneth Solomon, M.D. 310
18. PSYCHODYNAMIC ASPECTS OF PERSONALITY
    DISTURBANCES. *Louis A. Leaff, M.D.* 339
19. SOCIOCULTURAL DETERMINANTS OF PERSONALITY
    PATHOLOGY. *Joel S. Albert, M.D.* 361
20. THE PROBLEM OF IMPULSIVITY IN PERSONALITY
    DISTURBANCES. *Russell R. Monroe, M.D.* 371
21. PSYCHOLOGICAL TESTING OF THE SEVERE
    PERSONALITY DISORDERS. *Francis L. Carney, Ph.D.* ... 393
22. THERAPEUTIC COMMUNITY AND MILIEU THERAPY OF
    PERSONALITY DISORDERS. *Mayer C. Liebman, M.D., and
    Douglas A. Hedlund, M.D.* 408
23. HOSPITALIZATION FOR PERSONALITY DISORDERS.
    Katherine Kemp, M.D. 448
24. BEHAVIOR THERAPY OF PERSONALITY DISORDERS.
    Joseph H. Stephens, M.D., and Susan L. Parks, B.A. ... 456
25. FAMILY THERAPY WITH PERSONALITY DISORDERS.
    Henry T. Harbin, M.D. 472
26. PERSONALITY DISORDERS IN PRIVATE PRACTICE.
    Ellen McDaniel, M.D. 498
27. PSYCHOPHARMACOTHERAPY IN THE PERSONALITY
    DISORDERS OF ADOLESCENCE AND ADULTHOOD.
    Lino Covi, M.D., and Ronald S. Lipman, Ph.D. 511
28. PERSONALITY DISORDERS IN THE MILITARY SERVICE.
    Robert E. Strange, M.D. 523
29. PERSONALITY DISORDERS IN PRISONS.
    George Bach-y-Rita, M.D. 540
30. PESONALITY DISORDERS IN THE COURT.
    Jonas R. Rappeport, M.D. 551

Appendix A 579
Appendix B 588
Index 589

1

A COMPARISON BETWEEN DSM III AND DSM II PERSONALITY DISORDERS

John R. Lion, M.D.

Readers of DSM III (4) will be surprised to find the absence of four "old" personality disorders and the creation of four new terms (Table 1.1). Where did the previous personality disorders go? From where did the new terms emerge? Is there data to support the new terms or are these capricious fabrications of a committee reconceptualizing entities for a new statistical manual?

Some terms have logically disappeared because of new knowledge. For example, the cyclothymic personality was included in DSM I (2) and DSM II (3) but deleted from DSM III as a personality disorder; it is now included among the affective disorders as the formal Cyclothymic Disorder. It is interesting to note that the availability of lithium in the United States has probably shaped this diagnosis. Cyclothymic personalities were always seen as premorbid variants or precursors of manic depressive illness. However, when lithium became available in the early 1970s, it became apparent that some cyclothymic personalities could be treated with the drug. Accordingly, the cyclothymic personality was seen as someone suffering from a mood disorder and appropriately placed in that group of disease entities. It should be noted that the diagnosis of a Chronic Depressive Disorder can still be made among the affective disorders. Earlier draft versions of DSM III contained a "hypomanic" personality but that term was deleted because of lack of consensus about the validity of the term. Nevertheless, there are many clinicians who encounter patients with affective swings who do not have family histories of bipolar diseases and whose moods do not esculate to hypomania or plunge to true clinical depression. These patients may conceivably be diagnosed as narcissistic or histrionic, particularly if the mood is in response to small environmental changes reflecting issues of self-esteem. Should the clinician still privately feel that cyclothymic traits are the issue, he can use the terms of Atypical, Mixed, or Other personality. It should be noted that the International Classification of Diseases (ICD-9) uses the term "affective personality disorder," within which is subsumed the old cyclothymic personality as well as the depressive personality. Many terms from DSM II are retained in the World Health Organization's Ninth

TABLE 1.1
DSM III and DSM II Personality Disorders

DSM II	DSM III	
Paranoid	Paranoid	
Cyclothymic	──────────→	Cyclothymic Disorder
Schizoid	Schizoid	
Explosive	──────────→	Intermittent Explosive Disorder
Obsessive-Compulsive	Compulsive	
Hysterical	Histrionic	
Asthenic	( )	
Antisocial	Antisocial	
Passive-Aggressive	Passive-Aggressive	
Inadequate	( )	
	Narcissistic	
	Dependent	
	Avoidant	
	Borderline	
	Schizotypal	

Revision of ICD (15) because this classification went to press before the DSM III was completed.

The DSM II terms of inadequate personalities and asthenic personalities have been deleted. In the previous edition of this book (8), extensive discussion was given to these entities and their tentative place in the nomenclature. The inadequate personality, most prevalently seen within the military, has been viewed by many workers as belonging to the schizophrenic spectrum of disorders (7). But more important for the phenomenologic characteristics of DSM III, the inadequate personality has always been defined primarily in terms of functional impairment instead of representing a distinctive pattern of behavior. For this reason alone it was dropped from DSM III. Once again, many clinicians may prefer this term when they see individuals dysfunctional within tightly structured and bureaucratic settings such as the military. In such cases, the term Dependent Personality may perhaps be used or the adjective "inadequate" can be used with the formal term Atypical Personality. As with the cyclothymic personality, the term inadequate is retained in ICD-9 under the "asthenic personality disorders."

This latter term, asthenic personality, has also been dropped from DSM III because it was so rarely used. It was introduced into the nomenclature in the 1968 edition of DSM II and reflected the characterologic counterpart of the neurasthenic neurosis. An extensive review of this term has been made by Azcarate (1) in a previous edition of this volume. The hallmarks of the asthenic personality were easy fatigability and a diagnosis, almost always, of exclusion of other physical diseases. The differential diagnosis between the old asthenic personality and the inadequate personality was problematic; the anhedonia and despondency of the former was always difficult to distinguish from an affective disorder. It is perhaps best that the ambiguous term was dropped from DSM III.

The Dependent Personality appears again in DSM III, having been present in the 1952 edition of DSM I as a variant of Passive-Aggressive Personality. However, only the Passive-Aggressive Personality appeared in DSM II. This omission resulted from the confusion in combining the two very different traits into one disease entity.

The Schizoid Personality is retained in the DSM III. This term, introduced into the nomenclature with DSM I, continues through all versions, though it has different meanings at different times in the history of psychiatry. It was initially conceived of as a variant of schizophrenia but in DSM III, it is conceptualized more narrowly. Briefly, the Schizoid Personality is defined primarily by the absence of an individual's capacity to engage in social relationships. If there are alterations in perception or cognition or behavioral eccentricities, the term Schizotypal is used. The Schizoid Personality has always been seen as a defective person but these individuals have been capable of high performance in situations where there is social isolation. Indeed, some occupations involving little social input such as isolated military duty in outposts such as the Artic or solo performance with machines and computers may be very well carried out by schizoid individuals who do not need the nurturance and companionship of others. This positive trait is acknowledged in DSM III whereas it had not been acknowledged in DSM II.

As mentioned above, the Schizotypal Personality is a new entity which attempts to define the early schizophrenia or what was previously known as the borderline schizophrenic or latent schizophrenic. There is sufficient controversy over the nuances of these terms that the reader is best referred again to the chapter on Schizoid and Schizotypal Personalities. The main point to be made here is that the "new" term of Schizotypal is an attempt to delineate among concepts of latent schizophrenia, the Borderline Personality, and a Schizoid Personality disturbance. To the clinician in practice, it may seem that Schizotypal is a very stilted word and represents the splitting of hairs, yet there seems to be sufficient interest in schizophrenia and its clinical heritage and prognosis to make these terms important.

Schizoid and Schizotypal are related terms; a third related term is the Avoidant Personality Disorder, which is again a new entity in DSM III. The Avoidant Personality wants to engage in social relationships but is fearful, whereas the Schizoid is detached and indifferent to social relationships. It may strike the clinician that this distinction is quite arbitrary and based upon intrapsychic considerations. However, DSM III focuses principally on the observable and thus delineates between those who have no interest in being with people as opposed to those who are simply shy. The difference may be significant with respect to prognosis or work impairment. The Avoidant Personality is also a less pejorative term; calling someone "schizoid" connotes schizophrenia in the minds of the lay public, and the term "avoidant" may be a softer title which carries less social stigma. However, the terms are still very similar. ICD-9 retains the term "schizoid personality disorder."

The borderline syndrome is perhaps one of the most frequently studied entities in psychiatry. Like the Narcissistic Personality to be described below, there is much more information available on this subject than there was at the time of DSM II. In DSM III, the Borderline Personality is given formal recognition as a discrete entity with disturbances of mood, interpersonal relationships, and the existence of self-destructive acts. The core disturbance of this borderline personality is that of identity and the inclusion of the term borderline reflects the need to differentiate between it, the more stable Schizoid disorders, and the more unstable Schizotypal disorders. The diagnostic criteria are quite well defined but the clinician may still experience much difficulty in making a differential diagnosis among all of the above personality disorders. Combined diagnoses may be inevitable. The profession seems to grapple endlessly with the concept of borderline, almost as though redefinition would alter treatment and prognosis.

Because the adjective "hysterical" was often used together with Borderline Personalities, the term has been replaced in DSM III by the Histrionic Personality. This avoids the ambiguity associated with the literature on borderline hysteria which dealt with "good" and "bad" hysterics; the reader is referred to the chapter on the Histrionic Personality for clarification.

There is a new DSM III entity called the Narcissistic Personality. The term reflects extensive writings by Kernberg and Kohut on this disorder which are referred to within the chapter on this disorder. In answer to the questions raised at the beginning of this chapter, it can be said that there is more "data" about the Narcissistic Personality due to interest in the processes of narcissism itself. Those clinicians interested in this problem took an active interest in the issue and collectively conceptualized the Narcissistic Personality, begging for its inclusion in DSM III. Those practitioners who encounter the grandiosity of psychopaths and seek a place to make the diagnosis of psychopathy might conceivably use the Narcissistic Personality. However, "bad" psychopaths might best be placed in the Atypical Personality groupings. The ICD-9 lists a "personality disorder with predominantly sociopathic or asocial manifestation." Subsumed within this group are such things as amoral personality, an asocial personality, and the ubiquitous antisocial personality seen in DSM I and DSM II as well as DSM III.

Most clinicians will miss the explosive personality. That disorder has been subsumed under the new class of Disorders of Impulse Control in DSM III. There are five such disorders: Intermittent Explosive Disorder, Isolated Explosive Disorder, Pyromania, Kleptomania, and Pathologic Gambling.

The main reasons for removing the term of explosive personality was that the explosiveness itself was in contrast to the individual's normal mode of behavior and represented a paroxysmal deviation from what was usually a quiescent base line state. From the phenomenologic point of view, it was felt that explosiveness represented a impulse disorder which was similar to impulsive stealing, gambling, or firesetting. In DSM III, then, an individual suffering from explosive outbursts of aggression is now seen as suffering from a Disorder of Impulse Control. An advantage of the new conceptualization of Intermittent Explosive Disorder is the expanded essential and associated features. In DSM II where the explosive personality first appeared, it was implied that this disorder might represent central nervous system dysfunction. The term itself had a heritage in the old epileptoid notion of behavior. In DSM III, such parameters as neurologic signs and symptoms and electroencephalographic findings enables the clinician to make this diagnosis more precisely. The therapeutic implications are also more apparent. The Intermittent Explosive Disorder diagnostic criteria are included within the appendix of this book for reference. The disorder is distinguished from the Isolated Explosive Disorder in that the latter is a onetime catastrophic crisis or leading to a single violent act. For example, an individual who runs "amuck" and kills large numbers of people would be classified here whereas a person with an extremely bad temper of the old explosive personality type would be classified in the Intermittent Explosive Disorder category. It should be noted that explosive personality disorder is retained in ICD-9 where the alternative term, emotionally unstable personality, is subsumed. The emotionally unstable personality is a DSM I notation. In DSM II, it was subsumed within several categories such as the hysterical, explosive, and passive-aggressive personalities.

The clinician who uses DSM III will note that some personality disorders are described quite prosaically and almost poetically, while others, such as the Antisocial Personality, are more rigorously defined. For example, the Avoidant Personality is defined as an individual "who is hypersensitive to rejection unless given unusually strong guarantees of uncritical acceptance." This may strike the reader as applicable to almost everyone and puts the diagnostic features very "soft." In contrast, much "harder" diagnostic criteria are available for the Antisocial Personality. For example, the Antisocial Personality has as its distinguishing characteristics the fact that the patient must be at least 18 and must have the onset, before age 15 of three or more behavioral features such as "truancy which is positive if it amounted to at least five days per year for at least two years not including the last year of school." The remainder of the diagnostic criteria also contain numbers and qualifying parameters which reflect the fact that this personality disorder has been exhaustibly studied by the disciplines of psychiatry, psychology, sociology, and criminology. A large computer generated data base is available for it so as to make the diagnostic process much more precise than that for other personality disorders.

DSM III describes certain disorders in children and adolescents which correspond to personality disturbances of later life. The most obvious is the Antisocial Personality, referred to as a Conduct Disorder. This can be detected quite early. Indeed, the operational criteria of adulthood specify parameters which appear before the age of 15. Two other childhood and adolescent disorders have the same name as the adult counterparts: the Schizoid and the Avoidant. The Passive-Aggressive Personality is referred to as an Oppositional Disorder when it is seen in younger age groups while the Borderline Personality is identified as an Identity Disorder. The reader is referred to the chapter on the subject of personality formation in childhood and adolescence; it can be stated here that many clinicians will take issue with the existence of an Identity Disorder in a child or adolescence, claiming that adolescence in particular has as its developmental hallmark an identity disturbance which is an integral part of this phase of life.

In DSM III field trials, clinicians were invited to participate in a reliability study utilizing draft versions of the DSM III nomenclature. The details of this can be found in Appendix F of DSM III but the results indicate only a moderate reliability for the personality disorders, lower than that for the schizophrenias and affective disorders. No doubt much of this comes from the vagueness of the definitions as mentioned above.

Are personality disorders diagnosed with any frequency? This depends. It is generally known from epidemiological studies that the maximum rates of diagnoses are found among males and in lower socioeconomic classes (5). Thus the Antisocial Personality is a frequent diagnosis in prison. In private practice, however, the Compulsive, Borderline, and Histrionic Personality may be over-represented as diagnoses by clinicians who engage in long-term psychotherapy with these patients. Examination of diagnostic categories of patients entering a private psychiatric hospital in the Baltimore area during the year 1979 revealed these disorders to constitute approximately 11 percent of the total population (12). The percentages were higher at younger age groups and dropped as a function of age when depression was a more popular diagnosis. On a national level, approximately five percent of admissions to public mental hospitals in the United States during the year 1971 were diagnosed as having personality disorders while the same percentages applied to patient admissions to private mental hospitals (14). Older data indicates that in 1969, about 11 percent of admissions to outpatient psychiatric facilities in the United States, excluding federally funded community mental health centers and those of the Veterans Administration, fell into the classification of personality disorders (13). One study comparing the distribution of psychiatric diagnoses made in emergency rooms in a variety of American City general hospitals and one European City hospital (Helsinki,

Finland) revealed character disorders constitute approximately 7 to 17 percent of patients seen (10). Obviously, these differences in percentages reflect a host of variables such as physician training and culture. With respect to the diagnostic process itself, some facilities urge clinicians to make two diagnoses, a symptomatic and a characterologic diagnoses. For instance, psychotic disorders when treated often resolve into personality disorders. For example, paranoid psychoses when treated show the individual to be a Compulsive Personality and paranoid psychoses can, when ameliorated, show a Paranoid Personality.

In outpatient settings, assessment of personalities is often hampered by the need for rapid assessment and disposition and biases rapidly develop and attain solidification in the patient's chart. For example, a patient repeatedly entering the emergency room with a Dependent Personality and alcoholism may be repeatedly so diagnosed; clinicians are apt to forget that personality disorder is not immune from psychosis and affective disorders and hospitalization often brings out a truer picture of the patient's personality characteristics. Sometimes, patients present repeatedly in an outpatient setting because of impending decompensation (9). Characterologic defenses are by definition lifelong, but they may fail the patient during crises, and such patients may use emergency room facilities in times of stress (11). In the outpatient clinic, emergency room, and on the ward, countertransference elements play a role in shaping of diagnosis. If the patient is a rather noxious individual, the primary diagnosis made by the clinician may be that of a personality disorder and the symptomatic diagnosis may be secondary.

DSM III groups the personality disorders into three clusters. The Paranoid, Schizoid, and Schizotypal disorders are labelled as those appearing as odd or eccentric; the Histrionic, Narcissistic, Antisocial, and Borderline disorders appear emotional and dramatic; the Avoidant, Dependent, Compulsive and Passive-Aggressive individuals appear anxious or fearful. Such a classification overgeneralizes but these traits would appear to have some heuristic value from the standpoint of treatment. For example, the eccentricities of one group of personality disturbances could be correctable through exposure to a social milieu such as group therapy. The emotional lability and dramatic nature of another group of personality disorders might benefit from some psychopharmacologic dampening process, while fearfulness and anxiety of yet another group of disorders would warrant a supportive therapeutic intervention. But these issues are more complex. For example, Borderline and Schizotypal patients are often quite fragile and may require individual therapy, possibly with medication. The dampening of excessive emotionality such as that seen in the Antisocial Personality is far from an easy task. And the pulling of the anxious Compulsive or Dependent Personality from his protective characterologic shell may be more detrimental than initially realized.

Crisis intervention in the case of personality disorders who are hospitalized and pose management problems has been described by Kahana and Bibring (6). These workers have discussed, for example, tactics of managing the obsessive-compulsive individual who becomes anxious in a medical or surgical hospital setting as the result of not having any control over his environment. One treatment technique in such cases involves returning to the patient some mastery over his medical management by requiring that he approach the nursing station at definite times to receive medication. Likewise, intervention in the case of the masochistic personality involves acknowledgment of the patient's suffering, rather than an attempt to bolster his spirits. These strategies of supporting the characterological defenses of patients with personality disturbances are useful not only in a nonpsychiatric setting, but also in office psychotherapeutic practice. The aim of supportive therapy with many patients is to aid in strengthening weakened defenses which occur under stress. The therapist needs to know what kinds of stresses cause problems for patients with certain personality configurations. Thus, it should be remembered that the obsessive-compulsive person becomes anxious when his environment is not structured; the masochist when people and events are too nice; the paranoid and schizoid, when there is too much intimacy. It also requires recalling that the upholding of character defenses as described above has a therapeutic goal different fom a more psychoanalytical and long-term-oriented therapy which involves the analysis of defenses and the restructuring of personality defense formation.

REFERENCES

1. Azcarate, C. Schizoid, asthenic and inadequate personalities. In Personality Disorders, J. R. Lion (Ed.). Williams & Wilkins, Baltimore, 1974.
2. Diagnostic and Statistical Manual of Mental Disorders, First Edition. American Psychiatric Association, Washington, D. C., 1952.
3. Diagnostic and Statistical Manual of Mental Disorders, Second Edition. American Psychiatric Association, Washington, D. C., 1968.
4. Diagnostic and Statistical Manual of Mental Disorders, Third Edition. American Psychiatric Association, Washington, D. C., 1980.
5. Dohrenwend, B. P., and Dohrenwend, B. S. Social Status and Psychological Disorder: A Causal Inquiry. Wiley-Interscience, New York, 1969.
6. Kahana, R. J., and Bibring, G. L. Personality types in medical management. In Psychiatry and Medical Practice in a General Hospital, N. E. Zinberg (Ed.). International Universities Press, New York, 1964.
7. Kety, S. S., Rosenthal, D., Wender, P. H., and Schulsinger, F. The types and prevalence of mental illness in the biological and adoptive families of adopted schizophrenics. In: *The Transmission of Schizophrenia*, D. Rosenthal and S. S. Kety (Eds.). Pergamon Press, Oxford, 1968.
8. Lion, J. R. (Ed.). Personality Disorders. Williams & Wilkins, Baltimore, 1974.
9. Lion, J. R., and Leaff, L. A. On the hazards of assessing character pathology in an outpatient setting. Psychiatr. Q., 47:104, 1973.
10. Muller, J. J., Chafetz, M. E., and Blane, H. T. Acute psychiatric services in the general hospital. III. Statistical survey. Am. J. Psychiatry, 124 (Suppl.): 46, 1967.

11. Raphling, D., and Lion, J. R. Patients with repeated admissions to a psychiatric emergency service. Community Ment. Health J., 6: 313, 1970.
12. Sheppard and Enoch Pratt Hospital, 1978/1979 Annual Report, Baltimore, Md.
13. Statistical Note 48, April 1971. Survey and Reports Section, Biometry Branch, OPPE, N.I.M.H., Bethesda, Md.
14. Unpublished statistical data, Biometry Branch, OPPE, N.I.M.H., Bethesda, Md., 1973 (Dr. M. Kramer).
15. World Health Organization International Classification of Diseases, Ninth Revision.

2

CLASSIFICATION OF PERSONALITY DISORDERS

Manoel W. Penna, M.D.

No serious scientific endeavor can proceed if the investigator lacks the means to catalog the object of his observations in accordance with a systematic principle. In medicine, diagnosis is the equivalent of this process of classification.

In addition to theoretical considerations, an accurate diagnosis has important practical implications for effective patient care. The greater the precision with which it reflects etiological knowledge, the more accurate is its contribution toward establishing clear prognosis and determining precise treatment plans.

The lack of fundamental knowledge about the etiology of mental disorders requires that psychiatry look for different criteria in establishing a taxonomic system for the majority of its disturbances. Following the Kraepelinian tradition, mental disturbances are classified mostly on the basis of symptom characteristics and a rather elusive concept called the natural course of the disease. The considerable subjectivity of such a system leads to a good deal of disagreement when different psychiatrists try to assign patients to the various categories. This problem is experienced very acutely in the area of personality disorders where the differences between people are expressed in terms of traits which vary in a continuum, and where the boundaries between normal and abnormal can hardly be determined with objectivity. Existing systems are almost universally felt to be inadequate, and no definite resolution appears forthcoming. Meanwhile, a review of old and new approaches, with an analysis of the obstacles they attempt to surmount, may shed some light into the conceptual and methodological pathways which have the potential to lead to better-defined and more homogeneous groupings of personality disorders.

Isolating the Concept

The class of disturbances that we now designate as personality disorders has been recognized in the psychiatric literature for well over a century.

Pinel's description of a "manie sans délire" is a well-known example. Like many of the earlier psychiatric reports it is considered to delineate a rather heterogeneous group containing not only various types of personality disorders but also conditions more probably related to paranoid states and psychomotor epilepsy. Prichard refocused on the problem when he proposed in 1835, in England, the more circumscribed concept of "moral insanity." This publication drew considerable attention not only from psychiatrists but also from jurists, for it raised complex legal questions, notably in the area of criminal responsibility, an issue that receives detailed treatment in another section of this book. It is interesting to notice that the discovery of patients whose behavior was so severely maladapted as to suggest the disorganization of psychotic processes (11) and yet remained lucid and could use logic and reason quite competently has continued to be a source of bewilderment across time to our present day.

As a preliminary step toward classifying personality disorders, it is necessary to determine the scope and limits of our subject matter and decide on its appropriate place in the psychiatric nosological system alongside other categories of mental disorders. Two models are proposed.

Championing one, Cleckley (11) argues vehemently against a class at large of personality disorders. He considers it only a haphazard aggregate of unrelated clinical entities serving no purpose other than adding further confusion to the issue. Instead, he asks for recognition of the Psychopathic Personality as a category in its own right alongside the other major groups of psychiatric disorders. The remaining proposed subdivisions of personality disorders should be placed where, as he sees it, they rightfully belong: the Schizoid Personality under the group of the schizophrenias, the Cyclothymic Personality with the manic-depressive group, etc. (11).

The current trend follows a different approach. Reasoning that a lifelong, enduring pattern of maladaptive behavior is a common characteristic of these disorders, most authors feel that they belong together as subgroups of a major category of personality disorders. This viewpoint has received official sanction in the classification system approved by the American Psychiatric Association (2–4) and is implicit in the organization of this book.

The Diagnosis of Personality Disorder

It is a truism that the diagnostic process in psychiatry is often cumbersome and fails to reach the desired accuracy, a problem that stems from the absence of a specific pathological and etiological foundation. Psychiatrists are accused of mimicking their medical colleagues in taking their various nosological groups at face value, as if they were real and well-defined disease entities. It appears scientifically more sound for psychiatrists to regard diagnosing as an operational process, in which the purpose of the operation is an integral part in the definition of terms. For, in actual practice, when we diagnose we consider, implicitly or explicitly, which function the diagnosis is going to fulfill. A military organization uses psychiatric diagnoses to meet needs that are far different from those experienced by a researcher investigating a specific drug effect. Their concerns again are markedly different from those of a clinician trying to decide which form of treatment to institute with a given patient. Time and again they are led to design different classification systems which have a certain degree of interdependency but are still more or less tailored to their specific needs.

As we narrow down our interest to the specific case of the personality disorders we come to face another order of considerations which is rather unique in the whole field of medicine. Since many of these patients have no complaints but are brought to the attention of the clinician because of the disturbing effect that their behavior has on others in their human environment, the question about the diagnosis serving only as a disguise for a value judgment cannot be circumvented. Some flatly state that the personality diagnosis is "fundamentally social" (5). In a similar vein, Redlich and Freedman, based on the view that the neuroses, the normal, and the disordered personalities represent only quantitative variations of the same dimension, contend that these diagnostic distinctions rest not on significant psychopathological differences but on the ways that culture regulates the assignment of the sick role (34).

The problem is not a new one. In his monograph of 1923 Schneider (36) was very explicitly aware of this danger and made a painstaking effort at trying to extricate his classification from any influence that social values and attitudes may have on personality diagnosis. He reconsidered the possible ways in which normality can be conceptualized and concluded that only a definition in statistical terms was compatible with the practice of psychiatry as a medical specialty. On that basis he defined abnormal personality as a category at large, under which he isolated the group of psychopathic personalities, characterized by the fact that they either suffer or cause suffering to others because of their disordered personality. He then proceeded to describe 10 different types of psychopathic personalities: (1) the hyperthymic psychopath; (2) the depressive psychopath; (3) the insecure psychopath (with two subtypes: the sensitive and the anancastic); (4) the fanatic psychopath; (5) the self-seeking psychopath; (6) the emotionally unstable psychopath; (7) the explosive psychopath; (8) the affectless psychopath; (9) the weak-willed psychopath; (10) the asthenic psychopath. Schneider's approach appears logically sound but, as we will presently see, it does not eliminate all the difficulties.

Let us consider first the concept of abnormal personality. Jaspers' definition is a fairly typical example of such a concept as described by Schneider and others who follow a similar approach. According to him they "represent dispositions which deviate from average and appear as extreme variations of human nature" (20). As we lack a system of classification for normal people, it is immediately clear that such a definition does not preclude an arbitrary demarcation of the limits of the average and still leaves room for value judgments to crop up. Furthermore, it is not tied in with the concept of illness since it is possible to have an abnormal personality without necessarily being afflicted with a psychiatrically defined disorder. Therefore, as Schneider himself noticed (36), the description of personality types as if they were diagnostic categories is unwarranted.

There is another complication of a practical nature: because the categories encompass so much of the variance in human nature, they become too broad to maintain their clinical usefulness. Consequently, many of the systems proposed (19, 21, 36) have been largely abandoned in clinical practice.

Conceptualizing personality disorders as variations of the normal seems to make their distinction from neurotic processes very awkward and has led many authors to couch their clinical descriptions in terms of modes of reaction (31) or types of neurotic behavior (34) which put together the so far separate groups of neurotic and personality disorders. McCall (32) goes a step further, and while maintaining the group of personality disorders he argues for the neuroses to be considered "symptom-complexes" which can be found in other major categories of psychiatric disorders and even in normal persons under stress.

Morphology, Temperament, and the Typological Approaches to Classification

Even though people show wide variation in both physical and psychological attributes, the idea that persons who look alike might have similar kinds of temperaments and might also be more susceptible to certain kinds of pathological processes is an ancient one. Throughout the recorded history of medicine, innumerable attempts have been made to determine whether these relationships exist and, if so, to identify the variables which regulate them. They have led to just as many classification systems.

In general, the problem has been studied under two different methodological approaches. One tries to select and measure a set of dimensions and look for the laws which determine how they vary and interrelate. The other concerns itself with the ways a number of characteristics group together defining a type. The choice, as elegantly put by Eysenck (15), is between a dimensional versus a categorical approach. In personality studies the dimensions are commonly presented as traits which refer to tendencies to feel, experience, or act in certain ways. The typological approach has a much older history.

One of the oldest typologies stems from the work of Hippocrates. He described two constitutional types, the habitus apoplepticus, made of short and muscular individuals, and the habitus phthysicus, characterized by persons who are tall and thin. In parallel with these morphological types Hippocrates put forth his humoral theory of temperament. He postulated that the body contained four types of humors and that the qualities of an individual's temperament were determined by the differential distribution of these fluids. Thus, an excess of yellow bile was associated with a choleric temperament, black bile with a melancholic one, phlegm with the phlegmatic, and blood with the sanguine.

To the contemporary physician the Hippocratic theory appears naive. However, his descriptions of polar types, with a rather rigid pigeonholing of individuals in one or another of his mutually exclusive categories, exerted a profound influence in all subsequent attempts to describe constitutional types down to present times. They have invariably consisted of a combination of two, three, or four types such as the digestive, muscular, cerebral, and respiratory types of the French school, or Viola's microsplanchnic, normosplanchnic, and macrosplanchnic in the Italian school.

Regarding the second order of relationships mentioned above, i.e., the one between constitutional type and special vulnerabilities to disease, a most impressive contribution was made by Kretschmer (23) in 1921. Derived initially through clinical observation, his system gradually developed a variety of anthropometric measurements and grew in complexity as he struggled desperately to explain an increasingly diversified body of data under his original concepts.

Kretschmer started by describing three morphological types: the leptosomic, the pyknic, and the athletic and later on added several dysplastic types. Then, he complied a variety of personality traits and studied their distribution among his morphological types. The difficulties he ran into in carrying out this endeavor are a good illustration of the conceptual and methodological shortcomings of the typological approach. Like many others before and after him, Kretschmer found it useful to report his findings in terms of descriptions of types. However, the more he tried to systematize the measurements he obtained, the more apparent it became that the variables were spread out in a continuum, and that trying to fit dimensional variation into polar types was a truly herculean task. As a consequence, Kretschmer's description of types was soon loaded with so many qualifications that they were quickly criticized as having become meaningless. What has remained from his efforts is the association between the pyknic type, the Cyclothymic Personality, and the manic-depressive psychosis, and the relationship between the leptosomic physique, the Schizoid Personality, and the schizophrenic disorders (23).

Another well-known contribution was the one made by Sheldon et al. (38). They developed a photographic technique for anthropometric measurements which proved reliable and had the additional advantage of making possible longitudinal studies due to the ease with which they could be stored. Their typology again rested on three basic components: endomorphy (predominance of roundness of the body), mesomorphy (predominance of bone, muscle, and connective tissue), and ectomorphy (fragile body build). To avoid typological rigidity they scored their measurements in seven-point scales, thus allowing for variation along dimensional axes. With this device their types were described by a three-digit number. As an illustration, extreme endomorphy would be represented by 7-1-1, indicating extreme obesity, reduced distribution of bone and muscles, and absence of thin, fragile body structure.

They followed a similar methodology in scoring temperament traits. Once again they came up with three components: viscerotonia, somatotonia, and cerebrotonia. Among the traits defining the first component (viscerotonia) are relaxation in posture and movement, love of physical comfort, pleasure in eating, sociophilia, and extroversion of affect. Somatotonia is defined by traits such as assertiveness of posture and movement, love of physical adventure, physical energy, lust for power, competitive aggressiveness, agoraphilia, and indifference to pain. Cerebrotonia is defined by traits like tightness of posture and movements, physiological overresponse, love of privacy, mental oversensitivity, apprehensiveness, emotional restraint, sociophobia, and hypersensitivity to pain (37).

The system appeared promising and initially aroused a good deal of enthusiasm. Nevertheless, it has had little influence in clinical practice. This may be explained by a problem which has plagued all attempts at personality classification, namely, that they turn out a disparagingly impoverished picture of human nature which in actuality is enormously rich and complex in variation.

Research Models

The general dissatisfaction with existing systems of classification has led a number of investigators, mostly psychologists (a fact probably explained by the psychiatrist's lack of research training and ignorance of the mathematical foundation necessary for complex statistical analysis), to address themselves to the task of designing a model adequate for research purposes, or useful for clinical work, or both. The variety of approaches they use is too large to allow a comprehensive review of even the most important contributions. We will limit ourselves to a brief overview of only a few which appear more relevant to clinical practice, unavoidably influenced by our own biases.

Cattell is undeniably the best known among the group of investigators who have been approaching the study of personality through trait analysis. He uses measurements which reflect the variations of personality traits along a dimensional axis.

As a researcher he takes the stand that any body of theory does not merit to be called scientific unless it presents testable hypotheses which can be expressed in mathematical language. This stance deviates markedly from the approach of the clinician who is dealing with complex human problems unraveling in a varied physical and human environment. He is concerned with practical matters and has a tendency to perceive the more rigorous language of the scientist as an oversimplification. Explicitly aware of this dichotomy, Cattell has made a remarkable attempt at bridging the gap and bringing the two together (8).

He starts out by identifying surface traits, which are variables that group together in a correlation cluster.

From an original list of 181 variables he obtained 42 traits of which we give a few examples (6):

1. Adaptable: flexible; accepts changes of plan easily; satisfied with compromises; is not upset, surprised, baffled, or irritated if things are different from what he expected. vs Rigid: insists that things be done the way he had always done them; does not adapt his habits and ways of thinking to those of the group; nonplussed if his routine is upset.

2. Emotional: excitable; cries a lot (children), laughs a lot, shows affection, anger, all emotions, to excess. vs Calm: stable; shows few signs of emotional excitement of any kind; remains calm, even underreacts, in dispute, danger, social hilarity, etc.

3. Conscientious: honest; knows what is right and generally does it, even if no one is watching him; does not tell lies or attempt to deceive others; respects others' property. vs Unconscientious: somewhat unscrupulous; not too careful about standards of right and wrong where personal desires are concerned; tells lies and is given to little deceits; does not respect other's property.

4. Conventional: conforms to accepted standards, ways of acting, thinking, dressing, etc.; does the "proper" thing; seems distressed if he finds he is being different. vs Unconventional, Eccentric: acts differently from others; not concerned about wearing the same clothes or doing the same things as others; has somewhat eccentric interests, attitudes, and ways of behaving; goes his own rather peculiar way.

5. Prone to Jealousy: begrudges the achievement of others; upset when others get attention, and demands more for himself; resentful when attention is given to others. vs Not Jealous: likes people even if they do better than he does; is not upset when others get attention, but joins in praise.

6. Considerate, Polite: deferential to needs of others; considers others' feelings; allows them before him in vs Inconsiderate, Rude: insolent, defiant, and "saucy" to elders (in children); ignores feelings of others;

	line, gives them the biggest share, etc.	gives impression that he goes out of his way to be rude.
7.	Quitting: gives up before he has thoroughly finished a job; slipshod; works in fits and starts; easily distracted, led away from main purposes by stray impulses or external difficulties. vs	Determined, Persevering: sees a job through in spite of difficulties or temptations; strong-willed; painstaking and thorough; sticks at anything until he achieves his goal.
8.	Tender: governed by sentiment, intuitive, empathetic, sympathetic, sensitive to the feelings of others; cannot do things if they offend his feelings. vs	Tough, Hard: governed by fact and necessity rather than sentiment, unsympathetic; does not mind upsetting others if that is what has to be done.
9.	Self-effacing: blames himself (or nobody) if things go wrong; reluctant to take credit for achievements; does not seem to think of himself as very important or worthwhile. vs	Egotistical: blames others whenever there is conflict or things go wrong; often brags; quick to take credit when things go right; has a very good opinion of himself.
10.	Languid, Fatigued, Slow: lacks vigor; vague and slow in speech; dawdles, is slow in getting things done. vs	Energetic, Alert, Active: quick, forceful, active, decisive, full of pep, vigorous, spirited.

He then uses factor analysis to determine the source of change variance in these variables. His analysis yielded 16 factors which he designated source traits (6, 7) (Table 2.1).

While in clinical practice the data are obtained in an interview situation, Cattell derived his factors from observations made under three different conditions: in natural life situations, in a questionnaire type of test, and in an objective test situation, which he called L, Q, and T data, respectively (6). Therefore, it is not surprising to find that his factors differ in number and may differ in meaning from variables obtained through clinical observations. It also accounts for the fact that some of them are simply represented by notations similar to the alphabetic system first used to characterize the vitamins (6). This can indeed appear esoteric enough to keep most clinicians away no matter how carefully Cattell defines his terms.

So far Cattell's model has the limitations of a cross-sectional scheme when compared with the historical and psychodynamic data obtained by the clinician. The latter give him a longitudinal perspective while arriving at a diagnosis. Being comprehensive, Cattell set out to design an equivalent complement to his trait model by proposing three additional models: state, process, and type.

He conceptualized a psychological state as being "recognizable by a set of variables which alter together, rising and falling over time, independently of other states" (9). It is derived from the differences between two sets of measurements separated by a time interval during which the subjects were affected by disturbing stimuli (8).

TABLE 2.1*
Brief Descriptions of Some Primary Source Traits Found by Factor Analysis†

Low Score Description	Technical Labels Low Pole	Technical Labels High Pole	Standard Symbol	High Score Description
Reserved, detached, critical, cool	Sizothymia	Affectothymia	A	Outgoing, warm-hearted, easygoing, participating
Less intelligent, concrete thinking	Low general mental capacity	Intelligence	B	More intelligent, abstract thinking, bright
Affected by feelings, emotionally less stable, easily upset	Lower ego strength	Higher ego strength	C	Emotionally stable, faces reality, calm
Phlegmatic, relaxed	Low excitability	High excitability	D	Excitable, strident, attention-seeking
Humble, mild, obedient, conforming	Submissiveness	Dominance	E	Assertive, independent, aggressive, stubborn
Sober, prudent, serious, taciturn	Desurgency	Surgency	F	"Happy-go-lucky," heedless, gay, enthusiastic
Expedient, a law to himself, bypasses obligations	Low superstrength	Superego strength	G	Conscientious, persevering, staid, rulebound
Shy, restrained, diffident, timid	Threctia	Parmia	H	Venturesome, socially bold, uninhibited, spontaneous
Tough-minded, self-reliant, realistic, "no nonsense"	Harria	Premsia	I	Tender-minded, dependent, overprotected, sensitive
Trusting, adaptable, free of jealousy, easy to get on with	Alaxia	Protension	L	Suspicious, self-opinionated, hard to fool
Practical, careful, conventional, regulated by external realities, proper	Praxernia	Autia	M	Imaginative, preoccupied with inner urgencies, careless of practical matters, Bohemian
Forthright, natural, artless, sentimental	Artlessness	Shrewdness	N	Shrewd, calculating, worldly, penetrating
Placid, self-assured, confident, serene	Untroubled adequacy	Guilt proneness	O	Apprehensive, worrried, depressive, troubled
Conservative, respecting established ideas, tolerant of traditional difficulties	Conservatism	Radicalism	Q_1	Experimental, critical, liberal, analytical, free thinking
Group-dependent, a "joiner" and sound follower	Group adherence	Self-sufficiency	Q_2	Self-sufficient, prefers to make decisions, resourceful
Casual, careless of protocol, untidy, follows own urges	Weak self-sentiment	Strong self-sentiment	Q_3	Controlled, socially precise, self-disciplined, compulsive
Relaxed, tranquil, torpid, unfrustrated	Low ergic tension	High ergic tension	Q_4	Tense, driven, overwrought, fretful

* Reprinted from Cattell (7, p. 392).
† In ratings and questionnaires, and now embodied in the Sixteen Personality Factor Test.

Several state dimensions have been described such as high anxiety vs. low anxiety, stress vs. repose, depression vs. elation, torpor vs. excitation, regression vs. mobilization, etc. Cattell emphasizes in particular the finding that the state of anxiety is distinct from a state of stress (9). If successive measurements of both source traits and psychological states show a characteristic pattern of sequences, then a process is identified. A type, theorizes Cattell, is a "modal collection of people in multidimensional space," in analogy with the biological concept of species (8). The latter two models require complex mathematical treatment to be worked out. They are also newer and have not had the thorough investigation that the source traits and the psychological states have had.

It is of interest to clinicians that many of the findings reported by Cattell are in agreement with clinical observations. In some instances they also mirror the dilemma faced by the psychiatrist conducting the everyday business of treating patients supported by conflicting theories of human behavior. For example, the finding of similar factors in groups of both normal and abnormal populations—even though abnormal individuals can be easily identified through the differential variation of certain traits—lends support to the view that the difference between normal and abnormal is a quantitative one (8). In contrast, those who maintain that the psychoses are qualitatively different will find solace in the finding that psychotic groups revealed a set of almost purely pathological factors (10)—Cattell's "pathology supplement scales"—previously undetected in normal populations.

Another outspoken critic of the inadequacies in existing psychodiagnostic systems is Eysenck. He deplores their lack of an etiological foundation, their low interrater reliability, and their low relevance for treatment choices. Like Cattell, he is dissatisfied with hypotheses stated in ways not conducive to empirical research. Vague hypotheses, he emphasizes, lead to equally vague testing techniques (projective tests) and treatment methods (psychotherapy) (12, 15). So far his studies have borne out the absence of qualitative differences between normal, neurotic, and psychotic. He sees them, tentatively, as occupying different quantitative dimensions. On these grounds he argues for the abandonment of categorical descriptions of behavior disorders in favor of a dimensional approach (12). Basic to Eysenck's theory is the relationship between certain personality variables and conditionability. He described a general factor of neuroticism—stability, and another dimension of extroversion—introversion, "which finds its prototype in the neurotic population in the hysteric-psychopathic (extroverted) and the anxious-obsessional (introverted) type of personality" (12).

Eysenck finds that under specified circumstances extroverts are more difficult to condition than introverts. He also contends that introverts are more susceptible to neurotic disorders while extroverts are more liable to suffer from personality disorders (13). Given these postulates, it is easy to follow Eysenck's theorizing. Neuroses are constituted by conditioned autonomic responses to normally neutral stimuli and the motor movements are made in response to them, whereas psychopathic disorders are determined by the lack of the conditioned responses which lead to the development of the values and attitudes commonly recognized as "conscience" (15).

To do Eysenck justice it needs to be emphasized that this brief description fails to reflect the comprehensiveness of his theoretical model. In fact, he ties the variables discussed with the neurophysiological mechanisms underlying conditioning, taking into consideration the functional interrelations between the ascending reticular activating system, the visceral brain, and the cerebral cortex (15).

A very important aspect of Eysenck's model is its immediate relevance for behavior therapy, to which, in fact, it appears to have been limited so far. It becomes important to determine, prior to treatment, the individual patient's position in the above-mentioned personality dimensions related to conditioning and the ease or difficulty with which he forms conditioned responses in more than one field.

Maurice Lorr brings us back to a typological approach to psychodiagnostics. He justifies his choice with three major reasons: (1) a typological description conveys more information about the characteristics of the type than would be available in the measurement of a single attribute; (2) the total configuration of the type, being more than the sum of its profile of scores, increases our ability to make predictions to outside criteria; (3) as subtypes are detected, new hypotheses can be developed and tested, leading to new theoretical developments (28).

Lorr's approach begins with what is essentially clinical observation and maintains a close relationship with clinical reality. It is true that he carried out his research with acute psychotic patients but it is easy to see how his methodology can be applied to personality classification. His raw data were obtained in a 30- to 60-minute interview conducted by a skilled observer. The results consist of rates of observable behaviors and patients' self-reports, previously determined to be indicators of a behavior disturbance. These measurements are grouped, through factor analysis, into clusters which represent relatively unitary dimensions of behavior. Ten such factors—Lorr calls them syndromes, which he defines as a group "or complex of symptoms that tend with high frequency to go together" (27)—are thus identified and constitute Lorr's Inpatient Multidimensional Psychiatric Scale (27, 29):

1. Excitement: excessive and accelerated speech. Elevated mood and self-esteem. Emotional expression tends to be histrionic.
2. Hostile belligerence: patient shows disdain for others. He is likely to manifest much hostility, resentment, and a complaining bitterness.
3. Paranoid projection: fixed beliefs that attribute a hostile, persecuting, and controlling intent to others around him.
4. Grandiose expansiveness: attitude of superiority toward others. Fixed beliefs that he possesses unusual powers. Reports divine missions and may identify himself with well-known or historical personalities.
5. Perceptual distortions: hallucinations that threaten, accuse, or demand.
6. Anxious intropunitiveness: vague apprehension as well as specific anxieties. Disparaging attitudes toward himself. Prone to guilt for real and imaginary faults. Mood is typically dysphoric.

7. Retardation and apathy: speech, ideation, and motor activity are delayed, slowed, or blocked. Apathy and disinterest in future.
8. Disorientation: disorientation to time, place, and season.
9. Motor disturbances: assumes bizarre postures and makes repetitive facial and body movements.
10. Perceptual disorganization: thought disturbances are manifested in irrelevant, incoherent, and rambling speech. Stereotyped phrases and neologisms.

Within this framework he then proceeds to explore the full range of behaviors recorded in order to determine whether he can group his subjects into homogeneous subtypes. With this procedure he identifies several acute psychotic types which are named excited-hostile, hostile paranoid, hallucinated paranoid, grandiose paranoid, anxious-depressed, retarded motor disturbed, disoriented, anxious-disorganized, excited-disorganized, and retarded-disorganized (27). Comparing these types with the standard categories of the American Psychiatric Association's nosological system, Lorr verifies that they are largely in harmony. For example, 64% of the male patients typed as hostile paranoid, 78% of the hallucinated paranoid, and 71% of the grandiose paranoid had received the clinical diagnosis of paranoid. This contrasts with the base rate of 41% diagnosed as paranoid in the entire male sample. This indicates, in general, research support to the clinically derived subdivisions. On the other hand, 67% of the patients typed as excited-hostile were also diagnosed as paranoid. This led Lorr to suggest that the diagnosis of paranoid schizophrenia in actuality includes several identifiable subgroups which can be isolated and defined with more rigor with his approach (27).

In a radical departure from the more or less conventional approaches described so far, Timothy Leary proposes a model which introduces new dimensions to the problem of classifying personality and, for that reason, deserves consideration here. He contends (26) that the philosophical orientation of the investigator or clinician is not unrelated to his work, as has been often stated. It is rather a foundation that strongly determines the choice of theoretical constructs and measurement devices. Therefore, it is necessary first to establish the basic premises.

Leary sees the life of an individual as a continuous, ever-changing flow of unique situations that cannot be studied except by a truly existential psychology which demands conceptual and methodological flexibility that will arise from, and will constantly adjust to, the ever-changing character of its subject.

Another important consideration is that both research and therapy are an encounter of individuals sharing time and space. On this account psychology also needs to be transactional, and that requires an open and intense collaboration between the partners involved.

Two conventional elements of investigation, the test and the experiment, are alien to an existential approach inasmuch as it is necessary to study the individual as he experiences and acts in naturally occurring situations. Records, concepts, and methods will grow out of the unique nature of the particular situation instead of being superimposed on them.

In order to make the transactional approach actually operative, the therapist-investigator and the patient-subject need to work together as true partners. They need to have an equal voice in choosing the problem to be studied, in determining the variables to be considered, and in designing and constructing the recording and measuring devices. Secrecy is a hazard to be avoided because only absolute frankness may ensure the full cooperation of the patient.

A keystone in Leary's model is the need to keep separate, and deal differently with, internal and external events (25, 26). He proposes that psychology has failed to realize clearly that any given moment of a man's life is actually a composite of an inner life of consciousness and an external life of behavior, perennially influencing each other. As a result, many descriptions of interpersonal events are contaminated with motivational assumptions. In order to avoid this pitfall we need to be constantly aware of which realm we are dealing with. First, there is the internal, subjective, and experiential, where we define the real, the true, the right and the wrong, and where logic is shaped by associational processes. Next comes the external behavioral, which can be observed, where we can determine and agree on subject matter, facts, or the concept of right and wrong and where logic is regulated by the relationship of external symbols. Dealing with these two different realms requires different concepts, different models, and different measures (26).

Having separated these two levels, Leary proceeds to map out the methodological foundation necessary to describe and measure the behavioral level. He proposes that the natural field where behavior occurs can be better recorded and measured in terms of two simple dimensions: space (the locale where the behavior takes place) and time (the length of time and frequency a person occupies a given space). In his view the interpersonal aspect of behavior is really a simple issue: the sharing of space and time by two or more people, be it the home, the office, the hospital, the prison, or any other location. The sequences evolved reflect what he calls intimacy (26). He warns us that to try to "measure" behavior directly, via observation, labeling, or naming, leads us back to the old confusion of internal/external (25).

Concurrently, we need to record the movements made by the actors in their space-time. Their measurement is a complex problem and Leary reminds us that we do not actually measure movements per se but only the records that we produce (25). Any number of them can be defined, recorded, and counted. Statistical indices can be developed which Leary visualizes leading to a system of notations that describe behavior more accurately than is possible with verbal language (26).

A nagging problem remains: how to sort out which behaviors are to be recorded. This can only be answered, emphasizes Leary, if we know at which experiential level the person is. Here is where our knowledge falters the most. At our present level of information, Leary postulates the existence of seven levels of consciousness. He firmly believes that if the psychiatrist ignores and does not recognize them the diagnostic process may become irrelevant.

In the diagnosis of consciousness we need better concepts, better language, and better instruments. Here is where Leary's model meets its greatest difficulties. Probably it is also where it will find the most controversy.

The Clinical Approach and the Standard Diagnostic System

In an attempt to impose order in a field which had become rather chaotically split by a variety of competing systems of classification, the American Psychiatric Association proposed its own system. Published in 1952 as the Diagnostic and Statistical Manual of Mental Disorders (2), it became the standard classification model for the United States. It aroused a good deal of criticism, and two of the major points have been summarized by McCall (32). One was the decision to group together, under one single large category, disorders of psychogenic origin or without clearly defined physical cause or structural change in the brain—conditions as disparate as the affective and schizophrenic disorders, the psychoneuroses, the personality disorders, and the transient situational personality disorders. That is a logical tour de force, comprehensive but hardly exact.

The second criticism was the failure to maintain clinical descriptions separate from underlying assumptions about the nature and etiology of different conditions. This was specially relevant in the many instances where psychoanalytic assumptions became criteria for classification.

Some objections can also be raised regarding the way the Manual treated personality disorders. Certain groups—personality pattern disturbance, personality trait disturbance, and sociopathic personality disturbance—were differentiated exclusively on the basis of psychoanalytic speculation about the course and vicissitudes of personality development. Thus, personality pattern disturbances are defined as "more or less cardinal personality types" whose deep-seated psychopathology leaves them little room for regression, except into a psychosis, whereas personality trait disturbances refer to individuals who show an inability "to maintain their emotional equilibrium under minor or major stress," a handicap which they acquired through fixation or regression. Furthermore, a therapeutic consideration of its sort, that individuals with a personality pattern disturbance "can rarely, if ever, be altered in their inherent structures by any form of therapy," is included in the description of the group.

In 1968 the American Psychiatric Association published a revised edition of the Diagnostic and Statistical Manual of Mental Disorders (3). It was a major attempt at bringing the American system into line with the World Health Organization's International Classification of Disease. At the same time, it tried to correct the mistakes of its first edition. Now it seems that most criticism has been directed toward the areas of the neuroses (32). It is important to consider, however, as Lorr has already pointed out (29), that different methodological criteria underlie the separation of the major groups of disorders. Thus, the psychoses are described as types or classes, the psychophysiological disorders as symptom complexes, the psychoneuroses as trait syndromes, the personality disorders again as types, and the organic brain syndromes in terms of the conventional medical model of disease.

Notwithstanding the fact that the problem of classifying personality is an important one for psychiatry and still remains far from being settled, a review of the psychiatric literature of the last years shows a surprising scarcity of papers on the subject. This may support the stand of many researchers who claim that the standard clinical categories do not lend themselves easily to investigation. Nevertheless, some of the studies reported deserve consideration here as they emphasize shortcomings in the use of the standard nosological system and also in the clinical validity of some of the accepted subdivisions.

How accurately do psychiatrists diagnostically assign patients to the different personality types? How does the diagnosis compare with their scoring of the same patients in terms of items selected on the basis of their description of traits and behaviors used in the clinical description of personality disorders? Not surprisingly, Walton et al. (43) concluded that the ratings were more reliable for the descriptive terms than for the diagnostic categories, despite the fact that the six psychiatrists who participated in his study worked together and frequently discussed the taxonomic system that they were using.

They also found that the degree to which the psychiatrists agreed on the diagnosis varied for the different categories. Agreement was higher in the diagnosis of Schizoid, Hysterical, and Sociopathic Personality. This could be interpreted as an indication of the conceptual validity or, perhaps, of a clearer clinical description of these conditions. They found, however, marked sexual differences in the way these diagnoses were used, which puts the problem in a different perspective. The label of sociopathy, for example, was applied with much higher frequency to men than to women. On the other hand, the interrater agreement regarding diagnosis reached its peak in the case of women. Hysterical Personality was the most common diagnosis for women (43).

Their report that the diagnosis of Cyclothymic Personality was relatively rare is of interest because it goes along with clinical experience. Their sample, however, is too small and restricted to hospitalized patients to allow for wide generalization.

Another phase of the work reported by Walton and his associates illustrates the trend to use statistical analysis in an attempt to determine more clearly defined clinical syndromes. Submitting to mathematical analysis their patients' scores on the 18 descriptive items that they used in order to determine their degree of association, they found that they were distributed in four different clusters. The first type was called Inhibited Personalities, characterized by a disturbance in interpersonal relationships with social maladaptation, anxiety, guilt, and absence of aggressive and sociopathic behavior. Type 2, designated by the general term of Personality Disorders, showed even greater disturbance in interpersonal relationships with poor social adaptation and great dependency. Clinically this appears to be a complex group since in standard nosology the women in the cluster were diagnosed as Hysterical Personality while the men were seen either as Schizoid or Obsessive Personalities. Type 3 represented the Aggressive Sociopath and Type 4 the Inadequate Sociopath with Addiction (43). Since there was higher interrater agreement in scoring the descriptive items which yielded these clusters, it is possible that they could be found to be more reliable than the standard diagnoses. These and similar statistically derived clusters have not been tested clinically, however, so that we cannot yet establish their usefulness.

One of the most controversial groups in the standard nosological system—whose use seems to be limited to North America—is the Passive-Aggressive Personality. Although frequently diagnosed (41), questions have been raised from many quarters about the existence of a syndrome whose very name reflects its conceptual and methodological ambiguity (44). Very little clinical research has been conducted on the subject, and the results are conflicting.

Investigators, based on factor analysis, have demonstrated that the traits of oral aggression and passivity appear isolated in two different factors (18, 24), a finding that places the concept of Passive-Aggressive Personality in a rather precarious position. As Lazare emphasizes, this coincides with the psychoanalytic subdivision of the oral stage into a sucking and biting stage, thus allowing for two different levels of fixation (24).

A more recent follow-up study of identified patients with the diagnosis of Passive-Aggressive Personality sought to determine whether such a syndrome could be justified on the basis of a typical clinical profile, clinical course, and outcome (41). The evidence elicited provides tentative confirmation of that hypothesis. The authors found that the patients studied, as a group, had "remarkably homogeneous" clinical features that remained stable over time. Among their main characteristics were disturbed interpersonal relationships, social maladaptation, affective reactions, and somatic complaints. In fact, analysis of the sample indicated a subdivision into three groups: one without other psychiatric diagnosis and two others complicated with alcoholism and depressive episodes, respectively. The clinical features and the clinical course of the disorder in the population studied suggested to the authors that the

Passive-Aggressive Personality occupies "an intermediate position between the extremes of sociopathic personality and the affective psychoses" (41).

Another diagnostic group—the Hysterical Personality—has been hotly debated in a long series of papers which are as voluminous as they are controversial. As it has been used by both professionals and laymen, the term hysteria has become a hodgepodge of characteristics stretching from personality traits such as vainness, egocentricity, emotional instability, and tendency to self-dramatization to many kinds of attention-getting, nonconforming, or demanding behaviors. The usefulness and validity of the concept has been repeatedly questioned (39) and the ambivalence about the use of the term is reflected in its conspicuous absence from the first edition of the Diagnostic and Statistical Manual and its subsequent reinstatement in the second edition.

The problem is further complicated by the use of the label hysteric to designate both symptom complexes and personality traits while the relationship between the two remains to be established with any degree of clarity (45). Designating conversion symptoms as hysterical—the course taken in the second edition of the Diagnostic and Statistical Manual of Mental Disorders—is not supported by follow-up studies that find a large incidence of organic disease in patients previously diagnosed as suffering from conversion reaction (40). It also stresses the danger of making a diagnosis by exclusion, calling a conversion symptom hysterical based exclusively on the presumptive absence of signs of physical illness.

Studying the Hysterical Personality per se, Lazare et al. found that traits described as hysterical in standard clinical textbooks and publications were in good agreement with the cluster they obtained through factor analysis (24). This lends support to the clinical description of the disorder. Other studies, however, underline a need for a clearer definition of the concept, notably when sociopathic behavior comes into the picture (43). The separation of two subgroups may be of great relevance toward establishing a more accurate prognosis and predicting the response to psychotherapy (16).

Methodological Problems

All the accumulated body of information in the psychiatric literature has made little headway in terms of rescuing the practicing clinician from his perceived need to wrestle with a nosological system felt by so many to be inadequate. Still there is no adequate replacement. The psychiatrist dealing with different personality disorders will be using a classification system based largely on clinical observations. The categories lack proven reliability and provide no information on the degree of severity of the disorder. Precarious is the doctor's position, indeed, if the diagnosis is of little help in determining the prognosis, in designing specific treatment plans, and in predicting the outcome of therapy.

One of the problems is that clinical observation ordinarily deals with selected and small groups of people, with no guarantee that they are representative of the population under consideration. Therefore, it may lead to unwarranted generalizations of findings obtained in a biased sample. One way of circumventing this pitfall is to submit clinical findings to the scrutiny of research. The belief that psychopaths had a tendency to improve with age (19), for example, has been seriously shaken by clinical research (30, 41, 42). In the same way, previous observations claiming that psychopaths were free from neurotic symptoms have not been confirmed by recent studies (35).

Clinical research with larger groups of population requires the utilization of certain devices which have problems of their own. Since inventories have been often used in personality studies, it seems timely to summarize here the criticisms raised by Orme (33). He argues that, in contrast with the clinical interview, personality inventories usually measure the range or scatter of symptoms or traits rather than their intensity. It is primarily on that basis that their scores are derived. Even if consideration is given to intensity, he questions the discriminative value of the inventory short of being used in the context of an interview, ultimately a defeat of its main purpose. He stresses two significant inadequacies of personality inventories when compared with intellectual assessment techniques: they fail to present problems in a graded order of difficulty, and they are unable to measure nonverbal abilities.

Another important aspect of the problem of personality classification is that the subdivisions are in actuality types. As has already been pointed out, the problem with type theory is that its categories are mutually exclusive. The evidence from trait analysis seems to indicate that the score obtained in one trait is not a good predictor of the scores in other ones, indicating that the individual is better represented by a profile (24). The evidence seems to weigh in the direction of accepting the trait approach as capable of a more accurate representation of human nature. Aware of the shortcomings of pigeonholing people in the typological approach, some authors have tried to classify behavior categories rather than types of people. Interestingly enough, many of them end up with a typological description of one sort or another (24, 27, 31). This trend is also true in psychoanalysis, despite its heavy reliance on the description of developmental and dynamic processes (17, 22).

Basic theoretical questions, explicitly or implicitly lying in the foundation of any personality theory, are still a source of controversy. Normal and abnormal behavior are conceptualized either as continuous or discontinuous categories. The medical model, as a prototype of the discontinuous model, meets a good many criticisms. In this regard the extreme position proposes the abandonment of all and any kind of classification scheme. One of the arguments is of an ethical nature: "mental illness" is still seen as an unaccepted social deviance, and as such the label can be devastating to the individual. Another argument has more of a behavioral quality: labeling a man sick may actually stimulate and reinforce the expression of more sick behavior (1).

DSM III

The dissatisfaction with the official nomenclature of psychiatric disorders embodied in the second edition of the Diagnostic and Statistical Manual propelled the Task Force on Nomenclature and Statistics of the American Psychiatric Association to renew its efforts at developing a new system of classification that would attempt to correct the shortcomings of the previous one. The final product—the third edition of the Diagnostic and Statistical Manual (DSM III) (4)—was published in 1980. Its most significant innovation was the introduction of operational criterial as guidelines for the construction of a diagnosis. This methodological change is expected to increase diagnostic reliability and facilitate communication. Close adherence to diagnostic criteria, even by practitioners of widely different theoretical orientations, will increase the likelihood that an individual receiving a given diagnosis, independent of its validity, will present a specific cluster of clinical elements that they would all recognize.

Another noteworthy feature in the development of DSM III was the extensive use of field trials as a mechanism to test the use of the provisional criteria in actual clinical practice and use this experimental feedback to further develop the criteria. This serves to highlight the obvious although often unrecognized fact that the formulation of a diagnostic system in psychiatry still remains an ongoing historical process only arbitrarily suspended at a given point in time in order to disseminate the current state of affairs at that point. One still needs to take into account, however, that the proposal was voted upon and approved by the general membership, thus bringing the force of the political process, with its unavoidable compromises, to bear on the final shaping of the official nomenclature.

DSM III places the category of personality disorder on Axis II, along with corresponding disorders of childhood and adolescence. Besides a residual type (atypical or mixed type), it puts forth 11 types of personality disorders grouped into three major clusters. The paranoid, the schizoid, and the schizotypal personality disorders constitute the first cluster, characterized by individuals who often appear "odd" or eccentric. The second group, where individuals often appear dramatic, emotional or erratic, includes the histrionic, the narcissistic, the antisocial, and the borderline personality disorders. Finally, the avoidant, the dependent, the compulsive, and the passive-aggressive personality disorders are grouped in a third cluster, where individuals often appear anxious or fearful. For comparison, it preserved six disorders previously described in DSM II (3): the paranoid, the schizoid (with modifications), the hysterical, the antisocial, the obsessive-compulsive, and the passive-aggressive. The cyclothymic was moved over to the group of affective disorders where it more appropriately belongs, and the explosive to a new and seemingly tentative cluster of disorders of impulse control. The asthenic and the inadequate personalities have made their perhaps definitive exit from the nomenclature system. In addition, DSM III introduces five new types of personality disorders: the schizotypal, the narcissistic, the borderline, the avoidant, and the dependent.

Critical Observation

The section on personality disorders is one of the most unsatisfactory links in DSM III. The manual itself acknowledges that the descriptive wealth and the specificity of the diagnostic criteria vary widely among the different personality types. On one extreme is the detailed behavioral profile—representing events which took place in the external world and as such became an object for observation and recording—which characterizes the criteria for the diagnosis of the antisocial personality. On the other are markedly subjective criteria such as the ones that orient the diagnosis of the narcissistic personality disorder. As a consequence, the assignment of a particular individual to one of the different disorders will be done with different degrees of certainty. The most typical cases present a not yet entirely defined quality conveyed by the total configuration of the individual that makes him perceived by most people as "crazy," "sick," or "in need of help." In many cases, however, the clinician may be required to make judgments on quantitative variations from the normal, a methodological difficulty already discussed in this chapter.

The old dilemma of diagnosing types or traits is not resolved but circumvented in DSM III by the allowance for multiple personality diagnoses. When this happens it will obviously reflect an inability to fit the individual patient into a given type, and the multiple diagnoses given will represent in practice quantitative trait differences from the normal in personality dimensions which are necessary but not sufficient to characterize a given type.

Thus, the problem of classifying personality disorders remains unresolved. By necessity, the clinician will be relying heavily on the standard taxonomy although he will still be able to resort to other models when specific problems, e.g., responses to psychotropic drugs, are being investigated. It appears as if the typological approach is here to stay because, as Lorr (28) points out, it facilitates the development of a testable hypothesis which leads to a new hypothesis in a process that continuously increases knowledge of the field.

However, the allowance for multiple diagnosis in DSM III is a testimony to the need to further refine and describe the attributes—traits, attitudes, emotional reactivity, observed behavior, etc.—relevant to the diagnosis of personality disorders. In particular, a great deal needs to be learned about the interactions of these variables, as exemplified by the different impact of specific psychosocial variables on the individual, depending on whether or not minimal brain dysfunction is also present. Such endeavor may lead to the development of more specific clinical subtypes. By the same token, treatment techniques need to be described with more clarity and specificity if we are to learn which personality dimensions determine response to therapy and how they do so. This obviously demands that the clinician assume some of the attitudes of the investigator for clinical research in combination with information derived from ongoing biological, psychological, and sociological investigation, offering a promising avenue to attain more refined clinical descriptions than are presently available.

REFERENCES

1. Albee, G. W. Notes toward a position paper opposing psychodiagnosis. In New Approaches to Personality Classification, A. R. Mahrer (Ed.). Columbia University Press, New York, 1970.
2. American Psychiatric Association. Diagnostic and Statistical Manual of Mental Disorders, Ed. 1. American Psychiatric Association, Washington, D. C., 1952.
3. American Psychiatric Association. Diagnostic and Statistical Manual of Mental Disorders, Ed. 2. American Psychiatric Association, Washington, D. C., 1968.
4. American Psychiatric Association. Diagnostic and Statistical Manual of Mental Disorders, Ed. 3. American Psychiatric Association, Washington, D. C., 1980.
5. Brody, E., and Sata, L. Trait and pattern disturbances. In Comprehensive Textbook of Psychiatry, A. M. Freedman and H. I. Kaplan (Eds.). Williams & Wilkins Co., Baltimore, 1967.
6. Catell, R. B. Personality and Motivation Structure and Measurement. World Book, New York, 1957.
7. Cattell, R. B. Personality theory derived from quantitative experiment. In Comprehensive Textbook of Psychiatry, A. M. Freedman and H. I. Kaplan (Eds.). Williams & Wilkins Co., Baltimore, 1967.
8. Cattell, R. B. The integration of functional and psychometric requirements in a quantitative and computerized diagnostic system. In New Approaches to Personality Classification, A. R. Mahrer (Ed.). Columbia University Press, New York, 1970.
9. Cattell, R. B., and Scheier, I. H. The Meaning and Measurement of Neuroticism and Anxiety. Ronald Press, New York, 1961.
10. Cattell, R. B., and Tatro, D. F. The personality factors, objectively measured which distinguish psychotics from normals. Behav. Res. Ther., 4: 39–51, 1966.
11. Cleckley, H. The Mask of Sanity. C. V. Mosby Co., St. Louis, 1964.
12. Eysenck, H. J. The Scientific Study of Personality. Routledge & Kegan Paul, London, 1952.
13. Eysenck, H. J. The Dynamics of Anxiety and Hysteria. Routledge & Kegan Paul, London, 1957.
14. Eysenck, H. J. Classification and the Problem of Diagnosis. In Handbook of Abnormal Psychology, H. J. Eysenck (Ed.). Basic Books, New York, 1961.
15. Eysenck, H. J. A dimensional system of psychodiagnostics. In New Approaches to Personality Classification. A. R. Mahrer (Ed.). Columbia University Press, New York, 1970.
16. Forrest, A. D. The differentiation of hysterical personality from hysterical psychopathy. Br. J. Med. Psychol., 40: 65–78, 1967.

17. Frosch, J. Psychoanalytic considerations of the psychotic character. J. Am. Psychoanal. Assoc., 18: 24–50, 1970.
18. Goldman-Eisler, F. Breastfeeding and character formation. In Personality in Nature. Society and Culture. C. Kluckohna and H. A. Murray (Eds.). Alfred A. Knopf, New York, 1953.
19. Henderson, D. K. Psychopathic States. W. W. Norton, New York, 1939.
20. Jaspers, K. General Psychopathology. University of Chicago Press, Chicago, 1963.
21. Kahn, E. Psychopathic Personalities. Yale University Press, New Haven, 1931.
22. Kernberg, O. F. A psychoanalytic classification of character pathology. J. Am. Psychoanal. Assoc., 18: 800–522, 1971.
23. Kretschmer, E. Physique and Character. Harcourt, Brace and World, New York, 1925.
24. Lazare, A., Klerman, G. L., and Armor, D. J. Oral and obsessive and hysterical personality patterns. Arch. Gen. Psychiatry, 14: 624–630, 1966.
25. Leary, T. The effects of test score feedback on creative performance and of drugs on creative experience. In Widening Horizons in Creativity, C. W. Taylor (Ed.). Wiley, New York, 1964.
26. Leary, T. The diagnosis of behavior and the diagnosis of experience. In New Approaches to Personality Classification. A. R. Mahrer (Ed.). Comlumbia University Press, New York, 1970.
27. Lorr, M. Explorations in Typing Psychotics. Pergamon Press, London, 1966.
28. Lorr, M. A typological conception of the behavior disorders. In New Approaches to Personality Classification. A. R. Mahrer (Ed.). Columbia University Press, New York, 1970.
29. Lorr, M., Klett, C. J., and McNair, D. M. Syndromes of Psychosis. Pergamon Press, Oxford, 1963.
30. Maddocks, P. D. A five year follow-up of untreated psychopaths. Be. J. Psychiatry, 116: 511–515, 1970.
31. Mayer-Gross, W., Slater, E., and Roth, M. Clinical Psychiatry. Cassell and Co., Ltd., London, 1960.
32. McCall, R. J. The dispensable and the indispensable in psychopathological classification: Neurosis and character disorder in the 1952 and 1968 DSM's. Int. J. Psychiatry, 7: 339–403, 1969.
33. Orme, J. E. Are obsessionals neurotic or are neurotics obsessional? Br. J. Med. Psychol., 41: 415–416, 1968.
34. Redlich, F., and Freedman, D. The Theory and Practice of Psychiatry. Basic Books, New York, 1966.
35. Robins, E. Antisocial and dyssocial personality. In Comprehensive Textbook of Psychiatry, A. M. Freedman and H. I. Kaplan (Eds.). Williams & Wilkins Co., Baltimore, 1967.
36. Schneider, K. Psychopathic Personalities. Charles C Thomas, Springfield, Ill., 1958.
37. Sheldon, W. H., and Stevens, S. S. The Varieties of Temperament, Harper, New York, 1942.
38. Sheldon, W. H., Stevens, S. S., and Tucker, W. B. The Varieties of Human Physique. Harper, New York, 1940.
39. Slater, E. Hysteria 311. J. Ment. Sci., 107: 359–381, 1961.
40. Slater, E. Diagnosis of "hysteria." Br. Med. J., 1: 1395–1399, 1965.
41. Small, I. F., Small, J. G., Alig, V. B., and Moore, D. F. Passive-aggressive personality disorder. A search for a syndrome. Am. J. Psychiatry, 126: 973–983, 1970.
42. Tolle, R. The mastery of life by psychopathic personalities. Psychiatr. Clin., 1: 1–14, 1968.
43. Walton, H. J., Foulds, G. A., Littmann, S. K., and Presly, A. S. Abnormal personality. Br. J. Psychiatry, 116: 497–510, 1970.
44. Whitman, R. M., Trosman, H., and Koenig, R. Clinical assessment of passive-aggressive personality. Arch. Neurol. Psychiatry, 72: 540–549, 1954.
45. Ziegler, F. J., Imboden, J. B., and Rodgers, D. A. Contemporary conversion reactions. III. Diagnostic considerations. J. A. M. A., 186: 307–311, 1963.

3

SCHIZOID AND SCHIZOTYPAL PERSONALITY DISORDERS

Larry J. Siever, M.D.

Introduction

There has historically been a great deal of ambiguity surrounding the application of the diagnosis "schizoid personality." As the term gained prominence in the early part of this century, its usage broadened and thus lost much of its salience and specificity. As Manfred Bleuler points out, it is remarkable "how quickly the concept dominated the whole of psychiatric thought, and how interest in it gradually vanished—all within half a century" (5). The new DSM III classification reflects an attempt to clarify this diagnostic area by demarcating it into two distinct diagnoses: the familiar "Schizoid Personality Disorder" and a new diagnosis, "Schizotypal Personality Disorder," introduced by the architects of DSM III. The diagnostic criteria for the two diagnoses are shown in Appendix A. In order to understand the impetus for this new diagnostic usage and the thinking behind it, it is useful to review the history and evolution of the parent diagnosis "Schizoid Personality Disorder," for the history of the more recent term "Schizotypal Personality Disorder" is closely intertwined with it.

The origin of the term "schizoid personality" and the concept behind it took shape, with the term "schizophrenia," in the discussions of the doctors of the Swiss Burgholzi Clinic working under the direction of Eugen Bleuler. It was later popularized by Kretschmer of the "Tubing school of psychiatry" and elaborated by psychiatrists of the "Munich school." The concept evolved from the clinical impression that there exists a specific personality profile observed in many individuals who later develop chronic schizophrenia. Kraepelin originally noted retrospectively that children who later became schizophrenic were particularly "quiet, shy, reserved" (41), qualities one might associate with the schizoid personality. This picture was also frequently characteristic of schizophrenics who had partially recovered from their psychosis. Thus it was conceived that these qualities represented the character style most closely associated with schizophrenia, only apparent when the overt psychosis is absent or quiescent. Clearly, the more florid manifestations of the schizophrenic psychosis overshadow the less striking chronic schizoid picture. This characteristic picture was seen as an adaptation to a vulnerability to psychosis, which might emerge when a decompensation occurred in the face of stress or the increased demands of adulthood. Most of the European psychiatrists of this period interested in schizophrenia felt that this characterological abnormality had its origin in the same hereditary substrate that they hypothesized as providing the basis for schizophrenia itself. Similar clusters of characteristics and peculiarities were observed in the relatives of schizophrenics, supportive evidence for such a genetic hypothesis. Clinicians interested in possible psychosocial aspects of the etiology of schizophrenia also remarked on this association. They also conceived of the schizoid as closely related diagnostically to the schizophrenic, but tended to emphasize what they saw as the common developmental origins of these two syndromes.

Over time, the term "schizoid" came to apply to a personality profile that, although derived from its hypothesized relationship to schizophrenia, designated a more general population marked by social withdrawal. Psychoanalytically oriented clinicians focused on the dynamics and defensive aspects of the "schizoid position" and its role in personality development, while more biologically oriented investigators continued to explore the relationship of schizoid personality to schizophrenia. Thus at the present time the term "schizoid personality" is used variously to indicate (a) a personality style characterized by social isolation, (b) a stage of personality development, (c) a syndrome identified as a premorbid precursor of schizophrenia, or (d) a character type associated genetically with schizophrenia. The origins and the various usages of the term "schizoid" will be examined in more detail, with particular emphasis on the features included in the personality style.

The origins of the term "schizotypal," introduced over two decades ago, and its recent revival and usage as designating (a) a personality disorder characterized by cognitive-perceptual disturbances, and (b) a symptom cluster genetically associated with schizophrenia are then reviewed.

The next section is an explanation of the DSM III criteria for these two diagnoses in the light of the previous discussion and an attempt to clarify the issues of differential diagnosis for these two disorders. Finally, there is a discussion of the options for the treatment of patients who meet the diagnostic criteria for either of these disorders.

Origin and Usage of "Schizoid Personality Disorder"

Background

As noted above, the earliest concepts of the schizoid character took their form from the clinical observations and theoretical views of the German and

Swiss psychiatrists of the early 20th century. They were interested in the phenomenology, nosology, and constitutional underpinnings of schizophrenia. Thus it was of great interest to them to note that the nonpsychotic relatives of schizophrenics had a number of peculiar features, including social isolation and an eccentric communicative style, apparently not seen as frequently in families of psychiatric patients with other diagnoses. Although the character of those features suggested a nosologic relationship to schizophrenia, their manifestation might range in severity from a character style to a clear psychopathological disorder (57). Thus its importance rested as much on the presumed constitutional relation to schizophrenia as on its utility as an independent uniform psychopathological entity. Kahn of the Munich school (29) referred to it as a "psychopathologic-genealogic disorder" and attempted to demonstrate the syndrome in his studies of schizophrenic families. Eugen Bleuler similarly conceived of "schizoid" as a dimension of all personalities, with schizophrenia as its extreme prototype, stating "every man then has one syntonic and one schizoid component, and through closer observation one can determine its force and direction and can also put it in relation to his heredity, if the members of the family are known ... Exaggerations or caricatures of this reaction come into existence as schizophrenic manifestations" (4). For him, the line between the "normal" individual with his schizoid component and the schizoid character of schizophrenic was not a clearly differentiated one. Furthermore, on the more psychopathologic side of the spectrum he states, "At what state of the anomaly anyone should be designated as only a 'schizoid' psychopath, or as a schizophrenic mentally diseased—cannot at all be decided as yet" (4). He considers schizoid peculiarities of character as within normal limits, while latent schizophrenia carries stigmata of more serious psychopathology with its symptoms of thought disorder and social dysfunction—presaging the later distinction between Schizoid and Schizotypal Personality Disorders. At its very inception, therefore, the term "schizoid" described the character of a dimension of personality and, as such, did not lend itself to being defined as a clearly demarcated diagnostic entity. This conception has been the source of continuing difficulty in the use of the term for a diagnosis.

Bleuler refers to the schizoid characters in families of schizophrenics as "people who are shut-in, suspicious, incapable of discussion, people who are comfortably dull at the same time sensitive, people who in a narrow manner pursue vague purposes, improvers of the universe, etc." (4). The latter part of the description illustrates another continuing issue in the diagnosis of schizoid personality, its contradictions and subtleties. The schizoid appears insensitive, yet there is a sense of acute sensitivity underlying this bland aloofness. There appears a constriction, even pettiness of purpose, that may seem to conceal a vaguely defined grandiosity. These behavioral paradoxes illustrate the complexity of applying diagnostic criteria even to the early most phenemonologically oriented descriptions of this character type.

Kretschmer was one of the first authors to delineate in detail a schizoid typology. He characterized the schizoid as variously possessing three clusters of characteristics (42):

a) "Unsociable, quiet, reserved, serious (humorless), eccentric"
b) "Timid, shy, with fine feelings, sensitive, nervous, excitable, fond of nature and books"
c) "Pliable, kindly, honest, indifferent, dull-witted, silent."

He summarizes his impressions by stating that the schizoid temperament lies between the extremes of excitability and dullness—these contrasts creating a continuing paradox in the characterization of the schizoid personality. As an example of these contradictions, he quotes the playwright Strindberg: "I am hard as ice, and yet so full of feeling I am almost sentimental." He calls the mixture of these two elements, the "hyperesthetic" (or sensitive) and the "anesthetic" (insensitive) elements, co-existing in a "psychoasthetic proportion," which is frequently "jolted" out of its equilibrium state in the life of the schizoid. Over time the hyperesthetic component may become dulled, as in the example Kretschmer cites of an excitable, passionate young poet who later becomes a "dull-witted catatonic" (42). In their social relations, they are timid, an expression of their hyperesthetic dimension according to Kretschmer, fearing the intrusion of a stranger into their rigidly bounded autistic inner life, although they may have an "electic sociability within an exclusive circle" (42). Their affective expression may appear unusual and difficult to comprehend. Kretschmer considers the schizoid a fundamental biologically determined character type, as opposed to a more superficial personality style, fitting into his schema of biological types. He states "there is no doubt whatever that there are many 'nervous' and 'hysterical' individuals, many psychopaths and degenerates, who are biologically nothing other than schizoids" (42). The former terms he considers to be the names of convenient clinical classes whereas the "schizoid temperament" has deeper biological roots. This is another example of how the term "schizoid" was originally conceived to apply to a more fundamental property of human personality than a cluster of clinical characteristics.

Personality Characteristics

There are a number of characteristics, however, that are generally agreed to apply to the schizoid individual, that focus particularly on his psychosocial adaptation. The hallmark of the schizoid is his social isolation. The schizoid character is frequently described as reclusive, withdrawn, and uncompanionable. He often lives by himself and rarely interacts with the community around him. Arieti remarks "schizoid persons succeed without difficulty in decreasing their needs to an almost unbelievable extent. Many of them live alone in furnished rooms, away from their families, away from social contacts of any kind, except those which are absolutely necessary" (2). As a child they often are withdrawn with few friends and as an adolescent are more clearly set apart from their peers who are now interested in social events, dating, sports, while they pursue more solitary activies (e.g., watching TV, movies, reading, hobbies). However, it is important to note that all schizoid individuals do not conform to this picture, which by now has become stereotyped. They may have very superficially conforming lives with social and work acquaintances and thus may not appear to be isolated until an examination of the character of their contacts reveal few meaningfully close relationships with others. They may live or work in a group setting involving others, e.g., countercultural or religious groups that allow superficial contact without a true intimacy. Furthermore, other personality types may have periods in their life when they are quite isolated, for example, in response to a period of turmoil or a developmental lag in adolescence or as part of the picture of paranoid or avoidant personalities. Although these specific distinctions will be further explored later on, the crucial characteristic of people with a schizoid character, in contrast to these other personality types or developmental deviations, is that they consistently structure their lives to maintain a wide interpersonal distance between themselves and others that does not allow an opportunity of intimacy with another person to develop.

Thus it follows that such individuals have few, if any, close relationships. Those close relationships that do exist may involve a quite primitive often symbiotic dependence which is denied; for example, the young schizoid individual who is extremely dependent on parents or a spouse to maintain his self-esteem or even sense of identity. The loss of that important other person would bring on a severe decompensation or personality disintegration. However, the intensity of this dependence is not manifest in behavior towards or responses to the external presence of the other person. It may seem that they are minimally related to these important others. An example of this phenomenon is the schizoid patient who, while sitting reading in the same room with her husband, "became aware that she was thinking of an intimate relation with him and found she had slipped her hand inside her frock and was caressing her own breast" (23). As Guntrip points out she was "taking no notice of her husband as an external person; her relation with him was all going on inside herself and she felt contented." Another example would be the case of a young schizoid man who lives far from his parents and apparently disdains them but on news of a death of a parent abruptly decompensates. The valued object fulfills an important intrapsychic function for the schizoid but in a very narcissistic, introverted sense. Most commonly, these important others do not exist in the schizoid's social sphere, but are fragmentary intrapsychic representations of parental or other early important figures. At times, the schizoid may, in his wish to conform, or, in response to the initiative of another, become involved in a new important relationship. Arieti gives the example of a schizoid man living in isolation who comes into contact with an aggressive domineering woman who manages to involve him enough so that he agrees to marry her, perhaps out of sexual needs or other considerations (2). The most likely outcome of such a relationship is its dissolution as the spouse becomes a parental substitute and arouses, for example, fears in the schizoid of being swallowed up—fears that provided the basis for his isolation in the first place. Thus, close relationships are rarely enduring for the schizoid. When they do appear to exist, they are not based on shared intimacy, but on a narcissistic image of the other manipulated internally for a sense of security, or an insubstantial contact maintained for the appearance of social conformity.

Most of the contacts the schizoid has with others are thus superficial acquaintances at work or in their community. There may be a facade of sociability, but it only masks a sense of emptiness and playacting at social roles (23). The more severe schizoid's lack of social skills often precludes any convincing attempt at playacting. Even brief, impersonal contacts may be awkward and halting. It is this latter group that is usually referred to when the schizoid character is discussed in relation to schizophrenia. However, dynamically oriented clinicians, who also tend to see the schizoid adaptation as a more widespread phenomenon, may see individuals more adept at going through the motions of a more active social life. It is important to note that, as of yet, it cannot be ruled out that some of these apparently healthier individuals may have a constitutional relatedness to schizophrenia as well.

The schizoid individual is often seen as compliant—illustrated in adjectives applied frequently to the schizoid such as "docile," "inoffensive," "obedient," or "pliable". He appears to go through the motions of doing what is expected of him. However, this is only to avoid conflict, which would arouse aggressive feelings in himself and others, thus creating a great deal of anxiety for him. He instead complies and represses his resentment and hostility (2). This phenomenon is in contrast to that of the individual who superficially complies because he realistically or unrealistically fears the consequences of his noncompliance, but is aware of the anger he experiences about his compliance. It is also in contrast to the more truly compliant personality, who may have repressed resentment, but complies primarily to elicit approval from an important other.

However, this characterization illustrates another area of apparent discrepancy in most descriptions of the schizoid person. The schizoid individual may be seen as having a "bizarre, uncompromising, and stubborn" nature, at best "a self-reliant independence" (5). Both compliant and stubborn characteristics are seen in the same individual at different times. If he has the opportunity, the schizoid structures his life so that he can operate fairly independently without the intrusion of others into his activities. Thus he may choose work that does not place a great deal of interpersonal demands on him, particularly in terms of carrying out the wishes of others, e.g., computer programmer, mathematician, night security guard. In this way he avoids the overt conflict that would stem from noncompliance but may be able to go about his activities self-sufficiently. Clearly it is more likely that the schizoid with greater intelligence or other strengths will be able to find such a situation for himself. It is in the paranoid personality that we may more likely see a rigid defiant stance towards the environment, but the schizoid, at times, if interfered with in a sphere that is essential for his narcissistic integrity, can be stubborn and unyielding. However, he is more likely to try and continue in his own way sidestepping the demands of the other rather than confronting the authority directly.

The whole issue of sensitivity in the schizoid as discussed earlier epitomizes the seeming contradictions in the descriptions of this disorder. The schizoid may respond to insults or stinging criticism as if they were comments about the weather, apparently totally insensitive to the remarks of others. They do not seem to derive any pleasure from praise or approval and appear to lack a capacity for empathy with others. Nevertheless, particularly when younger, they may appear to be hypersensitive and even when distant, appear to have a tenuous fragility. Dynamically oriented theoreticians view the schizoid individual's appearing uninvolved and insensitive on the surface as a defense against a profound unconscious vulnerability (2). The effects of emotional arousal are so anxiety-producing and potentially destructive to the personality that it is avoided at all costs. This defense is in contrast to the avoidant personality who is hypersensitive to rejection and thus may spend a great deal of effort avoiding intimacy but is acutely aware of the pain of rejection, while it happens largely unconsciously in the schizoid patient. It may seem to the interviewer that the schizoid individual has, in effect, created an impenetrable "bubble" between himself and the rest of the human world. Interpersonal emotional events that one might expect to affect others seem to have no impact on him.

Thus insensitivity is part of a generalized disturbance in the quality and expression of affect in the schizoid person. He will lack any emotional display, in fact, deliberately withdrawing emotionally from his environment. He appears humorless, aloof, and detached. Frequently, he is described as quiet. Whether this lack of emotional expression is entirely defensive or part of a more constitutional predisposition is still a matter of controversy. Manfred Bleuler (5), in his study of the relatives of schizophrenics, saw many children of schizophrenics who were "secretive, cold, unpredictable, or bizarre," but could not be certain whether this was in response to their often traumatic experiences with their sick parents or to a constitutional factor. Current evidence from adoptive studies is not clear as to whether this characteristic is genetically related to schizophrenia. However, there is evidence that there is a lack of psychologic perceptiveness and capacity for empathy in schizoid children when diagnosed and later followed as adults (9, 81). Whether defect or defense, this difficulty seems to represent an integral part of the schizoid picture.

One area particularly difficult for someone with a schizoid personality is the management of aggression. He has difficulty expressing aggression and avoids situations where it is expressed. Some consider the schizoid less well integrated than the paranoid, who is better able to express hostility. However, difficulty in expressing aggression is not unique to the schizoid, being characteristic of the depressive who fears that his hate will destroy its object. The schizoid character fears the impact of his positive feelings as well, according to Fairbairn (11) and Guntrip (23). It is certainly true that all aspects of emotionality seem threatening to the schizoid person where a certain warmth and relatedness is more in evidence in the depressive. However, the schizoid individual's avoidance of aggression leads to a stance of passivity and a quiet demeanor.

A rich inner fantasy life is considered by many to be an integral part of the schizoid, so much so that it is almost as often associated with the schizoid concept as the characteristic of social isolation. People with schizoid character are certainly introverts rather than extroverts. Their inner life at its most adaptive may be "creative . . . the kind of life that generates new things, and that is necessary for cultural development" (4). Often it manifests itself as an inordinate absorption with abstract principles or vague products of the imagination that have an emotional value that is difficult for others to comprehend. This may be in relation to a cause, an idiosyncratic personal belief system, or an imaginary fantasy world. In any case, this investment in an idiosyncratic personal world represents a withdrawal from a subjectively perceived more dangerous investment in the external world. Wolff et al. (81) describe this phenomenon in schizoid children who are "often preoccupied with their own systems of ideas and interests such as electrons, dinosaurs, and politics, and it was a feature of their preoccupations that these did not change over the years." Thus, in contrast to healthier creative individuals with a rich inner life, the schizoid character's investment coexists with an apparent disinterest in external events and has an inflexibility or rigidity about it that tends to diminish its potential generativity of new and relevant contributions to human knowledge. Wolff gives an example of one 4-year-old boy who "invented and peopled a square island on the ocean floor" and daydreamed about this island even when seen 10 years later (81). However, there may be an imaginativeness and originality about these productions and many consider a number of outstanding artists and scientists to have had marked schizoid features. The schizoid adolescent is frequently characterized as a withdrawn person who likes to go to movies, watch television, or listen to hi-fi music and may be an avid reader of books on philosophy and psychology. The tremendous power of the inner fantasy and capacity to exclude external reality is illustrated by the case of a schizoid patient who could close his eyes in therapy sessions and plunge into a personal fantasy, apparently oblivious to the therapist or any reminder of the external world. Thus the schizoid patient seems not only to have the wish to withdraw from the world around him to avoid the conflicts he experiences there but often has an extraordinary capacity to enliven his inner world and block out the pressing stimuli of his environment, so that at times he seems more effective in this withdrawal than other patients.

Both his pervasive tendency to withdraw into his own fantasy world and his idiosyncratic approach to life often give the schizoid person an eccentric quality. This is even more pronounced when there is a suggestion of mild thought disorder with some cognitive slippage and referential thinking. These are characteristics that have been noted in the relatives of chronic schizophrenics and thus have often been associated with the schizoid concept in the past. However, the current DSM III terminology would treat these features as indicative of Schizotypal Personality Disorder and in fact as excluding the diagnosis of Schizoid Personality Disorder. Thus the eccentricities of the schizoid without evidence of cognitive distortions tend to be more a function of his isolated life style and inner-orientation. He may keep unusual hours, have interests that are not shared by his peer group, wear clothes that, although not provocative, set him apart from others by their plainness. These kinds of characteristics tend to make others consider him somewhat odd or strange. The more superficially conforming schizoid, however, may not appear eccentric at all and may be, in fact, noteworthy for his bland conformity.

Schizoid characters may have neurotic characteristics associated with other disorders, such as obsessive-compulsive defenses or psychosomatic symptoms (2). These, however, are ancillary to the major characteristics discussed here. They serve to protect him against anxiety and frequently become more pronounced under situations of stress or impending decompensation. Furthermore, the disturbances in the affective and interpersonal sphere are more severe than in the DSM III Obsessive-Compulsive or the Compulsive Personality Disorder.

While the features discussed above are characteristic of the behavior of the person with a Schizoid Personality Disorder, there are also subjective complaints that one hears more frequently from the schizoid individual. It is certainly true that these people often will not seek treatment, as the possible intimacy and exposure it represents may be threatening to them, and their restricted life-style may shield them from overwhelming anxiety. If they do, however, they frequently speak of "missing the bus," feeling that life is passing them by (23). They complain of feeling "cut off, shut off, out of touch, feeling apart or strange, of things being out of focus or unreal, of not feeling one with people, or of the point having gone out of life" (23). These complaints differ from those of the depressive who prominently speaks of his low mood, inability to function or experience pleasure, and often anger or guilt. The schizoid patient's complaints, if he articulates them, are complaints of observing life at a distance, experiencing a lack of feeling.

The schizoid person is likely to gravitate towards one of several social milieus which provide an environment complementary to their needs. One example is that of an encapsulated existence where their work situation has few interpersonal ramifications as discussed previously. In fields where social demands are few, they may, in fact, excel. Often they are attracted to cults or quasireligious movements that offer an organizing philosophy, encompassing structure, and opportunity for interpersonal contact without the threat of intimacy. A number of studies (15, 76) have noted the personal distress and frequent difficulty in managing hostility in individuals prior to their entry into a cult and the relief that cult may provide with its "structured opportunities to make emotional connections with others, which they viewed as highly difficult before they joined the groups" (76). The drug culture also may provide a way out of the "schizoid dilemma." Brown describes this dilemma as the fact that "the schizoid individual can neither be in a relationship with another person or out of it without risking the loss of both his object and himself." She goes on to describe how both the drug usage itself and the context of that use allow a feeling of warmth and relatedness with others without the threat of many of the conflicts deriving from a deeper intimacy. It is important to emphasize, of course, that all of these life-styles and occupations may attract a broad range of personality types, of which the schizoid personality may represent only a small subgroup.

Psychodynamic Developmental View

The term "schizoid" is used by psychodynamically oriented writers as a more specific mode of relating to others and the internalized representation of others. Melanie Klein (39) was one of the first to elaborate this perspective on the schizoid concept. She postulated that there is a paranoid-schizoid position which every infant experiences as part of his psychic development. This is characterized by a basic fear of losing his capacity to preserve his ego. When the infant experiences early oral and sadistic impulses, these impulses, felt as dangerous to the ego's integrity, are split off. They may then be projected onto the other person, i.e., the mother caring for the infant. Thus the other becomes dangerous and is a source of intense persecutory anxiety. There are a variety of defense mechanisms that develop as a consequence of this anxiety. One is splitting, in which the ojects and feelings towards them experienced as pleasurable or "good" are kept separate in consciousness from those objects and feelings experience as "bad." The "bad objects" are projected, perceived as part of a threatening external environment, while the "good objects" are introjected, experienced as part of the infant's internal world. Another defense is idealization, in which there is an exaggerated view of the object as "all good" and any "bad" qualities that might be realistically perceived are denied and split off. These idealized objects promise both unlimited gratification and protection against frustration and persecution. The schizoid character retains primitive defensive modes derived from this period of development. Their splitting is so pervasive that "all emotional, one might even say, human elements of the patient-therapist relationship may appear to be completely destroyed or dispersed, thus producing an atmosphere of emotional shallowness and emptiness which is very hard for the therapist to tolerate over a long period of time" (32). Thus relatedness for the schizoid arouses impulses experienced as so dangerous that the alternative of not allowing any experience of relatedness seems preferable.

Fairbairn (11) characterized the problem of the schizoid position as the fear of love. The schizoid person, he stated, is terribly fearful that the intensity of his love will devour its object, thus destroying it. This is in contrast to the depressive's fear of the destructive power of his hate. As a response to frustration from uncertainty as to the caretaking object's availability to provide for the infant's needs, the infant may desperately crave to make certain of the love object by swallowing and incorporating it. This fantasized act, however, would lead to the loss of the object. Thus the schizoid individual is frightened to allow himself to experience the need for relatedness to another. There ensues a massive withdrawal from any opportunity for relatedness.

Guntrip (23) has elaborated this view in his book *Schizoid Phenomena, Object Relations, and The Self.* He gives an example of a patient who "fantasized standing with a vacuum cleaner (herself, empty and hungry) and everyone who came near she sucked into it ... (she stated) 'I'm afraid I couldn't make moderate demands on people so I don't make any demands at all'" (23). The schizoid fears devouring the object of his affections or being devoured by the object.

It is important to note that those formulations describe a hypothesized developmental phase and a dynamic position rather than a descriptive character type. Thus these schizoid dynamics may exist in an individual who does not correspond to the character type described in the previous section or does not fulfill DSM III criteria.

Relationship to Schizophrenia

Premorbid Forerunner. The third usage of the term schizoid is that of the premorbid character type of individual who goes on to develop schizophrenia. The issue raised by this definition is whether there is empirical evidence that there is a clinical profile related to schizophrenia and whether this profile corresponds to characteristics historically associated with the "schizoid character." There have been two general approaches to this issue. The first has been to examine retrospectively the premorbid personality picture of chronic schizophrenics or, the second, to look prospectively at children with psychopathology. Early studies failed to support the hypothesis that a schizoid premorbid picture was at all characteristic of schizophrenia (3, 13, 49, 50). In fact a number (50, 55, 62) indicated, based on prospective data on a child sample, that children with highly aggressive behavior were much more likely to develop schizophrenia than delinquent, neurotic, or healthy control children. In a study by Bower (6) of childhood characteristics of schizophrenics, only 9% were regarded as "seclusive, sensitive, shy," the characteristics more commonly associated with the schizoid. Mellsop (47, 48) found that of a group of 384 psychiatric patients seen as children and as adults in Melbourne, 40% of the adult schizophrenics had presented in childhood as "neurotic," 21% with "adaptation reaction," 10% with "specific developmental disorders," and only 4% with personality disorders, none of these "schizoid" in type. More definitive studies that would involve taking a large cross-section of the childhood population and subsequently ascertaining the incidence of schizophrenia in that population remain to be done for obvious logistic reasons.

However, there are several studies which shed some further light on this issue. Gittelman-Klein and Klein (16) looked at the relationship of premorbid social adjustment and prognosis in schizophrenia confirming the theory that those schizophrenics with a schizoid personality prior to the onset of their schizophrenia have a poorer chance for a favorable outcome than other schizophrenics. Roff et al. (63) studied a sample of child guidance clinic patients who received an adult diagnosis of schizophrenia and found that schizoid childhood symptoms were related to a poor outcome, as were neurotic symptoms with low IQ, while unsocialized aggressive symptoms and neurotic symptoms alone were associated with a more favorable outcome.

Longabaugh and Eldred (45), in a later study of schizophrenics, confirmed the results of Gittelman-Klein and Klein, finding that a schizoid premorbid maladjustment significantly correlated positively with severity of illness, a chronic undifferentiated diagnosis, and less frequent interaction with staff and other patients, and correlated negatively with a paranoid reaction and MMPI ego strength. Illness onset was not consistently related to any of the posthospitalization measures.

Thus these studies do not support the hypothesis that a schizoid premorbid adjustment is the usual antecedent of adult schizophrenia or that a childhood schizoid picture will predict a later schizophrenic adjustment, but suggest that this type of premorbid adjustment in a schizophrenic, when present, correlates with a poorer outcome. However, a more restrictive definition of schizophrenia, such as is found in DSM III, which selects for a more severe chronic population may be more closely associated with a schizoid premorbid picture.

Genetic. Family studies also do not support a uniform relationship between the schizoid personality and schizophrenia. Interest was stimulated by early family studies of schizophrenics by Slater (69), Kallman (30), and Bleuler (5), suggesting not only are relatives of schizophrenics more likely to have schizophrenia than the general population, but also others who have not been clinically schizophrenic may show schizophrenia-like characteristics. For example, Kallman found 22.8% of the grandchildren of schizophrenics could be classified as schizoid personality.

Kety et al. (33, 35), in their adoption studies, which allow a better separation of genetic and environmental influences, did not find evidence for a genetic relationship of schizoid personality to schizophrenia, but did find evidence for the existence of a "schizophrenic spectrum" which included "borderline states," defined somewhat differently than current conceptions of borderline personality. Their borderline states included individuals with indications of cognitive disorganization without overt psychosis or clear formal thought disorder, e.g., strange or atypical mentation, brief episodes of cognitive distortion as well as characteristics such as ahedonia, personality lacking in depth, and multiple neurotic manifestations. The diagnosis of schizoid personality, corresponding to more general conceptions of the schizoid individual as shy and reclusive, did not show an increased prevalence in the biological relatives of schizophrenics, as opposed to their adoptive relatives or to the biological relatives of controls. Thus "borderline schizophrenia" which did show such an increased prevalence, in fact, was not defined in terms of social isolation, thus clearly pointing to the odd cognitive-perceptual characteristics as a better marker for a relationship to schizophrenia than characteristics of social withdrawal. However, the social adaptation of these borderline schizophrenics was less impulsive with less internal turmoil and more social isolation than current conceptions of borderlines (Gunderson and Siever, unpublished data).

Stephens et al. (73), in their study of the relatives of schizophrenics, again found no support for a genetic relationship between schizoid personality and chronic schizophrenia. They found instead that the psychiatric disorders among the first degree relatives of schizophrenics range over a broad spectrum of psychopathology. Such data (31) did not fit well with the model of either schizophrenia or schizoid personality as manifestations of the same dominant gene with variable penetrance proposed by Heston (25).

Twin studies also offer no clear support for a specific relationship between the schizoid personality and chronic schizophrenia. Gottesman and Shields (18) were unable to find any significantly increased prevalence of schizoid personality in the monozygotic twins of schizophrenics compared to the dizygotic twins of schizophrenics, a comparison that should reveal such a genetic relatedness if it exists. In fact, Shields et al. (67) found that any concept of "schizoidia", i.e., a specific personality type related to chronic schizophrenia, which represented the presence of a dominant gene with varying degrees of penetrance, would be much too broad to be clinically useful. Essen-Moller was more successful in his attempt to identify "schizoidia" in the twins of the schizophrenics in this study and was able to blindly identify at least schizophrenia-related characteristics in 100% of the co-twins of probands. Unfortunately, he has never codified and published the cues on which he based his clinical judgment of the diagnosis of "true schizophrenia." Other twin studies such as those of Kringlen (43), Inouye (28), Essen-Moller (10), Fischer (12), and Tiernari (75) found certain co-twins of schizophrenics, who were not schizophrenic themselves, to have "odd" characteristics leading to various diagnoses, including schizoid personality or borderline personality. However, the picture in these cases was hardly uniform and, in most cases, subsumed only a minority of the cases (68). Mosher et al. (51) specifically looked for schizoidness, defined as avoidance of close relationships and detachment, in the co-twins of the schizophrenics, and they found no evidence for its increased incidence in the co-twins of the schizophrenics compared to normal twins. However, several co-twins of schizophrenics were described as having a tendency to disorganization and rambling speech which one might consider as evidence of the odd communicative characteristics of the Schizotypal Personality Disorder discussed later. Other evidences of personality disturbances in these individuals, in most cases, were not present. From these genetic studies, it seems that there is no clear relationship between the diagnosis of schizoid personality and chronic schizophrenia, although there may be characteristics of those individuals related to schizophrenics that are "schizophrenia-like."

Origins and Usage of "Schizotypal Personality Disorder"

Background

Our of the ambiguity surrounding the concept of schizoid personality, i.e., its current designation as a more general introverted, socially isolated personality style which has no demonstrable relation to schizophrenia, there emerged an interest in the last 30 years in defining a personality disorder that did capture the schizophrenia-like characteristics remarked in the genetic studies of schizophrenia. Both clinicians, who worked with patients who were not schizophrenic but presented many of the psychotic-like features of schizophrenia, and researchers, who were interested in isolating the genotype underlying schizophrenia, proposed diagnostic terms and characterizations for such a disorder.

It was actually Sandor Rado in 1953 who introduced the term "schizotype" as an abbreviation for "schizophrenic genotype" and applied it to a similar group of patients (58). According to Rado, individuals with this genotype may or may not be clinically schizophrenic but will always manifest an ensemble of psychodynamic traits called the "schizotypal organization." This organization is a predictable consequence of what Rado views as the two inherited defects of schizophrenia: (a) an integrative pleasure deficiency limiting the experience of pleasure, and (b) a proprioceptive disorder leading to a distorted awareness of bodily self. Thus the "schizotype" has the characteristics of (a) a profound vulnerability to any loss of pleasurable pursuits and heightened attachment to whatever sources of pleasure are available, (b) an overdependence on others, particularly parents of parental surrogates, and (c) an intellectual approach to understanding others compensating for the deficient guidance of internal affective cues. Such patients exhibit an excess of the negative affects, suffer from low self-confidence, are self-conscious and preoccupied, lack emotional spontaneity, have inconsistent social perceptions, and are perceived by themselves and others as different (59). Interestingly, Rado does not emphasize cognitive distortions of these patients, in contrast to the DSM III author's conception which focuses on these characteristics primarily.

Rado's schizotype may show any of four adaptations: (a) compensated—a relatively stable adaptation, although the previously described characteristics are clearly recognizable, (b) decompensated—an adaptation marked by dyscontrol of the painful affects, secondary neurotic symptoms, and overdependence and which Rado equates with Hoch and Polatin's "pseudoneurotic schizophrenic", (c) disintegrated—the overt schizophrenic psychosis, and (d) deteriorated—end-stage chronic schizophrenia. The first two adaptations would presumably correspond most closely to the DSM III conception of schizotypal personality.

Such a model has clear heuristic value for research attempting to understand the genetic antecedents of schizophrenia. Paul Meehl (46) refined and elaborated a similar formulation from a more sophisticated research vantage point. He advocated the use of the term "schizotype" for the personality organization observed in an individual with a genetic predisposition to become schizophrenic. According to his hypothesis, all individuals with such a predisposition have an inherited "integrative neural detect," termed "schizotaxia," which, through social learning, develops into the schizotypal personality organization. The four cardinal traits of this personality type are (a) cognitive slippage, an associative dyscontrol that finds its most extreme manifestation in the formal thought disorder of the schizophrenic, (b) social aversiveness, based on an expectation of rejection and asocial distrust "which cannot be matched ... by any other diagnostic group (46)," (c) anhedonia, a perversive and refractory defect in the capacity for pleasure, and (d) ambivalence, one of Bleuler's cardinal four characteristics of schizophrenia. Meehl considers "autism" and "dereism," considered core characteristics by Bleuler, to be derivative from the combination of slippage, anhedonia, and aversiveness. The degree of success of the schizotypal's adaptation will be variable. In more fortunate individuals, compensatory strengths such as high thresholds for anxiety and physical vigor, partially compensate for the vulnerability to psychosis, and they may never manifest clinical schizophrenia. Others less fortunate with other constitutional weakness and a less adequate childhood environment will become clinically schizophrenic. All will have, however, to varying degrees the schizotypal characteristics.

Meehl speculates on possible origins of the neural defect or "schizotaxia," considering either the anhedonia as primary, the cognitive slippage as primary, or a failure of inhibitory processes in the nervous system as primary and considering how any of these defects might lead to the above constellation. He points out the potential power of a research strategy which could identify indicators of compensated schizotypes and apply such indicators to family studies.

Golden and Meehl (17) attempted to detect the "schizoid taxon" in a hospitalized psychiatric sample not including schizophrenics. They chose items on the MMPI that distinguished between schizophrenics and normals deleting decompensation-related items and applied them to a group of inpatients with personality disorders, neurosis, and transient situational disorder and detected a latent homogeneous class of schizoid individuals. These items tapped into characteristics of disappointment in life and love, interpersonal aversiveness, and anhedonia. Another study attempting to characterize "schizotypic" patients examined a group of individuals selected on the basis of an elevation of the schizophrenia scale of the MMPI. The schizotypal subjects showed progressive loosening of their perceptions of photographs representing personality attitudes or personal constructs over several trials (26), apparently reflecting a looser cognitive organization.

While researchers focused on possible behavioral concomitants of a schizophrenic genotype, a number of clinicians were concerned about the psychotherapeutic difficulties encountered in patients with micropsychotic phenomena who were not clinically schizophrenic. Hoch and Polatin (27) described the "pseudoneurotic schizophrenic" who presents with prominent neurotic symptoms but, on closer scrutiny, manifests short-lived psychotic phenomena, where fantasy merges imperceptibly with delusional material. Knight (40) used the term "borderline" for such individuals and warned of the danger of overly intrusive exploratory psychotherapy for these people. Frosch (14) proposed the term "psychotic character" for a similar group of patients, also emphasizing their psychotic-like characteristics. Their exposition of these disorders was more reminiscent of the subclassifications of schizophrenia, "latent schizophrenia" as used by Bleuler (4) or "ambulatory schizophrenia" as used by Zilborg (83), than of the early descriptions of schizoid personality. This is primarily because they focused on distortions in the cognitive perceptual sphere rather than on social behavior.

While the term schizotypal personality did not become immediately popular, the term borderline personality (19, 20, 22, 32, 56) largely supplanted such diagnostic labels as "psychotic character" or "pseudoneurotic schizophrenic." The term "borderline schizophrenia," later replaced by "latent schizophrenia," was employed in the genetic studies of Rosenthal (65, 66), Kety (33, 35), Wender et al. (78, 79) and Reider et al. (61). Evidence in these studies did emerge relating such a disorder to chronic schizophrenia on a genetic basis. This disorder was differentiated from the schizoid personality, on the one hand, by the defining characteristics of perceptual-cognitive symptoms, not necessarily present in the schizoid, and from borderline personality, on the other hand, by the lack of intense affect, impulsiveness, and unstable personal relationships considered fundamental to this disorder by Gunderson and Singer (22). However, these distinctions are often not easy to make in practice. In most of Kety's cases, the cognitive symptoms will co-exist with a schizoid social adaptation, but as Reider points out "the borderline psychotic symptoms may occur in a variety of personality types" (60).

Spitzer et al. (71), as part of their work for the American Psychiatric Association Task Force on Nomenclature and Statistics, wished to develop criteria for one or more of the borderline concepts referred to in the literature. They felt that the term borderline is commonly used broadly in two contexts: the first as "a constellation of relatively enduring personality features of instability and vulnerability which have important treatment and outcome correlates" a la Gunderson and Kernberg (71), the second, as discussed above, in the concept "borderline schizophrenia," characterizing stable psychopathological characteristics observed in the relatives of chronic schizophrenics. They were concerned about the perceived lack of uniformity and accepted phenomenologic criteria for either of these usages. Spitzer et al. wanted to ask the question as to whether borderline was a unitary concept or actually more accurately conceptualized as two or even more subtypes. They set out to operationally define each of these two major concepts of borderline and study the relationship between them. They at that time used the term "Unstable Personality Disorder" to represent the concept of borderline personality (later changed back to the more common clinical usage of "Borderline Personality Disorder") with criteria derived from operational definitions of borderline personality and the term "Schizotypal Personality Disorder," a term revived from "schizotypy," to represent the concept of borderline schizophrenia, with criteria derived from the adoptive studies of

Kety et al. Thus it is of interest to note that the recent origins of the criteria for Schizotypal Personality Disorder were as much an attempt to differentiate this concept from other conceptions of "borderlines" as from the concept of "schizoid personality."

At present, there exists very little written on the schizotypal personality outside of the early clinical and theoretical formulations of Rado and Meehl and the more recent work of Spitzer, which has been translated into the DSM III criteria. There is even less critically designed research on this subject. A number of questions regarding this diagnosis then remain to be answered. It is not clear whether it exists as an entity independent of other personality disorders, whether it usually coexists with the social isolation associated earlier with the schizoid, or whether it may appear as well in patients with affective and other personality disorders marked by quite different social adaptations. It is not yet resolved whether and in what way DSM III captures its defining and discriminatory characteristics and what its course, origins, and treatment might be. There is no research as to whether it has an association with schizophrenia as a premorbid precursor. Data for a genetic relatedness to schizophrenia needs to be extended beyond the original studies from which the criteria were derived. Thus any attempt to characterize the personality characteristics of the schizotypal individual and the relationship of this diagnosis to schizophrenia, as has been done for the diagnosis of Schizoid Personality Disorder, must be considered tentative and unvalidated.

Personality Characteristics

Earlier conceptualizations of the schizotypal personality include disturbances in the cognitive, affective, and interpersonal domains. The DSM III defines the cognitive distortions as primary, implying that affective and interpersonal psychopathology are secondary.

One thus might conceptualize an individual with Schizotypal Personality Disorder as someone with poorly regulated cognitive controls that are particularly vulnerable to the disruption of affective interpersonal stimuli. The cognitive slippage that occurs with even low levels of anxiety may give the patient's speech a digressive or vague quality such that it is difficult to follow. The patient may find it difficult to find the right words to express himself and thus realistically perceives the trouble others have in understanding him. This dysregulation may exist not only in the cognitive sphere but also in the motor sphere as well, giving the individual's movements an asynchronous awkward quality.

As a corollary, these individuals may be more vulnerable to the intrusion of primary process thinking, particularly under stress, and may be less capable of distinguishing such perceptions from reality. This may manifest itself in feelings of unreality, recurrent illusions, magical thinking, feelings of having special powers, and self-referential thinking. Although examples of such intrusions may be found in any individual, they are presumably more pervasive and occur with greater intensity in the schizotypal patient.

Patients with Schizotypal Personality Disorder usually have affective psychopathology as well. Often they appear to have a constricted affect and appear distant and difficult to relate to. However, it is quite possible that individuals satisfying these criteria have a more labile affect and appear to have psychopathology more akin to the affective disorders.

They often are socially isolated with few close relationships. This may be related to a primary anhedonia, a possibility Meehl has discussed, or a defensive withdrawal from others because of the potential disruptive power of interpersonal relatedness. When confronted with social situations, their anxiety may be evident. As a way of protecting themselves, distancing themselves from others, and organizing their perceptions of the external world, they may be suspicious and paranoid.

Genetic Relationship to Schizophrenia

The interest in the current DSM III diagnosis of Schizotypal Personality Disorder evolved from the possible relatedness of this disorder to schizophrenia. The DSM III criteria reflect on empirical attempt to capture the characteristics of the borderline schizophrenic biological relatives of adopted schizophrenics.

Spitzer et al. developed their criteria by consulting Drs. Wender, Kety, and Rosenthal as to the cues they were using in making their borderline schizophrenia diagnoses. These cues had not been previously operationalized, as Wender, Kety, and Rosenthal made consensual diagnoses on the basis of a priori notions noted above (33) about the concept of borderline schizophrenia and applied them blindly to the biologic and adoptive relatives of schizophrenics and controls. Spitzer et al. then operationalized these cues after discussions with these investigators and applied them to 36 cases diagnosed by these authors as borderline schizophrenics. They modified and condensed these criteria so as to maximize their power to distinguish the borderline schizophrenics from other relatives and arrived at eight items relating to characteristics of communicative deviance, referential ideation, unusual perceptual experience, social isolation, and anxiety.

They combined these eight items with nine items from the literature on borderlines. These latter items pertained to concepts of identity disturbance, unstable and intense interpersonal relationships, impulsive and self-damaging behavior, and affective and anger dyscontrol, largely similar to the

Thus their inclusion might tend to contaminate the content with characteristics of individuals felt by the authors to be borderline schizophrenics, but having no demonstrated genetic relationship to chronic schizophrenia.

Furthermore the criteria were based on a factor analysis of a survey of 808 psychiatrists choosing a number of items from a very prelimited set. Although such an approach may point the direction for future research, it cannot be considered as a basis for a new diagnostic category.

At this time there is no independent evidence that individuals meeting the criteria for Schizotypal Personality Disorder will have a greater concentration of relatives who are schizophrenic in their families than individuals with other personality disorders. It may be for instance that the features of Schizotypal Personality Disorder may be associated with genetic relatedness to other types of psychopathology as well.

Nyman (53) has described an entity which he terms "nonregressive schizophrenia which appears similar in some of its features to the Schizotypal Personality Disorder. The diagnostic criteria for this disorder are dishabituation, or increase of perceptual intensity of stimuli normally screened from awareness, anhedonia, anxiety, and hypochondriasis. Such individuals do not go on to develop the overt psychosis of schizophrenia but retain these characteristics over a follow-up period of 5 to 8 years. The similarity of their age and sex distributions and social prognosis to classical schizophrenia in the families of these patients suggests a common genetic substrate for nonregressive and classical schizophrenia (53, 54). These studies further the notion that there are individuals who fail to satisfy the criteria for classical schizophrenia but who exhibit features similar to schizophrenia and have a higher familial risk for schizophrenia. However, the differences on emphases in the symptomatologic profiles of "nonregressive schizophrenia" and "Schizotypal Personality Disorder" suggest the need for more careful observational studies of such individuals with accompanying data as to family history and clinical course.

It is interesting how historically the definition of schizoid, originally closely linked to schizophrenia, evolved into a much more general diagnosis. Later "borderline" became the diagnosis most closely associated with schizophrenia, and this term too has achieved a somewhat different independent meaning. Thus "schizotypal" has taken up the banner of being the personality diagnosis most closely related to schizophrenia. However, the specificity and nature of such a relationship remains to be clarified and validated. It is not yet clear, in fact, whether there is a uniform personality picture genetically related to chronic schizophrenia (68). However, there is little question that there are individuals with the cognitive distortions encompassed in the schizotypal criteria, perhaps as a reflection of a genetic substrate related to schizophrenia, and the DSM III category "Schizotypal Personality Disorder" has attempted to fulfill the need to characterize such individuals.

DSM III Criteria

DSM III Criteria for Schizoid Personality Disorder

The DSM III criteria for Schizoid Personality Disorder find their fulcrum in the concept of a primary deficit in these individuals' "motivation and capacity for emotional involvement" (72) with a resultant lack of interpersonal relatedness. The characteristics correspond closely to the classical picture of the schizoid personality discussed earlier. However, the intent is to clearly differentiate these individuals from Schizotypal Personality Disorder and from schizophrenia. Thus the diagnosis is specifically excluded if there are symptoms of psychosis or even the more subtle cognitive-perceptual eccentricity of the schizotypal personality. If the individual is under 18, the disturbance must not meet the criteria for schizoid disorder of childhood and adolescence, as this disorder is described separately under childhood disorders.

It is important to note that the DSM III criteria specifically requires a marked lack of relatedness to others, as indicated in the criteria requiring that the patient have no more than one or two close friends and present a "cold, aloof" appearance. There are individuals who more dynamically inclined psychiatrists might consider schizoid in the quality of their relationships because, despite the appearance of closeness, they evince an underlying superficiality or role-playing quality in their relationships. Such individuals would not be considered schizoid by DSM III if they did not clearly satisfy these two criteria. The DSM III diagnostic classification represents an attempt to make empirical reproducible diagnoses which may result in a more narrow and clearly bounded diagnosis of schizoid than some previous usages.

The same considerations apply to the interpretation of the patient's indifference to praise or criticism. If the patient appears untouched by the feelings of others, including their positive and negative reactions towards him, he satisfies this criteria, even if there is an inferred underlying sensitivity. This apparent insensitivity is in contrast to individuals with avoidant personality disorder who are hypersensitive to rejection. These individuals may be socially isolated as well because, although they wish to involve themselves with others, they are reluctant to do so without the clear assurance of acceptance. This insensitivity also distinguishes the schizoid from individuals with paranoid personality disorder who show a hypersensitivity to criticism, often taking offense easily.

Patients with Narcissistic Personality Disorder may, like those with Schizoid Personality Disorder, seem indifferent to others' criticism and display a noticeable lack of empathy. However, their grandiosity and exhibitionism are not usually compatible with a schizoid social adaptation. Thus although the two personality disorders theoretically may coexist, it is unlikely that both sets of criteria will be found in the same individual.

Although the schizoid may have compulsive features, they are usually not seen to the degree one observes in those satisfying the criteria for Compulsive Personality Disorder. Furthermore, although compulsive characters may seem to have somewhat isolated lives, this is usually secondary to an excessive devotion to work.

Thus the diagnosis of Schizoid Personality Disorder will usually be applied as a sole diagnosis and the main differential is with Schizotypal Personality Disorder, which is established by the presence of a sufficiently odd cognitive and communicative style to satisfy the DSM III criteria discussed in the following section.

DSM III Criteria for Schizotypal Personality Disorder

The DSM III criteria for Schizotypal Personality Disorder reflect the emphasis on the perceptual cognitive distortions of this disorder. As noted in Appendix A, four of eight of the following criteria are required.

Many of these individuals evidence magical thinking, e.g., superstitiousness, clairvoyance, telepathy—a feeling that one has a "sixth sense" or "others can feel my feelings." This phenomena may be as subtle as an individual feeling that another close to him can understand what he is thinking without his verbally expressing these thoughts. On questioning, these people believe this understanding is not on the basis of nonverbal cues in a relationship of shared intimacy but rather happens in a more direct magical fashion. More obvious and extreme examples would be feelings that one can predict the future, that an angry thought about another might lead to their physical harm, or that strangers in a crowded place can read the patient's thoughts. The interviewer must often question the patient carefully or know him well over a period of time to find evidence of magical thinking, which may be encapsulated in specific areas of the patient's experience. This criterion was one of the best discriminators between those diagnosed borderline schizophrenia versus those diagnosed borderline personality in Spitzer's poll. Thus, although it is a difficult symptom to evaluate, it must be explored comprehensively and sensitively.

Ideas of reference or self-referential thinking are a central characteristic of the schizotypal. Thus the schizotypal character may have a sense that events in the environment unrelated to him, in fact, are directed towards him personally, e.g., an individual, while feeling anxious or angry, sees others talking and becomes convinced that they are speaking about him or while feeling sad hears a ballad on the radio and thinks it is meant especially for him. This symptom, of course, must be distinguished from more realistic perceptions that involve environmental events related to the patients.

The criteria of social isolation, (e.g., no close friends or confidants) in Spitzer's study did not discriminate the borderline group from the control group as well as other criteria. This is understandable, as the schizoid and avoidant characters will often be socially isolated as well. It points out an essential feature of the schizotypal diagnosis—it is a diagnosis consisting of perceptual-cognitive symptoms that are associated with a variety of interpersonal styles.

Perceptual distortions defined as recurrent illusions and depersonalization or derealization not associated with panic attacks provide the basis for another criterion. Such disturbances fall short of actual hallucinations but do have a quality akin to the distortions of the overt psychoses. These characteristics must be enduring as opposed to a symptom emerging during the stress of physical illness or the administration of a drug. Several clinical descriptions of borderline personality include this symptom as a characteristic phenomenon as well (21, 22). Thus although it is not included in the DSM III criteria for Borderline Personality Disorder it may in many instances correlate with the criteria for this disorder.

Odd speech, another criterion, is defined as speech that is digressive, vague, overelaborate, circumstantial, or metaphorical. It does not include incoherence which is too nonspecific and is seen in neurologic or demented patients or the loosening of associations seen in schizophrenia. It was another good discriminator between the schizotypal borderline and borderline personality disorders, with it being less common in the latter, as expected. Furthermore, the presence of odd speech was the best discriminator between the borderline group as a whole and the control group of all the schizotypal items. It appeared in 58 percent of the borderlines and only 11 percent of the controls. The unusual communication may manifest itself in the interview in a response that wanders away from the thrust of the interviewer's question so that the connection to the original material asked for is no longer clear, a vagueness that may come from leaving out details crucial to understanding the response, allusions to people or events not previously discussed, or idiosyncratic use of words or concepts with apparent unawareness of the peculiar usage. Certain of these qualities such as circumstantiality may be seen in temporal lobe epileptics while overelaborateness may be seen in the obsessional. However, the idiosyncratic nature of the speech distinguishes it from the speech of their other disorders.

Inadequate rapport in face-to-face interaction due to constricted or inappropriate affect is another apparently less specific criterion for the schizotypal. As discussed earlier, it is often a characteristic of the schizoid. The main difference is the emphasis on the inappropriate affect in the case of the schizotypal. Thus in an interview, the interviewer may feel the patient keeping him or her at a distance, as with the schizoid, but the unusual character of the affect makes it even more difficult to empathize with the patient. For example, the patient may laugh inappropriately around a very painful incident with a quality that goes beyond embarrassment or sound monotonous and flat when talking about an experience one might expect to be pleasurable. In the responses to Spitzer's questionnaire, this item also discriminated between the borderline and controls but was not one of the best discriminators. Although it was present in the majority of borderlines (66 percent) it was also present in a large number of controls (23 percent).

Suspiciousness or paranoid ideation is another characteristic which has in the past been associated with both borderline schizophrenia and borderline personality. In DSM III it is explicity included as a schizotypal criterion. It discriminates somewhat between the borderline schizophrenic and borderline personality in Spitzer's study, although not as well as odd communication or magical thinking. It may appear as a watchfulness or guarded quality on the part of the patient who may ask questions, revealing a suspicion of ulterior motives on the part of the interviewer. Although patients do not easily acknowledge suspiciousness, they may speak of their wariness in new situations and vigilance as to others' motives.

Finally, undue social anxiety or hypersensitivity to real or imagined criticism is one of the least specific criterion for schizotypal personality. In Spitzer's study, it was present in 85 percent of the borderline samples but also in 60 percent of the controls. It was extremely common in both borderline schizophrenics and borderline personalities. Characteristics similar to this one are included in other diagnostic categories, e.g., hypersensitivity to rejection in Avoidant Personality Disorder and anger in response to criticism in Narcissistic Personality Disorder.

Differential Diagnosis of Schizotypal Personality

One of the main difficulties involved in the differential diagnosis of the Schizotypal Personality Disorder is that it defines a limited range of characteristics with few from the behavioral or interpersonal spheres. The only item from this latter realm is "social isolation," which was one of the weaker discriminators in Spitzer's studies between borderlines and controls. Spitzer argues that these idiosyncratic styles of thinking and perceiving constitute the basis for a personality disorder if they are significant enough to impair adaptive functioning (70, 71). In any case, the character of the schizotypal traits makes it likely that this diagnosis will be frequently applied at the same time as another diagnostic category. However, it is not the DSM III authors' intention to consider these personality disorder diagnoses as mutually exclusive. In fact the authors state that "both schizotypal and borderline personality disorders are best conceptualized as independent dimensions of personality that can coexist within the same individual, rather than mutually exclusive diagnostic entities" (70).

Not infrequently, one will encounter individuals meeting the criteria for Schizotypal Personality Disorder who also satisfy the criteria for Borderline Personality Disorder and thus should be given both diagnoses. It is also quite likely that there will be individuals with antisocial personalities who have the cognitive-perceptual symptoms satisfying the criteria for Schizotypal Personality Disorder, corresponding to the older clinical term "schizoid psychopath." Such individuals, when prevented from engaging in acting out antisocial behavior, often appear more schizotypal but when given more freedom revert to their previous antisocial picture. Certain narcissistic characters may also have sufficient schizotypal features to satisfy that diagnosis as well. In principle, this diagnosis is compatible with a variety of other personality disorders, including Histrionic Personality Disorder, Compulsive Personality Disorder, Avoidant Personality Disorder, or Dependent Personality Disorder. If the schizotypal dimension represents manifestations of an enduring vulnerability to cognitive or perceptual distortion and disorganization, that may, in some instances, be related to chronic schizophrenia, it is not hard to imagine that such a vulnerability may coexist with a variety of quite different personality patterns. For example, a schizotypal woman who has been raised in an environment where dramatic behavior leads to approval and love may also carry the diagnosis of Histrionic Personality Disorder as well, while a schizotypal man who learns compulsive habits to contain feelings of aggression and compensate for a vulnerability to disorganization may also satisfy the criteria for Compulsive Personality Disorder.

However, the schizotypal diagnosis is defined as being mutually exclusive from Schizoid Personality Disorder, for the criteria for Schizoid Personality Disorder exclude any individuals with Schizotypal Personality Disorder. Spitzer states "the concent of Schizotypal Personality Disorder is merely a subdivision of what has for years been referred to as Schizoid Personality Disorder" (72). Thus schizotypal personalities may frequently have a schizoid social adaptation with a deficit in the capacity to form social relationships, but the term schizoid is reserved for individuals without the odd cognitive and perceptual features. The question which remains to be resolved by further research is whether schizotypal personalities usually have a schizoid adaptation or are as frequently associated with a variety of psychosocial characteristics or personality styles. Further research may also help us to characterize in a more refined manner those symptoms which particularly distinguish individuals with qualities seen to a more extreme degree in schizophrenia.

Treatment

Psychotherapeutic

Treatment of either the schizoid or schizotypal personality raises a number of difficult issues that have not been extensively addressed in the recent psychiatric literature. Both groups tend not to seek help initially and resist treatment once they have started. They may keep the therapist at such a distance that attempts to help may be met with failure. Sensitivity and tact are especially important in the treatment of such patients. A lapse of these qualities may lead to a flight from treatment by the patient.

The greatest experience in the treatment of these patients has occurred in the psychotherapeutic arena. Psychotherapy of the schizoid patient has been considered at some length by a variety of clinicians, particularly those from the "object-relations" school such as Fairbairn (11), Guntrip (23), and Kernberg (32). They emphasize the obstacles presented by the schizoid's withdrawal for, as Kernberg states, "Patients with strong, overt schizoid features may present such a persuasive distance and withdrawal from the therapeutic interaction that the therapist's ability and even his willingness to engage the patient in a meaningful relationship become seriously taxed" (32). Kernberg cites Guntrip's observation that the personality of the therapist becomes very important under these conditions. He must use his "natural warmth, emotional wealth, and his capacity for empathy" (32) to clarify the defensive nature of the patient's withdrawal and help him move beyond this position.

Guntrip states, "Psychotherapeutic success depends ultimately not on theory, and not on a stereotyped technique, but on the individual therapist's ability to understand intuitively and accurately this particular patient, and to sense what is truly this patient's problem" (23). He emphasizes the importance of continuing availability and regard despite acting out or feelings of isolation on the part of the patient.

Appel sees the ultimate task of therapy as "rekindling the hope that the needs of the primitive ego can be met without ego collapse or suffocation," thus helping the patient to accept his own inner needs. He agrees with Guntrip and Fairbairn that the psychotherapeutic role is constructive rather than primarily interpretive. However, the countertransferential reactions of the therapist may get in the way of such a reconstructive role. When faced with the intense hunger and ambivalence of these patients, the therapist may experience sensations of "fogginess," sleepiness," "confusion," "dissociation," or even "murderous rage" (1). The therapist must understand his own reactions and use them to understand the patient's feelings of being cut off, a defense against intensely painful emotions. He must attempt to ally himself with the healthy parts of the patient's ego. By the therapist's appreciation that the patient has something to offer in any sharing he does of himself with the therapist, the therapist helps the patient accept his or her needs, thus validating the sense that the patient can give without destroying or being destroyed.

However, it is perhaps more frequent that the schizoid has developed a stably isolated defensive style and will not seek treatment for the purpose of longer-term change. It may be though that, despite their reclusive life style, they find themselves in a situation where they develop a meaningful relationship with another which stirs up a variety of tumultuous feelings. This could be a colleague at work or a roommate at school who, for any number of reasons personal and situational, penetrates beyond the defensive barrier the schizoid has so successfully maintained. If this person is of the same sex, homosexual fears may surface. Intense fears of intimacy, long avoided, might emerge. At this point, the schizoid may seek treatment for symptoms of anxiety. The therapist may elect to help the patient in a short-term crisis-oriented manner, restoring his equilibrium without embarking on a longer-term treatment with questionable prognosis. The more crisis-oriented approach may help the patient achieve limited insight, where more extensive exploratory work may be so threatening that he would leave treatment. It can also buttress any healthier defenses that have been overwhelmed by regressive feelings.

There are indications that at least some schizoid patients may benefit from group therapy. However, as Yalom (82) suggests, "An individual who, in the screening procedure, is a severely schizoid, isolated individual with a pervasive dread of self-disclosure is an unfavorable candidate for interactional group therapy." Those with less severe schizoid disturbances, however, may be able to tolerate the experience with the help of short-term individual psychotherapy at the beginning of the group. This will afford them an opportunity to establish intimacy within the confines of the group as a step towards further growth. For the schizotypal personality, the threat of decompensation or flight from the group precludes the consideration of group therapy in most instances.

Most of these considerations involved in the therapy of schizoid patients apply to schizotypal patients as well. Knight (40), in his discussion of the "borderline states" (which may include individuals categorized as having a borderline personality disorder in DSM III but probably are closest to the current concept of a schizotypal personality), points out the need for the therapist not to attack the psychoneurotic defenses and symptoms, for they protect the patient from psychotic disorganization. Therapy should "act as a rescue force for the main army of ego functions" (40) and help convert more maladaptive defenses to adaptive defenses. This may help protect the patient from the disruption of ego functions under stress that exacerbate the psychotic-like symptoms.

Psychopharmacologic

Pharmacologic treatment has not appeared to be a promising avenue of treatment for either the schizoid or schizotypal group. Klein (38) suggests that when anticipatory anxiety or social inhibition are present the schizoid may respond to minor tranquilizers. Depressive episodes may respond to antidepressants. However, these measures are not recommended for routine maintenance therapy of schizoid individuals. Phenothiazines can be used for incipient psychotic episodes for either the schizoid or schizotypal patient, but are not indicated for chronic treatment.

Although pharmacologic treatment of the recent diagnosis of schizotypal personality has not been discussed in the literature, there have been studies of response to treatment in pseudoneurotic schizophrenics, a forerunner of this diagnosis. Klein (36, 37) administered chlorpromazine, imipramine, and placebo in a double-blind design to hospitalized patients, including 32 pseudoneurotic schizophrenics. Imipramine showed significant differences from placebo while chlorpromazine did not. Tranylcypromine, a MAO inhibitor, produced surprising improvement in another study of 28 pseudoneurotic schizophrenics (24). Klein feels that these patients may be more closely related to the affective disorders than to schizophrenia, in part on the basis of these pharmacologic findings.

Patients diagnosed borderline, the basis of the diagnosis being unclear, have shown better symptom relief with diazepam than trifluoperazine, according to Vilkin (77). However, Brinkley et al. (7) have treated borderline patients with low-dose neuroleptic regimens. Most of these patients had symptoms of thought disorder, brief delusions, and thought "slippage" that would seem to qualify them for the diagnoses of Schizotypal Personality Disorder as well as Borderline Personality Disorder. These patients responded to low-dose phenothiazines with a decrease in both acute symptomatology and, in several cases, improvement in their more chronic cognitive disorganization.

At present, however, there are no definitive indications for psychopharmacologic intervention in these personality disorders, except when coexisting with other more acute state diagnoses. The field awaits further research in this area.

Summary

Both diagnostic categories, Schizoid Personality Disorder and Schizotypal Personality Disorder, emerged in the context of studies of schizophrenia. Schizoid Personality Disorder developed into a diagnosis applied to individuals who have little capacity for close relationships, a usage that had wide currency through much of this century. It has proved a fruitful concept in both biological research and psychodynamic investigation. However, its application became so broad it lost any specificity in relation to schizophrenia. The term Schizotypal Personality Disorder was introduced by Spitzer to characterize individuals with the cognitive oddities often found in the relatives of schizophrenics. This diagnosis has yet to be researched and validated as a distinct category, and little is known about its origin, cause, and treatment. Both disorders are difficult to treat by either psychotherapeutic or psychopharmacologic intervention.

REFERENCES

1. Appel, G. An approach to the treatment of schizoid phenomena. Psychoanal. Rev., *61:*99–113, 1974.
2. Arieti, S. *Interpretation of Schizophrenia,* pp. 61–63, 65, and 72. Robert Brunner, New York, 1955.
3. Birren, J. Psychological examinations of children who later become psychotic. J. Abnorm. Soc. Psychol., *39:*84–96, 1944.
4. Bleuler, E. *Textbook of Psychiatry,* translated by A. A. Brill, pp. 125, 175, 437, and 441. Allen & Unwin, London, 1924.
5. Bleuler, M. *The Schizophrenic Disorders,* pp. 434–435, 455. Yale University Press, New Haven and London, 1978.
6. Bower, E. M., Shellhamer, T., and Daily, J. M. School characteristics of male adolescents who later become schizophrenic. Am. J. Orthopsychiatry, *30:*712–729, 1960.
7. Brinkley, J. R., Beitman, B. D., and Friedel, P. O. Low-dose neuroleptic regimens in the treatment of borderline patients. Arch. Gen. Psychiatry, *36:*319–326, 1979.
8. Brown, V. Drug people: Schizoid personalities in search of a treatment. Psychother. Theory Res. Pract., *8:*213–215, 1971.
9. Chick, J., Waterhouse, L., and Wolff, S. Psychological construing in schizoid children grown up. Br. J. Psychiatry, *135:*425–430, 1979.
10. Essen-Moller, E. Twenty-one psychiatric cases and their MZ co-twins: A thirty years' follow-up. Acta Genet. Med. Gemellol. (Roma), *19:*315–317, 1970.
11. Fairbairn, W. *An Object-Relations Theory of the Personality.* Basic Books, Inc., London, 1952.
12. Fischer, M. A Danish twin study of schizophrenia. Acta Psychiatr. Scand. (Suppl.), *238:*1–158, 1973.
13. Frazee, H. E. Children who later become schizophrenic. Smith College Studies Soc. Work, XXIII:125–149, 1953.
14. Frosch, J. The psychotic character: Clinical psychiatric considerations. Psychiatr. Q., *38:* 81–96, 1964.
15. Galanter, M., Rabkin, R., Rabkin, J., and Deutsch, A. The "moonies": A psychological study of conversion and membership in a contemporary religious sect. Am. J. Psychiatry, *136:*165–170, 1979.
16. Gittelman-Klein, R., and Klein, D. Premorbid asocial adjustment and prognosis in schizophrenia. J. Psychiatr. Res., *7:*35–53, 1969.
17. Golden, R., and Meehl, P. Detection of the schizoid taxon with MMPI indications). J. Abnorm. Psychol., *88:*217–233, 1979.
18. Gottesman, I., and Shields, O. *Schizophrenia and Genetics: A Twin Study Vantage Point.* Academic Press, Inc., New York, 1972.
19. Grinker, R. R., Sr., and Werble, B. *The Borderline Patient* Jason Aronson, Inc., New York, 1977.
20. Grinker, R. R., Sr., Werbel, B., and Dye, R. *The Borderline Syndrome.* Basic Books, Inc., New York, 1968.
21. Gunderson, J. G., and Kolb, J. E. Discriminating features of borderline patients. Am. J. Psychiatry, *135:*792–796, 1978.

22. Gunderson, J. G., and Singer, M. T. Defining borderline patients: An overview. Am. J. Psychiatry, *132:*1–10, 1975.
23. Guntrip, H. *Schizoid Phenomena Object-Relations and the Self*, J. D. Sutherland, (Ed.), pp. 17–18, 26, 43, 62–63, and 316. Hogarth Press, London, 1968.
24. Hedberg, D. L., Houck, J. H., and Glueck, B. C. Tranylcypromine-trifluoperazine combination in the treatment of schizophrenia. Am. J. Psychiatry, *127:*114–1146, 1971.
25. Heston, L. L. The genetics of schizophrenia and schizoid disease. Science, *167:*249–256, 1970.
26. Higgins, K., and Schwartz, J. C. Use of reinforcement to produce loose construing: Differential effects for schizotypic and nonschizotypic normals. Psychol. Rep., *38:*799–806, 1976.
27. Hoch, P., and Polatin, P. Pseudoneurotic forms of schizophrenia. Psychiatr. Q., *23:*248–276, 1949.
28. Inouye, E. Similarity and dissimilarity of schizophrenia in twins, In *Proceedings of the Third International Congress of Psychiatry*, Vol. 1, pp. 524–530, 1961. University of Toronto Press, Montreal, 1963.
29. Kahn, E. *Psychopathic Personalities*, translated by H. F. Dunbaar. Yale University Press, New Haven, 1931.
30. Kallman, F. J. *The Genetics of Schizophrenia*. Augustin, Locust Valley, New York, 1938.
31. Kay, D. W. K., Rothe, M., Atkinson, M. W., Stephens, D. A., and Garside, R. F. Genetic hypothesis and environmental factors in the light of psychiatric morbidity in the families of schizophrenics. Br. J. Psychiatry, *127:*109–118, 1975.
32. Kernberg, O. *Borderline Conditions and Pathological Narcissism*, pp. 118–119. Jason Aronson, Inc., New York, 1975.
33. Kety, S. S., Rosenthal, D., Wender, P. H., and Schulzinger, F. The types and prevalence of mental illness in the biological and adoptive families of adopted schizophrenics. In: *The Transmission of Schizophrenia*, D. Rosenthal and S. S. Kety (Eds.). Pergamon Press, Oxford, 1968.
34. Kety, S. S., Rosenthal, D., Wender, P. H., and Schulsinger, F. Mental illness in the biological and adoptive families of adopted schizophrenics. Am. J. Psychiatry, *128:*302–306, 1971.
35. Kety, S. S. Rosenthal, D., Wender, P. H., Schulsinger, F., and Jacobsen, B. Mental Illness in the biological and adoptive families of adopted individuals who have become schizophrenics: A preliminary report based on psychiatric interviews. In: *Genetic Research in Psychiatry*, R. Fieve, P. Rosenthal, and H. Brill, (Eds.). Johns Hopkins University Press, Baltimore, 1975.
36. Klein, D. F. Importance of psychiatric diagnosis in the prediction of clinical drug effects. Arch. Gen. Psychiatry, *16:*118–126, 1967.
37. Klein, D. F. Psychiatric diagnosis and a typology of clinical drug effects. Psychopharmacologia (Berlin), *13:*359–386, 1968.
38. Klein, D. F. Psychiatric case studies: Treatment, drugs, and outcome. Williams & Wilkins Co., Baltimore, 1972.
39. Klein, M. Notes on some schizoid mechanisms. In *Developments in Psychoanalysis*, M. Klein, P. Heinmann, S. Isaacs, and J. Riviere (Eds.), pp. 292. Hogarth Press, London, 1952.
40. Knight, R. Borderline states. Bull. Menninger Clin., *17:*1–12, 1953.
41. Kraepelin, E. *Psychiatrie*. Barth, Leipzig, 1913.
42. Kretschmer, E. *Physique and Character*, translated by W. J. Sproti, pp. 151, 154, 161, and 179. Kegan Paul, London, 1925.
43. Kringlen, E. *Heredity and Environment in the Functional Psychoses*. Heinemann, London, 1967.
44. Liebowitz, M. Is borderline a distinct entity? Schizophr. Bull., *5:*23–38, 1979.
45. Longabaugh, R., and Eldred, S. H. Premorbid adjustments, schizoid personality and onset of illness as predictors of post-hospitalization functioning. J. Psychiatr. Res., *10:*19–29, 1973.
46. Meehl, P. E. Schizotaxia, schizotypy, schizophrenia. Am. Psychol., *17:*827–838, 1962.
47. Mellsop, G. W. Psychiatric patients seen as children and as adults: Childhood predictors of adult illness. J. Child Psychol. Psychiatry, *13:*91–101, 1972.

48. Mellsop, G. W. Adult psychiatric patients on whom information was obtained during childhood. Br. J. Psychiatry, *123:*703-710, 1973.
49. Morris, D. P., Soroker, E., and Burrus, G. Follow-up studies of shy, withdrawn children. I. Evaluation of later adjustment. Am. J. Orthopsychiatry, *24:*743-754, 1954.
50. Morris, H. H., Escoll, P. J., and Wexler, R. Aggressive behaviour disorders of childhood: A follow-up study. Am. J. Psychiatry, *112:*991-997, 1956.
51. Mosher, L. R., Stabenau, J. R., and Pollin, W. Schizoidness in the non-schizophrenic co-twins of schizophrenics. In: *Proceedings of the Vth World Congress of Psychiatry*, pp. 1164-1175. Excerpta Medica Foundation, Amsterdam, 1973.
52. Nyman, A. K. Non-regressive schizophrenia. Clinical course and outcome. Acta Psychiatr. Scand. (Suppl.), *272:*1-143, 1978.
53. Nyman, G. E. The clinical picture of non-regressive schizophrenia. Sartryck Nordisk Psykiatrisk Tidsskrift., *29:*249-258, 1975.
54. Nyman, G. E., Nyman, A. K., and Nylander, B. I. Non-regressive schizophrenia. I. A comparative study of clinical picture, social prognosis, and heredity. Acta Psychiatr. Scand., *57:*165-192, 1978.
55. O'Neal, P., and Robins, L. N. The relation of childhood behavior problems to adult psychiatric status: A thirty year follow-up study of 150 subjects. Am. J. Psychiatry, *114:* 961-969, 1958.
56. Perry, J. C., and Klerman, G. L. The borderline patient: A comparative analysis of four sets of diagnostic criteria. Arch. Gen. Psychiatry, *35:*141-152, 1978.
57. Planansky, K. Conceptual boundaries of schizoidness: Suggestions for epidemiological and genetic research. J. Nerv. Ment. Dis., *142:*318-331, 1966.
58. Rado, S. Dynamics and classification of disordered behavior. In: *Psychoanalysis and Behavior*, pp. 268-285. Grune & Stratton, New York, 1956.
59. Rado, S. Schizotypal organization preliminary report on a clinical study of schizophrenia. In: *Psychoanalysis and Behavior*, Vol. II, pp. 1-10. Grune & Stratton, New York, 1962.
60. Rieder, R. O. *Borderline Schizophrenia*: *Evidence of Its Validity*. Schizophr. Bull., *6:*39-46, 1979.
61. Rieder, R. O., Rosenthal, D., Wender, P. H., and Blumenthal, H. The offspring of schizophrenics. Fetal and neonatal deaths. Arch. Gen. Psychiatry, *32:*200-211, 1975.
62. Robins, L. N. *Deviant Children Grown Up.* Williams & Wilkins, Baltimore, 1966.
63. Roff, J. D., Knight, R., and Wertheim, E. A factor analytic study of childhood symptoms antecedent to schizophrenia. J. Abnorm. Psychol., *85:*543-549, 1976.
64. Rosenthal, D. Discussion: The concepts of subschizophrenic disorders. In: *Genetic Research in Psychiatry*, R. R. Fieve, D. Rosenthal, and H. Brill, (Eds.), pp. 199-209. The Johns Hopkins University Press, Baltimore, 1975.
65. Rosenthal, D., Wender, P. H., Kety, S. S., Welner, J., and Schulsinger, F. The adopted-away offspring of schizophrenics. Am. J. Psychiatry, *128:*307-311, 1971.
66. Rosenthal, D., Wender, P. H., Kety, S. S., Schulsinger, F., Welner, J., and Ostergaard, L. Schizophrenics' off-spring reared in adoptive homes. In: *The Transmission of Schizophrenia.* Pergamon Press, Oxford, 1968.
67. Shields, J., Heston, L. L., and Gottesman, I. I. Schizophrenia and the schizoid: The problem for genetic analysis. In: *Genetic Research in Psychiatry*, R. R. Fieve, D. Rosenthal, and H. Brill, (Eds.), pp. 167-197. The Johns Hopkins University Press, Baltimore, 1975.
68. Siever, L. J., and Gunderson, J. G. Genetic determinants of borderline conditions. Schizophr. Bull., *5:*59-86, 1979.
69. Slater, E., with the assistance of J. Shields. Psychotic and neurotic illness in twins. Special Report Series, No. 278, Medical Research Council (Great Britain), 1953.
70. Spitzer, R., and Endicott, J. Justification for separating Schizotypal and Borderline Personality Disorders. Schizophr. Bull., *5:*95-100, 1979.
71. Spitzer, R. L., Endicott, J., and Gibbon, M. Crossing the border into borderline personality and borderline schizophrenia. The development of criteria. Arch. Gen. Psychiatry, *36:* 17-24, 1979.
72. Spitzer, R. L., Williams, J. B., and Skodol, A. G. DSM-III: The major achievements and an overview. Am. J. Psychiatry, *137:*151-164, 1980.
73. Stephens, D. A., Atkinson, M. W., Kay, D. W. K., Roth, M., and Garside, R. F. Psychiatric morbidity in parents and sibs of schizophrenics and non-schizophrenics. Br. J. Psychiatry,

*127:*97–108, 1975.
74. Stone, M. H. The borderline syndrome: Evolution of the term, genetic aspects and prognosis. Am. J. Psychother., *31:*345–365, 1977.
75. Tiernari, P. Schizophrenia and monozygotic twins. In: *Psychiatria Fennica*, K. A. Achte (Ed.), pp. 97–104. Psychiatric Clinic of the Helsinki University Central Hospital, Helsinki, Finland, 1971.
76. Ungerleider, J. T., and Wellisch, D. Coercing persuasion (brainwashing), religious cults, and deprogramming. Am. J. Psychiatry, *136:*279–282, 1979.
77. Vilkin, M. I. Comparative chemotherapeutictrial in treatment of chronic borderline patients. Am. J. Psychiatry, *120:*1004, 1964.
78. Wender, P. H., Rosenthal, D., Kety, S. S., Schulsinger, F., and Welner, J. Crossfostering: A research strategy for clarifying the role of genetic and experiential factors in the etiology of schizophrenia. Arch. Gen. Psychiatry, *30:*121–128, 1974.
79. Wender, P. H., Rosenthal, D., Zahn, T. P., and Kety, S. S. The psychiatric adjustment of the adopting parents of schizophrenics. Am. J. Psychiatry, *127:*1013–1018, 1971.
80. Wender, P. H., Rosenthal, D., Rainer, J. D., Greenhill, L., and Sarlin, B. Schizophrenics' adopting parents: Psychiatric status. Arch. Gen. Psychiatry, *34:*777–784, 1977.
81. Wolff, S., and Barlow, A. Schizoid personality in childhood: A comparative study of schizoid, autistic and normal children. J. Child Psychol. Psychiatry, *20:*29–46, 1979.
82. Yalom, I. D. *The Theory and Practice of Group Psychotherapy*, pp. 167–169. Basic Books, Inc., London, 1970.
83. Zilboorg, G. Ambulatory schizophrenics. Psychiatry, *4:*149–155, 1941.

4

NARCISSISTIC PERSONALITY

Jay A. Phillips, M.D.

Narcissistic Personality Disorder as a diagnostic entity is a relatively recent phenomenon, emerging over the last 15 years from work in psychoanalysis. As stated in DSM III, as a comment on prevalence:

> This disorder appears to be more common recently than in the past, although this may only be due to greater professional interest in the category.

Within psychoanalysis, several factors appear to contribute to the dramatic increase in interest. Since late in Freud's life, analysts have refined their understanding of early development, especially as it related to patients for whom standard technique has seemed inadequate. The focus on narcissism can be traced from Freud's formulations on both psychic development, in which narcissism is a very early developmental phase, and severe psychopathology, in which it prevents psychothepeutic treatment. Work by Sullivan and his followers in the United States, and by Melanie Klein and others elsewhere, included doubts about Freud's formulations on narcissism, especially regarding the accessibility to treatment of pathology judged more disturbed than "neurotic." It was with this intellectual background that papers appeared in the mid 1960s delineating a group of patients whose traits seemed to justify the label naming this chapter.

In Greek mythology, Narcissus was a beautiful youth who refused all offers of love. In punishment for his indifference to the attentions of Echo, he was made to fall in love with his image in a pool. When he tried to embrace his beloved, the object disappeared. Unable to possess the beloved, he pined away and was transformed into the flower that bears his name. It is notable for the discussion that follows to pay more attention to Echo. She was a mountain nymph who had assisted Zeus in distracting Hera during one of his dalliances. Hera retaliated by making her unable to speak but to repeat the last words. When spurned by Narcissus, she pined away until only her voice was left, the echo (1).

In what follows, I will trace the concept of narcissism from its introduction by Freud, through its clarification by certain prominent followers, into its elaboration as the defining characteristic of a personality disorder. In particular, the major contending views will be stated, followed by current attempts to reconcile the incompatibilities suggested. DSM III description and criteria will be compared with these formulations, including differential diagnostic issues. Finally, treatment will be discussed in light of the work presented.

Freud published his groundbreaking "On Narcissism: An Introduction" in 1914, though his editor cites indications of his using the term as early as 1909 (2). Although the German equivalent of the term was coined by Nacke a decade earlier "to describe a sexual perversion," Freud's earliest reported references are to the concept as a developmental phase, and the paper begins by elaborating the concept as justifiably broader in reference than a perversion.

Observations of young children and application of his libido theory led Freud to assert that "primary narcissism" describes the earliest emotional life of the child. Reasoning from the data of psychotic detachment from reality, he suggested that before the developing child invested in others, all libido was invested in "the ego." Psychotic symptoms represented an aberrant expression of "secondary narcissism" according to this reasoning, as did the preoccupations of hypochondria (or of physical illness). Freud felt the investments in objects and ego opposed one another, interpreting manifestations of being in love as one extreme and paranoid delusions of world destruction as the other. He speculated that the child turns to objects when the excitement of investment in his own ego becomes unpleasurably intense, that inability to love another will lead to pathogenic manifestations of excessive "egoism," i.e., illness. These latter are examples of ideas that have been applied to nonpsychotic, personality-disordered patients: paranoid or hypochondriacal trends are thought to be illuminated or obscured by Freud's formulations, according to different writers.

Freud saw remnants of the child's original narcissism in the ego-ideal of the adult, i.e., when one's standards and values are treated as inviolable and commanding admiration and devotion. In this formulation, healthy development was characterized by a shift from primary narcissism to object love, with secondary narcissism as a consequence of adherence to one's ego-ideal.

He discussed the later choice of a love-object based on the self, in contrast to choices based on significant others from childhood, and called the former narcissistic. He went on to comment on the erotic significance to adults of degrees of narcissistic elements in object choice. These thoughts were based on the above-mentioned notions of mutual exclusion (so-called U-tube idea) of object-libido and ego-libido as well as on certain assumptions of masculinity and femininity that have since been reformulated.

Thus, for Freud, narcissism referred to the object of libidinal investment being the person's own "ego" or self. Freud used "ego" and "self" somewhat interchangeably and casually in this essay. Much of what was new in this required reevaluation as the structural theory emerged in the 1920s. The theoretical literature since Freud has been reviewed recently (18) and much of what follows enumerating this is elaborated there.

A crucial refinement was accomplished by the progressive distinction between ego and self (3, 4). In structural terms, the ego is a major division of the personality, responsible for adaptation including mediation between drives, superego, and external reality. The self is a substructure of the ego, although alternative views of the self within the context of structural theory have been offered (10–12). This substructure concept was further elaborated: conscious, preconscious, and unconscious representations of the individual were included. It was Hartmann in particular who emphasized the self as the target of libidinal investment in narcissism.

As Teicholtz emphasizes, all of the theoretical problems of psychoanalysis have overlapped with the concept of narcissism, several with important consequences for the entity Narcissistic Personality Disorder, as it has come to be defined. Ambiguities persist around the relation between the self as a substructure and the self as an experience, around the development of the self as both substructure and experience, around the differentiation between self- and object-representations developmentally and experientially, and around the relations between self- and object-representations and real objects, to list some simplistically. Several of these areas will be elaborated below, as they figure importantly in the work of Kernberg and Kohut, often as areas of disagreement. One easily summarized result of much of this thinking is fairly widespread rejection of the U-tube formulation of libidinal investment in favor of a more complex view. Some authors have, for example, noted a mutually enhancing tendency of libidinal investment in objects and the self.

Narcissistic Personality Disorder as a diagnostic entity first appears in the analytic literature in the 1960s. Rothstein has recently reviewed the clinical literature relevant to this concept in a work which complements that by Teicholtz referred to above. Many of the thoughts that follow may be found there in greater detail (15). The concept owes much of its prominence and controversy to the work of Kernberg and Kohut. I will, therefore, devote more detailed consideration to their contributions (7, 8).

Both workers cite certain common features among the patients they designate as Narcissistic Personality Disorder. These include (a) chronic, pervasive problems underlying a spectrum of chief complaints, (b) grandiosity (exaggerated sense of self-importance, unrealistic assessment of capabilities), and (c) lack of empathy for others, viewing others only for the gratifications they provide, relating with shallowness. In addition to these attributes, each author emphasizes other qualities in association to theoretical formulations and technical recommendations.

Kernberg describes additional qualities referring heavily to relations with others. He cites a superficial appearance of little disturbance with good impulse control. There is extreme self-reference, self-absorption, a need to be loved, admired, paid tribute, with restlessness and boredom in the absence of constantly renewed supplies. The inflated self-concept is accompanied and maintained by a devaluation of others, intense envy, and threatening feelings of inferiority. Idealization may be present in those relationships providing the above-mentioned supplies; relations in general are marked by exploitiveness and a cold ruthless entitlement to absolute control. This is said to stem from an essential inability to depend on others out of profound distrust. Kernberg emphasizes the defensive reliance on splitting (of representations into all-good and all-bad), denial, and idealization/devaluation to manage conflicts predominantly aggressive in drive aspects. He dates these conflicts and the quality of the aggression to the oral stage. These formulations are crucial in Kernberg's view; they dictate his view of Narcissistic Personality Disorder as so many manifestations of pathological narcissism, derailed from normal development by experiences provoking unmanageable rage and aggression in the young child. This in turn points toward the technical recommendations he makes.

Kohut emphasizes subtly different phenomena and discusses these using some less widely held definitions. He cites a pervasive sense of emptiness in his patients, frequent depression, and feelings of unreality. There is hypochondriacal brooding, often responsive to interest from the environment; these may include organ function disturbances (i.e., somatic symptoms with strong evidence relating them to psychological conflict). The patient is extremely sensitive to rebuff, and displays a dependence on objects for equilibrium in which the object is experienced as an extension of the self. There may be perverse trends and otherwise a lack of interest in sex, work inhibitions, delinquent activity, and lying. A tendency to rage may be seen. Kohut does not emphasize diagnosis by behavior or by defensive hierarchy, or even by reported relations to others, but rather by certain manifestations of the transference in the analytic situation. Another idiosyncratic idea of Kohut's is conceiving narcissism as a quality of libidinal energy. Another is his formulation of the developmental line of narcissism, independent of object-love and independent of considerations of aggression (except as a rage-response to frustration of stage-appropriate narcissistic needs). Thus, for Kohut, Narcissistic Personality Disorder refers to a developmental arrest and indicates technical steps consistent with this.

Several authors have questioned whether Kernberg and Kohut are discussing the same patients (13, 14). It seems most likely that each is discussing a spectrum and that one overlaps the other. A notable attempt to synthesize the two has been offered by Rothstein. He proposes to define the diagnosis "by the predominant mode of investment of narcissism in the self-representation." Unfortunately, this statement is redundant in its use of the concept narcissism as denoting a special kind of libidinal energy, a view espoused only by Kohut among the major contributors to this area. A minor modification would reconcile the conclusions of Teicholtz with Rothstein's clinical formulations. Narcissistic Personality Disorder would be defined by *a pre-*

dominant mode of investment in the self-representation. This is simply a transposition of the definition of the concept narcissism into the realm of chronic, life-complicating, character-disordered behavior. Rothstein emphasizes another dimension important for the diagnosis, namely, "the state of structural integration" of narcissism. By this he aims to bridge the spectra of Kernberg and Kohut: many of Kernberg's patients seem much more fragile in the coherence and stability of their self-representation (however grandiose it may be) than Kohut's. This would reconcile the definition with the common clinical experience of dominant narcissistic traits in patients with symptom constellations ranging from psychotic through borderline and neurotic to apparently asymptomatic.

DSM III

The most recent edition of the *Diagnostic and Statistical Manual of Mental Disorders* published by the American Psychiatric Association distinguishes personality traits from Personality Disorders. Traits are "enduring patterns of perceiving, relating to, and thinking about the environment and oneself ... exhibited in a wide range of important social and personal contexts." Traits are said to constitute Personality Disorders "only when [they] are inflexible and maladaptive and cause either significant impairment in social or occupational functioning or subjective distress. . . . " It goes on to indicate the appearance of both traits and disorders by adolescence or earlier (16).

Narcissistic Personality Disorder is characterized here by "a grandiose sense of self-importance or uniqueness; preoccupation with fantasies of unlimited success; exhibitionistic need for constant attention and admiration, characteristic responses to threats to self-esteem; and characteristic disturbances in interpersonal relationships." These latter are illustrated by "feelings of entitlement, interpersonal exploitiveness, relationships that alternate between the extremes of overidealization and devaluation, and lack of empathy."

It will be noticed that this description is heavily behavioral in comparison to the psychoanalytic work from which it was derived. This becomes more obvious and potentially problematic in the operational *Diagnostic criteria*, seen in Appendix A. It is clear that a rigid application of the *diagnostic criteria* prescribed by the manual, i.e., all of the lettered criteria, including two of those numbered under E, would exclude many patients with disturbing self-preoccupation who, for other dynamic reasons, all related in complex ways, would fail to meet one or more. While the greater familiarization associated with treatment might ultimately reveal all the criteria in various sectors of the patient's life, such traits as exhibitionism and interpersonal exploitiveness may be effectively disguised.

One patient prided himself on his sensitivity toward and concern for others. Only through many months of therapy for variably intense depression did it become clear that his concern was based on an exquisite vulnerability to indifference and competition from those he worked and lived with. He required positive affective quality in these relationships, and in its absence felt depleted and immobilized. The others functioned as necessary extensions of himself in maintaining his ability to work and relate.

Associated Features. DSM III cites the frequent appearance of "features of Histrionic, Borderline, and Antisocial Personality Disorders.... " The analytic work abstracted above indicates features of Paranoid, Schizoid, Avoidant, and Compulsive Personality Disorders as defined in the manual. For example, the cool indifference of the Narcissistic Personality Disorder will overlap the coldness and suspiciousness of Paranoid Personality Disorder; the perfectionism and expecting others to do things as the patient demands of Compulsive Personality Disorder will also refer to the grandiosity and exploitiveness of others as extensions of Narcissistic Personality Disorder.

Transient psychotic symptoms and depressed mood are cited and may be the presenting symptoms; the latter is especially common in the clinical experience of this writer. The preoccupation with the self will often include somatic complaints. When these are dominant, the patient frequently rejects psychiatric referral despite dissatisfaction with a series of physicians.

Impairment. Besides the definitional disturbance of interpersonal relations, symptoms may interfere with occupational functioning. Depressed mood, relationship problems, and the pursuit of unrealistic expectations are cited as common examples in the manual.

Complications. DSM III cites Dysthymic Disorder, Major Depression, and Brief Reactive Psychosis as possible complications, but it can be seen from the above discussion that many other Axis I disorders could represent symptomatic expression of Narcissistic Personality Disorder. The whole class of Anxiety Disorders, several Somatiform Disorders, and certain of the Psychosexual Disorders seem to this writer important possibilities not mentioned by the manual. Hypochondriasis in particular presents in this association, an observation first linked by Freud. Paraphilias are cited by Kohut.

Differential Diagnosis. It is difficult to limit this to Borderline and Histrionic Personality Disorders as DSM III does. To do so would limit the diagnosis to the more obviously disturbed or dramatic cases. As indicated above, many Axis II diagnoses have narcissistically tinged traits among their diagnostic criteria; the extent of narcissistic dominance of the personality often can be determined with confidence only after a period of treatment.

Philosophy of diagnosis arises as an issue in these considerations. Making a diagnosis is a medical act which takes place in several social and political contexts simultaneously. Differing attitudes among clinicians vis-à-vis these contexts will lead to varying emphases in diagnosis by equally skilled observers. Doing justice to the complexity of the patient may be incompatible with asserting a patient's conformity with *Diagnostic criteria*. DSM III implicitly acknowledges this by allowing multiple Personality Disorder diagnoses and by defining Atypical and Mixed Personality Disorders.

Therapy

Crises, Decompensations, and Associated Symptoms. These should in general be approached supportively. In this paradigm the patient comes in symptomatic distress with a complaint which the clinician assesses as disrupted self-esteem. The basis may be the loss of a need-gratifying object who has been functioning as an extension, a disappointment in previously successful pursuit of ambition, or some other deflation.

Horowitz has written on the therapy of what he calls Stress Response Syndromes in various personality types (5). He details the supportive approach necessary for allowing Narcissistic Personality Disorders to use contact with the therapist to repair the injured self-esteem and reconstitute the disrupted self-image. The therapist must refrain from confronting grandiosity or self-aggrandizing externalization. The therapist must be willing to participate in the patient's need to be admired, which in turn can allow the eventual tactful address of threatening aspects of reality. Horowitz cites the difficulty encountered by the therapist accustomed to relying on positive transference and alliance to support work on threatening issues. Tact and forbearance are stressed by the patient's frequent nonacknowledgment of the therapist as fully human. One apparently paradoxical manifestation of this is the attribution of greatness and specialness to the therapist (idealization), which can be very discomforting. This may alternate with scathing devaluation. It will be useful for the therapist to keep in mind the function these behaviors serve: to reconstitute the self-image as intact and good under conditions in which it has been damaged, thereby threatening the patient with fragmentation. Horowitz details specific therapeutic counters for various elements of narcissistic style. A table from his work is included below (Table 4.1).

It may be useful here to recall the fate of Echo in her suit of Narcissus: the therapist who offers only reflection of the patient's last words will surely be spurned as unempathic to the dictates of his fragile self-esteem. Conversely, the therapist may come to feel personally spurned despite his most empathic efforts by a patient who is fundamentally unable to acknowledge another's humanity or feelings. With Narcissistic Personality Disorders at least as much as with other patients, the therapist's self-awareness and self-analytic efforts will be essential.

Treatment of the Personality Disorder. Some patients will be responsive

TABLE 4.1
Some of the "Defects" of Narcissistic Style and Their Counteractants in Therapy

Function	Style as "Defect"	Therapeutic Counter
Perception	Focused on praise and blame	Avoid being provoked into either praising or blaming.
	Denial of "wounding" information	Tactful timing and wording to counteract denials.
Representation	Dislocates attributes as to whether of the self or another person	Clarify who is who in terms of acts, motives, beliefs, and sensations.
Translation of images into words	Slides meanings	Consistently define meanings, encourage decisions as to most relevant meanings or weightings.
Associations	Overbalanced in terms of finding routes to self-enhancement	Hold to other meanings; cautious deflation of grandiose meanings.
Problem solving	Distortion of reality to maintain self-esteem, obtain illusory gratifications, forgive selves too easily.	Point out corruptions (tactfully), encourage and reward reality-fidelity. Support of self-esteem during period of surrender of illusory gratification (real interest of therapist, and identification with therapist as noncorrupt person, helps). Help develop appropriate sense of responsibility. Find out and discourage unrealistic gratification from therapy.

to the approach outlined above and will terminate after symptom relief has been obtained. Others will have identified long-standing symptoms (loneliness, depression) for which they may want more help. Still other patients will present with vague symptomatology requesting psychoanalysis. When the patient shows signs of good ego strength, after careful assessment by an experienced analyst, the recommendation of analysis may be made with the aim of definitive treatment of the underlying disorder by reconstruction of the patient's personality development.

As indicated above, the works of Kernberg and Kohut have come to stand for technical approaches that have important differences. Both stress the need for long periods of forbearance and noninterpretation of grandiosity or idealization as a defense. Kohut's position is that this empathic stance should be maintained, in acknowledgment of the arrested narcissistic development which can then proceed through the transference. Kernberg's position is that ultimately these attitudes and behaviors must be drawn to the patient's attention as pathologically elaborated defenses against destructive urges toward significant others from the oral and anal stages. Kohut sees the successful analysis leading to more adaptive and productive forms of narcissism, with improved personal relations as a possible byproduct. Kernberg sees the patient passing through depression on the way to relationships in which the other's humanity and needs can be tolerated and responded to empathically. The differences between these positions are substantial, and each has a significant following in analytic literature and discussions. The so-far overwhelming complexity of outcome assessment in analysis has precluded definitive research. Probably both approaches will be used by various practitioners for many years before some consensus is achieved. There is widespread agreement that Kohut's descriptions have brought order to a range of clinical phenomena previously judged beyond the reach of analytic intervention. Whether this order actually changes that reach, or provides a new basis for clinical psychoanalysis, as he suggests in his most recent work (9), is widely disputed (17).

Narcissistic Personality Disorders have brought into focus many aspects of psychoanalysis as theory and treatment. These patients, with their uncomfortable and often disturbing characteristics, will continue to stimulate work aimed at offering them more satisfying lives.

REFERENCES

1. Bulfinch, T. Echo and Narcissus. In: *Bulfinch's Mythology*, pp. 101–103. Avenel Books, New York, 1978.
2. Freud, S. On Narcissism: An introduction. In: *The Standard Edition of the Complete Psychological Works of Sigmund Freud*, Vol. 14, pp. 69–102. J. Strachey (Ed.), Hogarth Press, London, 1957.
3. Hartmann, H. Comments on the psychoanalytic theory of the ego. In: *Essays on Ego Psychology*, pp. 113–141. International Universities Press, New York, 1964.
4. Hartmann, H., and Lowenstein, R. Notes on the superego. In: *Papers on Psychoanalytic Psychology [Psychological Issues]*, Monograph 14], pp. 144–181. International Universities Press, New York, 1962.
5. Horowitz, M. *Stress Response Syndromes*, pp. 181–184. Jason Aronson, New York, 1976.
6. Jacobson, E. *The Self and the Object World*, International Universities Press, New York, 1964.
7. Kernberg, O. *Borderline Conditions and Pathological Narcissism*, Jason Aronson, New York, 1975.
8. Kohut, H. *The Analysis of the Self*, International Universities Press, New York, 1971.
9. Kohut, H. *The Restoration of the Self*. International Universities Press, New York, 1975.
10. Klass, D., and Offenkrautz, W. Sartre's contribution to the understanding of narcissism. *Int. J. Psychoanal. Psychother.*, 5:547–565, 1976.
11. Lichtenberg, J. The development of the sense of self. *J. Am. Psychoanal. Assoc.*, 23:453–484, 1975.
12. Modell, A. *Object Love and Reality*. International Universities Press, New York, 1968.
13. Moore, B. Toward a clarification of the concept of narcissism. In: *The Psychoanalytic Study of the Child*, Vol. 30, pp. 243–276. Yale University Press, New Haven, 1975.
14. Pulver, S. Narcissism: The term and the concept. *J. Am. Psychoanal. Assoc.*, 18:319–341, 1970.
15. Rothstein, A. An exploration of the diagnostic term "Narcissistic Personality Disorder." *J. Am. Psychoanal. Assoc.*, 27:893–912, 1979.
16. Spitzer, R. et al. Personality Disorders; Narcissistic Personality Disorder, in *Diagnostic and Statistical Manual*, Third Edition, pp. 305, 315–317. American Psychiatric Association, Washington, D. C., 1980.
17. Stein, M. Book review: Kohut's *Restoration of the Self*. *J. Am. Psychoanal. Assoc.*, 27:665–681, 1979.
18. Teicholz, J. A selective review of the psychoanalytic literature on theoretical conceptualizations of narcissism. *J. Am. Psychoanal. Assoc.*, 26:831–863, 1978.

5

BORDERLINE PERSONALITY DISORDERS

George E. Gallahorn, M.D.

Introduction

In the past 30 years many articles and books have been written about Borderline Personality Disorder. The list of diagnostic labels applied to these patients suggests the difficulties encountered when an attempt is made to diagnose such patients primarily on the basis of symptoms. A partial list of diagnoses includes: Ambulatory Schizophrenia (24), "As-If" Personality (5), Borderline Schizophrenia (16), Borderline State (15), Incipient Schizophrenia (22), Latent Schizophrenia (2), Pseudoneurotic Schizophrenia (12), Pseudopsychopathic Schizophrenia (6), and Psychotic Character (18). In recent years articles by Gunderson and Singer (9) and Spitzer et al. (23) compiled data to clarify the concept of Borderline Personality. A broad heterogeneous group of patients who were called "Borderline" were subdivided into several Personality Disorders. Most of the patients fell into the categories of Schizotypal or Borderline Personality Disorder in DSM III (3). These diagnoses are made almost exclusively on behavior. Kernberg (13), who has written extensively on Borderline patients, utilizes a broader concept of a personality organization which could be found in a number of personality disorders as defined in DSM III. Many features, such as defenses which Kernberg describes in borderline personality organization, also may be found in the Borderline Personality Disorder. Thus, this chapter will focus on both the Borderline Personality Disorder as defined in DSM III and Borderline Personality Organization.

Diagnosis

The term "Borderline" does not refer to fluctuations in the patient's underlying pathology. There is no shifting from neurosis to psychosis and back again. There may be elements of neurotic and/or psychotic disturbances together with an underlying character organization which is resistant to change (13). This underlying personality disorder is manifested by intense fluctuations in interpersonal relations, mood, and self-image. In a review by

Gunderson and Singer of the descriptive literature on Borderline patients, these fluctuations were identified as significant features of the Borderline personality (9). The DSM III lists the following characteristics of the Borderline patient's long-term functioning:

A. At least five of the following are required:

1.) Impulsivity or unpredictability in at least two areas that are potentially self-damaging, e.g., spending, sex, gambling, substance use, shoplifting, overeating, physically self-damaging acts.
2.) A pattern of unstable and intense interpersonal relationships, e.g., marked shifts of attitude, idealization, devaluation, manipulation (consistently using others for one's own end).
3.) Inappropriate, intense anger or lack of control of anger, e.g., frequent displays of temper, constant anger.
4.) Identity disturbance manifested by uncertainty about several issues relating to identity, such as self-image, gender identity, long-term goals or career choice, friendship patterns, values, and loyalties, e.g., "Who am I?" "I feel like I am my sister when I am good."
5.) Affective instability: Marked shifts from normal mood to depression, irritability, or anxiety, usually lasting a few hours and only rarely more than a few days, with return to normal mood.
6.) Intolerance of being alone, e.g., frantic efforts to avoid being alone, depressed when alone.
7.) Physically self-damaging acts, e.g., suicidal gestures, self-mutilation, recurrent accidents or physical fights.
8.) Chronic feelings of emptiness or boredom.

B. If under 18, does not meet the criteria for Identity Disorder (3).

There are a number of other features which are frequently associated with the Borderline Personality. Transient psychotic episodes may occur. These are precipitated by stress, drugs, alcohol, or the transference (13). There usually is a paranoid quality to these episodes (9). Other features may be present. They are delinated most clearly by Kernberg's description of symptom constellation and ego defenses. The following material is a summary of Kernberg's concepts of Borderline Personality Organization (13).

Kernberg feels that two or more of the following symptom constellations are suggestive of Borderline personality organization, but none are pathognomonic. The constellations are: anxiety, polysymptomatic neurosis, polymorphous perverse sexual trends, classical prepsychotic personality structures, impulse neurosis and addictions, infantile, narcissistic, and masochistic personalities.

The type of anxiety experienced by Borderline patients is free floating, chronic, and diffuse. It can be extremely devastating to the patient suffering from it. This anxiety is difficult to distinguish from anxiety associated with anxiety states (3), and other symptoms must be present if the patient is to be diagnosed as Borderline.

Polysymptomatic neurosis includes:

a.) Multiple phobias especially those involving severe social inhibition.
b.) Obsessive-compulsive symptoms with rationalizing about the symptoms.
c.) Multiple elaborate bizarre conversion symptoms—especially those bordering on bodily hallucinations.
d.) Dissociative reactions, especially hysterical twilight states.
e.) Hypochondriasis of a severe nature, with social withdrawal.
f.) Paranoid hypochondriacal trends with any other symptomatic neurosis.

Classical prepsychotic personality structures include the Paranoid, Schizoid, and "hypomanic" (13) personalities. Paranoid and Schizoid are discussed in other chapters and will not be elaborated on here.

Impulse neurosis and addictions represent chronic repetitive ego syntonic outlets for instinctual needs. The impulses experienced by the patient are ego-dystonic when he is not in the throes of an impulsive episode. Patients with this symptomatology should be distinguished from "acting out" personality disorders. This latter group present a more generalized lack of impulse control and chaotic life-style.

Kernberg feels that the Borderline personality organization can exist as part of other personality disorders. The DSM III presents a somewhat similar view, although the Borderline patient is seen as having a personality disorder, rather than a personality organization. In Kernberg's view personality disorders with "infantile," "narcissistic," or "masochistic" traits may have a Borderline personality organization. He feels that these personalities are "lower level character disorders." The personality with infantile traits presents with marked oral conflicts and an aggressive demanding dependency on others. The personality with narcissistic traits has a strong need to be loved and admired. Relationships are superficial. There is little empathy for others, and they are valued only if they provide the narcissistic supplies needed by these patients. Personalities with masochistic traits exhibit marked self-destructiveness with self-mutilation. Relief of anxiety is associated with the act of self-mutilation, and there is often a mixture of primitive sexual and aggressive feelings discharged through this act.

All of the symptom constellations previously described are manifestations of ego weaknesses. A structural analysis of ego weaknesses is another approach to the diagnosis of Borderline personality. Kernberg states that there are three nonspecific manifestations of ego weakness:

1.) Lack of anxiety tolerance.
2.) Lack of impulse control.
3.) Lack of developed sublimatory channels.

Lack of anxiety tolerance may be difficult to determine in patients with chronic severe anxiety. However, Borderline patients often respond to any increase in anxiety with additional symptoms, alloplastic behavior, or ego repression (13).

Lack of impulse control was discussed previously. It should be reemphasized that this lack of impulse control is ego-syntonic during the act and usually is repetitive in nature. After the act, the patient dissociates this aspect of his personality from himself.

The lack of sublimatory channels is most curious. At times this appears to be a constitutionally determined weakness. Sociocultural factors must be considered also. The difficulties encountered in mobilizing hospitalized Borderline patients to participate in the occupational and recreational therapy programs attests to an incapacity to make use of sublimation. There is an almost phobic avoidance of sublimatory activities. Some patients may participate but their involvement is quite grim and compulsive.

An additional manifestation of ego weakness is the presence of primary process thinking. This thought disturbance occasionally may manifest itself during times of stress. In many cases, however, formal projective psychological testing is needed to demonstrate the pathological thought processes (9). Other types of psychological tests are not generally useful in the diagnosis of Borderline Personality.

There are five defensive operations that frequently are used by the Borderline patient. These are: splitting, primitive idealization, projective identification, denial, omnipotence, and devaluation (13). Splitting is the primary defense. Splitting refers to the active separation of mental representations of self and others into all good or all bad images. Consequently, at any particular time, the therapist and others may be seen by the patient as all good; and at another time, they may be seen by the patient as all bad.

In primitive idealization, external good objects are seen by the patient as all good. These good objects protect the patient from hostile bad objects.

Projective identification occurs when there is loss of self-object differentiation, and the unacceptable impulses which were originaliy projected onto the external object continue to be experienced by the patient. The patient consequently feels a need to overwhelm and control the object before the objects destroys him.

Omnipotence and devaluation are a result of the splitting in which the patient engages. Omnipotence is due to introjection of, and identification with, the idealized object. There also is a strong need to control the good object. This can be done in fantasy by omnipotence. When the good external object frustrates and disappoints, it is no longer useful to the patient, and devaluation of the object occurs.

The denial used by the Borderline patient is manifested by a lack of emotional appreciation by the patient of different and often opposite affective states. The patient is aware of his different reactions but cannot integrate these opposite affective states as coming from him and as relevant parts of him.

In summary, the Borderline patient has contradictory images of self and others. Consequently, there is no whole concept of self or others. External objects are idealized or devalued, and consequently are not dealt with realistically. In addition there is no realistic sense of self.

A clinical example will illustrate some of the personality characteristics of the Borderline patient as well as some associated symptomatic features.

> A. was a 19-year-old single Caucasian female who had been symptomatic since the age of 13. She had rage reactions towards her parents and friends. She would shift back and forth from idealization to devaluation of her parents and others as well as herself. She abused drugs. She had no sense of her own identity, and felt at times as if she might merge with others. The patient felt chronically empty and bored. A. also had compulsive bedtime rituals, dissociative episodes with wrist cutting, hypochondriacal worries about vomiting, and chronic severe anxiety.
>
> After several unsuccessful brief hospitalizations, the patient was admitted to a long-term hospital when she was 15 years old. During her inpatient treatment, there were intense affective shifts in relation to the therapist and other staff and patients. Only after significant therapeutic work was done on these shifts was A. able to be discharged and treated as an outpatient. She was 18 years old at the time of discharge.

Differential Diagnosis

Despite attempts to clarify the differential diagnosis of Borderline Personality, many problems in this area remain. The Borderline patient may have elements of psychosis, neurosis, and other personality disorders in his symptom picture. At times, Borderline patients may experience Brief Reactive Psychosis as an associated feature. In a general way, Borderline patients with this type of psychosis may be distinguished from other psychotic patients by the degree and intensity of the impairment of reality testing. Borderline patients maintain their capacity for reality testing until they are stressed, or under the influence of drugs or alcohol, or experience an intense transference reaction. The lack of reality testing in the Borderline patient is transient, while in other psychotic patients it is more pervasive and generalized.

Schizophrenia and Borderline Personality Disorders are confused more often than other psychoses. Perhaps this is why Schizophrenia is tied to the many diagnostic labels applied to the Borderline patient (e.g., Borderline Schizophrenia). Some patients in this Borderline Schizophrenic group are now categorized as Schizotypal Personality Disorders in DSM III (3). There are common periods of stress for both the Schizophrenic and the Borderline patient. Symptoms appear usually in late adolescence or early adulthood as patients attempt to master age-appropriate tasks, including separation from home and career choice. There are Borderline patients who arrive at partial solutions to these and other tasks, but then fall prey to the inevitable losses and disappointments of middle-age, such as children leaving home. Under these latter stresses patients initially may appear to be suffering from a major depression, but there is a hollow empty quality to the depressive affect. Kernberg feels this is a reflection of superego pathology on the part of the Borderline patient who cannot experience genuine depressive feelings (13).

Patients suffering from a full-blown Bipolar Disorder, Manic Type, are seldom confused with Borderline patients. However, if the patient is hypomanic or suffering from a Schizoaffective Psychosis, some problems of differential diagnosis may be encountered. However, in these diagnostic entities, the difficulties in object relations are of a type not encountered in Borderline patients.

Paranoid Disorders might be confused with Borderline patients because both groups of patients may have paranoid delusions and intense anger if a Borderline patient is experiencing a Brief Reactive Psychosis. However, once the patient reveals his well-formed delusional system, Borderline personality with a Brief Reactive Psychosis can be excluded.

Neurotic (Anxiety, Somatoform, Dissociative Disorders) patients are more difficult than psychotic patients to differentiate from Borderline Disorder patients. Neurotics may present with symptoms similar to those in the polysymptomatic neuroses mentioned previously. Unless the patient is under significant stress at the time of his evaluation, presence of a Borderline Personality may be missed. It is only under the influence of stress, alcohol, drugs, or the transference later in the therapeutic relationship that the patient manifests problems in ego boundaries. The neurotic maintains intact ego boundaries. This problem of boundaries and close interpersonal involvement leads to extremely chaotic interpersonal relationships. Ordinarily, these types of relationships are not found in the usual neurotic patient.

The differential diagnosis of Borderline Personality Disorder from other personality disorders is difficult at times. The DSM III (3) indicates that patients may be given the diagnosis of Borderline Personality as well as other personality disorders simultaneously. The personality disorders most likely to be confused with Borderline Personality are the Schizotypal, Histrionic, Narcissistic, and Antisocial Personality Disorders. Previously, "Borderline" probably included patients who are diagnosed now as Borderline Personality Disorder or Schizotypal Personality Disorder (3). The DSM III has separated these two groups of patients but some points of similarity remain. In the Schizotypal Personality, there are ideas of reference and paranoid ideation. These may be confused with the transient psychotic episodes of the Borderline patient. Perhaps the absence of precipitating factors could be helpful in suggesting a Schizotypal Personality. The social isolation of the Schizoptypal Personality may appear similar to a Borderline Personality who is viewing almost every individual as all bad. If there is a history of seeing others as all good, this would suggest that the patient is using the defense of splitting and is a Borderline Personality. Finally, affective instability would appear to be more consistent with the diagnosis of Borderline Personality.

A major feature of the Histrionic Personality Disorder is intense affective shifts. These shifts may appear similar to the affective instability seen in the Borderline patient. An identity disturbance which is frequently seen in Borderline patients usually would not be present in the Histrionic Personality Disorder.

The Narcissistic Personality Disorder utilizes ego defenses which are similar to those of the Borderline Personality Disorder. As a consequence the grandiosity, idealization, and rage of the Narcissistic Personality Disorder may be similar to the images of all good or all bad self and others found in the Borderline patient. The presence of an identity disturbance and physically self-damaging acts which are repetitive would be more consistent with the diagnosis of Borderline Personality Disorder.

Impulsivity, recklessness, and aggression may be found in the Antisocial Personality Disorder. There are similar traits in Borderline patients. The specific history of behavioral problems before the age of 15, as well as absence of guilt, would suggest any Antisocial Personality Disorder rather than a Borderline Personality Disorder.

Adolescence is a time of rapidly shifting emotions and exploring various identities, or, conversely, the adolescent may adopt the role of asceticism and renounce all feelings and impulses. In either instance the adolescent may appear to be suffering from an Identity Disorder (3) rather than the normal adolescent identity confusion (7). The diagnosis of Identity Disorder in an adolescent should be made only after it is seen that he lacks an integrated self-concept. This matter is discussed further in another chapter on childhood and adolescence.

The differentiation of organic states from the Borderline Personality may be difficult at times. Patients who have psychomotor epilepsy can experience outbursts of rage, anxiety, and feelings of unreality. These symptoms are commonly found in Borderline Personalities. An EEG with a sleep record may be helpful, although temporal lobe spikes may not appear. The examiner in any case should closely evaluate the patient's ego function and object relations. Even if they are suggestive of a Borderline Personality Disorder, the patient may still have psychomotor seizures, and a trial of anticonvulsants should be considered.

Minimal brain dysfunction (Attention Deficit Disorder) as a major factor in a patient's appearing to have a Borderline Personality has been discussed by Hartocollis (10). In his series of 15 minimally brain-damaged patients most would have been considered Borderline Personalities. He feels that these patients suffer from congenital ego defects. They can be distinguished from Borderline patients by mild signs of organicity on psychological testing and soft neurologic signs. This group responds very poorly to conventional psychotherapeutic methods. They seem to respond better to a directive-supportive approach which includes an acknowledgment of possible organicity by the patient and his parents.

The use of consciousness-altering drugs poses a problem in the differential diagnosis of Borderline Personality. Patients who are experiencing the effects of drugs such as LSD may appear Borderline because of the feelings of unreality that are common effects of drug ingestion. These patients also may develop new neurotic symptoms to compensate for the ego boundary disruption that acute ingestion of hallucinogens may precipitate. Patients who are experiencing flashbacks manifested by anxiety and feelings of unreality may be confused with the Borderline patient. Conversely, Borderline patients who are suddenly stressed may rationalize their symptoms as a flashback. Finally, there is little doubt that hallucinogenic drugs which disrupt ego boundaries can be responsible for making a Borderline patient markedly symptomatic.

Psychodynamics

Psychodynamic theories of the Borderline patient are based partly on the patient's interactions in psychotherapy or psychoanalysis, and partly on the interactions between parents and Borderline adolescents. From these interactions, certain inferences are drawn about the patient's development in infancy and early childhood. Kernberg feels that Borderline patients have either a constitutional excess of aggression or a history of extreme frustration in the first year of life (13). In either case, there are intense aggressive feelings. These intense feelings interfere with the normal process that takes place between 18 and 36 months of life in which the infant integrates images of an all good mother and an all bad mother into a single entity—mother. There is similar integration of mental representations of others as well as the self. Because the aggression is so intense, the child who will eventually become Borderline fears that its rage and hate towards the all bad mother will overwhelm its love for the all good mother, and she will be annihilated. Therefore, in order to preserve the all good mother, the child maintains two separate mental images—the all good mother and the all bad mother (splitting). A similar process takes place with mental representations of others and self.

Masterson and Mahler state that the trauma occurs during the rapprochement subphase of separation—individuation (18 to 36 months) (17, 20). They feel that the child has a mother who is Borderline. This mother cannot tolerate the child separating, and whenever the child makes an attempt at separation, the mother withdraws her love. This results in the child feeling abandoned, and there are accompanying affects of depression, rage, guilt, fear, passivity, helplessness, emptiness, and void (19). Whenever there is a separation problem in later life, the patient experiences similar feelings.

Although Kernberg and Masterson and Mahler disagree on the etiology of the psychodynamics, all recognize the primitive affects and defenses that are present in adolescence and adulthood.

Therapy

Anna Freud has commented that if she presents two cases from which a resident in her clinic is to choose—almost invariably a Borderline patient is selected in lieu of a classical neurotic patient (21). The ever increasing numbers of articles and books on Borderline patients also bespeaks such interest. I suspect that most therapists are challenged by the Borderline Personality because of these patients' potential for improvement. The presence of transient psychosis and intense shifting affects conveys to the therapist an impression of severe regression and illness. Yet, the intact aspect of the patient's ego is evidence of a much higher level of functioning that can be attained. Thus, the stage is set for those of us not heroic enough to undertake long-term work with chronic schizophrenics to act out rescue fantasies with Borderline Personality Disorder patients. It is imperative that the therapist of a Borderline patient closely examine his countertransference feelings to avoid using the patient as the object of omnipotent fantasies, or retaliating against the patient when he is seen as a devalued object by the patient.

Most authors feel that classic psychoanalytic treatment with the patient lying on the couch and free associating is risky. Some authorities such as Giovacchini (4) and Kernberg (13) do recommend this form of therapy for selected Borderline patients. However, Kernberg feels that the majority of Borderline patients are best treated in psychoanalytic psychotherapy. In summarizing his approach, Kernberg states, "In short, technical neutrality, attention to abstinence in the transference, preservation of the internal freedom for analyzing the transference, and, introspectively only, the countertransference components of the analyst's emotional reaction are intimately linked aspects of the overall technical approach to Borderline patients" (14).

Psychotherapy can be intensive with a strong emphasis on change or it can be supportive of the patient through many crises over an extended period of time. Reality issues must be attended to in therapy. At times the patient may neglect the demands of reality and not discuss such important issues as the loss of a job or school difficulties.

Another important issue in psychotherapy is limit setting. Borderline patients frequently are involved in destructive acting out, and it is imperative that the therapist let the patient know that such behavior is unacceptable and will not be tolerated. In one's outpatient office it may be necessary to restrain a patient who is attempting to destroy something, or injure himself or the therapist. Often though, the acting out takes place outside of the office. The therapist must be on guard to intervene against any such regressive behavior. At the same time the patient must be allowed autonomy and freedom to grow.

One final aspect of the individual psychotherapy of the Borderline patient must be reemphasized—the transference and countertransference. These patients may develop a psychotic transference of a transient nature. Usually the therapist is the idealized object. However, this positive relationship can shift rapidly to a strong negative reaction, with the therapist being perceived as all bad. It requires much self-awareness on the part of the therapist to survive the onslaught of these transference feelings and strike the right balance between empathy and detachment, between limit setting and nondirectiveness.

Borderline patients can be treated with group therapy. Often the group is composed of a number of seriously ill patients, and the group's task is a supportive one. The difficulty in managing an emerging psychotic transference in a more exploratory group setting mitigates the inclusion of Borderline patients in this type of group. If they are included, they often drop out as problems around feelings of intimacy emerge.

The Borderline patient often is hospitalized because of the appearance of psychotic symptoms during times of stress. Some patients do well with brief crisis-oriented hospitalization during which environmental manipulation can lead to at least a partial resolution of the crisis.

Short- and long-term hospitalization usually are precipitated by a gradual decline in functioning during a life crisis such as graduation from school. In the case of short-term hospitalization, a therapeutic alliance can be established with the patient, and an attempt can be made to add some structure and stability to the patient's life before discharge. Long-term hospitalization (6 months to several years) is indicated for those patients with extremely weak egos—particularly those that engage in chronic self-destructive behavior. The milieu of the long-term hospital provides a situation in which the patient engages in splitting with significant staff. All staff must work hard to avoid being caught up in this splitting (Main's Syndrome) (1, 18).

Medication can sometimes aid in the treatment of the Borderline patient. However, because authors have had difficulty agreeing to specific characteristics of the Borderline patient, no thorough studies regarding the use of medication have been done. It has been observed that during periods of stress when the patient is experiencing a transient psychotic episode, one of the major tranquilizers can be useful in decreasing anxiety and firming up loose ego boundaries. Borderline patients usually do not do well on major tranquilizers when things are going relatively smoothly. They complain of distortions of body image and feelings of depersonalization. For this reason it is inadvisable to insist that the patient remain on major tranquilizers chronically. Also patients complain that medications interfere with their attempts at adaption and problem solving (11).

The apparent depression that is experienced by Borderline patients often tempts the therapist to use tricyclic antidepressants. There are no studies showing these two medications to be effective with this group of patients. Needless to say, amphetamines should never be used because of their potential for abuse. Finally, the minor tranquilizers are not recommended for most Borderline patients. These patients have a high potential for drug abuse. The antianxiety effect of minor tranquilizers provides some initial relief from anxiety. However, because of the chronic nature of the patient's disorder, the medication must be taken regularly. As tolerance develops, the dose is increased—often to addictive levels.

REFERENCES

1. Adler, G. Hospital treatment of borderline patients. Am. J. Psychiatry, *130:*32–36, 1973.
2. American Psychiatric Association. Diagnostic and Statistical Manual of Mental Disorders, II. American Psychiatric Association, Washington, D. C., 1968.
3. American Psychiatric Association. Diagnostic and Statistical Manual of Mental Disorders, III. American Psychiatric Association, Washington, D. C., 1980.
4. Boyer, L., and Giavacchini, P. *Psychoanalytic Treatment of Characterological and Schizophrenic Disorders.* Science House, New York, 1967.
5. Deutsch, H. Some forms of emotional disturbance and their relationship to schizophrenia. Psychoanal. Q., *11:*301–321. 1942.
6. Dunaif, S. L., and Hoch, P. H. Pseudopsychopathic schizophrenia. In: *Psychiatry and the Law,* P. Hoch and J. Zubin (Eds.). Grune & Stratton, New York, 1955.
7. Erikson, E. H. *Identity, Youth, and Crisis.* W. W. Norton, New York, 1968.
8. Frosch, J. The psychotic character: Clinical psychiatric considerations. Psychiatr. Q., *38:* 81–96, 1964.
9. Gunderson, J., and Singer, M. Defining Borderline patients: An overview. Am. J. Psychiatry, *132:*1–10, 1975.
10. Hartocollis, P. The syndrome of minimal brain dysfunction in young adult patients. Bull. Menninger Clin., *32:*102–114, 1968.
11. Havens, L. Some difficulties in giving schizophrenic and borderline patients medication. Psychiatry, *31:*44–50, 1968.
12. Hoch, P. H., and Polatin, P. Pseudoneurotic forms of schizophrenia. Psychiatr. Q., *23:*248–276, 1949.
13. Kernberg, O. Borderline conditions and pathological narcissism. Jason Aronson, New York, 1975.
14. Kernberg, O., Technical considerations in the treatment of borderline personality organization. J. Am. Psychoanal. Assoc., *24:*793–829, 1976.
15. Knight, R. P. Borderline states. Bull. Menninger Clin., *17:*1–12, 1953.
16. Knight, R. P. Management and psychotherapy of the borderline schizophrenic patient. Bull. Menninger Clin., *17:*139–150, 1953.
17. Mahler, M. A study of the separation-individuation process and its possible application to borderline phenomenas in the psychoanalytic situation. Psychoanal. Study Child, *26:* 403–424, 1971.
18. Main, T. The ailment. Br. J. Med. Psychol., *30:*129–145, 1957.
19. Masterson, J. Psychotherapy of the borderline adult. Brunner/Mazel, New York, 1976.
20. Masterson, J., and Rinsley, D. The borderline syndrome: The role of the mother in the genesis and psychic structure of the borderline personality. Int. J Psychoanal., *56:*163–178, 1975.
21. Philadelphia Academy of Psychoanalysis. *Panel on the Ego and the Mechanisms of Defense.* Philadelphia, April 1973.
22. Pious, W. Obsessive-compulsive symptoms in an incipient schizophrenic. Psychoanal. Q., *19:*327–351, 1950.
23. Spitzer, R., et al. Crossing the border into borderline personality and borderline schizophrenia. Arch. Gen. Psychiatry, *36:*17–24, 1978.
24. Zillborg, G. Ambulatory schizophrenia. Psychiatry, *4:*149–155, 1941.

6

HISTRIONIC PERSONALITY

Joe P. Tupin, M.D.

Histrionic Personality

The concept of hysteria dates from ancient times; the history has been reviewed by Veith (36). The syndrome has been recently reviewed by Horowitz and others (17). In Diagnostic and Statistical Manual III (3), the term Histrionic Personality replaces the Hysterical Personality of DSM II (2). Furthermore, the term hysterical is removed from the DSM III in other areas also. Confusion about the concept of the terminology was the cause of these changes (18). In order to discuss, histrionic personality in the various uses of the related terms must be briefly considered.

Hysteria may denote a transient loss of control, usually with both affective and behavioral elements, often resulting from an overwhelming stress. This use of "hysteria" is often found in the lay press and related publications. Epidemic hysteria is used to denote shared, transient complaints in groups, usually with no physical findings which are often associated with some stressful event.

Hysterical neurosis is defined in DSM II nomenclature (2) as a condition "characterized by an involuntary psychogenic loss or disorder of function." This diagnosis includes two syndrome types, conversion reaction, and dissociative reaction.

In DSM III the hysterical neuroses have been divided, and the term "hysteria" is no longer associated with them. Some appear in the somatiform disorders group which includes somatization disorder (Briquet's) (8), conversion disorder, psychalgia, and hypochrondiasis. The main point of this separation is to remove the term hysteria which has been badly contaminated in the past, being used to refer both to the personality disorder and neuroses. Furthermore, conversion disorder and Briquet's are considered not to significantly overlap with histrionic personality disorder, although there is some debate about this matter. Hysterical Neuroses, dissociative type (DSM III), are grouped in a separate category, Dissociative Disorders, which includes psychogenic amnesia, psychogenic fugue, multiple personality, and depersonalization disorder.

Another relevant DSM III category is factitious disorder conditions which are characterized by physical or psychological symptoms that are voluntarily initiated by the patient. The motivation behind this may vary—there may be no apparent goal other than to assume the role of patient. It is presumed that motivation to become a patient bears a significant psychological root. The symptoms may be either psychological or physical. Malingering, on the other hand, refers to the patient who produces symptoms voluntarily but for a goal that is obviously recognizable.

Hysterical Personality was defined in the American Psychiatric Association Diagnostic and Statistical Manual of Mental Disorders II as a disorder "characterized by excitability, emotional instability, over-reactivity, ... self-dramatization, ... attention-seeking [immaturity, vanity, and unusual dependence]." This diagnosis is made from observations of manifest personality traits. Levels of libidinal fixation, mechanisms of defense, and ego structure are not relevant in establishing the diagnosis. In DSM III, hysterical personality disorder no longer appears, rather it is replaced with the term "histrionic personality disorder." The essential feature "is behavior that is overtly dramatic, reactive, and intensely expressed, with characteristic disturbances in interpersonal relationships." The individual may "act out a role such as 'victim' or 'princess' without being aware of it." The person is described as being excitable, irrational, and with angry outbursts or tantrums. They may be seen by others as being shallow and lacking in genuineness, although superficially charming and appealing. They may become demanding and egocentric, inconsiderate, and may exhibit manipulative suicidal threats, gestures, or attempts. Often the individuals are attractive and seductive. Overt behavior in both both sexes is often a caricature of femininity. Dysphoric moods, disinterest in intellectual achievement, impressionability, suggestibility, obstinance, and complaints of poor health are common.

They may exhibit substance abuse, depressed mood, brief reactive psychosis, conversion disorders, somatization disorder, and suicide attempts.

Diagnostic criteria for Histrionic Personality Disorder can be found in Appendix A. These criteria are characteristic of the individual's current and long-term functioning, are not limited to episodes of illness, and cause either significant impairment in social or occupational functional or subjective distress. Blacker and Tupin (6) have suggested that the diagnosis be based on the finding of aggression, dependency, sexual problems, sexual provocativeness, obstinacy, exhibitionism, egocentricity, and emotionality. These behaviors will have different manifestations in males and females.

Hysterical psychosis is not included in the American Psychiatric Association's official nomenclature. However, recent interest (16, 21, 24) in this syndrome has documented its existence and emphasized the differentiation from other psychogenic psychoses. It is usually short lived, is precipitated by actual object loss or other significant stress, and has no long-term sinister prognosis of deterioration. In DSM III hysterical psychosis does not exist, but brief reactive psychosis has been introduced as characterized as a brief psychosis of at least a few hours' duration but lasting not more than 1 week. The sudden onset immediately after severe emotional stress and eventually terminating in complete recovery to the prepsychotic state. There may be an occasional symptomatic similarity to schizophrenia, but the course and prognosis are different.

Histrionic Personality Disorder

Early writers, Abraham (1) and Reich (33), stressed the libido theory and postulated that the Histrionic Personality disorder was a result of fixation at the level of early genital experience. Others, particularly Freud (13) and Marmor (29), argued that oral traits were also important in understanding the Histrionic Personality. Lastly, Marmor (29) and Knight (20) emphasized the contribution of the ego to the complete understanding of this personality disturbance. These authors set the stage for a debate about whether there are two types of Histrionic Personality disorders—one "genital" (the true disorder), and the other "oral" in origin, or only one "disorder" with a mixture of the traits.

More recently, experts have emphasized that hysterical traits may characterize a variety of psychosexual levels of development. Their arguments have been summarized by Lazare (23), who suggests that there is a continuum of personality pathologies exhibiting hysterical traits. He suggests that this spectrum of disturbance may be understood by considering the two polarities of the continuum—the good or healthy hysteric (genital) and a bad or sick hysteric (oral).

Chodoff and Lyons (10), in their 1953 review, identified the following personality traits associated with the personality disorder: (a) dependence; (b) egocentricity; (c) emotionality; (d) exhibitionism; (e) fear of sexuality; (f) sexual provocativeness; and (g) suggestibility. Cognitive and interpersonal characterizations have been suggested by Berblinger (5) and Horowitz (17).

The first seven of these traits have been demonstrated to occur consistently in women receiving the diagnosis. Lazare et al. (24) was able to distinguish between Oral, Obsessive, and Histrionic Personality patterns, although a number of oral and obsessive personality traits were noted to typify patients with Histrionic Personality disorders. This observation is compatible with the view that the Histrionic Personality disorder is a continuum crossing a number of psychosexual levels. This research used rating scale data which was then factor-analyzed, revealing three factors which correspond closely with the diagnosis of Histrionic, Oral, and Obsessive Personality.

The characteristics of the two ends of the continuum were carefully reviewed by Lazare (23) in 1971. Tables 6.1, 6.2, and 6.3 summarize Lazare with added information from Berblinger (5), Blinder (7), Cleghorn (11), Halleck (15), and Blacker and Tupin (6).

TABLE 6.1
Personality Traits

Healthy (good or assertive)	Ambitious, competitive, buoyant, energetic, strict standards of behavior, aggressive, vain, histrionic, insensitive, overtalkative, coquettish, young appearing, emotionally expressive and labile, suspicious, impulsive, uneasy with women, competitive-destructive with men, successful, accomplished, caricature of femininity.
Sick (bad or dependent)	Low self-esteem, passive, dependent, helpless, withdrawn, pouty, obstinate, unpredictable, flighty, tentative, shy, sensitive, communicatively unclear, suggestible, compliant, frequent complaints of physical problems, feels over-whelmed, demanding, diminished guilt.

TABLE 6.2
Life History

Healthy (good or assertive)	Frequently oldest, father's favorite, mother's assistant, responsible and engrossed in home perceives mother as uninteresting, sexually frigid, nonworthy of emulation; the family may regard the patient as juvenile, inefficient, and cute. Ingratiating, emotional, often sexually inhibited, chooses older or unavailable men, may dominate in marriage; communicatively vague, strong emphasis on femininity, often successful in academics and vocations. Makes striking use of cosmetics, clothes to emphasize femininity and attractiveness, retains friendships, may belong to clubs or gangs in preadolescence, achievement and peer success in latency.
Sick (bad or dependent)	Often youngest child in family, described as cold, quarrelsome, ungiving, remote, mother perhaps absent, passive, or depressed, may have died early or have been ill; father may be seductive, dominant, or inaccessible; marital instability or great tolerance for abusive spouses, continued no true latency; preadolescence characterized by withdrawal, distorted peer relations with regression and demandingness, much fantasy, little achievement, poor peer relationships based on expectations of rescue and nurture, fears of rejection, childish, sexual promiscuity in exchange for nurturance and protection, academically and educationally eratic, poor tolerance of inner personal stress, and reacts with impulsivity, depression, psychosis, or conversion symptoms.

The personality type described by Perley and Guze (30) was initially labeled "hysteria," subsequently Briquet's Syndrome, and in DSM III is called Somatization Disorder. It is defined as a stable syndrome distinct from conversion reactions and other psychiatric disorders. It is characterized by an early onset, usually before age 20, almost invariably before age 30, appearing most exclusively in females and involving multiple physical complaints, sexual symptoms, anxiety and depression, multiple hospitalizations, and a high incidence of surgery. Six-year follow-up studies done by this group emphasize the stability of this syndrome and point to the early onset of this pattern of behavior. They argue that this syndrome is closely related to hysterical disorders on the basis of the physical preoccupation, exhibitionism, sexual difficulties, suggestibility, dependence, and emotionality.

These authors (14) have identified 10 categories of the symptoms and make the diagnosis on the presence of at least 25 symptoms in nine of the 10 categories (see Table 6.4).

TABLE 6.3
Psychodynamics

Healthy (good or assertive)	Oedipal conflicts predominate, obsessional defenses frequent, sexual issues are prominent, regression, manipulation, and control common, external reality, integrated ego and superego functions, has basic trust, can retain object relations, effective in insight-oriented psychotherapy.
Sick (bad or dependent)	Oral conflicts prominent, condensation of genital and pregenital aims, poor integration of ego function, primitive sexually, confusion of internal and external reality, poor tolerance of tension, poor object relationships, periodic emotionality, may use alcohol or drugs, physical complaints and operations common, suicidal gestures, frigid, unaware of emotional problems within themselves, defensive failure leads to acting out, depression, distortions in internalized object relations.

TABLE 6.4
*Criteria for Hysteria**

Group 1	Group 4	Group 8
Headaches	Breathing difficulty	Sexual indifference
Sickly	Palpitation	Frigidity
Group 2	Anxiety attacks	Dyspareunia
Blindness	Chest pain	Other sexual difficulties
Paralysis	Dizziness	Vomiting during 9 months of pregnancy or hospitalized for hyperemesis gravidarum
Anesthesia	Group 5	
Aphonia	Anorexia	
Fits or convulsions	Weight loss	Group 9
Unconsciousness	Marked fluctuations in weight	Back pain
Amnesia		Joint pain
Deafness	Nausea	Extremity pain
Hallucinations	Abdominal bloating	Burning pains of the sexual organs, mouth, or rectum
Urinary retention	Food intolerances	
Trouble walking	Diarrhea	Other bodily pains
Other conversion symptoms	Constipation	Group 10
	Group 6	Nervousness
Group 3	Abdominal pain	Fears
Fatigue	Vomiting	Depressed feelings
Lump in throat	Group 7	Need to quit working or inability to carry on regular duties because of feeling sick
Fainting spells	Dysmenorrhea	
Visual blurring	Menstrual irregularity	
Weakness	Amenorrhea	Crying easily
Dysuria	Excessive bleeding	Feeling life was hopeless
		Thinking a good deal about dying
		Wanting to die
		Thinking of suicide
		Suicide attempts

* Reprinted from Guze et al. (14).

Origins of Behavior

Psychodynamics. MacKinnon and Michels (27) and Blacker and Tupin (6) have summarized the psychoanalytic theory and note that the future hysteric developed an early pattern where infantile struggles with parents were decided in her favor on the basis of dramatic or troublesome behavior. There may be conflict between the parents which the patient learns to exploit.

For the *female* the mother may have been a weak identification model with conflict about her own femininity or she may actually be unavailable through illness, death, or severe psychiatric difficulty. The father may be withdrawn and critical of the mother's behavior. The mother may be resentful or envious of men. Affection is difficult for both parents and may be prominent only when the child is ill. Misbehavior may go unpunished through the child's manipulative skills and conflict between parents, thus paving the way for impulsive acting out as an adult. Early deprivation may make the child vulnerable to subsequent parental conflict.

As manipulative and often seductive skills develop in the female child, these are used to capture the father's attention. The father himself may be more comfortable with a female child than with his adult, envious, perhaps castrating wife. Furthermore, he may be flattered by the child's attention and subtly reward the sexual characteristics of the manipulation. This attention may bolster his sagging adult image; he is a victim of the wife's hostility.

As the female hysteric approaches puberty, the father becomes increasingly uncomfortable with her femininity. Since she may lack the firm feminine identity because of the faulty relationship with the mother, she may develop a period of tomboyish behavior. The erotic relationship between the father and daughter becomes further denied during puberty, and she may see father as more capricious and unpredictable. Thus she feels unwanted by both parents and may turn to membership in clubs, early dating, heterosexual behavior, and other uses of her manipulative and seductive skills to make up for this lack. Frequently, this may lead to popularity with her peers but often these relationships may be superficial and unrewarding since they do not comfort the deep need for affection and closeness that stems from early childhood. She maintains relationships at a superficial level for fear of disappointment and rejection, as with the parents, and thus tends to exploit and manipulate those around her for temporary satisfaction. The manipulations, if unsuccessful, may lead to more emotional and dramatic outbursts which may serve the purpose of controlling the people around her. The unresolved oedipal situation, which was characterized by a faulty identification with mother and an ambivalent sexualized relationship with father, has not left the female hysteric with her skills for establishing appropriate peer relationships. She frequently finds herself more comfortable in the company of men although she is fearful of the sexual implications of an intimate involvement, leading to sexual problems, often frigidity. Paradoxically, her most successful technique with men is one of nonverbal, coy seductiveness—a behavior she is frequently unaware of—and she may be quite surprised when responded to. Likewise, her distant relationship with mother leaves her ill prepared for genuine relationships with feminine peers by whom she feels threatened and potentially attacked because of her success with men. In some patients there may even be a deeply repressed sexual desire for women.

As she becomes more obviously feminine and sexual, the family imposes more strenuous controls. The girl in turn feels internal pressures to regress. She wants to avoid being the feminine object in direct conflict with mother for father's affection. This emerging sexuality further stimulates the latent eroticism between herself and father which, of course, must be denied. In the more primitive or oral hysteric this may be a time of significant regression marked by social withdrawal, extremely unsatisfying personal relationships, and sexual promiscuity. The latter serves the purpose of attracting some attention and nurturance from those around her.

In an effort to solidify her shaky feminine identity, the patient may be particularly preoccupied with adopting feminine characteristics to the point of bizarreness or exaggeration. This stance may be characterized by the overuse of cosmetics, flamboyant, sexual dress, and mannerisms inappropriate to the social situation. Adolescense and early adulthood may be marked by a variety of turbulent "love affairs," transient physical complaints, and alternating periods of gregarious socialization, and withdrawal-depression. The more aggressive and stable (good) the hysteric, the more likely she is to achieve success in college or work during this period; the more passive and regressed (oral) the individual, the more chaotic and desperate the behavior becomes. It frequently culminates in an early marriage to the first available suitor in a desperate effort to seek nurturance and stability.

The male may have a stronger admixture of obsessive traits or he may be an overt homosexual. Identification is more with mother who herself may be a hysteric and so mannerisms follow a caricature of femininity. Father may be withdrawn, hypercritical, and subtly aggressive toward the son, alternating his behavior with periods of disinterest, withdrawal, and absence.

Biological. A neurobiological theory has been advanced by Ludwig (29). That author believes that the basic defect in hysteria is biological, stemming from two instinctive patterns: (a) violent motor reaction, and (b) sham death reflex. The violent motor reaction is described as an "instinctive defense reaction against disturbing or external stimuli." A dangerous situation may be real or fantasied and once the "overproduction of aimless motions" occurs and is successful it is then reinforced. Examples of symptoms arising from this matrix include fugue states, convulsive paroxysms, and similar states. The sham death reflex is noted in animals to be "characterized by partial loss of reaction to outer stimuli and often a well marked analgesia." Symptoms arising from this characteristic include twilight and dreamy states, various spells and fits, blindness, deafness, and analgesia. Ludwig then goes on to suggest that operant conditioning and regressive activity then complete this symptomatic picture. However, he is not clear in differentiating conversion reactions and Hysterical Personality.

He draws from a number of other investigators a concept of "selective depression of awareness of a bodily function brought on by corticofugal inhibition of afferent stimulation at the level of the brain stem reticular formation." This, he concludes, is an attention dysfunction representing the neurophysiological basis for the hysterical disorder leading to "a constant state of distraction manifested by a disassociation between attention and certain sources of afferent stimulation with a simultaneous diversion of attention to non-symptom related areas." He then points out how this might account for memory dysfunction, dysfunctions of attention, gaiting control, and field articulation, all of which he believes to be characteristic of the hysteric. This is an interesting, new hypothesis which merits extensive review.

General Information

Incidence. Arkonac and Guze (4) have suggested the incidence of hysteria to be about 2% in the general population and about 15% among female relatives of hysterics. He also pointed to the high incidence of alcoholism and sociopathy in male relatives. There is no incidence data for Hysterical Personalities per se. Clinical experience would suggest that it is a rather common entity. Halleck (15) suggests that the high incidence reflects the feminine role expectations in American society which, when translated through childrearing practices, produce a continuum from normal femininity to pathological characteristics. Detailed material is presented in Horowitz (17).

Presenting Complaints. Somatic complaints, sexual difficulties, depression, "nervousness," suicidal gestures, or marital difficulties are common initial complaints. These symptoms frequently occur when the hysteric's life-style causes interpersonal conflict or when cherished attributes begin to fail from age or other causes.

Family History. It has been previously noted that there is a high incidence of alcoholism and sociopathy in male relatives, and hysteria and some sociopathy in female relatives (4).

Prognosis and Complications. As with all personality disorders, the pattern ordinarily begins at adolescence, is well established by the mid-20s and early 30s, and persists throughout life. Aging presents particular difficulties to these people with the narcissistic, exhibitionistic characteristics. Often in the early 40s or 50s, as beauty fades and sexual desirability lessens, depression and anxiety develop. Physical complaints become more prominent, and sexual promiscuity may ensue, further complicating marital difficulties. Other complications include the emergence of brief reactive psychosis, conversion reactions, suicidal gestures, depression, and alcohol and drug abuse.

Although a common complication of Hysterical Personality disorder, conversion reactions may occur in association with various types of psychopathology (10, 35).

Incidence in Men. Much has been made in literature about the puzzling absence of this personality type in men. Attention has been drawn by some authors (11) to the fact that this disturbance is associated with male homosexuality. Luisada et al. (19) reviewed the history of the diagnosis of histrionic personality and hysteria generally in men and made several important points. Chodoff and Lyons (10) first suggested that personality disorder should be separate from conversion reactions and furthermore felt that the male with the personality disorder would be a passive homosexual. Conversely, Cameron (9) suggested that, rather than femininity, the "Don Juan" factor would dominate a type of supermale. Malmquist and Halleck (15, 28) supported this, and furthermore Halleck suggested men might tend toward sociopathy. Other authors, Lindberg and Lindgard (25) and MacKinnon and Michels (27), furthered the development of the understanding of the male with histrionic personality disorder. Luisada concludes the summary of the history with the following: "Those who agree about the existence of the male hysterical personalities have thus described passive, effeminate, homosexuals or Don Juans, exuding masculinity."

Luisada, in his own study of 27 men who fitted the DSM III criteria, found that they generally came in for treatment between the ages of 15 and 25 from the cause of pressure from others. Frequently, there were suicidal gestures, often with an alternate diagnosis of passive-aggressive personality or alcohol or drug abuse problems. Brief psychosis occurred in some. Conversion symptoms were rare, as were other physical complaints. Excess surgery was not seen. In the family history the father was described as unassertive or absent and there was a high incidence of mental illness, particularly alcoholism.

These patients had a low educational achievement with occupational instability and trouble in the military, often with a dishonorable discharge. Most were heterosexual and 50% had been married; however, there were only 2 stable marriages at the time of this study. Generally, the sexual relationships were unrewarding. There was a high incidence of alcohol and criminal behavior in this population drawn from a state hospital and community clinics. There was some exaggeration of both feminine and masculine traits, but this was not typical of all of the patients.

Findings of Luisada et al. (19) and subsequent review by Blacker and Tupin (6) suggested that the male with histrionic personality disorder is not the "caricature of femininity" previously suggested by earlier authorities, but rather is present as two types—both a caricature of femininity and masculinity, with some patients not achieving an excessive expression of behavior. Blacker and Tupin (6) have reviewed the psychodynamics associated with the male hysteric and in fact they are the reciprocal of the female—the failed relationship with the father and subsequent identification or sexualization of the relationship with the mother. It may be well to suggest that these insights may seem to suggest that the central defect is with the development of an appropriate gender role identification and thus disturbance can be conceived as a caricature of sexuality. For males, of course, this will have a predominance of antisocial features in our culture. A more thorough review is contained in Blacker and Tupin (6).

Treatment

Psychotherapy is the basic treatment for personality disorders. The healthier, good hysteric seems to respond well to psychoanalytically oriented psychotherapy and probably also will benefit from appropriate group therapies, including marital and family therapy. The more primitive, bad or sick hysteric may respond better to goal-limited, supportive psychotherapy. Decompensation to depression or psychosis should justify the judicious use of appropriate psychopharmacological agents. Transference and cognitive issues must be carefully managed (17).

Differential diagnosis should include primary depression, anxiety reactions, organic disease, malingering, psychophysiological-psychosomatic reaction, drug and alcohol abuse, somatization disorder, and personality disorders including Borderline, Narcissistic, Antisocial, and Dependent types.

Anxiety reactions center on cardiovascular and respiratory findings and are only confused with hysteria because of the somatic complaints.

Depression, likewise, can focus on somatic complaints with fatigue, anorexia, weight loss, insomnia, constipation, and pain syndromes. Depressed affect and the absence of preexisting hysterical personality traits aid in the diagnosis of depression, although they may coexist.

Organic disease must always be considered when physical complaints are involved. Conversely, overemphasis on organic etiology of the complaint to the exclusion of the psychogenic aspects can produce inordinate bias in both the patient and the physician.

Malingering, the most difficult situation of all, must be judged against previous personality patterns and outside validation.

Hypochrondriasis, a term denoting a preoccupation with physical complaints and body function, has been related to a number of primary diagnoses, e.g., Hysterical Personality, involutional psychosis. In the context of this review it would probably best fit as another term of hysteria as described by Perley and Guze.

REFERENCES

1. Abraham, K. Selected Papers on Psychoanalysis. Basic Books, New York, 1960.
2. American Psychiatric Association. Diagnostic and Statistical Manual of Mental Disorders, Ed. 2. American Psychiatric Association, Washington, D. C. 1968.
3. American Psychiatric Association. Diagnostic and Statistical Manual of Mental Disorders, Ed. 2. American Psychiatric Association, Washington, D. C. 1980.
4. Arkonac, O., and Guze, S. A family of hysteria. N. Engl. J. Med., 268:239–242, 1963.
5. Berblinger, K. W. The quiet hysteric and her captive respondent. Dis. Nerv. System., 21:1–4, 1960.
6. Blacker, K. H., and Tupin, J. P. Hysteria and hysterical structures: Developmental and social theories. In: *Hysterical Personality*, M. J. Horowitz (Ed.), Ch. 2, pp. 95–142. Jason Aronson, New York, 1977, pp. 95–142.
7. Blinder, M. G. The husterical personality. Psychiatry, 29:227–235, 1966.
8. Briquet, P. *Traite' Clinique et Thérapeutique à l'Hystérie.* Baillière, Paris, 1859.
9. Cameron, N. Personality development and psychopathology: A dynamic approach, Houghton-Mifflin, Boston, 1963.
10. Chodoff, P., and Lyons, H. Hysteria—the hysterical personality in hysterical conversion. Am. J. Psychiatry, 114:734–740, 1958.
11. Cleghorn, R. A. Hysterical personality and conversion-theoretical aspects. Can. Psychiatr. Assoc. J., 14:553–567, 1969.
12. Easser, B. R., and Lesser, S. R. Hysterical personality—a reevaluation. Psychoanal. Q., 34: 389–405, 1965.
13. Freud, S. Hysteria. In: *Collected Papers*, Vol. 1. Hogarth Press, London, 1955.
14. Guze, S. B., Woodruff, R. A., Jr., and Clayton, P. J. Sex, age, and the diagnosis of hysteria. Am. J. Psychiatry, 129:747–748, 1972.
15. Halleck, S. L. Hysterical personality traits—Psychological, social and introgenic determinants. Arch. Gen. Psychiatry, 16:750–757, 1967.
16. Hollender, M. H., and Hirsch, S. J. Hysterical psychosis. Am. J. Psychiatry, 120:1066–1076, 1964.
17. Horowitz, M. J. *Hysterical Personality.* Jason Aronson, New York, 1977.
18. Hyler, S. E., and Spitzer, R. L. Hysteria split asunder. Am. J. Psychiatry, 135:1500–1504, 1978.
19. Luisada, P. V., Peele, R., and Pittard, E. A. The hysterical personality in men. Am. J. Psychiatry, 131:518–521, 1974.
20. Kernberg, O. Borderline personality organization. J. Am. Psychoanal. Assoc., 15:641–685, 1967.
21. Knight, R. P. Borderline states, Bull. Menninger Clin., 17:1–12, 1953.
22. Langness, L. L. Hysterical psychosis—The cross cultural evidence. Am. J. Psychiatry, 124: 143–151, 1967.
23. Lazare, A. The hysterical character in psychoanalytic theory—an evolution and confusion. Arch. Gen. Psychiatry, 25:131–137, 1971.
24. Lazare, A., Klerman, G. L., and Armor, D. J. Oral, obsessive and hysterical personality patterns. J. Psychiatr. Res., 7:275–290, 1970.
25. Lindberg, B. J., and Lindgard, B. Studies of the hysteroid personality attitude. Acta Psychiatr. Scand., 39:170–180, 1963.
26. Ludwig, A. M. Hysteria. Arch. Gen. Psychiatry, 27:771–786, 1972.
27. MacKinnon, R. A., and Michels, R. R. *Psychiatric Interview in Clinical Practice.* W. B. Saunders Co., Philadelphia, 1971.
28. Malmquist, C. P. Hysteria in childhood. Postgrad. Med., 50:112–117, 1971.
29. Marmor, J. Orality in the hysterical personality. Am. J. Psychoanal. Assoc., 1:656–671, 1953.

30. Perley, J. M., and Guze, S. B. Hysteria—The stability and usefulness of clinical criteria. N. Engl. J. Med., *266:*421–426, 1962.
31. Polatin, P., and Fieve, R. R. Patient rejection of lithium carbonate prophylaxis. J. A. M. A., *218:*864–866, 1971.
32. Purtell, J. J., Robins, E., and Cohen, M. E. Observations on clinical aspects of hysteria—A quantitative study of fifty patients and one-hundred and fifty-six control subjects. J. A. M. A., *146:*902–909, 1951.
33. Reich, W. *Character Analysis.* Orgone Institute Press, New York, 1949.
34. Richman, J., and White, H. The family view of hysterical psychosis. Am. J. Psychiatry, *127:*280–285, 1970.
35. Slavney, P. R., and McHugh, P. R. The hysterical personality, a controlled study. Arch. Gen. Psychiatry, *30:*325–329, 1974.
36. Veith, I. *Hysteria—History of a Disease.* University of Chicago Press, Chicago, 1963.
37. Warner, R. The diagnosis of anti-social and hysterical personality disorders. J. Nerv. Ment. Dis., *166:*839–845, 1978.
38. Zetzel, E. R. So-called good hysteric. Int. J. Psychoanal., *49:*256, 1968.

7

DEPENDENT PERSONALITY

Kenneth L. Malinow, M.D.

Much of what has been written in the previous chapter on the passive-aggressive personality, both generally and specifically, also applies to the dependent personality. Although its antecedents were more clearly seen in early psychoanalytic literature and the underlying psychodynamics more clearly worked out, the two personality types share much in common. Both diagnostic categories evolved from a more primitive nomenclature that changed with the American neuropsychiatric experience of World War II. It was during this war that the old diagnostic category "psychopathic personality" was eliminated and replaced by "character and behavior disorders." This was further divided into "pathologic personality, the addictions and immaturity reactions." The latter was defined as a "neurotic type reaction to routine military stress, manifested by helplessness or inadequate responses, passiveness, obstructionism or aggressive outbursts" (22) This subtype, which was responsible for over 6 percent of all Army hospital admissions in World War II (22,), was the clear forerunner of all subsequent attempts to categorize passive-aggressive/dependent type behaviors (27). By 1952 the passive-aggressive personality appeared as a separate diagnostic category in DSM I with the now classic three subtypes: passive-aggressive subtype (characterized by stubborness, procrastination, pouting, passive-obstructionism, and inefficiency); passive-dependent subtype (characterized by inappropriate clinging in the face of environmental frustration); and aggressive subtype (characterized by aggressive temper tantrums and destructive behaviors in the face of frustration) (4). The authors of DSM I clearly recognized the frequent concomitant expression of any combination of those behaviors in any particular individuals at any one time or over a period of time and stressed the similar underlying psychopathology.

In DSM II, while passive-aggressive subtype rose to a separate diagnostic category with the addition of a dynamic description, both passive dependent and aggressive subtypes fell into a category of "other personality disorders of unspecified types" (5).

With the advent of DSM III dependent personality became a separate category with three diagnostic criteria. These are as follows.

A. Passively allows others to assume responsibility for major areas of one's life because of an inability to function independently (e.g., lets spouse decide what kind of job one should have).

B. Subordinates own needs to those of supporting person in order to avoid any possibility of having to rely on self (e.g., tolerates abusive spouse).

C. Lacks self confidence (e.g., sees self as helpless, stupid). The differential diagnosis consists of "chronic schizophrenia, affective disorders, histrionic personality disorders" (6).

What is lacking in this clinical description and differential diagnosis is the clinical and historical link to passive-aggressive personality. This becomes clearer with examination of the patient's behavior, which must necessarily begin with the analysis of an act. The passive-aggressive act is that peculiarly hostile, angry, and aggressive action that lies just within the bounds of what is legal, socially acceptable, and yet remains provocative (13). On the other hand a dependent act is much more difficult to identify and delineate (15, 19). The reasons for this is the very nature of the interpersonal meaning of that act. Up to a point, the dependent act may be unrecognized or seen as a flattering or even friendly gesture. It may be interpreted as both normal and acceptable in a person at one time (for example, when a person is ill) while later on being seen as irritating, and pathological. It is when the dependent act becomes perceived as abnormal that it is also frequently perceived as irritating, abusive, and hostile. Thus the very recognition of an act of dependency in many cases also involves recognition of its hostile and aggressive components. Thus the most basic behavior of passive dependency involves the most basic component of passive aggressivity. One then can see the dependency of truly passive dependent persons is a truly hostile dependency with "latent aggression." It is along these lines that Whitman et al. suggested we view the behavior on a continuum between passive dependent on one pole to passive-aggressive actions at the other pole (28).

Further both Whitman *et al.* and Small *et al.*, in their respective papers on passive-aggressive behavior, show how similar these subtypes really are (25, 28). Patients in one category at one time may exhibit characteristics of the other at a later date. Both categories show a high frequency of concurrent dysphoric reactions of anxiety and depression. Also, alcoholism is frequently seen in both groups. It is with in depth analytic material that one can truly appreciate the difficulty in separating the categories. In such reports as Berman's (2) or DeRosis' (3) the patients show their aggressive and dependent behaviors as mixed and inseparable. Indeed, in therapy the personality distinction blurs even further. The mere act of isolation on the couch may be experienced with such intense discomfort that a passive-dependent individual will begin coming late, missing sessions, or having "difficulty" with other boundaries of therapy. On the other hand, a passive-aggressive individual trapped by his own devices and confronted with his actions may begin to regress to a dependent, clinging stance in order to avoid both the conscious threat of paying the piper and the unconscious conflict touched upon. It is with all this in mind that one should exercise caution in making the diagnosis.

The rest of the differential is not extensive but still important to make. It involves careful and comprehensive psychiatric evaluation and medical work-up. Chronic schizophrenia is usually easy to recognize by a lack of reality testing and socialization, and withdrawal. A passive-dependent may exhibit psychotic behavior and show evidence of thought disorder during a crisis without benefit of a supporting adult, but this is usually brief and dealt with by supportive psychotherapy. Passive-dependent persons are also not socially withdrawn or self isolated but instead crave some companionship. The distinction between the introverted personality, schizotypal and passive-dependent, is also rarely difficult to make. While the introvert has few friends and a bland constricted affect, this is not commonly seen in passive-dependents. Likewise, the passive-dependent does not usually show the odd metaphorical communication, illusions, magical thinking, or withdrawal of the schizotypal. It should be noted that all of the above diagnostic categories include persons with severe impairment of social and occupational skills.

It is the distinction from the histrionic personality that may prove most difficult to make. Both can appear as clinging, child-like, and immature. Just like the histrionic, the passive-dependent may also exhibit self-dramatizing, manipulative, and attention-seeking behavior, especially in times of crisis. What eventually distinguishes the two is the flamboyant sexuality, vain, egocentric, and self-absorbed behavior, and shallowness of the histrionic.

Since dependent persons in crisis are frequently depressed, a diagnosis of an affective disorder may be entertained.

Just as important as the psychological work-up is a careful medical and neurological investigation to discover covert brain damage or disease. Passive-dependent behavior is commonly seen in mentally retarded individuals, and it behooves any investigator to make the diagnosis. In fact retarded individuals who exhibit passive-dependent traits irrespective of IQ are less successful than otherwise (8). Also impairment of vision, hearing, or communication ability may present as either passive-aggressive or dependent behavior.

Dependent characters usually present to therapy as referrals because of failure to achieve expected optimal functioning on the job, socially (7, 9, 23), or in a hospital setting (16). Frequently, these persons may present themselves in therapy because of depression or anxiety when a person they are highly dependent upon leaves or dies. When referral is from the medical/surgical units in a hospital because of failure to progress in rehabilitation because of anxiety or medical reasons, the prognosis in patients with passive-dependent characteristics is usually poor (1, 14). In fact alcoholics with peripheral neuropathy have passive-dependent traits that seem to distinguish them from alcoholics who neither have passive-dependent characteristics nor develop peripheral neuropathy (24). Passive-aggressive character traits are also central findings in patients with ileitis and bronchial asthma (18, 29).

Treatment is difficult but rewarding. Whitman et al. found in his study that patients with a clear diagnosis of passive-aggressive did better in therapy than passive-dependents. They felt this was in part due to the older age of presentations of the passive-aggressive group at onset of therapy, lack of need for hospitalization, and more complex ego defensive patterns.

Successful treatment has been demonstrated using a variety of modalities: dynamic (2, 3, 10–12), pharmacologic (20), and group (21). Therapy in all cases consists of establishing a trusting relationship with the patient with a gradual transferring of dependency onto the therapist and therapy. Therapists should support attempts at a separate and independent life-style along with attempts to help the patient modulate the intense anxiety that goes along with such decision making. Critical in the therapy is the point where the patient's support system (family, therapy) fails him either in real or imagined ways. If "expectations" have been too great, then disillusionment will lead to a sense of loss. At this point the compliant and dependent patient becomes depressed. "The depression usually takes the form of passive-resistance" (26). What must be remembered is that while the patient's group experiences passive resistance, the depressed patient is experiencing his own despised passivity. Therapy should be supportive with the use of anxiety agents and antidepressants if there is the possibility of the patient being overwhelmed by negative affect. As Kiev points out, one should not underestimate the depth and seriousness of the patient's depression since passive aggressive/dependent suicide attempts are solitary and serious (17). Needless to say, clarification and interpretation over a number of these crises will hopefully result in genuine insight on the part of the patient and substantial growth of the personality (12).

In an open clinical study of 50 passive-dependent women Hill reports on a number of characteristics these patients had in common that had important bearing on therapy (12). Generally they all acted as if ruled from afar by their parents through their own powerful superego. They presented as a group as rigid, compulsive, judgmental, and moralistic, and were frequently at odds with a man in their life. There was a strong undercurrent of hostility toward what they perceived as a controlling world. Stress was poorly tolerated and experienced as anxiety and depression with marked somatization. Patients frequently presented medically with a multitude of bodily complaints. Hill sees hospitalization as necessary in severely depressed or anxious patients but when not needed it should be discouraged since it leads to a powerful regression toward dependency. Treatment as a whole is seen as supportive of a patient's attempts to trust the therapist and make gains toward independence. Early on, she allowed patients to become dependent on the therapist but "with the conviction and expectation that (the patient) will grow into functioning independently. This is a long and involved process with many setbacks. The patients invariably try to manipulate the therapist into making decisions for them and this needs to be identified each time. At points of decision making, patients may be overcome by severe and disabling panic attacks. These frequently spread to the patient's family with all becoming desperate to have the therapist take over and make things right. It is difficult but essential to maintain calmness so insight can be applied. Improvement is noted by a decreasing frequency of attacks and a lessening of their severity. Termination should be a joint decision, with therapists keeping their door open so that patients may return. In Hill's study, therapy ran anywhere from 5 sessions over a few months to 63 sessions over 2 years. Only 2 of 50 patients showed no improvement.

Group therapy has been utilized with success in passive-dependent patients referred from a medical setting. Whether therapy was monthly, bimonthly, or weekly, all patients improved. As expected, the greatest therapeutic gains are seen in the groups that meet more frequently so that symptoms do not become the groups only concern (21).

Psychopharmacotherapy consists of the judicious use of antianxiety drugs when needed in patients crippled by overwhelming anxiety. Occasionally, a major tranquilizer will be needed in the dependent patient who has a psychotic decompensation. This, though, can usually be handled by hospitalization and transfer of dependency onto the therapist. Caution should be exercised that the dependent patient does not become a drug-dependent patient. In a well-constructed study of the use of antidepressants in passive-dependent patients, Lauer used tricyclic antidepressants in anxious, anergic, and somatizing patients prior to their experiencing subjective depression (20). He hypothesized that prior to subjective experiencing of overt depression, passive-dependent persons will begin to overtly express their dependent needs either by "pseudoaggression" mediated by overcompensation and reaction formation or by repression and somatization. In his study, patients experienced decreased anxiety and an increased availability of energy, resulting in increased self-assertiveness, and outgoing behavior. The patients themselves commented that while taking medications they were more comfortable with better interpersonal relationships.

REFERENCES

1. Anderson, K., and Berg, S. The relationship between some psychological factors and the outcome of medical rehabilitation. Scand. J. Rehabil. Med., 7:166–170, 1975.
2. Berman, S. A type of academic failure among male adolescents: a problem of early identification. Am. Acad. Child Psychiatry, 10(3):418–443, 1971.
3. DeRosis, H. Two cases of fictional living. J. Psychiatry Q., 46(1):125–135, 1972.
4. Diagnostic and Statistical Manual of Mental Disorders (DSM I), p. 37. American Psychiatric Association, Washington, D. C., 1952.
5. Diagnostic and Statistical Manual of Mental Disorders (DSM II), pp. 43–44. American Psychiatric Association, Washington, D. C., 1968.

6. DSM III, Diagnostic Criteria Draft. Task Force on Nomenclature & Statistics, American Psychiatric Association, January 1978.
7. Fischer, G. Psychological needs of heterosexual pedophiliacs. Dis. Nerv. Syst., *30*:419–421, 1969.
8. Floor, L., and Rosen, M. Investigating the phenomena of helplessness in mentally retarded adults. Am. J. Ment. Deficiency, *79*(5):565–572, 1975.
9. Gardner, L. I., and Neu, R. L. Evidence linking an extra Y chromosone to sociopathic behavior. Arch. Gen. Psychiatry, *26*:220–222, 1972.
10. Gralnick, A. Management of character disorders in a hospital setting. Am. J. Psychother., *33*(1):54–66, 1979.
11. Hartman, B. J. Treatment of psychogenic heart syndrome by psychotherapy. J. Natl. Med. Assoc., *69*(1):63–65, 1977.
12. Hill, D. E. Outpatient management of passive-dependent women. Hosp. Community Psychiatry, *21*(12):402–405, 1970.
13. Hodge, J. R. The Passive-Dependent versus the Passive-Aggressive Personality, U. S. Armed Forces Medical Journal, *6*(1):84–90, 1955.
14. Hirschenfang, S., Shulman, L., and Berriton, J. Psychosocial factor influencing the rehabilitation of the hemiplegic patient. Dis. Nerv. Syst. *29*(6):373–379, 1968.
15. Kagan, J., and Moss, H. The stability of passive and dependent behavior from childhood through adulthood. Child Dev. *31*:577–591, 1960.
16. Kahana, R., and Bibring, G. Personality types in medical management, In: *Psychiatry in Medical Practice in a General Hospital*, Norman Zimbing (Ed.) pp. 168–173. International Universities Press, New York, 1964.
17. Kiev, A. Cluster analysis profiles of suicide attempts. Am. J. Psychiatry *133*(2):150–153, 1976.
18. Knapp, P., and Nemetz, S. J. Sources of tension in bronchial asthma. J. Psychosom. Med., *19*(6):466–485, 1957.
19. Lansky, L., and McKay, G. Independence, dependence, manifest and latent masculinity femininity: Some complex relationships among four complex variables. Psychol. Rep., *24*:263–268, 1969.
20. Lauer, J. The effect of tricyclic antidepressant compounds on patients with passive-dependent personality traits. Curr. Ther. Res. *19*(5):495–505, 1976.
21. Montgomery, J. Treatment management of passive-dependent behavior. Int. J. Soc. Psychiatry, *17*(4):311–319, 1971.
22. Neuropsychiatry in World War II, Vol I. Zone of the Interior. Col. Roberts Anderson, MCUSA (Ed.), pp. 140 and 756. Office of the Surgeon General, Dept. of Army, Washington, D. C., 1966.
23. Sadoff, R. L., and Collins, D. J. Passive dependency in stutterers. Am. J. Psychiatry, *124*(8): 1126–1127, 1968.
24. Silber, M., Hirschenfang, S., and Benton, J. Psychological factors and prognosis in peripheral neuropathy. Dis. Nerv. Syst., *29*:688–692, 1968.
25. Small, I., Small, J., Alig, V., and Moore, D. Passive-aggressive personality disorder: A search for a syndrome. Am. J. Psychiatry, *126*(7):973–981, 1970.
26. Symonds, M. Emotional hazards of police work. Am. J. Psychoanal. *30*(2):155–160, 1970.
27. *U. S. Joint Armed Services Nomenclature and Methods of Reducing Mental Conditions.* Washington, D. C., 1949.
28. Whitman, R., Trossman, H., and Koenig, R. Clinical assessment of passive-aggressive personality. Arch. Neurol. Psychiatry, *72*:540–549, 1954.
29. Whybroww, P., Kane, F., and Lipton, M. Regional ileitis and psychiatric disorders, Psychosom. Med. *30*(2):209–221, 1968.

8

THE AVOIDANT PERSONALITY

Theodore Millon, Ph.D.

The label "avoidant personality" is a new term in the official psychiatric nomenclature, having been coined by Millon (28) as a descriptive designation for patients characterized by a long-standing, pervasive and active withdrawal from social relationships. Although derived theoretically—deduced as a syndrome from a biosocial-learning model—the features hypothesized as characteristic of the avoidant accurately portray cases well known to everyday practitioners and correspond in most details to descriptively similar, though conceptually and metapsychologically diverse, entities reported in the nosological literature. Before we examine some of the syndrome's historical precursors, it will be useful to summarize its major clinical features and clarify points of a differential diagnostic nature.

Major Clinical Features

The DSM III considers the essential features of avoidants to be their "hypersensitivity to potential rejection, humiliation and shame." They exhibit an unwillingness to enter into social relationships unless there is assurance that they will be uncritically accepted. Particularly significant is the fact that they withdraw socially despite strong desires for affection and acceptance. Devastated by disapproval, they distance from others for fear that they will be denigrated and rejected.

As described by Millon (28, 30), avoidants feel their loneliness deeply, experience being out of things, and have a strong, though often repressed, desire to be accepted. Despite their longing to relate and participate actively in social life, they fear placing their welfare in the hands of others, or trusting and confiding in them. Thus, the social detachment of avoidants does not stem from deficit drives and sensibilities, as in the schizoid personality, but from an active and self-protective restraint. Although experiencing a pervasive estrangement, they do not expose themselves to the defeat and humiliation they anticipate.

Since their affective longings cannot be expressed overtly, they cumulate and are vented in an inner world of rich fantasy and imagination. Their need for contact and relatedness may pour forth in poetry, be sublimated in intellectual pursuits or a delicate taste for food and clothing, or be expressed in finely detailed and expressive artistic activities.

Their isolation and protective withdrawal result in a variety of secondary consequences which compound the avoidants' difficulties. Their apparently tense and fearful demeanor often "pulls" ridicule and deprecation from others, that is, leaves them open to persons who gain satisfaction in taunting and belittling those who dare not retaliate. To most observers who have but superficial contact with them, avoidant personalities appear timid and withdrawn or perhaps cold and strange—not unlike the image conveyed by the schizoid personality. However, those who relate to them more closely recognize that they are anxious, hypersensitive, evasive, and mistrustful.

Avoidant personalities are alert to the most subtle feelings and intentions of others. Although this vigilance serves to protect them against potential danger, it floods them with excessive stimuli and distracts them from attending to the ordinary features of their environment. In the course of a typical day, avoidants may be so attuned to matters that bear on how others feel toward them that they can attend to little other than the routine aspects of their daily life. Cognitive processes of avoidants are not only interfered with by this flooding of irrelevant environmental details, but also are complicated further by an inner emotional disharmony. These feelings upset their cognitive processes and diminish their capacity to cope effectively with many of the tasks of ordinary life. This "cognitive interference," a cardinal feature of the avoidant personality, is especially pronounced in social settings. It is here that they must protect themselves from anticipated humiliation and rejection.

Avoidant personalities are beset by several conflicts. They have difficulty acting on their own because of marked self-doubt. On the other hand, they are unable to depend on others because of their social mistrust.

In a descriptive summary of the avoidant personality written for his colleagues on the DSM III Task Force, the author specified the following five diagnostic criteria as the prime features of the syndrome (29):

1. Affective dysphoria (e.g., describes a constant and confusing undercurrent of tension, sadness and anger; vacillates between desire for affection, fear and numbness of feeling).

2. Mild cognitive interference (e.g., is bothered and distracted by disruptive inner thoughts; irrelevant and digressive ideation disrupts social communication).

3. Alienated self-image (e.g., describes life as one of social isolation and rejection; devalues self and reports periodic feelings of emptiness and depersonalization).

4. Aversive interpersonal behavior (e.g., tells of social pan-anxiety and distrust; seeks privacy to avoid anticipated social derogation).

5. Perceptual hypersensitivity (e.g., vigilantly scans for potential threats; overinterprets innocuous behavior as a sign of ridicule and humiliation).

Issues of Differential Diagnosis

Because it is a syndrome that is new to mental health practitioners, and because several of its features are similar to those of other personality disorders, the avoidant diagnosis requires greater differential clarification than usual. Especially problematic may be distinctions that need to be drawn among avoidant, schizoid, and schizotypal personality diagnoses; to a lesser extent, difficulties might occasionally arise in differentiating among avoidant, dependent, and borderline designations. Detailed consideration of these diagnostic issues has been provided in a recent text (30). We will summarize only a few of the more salient points here. The following quote may serve as a useful précis of this discussion (30):

> In the past, the label schizoid was applied to individuals with a mix of features that the DSM-III now differentiates into three separate personality syndromes: the schizoid, the avoidant, and the schizotypal. The designation "schizoid" is limited to personalities characterized by an *intrinsic defect* in the capacity to form social relationships. The label "avoidant" represents those who possess both the capacity and desire to relate socially, but who *fear humiliation and disapproval* and, hence, distance themselves from such relationships. The term "schizotypal" is reserved for individuals who are noted by the *eccentric character of their social communications and behaviors*, and for an ostensive genetic linkage to schizophrenia.

Let us elaborate these distinctions further.

Avoidant-Schizoid Distinction. Schizoids differ from the similarly appearing avoidant personalities in that they possess a defect or deficit in their capacity to relate socially and empathically. By contrast, avoidants are excessively sensitive to social feelings and defensively withdraw from interpersonal relationships for fear of experiencing humiliation and rebuff. Unfortunately, many clinicians, especially those of an analytic persuasion, consider any overt lack of affect or social blandness to signify a protective emotional blunting and isolation owing to repressed childhood disappointments, conflicts, or anxieties. The notion that affect and social insensitivity signifies an adaptive defensiveness does not apply to the DSM III conception of the schizoid personality, but does apply to the avoidant personality. Although the DSM III avoids specifying etiologies for its syndromes, the schizoid category was formulated to represent asocial and affectless individuals who are neither conflicted, nor suffer social anxieties nor the desire for interpersonal warmth or closeness; their detached and unemotional characteristics derive from inherent deficits in personal sensitivity and empathy. Clinicians who correctly ascribe their patients' bland exteriors to defensive actions consequent to conflict or disillusion should employ the new avoidant personality designation to represent their views. These patients are emotionally sensitive and, despite their restraint and withdrawal, do desire interpersonal warmth and social acceptance. Upon first examination, avoidants may appear to be cooly detached; their warmth and neediness will be exhibited upon closer contact. Schizoids, however, continue to be distantly connected and emotionally disengaged.

Avoidants may be spoken of as being *actively detached* (28, 30). They are oversensitive to social stimuli and hyperreactive to the moods and feelings of others, especially those which portend rejection or humiliation. By contrast, schizoids are best considered *passively detached*. They are underaroused, undermotivated, and insensitive. As a consequence of their deficits they simply fail or are unable to respond to the incentives that activate interpersonal behaviors and stimulate relevant and mutually rewarding social relationships.

It may be useful for purposes of further comparison to reproduce the five diagnostic criteria that the author wrote for his DSM III colleagues as a means of highlighting the prime features of the schizoid personality; the reader may contrast them to the previously excerpted avoidant personality criteria (29).

1. Affectivity deficit (e.g., exhibits intrinsic emotional blandness; reports weak affectionate needs and an inability to display enthusiasm or experience pleasure).

2. Mild cognitive slippage (e.g., evidences impoverished and obscure thought processes inappropriate to intellectual level; social communication often tangential and irrelevant).

3. Interpersonal indifference (e.g., possesses minimal "human" interests; prefers a peripheral role in social and family relationships).

4. Behavioral apathy (e.g., experiences fatigue, low energy and lack of vitality; displays deficits in activation, motoric expressiveness and spontaneity).

5. Perceptual insensitivity (e.g., reveals minimal introspection and awareness of self; is impervious to subtleties of everyday social and emotional life).

Avoidant-Schizotypal Distinction. In general, the behaviors, perceptions, and thought processes of the schizotypal suggest that he possesses a more severe form of pathology in personality organization than is found in the avoidant (18, 28, 30). More specifically, schizotypals exhibit obvious eccentricities such as odd speech, ideas of reference, magical thinking, and recurrent illusions—essentially, features that often typify schizophrenia without the characteristic delusions and hallucinations. Avoidants exhibit fewer dramatic peculiarities and bizarre behaviors, expressing instead an anxious anticipation of humiliation, a fear of interpersonal rejection, low self-esteem, and an unrequited desire for social acceptance.

According to Millon (30), the schizotypal personality may be best understood as a more severe or decompensated variant of the avoidant and schizoid personalities. Endowed with a less advantageous constitutional makeup, or subjected to more deleterious life experiences, the schizotypal pattern may gradually and insidiously unfold through earlier and milder avoidant or schizoid phases.

For purposes of comparison, and toward the end of facilitating recognition of the greater severity of the schizotypal, as contrasted to the avoidant and schizoid personalities, we will reproduce the five prime diagnostic criteria the author drafted for his DSM III Task Force associates to characterize the syndrome that ultimately was labeled "schizotypal" (29):

> 1. Social detachment (e.g., prefers life of isolation with minimal personal attachments and obligations; over time, has drifted into increasingly peripheral social and vocational roles).
> 2. Behavioral eccentricity (e.g., exhibits peculiar habits frequently; is perceived by others as unobtrusively strange or different).
> 3. Non-delusional autistic thinking (e.g., mixes social communication with personal irrelevancies, obscurities and tangential asides; appears self-absorbed and lost in daydreams with occasional blurring of fantasy and reality).
> 4. Either (a) anxious wariness (e.g., reports being hypersensitive and apprehensively ill-at-ease, particularly in social encounters; is guarded, suspicious of others and secretive in behavior); or (b) emotional flatness (e.g., manifests a drab, sluggish, joyless, and spiritless appearance; reveals marked deficiencies in activation and affect).
> 5. Disquieting estrangement (e.g., reports periods of depersonalization, derealization and dissociation; experiences anxious feelings of emptiness and meaninglessness).

Avoidant-Dependent Distinction. Dependents are trusting souls; they seek out intimate and affectional relationships in both the hope and the assumption that they will be secured. In contrast, avoidants are rarely trusting; they anticipate social rejection and, hence, fail to seek warmth and maintain distance from personal closeness. They withdraw from affection and intimacy, whereas dependents are at their most comfortable and secure when experiencing a bond and a sharing with another. Should a dependent sense that he may be abandoned or rejected by a "significant" other, he will do anything to regain his favored place, increasing his compliance and submitting to whatever the other wishes, throwing all caution to the winds and exposing himself to even further deprecation. Not only does the avoidant rarely chance a bond which may result in rejection or humiliation, but should such signs become evident in a formerly secure affiliation, he will neither submit nor demean himself to regain favor, but quickly and protectively withdraw, repressing his pain and closing off all avenues that might reactivate it.

It may be useful again to reproduce the diagnostic criteria drafted by the author to represent the salient features of the syndrome under discussion, the dependent personality (29). Comparison with the criteria for the avoidant that were presented earlier may aid the reader's differential diagnostic efforts in ways other than those supplied by the DSM III criteria:

1. Pacific temperament (e.g., is characteristically docile and noncompetitive; avoids social tension and interpersonal conflicts).
2. Interpersonal submissiveness (e.g., needs a stronger, nurturing figure, and without one feels anxiously helpless; is often conciliatory, placating, and self-sacrificing).
3. Inadequate self-image (e.g., perceives self as weak, fragile and ineffectual; exhibits lack of confidence by belittling own aptitudes and competencies).
4. Pollyanna cognitive style (e.g., reveals a naive or benign attitude toward interpersonal difficulties; smooths over troubling events).
5. Initiative deficit (e.g., prefers a subdued, uneventful and passive life-style; avoids self-assertion and refuses autonomous responsibilities).

Avoidant-Borderline Distinction. As with the schizotypal personality, the borderline syndrome signifies a pathological level of personality organization that is usually more severe and dysfunctional than that observed among avoidants. The affective instability, repetitive impulsivity, and pervasively erratic relationships of the borderline signify a long-standing and weak level of social and personal adaptation. Although borderlines occasionally exhibit a loneliness and an anticipation of social failure that is akin to that seen in the avoidant, these signs are transient symptoms rather than persistent traits, a minor and passing facet of a larger spectrum of unregulated emotions and conflict-filled relationships. The criteria reproduced below represent the author's judgment of this syndrome's most salient features and were drafted prior to the committee's vote to select the borderline designation (29). It clearly aligns the syndrome within the affective disorders spectrum. It represents a moderately severe affective personality pattern in the same sense as the schizotypal syndrome represents a moderately severe personality within the schizophrenia spectrum.

1. Intense endogenous moods (e.g., continually fails to accord mood with external events; is either depressed or excited or has recurring periods of dejection and apathy interspersed with spells of anger, anxiety, or euphoria).
2. Dysregulated activation (e.g., experiences desultory energy levels and irregular sleep-wake cycle; describes time periods which suggest that affective-activation equilibrium is constantly in jeopardy).
3. Self-condemnatory conscience (e.g., reveals recurring self-mutilating and suicidal thoughts; periodically redeems moody behavior through contrition and self-derogation).
4. Dependency anxiety (e.g., is preoccupied with securing affection and maintaining emotional support; reacts intensely to separation and reports haunting fear of isolation and loss).
5. Cognitive-affective ambivalence (e.g., repeatedly struggles to express attitudes contrary to inner feelings; simultaneously experiences conflicting emotions and thoughts toward others, notably love, rage and guilt).

Theoretical Precursors

The clinical features that characterize the avoidant personality have been observed and reported in the literature since the turn of the century, most often in conjunction with what has been labeled the schizoid character. We will subdivide our presentation of these historical precursors into three groups: writers who have been guided by a constitutional viewpoint, clinicians inclined toward psychoanalytic interpretations, and theorists of a biosocial-learning orientation.

Constitutional Views. Having coined the term "schizophrenia," Bleuler (4) was also the first to employ the label "schizoid." However, the view that the symptoms of "dementia praecox" were dramatic accentuations of pre-existing traits was recorded earlier in the clinical literature by Kahlbaum (16), Binet (3), and Hoch (14). For example, in describing his "shut-in" type, Hoch wrote, "what is, after all, the deterioration in dementia praecox if not the expression of the constitutional tendencies in their extreme form."

Kraepelin (21) also wrote of a prodromal form of dementia praecox, describing it as "certain abnormal personalities with mild defect states ... a product of dementia praecox experienced in earliest childhood, and then brought to a standstill." He elaborated this view in later texts (22), speaking of these patients as "autistic personalities," characterizing them as inclined to "narrow or reduce their external interests and contacts and their preoccupation with inward ruminations."

Bleuler coined the term "schizoidie" (5, 7) to represent a cluster of prepsychotic traits akin to Hoch's "shut-in" and Kraepelin's "autistic" types. He described them as "people who are shut in, suspicious, incapable of discussion, people who are comfortably dull at the same time sensitive" (6).

It was not until Ernst Kretschmer (23) that the constitutional view reached its clearest formulation. More important perhaps was his recognition that the schizoid character may arise from a combination of two, diametrically opposite levels of sensitivity. The seeming contradiction in Bleuler's quote in the previous paragraph—"comfortably dull at the same time sensitive"—was explained by Kretschmer in his distinction between hyperaesthetic and the anaesthetic constitutional proclivities. Although most individuals exhibit a mix of these temperament extremes, clear-cut clinical entities are seen among those who fall at one or the other polarity of the continuum. This distinction of Kretschmer's is the prime forerunner of the differentiation that has been made between the DSM III schizoid and the DSM III avoidant personalities. Those at the anaesthetic pole, similar to the DSM III schizoid, are characterized by Kretschmer as indifferent, affectively insensitive, flavorless, boring, unfeeling, lacking in an emotional life, phlegmatic, tepid, strange, unsympathetic, emotionally empty, cold, and soulless. In contrast, those at the hyperaesthetic pole are clinical types that clearly anticipate the features of the DSM III avoidant personality. Kretschmer describes them as abnormally tender, constantly wounded, sensitively susceptible, feeling all the harsh, strong colors and tones of life, wishing to deaden all outside stimulation; beneath the "cover of a sulky silence" is an inner tension which "gets heaped up" and "which cannot be spoken out."

Similar formulations suggesting a constitutional base for the avoidant's hypersensitivity were presented by genetic researchers. For example, Kallmann (17) spoke of patients who suffered "schizoidia" as being both autistically introverted and exhibiting "surges of temperament and inappropriate responses to emotional stimuli."

An explicit biological formulation that differentiates the schizoid character into two such types has recently been proposed by Klein (19). One group, that fitting the current DSM III schizoid portrayal, is noted by its intrinsic and ego-syntonic asocial qualities. The second type, described in a manner that foreshadows the features of the DSM III avoidant personality, is characterized as "shy, socially backward . . . fearful and therefore isolated, but appreciates sociability and would like to be part of the crowd . . . seems to have an emotional state compounded of anticipatory anxiety (and) low self-esteem" (19).

Psychoanalytic Conceptions. There have been a number of analytic descriptions and explanatory schemas that clearly correspond to the characteristics and etiology of the avoidant personality; these formulations have invariably been associated with the designation "schizoid character." Now that the traditional schizoid concept has been subdivided into several DSM III personality types—schizoid, avoidant, and schizotypal—it is necessary that we re-assess the earlier literature on the schizoid and identify those propositions that are most relevant and applicable to modern formulations of the avoidant and schizotypal syndromes. What follows is a summary of analytic proposals that were initially addressed to the schizoid character, but which appear today to be more pertinent to the avoidant personality; a detailed historical review and comparison of this literature may be found in Millon (30).

The essential theme of analytic theorists is that the "schizoid character" evolves as a defensive consequence of early parental rebuff or indifference. As noted earlier, the defense and disillusion model of development seems most applicable in the background of avoidants, whereas the defect and deficit model appears relevant to the history of schizoids. To the English analyst Fairbairn (10), these character types have experienced an "unsatisfactory emotional relationship with their parents and particularly with their mothers." As a consequence, they are incapable of either giving love or being loved, having learned to depersonalize and "de-emotionalize" object relationships. Deutsch's (9) proposal of an "as if " type is similar to that presented by Fairbairn. However, "as if" personalities seem intrinsically lacking in affect, that is, devoid of empathic and emotional sensitivity.

Because they exhibit no social apprehension, nor an awareness of their social insensitivity, this type appears to be more properly a forerunner of the DSM III schizoid, rather than avoidant character. Closer to the avoidant concept is Winnicott's (32, 33) proposal of a "false self" personality. These seemingly unfeeling and detached individuals protect their deeper sensitivities or "true self" by interposing a false self between it and the outer world. This front hides and protects the true self from the pains and failures of life, shielding it with a false ego-strength, so to speak, so that it can be preserved in an unaffected state. Guntrip (12) and Laing (24) have elaborated the proposals of Fairbairn and Winnicott; in the works of both are sensitive portrayals of the inner feelings and defensive struggles that typify the avoidant personality, although the label they append to their writings is that of schizoid.

Similar analytic formulations have been offered by Horney (15), Arieti (2), and Burnham (8). Horney characterizes her "detached" type as one who has learned to "move away" from people. She speaks of him as experiencing an "intolerable strain in associating with people and solitude becomes primarily a means of avoiding it." There is a need to put distance between self and others, and to follow a set of negative goals in life, such as *not* to be involved, *not* to need anyone, and *not* to let anyone intrude or be influential. To Arieti, the lack of involvement and overt insensitivity of these patients is a defense against their profound vulnerability to personal and social pain. What distinguishes Arieti's view is his contention that this vulnerability is repressed so successfully that there is no awareness of personal needs, nor is there any pain or longing for social affection. Burnham, following an object-relations framework, attributes the syndrome to a so-called "need-fear dilemma." To him, this patient's "very psychological existence depends on his maintaining contact with objects," but the excessiveness of his need makes others inordinately dangerous since they "can destroy him through abandonment." His only recourse to alleviate the pain of his dilemma is "object avoidance."

Biosocial-Learning Theory. In a recent formulation a deductive system was proposed by Millon for generating and coordinating personality syndromes (28–31). Drawing upon three polarities that were posited by several European theorists early in the century (11, 13, 20, 25, 26), Millon employed the dimensions of active-passive, subject-object, and pleasure-pain as the basis for constructing a full-range personality typology. For example, Freud (11) wrote "our mental life as a whole is governed by three polarities, namely, the following antitheses:

   Subject (ego)-Object (external world)
   Pleasure-Pain
   Active-Passive."

Despite their early promise as a conceptual basis for deriving personality disorders, the systems that were developed by the aforementioned theorists lay fallow until they were "rediscovered" in the biosocial-learning theory proposed by the author. The present theory generates eight styles of basic pathological personality functioning, as well as several severe or more dysfunctional personality types. A 4 × 2 matrix consisting of two basic dimensions was construced to derive the eight basic personalities.

The first dimension pertains to the primary source from which patients gain comfort and satisfaction (pleasure or positive reinforcement) or attempt to avoid emotional distress (pain or negative reinforcement). Patients who experience few rewards or satisfactions in life, be it from self or others, are referred to as *detached* types. Those who measure their satisfactions or discomforts by how "others" react to or feel about them are described as *dependent*. Where gratification is gauged primarily in terms of "self," that is, one's own values and desires, with little reference to the concerns and wishes of others, the patient is said to exhibit an *independent* personality style. Finally, those who experience considerable conflict over whether to be guided by what others say and wish or to follow their own opposing desires and needs are referred to as *ambivalent* personalities.

The second dimension of the theoretical matrix reflects the basic pattern of instrumental or coping behavior the patient characteristically employs to maximize rewards and to minimize pain. Those patients who seem aroused and attentive, arranging and manipulating life events to achieve gratification and avoid discomfort, display an *active* pattern. In contrast, those who seem apathetic, restrained, yielding, resigned, or seemingly content to allow events to take their own course without personal regulation or control possess a *passive* pattern.

Before we outline the principal personality syndromes, let us be mindful that the schema is a theory-derived synthesis, a set of abstract prototypes that corresponds well to personality entities observed in clinical practice. However, it is a typology documented only in part by systematic empirical research, a provisional tool which aids us in organizing our subject more clearly and with greater understanding.

1. The *passive-detached* style is characterized by social impassivity. Affectionate needs and emotional feelings are minimal, and the individual functions as a passive observer detached from the rewards and affections, as well as from the dangers of human relationships. This patient is closest to the DSM III schizoid personality.

2. The *active-detached* style represents an intense mistrust of others. The individual maintains a constant vigil lest his impulses and longing for affection result in a repetition of the pain and anguish he has experienced previously. Distance must be kept between himself and others. Only by an active detachment and suspiciousness can he protect himself from others. Despite desires to relate to others, he has learned that it is best to deny these desires and withdraw from interpersonal relationships. This patient corresponds to the DSM III *avoidant* personality.

3. The *passive-dependent* style is characterized by a search for relationships in which one can lean upon others for affection, security, and leadership. This patient displays a lack of both initiative and autonomy. As a function of early experience, he has learned to assume a passive role in interpersonal relations, accepting whatever kindness and support he may find, and willingly submitting to the wishes of others in order to maintain their affection. This patient is most like the DSM III *dependent* personality.

4. In the *active-dependent* style we observe an insatiable and indiscriminate search for stimulation and affection. The patient's gregarious and capricious behavior gives the appearance of considerable independence of others, but beneath this guise lies a fear of autonomy and an intense need for signs of social approval and affection. Affection must be replenished constantly and must be obtained from every source of interpersonal experience. This patient is highly similar to the DSM III *histrionic* personality.

5. The *passive-independent* style is noted by narcissism and self-involvement. As a function of early experience the individual has learned to overvalue his self-worth; however, his confidence in his superiority may be based on false premises. Nevertheless, he assumes that others will recognize his worth, and he maintains distance from or exploits those whom he views to be inferior to himself. This patient is essentially the same as the DSM III *narcissistic* personality.

6. The *active-independent* style reflects a mistrust of others and a desire to assert one's autonomy; the result is an indiscriminate striving for power. Rejection of others is justified because they cannot be trusted; autonomy and initiative are claimed to be the only means of heading off betrayal by others. This patient is most similar to the DSM III *antisocial* personality.

7. The *passive-ambivalent* style is based on a combination of hostility toward others and a fear of social rejection and disapproval. The patient resolves this conflict by repressing his resentment. He is rigid and perfectionistic, and tends to overconform and overcomply to others on the surface; however, lurking behind this front of propriety and restraint are intense contrary feelings which, on rare occasion, seep through his controls. This patient exhibits traits akin to those of the DSM III *compulsive* personality.

8. The *active-ambivalent* style represents an inability to resolve conflicts similar to those of the passive-ambivalent; however, these conflicts remain close to consciousness and intrude into everyday life. The individual gets himself into endless wrangles and disappointments as he vacillates between deference and conformity at one time and aggressive negativism the next. His behavior displays an erratic pattern of anger or stubbornness intermingled with hopeless dependency, guilt, and shame. This patient is a more complex variant of the narrowly conceived DSM III *passive-aggressive* personality.

A major theme stressed in the theory is the intrinsic continuity of personality development. Thus, the more severe forms of psychopathology are seen as elaborations and extensions of a patient's basic personality style. More advanced or decompensated states are viewed as outgrowths of one of the basic eight personality styles seen under the pressure of intense or unrelieved adversity. No matter how dramatic or maladaptive a patient's behavior may be, it is viewed as an accentuation or distortion that derives from, and is fully consonant with, his personality pattern.

Three additional personality patterns were derived for the moderately severe or advanced level of dysfunction. They differ from the first eight by several criteria, notably deficits in social competence and periodic, but reversible, psychotic episodes. Their personality organization or structure is less integrated than their milder counterparts, and they are more vulnerable to the strains of everyday life. Their features and corresponding DSM III syndromes will be noted briefly.

9. The advanced and *dysfunctional detached* style is characterized by a marked isolation with minimal personal attachments or obligations. Behavioral eccentricities are notable, and the individual is often perceived by others as strange or different. Depending on whether the basic or early pattern was essentially passive or active, there will be either an anxious wariness and hypersensitivity, or an emotional flattening and deficiency of affect. This patient parallels the DSM III *schizotypal* personality.

10. The advanced and *dysfunctional dependent* style is typified by intense endogenous moods with recurring periods of dejection and apathy interspersed with spells of impulsive anger, anxiety, or euphoria. Many reveal persistent self-mutilating and suicidal thoughts, appear preoccupied with securing affection, and display a cognitive-affective ambivalence evident in simultaneous feelings of rage, love, and guilt toward others. This patient corresponds to the DSM III *borderline* personality.

11. The advanced and dysfunctional independent style is noted by a vigilant mistrust of others and an edgy defensiveness against anticipated criticism and deception. There is an abrasive irritability and a tendency to precipitate exasperation and anger in others. Expressed often is a fear of losing autonomy, leading to a tense resistance to external influence and control. This patient is similar in most respects to the DSM III *paranoid* personality.

The biosocially learned origins of these styles are detailed in Millon (28, 30). In the following paragraphs we will summarize a series of hypotheses from the theoretical model as they apply to the developmental background of the avoidant personality.

Developmental Hypotheses

For pedagogical purposes, it is often necessary to separate biogenic from psychogenic factors as influences in personality development. This bifurcation does not exist in reality. Biological and experiential determinants combine and interact in a reciprocal interplay throughout life. This sequence of biogenic-psychogenic interaction evolves through a never-ending spiral. Each step in the interplay builds upon prior interactions and creates, in turn, new potentialities for future reactivity and experience. Etiology in psychopathology must be viewed as a developmental process in which intraorganismic and environmental forces display not only a reciprocity and circularity of influence but also an orderly and sequential continuity throughout the life of the individual.

The circular feedback and serially unfolding character of the developmental process defy simplification, and must be kept in mind when analyzing the background of personality pathology. There are few unidirectional effects in development; it is a multideterminant transaction in which a unique pattern of biogenic potentials and a distinctive constellation of psychogenic influences mold each other in a reciprocal and successively more intricate fashion.

Each individual is endowed at conception with a unique set of chromosomes that shapes the course of his physical maturation and psychological development. The physical and psychological characteristics of children are in large measure similar to those of their parents because they possess many of the same genetic units. Children are genetically disposed to be similar to their parents not only physically but also in stamina, energy, emotional sensitivity, and intelligence.

Each infant displays a distinctive pattern of behaviors from the first moments after birth. These characteristics are attributed usually to the infant's "nature," that is, his constitutional makeup, since it is displayed prior to the effects of postnatal influences. Unfortunately, there has been little systematic attention paid to the child's own contribution to the course of his development. Environmental theorists have viewed disorders to be the result of detrimental experiences that the individual has had no part in producing himself. This is a gross simplification. Each infant possesses a biologically based pattern of reaction sensitivities and behavioral dispositions which shape the nature of his experiences and may contribute directly to the creation of environmental difficulties.

The biological dispositions of the maturing child are important because they strengthen the probability that certain kinds of behavior be learned. It appears clear also that constitutional tendencies evoke counterreactions from others which accentuate the initial dispositions. The child's biological endowment shapes not only his behavior but that of his parents as well. If the child's primary disposition is cheerful and adaptable and has made his care easy, the mother will tend quickly to display a positive reciprocal attitude; conversely, if the child is tense and wound up, or if his care is difficult and time consuming, the mother will react with dismay, fatigue, or hostility. Through his own behavioral disposition then, the child elicits a series of parental behaviors which reinforce his initial pattern.

The reciprocal interplay of biologic patterns and parental reactions has not been sufficiently explored. The biosocial-learning approach presented in this paper stems largely from the thesis that the child's constitutional pattern shapes and interacts with his social reinforcement experiences.

The fact that early experiences are likely to contribute a disproportionate share to learned behavior is attributable in part to the fact that their effects are difficult to extinguish. This resistance to extinction stems largely from the fact that learning in early life is presymbolic, random, and highly generalized. Additional factors which contribute to the persistence and continuity of early learnings are social factors such as the repetitive nature of experience, the tendency for interpersonal relations to be reciprocally reinforcing, and the perseverance of early character stereotypes.

Beyond these are a number of self-perpetuating processes which derive from the individual's own actions. Among them are protective efforts which constrict the person's awareness and experience, the tendency to perceptually and cognitively distort events in line with expectancies, the inappropriate generalization to new events of old behavior patterns, and the repetitive compulsion to create conditions which parallel the past.

Children learn complicated sequences of attitudes, reactions, and expectancies in response to the experiences to which they are exposed. Initially, these responses are specific to the particular events which prompted them; they are piecemeal, scattered, and changeable. Over the course of time, however, through learning what responses are successful in obtaining rewards and avoiding punishments, the child begins to crystalize a stable pattern of instrumental behaviors for handling the events of everyday life. These coping and adaptive strategies come to characterize his way of relating to others, and comprise one of the most important facets of what we may term his personality pattern.

With the foregoing as a précis and perspective, let us proceed to outline a number of both biologic and psychosocial factors which we believe interact to shape the avoidant personality pattern.

Heredity. Genetic predispositions to avoidant behavior must not be overlooked, despite the lack of empirical data. Many physiological processes comprise the physical substrate for complex psychological functions. It would be naive to assume that these substrates do not vary from person to person. Studies which demonstrate a high correspondence within family groups in social apprehensiveness and withdrawal behavior can be attributed in large measure to learning, but there is reason to believe, at least in some cases, that this correspondence may partially be assigned to a common pool of genotypic dispositions within families.

Fearful Infantile Pattern. Infants who display hyperirritability, crankiness, and withdrawal behaviors from the first days of postnatal life may not only possess a constitutional disposition toward an avoidant pattern but may prompt rejecting and hostile attitudes from their parents. Such tense infants typically induce parental dismay, an attitude which may create a stereotype of a difficult-to-manage child. In these cases, an initial tendency toward anxiety may be aggravated further by parental rejection.

Neurological Imbalances. Quite possibly, avoidant personalities experience aversive stimuli more intensely than others because they possess an especially dense substrate in the "aversive" center of the nervous system. Another plausible speculation regarding the aversive feature of this personality centers on a possible functional dominance of the sympathetic nervous system. Excess adrenalin may give rise to their hypervigilance, affective disharmony, and cognitive interference. Individual differences in brain anatomy have been well demonstrated, but we must recognize that speculations attributing complex forms of clinical behavior to biophysical variations are not only conjectural but also rather simplistic. Even if biological differences in aversiveness were found, the psychological form and content of these tendencies would take on their specific character only as a function of the individual's particular life experiences and learnings.

Parental Rejection and Deprecation. Even attractive and healthy infants may encounter parental devaluation and rejection. Reared in a family setting in which they are belittled and censured, youngsters will have their robustness and optimism crushed, and acquire in its stead attitudes of self-deprecation and feelings of social alienation. We can well imagine the impact of these experiences upon a child who was not especially robust to start with.

The consequences of parental rejection and humiliation are many and diverse. The opportunity for creating the basis for tension and insecurity through mismangement is greatest at the earliest stages of life. Infants of cold, rejecting parents will acquire a diffuse sense that the world is harsh and unwelcoming. They will learn, in their primitive way, to avoid attaching themselves to others. They will acquire a sense of mistrust of their human surroundings and, as a result, feel helpless and alone. Parents who scorn their offspring's first stumbling efforts will diminish markedly feelings of self-competence and the growth of confidence. Although normal language and motor skills may develop, the youngster will often utilize these aptitudes in a hesitant and self-doubting manner. He may accept as "valid" his parents' criticisms and begin to turn against himself. The roots of self-deprecation begun earlier in life may take firm hold over time. The image of being a weak, unlovable, and unworthy person may take on a strong cognitive base. The future avoidant may become increasingly aware of himself as unattractive, a pitiful person, one who deserves to be scoffed at and ridiculed. Little effort may be expanded to alter this image since nothing he attempts can succeed, given the deficits and inadequacies he sees within himself.

Peer Group Alienation. The give and take of friendship, school, athletic competitions, and heterosexual dating make demands that the healthy youngster is prepared to meet. Other youngsters, less fortunate, approach this era of life convinced of their inadequacies. The feeling is conveyed to peers and in turn is reinforced by them. Peer group interactions can be devastating for the future avoidant. Many such youngsters feel shattered by constant humiliation in the exposure of their scholastic, athletic, physical, or social inadequacies. Unable to prove themselves, they are not only derided and isolated by others, but become sharply critical toward themselves for their lack of worthiness and esteem. Feelings of loneliness and rejection are now compounded by severe self-judgments of personal inferiority and unattractiveness. They are unable now to turn either to others for solace and gratification or to themselves.

Aversive Coping Behaviors. The avoidant is guided by a need to put distance between himself and others, that is, to minimize involvements that can reactivate or duplicate past humiliations. Any desire or interest which entails personal commitments to others constitutes a threat to his security. To avoid the anguish of social relationships requires remaining alert to potential threat. This contrasts markedly with the style of the schizoid personality who is perceptually insensitive to his surroundings. The avoidant is keenly attentive to and aware of variations and subtleties in his stimulus world. He has learned through past encounters that the most effective means of avoiding them is to be hyperalert to cues which forewarn their occurrence.

Self-derogating Thinking. Turning away from one's external environment brings little peace and comfort. The avoidant finds no solace and freedom within himself. Having an attitude of self-derogation and deprecation, he not only experiences little reward in his accomplishments and his thoughts but also finds in their stead, shame, devaluation, and anguish. There may be greater pain being alone with one's despised self than with the escapable torment of others. Immersing oneself in one's thoughts and feelings is more difficult since the person cannot physically avoid himself, cannot walk away, escape, or hide from his own being. Deprived of feelings of self-worth, he suffers from painful thoughts about his pitiful state, his misery, and the futility of being himself. Efforts as vigilant as those applied to the external world must be expended to ward off the distressing thoughts and feelings that well up within him. He muddles his own ideas and emotions. Better to experience diffuse disharmony than the pain and anguish of thinking about oneself.

Restricted Social Experiences. Avoidants assume that the atypical experiences to which they were exposed in early life will continue to be their lot forever. In defense they narrow the range of activities in which they participate. By circumscribing their life, however, they preclude the possibility of corrective experiences, experiences which may show them that "all is not lost," that there are kindly and friendly persons who will not disparage and humiliate them. By detaching themselves from others they are left to be preoccupied with their own thoughts and impulses. Limited to these stimuli, they can only reflect about past events, with all the discomforts they bring forth. Since experience is restricted largely to their past, life becomes a series of duplications. They relive the painful events of earlier times rather than experience new events which might alter their attitudes and feelings.

Treatment Considerations

Because of the avoidant's basic mistrust of others, he is unlikely to be motivated either to seek or to sustain a therapeutic relationship. Should he submit to treatment, it is probable that he will maneuver to test the sincerity and genuineness of the therapist's feelings and motives. In many cases he will terminate treatment long before remedial improvement has occurred. The potential rewards of therapy may not only fail to motivate the avoidant but also may actually serve as a deterrent. It reawakens what he sees will be false hopes. It leads him back to the dangers and humiliations he experienced with others when he tendered his affections, but received rejection. Now that he has found a modest degree of comfort by detaching himself from others, he would rather leave matters stand, stick to his accustomed level of adjustment, and not "rock the boat" he so tenuously learned to sail.

A first therapeutic approach would be to assist the patient in managing a more rewarding environment. Here we might seek to discover opportunities which might enhance his self-worth. Supportive therapy may be all that can be tolerated until he is capable of dealing comfortably with his more painful feelings and thoughts. Psychopharmacologic treatment may be used to diminish or control anxieties. Behavior modification techniques may be useful as a means of learning less fearful reactions to formerly threatening situations. As the patient progresses in trust and security with the therapist, he may be amenable to cognitive methods which alter erroneous self-attitudes and distorted social expectancies. Deeper and more searching procedures can be useful in reworking unconscious anxieties and mechanisms. Lastly, group therapeutic approaches may be employed to assist the patient in learning new attitudes and skills in a more benign and accepting social atmosphere than he normally encounters.

REFERENCES

1. American Psychiatric Association. *Diagnostic and Statistical Manual of Mental Disorders* (DSM III). American Psychiatric Association, Washington, D. C., 1980.
2. Arieti, S. *Interpretation of Schizophrenia.* Brunner, New York, 1955.
3. Binet, A. Double consciousness in health. Mind, *15:*46–57, 1890.
4. Bleuler, E. *Dementia Praecox oder Gruppe der Schizophrenien.* Deuticke, Leipzig, 1911. English translation, *Dementia Praecox.* International Universities Press, New York, 1950.
5. Bleuler, E. Die probleme der schizoidie und der syntonie. Z. Gesamte Neurol. Psychiatr., *78:*373–388, 1922.
6. Bleuler, E. *Textbook of Psychiatry,* English translation. MacMillan, New York, 1924.
7. Bleuler, E. Syntonie-schizoidie-schizophrenie. J. Neurol. Psychopathol., *38:*47–64, 1929.
8. Burnham, D. L., Gladstone, A. I., and Gibson, R. W. *Schizophrenia and the Need-Fear Dilemma.* International Universities Press, New York, 1969.

9. Deutsch, H. Some forms of emotional disturbance and their relationship to schizophrenia. Psychoanal. Q., *11*:301–321, 1942.
10. Fairbairn, W. R. D. Schizoid factors in the personality. In: *Psychoanalytic Studies of the Personality*, Tavistock, London, 1952.
11. Freud, S. The instincts and their vicissitudes. In: *Collected Papers*, English translation, Vol. 4. Hogarth, London, 1925.
12. Guntrip, H. A study of Fairbairn's theory of schizoid reactions. Br. J. Med. Psychol., *25:* 86–104, 1952.
13. Heymans, G., and Wiersma, E. Beitrage zur speziellen Psychologie auf grund einer massenuntersuchung. Z. Psychol., *42, 46, 49, 51:*1906–1909.
14. Hoch, A. Constitutional factors in the dementia praecox group. Rev. Neurol. Psychiatry, *8:* 463–475, 1910.
15. Horney, K. *Our Inner Conflicts*. Norton, New York, 1945.
16. Kahlbaum, K. L. Heboidophrenia. Allg. Z. Psychiatrie, *46:*461–482, 1890.
17. Kallmann, F. J. *The Genetics of Schizophrenia*. Augustin, New York, 1938.
18. Kernberg, O. F. A psychoanalytic classification of character pathology. J. Am. Psychoanal. *18:*800–822, 1970.
19. Klein, D. F. Psychotropic drugs and the regulation of behavioral activation in psychiatric illness. In: *Drugs and Cerebral Function*, W. L. Smith (Ed.), Charles C Thomas, Springfield.
20. Kollarits, J. *Charakter und Nervositat*. Knoedler, Budapest, 1912.
21. Kraepelin, E. *Psychiatrie: Ein Lehrbuch*, Ed. 8, Vol. 3. Barth, Leipzig, 1913.
22. Kraepelin, E. *Dementia Praecox and Paraphrenia*. Livingstone, Edinburgh, 1919.
23. Kretschmer, E. *Korperbau und Charakter*. Springer Verlag, Berlin, 1925. English translation, *Physique and Character*. Kegan Paul, London, 1926.
24. Laing, R. D. *The Divided Self*. Quadrangle, Chicago, 1960.
25. McDougall, W. *Introduction to Social Psychology*. Scribners, New York, 1908.
26. Meumann, E. *Intelligenz und Wille*. Barth, Leipzig, 1910.
27. Millon, T. (Ed.) *Theories of Psychopathology*. W. B. Saunders, Philadelphia, 1967.
28. Millon, T. *Modern Psychopathology: A Biosocial Approach to Maladaptive Learning and Functioning*. W. B. Saunders, Philadelphia, 1969.
29. Millon, T. *Millon Clinical Multiaxial Inventory Manual*. National Computer Systems, Minneapolis, 1977.
30. Millon, T. *Disorders of Personality: DSM-III: Axis II*. Wiley, New York, 1981.
31. Millon, T., and Millon, R. *Abnormal Behavior and Personality*. W. B. Saunders, Philadelphia, 1974.
32. Winnicott, D. W. Primitive emotional development. In: *Collected Papers*. Tavistock, London, 1958.
33. Winnicott, D. W. On transference. Int. J. Psychoanal., *37:*382–395, 1956.

9

PASSIVE-AGGRESSIVE PERSONALITY

Kenneth L. Malinow, M.D.

Introduction

The difficulties in forming an adequate conceptualization and treatment strategy for patients with passive-aggressive personality disorders reflect similar problems in the entire field of personality theory. There are a lack of common definitions, diagnostic criteria, and well-structured and replicated research. The term itself, passive-aggressive, is ambivalent and suggests paradox. No other label of personality suggests seemingly opposite and exclusive behaviors occurring simultaneously. Does the term denote behavior occurring on a single axis with two opposite poles or is it referring to multiaxial and orthoganol behaviors? Is it the behavior that is being described or is the the psychodynamics? Are the behaviors or dynamics truly stable over the long term or are they circumstantial and state dependent? The very basic nature of these problems and questions must be viewed in contrast to the ubiquity of passive-aggressive as a label, explanatory concept and diagnostic category in modern psychiatry. This concept is found in the child (2, 9, 12, 17, 20, 30), adolescent (24), and adult (29, 30) literature. It is of importance to both civilian and military psychiatry (16, 32), consultation-liaison psychiatry (21), medical-surgical nursing (26), suicidology (22), the study of morbid behavior (1), psychiatry testing and profiling (23, 29), psychoanalysis (3, 19), drug abuse and alcoholism (5, 10, 18), family therapy (25), paraphilias (15), mental retardation (11), and neurology (31). The usefulness of the concept extends beyond the confines of pathologic behaviors into areas of normal and appropriate action. The executive who uses his secretary to consistently interrupt and cut short unpleasant meetings does so with the covert understanding of all involved, and would be popularly labeled as acting in a passive-aggressive manner. This type of behavior in highly structured and dependent groups such as large corporations or the military is not just common, but indeed, is both acceptable and normal. Patients in therapy who frequently act violently against others or their selves and subsequently change to exhibit more passive forms of aggression are considered to be improving. Indeed, Freud's dictum that hurling a curse word instead of a spear is the first step toward civilization is a basic example of acceptable passive-aggressive action.

Yet, in the face of such extensive utility one finds a pitiful lack of useful knowledge concerning etiology and treatment. This chapter will review the history and literature on passive-aggressive personality and attempt a reformulation.

History

Historically, passive-aggressive personality is a term and concept that evolved directly from the American military neuropsychiatric experience of World War II. Although the concept of passive-dependent and passive-aggressive characters had some antecedents in early psychoanalytic writing, its usefulness as a descriptor of behavior and diagnostic category was not demonstrated until World War II.

As a point of origin, elucidation, and contrast, one can examine the American psychiatric experience of World War I. It was a war that lasted 1½ years for this country. It was fought on one front, and put only minimal strain on our personnel and economy. The country had more than adequate resources to meet the challenge. The neuropsychiatric problems were situational (because of short time span of war) and were related to catastrophic physical and emotional stress, e.g., combat neurosis. The etiology and dynamics were cast in the recently formulated concepts of psychoanalysis. It was during this European experience that American psychiatry left the confining walls of the asylum and began to examine man in his world. American psychiatry was exposed to the revolutions taking place in European psychiatry and found tools that were powerful as both research and therapeutic techniques (hypnosis, psychoanalysis).

In contrast, World War II lasted almost 5 years, and this country had combat troops in every hemisphere under all sorts of climatic and social conditions. This war required total mobilization of American manpower and economic resources. People were needed not just in combat but in a myriad of supporting roles. This war taxed the American system in a way that nothing else had since the Civil War 80 years prior to it. It was out of these circumstances that efficiency and effectivity became important. It wasn't just a soldier's ability to cope with combat that was important but also his ability to *adapt* to a wide range of cultural and social conditions and to the many roles that he would be called on to perform. This adaptability and role flexibility was also important in the civilian war effort. The images of men washing, cooking, and caring for themselves and other men, while a woman back home was riveting an airplane, were rallying concepts for a society hurtling through cataclysmic psychologic change. It was here that the concept of role emerged in American psychiatry. According to Colonel A. J. Glass, there was a change in "orientation of psychiatry as a result of wartime experience toward considering the emotional problems of the individual within the context of his group, and social culture, instead of almost exclusive preoccupation with intrapsychic conflict or pathology ... (it) provided a firsthand opportunity for the psychiatrist to observe effects of the group process and its impact upon attitude, values and finally symptoms and behaviors of individuals (13).

It was this need to get maximum effort out of a finite and exhaustible pool of personnel that necessitated change in other aspects of psychiatry relating to personality theory. Accurate diagnostic categories for the purpose of screening and prediction of behaviors became important. The beginning of our modern psychiatric nomenclature was being formulated, and the final step in its modernization was taken in 1945 by Colonel Menniger in a bulletin TB M.D. 203 dated October 19, 1945, that was the revised nomenclature and list of psychiatric standards (28). This was the clear precursor of the DSM I issued 7 years later. In this manual the term "psychopathic personality" was eliminated and replaced by character and behavior disorders. These were subdivided into "pathologic personality, addiction and immaturity reactions." The latter was defined as a "neurotic type reaction to routine military stress, manifested by helplessness, or inadequate responses, passiveness, obstructionism or aggressive outbursts" (4). This is essentially the forerunner of all subsequent definitions of passive-aggressive personality. It was this diagnosis that accounted for 6.1 percent of all psychiatric admissions to military hospitals (Army), the largest of any of the character and behavior disorders diagnostic categories (27). One suspects that if outpatient records had been kept and tabulated, they would have accounted for an even higher percentage of that statistic.

As a label for a mental disorder and pattern of behavior, passive-aggressive was only officially recognized in 1949 in a technical bulletin of the Veterans Administration Armed Services Nomenclature and Method of Recording Psychiatric Conditions (28). By 1952, DSM I was created out of these preceding military manuals, and passive-aggressive appeared as a syndrome with three subtypes: passive dependency (characterized by inappropriate clinging behavior in the face of even trivial frustration); passive-aggressive subtype (characterized by stubborness, procrastination, pouting, passive obstructionism, and inefficiency); and aggressive subtype (characterized by aggressive temper tantrums and destructive behaviors in the face of frustration). DSM I recognized the diagnostic and temporal overlap between these subtypes as "manifestations of the same underlying psychopathology ... (that) frequently occur interchangeably in a given individual falling into this category" (6).

In DSM II, passive-aggressive personality rose to a separate diagnostic category, with the other two diagnostic subtypes, passive-dependent and aggressive, relegated to a catch-what's-left category of "other personality disorders of unspecified types." In this manual passive-aggressive behavior is described in terms similar to those used in the previous manual, but dynamics are more clearly described. "This behavior commonly reflects hostility which the individual feels he dare not express openly. Often the behavior is one expression of the patient's resentment at failing to find gratification in a relationship with an individual or institution upon which he is overdependent" (7). This was a significant step in that it freed the diagnosis from purely behavioral descriptors and elevated dynamic considerations to diagnostic criteria. The category could not be applied to patients whose behaviors consisted of a wide variety of symptoms such as the chronic expression of pain. The category was diagnostically appropriate for 9.1 percent of patients in a study conducted during the period that DSM II was in effect (28). Thus it seems surprising that originally passive-aggressive personality was left out of the first draft of DSM III (36).

In a letter dated 9/20/77 from Robert Spitzer, M.D. to Members of the Advisory Committee on Personality Disorders, he states, "One of the persistent questions that we have had about that proposed DSM III classification is that of the absence of the category Passive-Aggressive Personality Disorder . . . a category that was frequently used in DSM II . . . our major reason (for omitting this category) was questions regarding the syndromal nature of the disorder, and whether or not the passive-aggressive behavior was frequently merely an isolated defensive maneuver used by some individuals when in positions of relative weakness (for example, military settings)" (36). In fact, it was this concept of "situational reactivity" that was eloquently challenged in a letter to the Chairman of the Committee from one of its members, Erwin R. Smau, M.D. (35). He wrote that, "frequently the appreciation of this diagnosis per se develops only after years of clinical work, when it makes understandable behaviors that previously seen in isolated contexts, were too easily rationalized or remained mystifying." Eventually the category was included in DSM III in all of its phenomenological splendor as category 301.84. The diagnostic criteria are: "A. In both occupational and social areas of functioning, there is resistance to demands for adequate activity or performance. B. The resistance is not expressed directly but rather through at least two of the following: (*a*) Procrastination. (*b*) Dawdling. (*c*) Stubbornness. (*d*) Intentional inefficiency. (*e*) Forgetfulness. C. As a consequence of A and B there is pervasive and longstanding social or occupational ineffectiveness (including roles of housewife, student), e.g., intentional inefficiency has prevented job promotion. D. Does not meet the criteria for any other Personality Disorder" (8). The differential diagnosis includes only oppositional disorder and passive-aggressive maneuvers used in certain isolated situations. It seems worth noting that the exclusionary criterion "D. Does not meet the criteria for any other Personality Disorder" makes its only appearance on the personality axis under this category. Also, this is the only category where the first differential is a childhood or adolescence disorder.

Committees, like other highly dependent groups, are not excluded from the expression of opposition passively.

Differential Diagnosis

Oppositional and obstructive behaviors are the frequent causes of referral to a psychiatrist, and more consideration must be given to the ubiquity of the symptoms in a wide range of character disturbances. Indeed, phenomenologically, the inappropriate preoccupation with trivial details, rules, lists, etc. in a compulsive personality, or the lying, truancy, and aggressiveness of the antisocial personality disorder may present as obstructive or oppositional behavior.

Just as important is the consideration of an underlying organic brain syndrome or unacknowledged physical defect. Poor vision or hearing, unrecognized or denied by the person, could easily manifest itself as a series of increasingly frustrating, ineffective, and oppositional encounters with authorities in the school, armed forces, or other task-oriented organizations. The mental retardations or more specific brain lesions can also present with "forgetting," ineffectiveness, and frustrating behavior that may be perceived as oppositional. Therefore, the diagnostic considerations must range wider than those mentioned by the DSM III unless other serious behavioral problems or serious physical pathology be overlooked.

Clinical Characteristics and Diagnostic Considerations

It is clear that although there is little disagreement that a core of characteristic signs exist, there has been great disagreement what, if anything, they mean. It was with this in mind that Whitman and his group attempted a clinical study in order to understand the diagnosis. This, and the subsequent study by Small, are the only two well-constructed studies on this subject to be found in the modern English literature.

Between 1952 and 1953, Whitman et al. (38) examined 400 patients coming into an outpatient clinic and found the most common personality diagnosis was passive-aggressive dependent types (passive-aggressive, 18.5% dependent type, 23%) at 41.5%. The next most frequent with 19.5% was hysterical type. A tabulation of associated symptoms revealed that the two most frequent associated symptoms with passive-aggressive types were anxiety (41%) and depression (25%). For dependent type these also were the two most frequent associated symptoms, but the frequency was reversed with anxiety, found 29% of the time, while depression was found 36% of the time. They also noted a male/female ratio of 2 to 1. The paper suggests that although passive-aggressive may describe a particular type of aggression, an alternative perspective was to see it as a "continuum of behavior, the two extremes being passivity and aggressivity." The behavior dynamics are subtly intertwined, but, they caution us, still distinct. The behavior consists of 'normal' American assertiveness" transformed by an ambiguous situation to passivity. The shame over this passive stance is expressed by hostile behavior. The dynamic correlates are aggression transformed by guilt and fear of retaliation into dependency transformed again by guilt and external need frustration into a pseudoaggressive drive. The most effective therapy they suggest is an interpretive approach where the general goal is to differentiate hostile from assertive behavior and encourage acceptance of the realistic dependency of the psychotherapeutic situation. The patient's fear of aggression and dependency must be dealt with relatively early in therapy on a superficial level, or the patient may discontinue treatment after only a few visits. They generally feel that the passive-aggressive subtype has a better prognosis than the passive-dependent subtype, based on a lack of hospitalization, more complex ego defense patterns, and occurrence of the initial visit at a later age.

In a well-constructed longitudinal study of 100 patients with a diagnosis of passive-aggressive personality with up to 15 years follow-up, Small and Small et al. (34) found three distinct groups of patients with this diagnosis. The first group consisted of 52% who met operational criteria for an additional significant mental disorder—but no specific psychiatric diagnosis emerged. The second group of 18% displayed similar findings but in addition met the criteria of alcoholism. Group three had attributes similar to the other two groups but showed the signs and symptoms of clinical depression at the time of assessment. In general, for all three groups the areas most disturbed in rank order were: (a) social and interpersonal reaction, (b) affect, and (c) somatic complaints. All three groups displayed impulsive behavior. Frequent outbursts of verbal aggression and tearfulness, suicidal gestures, and numerous physical complaints in the face of no organic pathology were present.

As a whole, Small's patients did fairly well on follow-up. A small percentage accounted for most of the rehospitalization, while the majority of patients' symptoms seemed to remain stable or progress in ways consistent with their increasing age. For this larger group the disease was only "intermittently incapacitating." There was only one successful suicide. The more serious disabilities occurred with greater frequency in the depressed and alcoholic groups as might be expected.

An Analysis

In order to attempt a reformulation of this data let us start by asking what about the behavior of the passive-aggressive person is compulsive, unadaptable, inflexible, and repetitive? In general, a number of different symptoms emerge. The first is a particular form of expressed hostility. The hostility, anger, and aggression are expressed in behavior that lies just within the bounds of what is legal, socially acceptable, yet still provocative. That is, the passive-aggressive act is an act of aggression that has been modified and restrained by reality and social judgment. What can be inferred, then, is the passive-aggressive personality retains a core of well functioning, reality testing, and social judgment. What is pathologic about this behavior is that it is compulsively repeated in a variety of inappropriate situations. It is neither flexible nor adaptable. The behavioral motives are frequently conscious but just as frequently preconscious or unconscious. What is never conscious in these persons is the defensive nature of the passive-aggressive act. The original conflict of hostile dependency is externalized. The passive intrapsychic conflict is displaced into the world and social group and is then acted upon as a means of controlling anxiety and depression. This externalization of the conflict with its attendant involvement of others and their reactions ensures that the intrapsychic conflict is obscured and focus is maintained on external reality. Therapy relies heavily on refocusing the patient toward his intrapsychic reality.

Other repetitive observable behaviors are the dysphoric reactions and frequent somatic problems with which this group frequently presents. It is anxiety and depression that are the most frequent seen accompanying psychological disturbances in these personalities as observed by both Small and Whitman. Sifneos (33) remarks in one of his papers on psychosomatic medicine that alexithymic individuals also frequently present with passive-aggressive or dependent personality structure. This all suggests that alexithymia may be a concomitant and underlying constellation that can explain much of what is confusing about these persons' behavior.

Alexithymia was a word coined by Sifneos et al. in 1972 (33) to describe the finding that many psychosomatic patients are "without words (alexi) for their feelings (thymia). " The observations were extended by Sifneos, Nemiah, Krystal, and others to include disturbances in cognitive, affect, and bodily functioning. Cognitive disturbances are manifested by a minutiae-laden, concrete, and externally or somatically rooted thinking called pensee' operatoire. The patients seem to be able to endlessly describe their illness or circumstances that surround their behavior without any apparent affect. There is a paucity of symbolization, fantasy, or dream material. Affect disturbance consists of the inability to experience any well-differentiated affect other than a generally regressed and primitive form of anxiety-depression. There is also an inability to recognize differences in affects or that affect has concomitant autonomic arousal in the body. Thus, unpleasant feelings are not and cannot be expressed in rich, well-differentiated terms but instead are experienced as unpleasant autonomic arousal without any intrapsychic connections. Another common affect disturbance is the sudden release of depressed and angry emotions onto the body and the environment as short and intense bouts of sadness, anger, and violence. The third realm of disturbances is somatic. The body is held in a stiff and rigid posture, and is experienced as fragmented and ill. There is an increased frequency of psychosomatic illness in these people. The explanation for this syndrome has been variously postulated as anatomic defects or biochemical defects, or has been formulated along more classic psychoanalytic concepts, as by Krystal. He suggests an inability, prohibition, or taboo about tolerating unpleasant feelings and autonomic arousal. Faced with a conflict and its unpleasantness, affects (depression, sadness, boredom, shame, guilt, etc.) begin to dedifferentiate and become obscured in a matrix of anxiety-arousal. This anxiety/depression is defended against by somatic displacement and externalizations.

The patients described by Whitman and Small manifest these findings to a greater or lesser extent. They clearly experience anxiety/depression as the most prevalent feeling. There is concomitant somatization and hypochondriasis that seem to be related to periods of increased intrapsychic stress when anxiety/depression become overwhelming. It is controlled by the discharge of tension by acts of passive-aggressive, outright violence, alcohol or drug abuse, or a sudden burst of sadness or crying. The relevance of this formulation lies in the need to modify therapy from a purely interpretive stance to being supportive of affect modulation and control. Confrontation and interpretation will only increase anxiety and cause an increase in somatic complaints and passive-aggressive acts or other external action-oriented defenses. This will keep the focus of therapy on action and not the underlying conflicts.

Treatment

Treatment is, as imagined, difficult but not impossible, nor without its personal rewards. The difficulties lie in two separate aspects of therapy. First, "the resistance of the patient is especially strong, and the countertransference pitfalls are many" (14). The second consideration is the relative frequency of serious depression and anxiety and the patient's difficulties in dealing with it. These will be discussed separately, and a case example will be presented.

The problem of resistance to therapy is usually present at a conscious level from the start and must be dealt with. These personality types find their way into therapy usually via referral from a superior because of job ineffectivity and disruptive social relationships. The referring source, job supervisor, teacher, etc. may even have been directly involved in frustrating and conflict-laden situations with the patient. Thus, entrance into therapy is usually under duress and is characterized by hostile compliance. The very nature of therapy, with its boundaries of time and money, complicated by a prior distrust, will allow a rapid establishment of the negative transference and thwart a therapeutic alliance. Therapy therefore consists of "the painstaking effort of aiding the patient to see his behavior in very concrete terms and leading him step by step to understanding the predicament he is really in, as well as, change. His ability to do so must ultimately spring from the birth of some trust" (38). Those people need to see that they are ultimately responsible for many of their failures, inadequacies, frustrations, and behavior. They need to reclaim the anger hidden by a cloak of marginal compliance and superficial friendliness. The opportunity for the therapist will not be lacking since the therapeutic boundaries will be tested and transgressed over and over again. The practical problem of being on time, and missing sessions, payment, or even talking in therapy are serious reflections of the underlying conflict between a need to be dependent and protected by someone and the anger and rage directed at the very same person. The boundaries of therapy can be protected and the patient's best interest served by direct and repeated interpretation of the behavior as angry acts directed at the therapist in order to provoke a punishing response and ultimately defeat therapist and therapy. This can be shown to the patient as just the latest actions in a long historical pattern. Interpretation of behavior as resistance will in the long run, promote a positive transference and a working alliance. Need must also be taken to help the patient deal, not just with his anger, but also the hidden affects of depression and anxiety. In fact, it is the problem of tolerating and modulating unpleasant affect that comprises the other serious side of therapy.

As pointed out earlier, anxiety and depression are frequent presenting complications of patients with passive-aggressive personalities. Frequently, this results from a failure of the defensive aspects of their behavior to contain and modulate these feelings. In therapy as the patient becomes conscious of his part of his frustrations and failures he frequently becomes depressed and anxious. As an example, a middle-aged drug addict was referred for evaluation because of poor memory and suspected organic brain disease. The examination of cognitive functioning revealed that his short-term and long-term memory were intact. He agreed to come into thrice-weekly psychotherapy in order to understand why he forgot appointments, medications, etc. He would frequently answer the therapist's questions about his life-style with, "I forgot," or "I can't remember." After months of my pointing out to him that his memory was indeed functioning well and maybe something else was involved with his "forgetting," he finally stated that maybe he couldn't remember because he didn't want to remember what took place. At this point he began to miss and come late for appointments and when he did show up he would repeat over and over, "I've got nothing to say." His affect was sullen and angry. When confronted with the angry aspects of his behavior he blurted out how, in the beginning of therapy, he showed up in clinic early for an appointment and found the hall deserted of people. He felt abandoned, panicky, and angry and left before his therapist arrived. This acknowledgement of anger was followed by him becoming depressed about the whole of his life and anxious that he may "kill himself."

The depths of depression and suicidal potential should not be underestimated in passive-aggressive characters. As Kiev pointed out, these patients usually "attempted suicide in a remote and private way, using irreversible means and making no effort to obtain help ... (making them) a high-risk group" (22). Daily therapy sessions, brief hospitalization, and chemotherapy all may be needed at this point. Although the depression is reactive and characterological and vegetative signs and symptoms may be absent, antidepressant therapy with a drug that has selective properties, such as Elavil or Sinequan, may be useful. Caution must be exercised about the amount of medication given to this, as well as any suicidal individual. It can be useful to interpret and support the patient's depression in order to promote both psychological and behavioral change. A minor tranquilizer is useful at this point to help deal with anxiety, sleeplessness, etc. Vistaril or a benzodiazepam, such as Librium or Valium in small amounts, are useful. The key to treatment concern remains in promoting verbalization, symbolization of fantasy and dreams, to bond anxiety and depression. This is done by directing these normally nonpsychologic patients to look at their dreams and fantasies, etc.

The major complication in prescribing medication is that compliance to a regimen usually becomes another boundary to transgress or manipulate.

Other methods to support affect and tolerance can usefully include biofeedback, relaxation training, guided imagery, and affect desensitization.

Patients will frequently dropout of therapy by not showing up, and it behooves the therapist to set up guidelines with the patient early in therapy about this. Therapy need not be continued, and a patient who has done well for 3 or 4 months may need to leave, only to return later and quickly pick up where therapy left off. These separations are usually ways of self-modulation of depression and anxiety and anger.

REFERENCES

1. Akhtar, S., a id Hastings, B. W. Life threatening self-mutilation of the nose. J. Clin. Psychiatry, 39(8):676–677, 1978.
2. Bemporad, J. R., Kresch, R. A., Asnes, R., and Wilson, A. Chronic neurotic encopresis as a paradigm of a multifactorial psychiatric disorder. J. Nerv. Ment. Dis., 166(7):472–479, 1978.
3. Blacker, K. H. Tracing a memory. J. Am. Psychoanal. Assoc., 23(1):51–68, 1975.
4. Brill, N. Q. Hospitalization and disposition. In: neuropsychiatry in World War II, Vol. 1, Zone of the Interior R. J. Anderson, Col., MC USA, p. 140. Office of the Surgeon General, Dept. of the Army, Washington, D.C., 1966.
5. Calogeras, R. C., and Camp, N. M. Drug use and aggression. Bull. Menninger Clin., 39(4): 329–344, 1975.

6. Diagnostic and Statistical Manual of Mental Disorders (DSM I), p. 37. American Psychiatric Association, Washington, D. C., 1952.
7. Diagnostic and Statistical Manual of Mental Disorders (DSM II), pp. 43–44. American Psychiatric Association, Washington, D. C., 1968.
8. Diagnostic and Statistical Manual of Mental Disorders (DSM III). Diagnostic Criteria Draft. Task Force on Nomenclature and Statistics. American Psychiatric Association, Washington, D. C. January 1978.
9. Dreger, R. M. The children's behavioral classification project: An interim report. J. Abnorm. Child Psychol., 5(3):289–297, 1977.
10. Eshbaugh, D. M., Hoyt, C., and Tosi, D. J. Some personality patterns and dimensions of male alcoholics: A multivariate description. J. Pers. Assess., 42(4):409–417, 1978.
11. Floor, L., and Rosen, M. Investigating the phenomenon of helplessness in mentally retarded adults. Am. J. Ment. Defic., 79(5):565–572, 1975.
12. Freeman, E. D. The treatment of enuresis: An overview. Int. J. Psychiatry Med., 6(3):403–412, 1975.
13. Glass, A. J., Col. MC USA (Ret.): Neuropsychiatry in World War II, Vol. 1, Zone of the Interior. Col. R. S. Anderson, MC USA, p. 759. Office of the Surgeon General, Dept. of the Army, Washington, D. C., 1966.
14. Gralnick, A. Management of character disorders in a hospital setting. Am. J. Psychother., 33(1):64–66, 1979.
15. Hackett, T. P. The psychotherapy of exhibitionists in a court clinic setting. Semin. Psychiatry, 3(3):297–306, 1971.
16. Hodge, James R., Lt. (MC) USNR. The passive-dependent versus the passive-aggressive personality. U. S. Armed Forces Med. J. 6(1):84–90, 1955.
17. Hoffman, E., Marsden, G., and Kalter, N. Children's understanding of their emotionally disturbed peers: A replication. J. Clin. Psychol., 33(4):949–953, 1977.
18. Horwitz, J. I., Daya, D. K., and Dalpat, K. Non-help-seeking wives of employed alcoholics. J. Stud. Alcohol, 38(9):1735–1739, 1977.
19. Hutzler, J. C., and Pinta, E. R. False-acknowledgment phenomenon in psychotherapy. Am. J. Psychoanal. 37(2):167–171, 1977.
20. Kagan, J., and Moss, H. The stability of passive and dependent behavior from childhood through adulthood. Child Dev., 31:577–591, 1960.
21. Kahana, R. B., and Bibring, C. Personality types in medical management. In: *Psychiatry and Medical Practice in a General Hospital*, Norman Finberg (Ed.), pp. 108–123. International Universities Press, Inc. New York, 1964.
22. Kiev, A. Cluster analysis profiles of suicide attempters. Am. J. Psychiatry, 133(1):150–153, 1976.
23. King, G. D., and Kelley, C. K. Behavioral correlates for spike-4, spike-9, and 4-9/9-4 MMPI profiles in students at a university mental health center. J. Clin. Psychol., 33(3):718–724, 1977.
24. Long, W. A. Adolescent maturation. A clinical overview. Postgrad. Med., 57(3):54–60, 1975.
25. Mann, A. M., and Lundell, F. W. Further experience in conjoint psychotherapy of marital pairs. Can. Med. Assoc. J. 116(7):772–774, 1977.
26. Murphy, P. L., and Schultz, E. D. Passive-aggressive behavior in patients and staff. J. Psychiatr. Nurs., 16(3):43–45, 1978.
27. Neuropsychiatry in World War II. In: Zone of the Interior, p. 756. Office of the Surgeon General of the U. S. Army, Wash., D. C.,
28. Pasternak, S. A. The explosive antisocial, and passive, aggressive personalities. In: *Personality Disorders*, J. R. Lion (Ed.) p. 63. Williams & Wilkins, Baltimore, 1974.
29. Plutchik, R., and Platman, S. R. Personality connotations of psychiatric diagnoses. Implications for a similarity model. J. Nerv. Ment. Dis., 165(6):418–422, 1977.
30. Rich, C. L. Borderline diagnoses. Am. J. Psychiatry, 135(11):1399–1401, 1978.
31. Schneck, J. M. Sleep paralysis and microsomatognosia with special reference to hypnotherapy. Int. J. Clin. Exp. Hypn., 25(2):72–77, 1977.
32. Schuckit, M. A., and Gunderson, G. K. The clinical characteristics of personality disorder subtypes in naval service. J. Clin. Psychol., 40:178–179, 1979.

33. Sifneos, P., Apfel-Savitz, R., and Frankel, F. The phenomena of alexithymia. Psychother. Psychosom., 28:45–47, 1977.
34. Small, I. F., Small, J. G., Alig, V. B., and Moore, D. F.: Passive-aggressive personality disorder: A search for a syndrome. Am. J. Psychiatry, 126(7):973–983, 1970.
35. Smau, E. R. Letter to Robert Spitzer, November 4, 1977.
36. Spitzer, R. Memorandum to Members of the Advisory Committee on Personality Disorders. September 20, 1977.
37. U. S. Joint Armed Services: Nomenclature and Methods of Recording Mental Conditions. Washington, D. C., 1949.
38. Whitman, R., Trousman, H., and Koenig, R. Clinical assessment of passive-aggressive personality. AMA Arch. Neurol. Psychiatry, 72:540–549, 1954.

10

THE ANTISOCIAL PERSONALITY AND RELATED SYNDROMES

William H. Reid, M.D., M.P.H.

Introduction

The phrase "antisocial personality" represents the most used diagnostic concept in forensic psychiatry and one of the more common syndrome stereotypes in general psychiatry and psychology. Even with increasing efforts toward specific syndrome definition in the mental health professions, it seems safe to say that each clinical or forensic professional has his or her own definition of antisocial personality, as well as a set of impressions—often derived from extensive experience—regarding treatment and prognosis.

This chapter will first address the history of the concepts of psychopathy, sociopathy, and antisocial personality. Appropriate processes for evaluation of severe antisocial syndromes will then be discussed, with emphasis on the current operational criteria of the American Psychiatric Association's *Diagnostic and Statistical Manual III (DSM III)*. Differential diagnosis will be addressed in the light of both of these stringent criteria and the practicality necessary for clinical prediction with regard to treatment and management. Developmental, psychodynamic, genetic/familial, organic, and social correlates will be presented, and the question of etiology will be discussed. Finally, since a number of individuals with severe antisocial syndromes, including antisocial personality, do seek treatment either voluntarily or involuntarily—and many feel direct or indirect psychic pain—some basic principles for intervention will be discussed. Detailed descriptions of treatment modalities and programs may be found elsewhere in this volume, as well as in other works by various authors (69, 73).

The diagnosis "antisocial personality" is, since 1980, rather rigidly defined. Nevertheless, most reports and much research prior to that time (and a significant amount since) use different criteria. Sometimes the requirements for diagnosis are clearly outlined in the work reviewed below; at other times such reports address antisocial *symptoms* or *behaviors* which are separate from the true personality disorder. Often, however, clarification or differentiation is lacking. The reader is thus cautioned to read the following pages with a careful eye toward the syndromes being discussed, and to be continually aware of important separations among antisocial behavior, symptoms, syndromes, and the antisocial personality itself.

History of the Concepts

Most authors agree that Pinel was the first Western medical scholar to recognize certain kinds of antisocial behavior as mental illness (*Manie Sans Delire*) (64). Prichard's "moral insanity" of some years later was described in terms similar to mid 20th century descriptions of sociopathy (65). Later in the 19th century the vague diagnosis assumed more medical dimensions, being described by Koch as "constitutional psychopathic inferiority" (26). Extrapolations backward of clinical descriptions led to various etiologic hypotheses, both organic and psychodynamic, including that of Kraepelin (46), who described inhibition of development leading to infantilism.

During the 1930s Franz Alexander (1) described some antisocial individuals as "neurotic characters" whose conflict was ineffectively resolved through alloplastic activity rather than classic neurotic symptoms. Alexander spoke of the possibility of the existence of a "pure psychopath" who would lack any guilt or self-destructive activity; however, he doubted the real presence of this syndrome. Karpman (39) later described such persons and coined the term "anethopath" to separate them from those who lacked the complete psychopathic syndrome.

A number of authors have spoken of psychopathy* to describe characteristics of creativity, charm (32), a pioneering spirit (35), and even a messianic respite from the problems of our troubled world (31). On the one hand, this kind of classification lends itself to the concept of "degrees" of psychopathy, and allows for antisocial traits within persons not usually associated with causing pain and suffering in others. Another view, most aptly described by Cleckley over the past 40 years, is that although some psychopaths/sociopaths may disguise their pathology in a number of ways (business, academic, political, military), their pathology is present nonetheless. That is, although social functioning may be present, there is a serious developmental and/or organic defect. The Cleckian viewpoint is consolidated in his concept of "semantic aphasia" which, in spite of early interpretations by Cleckley and others, is not synonymous with psychosis or verbal defect (12).

In the 1940s and 1950s criminality and delinquency were inextricably

---

* The term "psychopath" was considered acceptable and descriptive between about 1910 and 1960. Although sometimes considered outdated or overly vague at present, it (and the companion term "sociopath") will be used in specified ways throughout this chapter. Although Halleck wrote that the term has been retained for anecdotal use because of its communicative value, misunderstanding of its various definitions from decade to decade and clinician to clinician would suggest that the term should be used cautiously.

interwoven with concepts of psychopathy. In 1956 William and Joan McCord described the psychopath as an "antisocial, aggressive, highly impulsive person who feels little or no guilt and who is unable to form lasting bonds of affection with other human beings" (57). Their work, along with that of Cleckley, formed much of the foundation for the official Western diagnostic nomenclature prior to 1980 (c.f., ref. 2).

Thus there are primarily two ways of viewing the concept of antisocial personality: as a discernible personality disorder with symptoms which may be present to a greater or lesser degree (c.f., ref. 57), and as a largely hypothetical "pure" state of character pathology (cf., refs. 1, 39, and 70). The bulk of this chapter addresses the former concept, as well as some antisocial behavior which is clearly not part of the "official" antisocial personality disorder.

Diagnosis

Subjective and Pre-1980 Criteria

The basis for diagnosis of antisocial ("psychopathic," "sociopathic") personality between 1940 and 1970 is in large measure found in the work of Cleckley. The fifth edition of the venerable *The Mask of Sanity* repeats his 16 diagnostic characteristics in terms similar to those of the first edition:

(1) Superficial charm and good "intelligence"
(2) Absence of delusions and other signs of irrational thinking
(3) Absence of "nervousness" or psychoneurotic manifestations
(4) Unreliability
(5) Untruthfulness and insincerity
(6) Lack of remorse or shame
(7) Inadequately motivated antisocial behavior
(8) Poor judgement and failure to learn by experience
(9) Pathologic egocentricity and incapacity for love
(10) General poverty of major affective reactions
(11) Specific loss of insight
(12) Unresponsiveness in general interpersonal relations
(13) Fantastic and uninviting behavior with drink and sometimes without
(14) Suicide rarely carried out
(15) Sex life impersonal, trivial, and poorly integrated
(16) Failure to follow any life plan.

These are described in elegant detail in later editions of that text (12).

Although some of these characteristics have been disputed on both theoretical and clinical grounds (70), the basic points were represented in both anecdotal and more scientific reports following their publication. Lindner used similar words to describe his "criminal psychopath(ic)" patient in *Rebel Without a Cause* (49), although he was also one of those who felt that the prevailing cultural ethics and morality were crucial to the definition of psychopathy. He differed with Cleckley in this regard. The Clecklian influence, no doubt supported by clinical and social experience, flourished in the descriptions of the McCords (57, 58), and figured heavily in Cameron's (8) description of "sociopathic personality". It should be noted that these characteristics were frequently applied to juveniles (which is not done today—see below) and even to young children by some authors.

In *Personality Development and Psychopathology*, Cameron (8) gives a predominately phenomenological description of "sociopathic personality." The author divided the overall disorder into a number of subsets, including "irresponsible" and "emotionally shallow" sociopaths and "antisocial sociopathic personality reactions." This allowed for the statement that not all sociopaths are criminal, and vice versa; antisocial reactions may occur in sociopathic personalities for different reasons, mostly rooted in childhood family life. The author also noted that crimes committed by persons with "antisocial sociopathic personality" were by and large the same as those committed by other criminals (i.e., a wide variety). The topic of antisocial personality and crime is discussed later in this chapter.

The chapter on personality disorders in *Comprehensive Textbook of Psychiatry*, Ed. 2 (94), devotes more time to antisocial personality than to all of the others combined. The authors cite the 1968 American Psychiatric Association nomenclature (DSM II) as the basis for diagnosis. Necessary criteria include "Basically unsocialized ... conflict with society ... incapable of significant loyalty ... selfish, callous, irresponsible, impulsive, and unable to feel guilt or to learn from experience and punishment." They note such individuals' low frustration tolerance and tendency to rationalize their behavior and blame others.

During the 1970's research diagnostic criteria similar to the objective operational criteria described below and in DSM III began to be used in large-scale population studies. Nevertheless, Guze (23), an outspoken proponent of careful objective diagnosis, gave credence to "the nature of sociopathy" as reflecting two (compatible) views, one sociological and one related to personality pattern.

Before moving on to the operational criteria of the current nomenclature, it should be understood that scholarly inquiries (and much useful data) do not always go hand in hand with changes in diagnostic rules. Even without leaving the field of psychiatry one can still find reports, for example in the psychoanalytic literature, which describe observations (and extrapolations of them) of parameters different from those found in the research diagnostic criteria, DSM III, or the International Classification of Diseases (ICD).

One such important report is that of Hott (35), in which he attempts to reconcile the differences among the various (e.g., violent and nonviolent) manifestations of antisocial personality which have been described above.

He describes "sick" antisocial individuals who are compulsively driven to be hostile to society's well-being and their own. Opposing this concept is that of the more healthy "antiviolence" antisocials who are not compulsively driven and who appear to be more spontaneously involved and interested in the good of society and their own welfare. Although seeing these latter persons as having the character disorder, Hott feels that they are less destructive, more rational, and may show spirit, purpose, and ability to work with groups. some live with other persons; companionship, work, and acceptance of duties can become very important. They have a capacity to form close personal and group attachments, and may be viewed on the surface as antisocial only in that their behavior reflects a specific sense of "here and now." Hott cites these people as the psychopaths who are often seen as pioneers, charming, or "good" in spite of their pathology.

The Current Diagnostic Nomenclature

All that glitters is not gold, and all that is antisocial, asocial, hedonistic, narcissistic, frustrating, or refractory to treatment is not antisocial personality. DSM III places antisocial personality disorder in the second of three "clusters" of personality disorders (3), along with the dramatic, erratic individuals who are described as histrionic, narcissistic, or borderline. The essential features of the diagnosis, number 301.7, include a history of continuous chronic antisocial behavior in which the rights of others are violated; a childhood-to-adulthood continuum of antisocial behavior patterns; and failure to sustain good job performance or competence in other equivalent areas of life (e.g., college, household activities) over several years. It should be noted that the antisocial behavior must not be the result of mental retardation, schizophrenia, or affective illness. It should further be pointed out that, in the author's opinion, violation of the rights of others does not necessarily imply criminality.

Criteria for diagnosis of antisocial personality according to the current American Psychiatric Association nomenclature (which is consistent with the ICD) can be found in Appendix A. It will readily be seen that statistically consistent diagnosis of antisocial personality is an easy matter compared with previously accepted methodologies. It is the author's hope that these criteria will also be found to separate a clinically distinct group of antisocial individuals from the much larger populations of sociopathic, criminal, or "mentally ill" antisocial persons.

In this light, a caveat should be added with regard to young adults. Although the operational criteria imply that persons over 18 who are engaged in full-time schooling can be given the diagnosis, it is apparent that one cannot really develop a chronic or persistent adult antisocial history until he has indeed been an adult for a few years. Further, the extended adolescence of college students and those in professional or graduate school gives some ground for caution in applying the diagnosis to, say, a 25-year-old medical student who has been in college since age 18.

The DSM III criteria make appropriate allowance for those individuals whose special situations require apparently antisocial behavior, such as some military personnel. One's particular motivation for such a life, however, may preempt this occupational exemption.

The matter of the sociopath's capacity for relationships is of such importance—in terms of both its intrinsic value as a characteristic and its position as a symptom of core personality defect involving basic trust or one's ability to internalize important parts of his infant environment—that the issue should be clear in the mind of the clinician or researcher before the diagnosis of antisocial personality is made (71). Absolute deficit in this "relationship" part of the diagnostic criteria forms part of the basis for the diagnosis of "core psychopathy" or "anethopathic personality", felt by the author to be a more severe subgroup of the antisocial personality (71), and is consistent with the earlier hypotheses of Alexander (1) and Karpman (39).

Finally, although a "burning out" of many symptoms after age 30 has often been described, one should continue to be strict in application of the diagnostic criteria. If the symptoms have indeed disappeared in large measure, and especially if they have been replaced with severe depression, then the clinical features at hand must be the most important consideration for diagnosis and treatment. Whether this represents personality change, new psychopathology, or the natural course of the character disorder has then become moot (70).

Differential Diagnosis

Differential diagnosis will be examined from two points of view. In the first, the psychiatric diagnosis of antisocial personality will be contrasted with social and behavioral syndromes which do not necessarily imply illness. Following that, antisocial personality will be contrasted with other diagnostic entities, both from DSM III and from traditional clinical practice.

The psychiatric literature has long held that chronic criminal behavior is not pathognomonic of an antisocial personality disorder. As was made clear earlier in this chapter, persons commit crimes, and lead criminal lives, for a variety of reasons. The presence of cultural subgroups within which even heinous criminality may be found is representative of dyssocial behavior within a deviant subculture. Although sociopaths may exist within that subculture, dyssocial behavior within it should not be regarded as evidence of antisocial personality. Examples may include organized criminal groups, cultural-religious groups such as the Thugs of India or Berserkers of the Middle East, and persons involved in "socialized aggressive reactions" (although these are usually juveniles). Similarly, situational antisocial activity as might occur during a war, and culturally determined assaultive syndromes such as the "amok" of Southeast Asia, should be differentiated from antisocial personality.

When differentiating antisocial personality from other psychiatric disorders, one should first rule out the presence of other cardinal diagnoses. Schizophrenia and chronic schizophreniform psychosis are fairly easy to establish, and effectively rule out antisocial personality. Brief psychotic episodes, if precipitated by organic or severe environmental events (e.g., drug abuse, intractable stress) may be consistent with the diagnosis. Severe affective illness may give rise to antisocial symptoms—for example, aggression or drug abuse in depressed patients; promiscuity and financial difficulty with hypomania—but these too are distinguishable by history, affect, and especially, incomplete fulfillment of the operational criteria listed above.

Substance abuse disorders, once seen as the hallmark of sociopathy, are now better understood as symptoms and/or illnesses in their own right. Again, the history is critical. Further, the author feels that antisocial behavior which has as its goal the maintenance of an addiction or the avoidance of related legal sanctions should be considered with caution when one is "counting points" in the operational criteria for antisocial personality.

With regard to mental retardation, the author disagrees with the DSM III position that "severe" mental retardation is necessary to eliminate the possibility of true antisocial personality. Although "borderline" and "mild" levels of intellectual deficit are not inconsistent with characterologic diagnosis, further impairment would lend serious doubt to either the operational criteria or the developmental/psychodynamic requirements outlined below.

Much more subtle is the differentiation of antisocial personality from other personality disorders and character pathology. Of the 11 specified personality disorders in DSM III, antisocial personality is the best delineated and most clear-cut in its diagnostic criteria. It is thus easier to rule in or out than the others.

Paranoid personality disorder (301.00), as differentiated from paranoid psychoses, shares with the antisocial personality a difficulty with close relationships and job performance; however, chronicity of antisocial behavior (especially beginning in childhood) is ordinarily absent in the former. Narcissistic personality disorder (301.81) may contain many features of antisocial personality (and, as with some other personality disorders, may coexist with it), but the chronic antisocial patterns and childhood criteria necessary for the antisocial personality diagnosis are not usually seen.

Borderline personality disorder (301.83), like many of the others described in DSM III, can present with impulsivity and an unpredictable temper. Unstable (but often very intense) interpersonal relationships and intolerance of aloneness or boredom are also similar to symptoms found in antisocial personality. The borderline patient, however, has greater affective instability and discomfort, as well as problems with self-image and a likelihood of deterioration under moderate stress (particularly loss). Self-damaging acts may be common, and seemingly antisocial behavior may have a transparent self-destructive theme. Passive-aggressive personality disorder (301.84) should rarely be confused with antisocial personality, but may include substance abuse or "resistive" features that appear antisocial.

The other personality disorders described in DSM III are unlikely to be confused with antisocial personality. Exceptions may be seen in individuals with antisocial personality whose clinical course has led to marked social deterioration, at which time there may be some similarity to, especially, schizoid (301.20) or avoidant (301.82) personality. Histrionic personality (301.50) rarely enters the differential; however, it occupies a special place in the familial/genetic study of antisocial personality (often as "hysterical personality"; see below).

Some character or "personality" disorders from other diagnostic methodologies are also of interest vis-à-vis differential diagnosis. Cameron (8) noted that the "inadequate personality" is similar to the old concept of "constitutional inferior psychopath." The same author describes "dyssocial sociopathic personality" as a subgroup of sociopathic personality disturbances. Most clinicians, however, differentiate the dyssocial individual from the person with antisocial personality (see above). Hott (35) agrees that the dyssocial person is capable of feelings of loyalty and closeness. This is consistent with Reid's (69) preference for the word "psychopath" over "sociopath," since the disorder is in the psyche, not in society. Hott and others, including the current nomenclature, also differentiate antisocial personality from asocial characters. The latter are described as unable to live in a social environment, narcissistic, and often pursuing lives that have little relationship to social reality.

Another diagnosis frequently described in the past was the impulse-ridden character or "impulsive personality." This disorder, most similar to "disorders of impulse control" in the current nomenclature, often involves drug abuse and may be manifested in pathological gambling (312.31), kleptomania (312.32), pyromania (312.33), intermittent explosive disorder (312.34), or other less common presentations. The driven quality of the behavior, frequent singularity of purpose, and lack of other criteria for a DSM III finding of antisocial personality are useful in differential diagnosis. In intermittent explosive disorder there is often an "organic"quality which may be seen in soft neurological signs, verbal or other "triggers," or hypersensitivity to alcohol or other substances.

"Emotionally unstable personality" has been addressed in at least two contexts. Cameron describes the disorder as quite different from antisocial personality: failure to achieve ego maturity, poorly controlled hostility and anxiety, considerable guilt, impulsiveness, and difficulty with interpersonal relationships. Although the immaturity and paucity of emotional integration are similar to the puerile characteristics often seen in some antisocial individuals, affective reactions to the emotionally unstable person's deficits quickly separate him from those with antisocial personality.

Rifkin et al. (78) described "emotionally unstable character disorder" (EUCD) as a chronic maladaptive pattern with short bipolar swings, usually not precipitated by environmental or interpersonal events. Although the diagnosis was deleted from DSM II and is not included in DSM III, it raised the interesting possibility of treatment of certain antisocial character disorders with lithium (36, 78). This syndrome, which may be seen in a demonstrable subgroup of patients, nonetheless is probably not closely related to antisocial personality (see *Course, Treatment, and Prognosis* below).

Many reports in the literature compare antisocial personality with simple aggression and juvenile antisocial behaviors. It should be clear that aggressive activity per se is insufficient evidence for antisocial personality. Many such behaviors or syndromes belong in the DSM III category "not attributable to mental disorder" (e.g., "adult antisocial behavior", V71.01), or "adjustment disorder with disturbance of conduct" (309.30). Antisocial behavior in children or adolescents, no matter how chronic or similar to antisocial personality, must be diagnosed as a childhood or adolescent syndrome, for example, a conduct disorder. Giovacchini (20) describes examples of "delinquent acting-out characters" whose behavior was subsequently found to be neurotic or to reflect other qualities inconsistent with antisocial personality.

The decision tree on p. 345 of the hardbound edition of DSM III will assist clinicians with different diagnosis.

Clinical Correlates

Given the operational criteria for the diagnosis of antisocial personality, certain functional, organic, familial, and childhood characteristics have been reported in association with the syndrome.

Functional

Criminality. In a large study of felons, both male and female, by Guze (23), very high rates of psychopathology were found. Seventy-eight percent (78%) of males met criteria for sociopathy similar to those of DSM III. Seventy-two per cent (72%) of that 78% were rearrested within 3 years, and 41% were reimprisoned. In the same study, the most frequent diagnosis among female felons was sociopathy as well (65%). It was usually associated with other diagnoses such as alcoholism, hysteria or substance dependence. Sociopathy alone was seen in only 19% of the females sampled. Twenty-six percent (26%) of the sociopaths gave a history of prior felony convictions, and previous female felony convictions were found only among sociopaths. All but one of the women with a history of homosexuality also fit criteria for sociopathy. Ninety-three percent (93%) of the reconvicted women were sociopaths, but only 30% of the strictly diagnosed sociopathic women were reconvicted within the follow-up period.

As the author points out, these percentages necessarily omit unconvicted criminals and those arrested for lesser crimes. Most had committed some sort of robbery or burglary; few had committed homicide or sex offenses. It must also be remembered that these data address only the question of how many criminals qualify for a diagnosis of antisocial personality, and not what portion of persons with antisocial personality engage in serious criminal behavior. The latter is presumably a smaller percentage.

Clinicians who have observed the relationship between personality disorders and criminals in forensic psychiatric settings often speak of the situational nature of many crimes, especially violent ones. They describe the "criminal psychopath" (here not necessarily conforming to DSM III criteria) as one who is persistently unable to adapt himself to social requirements because of impulsiveness and temperament (15) and/or serious defect in social skills (84, 90). Various authors differ in their feelings with regard to the likelihood of social deterioration, affective deterioration, or psychotic decompensation under stress.

In a study of 500 psychiatric patients, in which slightly different diagnostic criteria for sociopathy were used, 37% of 35 sociopaths had had felony convictions. In comparison, 23% of "drug addicts," 13% of alcoholics, and far lower numbers of mentally retarded, neurotic, and "undiagnosed" patients had had such convictions. The only retarded patient who had been convicted of a felony also met criteria for sociopathy and alcoholism. None of 200 patients with schizophrenic or primary affective disorders reported felony convictions. This study, reported in the same volume as the above work by Guze, is thus somewhat consistent with the results of his sample of convicted "property offense" felons.

In earlier studies, Glueck (21) found 19% of male admissions to Sing Sing to be "psychopaths" (diagnostic criteria are not available). Somewhat lower percentages have been found in studies of general criminality not limited to felonies. Bromberg and Thompson (6) found only about 7% "psychopaths" in almost 10,000 convicted criminals. In this study as well, diagnostic criteria were vague. Oltman and Friedman (63) reported psychopathy in about 14% of forensic psychiatric patients, using pre-DSM I criteria. More recently Tupin et al. (89) stated that most male murderers incarcerated at the California Medical Facility, Vacaville, a forensic psychiatric hospital in Northern California, had "personality disorders."

Histrionic Personality. Robins (79) reported that over one-fourth of adolescent girls referred to child guidance centers several decades ago for antisocial behavior eventually received adult diagnoses of hysteria. Guze et al. (25) reported a comparison of women with hysteria and women with anxiety neurosis which suggested a significant clinical and familial association between hysteria and antisocial behavior or sociopathy. This study was well controlled, although the number of patients was fairly small (30 in the hysterical group). The hysterical patients had considerable antisocial behavior in their personal histories, and their family histories contained significantly more delinquency and antisocial behavior than did those of controls. The data are particularly striking when it is noted that cases in which the subject had a diagnosis of sociopathy itself were excluded.

The 1976 Guze study cited above also studied rates of hysteria in subjects and their families, noting considerable association between hysteria and sociopathy in women, and very high rates of hysteria within the female relatives of both male and female sociopaths. The same study reminds us that although hysteria (often described by Guze and coworkers as Briquet's syndrome) is frequent among female felons, felony conviction is not common among hysterics. Until recently, serious crime has been far less frequent among women than men, leading one to the conclusion that the association between hysteria and felonies is less important than that between manifest sociopathy and felonies. Thus the lack of antisocial (or at least criminal) behavior among women with histrionic personality does not necessarily diminish the importance of the latter in our understanding of antisocial personality (see *Familial* correlates).

Organic

Neurological—especially post-traumatic and post-encephalitic—sources for antisocial behavior and personality change have been well described by Elliott (16). Specific association between antisocial personality and neurological disease or defect was predicted by Cleckley (11, 12). He invoked organic abnormalities concealed by intact surface function as a hypothetical basis for his concept of "semantic aphasia" in psychopaths, predicting subtle lesions in or near the supramarginal gyrus. Although Cleckley's hypothesis has never been proved, other neurological changes have been reported. Some of these are evasive and poorly replicated, some are apparently specific to certain syndromes, and still others appear to be fairly consistent correlates of carefully diagnosed antisocial personality.

Electroencephalographic (EEG) findings have frequently been sought but conventional techniques have rarely yielded consistent correlation with antisocial personality. Elliott (16) reported on the frequent EEG abnormalities found in psychopaths and their families. Knott et al. (44) and Hare (27) reported abnormal bilateral slow wave activity in about 50% of all antisocial patients. Hare noted that this is similar to normal tracings in children.

Activating procedures (including bemigride, photic stimulation) appear to increase positive findings in persons diagnosed as psychopathic, but the predictive usefulness of all of these studies seems low, especially considering their lack of diagnostic consistency. Schulsinger (82), in a comprehensive review, reported positive correlation between violence or impulsivity and one's chance of EEG abnormality. These changes, however, were nonspecific, not focal or epileptiform, and not enough evidence was present to describe any causative factor. In addition, in the light of newer diagnostic criteria and differences between European and North American descriptions at the time of the Schulsinger study (the data were collected between 1967 and 1969), one might reasonably assume that the increase in percentage of abnormal EEG's was related to larger proportions of neurological, impulsive, and "dyscontrol" (60) disorders. Syndulko (86) is similarly critical of much EEG research in antisocial syndromes.

Psychophysiological studies, reported primarily outside the usual psychiatric literature, have for some years built a more consistent case for neurological abnormality in antisocial personality. These reports center around autonomic nervous system data and, more recently, cerebral laterality. Many studies are still being replicated and because of their complexity and sometimes differing results, depending upon the technology used, should not yet be seen as completely reliable.

In general, psychophysiological data indicate lower baseline anxiety, probable lower anxiety when reacting to stress, and ambiguous evidence regarding speed of autonomic recovery from stressful situations (some studies indicating quicker "recovery time" and others slower). The results are usually used to explain the difficulty that antisocial individuals have in learning from experience, especially when such learning involves early conditioned responses mediated by fear or anxiety (27, 29, 30, 94). Hare has also studied cerebral laterality (28), and found no group differences in "left-sidedness" as expressed in right visual half-field (RVF) data. For further discussion of psychophysiological parameters, the reader is referred to the references just given.

Some biochemical parameters have recently been explored, although exhaustive early efforts at showing that psychopaths are "different" were by and large unsuccessful. Thus far unreplicated studies have described overproduction of phenylethylamine (81) and lowered serum cholesterol (91). Attempts to correlate psychophysiological findings with neurochemical abnormalities—including measurements of urinary MHPG, serum DBH, and platelet MAO—are in preliminary stages and include work in progress by the author, Copenhaver, Davis, and others.

Familial

Social inadequacy and antisocial behavior have been reported to run in families since long before the sagas of the Jukes and Kallikaks were described in the last century. Although the McCords (58) once held that psychopaths do not have a higher incidence of unusual ancestors than the general population, and that twin studies up to that time had not established an hereditary basis for the disorder, more recent work has demonstrated clear familial relationships. These include higher incidence of sociopathy within family trees, as well as consistent correlations with other diagnoses, some of which have been shown to have genetic components.

Schulsinger (82), in a large Danish adoption study using strict diagnostic criteria, noted that psychopathy was considerably overrepresented among biological relatives of psychopathic probands. Although none of the mothers of the group had a diagnosis of core psychopathy, it occurred more than five times as frequently among the biological fathers of index probands as among their adoptive fathers or fathers of controls. Females were poorly represented in this group, and sex differences were not as marked in siblings as in parent subgroups. The study differentiated drug and alcohol abuse from psychopathy per se. The author found no evidence that deprivation during infancy and brain damage caused by perinatal complications were correlated with later diagnosis of psychopathy. His conclusion was that genetic factors play an important role in the etiology of the disorder.

Crowe (14) studied 46 probands and 46 control adoptees, all of whom were adopted away from mothers at birth and followed up after 18 years of life. The mothers or probands were primarily felons (90%), with the majority having committed nonassaultive crimes. Criteria for diagnosis of antisocial personality in both mothers and probands were strict (Research Diagnostic Criteria). Controls were matched for age, sex, race, and approximate age at the time of adoption. A significantly higher rate of antisocial personality was found among probands, although the nonantisocial probands were no more deviant than controls. The antisocial probands experienced unfavorable conditions in infancy that may have been related to the development of the personality disorder (the most notable being significant time spent in temporary care prior to final placement); however, the control group was equally exposed to the same conditions and did not develop a higher rate of antisocial personality. These findings appear to illustrate an interaction between genetic and environmental factors in the development of antisocial personality.

Hypotheses of "genetic" influence as opposed to merely "familial" correlates are further supported—as is the probability of an ultimately biological propensity for antisocial personality—by work which strongly implies antisocial "equivalents" which are consistently found in the pedigrees of carefully diagnosed index psychopaths. These include hysterical syndromes (discussed above), severe alcohol abuse in the absence of criteria for a diagnosis of antisocial personality (66, 67), and evidence for relationships between genetic loadings for psychopathy and psychotic disorders (17, 72, 74).

XYY and Related Genotypes. Several genotypes involving the sexual chromosomes have been suggested as predisposing factors in criminal and/or aggressive behavior. To date no study has established a consistent relationship between these genotypes and strictly diagnosed antisocial personality. Moreover, it is now doubtful that even the most commonly implicated (XYY) is a valid predictor or consistent correlate of criminal behavior (4, 74).

Hook (34) agreed that the case for the XYY aggression/criminality syndrome has been overstated. He noted three potential hypotheses: an associative hypothesis in which XYY appears more often in groups in which, for independent reasons, deviant behavior is more frequent; a social hypothesis in which some physical or external correlate of the genotype (e.g., height) results in a phenotypic predisposition for social problems; and a neural hypothesis in which there is a direct or indirect genotypic aberration which leads to deviant behavior. While these are not necessarily mutually exclusive, evidence for each is elusive. Probably less than 1 percent of severe criminals with symptoms of antisocial personality have the XYY abnormality (82). Nonetheless, the total risk of an XYY individual eventually being psychiatrically hospitalized or placed in a correctional institution is about 18 times greater than for the normal Caucasian population at birth (assuming constant incidence and no differential mortality).

Childhood

Robins, in *Deviant Children Grown Up* (79), cited a number of childhood characteristics which were positively correlated with (although not necessarily predictive of) adult antisocial symptoms and criminality. Childhood theft, "incorrigibility," truancy, and frequent running away showed the strongest relationships. Over 80% of significantly antisocial adults in the follow-up group (who did not necessarily carry a diagnosis of antisocial personality) had reports of theft and incorrigibility in their child guidance clinic records. Some 65% of the adult antisocials had histories of significant truancy and running away. Conversely, over 30% of children who had symptoms of theft, incorrigibility, truancy, running away, "bad companions," "staying out late," physical aggression, poor employment records, or impulsivity had problems related to antisocial behavior as adults. This has led many authors to conclude that when predictions are made, the three most consistent forerunners of serious adult antisocial problems are number, frequency, and seriousness of juvenile antisocial symptoms.

The relationship between childhood "hyperactive" syndromes and adult antisocial disorders has recently been of considerable interest. Such a hypothetical relationship is consistent with some neurological theories of the etiology of sociopathy (e.g., implicating various forms of subtle nervous system deficit which either predispose one to certain kinds of behavior or make traditional socialization more difficult; "maturational lag"). This organic point of view is supported in several adoption studies (see above) which indicate inordinate numbers of sociopathic and/or hysterical relatives in the families of hyperactive children (25), a phenomenon not found in adoptive parents of such children (62). As with the behavioral correlates mentioned in the above paragraph, such findings are at this time of limited use in individual cases, although statistically significant predictive validity is found in group data.

It is interesting to note that at least one study reports little positive evidence in this regard. Weiss et al. (92) carried out a 10-year follow-up of hyperactive children in which social ability, responsibility, self-control, and socialization were evaluated by teachers, employers, and the individuals themselves. Antisocial personality or antisocial symptoms per se were apparently not specifically sought. Teachers tended to rate the young adults as inferior to normal controls, but employers did not. On self-rating scales they viewed themselves as inferior to controls on a personality test but no different on a psychopathological scale. Among questions on responsibility, self control, and socialization, the formerly hyperactive individuals rated themselves as worse than controls. This study raises the point that objective observation of hyperactive individuals may not disclose serious antisocial problems unless the investigators are particularly looking for them.

Emotional Development

Given that familial/genetic factors, prenatal and perinatal traumata, and other early organic problems may shape some important aspects of emotional development, the early experiences of the child are critical to the exacerbation, amelioration, and in some cases probably the etiology of the antisocial personality. These positive and negative experiences, the child's reactions to them, and the characteristics of early childhood environment which have been related to later adolescent and adult antisocial syndromes will now be discussed.

Because of the length of time necessary to follow a child from early development to adulthood, when antisocial personality can be diagnosed according to the current nomenclature, some reliance upon older concepts of "sociopathic" and "psychopathic" personality is necessary. In the author's opinion this developmental picture, although somewhat confused, can shed light upon treatment problems and studies of adult characteristics. Its correlation with discoveries through adoption studies, neurophysiological research, and the like strengthens the concept that psychodynamic and psychogenetic data are consistent with—not in opposition to—most available biological data.

Maternal deprivation has for decades been associated with antisocial character pathology in terms of the child's later inability to form meaningful relationships and develop trust and empathy (c.f. ref. 5). Leaff (48), in speaking of the narcissistic qualities of the antisocial personality, describes primitive distortions of ego and superego which arise from chaotic mother-child relationships, becoming evident around the rapprochement phase. Without an adequate "escape valve" for the child, usually found in the father, the traumatic maternal situation goes unattenuated. Inexperience with affectional bonds, due to deprivation or being rebuffed, leads to inability to empathize and a formation of "lovelessness" (58). Giovacchini (20) notes that psychoanalytic treatment of character disorders of this kind must be aimed at correction of the effects of early disruptive object relations.

In spite of apparent agreement among early reports, later studies have cast some doubt upon the consistency of the relationship between early deprivation and "affectionless" individuals. It is now felt that disorders related to such deprivation are neither as severe nor as specific as was suggested, and that a number of other experiential parameters are important. Nevertheless, increased interest in the literature with respect to effective (not physical) loss of parents, due to depression, for example, has opened some new avenues of inquiry about a number of adult socialization defects vis-à-vis development of empathy, mastery, and feelings of self-esteem (75).

Early Family Characteristics

The early family experiences of children destined to have serious problems with society appear to contain several overlapping—and far from pathognomonic—characteristics. These can be roughly grouped under two headings, one of which has to do with consistency of parenting (including parental separation, separation of parent from child, and chaotic family environment), the other with parental psychopathology, both subtle and gross. In the descriptions below the characteristics of the mother are overrepresented. This may be because of her almost ubiquitous position as primary early nurturer; it may also have to do with the relative lack of studies of the influence of fathering on early development.

Separation/Chaos. Robins (79), although putting considerable emphasis on parental psychopathology, was not strikingly impressed with the correlation between actual absence of one or the other parent and antisocial outcome in the child. Many of the effects reported were found whether or not the child was reared with the father in the home. Harmonious marriage was associated with better outcome when the father was not "sociopathic," but it did not protect the child from increased risk if the father was. Rutter (80) reviewed the effects of parental separation on children and concluded that separations due to family discord or psychiatric illness result in a much higher rate of antisocial behavior in offspring than do separations due to physical illness or vacation. This further emphasized the important and complex relationship among separation, parental pathology, and outcome in the child.

Rejection by parents, especially of unwanted or illegitimate children, was felt by Hewitt and Jenkins (33) to be a precursor of unsocialized aggression in children. Socialized aggression, on the other hand, was felt to be associated with neglecting or absent father figures. Other studies related to juvenile antisocial behavior (mostly delinquency), and not necessarily adult antisocial personality, have indicated that complete and permanent disruptions of family life (e.g., those resulting from illegitimacy, bereavement, desertion, or divorce) are better correlated with juvenile delinquency than are temporary separations (93).

Parental Psychopathology. As indicated above, parental pathology is probably more important than separation or chaos per se, and may of course contribute markedly to both. Robins' work revealed that having a sociopathic or alcoholic father (these were grouped together in that study) was a significant predictor of antisocial behavior in adult life. Leaff (47) described the presence of overt paternal brutality toward children, along with a mother who is antisocial, deprived, and clings fearfully to her children, as common in the development of grossly disturbed adults.

The literature is replete with references to maternal pathology. Mahler et al. (54) felt that separation and individuation were severely disrupted in the mothers of narcissists (closely related to antisocial individuals by Leaff (48)), and that this was related to difficulty in letting their children separate from them. Malone (55) described a number of factors in the mothers of antisocial children, most notably their narcissistic needs, devalued self-images, early conflicts, impulsivity, and ambivalence. These were felt to result in a delay in the transition from primary to secondary process (c.f., Cleckley's "sematic aphasia"), with predominate use of actions rather than words. This failure to have experienced comfort and protection from the mother leads hypothetically to defective development of internal attitudes of self-protection, and possible identification with her neglectful, nongiving, devaluing aspects.

Rexford (77) studied antisocial children for some years and observed the influence of mothers' unresolved oral conflicts upon the development of impulsive activity in their offspring. The feeling was that the mother's own oral dependent wishes had not been met, preventing her from meeting her child's needs for love and affection. The child's hostile feelings were not sufficiently overcome in later development to allow him to grow into a capacity for true object relationships. Maternal limits were poorly set, and frustration was lacking in the developmental experience of the child, leading to an inability to tolerate delay and frustration.

In studies of antisocial adolescents, Stubblefield (83) noted a general trend toward finding parents (especially mothers) overstimulating and inconsistent in their parenting attitudes. The parents frequently looked to the child for vicarious pleasure and gratification. Thus the antisocial behavior which the child/adolescent (or even adult) pursued both gratified the parents' needs for themselves and was part of their covert hostility toward the child, since such behavior is often self-destructive in the end.

Wilhelm Reich (68) described a number of typical symptoms in the parents of juvenile delinquents. He particularly cited histories of traumatic episodes, major disturbances in psychosexual development, and actual or effective loss of a parenting figure. Kaufman and Reiner (40) found considerable denial and anxiety in such parents, resulting in covert (but little overt) depression. Often the parent would engage in overt delinquency or show defiant attitudes that went hand in hand with the behavior of the child or adolescent. They believed that the majority of parents of juvenile delinquents studied in their child guidance centers had "impulse-ridden" character disorders. The adults in these families were "marginal", both socially and emotionally. They appeared selfish and hedonistic, with failure and rejection always nearby.

Johnson and Szurek (38) noted that a variety of kinds of parental pathology led to parents' accusations, warnings, and provocative suggestions which might constitute unwitting "permissions" for the adolescent to engage in sexual aberration, promiscuity, or other antisocial behavior. They felt that these adolescents were not "criminals out of a sense of guilt" (18), but were responding to unspoken parental prompting. Consistent with this line of reasoning, they felt that anxiety in the delinquent was related to anticipated punishment from the incorporated parent (and not to mature superego demands) (c.f., ref. 70).

A 1970 work of Glueck and Glueck (22) in the area of juvenile delinquency, citing in part the work of Jenkins and Argyle, offered three classifications of adolescent antisocial behavior and correlated them with family environment. Type 1, youth who are not particularly adventurous or defiant, was correlated with family backgrounds involving alcoholic, delinquent, or disturbed parents, and homes which were usually orderly and stable. The family unit is strong and parents compatible and attached to the child. The mothers are usually good disciplinarians, and relationships between boys and fathers are adequate. This author (W. H. R.) would tend to compare such individuals to the more neurotic characters described by Giovacchini (20).

Type 2 includes defiant and unconventional boys with little masochism. The families are frequently cohesive except for often delinquent mothers and incompatible parents. Supervision from the mother is inadequate, fathers tend to have vocational problems, and income is often poorly managed. Personality and family traits may be inconsistent from one individual to another. Type 3 represents the core group of serious juvenile delinquents. These are defiant, adventurous, unconventional, and irresponsible individuals whose families and households run the entire gamut of family pathology.

Within this group are subgroups who continue serious antisocial behavior into adulthood, as well as some who improve as they leave adolescence.

It should be reiterated that many of the careful developmental studies of the 1940s, '50s, and '60s arose out of a social mandate to understand and stem juvenile delinquency. The reader should be cautious when extrapolating these data into the realm of adult syndromes, especially true antisocial personality.

Mitigating Experiences

Fortunately for all concerned, the plasticity of neural mechanisms in the infant and young child, the variety of experiences available during development, the potential for change within parents and families, and the opportunity to repeat in adolescence some of the developmental processes of the first 6 years of life can all have mitigating and ameliorating effects on problems which may have been encountered during various stages of the child's development. Further, the presence of at least one healthy parent within the developmental environment seems to considerably decrease the child's risk for serious psychopathology of any kind (75). In addition, there is now evidence that certain children may be able to overcome serious parental/environmental deficits by virtue of their own "superkid" characteristics.

In a number of studies involving both follow-up of antisocial children (79) and psychoanalytic observation (38), discipline has been related to protection against development of antisocial personality. When both parents are lenient there appears to be less opportunity for the child to develop appropriate social controls and skills (or, from another viewpoint, reliable superego structures). Parental attitudes should be loving but well defined, with firmness in the shaping of the child's secondary process reactions to primary process impulses. Optimally, such firmness should not arise from hostility or sadism, and should not result in later masochistic gratification in the child (e.g., as is sometimes seen in family "scapegoating").

These concepts are also basic to one's mastery of mature interpersonal relations, especially with respect to tolerance of eventual loss. If, at some time during development, appropriate and realistic parental objects are internalized and oedipal conflicts are reasonably resolved, then supergo integration can further progress, and the potential for grief and mourning within the personality will increase. That is, as the individual's concept of self becomes more realistic, affects (especially those associated with loss and guilt) are more available, and loss (including narcissistic loss) can be tolerated without the fears of devastation which often lead to repression and denial of feelings.

Detailed exploration of the above, discussions of other views, and a review of many of the topics addressed in the Adult Psychodynamics section below may be found in extensive works by Leaff (48) and by Morrison (61).

Adult Psychodynamics

It has been noted that antisocial personality is not a psychotic disorder. Virtually every intensive observer of characterologic antisocial syndromes, however, agrees that the pathology of antisocial personality is more severe than that of most or all other character disorders. Cleckley speaks of "semantic aphasia" (11, 12); Leaff of severe deformations of the ego, superego, and instinctual integration (48); and Giovacchini of early disruption of object relations which leads to special problems of identity and dealing with reality (19). The level of pathology is comparable to that of the original description of borderline personality (43), although there is a basic— if pathological—integrity of self/object relations in the true psychopath.

Self-destructive and self-punishing concepts have been linked to antisocial character pathology for many years. Karl Menninger (59) described an indirect search for punishment. Lindner (49) saw the now-discredited death instinct (Thanatos) in his famous patient and related it to Oedipal and patricidal fantasies. Halleck (26) made similar observations without invoking the death instinct. He described links among psychopathy, masochism, and paranoia, with each being a different reaction to feelings of helplessness and needs to control and structure one's relationships with others. This, in his view, leads the psychopath to a search for painless freedom from object relations.

Other psychodynamic characteristics frequently described in persons diagnosed as having antisocial personality are more diverse. Leaff (48) notes that many structural and neurotic defects (e.g., superego pathology) can lead to antisocial behavior. Talley (87) observes from a Jungian point of view the regressive, puerile characteristics often described. Hott (35) found unconscious idealized images of perfectionistic behavior—with unrelenting "shoulds" of absolute moral standards and unconscious guilt—in individuals who were outwardly ruthless, guiltless, shameless, and without anxiety. These were felt to be so burdensome that the only way the person could relieve himself of internal pressures was to externalize them and overthrow the then social pressures felt from others.

This symptomatic concept of the aggression which is often seen in the antisocial personality is consistent with the views of the author (70) and others that the psychopath is not particularly aggressive per se. Rather, he may merely be acting within a world in which others are insignificant, or may be defending himself against real or fantasied aggression. Leaff describes that kind of aggression as related to a need to attack potential "providers" in order to prove that the world is not a place of trust or reliability. In each aggressive act, symbolic parental figures are unmasked and righteously destroyed.

One of the most attractive and internally consistent ways of conceptualizing the antisocial personality is that reviewed and elaborated by Louis Leaff (48). The "core psychopath" is described as suffering from a severe form of narcissistic personality structure, and his reactions are related to psychopathic modes of narcissistic repair (which can be differentiated from paranoid or borderline modes; c.f., ref. 6). The individual with an antisocial personality core—and thus this kind of narcissistic character—must be omnipotent and unable to invest in or depend upon others. His inner world of objects is one of shadows and persecutors in which the only way to know one is not being controlled by others is to be in total control of others and the environment. He thus attempts to control the aggression which he sees in others in a variety of ways, especially through projective identification and ingratiation. He may also be protected from this world of (projected) dangerous images by identification with an ideal, all-powerful person. Such powerful, giving figures can be valued, although they exist only in fantasy; eventually, almost all real participants in the psychopath's relationships frustrate him, are then perceived as worthless, and must be dispensed with.

The above paragraph implies that characterologically narcissistic persons—including those with antisocial personality—do love objects; however, the loved object is most often themselves. Given this fact, and recent elucidation of the characteristics and responses to psychoanalytic treatment of such patients (45), one can expect the formation of transference, albeit a special narcissistic kind, in intensive psychotherapy. This finding, in turn, increases the possibilities for successful psychoanalytically oriented treatment as we begin to better understand the psychology of the self.

Etiology

The etiology of the "pure" antisocial personality syndrome must still be described as unclear. Correlations, and occasionally causative relationships, may be drawn for certain specific kinds of antisocial behavior, which in turn may or may not be related to—or are incomplete manifestations of—the antisocial personality; however, our knowledge is incomplete.

Researchers from many fields have proffered theories. The McCords (58) cite parental rejection as an important causative factor which, if severe enough, can cause psychopathy by itself. With less severe rejection, neurological disorder and/or failure of the environment to provide developmental alternatives was felt to be necessary for development of "criminal psychopathy." Jenkins viewed antisocial personality as a failure of the socialization process (37), a stance adopted by Winokur and Crowe. The latter colleagues, in their 1975 chapter on personality disorders, speak of environmental deprivation and chaotic early family life (94). Other developmental potentially etiologic findings have been described above.

Guze (23) makes a tentative theoretical formulation that antisocial personality is a heterogeneous condition related to grossly disturbed families, who are often under adverse social conditions. As noted above, he feels that hereditary predisposition and organic CNS dysfunction may be involved in some cases. He notes the theoretical importance of the association between sociopathy and hysteria and concludes that there is a need for further very basic investigation to unravel the hereditary, other biological, and environmental puzzles that have appeared in the literature.

The author agrees with Guze that current biological implications cannot be ignored. It is exciting, however, to note that diverse groups of correlates—familial, biological, social, and developmental/psychodynamic—may come together and be found consistent and coherent. After all, information in each area is related to observation even more than to extrapolation and theorizing; it is unlikely that large groups of observers from different disciplines have misrepresented their data. Expansion of psychoanalytic concepts of the self, continuing refinement of neurophysiological techniques, and early forays into the neurochemistry of antisocial syndromes should all be helpful.

Epidemiology

Cleckley (1976 and earlier editions) and Halleck (26) described the scope of the various presentations of the "psychopath." Although both authors' comments are based upon pre-DSM III diagnostic criteria, the premise that antisocial personality appears in a number of ways in various segments of society holds true today. These people are found not only in prisons and on the "wrong side of the tracks," but also in virtually every social stratum and profession in which antisocial traits have a high survival value. In some circles such individuals—successful businessmen or politicians, for example—may go undiagnosed.

Estimates of actual prevalence vary from less than 1% to over 10%, depending in part upon criteria for diagnosis and in part upon the vigor with which a given investigator makes his or her search. This author feels that true antisocial personality, appropriately diagnosed, probably makes up only a small fraction of the general population (2% or less). In addition, the prevalence in high risk areas, such as among prisoners or mental patients, is probably well below commonly expected rates. In reviewing the international literature it should be recalled that the concept of psychopathy varies from country to country. This is especially important in light of the emphasis often placed upon Scandinavian population studies.

Estimates of sex differences have varied almost as much as those of prevalence. Most authors feel that the disorder is six to eight times more common in males, although some describe this difference as considerably less, based upon differences in presentation and social acceptance of the symptomatology in women. Still others, writing from strong foundations of familial observation and rigid diagnostic criteria, note that some classically "female" conditions may represent phenomenologic or even genetic equivalents of antisocial personality (e.g., some hysterical syndromes; c.f., ref. 13). The author leans toward the latter hypothesis, and sees little reason to assume that either the biochemistry or the psychodynamics necessary to produce severe antisocial syndromes is significantly associated with the presence of the Y chromosome. Similarly, the commonly cited finding that males who are destined to be diagnosed as having antisocial personality present symptoms far earlier than females is likely to be misleading.

There appear to be no significant differences in prevalence of the diagnosis with respect to race. Differences postulated between and among differing cultures may be more related to diagnostic criteria and social acceptance of symptomatology than to presence or absence of the disorder itself.

Course, Treatment, and Prognosis

Most authors who have observed large numbers of antisocial individuals over several years describe an unremitting course, although many observe remissions or changes in life-style (e.g., "burnout") as middle age approaches. Robins (79) found 12% of antisocial children to be free of symptoms, and 25% greatly improved, on follow-up after 30 years. Such natural improvement tended to occur during the fourth decade of life, and there appeared to be no means of predicting which individuals would be so fortunate. Among those who improved, interpersonal problems tended to remain, even though life-styles became more stable. This large study did not address antisocial personality per se and observed index cases who were too young for such a diagnosis were it to be applied today.

Other authors have studied untreated criminals over time. Guze (23) and Guze and Goodwin (24) reported sriking consistency of strict sociopathic diagnosis over 8 to 9 years. The study addressed a population very close to what is now described as antisocial personality, but limited itself to those sociopaths who were convicted male felons. Seventy-two percent (72%) of those who received the diagnosis originally received the same diagnosis at follow-up. Of those who did not receive it originally, 18% received it at follow-up. Three times as many men received the diagnosis at both original and follow-up interviews as received it at only one. Inconsistency of diagnosis appeared to be a manifestation of milder antisocial symptoms.

Maddocks (53) followed 52 British patients diagnosed as "psychopaths" on the basis of more or less Clecklian criteria. Using information from several sources, 33 males and 19 females were located after at least 5 years (6 years average). Significant and lasting reduction of impulsiveness and other symptoms was considered to be "settling down." The study found that five males and five females had "settled," 26 males and 13 females had not, and two males and one female had committed suicide. No clear pattern was seen, although two improved after a prison term, one after a severe fright, and one after a laminectomy. These data show a trend in the direction of this author's hypothesis of deterioration associated with confinement or restraint (see below). Within the group, men more commonly had symptoms related to breaking the law and money problems; women showed hysterical symptoms and suicide attempts. Only one person was found to have developed psychotic features during the follow-up period, and this was described as possibly either malingering or precipitated by confinement.

In the above study criteria for "settling down" were high. If conviction rate had been used, the outlook would have been better (only 21% were convicted after the first offense). The conclusion is a pessimistic one, with half of the individuals drifting into alcoholism or chronic invalidism.

Treatment

It is important to dispel the commonly held notion that antisocial syndromes—or antisocial personality—are untreatable. It is of almost equal importance that one not rationalize feelings of clinical impotence with the erroneous position that these people rarely seek treatment. The reader is referred to other writings and reports, both within and outside this text, for more extensive descriptions of treatment modalities (10, 50–52, 73). Some of these will be briefly discussed below.

The majority of antisocial syndromes either lead to discomfort in the patient or are dysphoric in and of themselves. As discussed above, the wide variety of behaviors that some clinicians and laymen call sociopathic are very often signs and symptoms of neurosis, affective disorder, functional psychosis, or organic central nervous system deficit, or a reaction to one of these. *These are conditions with which the psychiatrist is comparatively comfortable, which he or she is ordinarily used to treating, and for which prognostic optimism is often justified.*

The author often goes to some length to separate the syndromes described in the paragraphs above from true antisocial personality and other more characterologic disorders. Recent reports and modern treatment experience, however, should prevent one from assuming that the "true psychopath" who has been carefully diagnosed still fits the old stereotypes of lack of discomfort and virtual imperviousness to change. There is no question of the presence of at least "state" anxiety in antisocial personality, and careful evaluation reveals a potential for serious decompensation within even the apparently resilient character (c.f., the "anethopathic void"—refs. 39 and 70).

One precipitant of such (often depressive) decompensation is confinement. The individual with antisocial personality who, for reasons of illness, injury, incarceration, or even the aging process, finds himself intractably isolated and unable to use his ordinary resources for stimulation or denial may show a variety of symptoms of discomfort, including suicidal depression. Indeed, at this point he may be said to have lost many of the trappings of sociopathy and, because of his different affectual state, may be more amenable to both psychotherapeutic and pharmacologic treatment approaches. One of the positive signs described by Lion in the successful psychotherapy of antisocial individuals is the development of depression, which is at once frightening to the patient and an encouraging sign for the therapist (51).

The large number of characterologically antisocial persons who do not actively seek therapy (or who have not reached a meaningfully dysphoric point in the course of their continuing development) may come to treatment in other ways. One of the most familiar is the forensic setting, in which treatment may be involuntarily chosen or mandated. The truism that one must want psychotherapy in order to benefit from it does not apply here. Although psychic motivation is a necessary fuel for the efforts one asks in ordinary psychotherapy, it is not—or not in the traditional form—a requirement for the success of many treatment approaches for the antisocial offender.

Residential treatment programs may involve high security facilities which are prisons in themselves. These institutions are different from traditional mental hospitals in that they are not primarily designed to treat the mentally ill inmate but are therapeutic/rehabilitative programs for the ordinary criminal. Patients are usually chosen for their lack of cardinal mental illness (psychosis, severe affective disorder), and may be persons whose recidivism has made them "hopeless" cases. Admission to most such programs is voluntary in that an inmate who prefers prison life is free to choose it; however, in most cases "hospitals" are more comfortable than prisons. Examples include Patuxent Institution (Maryland), Bridgewater (Massachusetts), Broadmoor (England), and Herstedvester (Denmark). The programs and concepts used are discussed more fully in other chapters of this text, and in work by Stürup (84), Stürup and Reid (85), Carney (9, 10), and others.

Less institutional and often nonsecure programs have recently been developed to address rehabilitation needs on a community level. Such facilities usually have a population of less severe offenders (or at least less violent ones), although chronicity of criminal careers and rates of recidivism before admission may be marked. They frequently accept individuals as an alternative to probation, as part of programs of diversion from jail or courtroom prosecution, and/or to assist with the transition from institutional life to confident functioning within society. The latter has been recognized as extremely important to the prevention of reincarceration (85). Such programs, although they are ordinarily found within the community, should not be confused with ordinary "halfway houses." They are full-time, active treatment modalities. Examples include Tyce's P.O.R.T. (90) and Portland House, described in work by Reid and Solomon (76). Some other intensive group experiences are even less traditional, including the New Mexico "wilderness experience" described by Matthews and Reid (56) and similar programs.

Individual psychotherapy with severe antisocial characters is problematic, whether court-mandated or not. Lion (51, 52), has discussed this process in detail, noting special techniques which must be used and cautions which must be observed. Briefly, he recommends avoiding traditional therapeutic neutrality in favor of increased therapeutic stance as a real person, consistent confrontation tempered by acknowledgement of the patient's basic fragility, emphasis on the development of fantasy and affect (often depression), and the like. Countertransference and other feelings of the therapist are important issues in work with severely antisocial patients. Experienced supervision and frequent self-inquiry are recommended.

Medications and other organic treatments find little use in the treatment of antisocial personality. In fact, drugs often cause more problems than they help, including side effects and adverse reactions, abuse, and support for the patient's contention that he is "sick" or "can't help" his behavior.

Drug treatment for antisocial syndromes which are the result of underlying organic or other functional disorders, however, can be effective, provided one specifies a target syndrome or diagnosis before prescribing. Lithium is helpful in impulsive aggression (88); anticonvulsants are helpful in certain episodic or epileptiform conditions (16); and the several organic treatments available for depression will often alleviate sociopathic behavior which arises from depressive and self-destructive syndromes. Antidepressant therapy is also appropriate for the true sociopath who has developed the severe existential depression described earlier.

For a more complete review of pharmacologic approaches to treatment the reader is referred to two chapters by Kellner (41, 42).

Summary and Conclusions

The true antisocial personality is a distinct clinical entity. Other, sometimes behaviorally similar syndromes are more common as a whole; specific criteria such as those in DSM III should be used to differentiate patients.

Although such criteria may in some cases be insufficient, they help one avoid anecdotal labeling and stereotypic impressions which are detrimental to the understanding of the patient, his prognosis, and available treatment modalities.

The author has tried to describe the antisocial personality in a way that is realistic, and neither overly optimistic nor inappropriately pessimistic. It is clear that the current state of psychiatric/psychological evaluation and treatment has much to offer these individuals (and those around them who demand that they alter their behavior), even though much remains to be explored.

Many of the treatment methods described here and elsewhere are costly, and take considerable time and resources from individuals as well as society. One may reasonably ask whether such resources should be used for the treatment of the psychopath. Judgments must be made by individual clinicians, hospital administrators, judges, funding institutions, and politicians in this regard. The process of treatment/rehabilitation may seem inefficient, although this is not always the case. What must be stated is that such decisions should no longer be based upon the old notion that these patients are "untreatable." We can now address the sadness inherent in the psychopath, and in many cases lower his costs to society, his family, and himself.

REFERENCES

1. Alexander, F. The neurotic character. Int. J. Psycho-Anal., *11*:292–311, 1930.
2. American Psychiatric Association. *Diagnostic and Statistical Manual II*. American Psychiatric Association, Washington, D. C., 1968.
3. American Psychiatric Association. *Diagnostic and Statistical Manual III* American Psychiatric Association, Washington, D. C., 1980.
4. Baker, D. Chromosome errors and antisocial behavior. CRC Crit. Rev. Clin. Lab. Sci., *3:* 41–101, 1972.
5. Bowlby, J. Forty-four juvenile thieves. Int. J. Psycho-Anal., *25:*19–107, 1944.
6. Bromberg, W., and Thompson, C. B. The relation of psychosis, mental defect and personality types to crime. J. Crim. Law Criminol., *28:*70–89, 1937.
7. Bursten, B. *The Manipulator*. Yale University Press, New Haven, 1973.
8. Cameron, M. *Personality Development and Psychopathology*. Houghton Mifflin, Boston, 1963.
9. Carney, F. L. Inpatient treatment programs. In: *The Psychopath: A Comprehensive Study of Antisocial Disorders and Behaviors*, W. H. Reid (Ed.). Brunner Mazel, New York, 1978.
10. Carney, F. L. Residential treatment programs for antisocial personality disorders. In: *The Treatment of Antisocial Syndromes*, W. H. Reid (Ed.), Van Nostrand Reinhold, New York, 1981.
11. Cleckley, H. M. *The Mask of Sanity*. C. V. Mosby, St. Louis, 1941.
12. Cleckley, H. M. *The Mask of Sanity*, Ed 5. C. V. Mosby, St. Louis, 1976.
13. Cloninger, C. R., Reich, T., and Guze, S. B. The multifactorial model of disease transmission. III. Familial relationship between sociopathy and hysteria (Briquet's syndrome). B. J. Psychiatry, *127:*23–32, 1975.
14. Crowe, R. R. An adoption study of antisocial personality. Arch. Gen. Psychiatry, *31:*785–791, 1974.
15. Curran, D. A psychiatric approach to the offender. In: *The Roots of Crime*, N. East (Ed.). Butterworth, London, 1954.

16. Elliott, F. A. Neurological aspects of antisocial behavior. In: *The Psychopath: A Comprehensive Study of Antisocial Disorders and Behaviors*, W. H. Reid (Ed.). Brunner Mazel, New York, 1978.
17. Eysenck, H. J., and Eysenck, S. B. G. Psychopathy, personality and genetics. In: *Psychopathic Behavior: Approaches to Research*, R. D. Hare and D. Shalling (Eds.), Wiley, London, 1978.
18. Freud, S. Some character types met within psychoanalytic work (1916). In: *Standard Edition of the Complete Psychological Works of Sigmund Freud*, Vol. 14. Hogarth, London, 1957.
19. Giovacchini, P. L. Technical difficulties in treating some characterologic disorders: Countertransference problems. Int. J. Psycho-Anal., *51*:112–128, 1972.
20. Giovacchini, P. L. *Psychoanalysis of Character Disorders*. Jason Aronson, New York, 1975.
21. Glueck, B. A study of 608 admissions to Sing Sing prison. Ment. Hyg., *2*:85–151, 1918.
22. Glueck, S., and Glueck, E. *Towards a Typology of Juvenile Offenders*. Grune & Stratton, New York, 1970.
23. Guze, S. B. *Criminality and Psychiatric Disorders*. Oxford University Press, New York, 1976.
24. Guze, S. B., and Goodwin, D. W. Diagnostic consistency in antisocial personality. Am. J. Psychiatry, *128*(3):360–361, 1971.
25. Guze, S. B., Woodruff, R. A., Jr., and Clayton, P. J. Hysteria and antisocial behavior: Further evidence of an association. Am. J. Psychiatry, *127*(7):957–960, 1971.
26. Halleck, S. L. *Psychiatry and the Dilemmas of Crime*. Hoeber Medical Division, Harper & Row, New York, 1967.
27. Hare, R. D. *Psychopathy: Theory and Research*. Wiley, New York, 1970.
28. Hare, R. D. Psychopathy and laterality of cerebral function. J. Abnorm. Psychol., in press, 1980.
29. Hare, R. D., and Cox, D. N. Psychophysiological research on psychopathy. In: *The Psychopath: A Comprehensive Study of Antisocial Disorders and Behaviors*, W. H. Reid (Ed.), Brunner Mazel, New York, 1978.
30. Hans, R. D., and Schalling, D. *Psychopathic Behavior: Approaches to Research*. Wiley, London, 1978.
31. Harrington, A. The coming of the psychopath. Playboy, *18*(12):203, 1971.
32. Henderson, D. K. *Psychopathic States*. W. W. Norton, New York, 1939.
33. Hewitt, L., and Jenkins, R. C. *Fundamental Patterns of Maladjustment: The Dynamics of Their Origin*. State of Illinois, Springfield, 1946.
34. Hook, E. B. Behavioral implications of the human XYY genotype. Science, *179*:139–150, 1973.
35. Hott, L. R. The antisocial character. Am. J. Psychoanal., *39*(3):235–244, 1979.
36. Jefferson, J. W., and Greist, J. H. *Primer of Lithium Therapy*. Williams & Wilkins, Baltimore, 1977.
37. Jenkins, R. L. The psychopathic or antisocial personality. J. Nerv. Ment. Dis., *131*:318–334, 1960.
38. Johnson, A. M., and Szurek, S. A. The genesis of antisocial acting out in children and adults. In: *Experience, Affect, and Behavior*, D. Robinson (Ed.). University of Chicago Press, Chicago, 1969.
39. Karpman, B. On the need for separating psychopathy into two distinct types: The symptomatic and the idiopathic. J. Crim. Psychopathol., *3*:112, 1941.
40. Kaufman, I., and Reiner, B. S. *Character Disorders in Parents of Delinquents*, Family Service Association of America, New York, 1959.
41. Kellner, R. Drug treatment of personality disorders and delinquents. In: *The Psychopath: A Comprehensive Study of Antisocial Disorders and Behaviors*, W. H. Reid (Ed.). Brunner Mazel, New York, 1978.
42. Kellner, R. Drug treatment in personality disorders. In: *The Treatment of Antisocial Syndromes*, W. H. Reid (Ed.), Van Nostrand Reinhold, New York, 1981.
43. Kernberg, O. F. *Borderline Conditions and Pathologic Narcissism*. Jason Aronson, New York, 1975.
44. Knott, J. R., Platt, E. B., Ashby, M. C., and Gottlieb, J. S. A familial evaluation of the electroencephalograms of patients with primary behavior disorder the psychopathic personality. Electroencephalogr. Clin. Neurophysiol., *5*:363, 1953.

45. Kohut, H., and Wolf, E. S. The disorders of the self and their treatment: An outline. Int. J. Psycho-Anal., *59:*413–425, 1978.
46. Kraepelin, E. *Psychiatrie,* Ed. 8, Barth, Leipzig, 1915.
47. Leaff, L. A. Psychodynamic aspects of personality disturbance. In: *Personality Disorders: Diagnosis and Management,* J. R. Lion (Ed.), Williams & Wilkins, Baltimore, 1974.
48. Leaff, L. A. The antisocial personality: Psychodynamic implications. In: *The Psychopath: A Comprehensive Study of Antisocial Disorders and Behaviors,* W. H. Reid (Ed.), Brunner Mazel, New York, 1978.
49. Lindner, R. M. *Rebel Without a Cause: The Hypnoanalysis of a Criminal Psychopath.* Grune & Stratton, New York, 1944.
50. Lion, J. R. The role of depression in the treatment of aggressive personality disorders. Am. J. Psychiatry, *129:*347–349, 1972
51. Lion, J. R. Outpatient treatment of psychopaths. In: *The Psychopath: A Comprehensive Study of Antisocial Disorders and Behaviors,* W. H. Reid (Ed.). Brunner Mazel, New York, 1978.
52. Lion, J. R. Countertransference and other psychotherapy issues. In: *The Treatment of Antisocial Syndromes,* W. H. Reid (Ed.). Van Nostrand Reinhold, New York, 1981.
53. Maddocks, P. D. A five year follow-up of untreated psychopaths. Br. J. Psychiatry, *116:*511–515, 1970.
54. Mahler, M. D., Pine, F., and Bergman, A. *The Psychological Birth of the Human Infant.* Basic Books, New York, 1975.
55. Malone, C. Some observations on children of disorganized families and problems of acting out. J. Am. Acad. Child Psychiatry, *2:*22–49, 1963.
56. Matthews, W., and Reid, W. H. A wilderness experience treatment program. Int. J. Offender Ther. Comp. Criminol., *24* (2):171–178, 1980.
57. McCord, W., and McCord, J. *Psychopathy and Delinquency.* Grune & Stratton, New York, 1956.
58. McCord, W., and McCord, J. *The Psychopath: An Essay on the Criminal Mind,* Van Nostrand, Princeton, N. J., 1964.
59. Menninger, K. *Man Against Himself,* Harcourt, Brace, New York, 1938.
60. Monroe, R. R. *Episodic Behavioral Disorders.* Cambridge, Mass., Harvard University Press, 1970.
61. Morrison, H. L. The asocial child: A destiny of sociopathy? In: *The Psychopath: A Comprehensive Study of Antisocial Disorders and Behaviors,* W. H. Reid (Ed.), Brunner Mazel, New York, 1978.
62. Morrison, J. R., and Stewart, M. A. The psychiatric status of the legal families of adopted hyperactive children. Arch. Gen. Psychiatry, *28:*888–891, 1973.
63. Oltman, J. E., and Friedman, S. A psychiatric study of one hundred criminals. J. Nerv. Ment. Dis., *93:*16–41, 1941.
64. Pinel, P. *Abhandlung über Geisteverirrungen oder Manie.* Carl Schaumburg, Wein, 1801.
65. Prichard, J. C. *A Treatise on Insanity.* Sherwood, Gilbert and Piper, London, 1835.
66. Rada, R. T. Sociopathy and alcohol abuse. In: *The Psychopath: A Comprehensive Study of Antisocial Disorders and Behaviors,* W. H. Reid (Ed.). Brunner Mazel, New York, 1978.
67. Rada, R. T. Sociopathy and alcoholism: Diagnostic and treatment implications. In: *The Treatment of Antisocial Syndromes,* W. H. Reid (Ed.). Van Nostrand Reinhold, New York, 1981.
68. Reich, W. *Character Analysis.* Noonday Press Division of Farrar, Straus and Giroux, New York, 1949.
69. Reid, W. H. (Ed.) *The Psychopath: A Comprehensive Study of Antisocial Disorders and Behaviors.* New York, Brunner Mazel, 1978.
70. Reid, W. H. The sadness of the psychopath. Am. J. Psychother., 32(4):*496–509, 1978.
71. Reid, W. H. Diagnosis of antisocial syndromes. In: *The Psychopath: A Comprehensive Study of Antisocial Disorders and Behaviors,* W. H. Reid (Ed.). Brunner Mazel, New York, 1978.
72. Reid, W. H. Genetic correlates of antisocial syndromes. In: *The Psychopath: A Comprehensive Study of Antisocial Disorders and Behaviors,* W. H. Reid (Ed.). Brunner Mazel, New York, 1978.
73. Reid, W. H. (Ed.) *The Treatment of Antisocial Syndromes.* Van Nostrand Reinhold, New

York, 1981.
74. Reid, W. H., and Bottlinger, J. Genetic aspects of antisocial disorders. Hillside J. Clin. Psychiatry, *1* (1):87–95, 1979.
75. Reid, W. H., and Morrison, H. L. Children at risk. In: *Children of Depressed Parents*, H. L. Morrison (Ed.), Grune & Stratton, New York, 1981.
76. Reid, W. H., and Solomon, G. F. Community-based offender treatment programs. In: *The Treatment of Antisocial Syndromes*, W. H. Reid (Ed.), Van Nostrand Reinhold, New York, 1981.
77. Rexford, E. N. A developmental concept of the problems of acting out. J. Am. Acad. Child Psychiatry, *2:*6–21, 1963.
78. Rifkin, A., Quitkin, F., Carillo, C., Blumberg, A. G., and Klein, D. F. Lithium carbonate in emotionally unstable character disorder. Arch. Gen. Psychiatry, *27:*519–523, 1972.
79. Robins, L. *Deviant Children Grown Up.* Williams & Wilkins, Baltimore, 1966.
80. Rutter, M. Parent-child separation: Psychological effects on the children. J. Child Psychol. Psychiatry, *12:*233, 1971.
81. Sandler, M., Ruthven, C. R. J., Goodwin, B. L., Field, H., and Matthews, R. Phenylethylamine overproduction in aggressive psychopaths. Lancet, *8103:*1269–1270, 1978.
82. Schulsinger, F. Psychopathy: Heredity and environment. Int. J. Ment. Health, *1:*190–206, 1972.
83. Stubblefield, R. L. Antisocial personality in children and adolescents. In: *Comprehensive Textbook of Psychiatry*, A. M. Freedman, H. I. Kaplan, B. J. Sadock (Eds.), Ed. 2. Williams & Wilkins, Baltimore, 1975.
84. Stürup, G. K. *Treating the "Untreatable": Chronic Criminals at Herstedvester.* John Hopkins Press, Baltimore, 1968.
85. Stürup, G. K., and Reid, W. H. Herstedvester. An historical overview of institutional treatment. In: *The Treatment of Antisocial Syndromes*, W. H. Reid (Ed.). Van Nostrand Reinhold, New York, 1981.
86. Syndulko, K. Electrocortical investigations of sociopathy. In: *Psychopathic Behavior: Approaches to Research*, R. D. Hare and D. Schalling (Eds.). Wiley, London, 1978.
87. Talley, J. E. A Jungian viewpoint. In: *The Psychopath: A Comprehensive Study of Antisocial Disorders and Behaviors*, W. H. Reid (Ed.), Brunner Mazel, New York, 1978.
88. Tupin, J. P. Treatment of impulsive aggression. In: *The Treatment of Antisocial Syndromes*, W. H. Reid (Ed.), Van Nostrand Reinhold, New York, 1981.
89. Tupin, J. P., Mahar, D., and Smith, D. Two types of violent offenders with psychosocial descriptors. Dis. Nerv. Syst., *34:*356–363, 1973.
90. Tyce, F. A., Olson, R. O., and Amdahl, R. P.O.R.T. of Olmsted County Minnesota. In: Curr. Psychiatr. Ther., J. Masserman (Ed.), 1980.
91. Virkkunen, M. Serum cholesterol in antisocial personality. Neuropsychobiology, *5:*27–30, 1979.
92. Weiss, G., Hechtman, L., and Perlman, T. Hyperactives as young adults: School, employer, and self-rating scales obtained during 10-year follow-up evaluation. Am. J. Orthopsychiatry, *48*(3):438–445, 1978.
93. West, D. J. *Present Conduct and Future Delinquency.* International Universities Press, New York, 1969.
94. Winokur, G., and Crowe, R. R. Personality disorders. In: *Comprehensive Textbook of Psychiatry*, A. M. Freedman, H. I. Kaplan, and B. J. Sadock (Eds.), Ed. 2. Williams & Wilkins, Baltimore, 1975.

11

COMPULSIVE AND PARANOID PERSONALITIES

Walter Weintraub, M.D.

Introduction

In DSM III, the term "Compulsive Personality" is used in place of "Obsessive-Compulsive Personality." This nuance reflects phenomenological concerns of DSM III; compulsiveness can be observed behaviorally, whereas obsessions are more inferential in nature and reflect internal cognitive processes. Otherwise, the terms are identical and are described below.

There are a number of reasons why compulsive and paranoid states deserve to be considered together. Compulsive and paranoid traits or symptoms may coexist in the same individual. Both disorders have been described as diseases of the intellect by Rapaport (4) because of the pervasive use of reason for defensive purposes. Weintraub and Aronson have demonstrated a number of similarities in the speech patterns of compulsives and paranoids. For example, both groups make much use of verbal devices which seem to indicate high levels of denial and rationalization and the presence of a severe superego. The main difference in the speech of the two groups is the tendency of compulsives to "retract" remarks, an indication of their indecisiveness. Paranoids speak in a more guarded, but certain manner (7, 8).

Similarities between the compulsive and the paranoid extend to their life styles. Both are "loners" and tend to deal with strongly dependent needs by the reactive development of an "inner directed," autonomous way of life. In their interpersonal relationships both compulsives and paranoids are extraordinarily controlling and combative, the latter in very obvious, provocative ways, the former through the use of more subtle, disarming tactics. This is certainly one of the reasons why compulsives and paranoids often marry late or not at all.

Both groups contain many persons of high intelligence and impressive achievements. Their early histories often indicate precocious intellectual development. Psychoanalytic investigators have emphasized the importance of narcissism and magical thinking in both compulsives and paranoids as well as the importance of anal fixation in their psychosexual development.

Compulsive neurosis and personality disorder in their most severe forms not infrequently contain within them the potential for decompensation into paranoid psychosis. Perhaps the most common example of this transition is the involutional paranoid reaction occurring in women with compulsive personalities.

Similar psychotherapeutic strategies are often indicated in severe, chronic compulsive and paranoid states. Yet one must not push the parallel too far. Paranoid patients are much more fragile and resistant. They are less apt to seek help voluntarily and usually are in treatment only when overtly psychotic. Stable paranoid personalities are known to therapists less often as patients than as interfering spouses and relatives. Surveys of patients in psychotherapy and psychoanalysis show large numbers of compulsive characters but few paranoid personalities in treatment. For this reason, our knowledge of compulsive states is deeper and more secure than that of paranoid disorders. Indeed, our knowledge of paranoid characters has been obtained almost entirely from retrospective data gathered during their treatment after psychotic decompensation.

Despite the many bridges which connect compulsive and paranoid states, we shall consider them separately, emphasizing, however, those characteristics they have in common. The greater part of our attention will be focused on the diagnosis and treatment of Compulsive and Paranoid Personalities.

Compulsive Character

There is great confusion in the psychiatric literature concerning the classification of character disorders. This is for the most part due to the historical equation of character pathology with psychopathy. Psychoanalytic investigators have developed the concept of character neurosis in which the similarity in the development of personality traits and neurotic symptoms is stressed. Within this framework, hysterical and compulsive neuroses have their counterparts in specific well-defined hysterical and compulsive neurotic character disorders. Psychoneurotic symptoms are believed to develop as a result of inadequate ego defenses against id drive derivatives. The symptoms represent compromise formations which contain elements of disguised forbidden wishes, of defenses deployed against them, and of superego punishment. In compulsive neurosis the symptoms take the form of persistent, undesirable thoughts or urges to perform irrational acts. These thoughts (obsessions) and urges (compulsions) are experienced as foreign to the personality or "ego-alien." The compulsive person recognizes the pathological nature of his symptoms and is apt to seek help. His level of anxiety may be high because of fear that he will lose control and act out dangerous sexual or aggressive fantasies, a development which almost never occurs. Anxiety may also develop if the compulsive neurotic is prevented from carrying out his compulsive acts.

In character neuroses, because of more adequate repressive defenses, intrapsychic conflict is resolved by the development of personality traits which serve as stable barriers against unacceptable impulses. These traits tend to be rationalized and idealized and are so much a part of the person's character that he does not regard them as abnormal. Pathological character traits are, in other words, "ego-syntonic." Since the neurotic character does not usually suffer from severe anxiety, his motivation for treatment is often not great and his resistance to change may be formidable. The obsessive-compulsive personality pattern is characterized by excessive conformity, orderliness, stubbornness, and frugality. Difficulty in experiencing pleasure as well as controlled, inhibited behavior are also part of the clinical picture. People who live or work with compulsive characters find them reserved, cold, and controlling.

Many obsessive-compulsive traits are found in most normal people in all societies. Frugality and conscientiousness have great adaptive value. When, then, do we consider compulsive traits to constitute a disorder? Two factors are crucial here: the degree of disability and the extent of the character rigidity. If deviation from a set routine results in the mobilization of anxiety and guilt or if crippling inhibitions prevent the compulsive individual from enjoying even a moderate amount of pleasure from his activities, one is justified in speaking of a psychiatric illness.

Another criterion in deciding between normal and abnormal compulsivity is the degree to which the person can become intimate with others. If fear of closeness and a need to control others keeps the compulsive at a distance from family and prevents him from forming close friendships, it is reasonable to consider his behavior as deviant.

What is the evidence for the existence of a Compulsive Personality? In a thorough survey of relevant research, Kline has concluded that the existence of a compulsive character has been well established (2).

Epidemiological data have been difficult to obtain because most compulsive characters do not seek treatment. Although their lives are often drab and devoid of pleasure, they are generally successful in their careers and may experience little discomfort. Nemiah claims that compulsive characters exist in far greater numbers than compulsive neurotics (3); studies of patients in psychoanalysis and psychotherapy tend to confirm his assertion. These same surveys indicate that men far outnumber women in both compulsive categories (3).

It is important to note that there is no necessary relationship between compulsive symptoms and compulsive character traits. Most compulsive characters do not develop neurotic symptoms and many compulsive neurotics do not have compulsive character traits.

Psychoanalytic Theory of Character Formation

Modern psychoanalytic theories of character formation emphasize inherited, biological disposition, the interaction of id impulses, ego defenses, and early family influences, and identification with other significant figures. Psychoanalytic theory continues to stress the importance of fixation in the anal period of psychosexual development for the molding of obsessive-compulsive personality traits. The so-called anal character is believed to derive from anal erotism and the defenses against it. The anal triad—obstinacy, frugality, and orderliness—corresponds closely to the compulsive character, and its existence according to Kline, has been firmly established by well-executed investigations (2). However, if the existence of an anal character seems well established, systematic attempts to relate it to pot training have not been successful. The Freudian hypothesis that toilet training practices during the anal sadistic period of psychosexual development can influence character formation in a compulsive direction has not been confirmed. It is only fair to add, however, that negative studies have all been seriously flawed by methodological shortcomings. Much of Freudian psychosexual doctrine is theoretically testable but definitive investigations are still to be carried out.

Attempts by neo-Freudian analysts to explain compulsive personality development on the basis of social pressures or existential anxiety lack plausibility; their theories are even less subject to verification than those elaborated by classical psychoanalysts. There is no doubt, however, that post-Freudian analysts have added a phenomenological dimension to their case histories which has contributed to our understanding of the compulsive's inner world.

Compulsive Defense Mechanisms

The most important defense mechanisms found in the Compulsive Personality, those which give the disorder its characteristic flavor, are isolation and reaction formation. Isolation refers to the separation of ideas from the feelings which normally should accompany them. This enables hostile thoughts to appear in consciousness without feelings of guilt. Isolation is largely responsible for the cold, stilted manner of the compulsive. He may be inappropriately "objective" and "truthful" in his dealings with members of his family and friends.

> **Example.** F., a 45-year-old physician, reported the following incident to his therapist. He had gone to watch his 15-year-old play in a school basketball game on the previous day. The boy performed poorly and was publicly scolded by his coach. Humiliated, he burst into tears. In recounting the incident, F. dispassionately described the events in detail, giving a masterful psychological analysis of

the boy's behavior. One would not have thought he was talking about his own child.

Example. R., a successful 50-year-old businessman, reported in a somewhat irritated tone of voice that his wife continued to be upset by their estrangement from a 25-year-old son. Neither had seen him for 6 years, a state of affairs to which R. had become "well adjusted." He hardly ever thought about his son anymore. It was bothersome, however, to see his wife intermittently upset about him since this created a "bad atmosphere" in the home.

The defense mechanism of reaction formation leads to the development of attitudes and behavioral patterns opposite to repressed, objectionable impulses. These repressed urges are usually hostile in nature and, therefore, lead to the development of a consistent but rigid character trait of "kindness." Compulsively generous people often betray the origins of their selflessness by the controlling way in which they give. The beneficiaries of their generosity, sensing the underlying hostility, may feel uncomfortable in their presence without knowing exactly why.

Why Compulsive Characters Seek Treatment

Since most compulsive characters are successful in their work and do not suffer intolerable anxiety, why do they seek treatment? There are several reasons. First of all, the Compulsive Personality may decompensate in response to a severe environmental stress. He may develop neurotic symptoms, usually of a compulsive type, or become depressed or paranoid.

Example. J., a 25-year-old corporation executive, came for psychiatric treatment after physically assaulting his girlfriend. He reported that this was the first time he had ever struck a woman and was afraid that he might completely lose control of himself. All his adult life J. had led an extremely orderly existence, controlling to an incredible degree both his own behavior and that of people who came into contact with him. He refused to entertain in his apartment for fear that the precisely arranged furnishings might be moved out of place. When driving his car with his girlfriends, he wouldn't let them touch the glove compartment because its contents were meticulously arranged. Handsome and charming, he was attractive to many women, but he sooner or later found fault with them. The stress leading to his decompensation developed from an affair he was having with a psychiatric nurse. She reacted to his controlling behavior in the way trained professionals often do with people close to them. In self-defense, she began to interpret J.'s behavior to him. She told him that he had no control over his orderly way of life, that he could not act differently even if he wished. This is a challenge few obsessional characters can resist. He tried to change his ways, to become more "flexible" but found instead that he was developing classic symptoms of an obsessive-compulsive neurosis. He became preoccupied with the thought that his anus was unclean and began to wash it repeatedly after defecation. He couldn't make decisions and was unable to use his beloved hi-fi system because he was convinced the arm was exerting too much pressure on the records and was damaging them. These symptoms were insufficient to deal with the rage that was building against his girlfriend who was continuing with her "wild analysis." When he lost control and struck her, he became alarmed and sought treatment.

People with Compulsive Personality disorders may develop depressions following real or symbolic losses. These include death of a spouse or parent, retirement, separation from grown children, or loss of parental support in the case of college students living away from home Promotions, which deprive obsessional characters of important dependent gratifications or make them fearful of retaliation from envious competitors, may lead to depressive episodes. Depression is one of the principal reasons for obsessional characters seeking psychiatric help.

Individuals with compulsive personalities not infrequently are referred for psychiatric treatment in a state of incipient psychotic decompensation. If a full-blown psychosis does develop, it is usually a paranoid or acute schizophrenic reaction. Because of the danger of psychotic decompensation, obsessionals seeking psychotherapy should be carefully evaluated for severe ego damage before analytic forms of treatment are attempted.

Well-compensated obsessional characters may come for therapy because of pressure exerted upon them by others, usually unhappy spouses. Such patients may come to show their "good will" or get a "clean bill of health."

> **Example.** G., a 55-year-old businessman, came voluntarily for treatment when his wife threatened to leave him after 25 years of marriage. G.'s wife, a social worker, who was in therapy herself, had begun making more emotional demands on G. after their children had left home for college. Like many obsessionals, G. had reacted by withdrawing into more business and community activities. Active for many years in the mental health movement, G. had considerable psychiatric sophistication. During the first session, he gave an extremely organized, cogent, and insightful summary of his past life. He declared himself ready to do "whatever is necessary" to resolve his marital conflicts, for which he held himself entirely responsible. When, after several weeks, G.'s wife began to show signs of a more conciliatory attitude, G. decided that he had told me "everything there is to tell," that he was neither anxious nor depressed, but would come "as long as you think it is necessary." I agreed that further treatment was not indicated.

Often obsessional characters who are asymptomatic may come for therapy because of a vague sense that life is passing them by. They may complain that they derive little pleasure from their relationships and activities. Some obsessionals seek treatment because they cannot decide to marry, others because they've been divorced several times and realize something is wrong with them. Occasionally, an obsessional may choose treatment as a way of avoiding making an important decision.

> **Example.** S., a 22-year-old obsessive-compulsive character, found himself becoming more and more anxious as his fiancée began to pressure him to marry

her. In addition to the increased anxiety, S. also developed upper and lower gastrointestinal symptoms. He was advised by his family physician to seek psychoanalytic treatment. S. eagerly agreed and immediately informed his fiancée that they would have to postpone marriage plans since important decisions are unwise early in analysis.

In summary, individuals with compulsive characters may seek treatment because of vague and chronic dissatisfaction with life, because of pressures from persons close to them, or because of neurotic, depressive, paranoid, or schizophrenic decompensation.

Treatment of Compulsive Characters

Intensive psychoanalytic psychotherapy is the treatment of choice for the "pure" compulsive character: i.e., the individual who is relatively free of anxiety, who has no disabling neurotic symptoms, who has adequate ego defenses, and who is not severely depressed. There is an extensive literature on the psychotherapy of compulsive characters. In a short review article, one can only touch on some of the crucial issues.

Once rapport has been established, the principal therapeutic strategy is gradually and tactfully to bring to the patient's attention aspects of his behavior which are self-defeating. This usually means that many highly valued traits and attitudes, such as inflexible honesty and utopian expectations of self and others must be questioned. What has been ego-syntonic must be made ego-alien. When this has been successfully accomplished, the patient's anxiety level rises as intrapsychic conflict is created, and he can be treated like a neurotic. In practice, the process is usually extremely slow and difficult. This is partly due to the fact that we are dealing with very old, chronic patterns of behavior. Some of the difficulty can be attributed, however, to the countertransference distortions of the therapist.

The professions of psychoanalysis and psychotherapy tend to attract individuals with Compulsive Personalities. This is partly because the successful therapist has a degree of control over the vicissitudes of his professional life which is almost unique in the business world. He can plan his day to the minute, he charges for missed hours, he collects almost 100% of his bills, he is rarely disturbed after hours, and he can maintain a comfortable distance from his patients, who are indoctrinated into a highly stylized form of therapy.

However, a need to control both internal and external events is the most notable personality trait of the compulsive character. Indeed, his coming for therapy often stems from a fear that his impulses are getting out of hand and what he most wants from the therapist is help in this area. The obsessional character will generally deal with the problem of control in therapy in one of two ways. He may become overtly compliant and hope that by being a "good boy" he will share in the power and omniscience of the therapist. Covertly, however, he will struggle in a number of ways. He may, for example, assure the therapist of his "complete cooperation" at the onset of treatment. The therapist soon notices, however, that sessions with his "cooperative, compliant" obsessional patient are extremely exhausting. This is usually an indication that two compulsive characters, the patient and his therapist, have been struggling for control of the treatment situation.

Often the fight is out in the open. The obsessional patient may quickly seek out the therapist's weaknesses (which are usually very similar to his own) and begin to attack his intelligence, intellectual attainments, honesty, and fairness. The struggle between obsessional patients and therapists often ends in an impasse which may take the form of interminable analysis or therapy. Sometimes the patient simply quits in the early stages of treatment.

Various departures from conventional psychotherapy have been proposed to circumvent the struggle for control in the treatment of compulsive characters. Dramatic breaks in routine have been proposed, such as the therapist getting angry at the patient, confessing his feelings to him, treating him with "shock" encounter methods or even with psychedelic drugs. Without passing judgment upon the usefulness of these measures, it is important to note that the compulsive character is able to adapt to changes in the therapeutic environment. If the unexpected becomes the routine, he will learn to "play the game" or withdraw into a more guarded stance. If sufficiently threatened, he may quit treatment altogether. I know of a number of compulsive colleagues who can compulsively "express feelings" in encounter groups and then "turn it off" as soon as they return to ordinary life situations.

In the writer's opinion, compulsive characters can be successfully treated in conventional psychotherapy, provided that the therapist offers sufficient support and is able to avoid being cast in the role of an adversary. He must never set standards of performance which the patient cannot meet. At the beginning of treatment, the patient should never be told to reveal everything on his mind. He should rather be encouraged to tell his thoughts and feelings as best he can.

Therapists should not compete with obsessional patients. An insecure therapist, when attacked for being stupid or uncultivated, may react defensively and ask the patient to justify his remarks. This usually leads to an exhausting and fruitless "discussion." It is better to encourage the patient to consider his disappointment in the therapist's limitations.

Example. F., a 25-year-old physicist, spent a good part of the early sessions of analysis trying to establish his superiority to me in the areas of intelligence, general culture, and wit. At an appropriate moment, I pointed out to him that he was obviously a person of unusual gifts and that everything he said relative to our comparative talents and achievements might well be true. I suggested that the burden of proving his superiority must be a heavy one and encouraged him to consider the demands he was placing on himself.

Therapists should be candid with their patients about the need for the various rituals of therapy. If there are therapeutic reasons for the use of a couch or a 50-minute hour, they should be explained to the patient at the onset of treatment. If certain arrangements are for the therapist's convenience, this should also be made clear. Magical devices may entrance an obsessional patient, but they will do little to help him look at his own brand of magic.

In cases where compulsive characters seek psychiatric help in states of neurotic, psychotic, or depressive decompensation, the treatment of choice will, of course, vary. A severely depressed obsessional character, who was functioning satisfactorily prior to a massive environmental stress, should be treated symptomatically with electroconvulsive therapy or antidepressant medication. Supportive therapy is also appropriate for obsessional characters who have suffered paranoid or schizophrenic decompensation. In these cases, we are usually satisfied if we can restore the patient to his previous obsessional way of life. Obsessionals who have decompensated in a neurotic direction are often suitable for psychoanalysis or analytic psychotherapy if properly motivated.

The Paranoid Personality

General Considerations

The Paranoid Personality or character is on the benign end of a spectrum of disorders that also include, in increasing order of malignancy, paranoid states, paranoid schizophrenia, and paranoia. Of these psychopathological conditions, only the Paranoid Personality is considered to be nonpsychotic because delusional misinterpretation of reality is not part of the clinical picture. The paranoid character is described in the literature as suspicious, hypersensitive, argumentative, and, in some cases, litigious. He is frequently jealous and envious with a tendency to blame others for his shortcomings and to find excuses for his hostility. Although paranoid characters may decompensate into paranoid states or paranoid schizophrenia under stress, they generally maintain a stable adjustment, with little change, throughout their lives. They include in their numbers men of great talent and achievement.

Paranoid characters are usually loners; they often don't marry and have few or no close friends. They are intense, serious people. I disagree with those who say that paranoid characters have no sense of humor. They often have a devastating, cutting wit or a sardonic self-deprecating, gallows kind of humor. Some very successful and well-known comedians are paranoid characters.

As I have already indicated above, "pure" paranoid characters rarely seek psychiatric treatment. They come to our attention in several ways: as complaining or interfering spouses of patients in individual psychotherapy, as participants in family therapy in which other members of the family are designated as "sick", as perpetrators of violent crimes, or as plaintiffs in legal actions of various kinds, including malpractice suits.

Because the paranoid character is rarely treated in psychotherapy, we have few reliable introspective data. The student will search the psychiatric literature in vain for detailed case histories of Paranoid Personality disorders. Under what circumstances, then, do we have opportunities to learn about these people? There are several sources of useful information: (1) Since the principle paranoid defenses, denial, projection, and rationalization, are found in most people, we can learn a great deal about how paranoids think and feel from nonparanoid patients as well as from observing the "paranoia of everyday life" in ourselves, our families, and friends. (2) Paranoid characters sometimes do seek psychotherapy if they have other problems. Not infrequently, patients with compulsive symptoms or personality traits have strong paranoid tendencies which surface under stress. There are many such people in therapy and we can learn much about paranoid defenses from them. (3) Many patients given the diagnosis of paranoid state, paranoid schizophrenia, and paranoia have been studied in both inpatient and outpatient settings. We assume that prior to the development of their psychoses some of these patients had classic paranoid personalities. We are thus apparently in a position to gather valuable retrospective data from paranoid psychotics. In my experience, however, such data are often unreliable. When psychotic paranoids tend to deny or exaggerate previous pathology.

Example. A 35-year-old physician, referred to me in an acute delusional state, claimed that while he was in medical school he believed that he was the victim of a faculty plot to humiliate and destroy him. Since he had been president of his class with a record of friendly and constructive relationships with both professors and students, I doubted the accuracy of his remarks.

It may be of use to describe examples of paranoid thinking and behavior from the most benign varieties in normal people to the more severe manifestations in paranoid characters.

Examples of "the Paranoia of Everyday Life"

Children offer numerous and often amusing examples of "paranoid" behavior.

D., an 8-year-boy, assured his father that he was well prepared for a school recitation the following day and required no parental help. The next day he returned home from school distressed at having done poorly because of inadequate preparation. He angrily complained to his father, "I did bad because of you. You should have made me go over the assigment with you. It's your fault!"

W., a 30-year-old obsessive-compulsive intern, reported the following experience to his analyst. He was applying for a residency in psychiatry and was severely criticized by one of the interviewers for not showing sufficient commitment to his chosen specialty. Shaken by the experience and fearing rejection, W. returned home and blamed his indecisive state of mind on his wife who supposedly was making excessive demands on his time. The next day W. apologized to his wife for having unfairly attacked her.

The following example illustrates a more extreme use of projection by a compulsive character.

L., a 35-year-old research chemist, submitted a paper for publication in a scientific journal. He thought highly of it and was extremely disappointed when it was rejected with very critical comments. L. reacted angrily and wrote to the editor of the journal refuting the criticisms point by point. He told his therapist that he believed the rejection was due to the intervention of a powerful, envious colleague. Within a few days, L. was able to consider the matter more objectively and realized that he had overreacted.

In the following example, paranoid trends in a mixed hysterical-compulsive character are more prominent than in the previous case but not marked enough to deserve the diagnosis of Paranoid Personality.

J., a 30-year-old psychology graduate student, was completing his Ph.D. requirements and was hoping to stay on in the department as a faculty member. The department chairman was extremely friendly to him, as well as to the other doctoral candidates, and J. interpreted this to mean that he would be asked to stay on. He aggressively pursued his goal by flaunting his accomplishments before the chairman. When one of the other candidates was offered a faculty position and J. was not, he was wounded and reacted angrily. He insisted that the department chairman explain to him why he had been passed over after all the encouragement he had received. He declared that he was "puzzled" by the chairman's behavior and wondered about certain of the faculty being against him because they envied his ability.

The following episode occurred in the treatment of a genuine paranoid character. Although not psychotic, he can become delusional for short periods of time under stress.

S., a 30-year-old single, government lawyer, was referred to me for analysis because of chronic anxiety and interpersonal difficulties. Intelligent, competent, and very ambitious, S. was constantly at odds with his supervisor over the handling of cases assigned to him. Suspicious and intrusive, he always seemed to be provoking arguments. S. had a habit of walking into bars and baiting bigger and stronger men. When they would threaten to hit him, he would menace them with legal action for assault and battery. Although his supervisor never objected, S. felt uneasy about extending his lunch hours in order to come to see me. One day he had a particularly stormy encounter with his supervisor over the handling of a case just before leaving for an hour. On the way to my office, he developed the conviction that the F.B.I. was following him to see how he was using government time. After discussing the incident with me, S. realized that his suspicion was probably related to the argument with the supervisor and it quickly vanished.

Diagnosis

Typical paranoid characters present few diagnostic problems. A longstanding history of rigidity, suspiciousness, belligerence, and jealousy together with a tendency to blame others is a striking clinical picture which cannot easily be missed. To be sure, one cannot always draw the line between "normal projection" under severe stress and Paranoid Personality traits with great confidence. As in the case of the compulsive character, one will be guided by the extent to which the individual is prevented from deriving satisfaction and pleasure from his personal life and professional activities.

Ethnic and cultural factors must be carefully considered before making a diagnosis of Paranoid Personality. Latin pride, sensitivity, and histrionic display of jealousy may strike American observers as having a paranoid flavor. Such characteristics do not have the same significance in Mediterranean countries as they do in our own. Interpersonal competence among family and close friends will provide a more reliable criterion.

Certain normal individuals with strong projective defenses may behave like paranoid characters when forced to live in an alien culture. Orienting verbal and nonverbal signals which anchor them solidly to reality in familiar environments may be lacking in settings where their knowledge of native customs and language is limited. This is particularly true if few or no compatriots are present with whom doubts and suspicions can be aired and clarified.

Paranoid character traits are often present in individuals having psychotic and neurotic symptoms as well as traits of other personality disorders. As I have indicated above, compulsive and paranoid character traits frequently coexist in the same individual. In such cases, the compulsive traits are apt to predominate under ordinary circumstances with suspicious, aggressive, and sometimes "microdelusional" behavior provoked by severe threats to self-esteem.

Example. K., a 28-year-old resident in surgery with obsessive-compulsive and paranoid character traits, was criticized by his chief resident for taking too much time to complete his diagnostic work-ups. K. angrily replied that quality and not quantity of work was of chief concern to him. On the following day, upon entering the nurses' station, K. observed two interns whispering to each other. He became convinced that they were talking about him, that they knew of the chief resident's criticisms, and that he had become the "laughingstock" of the whole department. This conviction did not evolve into a fixed delusion but gradually faded away during the next few days when no further criticisms of his work were made.

At times, a difficult diagnostic problem is distinguishing the Paranoid Personality from more severe, delusional paranoid states. This is because delusional people are not always reliable reporters of their thoughts and feelings. Some wish to hide what they know others consider to be abnormal. Others simply cannot trust the psychiatrist; indeed, they may include him in their "pseudocommunities" of persecutors (1). Certain of these delusional patients may be erroneously diagnosed as paranoid characters simply because they withhold certain of their thoughts and feelings. Under severe stress, they may panic and become openly delusional.

> **Example.** J., a 45-year-old single, wealthy executive, lived with his aged mother in the family mansion. Distant and suspicious, he was considered eccentric but not "sick" by family and colleagues. He occasionally saw a psychiatrist who prescribed medication for "nervousness" associated with "job pressures." These "pressures" consisted of J. being encouraged to take on additional responsibilities for the company. J. was diagnosed as a Paranoid Personality. At a family party during the Christmas holidays, J. was teased by a cousin for leading "the life of a monk." J. became very upset, accused the cousin of calling him a homosexual, and made a suicidal gesture that evening. Psychiatric hospitalization was arranged and J.'s psychiatrist had the opportunity of speaking with his sister who provided information indicating that J. had been delusional for many years.

Etiology

Little is known about the etiology of the Paranoid Personality disorder. Because most paranoid characters are not available for study, many investigators assume that factors which appear to be associated with the development of delusional states are equally important in the genesis of the Paranoid Personality. In my judgment, we have no right, in our present state of knowledge, to make this assumption. There is no evidence to indicate that a majority or even a substantial number of people suffering from paranoid psychoses were paranoid characters prior to their breakdowns. This means that epidemiological data indicating that paranoid psychoses are most frequent among women and in the lower socioeconomic classes cannot be assumed to hold for paranoid characters.

Although the defense mechanisms associated with paranoid thinking and feeling, denial, projection, and rationalization can be detected in 2-year-old children, there is no evidence of a relationship between the extensive use of these adaptive devices in childhood and adolescence and the development of paranoid illness in adult life. After surveying the pertinent literature, Swanson et al. concluded, "... the retrospective history of the paranoid patient reveals little objective evidence of how his behavior evolves. In childhood 50% of such patients show a non-specific maladjustment which when present correlates with an early onset of paranoid disorder. When the maladjustment is schizoid in nature, it results in the most severe, adult paranoid disorder. In most adult subjects the first clearly specific evidence of paranoid behavior is that recognized as a paranoid personality which is probably the morbid state itself rather than a pre-morbid condition" (6).

A few remarks concerning possible etiological factors in paranoid psychoses are in order even though their relevance for paranoid characters is questionable. There is some evidence for a genetic factor in paranoid schizophrenia (5) but convincing data for biological inheritance in other paranoid disorders are lacking. There are no known neuroanatomic or neurophysiological concomitants of paranoid reactions. To be sure, paranoid behavior can result from many diseases which produce changes in the central nervous system, and certain drugs, such as the amphetamines, are capable of precipitating paranoid psychoses. There is no evidence, however, that the mechanisms by which physical damage to the brain leads to paranoid reactions play a part in the genesis of "functional" paranoid disorders.

The most influential psychological theory of paranoid reactions is Freud's analysis of delusional formation as denied and projected homosexual urges. Although a number of objective studies have confirmed a relationship between paranoid thinking and homosexuality (2), Freud's theory remains highly controversial and, in Cameron's words, "clinical evidence within the past 40 years has not consistently supported Freud's thesis" (1).

Klein made the most ambitious attempt to trace the development of paranoid thinking during the first year of life from a psychoanalytic point of view. She hypothesized the existence of a "paranoid position" in the 3-month-old infant because of the extensive use of projection as a defense against internal and external "persecutors." Most investigators believe that the elaborate fantasy life attributed by Klein to the infant is not compatible with its powers of conceptualization (9).

Neo-Freudian analysts have tended to follow Sullivan in emphasizing interpersonal rather than intrapsychic factors in the genesis of paranoid thinking. Much attention has been given to the vicissitudes of the early mother-child relationship, particularly with respect to the failure to develop basic trust and unambiguous communication. Direct observation of family interaction has been particularly useful in clarifying the development of a variety of distortions of communication in schizophrenic patients. It is not clear to what extent these findings can be generalized to include nonschizophrenic paranoids.

A number of social factors are believed to be associated with the development of paranoid disorders. The incidence of paranoid psychoses appears to be greater in the lower socioeconomic groups although the significance of this finding is not entirely clear.

Isolation from one's peer group may play a role in developing suspiciousness. Such isolation may be favored by parental overprotectiveness or secretiveness. Difficulties in socialization may occur among the children of immigrants and migrant workers. It is possible but by no means certain that these varieties of social isolation may favor the development of paranoid behavior. In evaluating psychosocial factors, one must keep in mind that isolation and a disadvantaged economic position can just as easily be the result as the cause of a paranoid disorder.

Precipitating Factors in Paranoid Reactions

It may appear paradoxical to speak of precipitating factors in character disorders, which are, by definition, long-standing, chronic conditions. Here we are concerned with those stresses which tend to mobilize existing defenses of denial and projection and may, on occasion, lead to decompensation into paranoid psychoses.

Precipitating factors can be divided into nonspecific and specific stresses. If one thinks of paranoid thinking and feeling as the projection of denied impulses onto others, it is clear that anything which stimulates forbidden wishes, such as exposure to temptation, impairs the ego's ability to deploy its defenses, such as physical illness, chronic brain disease, and drug ingestion, or increases superego severity, such as negative criticism, can activate paranoid defenses in a nonspecific way. There are certain events which appear to be particularly threatening to paranoids. Because of their lack of basic trust, their low tolerance for ambiguity, and their great fear of intimacy, paranoids are specifically vulnerable to interpersonal situations which lack candor and honesty or which contain elements of either homosexual or heterosexual seductiveness. As we shall see, these considerations are absolutely crucial in determining strategies and techniques of psychotherapy.

Psychotherapy of the Paranoid

The prognosis and treatment of the various paranoid psychoses has been widely discussed in the psychiatric literature and requires no additional comment here. The following remarks deal with the strategies and techniques of handling paranoid thinking and behavior in the psychotherapy of paranoid characters and patients of other diagnostic categories having significant paranoid trends.

Once denial and projection have established themselves as the primary defense mechanisms in the intrapsychic economy of adults, the chances of substantially diminishing their use by means of even prolonged, intensive psychotherapy are small. The rapid relief of anxiety, tension, and guilt provided by denial and projection greatly reinforces their continued use and this is why so few "pure" paranoid characters seek help. Attacking the patient's denial usually has the effect of increasing rather than decreasing its strength since the therapist's confrontation is experienced as criticism. If successful, breaking through the patient's denial runs the risk of provoking a depressive reaction which can be extremely dangerous and difficult to manage when the repertoire of defenses is so limited.

Over the years, clinicians have developed certain guidelines relative to the psychotherapy of paranoids. The following brief résumé reflects a consensus of current opinion.

Because of the paranoid's fear of seduction and intolerance of ambiguity, a firm, rigorously honest therapist is an absolute necessity. The therapeutic contract must be spelled out in sufficient detail so as to leave no room for misunderstanding. Messages from relatives and friends, if accepted, should be communicated in full to the patient. Interpretations should be infrequent, brief, and concrete. Therapists have to be particularly careful not to take sides when paranoid patients make accusations against other people. The temptation to take the patient's side or oppose him can both have the effect of strengthening the patient's defenses of denial and projection.

Countertransference difficulties arise from three principal sources: fear of the patient's hostility, disappointment in his slow rate of improvement, and inability to tolerate his dependent needs.

Paranoids are often provocative and threatening, and therapists who are not comfortable with their own aggressive feelings should not try to treat them. The most common errors are to withdraw from confrontation or to argue with the patient. Both reactions are seen as signs of weakness by the paranoid and his ability to control his own anger may as a result be lessened.

> **Example.** R., a 30-year-old married engineer I was treating beat up his mother in a fit of anger shortly before he was to have a session with me. While awaiting his arrival, his wife called warning me that he was armed and planned to "finish things." When R. arrived, I met him in the corridor outside the office, told him of his wife's call, and demanded that he turn over his weapon before going into the office. He at first refused, denying any intention to harm me. When I persisted, threatening to call the police, he handed me a knife. The session was held as planned.

Therapists treating paranoids must be content with modest gains attained slowly over long periods of time. Although paranoids often become loyal and grateful patients, trust develops at a snail's pace and rapport is easily ruptured. I know of several instances in which paranoid patients have broken off treatment after several years because their therapists forgot an appointment.

Underneath the paranoid's anger and "go-it-alone" approach to life lies an insecure, dependent person. Once rapport has been established, the therapist may find the paranoid making demands upon him for advice and guidance. Many psychiatrists are made uneasy when asked to be active and go from the extreme of taking over direction of the patient's life to allowing him to flounder in a state of indecision.

> **Example.** K., a 40-year-old paranoid lawyer, was unsure about the wisdom of giving up his solo practice and joining a firm. After mentioning his problem, he suddenly said, "You know my problem trusting people. I can't make this decision. You'll have to make it for me." I told him that I would be glad to help, but that I thought he was underestimating his own judgment. We took several sessions to discuss the problem in all its ramifications. I limited myself to bringing to his attention aspects of the proposed change he neglected to mention. He finally concluded that the stress of working in close contact with colleagues made collaborative practice unwise.

A word about how to deal with denial and projection when it arises in therapy. Most therapists agree that these defenses should not be directly challenged. As I have already indicated above, the loss of self-esteem which usually leads to their use is increased by direct attack. The most productive approach the therapist can take is to listen patiently to the complaints, refuse to take sides, and focus his attention on the patient's wounded feelings.

> **Example.** N., a 28-year-old textile engineer, came to a session one day in a rage. The family physician, who had been treating his father for a myocardial infarct, had made a "mistake in judgment." By delaying hospitalization, he had compromised his father's chances for recovery. N. went on attacking the doctor, threatening malpractice litigation, and triumphantly concluded that this experience "proved" that nobody can be trusted. It was obvious from N.'s account that no mistake in judgment had actually occurred; he was simply upset because the family doctor, whom he revered, had been unable to prevent his father's illness. The experience also stimulated N.'s fears about his own health. I told N. that his father's illness was obviously an extremely painful experience for him and that the realization that the family physician whom he had trusted might be powerless to prevent a tragedy must make things even worse. N. gradually calmed down and began to complain about how difficult it was to obtain security in a "cold, cruel world" no matter how hard one tried.

Even the most patient therapist will occasionally be provoked by the attacks of paranoid characters. The ability of paranoids to detect even small traces of hostility in others is proverbial. Therapists should not hesitate to tell such patients that they have been provoked to anger. The fact that the therapeutic relationship can survive such vicissitudes is deeply reassuring to paranoids.

Paranoid Patients and Medication

As a rule, well-compensated paranoid characters neither require nor desire chemotherapy. When psychotic decompensation threatens, however, prescribing major tranquilizers in adequate dosages becomes a most important part of the treatment program. If the need for drug therapy occurs in the context of a well-established patient-doctor relationship, the paranoid will usually be cooperative and even grateful for medication since he may be terrified by his increasing loss of control over emerging impulses. This is particularly true at night when weakened ego controls can lead to a state of severe insomnia. In such cases, paranoids may plead for sedation or tranquilization.

It is well known that paranoids are often resistant to the idea of chemotherapy, particularly when prescribed by physicians who have not yet gained their trust. Medication represents the threat of control by outside agents and a subsequent loss of autonomy. In extreme delusional states, the patient may fear that he is being poisoned by a malevolent persecutor.

Resistance of paranoids to medication will only be increased if the therapist himself is ambivalent about its use. Here as in other situations involving paranoids, the therapist must be firm, honest, and business-like. It is extremely important to try to include the patient in the process of prescribing medication, changing dosages, and monitoring physiological side effects. I make it a practice to explain to paranoid patients in great detail the purposes for which medication is being prescribed, the hoped for benefits, the possible side effects, and the criteria for reduction or discontinuance of the pharmacological agent. If paranoid patients are not encouraged to collaborate in their chemotherapy, they may take matters into their own hands and regulate dosages on their own without informing their therapists. This tends to happen when frightening physiological side effects occur and threaten the paranoid's sense of internal control. Paranoids should be encouraged to contact their therapists immediately if they become concerned about the effects of a particular drug. Often, a reassuring comment on the phone is enough to keep the patient from cutting his medication below an effective dosage level.

REFERENCES

1. Cameron, N. Personality Development and Psychopathology: A Dynamic Approach, pp. 470–515. Houghton Mifflin Co., Boston, 1963.
2. Kline, P. Fact and Fantasy in Freudian Theory. Methuen & Co., Ltd., London, 1972.
3. Nemiah, J. C. Obsessive-compulsive reaction. In: Comprehensive Textbook of Psychiatry, A. M. Freedman and H. I. Kaplan (Eds.), pp. 912–928. Williams & Wilkins Co., Baltimore, 1967.
4. Rapaport, D. Organization and Pathology of Thought, p. 627. Columbia University Press, New York, 1951.
5. Rosenthal, D. Genetic Theory and Abnormal Behavior, pp. 92–200. McGraw-Hill Book Co., New York, 1970.

6. Swanson, D., Bohnert, P. J., and Smith, J. A. The Paranoid, p. 307. Little, Brown & Co., Boston, 1970.
7. Weintraub, W., and Aronson, H. The application of verbal behavior analysis to study of psychological defense mechanisms. III. Speech pattern associated with delusional behavior. J. Nerv. Ment. Dis., *141:*172–179, 1965.
8. Weintraub, W., and Aronson, H. The application of verbal behavior analysis to the study of psychological defense mechanisms. VI. Speech pattern associated with compulsive behavior. Arch. Gen. Psychiatry *30:*297–300, 1974.
9. Klein, M. Contributions to Psychoanalysis, pp. 282–310. Hogarth Press, London, 1948.

12

ORGANIC PERSONALITY DISORDERS

Dietrich Blumer, M.D.

Introduction

DSM III lists "Organic Personality Syndrome" (310.10), characterized by a marked change in personality that is due to a specific organic factor but that is not due to any other organic brain syndrome. The personality change involves at least one of the following: emotional lability, impairment in impulse control, marked apathy and indifference, and suspiciousness or paranoid ideation. Both frontal and temporal lobe personality changes are to be listed in this insufficiently differentiated diagnostic category.

It is frequently assumed that diseases affecting the brain lead simply to either acute disorganization or chronic deterioration of personality, in delirum or dementia, respectively. The characteristic mental impairments with relatively widespread brain disorders are those of memory and intellect, with at times associated lability of affect; depressive or manic, paranoid or catatonic states may become manifest in previously well-adjusted individuals, and awareness of reality may be dimmed to various degrees with acute cerebral changes. It may be of considerable interest to compare the morbid mental changes in delirium or dementia to the overt or concealed facets of the premorbid personality. An inhibited, passive, and dependent man may openly display an autistic, aggressive, and inconsiderate "alter ego" once he is under a toxic influence; a conscientious and parsimonious person may become overscrupulous and miserly with the advent of senile cerebral changes. Thus, the premorbid personality may undergo a reversal to the opposite, or an exaggeration of former personality traits may take place with the patient displaying a caricature of his former self. However, there is no type of personality we can describe as characteristic for either the more acute or the more chronic stages of diffuse cerebral impairments.

Two types of localized cerebral changes, on the other hand, have been frequently found associated with certain characteristic personality changes. Both frontal and temporal lesions of the brain tend to leave intellectual functions fully intact, but may result immediately or gradually in prominent and highly characteristic personality changes. The frontal lesion is destructive in nature, while the temporal lobe lesion involved is of the irritative, epileptogenic type.

Psychiatrists may often fail to appreciate the role of organic factors in psychopathology, or may lose interest once the presence of a brain disease is established. Furthermore, patients with localized brain lesions tend to remain in the care of neurologists and neurosurgeons. It is then perhaps not so surprising that psychiatrists had remained content for so long to use the simplistic diagnostic scheme of either "acute or chronic brain syndrome" for any and all organic mental changes.

The "Frontal Lobe Personality"

Damage to the premotor frontal regions does not result in clear neurological changes. Patients with prefrontal lesions may show primarily "psychological" changes and may find their way to a psychiatrist. Frontal lobe disease can be recognized from its characteristic effects on personality and behavior, and with proper knowledge psychiatrists could avoid one of their most common errors of the category "missed neurological diagnosis." It is on the one hand obviously of crucial importance to make an early diagnosis in operable benign tumors of the brain, while on the other the autopsy finding of an inoperable tumor will provide little consolation to a psychiatrist who has treated the particular patient for months.

There is a fair understanding among neurologists and neurosurgeons as to the characteristic mental changes which are associated with lesions to the frontal lobes. A patient who presents with urinary incontinence and total lack of concern for the mishap, yet is intellectually intact, may be promptly diagnosed. However, clinicians who may be very familiar with the "frontal lobe syndrome" have not often detailed their behavioral observations on paper.

Various attempts of systematic correlation of frontal lobe lesions and mental changes have been undertaken over the past 100 years. The experience with psychosurgery, in the form of frontal lobotomies or topectomies, stimulated much interest in the mental changes related to frontal lobe lesions. It remains surprising, however, how little reflection the existing literature has found in psychiatric curriculum and textbooks.

The debate on the effects of frontal lobe disorder on personality has centered more on the question of specificity of lesions rather than on psychopathology. Mental changes similar to those characteristic for frontal lobe lesions may also be found under certain circumstances with lesions in other parts of the brain.

History

Possibly the earliest report documenting a change of personality following frontal lobe injury dates back to 1835 (9). A 16-year-old adolescent of morose, shut-in character and limited intellect had suffered a fit of jealously and had shot himself in the lower midforehead. He suffered extensive damage chiefly to the mesial-orbital parts of his frontal lobes and lost his sight entirely. He appeared now not only unconcerned over his blindness but assumed a gay, vivacious, and jocular disposition. He died 2 years later from unknown cause and no autopsy was reported.

The famous case of Phineas Gage, reported in 1848 and again in 1868 (16), aroused great interest at the time because at the age of 25 this foreman of a roadcrew *survived* an explosion which blasted a pointed iron bar (3 feet, 7 inches long, 1 ¼ inches in the largest diameter) through his head. It is well described, however, that after his injury he was "no longer Gage." Though untrained in the schools, he had previously possessed a well-balanced mind, was bright as well as "very energetic and persistent in executing all his plans of operation." His posttraumatic personality represented a radical change, described as follows: "the equilibrium or balance, so to speak, between his intellectual faculties and animal propensities seems to have been destroyed. He is fitful, irreverent, indulging at times in the grossest profanity, manifesting but little deference for his fellows, impatient of restraint or advice when it conflicts with his desires, at times pertinaciously obstinate, yet capricious and vacillating, devising many plans of operation, which are no sooner arranged than they are abandoned in turn for others appearing more feasible. A child in his intellectual capacity and manifestations, he has the animal passions of a strong man . . . ." His contractors, who regarded him as the most efficient and capable foreman in their employ previous to his injury, considered the change in his mind so marked that they could not give him his place again (when he halfheartedly applied for his former job, some 7 months after the accident). Phineas Gage died 13 years later. There was no autopsy, but the injury must have affected chiefly the mesial-orbital part of the left frontal lobe, upward to the convexity close to the midline and precentral area.

The first systematic attempt to correlate personality changes with frontal lobe lesions documented by postmortem examination was undertaken by a Swiss physican, Leonore Welt, in 1888 (29). She described the case of Franz Binz, a 37-year-old furrier who, while intoxicated, had fallen some 100 feet from a window of his apartment. He suffered a compound fracture of the frontal bones and severely injured the right frontal lobe. He was never unconscious, and was confused for only a brief period. Most striking was a subsequent change in his character with intellect well intact. He had been very good-natured, sociable, and gay, at all times when not drunk; for several weeks after the injury he was cantankerous, nasty, and threatening. Following discharge from the hospital 7 months after the accident, he appeared more quiet and would just sit on the same spot and stare for hours. He resumed his trade as a furrier and albeit slower he proved to be still a rather capable worker. He would, however, get drunk even more often than before. Less than 11 months after his injury, Franz Binz died from an acute infectious disease. The autopsy showed a deep scarring of the orbital part of both frontal lobes, more extensively on the right.

Leonore Welt (29) added 10 observations from the literature (including the two cases already quoted) to her own case and concluded that lesions of the frontal lobes left the intellect intact but resulted typically in a change of character: "... a tendency to harm others, a certain malice and heightened lack of consideration in implementing personal wishes and desires. Man becomes more bestial...."

In all observations the orbital gray matter was involved: five times bilaterally, five times the right side, and in one case perhaps the left side alone. In six cases the orbital part of the frontal lobes was solely involved. In the eight observations which included neuropathological findings, the median portion of the orbital brain was invariably involved. The right rather than the left orbital brain appeared as the probable site of the described character changes. The author points out, however, that such lesions have frequently been reported in the absence of character changes.

In the more recent literature, Karl Kleist's efforts to relate localized brain lesions to behavior and personality changes are noteworthy (20). He confirmed Leonore Welt's thesis of the significance of lesions to the orbital region, and related changes toward immoral, unfaithful, deceitful, thievish, and defiant behavior to orbital lesions. Kleist also noted puerile and facetious behavior in such patients. Euphoria was observed as a frequent early mental change in patients with frontal-orbital injuries; this was usually transient and at times later changed to a dysphoric mood. Kleist presumed that the unity of personality and man's self-determination were related to the orbital region and its connections.

In contrast, lesions of the upper portions of the frontal lobes (convexity) were frequently found to be associated with lack of psychic and motor initiative. Lack of thought formation was observed with impoverished and stereotyped modes of thinking.

Kleist pointed out that certain types of impulsivity or lack of initiative may be related to lesions of the brain stem, as had been well illustrated by behavioral effects of encephalitis lethargica.

The term "moria" was employed by Jastrowitz (19) for the childish, cheerful excitement of patients with frontal lobe lesions, and Oppenheim (24) referred to a similar attitude as "Witzelsucht" (facetiousness). The puerility of these patients has often been stressed. Urinary and rectal incontinence have been reported with marked regularity. Holmes (17) referred to three general types of changes associated with frontal lobe injury: (a) apathy and indifference; (b) depression, intellectual enfeeblement, automaticity, and incontinence; (c) restlessness, exuberance, euphoria, irritability, childishness, facetiousness, and marked egoism. Another group, according to Holmes, resembled cases of general paresis. Hypomanic states and moral derelictions were pointed out in the same patients by others.

Brickner, in an interesting monograph (7), discussed the intellectual functions of the frontal lobes in presenting one closely studied patient who had undergone amputation of the larger part of both frontal lobes. Almost the entire spectrum of "frontal lobe changes" was found present in this one patient. The author found nothing to suggest the occurrence of primary pathological changes of the emotions themselves, but noted that there was a mere lack of usual adult restraints in concealing apparently normal feelings. Only one function was considered as primarily affected: "the synthesis into complex structures of the simpler engrammic products associated in the more posterior parts of the brain."

Goldstein (13) described patients with frontal lobe lesions as markedly different in their everyday behavior: "Their faces are usually rigid, they lack expressive movements, they are slow and dull. In contrast to this usual behavior, they may suddenly react in an abnormal way and become abnormally excited." Goldstein felt that their mental condition could be best understood from the point of view that the patients were impaired in a special mental capacity, i.e., in the impairment of the "abstract attitude."

The perhaps earliest case on record of a frontal lobe injury with remarkable personality change (9) demonstrated the somewhat "beneficial" effect of a suicide attempt: formerly morose and shut-in, De Nobele's adolescent became vivacious, jocular, and insouciant. Both the apathetic-indifferent and the uninhibited-euphoric type of frontal lobe personality have in common a marked insouciance. Historically, the psychosurgical procedures were not developed on the basis of clinical observations, but from the findings in animal experiments. However, by placing a palliative frontal lobe lesion, the psychosurgeon indeed reproduces the reported effect of some accidental lesions: an otherwise intractable state of tension or anxiety is replaced by the insouciance of the frontal lobe syndrome.

While the effects of frontal lobotomy in psychotic patients are more difficult to assess, the postoperative behavioral patterns in patients operated upon because of intractable pain appear more clear-cut. In a lobotomy series reported by Dynes (14), one group of patients became uninhibited, euphoric, and tended to be somewhat restless, with a seemingly purposeless type of activity. Those with a second type of postoperative behavior pattern were slowed in thinking and acting, were dull, at times completely lacking in emotional expression or display, and showed a striking reduction in interest and driving energy. An admixture of the two sets of symptoms occasionally would occur. An inappropriate or misplaced emotional reaction appeared to be a regularly occurring personality trait characterizing all patients after lobotomy. Thus, one recognizes, in these two groups of patients, the two types of frontal lobe personality.

If one reviews the results of the more refined modern psychosurgical procedures, one is struck by a finding which tends to confirm Kleist's thesis of the differential effect of lesions to the orbital region and lesions to the convexity of the frontal lobes. Ström-Olsen and Carlisle (27) report the following serious side effects of four of 210 cases who underwent bifrontal stereotactic tractotomy (involving insertion of radioactive yttrium seeds bilaterally into the white matter of the posterior orbital cortex): one woman, aged 68, became very irritable, spiteful, and aggressive; two women developed excessive sexual demands and both eventually became promiscuous; another woman became hedonistic, uninhibited, overactive, and had a tendency to neglect her home because of her pleasure-seeking activities. Minor symptoms in 11 cases were irritability, outspokenness, and volubility, which did not noticeably affect family or social relationships, and three patients had begun to smoke excessively.

No "pseudopsychopathic" behavior is reported following bilateral cingulotomy, a modern psychosurgical approach sparing the orbital region. A brief period of confusion and giddiness may be observed postoperatively; Bailey et al. (1) report a transient lack of initiative in some of the cases from their Australian series. Carefully detailed follow-up studies, however, have not been reported in series of patients who have had cingulotomies.

Personal Cases

Case 1. A 45-year-old female physician had felt markedly listless. Several years earlier, at a time of stress in her family life, she had required psychotherapy and her current difficulty was thought to be due to the recurrence of a depressive reaction. When outpatient psychotherapy was unsuccessful, she was admitted to a psychiatric hospital. Three months later the need for a pulmonary check-up prompted her transfer to a general hospital, where somewhat fortuitously a brain scan was ordered, leading to the diagnosis of a large brain tumor. The husband described how increasing listlessness had started about 1 year earlier. She had started to take refresher courses, but this was soon felt to be too much of a burden to her. She would often sleep in classes. She would frequently stay in bed until noon and experienced a general difficulty in getting going. She became very slow in answering questions. About 8 months before the correct diagnosis was made, she had become incontinent of urine but displayed a remarkable lack of concern. The psychiatrist who treated her overlooked that she did not complain of any depressed feelings, hardly ever cried, and had none of the morbid thoughts which are customary in the depressed. Her appetite had remained good and her sleep was excessive. She also had stopped having dreams. She had remained affectionate toward her husband and was sexually responsive. When seen she was extremely apathetic. She never spoke on her own, was slow in response, and gave only very brief answers when queried. She described her state of mind as a lack of enthusiasm and energy for almost anything. EEG and brain scan confirmed a large space-occupying lesion in both frontal lobes. Angiography revealed a vascular tumor near the anterior portion of the corpus callosum and extending bilaterally. The preoperative ventriculography showed evidence of an intraventricular tumor. The meningioma which was removed upon right frontal lobectomy weighed approximately 125 gm.

Case 2. A 54-year-old male had been a very successful businessman, amassing a considerable fortune. Almost 4 years before he received proper medical attention, personality changes in the form of irritable and aggressive behavior began. He then became very careless concerning money, even with his income tax. His business associates and his wife left him, as his enterprises began to fail catastrophically. Regardless, he remained totally insouciant. The only friend who stayed with him reported how he kept humming to the tune of TV commercials even though internal revenue agents were knocking at the door. When he had lost his entire fortune—business, farm, horses, and all—he was finally arrested for passing a forged check. He seemed confused to the judge and was sent to a state hospital instead of to the jail. After 3 months of hospitalization, the diagnosis of an organic condition was made when it became apparent that he did not remember very much, and he was transferred to a general hospital. At the time of admission he had bilateral papilledema, symmetrically hyperactive deep tendon reflexes, and was intermittently incontinent of bowel and bladder. Brain scan revealed a large, midline frontal mass, which appeared to be arising from the floor of the frontal fossa, and arteriography showed marked posterior displacement of both anterior cerebral arteries. Upon craniotomy, a large bilateral olfactory groove meningioma was removed.

These two patients with bilateral frontal lesions presented a very different psychopathology, which, however, is known to be associated with frontal lobe damage in both instances. The hyperactive, irritable, and insouciant attitude of the one contrasts with the listless indifference and slowness of the other. The tumor chiefly affected the orbital region in the "pseudopsychopathic" or euphoric case, and chiefly the frontal lobe convexity in the apathetic patient who was "pseudodepressed."

Uniqueness of the "Frontal Lobe Personality"

Psychopathology. Two types of personality changes can be described after frontal lobe lesions: (a) changes toward apathy and indifference; and (b) changes toward puerility and euphoria. Admixtures of the two types seem to be more common than the pure types.

Patients of the apathetic type who have lost all initiative to move or to talk may still respond properly and intelligently. They function automaton-like. In most testing situations the initiative is provided by the examiner, and patients who are unable to function on their own in daily life may be able to produce perfectly normal test scores. Similarly, a patient of ours was able to perform sexual intercourse as long as his wife told him step by step what he had to do.

The puerile-euphoric type is characterized by a lack of adult tact and restraints. Such patients may be variously disinhibited: coarse, irritable, facetious, promiscuous, hyperactive. They may just lack social graces, or may on impulse commit antisocial acts. Paranoid-grandiose thinking may at times be manifest.

Differential Diagnosis. The apathy of a patient with frontal lobe lesion may be mistaken for the psychomotor retardation of the depressed. But the ideation of a frontal lobe patient with apathy is that of empty indifference, while the depressed reveals a morbid preoccupation with worrisome thoughts.

The puerile-euphoric type may look like a manic or hypomanic patient. The affect may be more shallow in the organic case. One may have to consider the course of the illness, the premorbid personality, and the presence or absence of previous episodes. The differentiation from an antisocial character disorder will be less of a problem. Patients who commit antisocial acts in marked contrast to the previous personality should be scrutinized for organic lesions.

Incontinence occurs very frequently with frontal lobe lesions, while seizures are less common. It should be stressed that incontinence occurs very rarely in functional psychiatric disorders. Both incontinence and seizures are definite indicators of an organic lesion.

Etiology. A strong argument can be made in relating the apathetic-indifferent type to lesions of the frontal convexity and the puerile-euphoric type to lesions of the frontal-orbital region. The common admixture of the two types would be related to the relative rarity of pure lesions of the convexity or of the orbital region, respectively. The lesion is usually bilateral in cases with personality changes.

There is strong evidence that various degrees of apathy may also result from lesions in other parts of the brain (thalamic, hypothalamic, and various subcortical lesions). Brain stem lesions, such as those of encephalitis lethargica, may be responsible for antisocial-hyperactive types of behavior as well as for akinetic behavior.

A great variety of lesions, including those of psychosurgery, may be responsible for the frontal lobe syndrome. Post-traumatic frontal lobe personality changes may be transient or they may become chronic. In the case of tumors, the frontal lobe syndrome will be supplanted in time by the signs of more diffuse brain disease, in particular with increase of the intracranial pressure. General paresis used to be a frequent cause of the frontal lobe type personality. Huntington's chorea and multiple sclerosis frequently present with the frontal lobe mental changes.

Treatment

There may be a treatment for the underlying disease, but there is no specific therapy for the frontal lobe personality. Of importance, however, for patients with the apathetic type of change, are early and steady rehabilitation efforts. As soon as possible, these patients should not be allowed just to sit around, but should be activated by occupational therapy and similar approaches.

Patients of the puerile-euphoric type tend to be very difficult for their families. The family may need much support and understanding in order to deal with the illness. Strict limit setting may be necessary.

The "Epileptic Personality"

Psychiatrists have ascribed a characteristic personality profile to epileptics since the latter part of the 19th century. Debates about the true or fictitious nature of the so-called Epileptic Personality have varied since that time, depending on the psychiatric expertise of the examiner and the type of epileptic population studied.

With the development of the EEG and new anticonvulsant drugs, neurologically oriented physicians led the advances in the field of epilepsy. The specificity of personality changes in epilepsy came frequently to be doubted. Institutionalization and ostracism from society were seen by some as the cause rather than as the result of mental changes; the presence of unspecified brain damage or excessive doses of anticonvulsants were implicated by others. When it was obvious that so many epileptics could have their seizures controlled and lead normal lives, the mention of Epileptic Personality became anathema as the very symbol of society's prejudice against epileptics.

The more differentiated opinion that mental changes in epilepsy were particularly associated with temporal lobe or psychomotor epilepsy—the one form of partial epilepsy involving the limbic system—has been almost as bitterly contested. Partial epilepsies involving the neocortex indeed tend to show no significant mental changes but patients with grand mal seizures may or may not show mental changes. Common generalized epilepsy in its pure form consists of grand mal, petit mal, and, rarely, myoclonic attacks, in the absence of brain damage. In most cases the seizures will be brought under control (23). If generalized seizures continue to be poorly controlled, the presence of brain damage and of temporal lobe involvement in particular is at least suspect and may well explain associated mental changes. Various types of epilepsy clearly merge into the stream of temporal lobe epilepsy which is the most intractable form of epilepsy. Apart from the infantile epileptic encephalopathy (West syndrome) and the childhood epileptic encephalopathy (Lennox-Gastaut syndrome) which both entail deterioration of intellect, temporal lobe epilepsy is the most malignant form of epilepsy because of its chronicity and high risk of mental changes.

The above reasoning may be plausible but needs to be corroborated by appropriate studies which would compare the psychopathology in temporal lobe epilepsy with the psychopathology in generalized epilepsy with and without signs of temporal lobe involvement. Such a study would be meaningful if one compared patients matched not only by age but also by duration and severity of seizure disorder; however, recent temporal lobe epileptics tend to be free of psychopathology and patients with long-standing common generalized epilepsy in its pure form tend to be free of seizures.

At this time we will only attempt to answer the question: are there indeed personality changes *unique* to epilepsy? We will assume that such changes would be related to involvement of the temporal-limbic system, without further belaboring this point. Personality changes unique to epileptics would need to be studied even though they might be present only in a few. We have reviewed elsewhere the evidence that such characteristic personality traits are indeed a rather common occurrence (4).

History

On the European continent, and particularly in the German-speaking countries, psychiatrists have traditionally included epilepsy in their efforts to arrive at precise descriptions and classifications of mental illness. The debate never centered around the concept of the "epileptic personality," but concerned the various mental manifestations occurring in the course of the disease. Samt, Kraepelin, Gruhle, and Schorsch represent the view on epilepsy of German psychiatry over the past 90 years. They describe what they recognized as typical symptoms of the disease. In contrast, Freud and Szondi attempt to elucidate the dynamic interaction of typical mental changes in order to understand the epileptic.

Samt was a psychiatrist at the Charité Hospital in Berlin. After Morel and Falret in France had begun to describe epilepsy with its psychiatric aspects, it was Samt who continued their work in Germany. He is almost forgotten now but deserves to be mentioned for his early descriptions of "forms of epileptic insanity." Under this title he published two papers in 1875 and 1876, respectively (25).

Samt describes habitual peculiarities in the character of certain epileptics, as follows: "I have seen such religious martyr-faces, epileptics who speak 'frankly and freely from the bottom of their heart' who beat their chests: 'As true as I live, from my heart I speak for emperor and king, dear God is with me'; epileptics who act like the most pious sufferers, who kneel down and swear to their angel-like innocence: 'Yes, I am sometimes a bit mean, but I don't attack, I want a pistol to my head if I do, but I love to live'; who if they are in the wrong, want to be 'crucified and condemned'; epileptics who see 'dear Jesus' in dreams and recognize a message from 'God the father' in a drawing on the wall, and who steal, strike and curse in a most vulgar manner—enough, those poor epileptics, such as one might meet in every institution, who have a prayer book in their pocket, dear God on the tongue, but an excess of viciousness in their whole body."

The last sentence in this paragraph has been cited in many of the German textbooks of psychiatry up to the present time. The authors usually assert that the picture fits only few extreme cases; however, Samt's powerful description of those poor and two-faced epileptics has exerted a particular fascination through almost 90 years.

Kraepelin, in 1904 (22), points out that a striking slowness and heaviness of intellectual process can be found in more than half of the epileptics who come to the attention of a psychiatrist. Frequently, a peculiar circumstantiality can be observed in addition to the slowness. Often their speech does not seem to move ahead at all; yet there is no incoherence, and they stubbornly finish their train of thought. Kraepelin reports that the memory suffers in advanced cases and that thinking may become impoverished. He goes on to consider the egocentricity of the patients: they may praise not only themselves but the other members of the family as well; worries about physical health may play a great role, while at the same time a striking optimism concerning the real ailment is maintained. Religious ideas are cultivated with very unusual predilection, and Kraepelin comments here that hope for salvation by a supernatural authority may find a particularly fertile soil in such helpless patients. The author goes on in his description of the personality of the epileptic, by saying: "The most dramatic changes brought about by epilepsy are in the emotional sector, even in cases where no impairment of the intellect can be recognized. Almost always an intensification of mental irritability occurs, which may be constantly present to a degree, but particularly manifests itself, to a pathological extreme, in attacks and under the influence of alcohol." Epileptics generally like to work; they may be slow but are often pedantically precise in the accomplishment of their tasks; some patients show a certain awkward helpfulness. They often do not remain steadily employed because of a peculiar restlessness which may be connected with episodic mood changes. Narrow-mindedness, selfishness, and irritability are looked upon by Kraepelin as the substratum favoring criminal tendencies in the epileptic.

Again about 30 years later, in 1930, Gruhle wrote the chapter on "Epileptic Reactions and Epileptic Diseases" in Bumke's *Handbook of Psychiatry* (15).

The epileptic, he states, is very slow in his comprehension; likewise it takes him great effort to express himself; "He is enormously circumstantial, it takes him a long time to get to the point, he uses expletives as well as an excessive number of polite expressions, fills in with quotations, and tries to insure himself in advance against any possible misunderstanding." The author continues to say that the epileptic is overly conscientious, even excessively pedantic, in the fulfillment of his religious duties; he is not just pious, he is hypocritical and full of bigotry; he is (basically) irritable and vengeful.

Gruhle reports how certain signs, differing from the aura, give long advance indication that an attack is approaching. The patient may be subdued, morose, and moody and doesn't feel like working, until the seizure occurs. "Yes, the physician and attendants hope for a seizure in these often very difficult patients, which comes like salvation for everybody involved: that patient is much more bearable for weeks thereafter."

There was also criticism of the attempts at isolating psychiatric symptoms in the epileptic. Bumke wrote in 1936 (8): "Earlier, in the case of so-called epileptoid psychopaths, explosiveness of affect was stressed as characteristic of the epileptic constitution. Nowadays, almost the opposite is pointed out as a specific type. The patients are said to be confiding, good-tempered and characterized by social solidity."

More recently, Schorsch (26), from the Bethel institutions for epileptics, gives a comprehensive summary of the modern knowledge about epilepsy, its clinical picture, and research. He says the following about "epileptic personality changes."

Commenting on the pathogenesis, he states that basically the course of mental processes is changed by the illness "toward slowness, adhesiveness, perservation"—in brief, toward the well-known "viscosity": "The patients lose their versatility, become awkward, circumstantial, pedantic. The difficulty in working through impressions and a delayed ability to react may well be of significance for the tendency toward damming up of affects and resentment." He also mentions the reaction of the environment to the illness—rejection on one hand, overprotection on the other—as important factors in the pathogenesis of the personality changes in epilepsy.

In describing the psychopathological picture presented by epileptic patients, Schorsch points out the marked emotional lability. They often display, changing with mood and situation, quite opposite behavior patterns: "stubbornness and abnormal suggestibility; quite marked respect for authority and a need for obtrusive familiarity without any sense for distance; devout, at times with sugar-coated manners, solemn formality, exaggerated politeness toward others, and the uninhibited use of foul language as well as outbursts of reckless brutality; arrogance and submissiveness. In the great majority of patients, such contradictory behavior is due to the illness and therefore cannot be assessed in the same way as the insincerity, hypocrisy and bigotry of healthy persons."

Samt's "poor epileptics" as well as certain asocial types of epileptics are rare according to Schorsch. A majority of idiopathic epileptics appear to be "hypersocial." And now the author says: "Most patients are basically good-natured, childlike-dependent, sincere; in their work they are industrious, thorough, conscientious. A true helpfulness is manifested in the institution, e.g. in the way that they help each other during attacks. Although some of them may initially be anxious to leave, they are basically at ease in the shelter offered by the institution, among fellow-sufferers, and are grateful for the chance to lead a life of meaningful activity at a place of employment where they do not risk being fired after a fit; grateful also for stimulation and pleasure which is offered during free time, but grateful mainly for all the sympathy, warmth, kind attention and respect for their human dignity. However, patients with severe personality changes, even without states of excitement, are difficult to bear, if the environment has no understanding for their peculiarities ...."

Freud (10), in his paper "Dostoevsky and Parricide" (1928), writes about the personality of Dostoevsky: "To consider Dostoevsky as a sinner or a criminal rouses violent opposition which need not be based upon a philistine assessment of criminals. The real motive for this opposition soon becomes apparent. Two traits are essential in a criminal: boundless egoism and a strong destructive urge. Common to both of these, and a necessary condition for their expression, is absence of love, lack of emotional appreciation of (human) objects. One at once recalls the contrast to this presented by Dostoevsky—his great need of love and his enormous capacity for love, which is to be seen in his manifestation of exaggerated kindness and which caused him to love and to help where he had a right to hate and be vengeful as, for example, in his relations with his first wife and her lover. That being so, it must be asked why there is any temptation to reckon Dostoevsky among criminals. The answer is that it comes from his choice of material, which singles out from all others violent, murderous and egoistic characters, thus pointing to the existence of similar tendencies within himself, and also from certain facts in his life, such as his passion for gambling and his possible confession to a sexual assault upon a young girl. The contradiction is resolved by the realization that Dostoevsky's very strong destructive instinct, which might easily have made him a criminal, was in his actual life directed mainly against his own person (inward instead of outward) and thus found expression as masochism and a sense of guilt. Nevertheless, his personality retained sadistic traits in plenty, which show themselves in his irritability, his love of tormenting and his intolerance even towards people he loved, and which appear also in the way in which, as an author, he treats his readers. Thus in little things he was a sadist towards others, and in bigger things a sadist towards himself, in fact a masochist—that is to say the mildest, kindliest, most helpful person possible."

Thus, Freud renders a coherent picture of the contradictory personality of the famous epileptic: the threat of repetitive, uncontrollable acts of murderous or near-murderous violence; the guilt and the need for atonement; seeking forgiveness and help from God; the attempt to adhere to a strict moral code; proving oneself as the "mildest, kindliest, most helpful person possible." Although Freud doubted that Dostoevsky could be thought of as a true moralist, he did not refer to him as a hypocrite. A hypocrite is a person who merely plays the role of a moral and pious person; Dostoevsky's religiosity and moral strivings appear to be of genuine nature.

Szondi, in 1963 (28), confirms what Freud said about the psychogenic factors in epilepsy. However, he considers the "epileptic reaction" as a genuine phenomenon which cannot be explained in terms of the sexual, sadomasochistic drives. He sees in the "epileptic reaction" the pathological variant of a general biological mechanism, whose goal is to rescue the individual from a dangerous situation by the paroxysm of a sudden, surprising action. In this mechanism, by necessity, there is a close correlation of psychic-emotional and physical-motor factors. The dynamic factor in this mechanism has the quality of a drive. Three phases can be differentiated in the drive-process: "First, the energies of the crude affects are pent up; rage or hate, anger or vengeance, envy or jealousy are incited.... Then follows the explosive discharge in some form of fit...." Then follows the phase during which the person tries "to make up," the "hyperethical, often hyperreligious phase." As an example for this process the author cites the case of an 18-year-old epileptic, who prior to an attack would throw lighted matches in his mother's face or would throw her clothing in a stove; after the seizure he would be exceedingly obedient, helped his mother wherever he could, and overwhelmed her with signs of his affection. In the phase of explosive discharge, the pent up energy is either turned actively outward or passively inward, against the self: a real or suspected enemy is attacked, or the person is "seized by an attack." In either case it is not just a case of anger but of anger at its pathological extreme: murderous intent.

In some patients with seizures, irritability with frequent explosive reactions may dominate the clinical picture. Such patients have been referred to as "asocial types." Others present a predominance of the "hyperethical phase," with many genuinely positive traits; they may be very conscientious, helpful toward others, never angry or unkind, and only the seizures betray that a different set of affects is also present. Often an emotional lability with sudden surprising changes of attitude may be characteristic.

Szondi remarks, after discussing the views of various authors: "It is astonishing to note how often the gluey-viscous affectivity was considered the core of the mental make-up of epileptics, and to what degree so many authors remained stuck themselves to this syndrome of adhesiveness, and with how many Greek words the same phenomenon was labeled." Szondi points out that epileptics constantly may have to hold back their anger, rage, and murderous intent: adhering to the very same sentence or thought or sticking to one and the same person represents a safety device in view of the threatening emotional lability and can be looked upon as a defensive maneuver to avoid the murderous intent.

More recently, Geschwind (12) has detailed the chronic personality constellation which tends to follow the onset of illness in temporal lobe epilepsy. He points out what he considers to be errors which have led some investigators to question the very existence of personality alterations in temporal lobe epilepsy. He describes the overall picture as that of a profound deepening of the patient's emotional responses. All events are serious to these patients, and there are no trivial occurrences. Patients may become increasingly concerned with cosmic issues, such as the fate of the world, or international politics. A surprising number among them begin to write extensively. They may become extensively concerned with moral issues and involve themselves with the rights and wrongs of rather trivial issues. Excessive religiosity frequently may be a striking feature of the temporal lobe epileptic. Paranoid ideation is sometimes present. Interictal aggressiveness is a common feature, but is relatively well tolerated by many of the families, probably because of the marked emotional warmth customarily displayed by these same patients toward the family members. Both the exaggerated aggressiveness and the unusual emotional warmth are seen as contrasting aspects of the deepened emotional responses. Changes in sexual behavior are a striking feature in many cases.

Bear (2, 3) developed an inventory for the assessment of the frequently noted interictal behavior and personality changes of temporal lobe epileptics. The Bear Inventory permitted, for the first time, a controlled quantitative analysis of these traits. The findings were highly significant, throughout the range of changes described earlier as characteristic for epileptics with temporal lobe involvement of some severity. Moreover, a clear difference between right and left temporal lobe epileptics could be demonstrated; the right temporal epileptic displayed emotional tendencies, in contrast to ideational traits of the left temporal epileptic. Right temporal epileptics exhibited "denial," while left temporal epileptics demonstrated an overemphasis of their own dissocial behavior.

Personal Cases

Case 3. G. P. is a 53-year-old white male who has suffered from psychomotor and generalized seizures since age 13. A right temporal lobectomy at age 40 was followed by decrease in frequency of psychomotor seizures and disappearance of grand mal attacks. Preoperative EEG's showed a spike focus in the right temporal tip and lesser spike activity in the right posterior temporal area. Postoperative EEG's showed spike activity in the right low central area and some more widespread spike activity occurring over the right hemisphere.

Following graduation from high school he worked steadily but in spite of his high intelligence never sought advancement. The seizures were chiefly nocturnal and he kept them a well guarded secret. While working some 20 years as a stock clerk in the same business nobody knew about his epilepsy.

He had married for companionship at about age 30, after showing little interest in dating. The girl had been pointed out to him as a good wife by his father. G. P. had never masturbated and had experienced nocturnal emissions on perhaps two occasions. The couple had intercourse a couple of times only during the first 8 years of the marriage and none since. G. P. would state that he respected women and that sex was of very small importance in his life. He abhorred "low talk" among his co-workers and in turn was often made the butt of their ridicule.

He had been irritable at times and moody for days, prior to the operation. His wife, who had not learned about his epilepsy prior to the marriage, threatened to leave him, and he made two suicide attempts. He then chose to undertake the operation for his epilepsy. In spite of the only partial success of the right temporal lobectomy, the patient's moodiness gradually subsided and he became much easier to get along with. He assumed an exuberant, enthusiastic attitude and participated now regularly in a number of community and church activities. He has been eager to help others and has volunteered for many good causes. However, there were occasional periods of anxiety, depression, and hypochondriacal concern, during which he was in much need of reassurance from his physician. He remained without any friends—not because of his seizures, which were nocturnal and unknown, but because he seeemed so different to others and knew himself to be different.

G. P. was followed over the years since his operation. He has never betrayed any anger, but has been gentle throughout. While calling at regular intervals he always presented himself in a most compliant manner. He was not merely a most cooperative patient, but eagerly volunteered for any new test or studies. He kept his physician informed by regularly forwarding a log of daily events as well as of his dreams. He was verbose but at the same time highly circumspect and meticulous in his statements. Thus, when he was asked what he would do if he saw a fire in a theater, or, if he found a stamped envelope in the street, he answered with good judgment, but made sure he had pinned down all the different possibilities involved, such as whether the stamp was cancelled or not, and whether the fire was large or small, had just begun or had been going for some time. Characteristic of his communications is the following *squirrel story*, which is an excerpt of one of G. P.'s regular letters to his physician.

"When we moved from an upstairs apartment to a first floor one (Dec. 1, 19- -) the squirrels I feed night and morning followed right with us. The squirrels are very tame and cute. They would feed out of my wife's and my hands. While I watch the door for a man to pick her up for work while she got ready I would prop the screen door open about four inches and feed them from inside by opening the inside door about an inch. They would come through the screen door opening and feed as I gave them food through the crack in the inside door. They would sit on the door sill and eat it (most of the time). It was Winter and this way I could feed them while inside. When I went walking I would prop the screen door open and place some food in a dish on the door sill and they would feed from that. One day I did not put the dish there, they had enough, and went walking. When I came back the screen door had not gone completely shut and they had chewed about 1/3 of the door away. I repaired this with water putty and painted it. Then to teach them to stay away from it I rubbed some Red Pepper on the repair with my finger. As I watched the next day one of them must have got into it. He just stood on the porch. You could see he was in awful pain, he quivered, cried and dripped from the mouth. It was awful to witness but they have not bothered the door since. The next day (June 5) I took a dish of peanuts out on the porch to feed them. They all acted normal until I saw one coming from the side to get in the dish. He upset it and I went to brush him away with my hand. As I did he gave me a good bite on the outside of the right hand at the little finger. I washed it good with soap and water and put on some Merthiolate. I have been taught to watch the animal. If it has Rabies it will die in 10 to 14 days giving time to start the Pasteur treatment. Also the further from the head the bite is the longer it takes. Rabies is a virus of the nerves following the nerves from the bite to the head where it is fatal.

Our squirrels are fed clean food and water. They do not get into any dead or rotten food. They all are as healthy as can be. Have a pretty coat and the cutest habits you would want to see. The litter they had this spring were the most domesticated I have ever seen. *Wouldn't you fight anything you knew treated you like he was with red pepper?* Squirrels are like other form of life. One alone you can train and it will respond without any trouble. But when another one or two show on the scene they are always fighting each other and chasing each other from the source of food. Also one always wants to be a bully. You should hear them growl and chase each other away when more than one tries to feed from the same dish.

I was a little alarmed about the bite because we have some neighbors who are scared of any animal at all. All they can say is "you know they can give you Rabies". Knowing circumstances I managed to conquer my nerves for a month and the squirrel was here and healthy as ever. After two weeks I felt safe, free and my nerves were quiet again.... August 12 a squirrel came to the door. I thought it was a meek one. I held a piece of Graham Cracker toward it. It looked at me and went for my hand as if to take the cracker. It ignored the cracker and bit my finger instead. This time it was the little finger of the left hand. Within 10 seconds the bottom of my stomach hurt, I got a headache and the base of my throat started to hurt and feel tight. As I write this it is bringing back memories and I can feel it again.

I stood it as long as I possibly could. The worry was making a wreck of me. Then I went to Dr. R. August 17. He is treating me as you did. Reassuring me it was my nerves. Proving my thoughts and worries wrong and in my own thoughts. He told me to increase my Valium to 1/2 tablet at 8:00 A.M. and 1/2 at 4:00 P.M. He also told me something I had read and forget. The state is considered Rabies free. There has not been a case I think he said in 5 or 7 years. This program of having dogs injected to prevent Rabies is purely political to make money and keep a record of dogs for licensing. Now I remember reading that in the paper when they started the program a few years ago.

I had not had a tetanus shot for an awful long time. He gave me one and said to have one every five years. Also do not feed the squirrels by hand. Toss the food to them or put it on a plate for them. They are wild animals and while no Rabies has been reported for a long time they can chew you up bad then infection maybe. He also reminded me that Bats are the ones that are full of Rabies. This I knew from childhood. Now I feed the squirrels in a dish on the porch. *No more by hand.* I slowly got ahold of myself again."

All details are meticulously recorded. The depth of the feeling for what went on between G. P. and the squirrels is remarkable, and remotely reminiscent of "Crime and Punishment."

Case 4. K. C. is a 43-year-old successful businessman, gifted with superior intelligence. In his early teens he had run away from a home bare of affection, and since then had made his career without further schooling on his own strength. He became a sponsor of the fine arts, and was well recognized for his cultivated taste.

His home life was less happy. He had remained loyally attached to a spouse who was little able to show affection, and the marital relationship was stormy. A closed head injury he had suffered in a car accident at age 20 was followed by seizures and personality changes which played a significant role in the vicissitudes of his interpersonal relationships.

Shortly after the head injury, he became off and on more prone to react with excessive anger to little provocation. A few years later he began to suffer from generalized seizures. The excessive irritability would now be very marked for hours or days preceding his grand mal attacks. At such times of heightened irritability he tended to react in a rather paranoid manner and to get in fights with friends or strangers "over nothing." Anxiety or feelings of unusual strength and inspiration would also frequently precede an attack. At times he would become unresponsive for a few moments and such events were followed by brief confusion. Anticonvulsants had been totally ineffective. EEG's showed at times temporal lobe abnormalities, but more often were within normal limits.

There was no decrease of sexual arousal and response, but, apart from the irritabililty, he developed after the head injury a peculiar difficulty in communicating with others. He had always been talkative but very much to the point; he became more verbose and bogged down with irrelevant details. His conversation was now so detailed that he was often in danger of losing his train of thought and he carried an anxiety about the competence of his memory. He would elaborate unnecessarily on secondary (and tertiary, etc.) facts before coming forth with the primary fact. He would, e.g., dwell at some length on "Friday noon" before coming to the point of a particular doctor's appointment (on Friday noon) he intended to make. He was often aware of this tendency to irrelevancy, but would still be unable to maintain fluent speech, and would rationalize his emphasis on small details. He wondered if "adrenalin" was able to offset this faulty mechanism of conversing as he found himself able to proceed properly from point to point at times when he was angry or when he spoke of a matter close to his heart.

His wife confirmed that he would talk very much, in direct conversation or over the phone, with exaggerated emphasis on all details—spending hours on little things, repeating himself over and over again. This tendency, perhaps more than K. C.'s irritability, contributed importantly to a near breakdown of their communication. The wife noted that K. C.'s inability to "let something go" would worsen during the heightened tension of the prodromal phase of a seizure.

K. C. would often get depressed, to the point of neglecting his work, over the discord in his marriage. It should be noted that K. C. had deep and very special religious feelings. He confessed to a deep awe of some force larger than himself, and struck friends by his mysticism, in the course of certain conversations.

Uniqueness of the "Epileptic Personality"

Psychopathology. A complex syndrome of personality and behavior changes follows (and rarely precedes) the onset of temporal lobe seizures, or of generalized seizures with presumed involvement of the temporal lobes. While sexual arousal and response tend to be often remarkably reduced, there is frequently a profound deepening of emotional responses (12). This deepening concerns an increased damming up and episodic discharge of anger and rage on the one hand, and an intensification of ethical-religious feelings on the other hand. The need to be good-natured, helpful, and God-fearing tends to be more predominant than the frequently publicized violence proneness.

The deepening of emotional responses affects much of the patient's psychic life. The so-called epileptic "viscosity" may be viewed as a result of the intensified ethical sense: there are no more trifles; the right or wrong of every item needs to be considered with all its ramifications; no issue can be easily dropped; these patients are then long-winded in speech and often feel the need to put down their thoughts in lengthy writings; they tend to be remarkably without humor, in general, and without appreciation of sexual humor in particular.

To others, such patients are very patently different. They themselves feel different from so many others and may tend to withdraw from ordinary social intercourse. They are indeed very good-natured and are most cooperative when they feel appreciated. To those about them daily, they may be difficult to bear; angry outbursts may be triggered, when others consider as irrelevant what to the patient is an important issue of right or wrong.

Paranoid attitudes are not infrequent and schizophrenia-like psychoses in temporal lobe epileptics are well known. They are often prone to depression, and manic mood swings also occur. Anxiety, hypochondriacal, and hysterical reactions in temporal lobe epileptics are not uncommon. In fact, this very vulnerability of epileptics to most of the well-known, functional mental changes has blinded observers to the fact that there are indeed very marked and peculiar personality and behavior changes which are unique to epileptics. It may be helpful to refer to the former as secondary symptoms and to the latter as primary symptoms of mental disorder in epilepsy.

Differential Diagnosis. The presence of traits of the "epileptic personality" has been described in patients with epileptogenic foci in the temporal lobes without overt seizures. But the significance of EEG changes alone in patients with Explosive Personality disorders or with global hyposexuality is not clearly established.

Patients with the described typical personality and behavior changes may at times suffer from temporal lobe seizures which have not been recognized. The diagnosis of temporal lobe seizures usually can be made clincially, based on the observations of the characteristic brief repetitive events which may be most variable but are highly stereotyped in a given patient, and are usually followed by a postictal confusional-amnestic phase (4, 6, 18). Repeat EEG's with sleep may have to be obtained. Cases of temporal lobe epilepsy with persistently negative EEG findings do exist but are rare. Generalized seizures are very frequent in temporal lobe epileptics, and their presence may make the diagnosis of epilepsy obvious.

Hysterical seizures are frequent among epileptics, and their recognition does not exclude the diagnosis of epilepsy. The schizophrenia-like psychoses which tend to occur in some patients after years of epilepsy are characterized by an intact affect and ability to relate. Otherwise, any of the symptoms of schizophrenia may be present. The other functional mental changes which so frequently are found in temporal lobe epileptics (secondary symptoms) are not different from those found in the psychiatric patient without epilepsy.

The unique personality and behavior changes have been described in the preceding section. Obviously, the entire spectrum of characteristic mental changes will only exceptionally be found in one individual patient. A combination of some of the traits is the usual finding.

Etiology. Personality changes are the exception in fresh cases of temporal lobe epilepsy, but are common in chronic cases. Some patients with generalized seizures may develop the traits of the "epileptic personality" earlier or later, presumably depending on the primary or secondary involvement of the temporal lobe structures.

Viscosity ("hypometamorphosis"), deepened anger and general emotionality, and hyposexuality can be described as the major changes of the Temporal Lobe Syndrome associated with relatively chronic temporal lobe epilepsy. They represent precisely opposite changes to those of the Temporal Lobe Syndrome after ablation of both temporal lobes (5, 11, 21): inability to maintain attention (hypermetamorphosis), lack of anger and fear, and hypersexuality (Klüver-Bucy Syndrome).

Treatment

Of primary importance is the treatment of the epilepsy. Temporal lobe epilepsy does not respond very well to anticonvulsant drugs, but if control of seizures is achieved, there may be a concomitant recovery from the global hyposexuality and from the heightened irritability. Dilantin, Tegretol, phenobarbital, and Mysoline are the anticonvulsant drugs of choice for temporal lobe epilepsy. On the other hand, some patients become more difficult when the seizures are suppressed. They may be more irritable, paranoid, or depressed, or may even become psychotic. It may be necessary to lower the anticonvulsasnts and allow some seizures for the mental well-being of some patients.

Unilateral anterior temporal lobectomy, performed in patients with primarily unilateral epileptogenic foci who have not responded to medication, may have a marked beneficial effect on some of the behavior changes. If the seizures are abolished, the sexuality and the episodic aggressivity tend to become normalized. The so-called "viscosity" seems not to be reversible. Various secondary symptoms of mental disorder in temporal lobe epilepsy may abate following successful surgery, but paranoid and schizophrenia-like changes tend to persist (30).

Psychotropic drugs may be tried in epilepsy according to their range of indication. In general, they are of limited effectiveness in epileptics. However, the phenothiazines are not contraindicated in epilepsy and may be helpful in paranoid, agitated, and schizophrenia-like states.

Psychotherapy, in general, is of limited value and usually has to be of the supportive type. The viscous type of speech often represents a significant obstacle for psychotherapy. Patient confrontation of the intelligent and cooperative patient with the problems created by his viscosity can lead to improvement (5). The patients tend to respond much better to a kind and understanding approach than to strict limit setting. Family members may need much support and help in understanding the patient.

Conclusion

Severe and unique personality changes can be described in certain patients with frontal lobe lesions on the one hand and some patients with epilepsy on the other. The terms "frontal lobe personality" and "epileptic personality" should only be used with implicit reservations. A frontal lobe lesion probably needs to be bilateral before it results in a personality change; lesions to the frontal convexity may tend to favor a different personality change from lesions to the orbital area; and lesions in other parts of the brain may, under certain circumstances, lead to similar personality changes. The "epileptic personality," far from being characteristic for most epileptics, appears to be associated with chronic involvement of temporal-limbic structures. A more precise etiology of the described organic personality changes will have to be established by careful neuropsychiatric studies.

The contrast between the two organic personality types is very striking. The frontal lesions are destructive in type and lead to immediate personality changes, while the temporal-limbic lesions are of an irritative-epileptogenic type and result in only gradually developing personality changes with peculiar psychodynamics of their own. The relative simplicity of the "frontal lobe personality" contrasts with the wealth of primary and secondary mental changes which may be associated with the "epileptic personality."

REFERENCES

1. Bailey, H., Dowling, J., Swanton, C., and Davies, E. Studies in depression: cingulotractotomy in the treatment of severe affective illness. Med. J. Aust., *1*:1971.
2. Bear, D. Temporal Lobe Epilepsy—a syndrome of sensory-limbic hyperconnection. Cortex, *15*(3):357–384, 1979.
3. Bear, D., and Fedio, P. Quantitative analysis of interictal behavior in temporal lobe epilepsy. Arch. Neurol., *34*:454–467, 1977.
4. Blumer, D. Temporal lobe epilepsy and its psychiatric significance. In: D. F. Benson, and D. Blumer (Eds.), *Psychiatric Aspects of Neurologic Disease*, pp. 171–198. Grune & Stratton, New York, 1975.
5. Blumer, D. Treatment of patients with seizure disorder referred because of psychiatric complications. In: *Psychiatric Complications in the Epilepsies: Current Research and Treatment.* McLean Hosp. J. (Special Issue):53–73, 1977.
6. Blumer, D. Neuropsychiatric aspects of psychomotor and other forms of epilepsy. In: *Comprehensive Management of Epilepsy in Infancy, Childhood and Adolescence.* S. Livingston (Ed.). Charles C. Thomas, Springfield, Ill., 1971.
7. Brickner, R. M. *The Intellectual Functions of the Frontal Lobes.* Macmillan Co., New York, 1936.
8. Bumke, O. *Lehrbuch der Geisteskrankheiten.* Bergmann, München, 1936.
9. De Nobele, E. Observation de suicide. Ann. Med. Belge, 115–117, 1835.
10. Freud, S. *Gesammelte Werke*, Vol. XIV. London, 1948.
11. Gastaut, H. Interprétation des symptômes de l'épilepsie "psychomotrice" en fonction des données de la physiologie rhinencephalique. Presse Med. *62*:1535–1537, 1954.
12. Geschwind, N. The clinical setting of aggression in temporal lobe epilepsy. In: *Neural Bases of Violence and Aggression*, W. Fields and W. Sweet (Eds.). Warren H. Green, St. Louis, 1975.
13. Goldstein, K. *Aftereffects of Brain Injuries in War.* Grune & Stratton, New York, 1948.
14. Greenblatt, M., Arnot, R., and Solomon, H. *Studies in Lobotomy.* Grune & Stratton, New York, 1950.
15. Gruhle, H. W. Epileptische Krankheiten. In: *Handbuch der Geisteskrankheiten*, O. Bumke (Ed.), Vol. 8, Ch. 4. Springer, Berlin, 1930.
16. Harlow, J. M. Recovery from the passage of an iron bar through the head. Publications Mass. Med. Soc., *2*:329–346, 1868.

17. Holmes, G. Mental symptoms associated with cerebral tumours. Proc. R. Soc. Med., *24:* 1931.
18. Janz, D. *Die Epilepsien.* Thieme, Stuttgart, 1969.
19. Jastrowitz, M. Beiträge zur Localisation im Grosshirn und über deren praktische Verwerthung. Dtsch. Med. Wochenschr., *14:*81, 1888.
20. Kleist, K. *Gehirnpathologie.* Barth, Leipzig, 1934.
21. Klüver, H., and Bucy, P. C. Preliminary analysis of functions of the temporal lobe in monkeys. Arch. Neurol. Psychiat., *42:*979–1000, 1939.
22. Kraepelin, E. *Psychiatrie.* Barth, Leipzig, 1904.
23. Niedermeyer, E. *Common Generalized Epilepsy.* Charles C Thomas, Springfield, Ill., 1970.
24. Oppenheim, H. Zur Pathologie der Grosshirngeschwülste. Arch. Psychiatr. Nervenkrankh., *21:*560, 1889.
25. Samt, P. Epileptische Irre-seinsformen. Arch. Psychiatr., *5:*1875; *6:*1876.
26. Schorsch, G. Epilepsie: Klinik und Forschung. In: *Psychiatrie der Gegenwart.* H. W. Gruhle (Ed.), Vol. II. Springer, Berlin, 1960.
27. Ström-Olson, R., and Carlisle, S. Bi-frontal stereotactic tractotomy: A followup study of its effects on 210 patients. Br. J. Psychiat., *118:*14, 1971.
28. Szondi, L. Schicksalsanalytische Therapie. Bern, 1963.
29. Welt, L. Ueber Charakterveränderungen des Menschen infolge von Läsionen des Stirnhirns. Dtsch. Arch. Klin. Med., *42:*1888.
30. Walker, A. E., and Blumer, D. Long term behavioral effects of temporal lobectomy for temporal lobe epilepsy. *Psychiatric Complications in the Epilepsies: Current Research and Treatment*, McLean Hospital (Special Issue), pp. 85–103, 1977.

13

DEPRESSIVE AND SADOMASOCHISTIC PERSONALITIES

Herbert S. Gross, M.D.

INTRODUCTION

Using DSM III, the depressive or sadomasochistic personality character can be diagnosed among the Atypical, Mixed, or Other types of personality disorders. There exist among the Affective Disorders the entities of Dysthymic Disorder in which the patient is depressed or anhedonic for 2 years; thus depressive and sadomasochistic personalities may be first detected when given this diagnosis. Atypical Depression might also alert the clinician to an underlying characterological depression.

Depressive and sadomasochistic personality as it is referred to in this chapter represents a psychopathological or maladaptive interpersonal strategy that is very common in clinical practice. These strategies are so characteristic of certain patients' behavior that the term personality disorder is justified. Such strategies are viewed as occurring in a "psychosocial field" which refers to interpersonal events in both the patient's daily life and as he/she presents in clinical situations. Diagnosis and psychotherapy are presented as overlapping interpersonal processes that have special characteristics when the patient presents these depressive and sadomasochistic strategies. The chapter includes a discussion of the (psycho) genetics of these disorders and the countertransference problems encountered in psychotherapy. The view of diagnosis as an interpersonal process could be contrasted to the diagnostic method that underlies DSM III. DSM III is based on grouping overt behavioral manifestations into syndromes. Psychiatric disorders are conceptualized as diseases with core processes that are manifest on the "surface" as symptoms that occur because the core processes are essentially similar across individuals. The more the disorders are related to pathophysiologic processes, the more applicable is the DSM III approach to diagnosis. Thus the symptoms of a depressive episode are clinically found to occur more often than the symptoms of personality disorders. The interpersonal strategies adopted by the person with a personality disorder are "chosen" from the repertoire of interpersonal strategies available in particular cultures. The personality disorders that result from such "choices" seem to have more variability than do the surface manifestations of pathophysiologic processes.

The term character or personality refers to those durable patterns of behavior that permit one to predict what another will do. Ordinarily such patterns permit us to reduce estrangement and maintain relationships (9). Disordered characters and personalities are terms that refer to similarly predictable behavior patterns seen in psychiatric consultation. In this chapter we will consider the Depressive and Sadomasochistic Personality disorders.

> The earliest memory of a young man was that of passing under a doorsill astride his father's shoulders. He grabbed for the sill and became terrified. He could trust neither his hands nor his father's shoulders, and he began screaming. He needed to be rescued by his mother. His life subsequent to the memory was full of disillusionment. He entered into a series of careers only to come to the threshold of graduation and fail to finish. As he walked out of what was to be our only interview, I was filled with an awful feeling of despair, the intensity of which I have rarely experienced. I later received a discouraged note from him confirming that he had perceived how vulnerable I was to his despair.

The depressive despair experienced by this group of patients is part of a way of life. The beginner is likely to underestimate the chronicity of these disorders. It is only after months of painful wrestling that he may question his diagnosis of Depressive Neurosis. He may or may not have learned that the depressive affect and the sadomasochistic behavior are a lifelong defense against feelings of loneliness and loss.

The central diagnostic question seems to be the extent to which the entire personality structure is organized around depressive and sadomasochistic interactive strategies.

> A couple presented themselves because of the depressive response of the wife to an extramarital affair of the husband. After 6 months of exploring the marital communications, the wife abruptly quit both the marriage and the therapy. It became apparent that her depression was more than an acute response to her husband's infidelity. Envy of the attention directed by her parents to a sister who was near death for 6 years during the wife's childhood had led to a use of depression and sadomasochism as a defense against more primitive threats. Two weeks after a success in the life of the sister, the wife began an affair that led to the break in treatment.

These people seem driven to failure and suffering, and have felt disillusion, mistrust, and despair all their lives. They also seem "entitled" to attention, to be hypercritical, and to morbidly worry about the future. They are exquisitely aware of social conventions and use such knowledge to criticize and predict doom. For people with such an exquisite sense of propriety they spread surprising amounts of unhappiness. If accomplishment threatens, the depressive and sadomasochistic character searches frantically for both flaws and bigger accomplishments in what seems like a perverse attempt to maintain dysphoric affect in a familiar equilibrium.

In contrast to the depressive affect that may provide information about losses, conflicts, and threats, the depressive character seems unable to "use" dysphoric affect. He seems to experience dysphoria as a requisite of life and not as a correlate of the stresses of life. At first contact the depressive character may, as mentioned above, be misdiagnosed as a reactive depressive. It is, of course, important to rule out the diagnosis of affective psychosis. The life of the Cyclothymic Personality is governed by mood swings. In contrast, the behavior of the depressive and sadomasochistic character determines the feeling states. In the affective psychoses and the cyclothymic personalities the mood state seems related to biological or constitutional factors. In the depressive and sadomasochistic character, the depressive affected seems a correlate of a life-style.

Dynamic psychiatry is, in part, predicated on the view that repetitive, "psychologically costly" behavior is a compromise formation that "really" advertises a "more basic problem" in living. It is my opinion that the depressive and sadomasochistic character uses depressive affect as a defense (12). The more basic underlying threat may relate to any developmental phase. In general, the more tenaciously does the person cling to the depressive life-style, the more primitive the threat against which he is defending.

The "making of a diagnosis" is a process that merits more attention, for it is often taken for granted. In the most serious disturbances, the psychoses, the "disposition," e.g., inpatient treatment, seems more crucial than diagnosis. It is characteristic of the neurotic disorders that patient and diagnostician can readily agree on which areas of living will be called symptomatic. In the character disorders there is no such agreement between patient and diagnostician. A behavior that seems symptomatic to one does not to the other. Yet, agreement of this issue is crucial to every form of therapy. In principle, any behavior that is repetitive, that causes pain to someone, and for which no utility can be found is symptomatic. The compelling quality and self-alien qualities of neurotic behavior form the basis for agreement between patient and therapist. Those qualities are not possible correlates of behaviors that are "part of" character structure, and the patient and diagnostician must work tolerantly toward making a diagnosis. Indeed, the very making of a diagnosis "with" the disordered character requires "therapeutic work." The behavior modifier and the analytic psychotherapist are very much alike in this stage before the "alleged work" begins.

The hallmark of the depressive and sadomasochistic character is that his behavior is directed at producing a depressive affective state. The depressive affect seems to have two sets of effects: one on the patient's self, the second on people with whom he had contact. The effects on the patient's self are the maintenance of certain familiar attitudinal states and bodily feelings. An expectation that things won't work out, a knitted brow, and hunched shoulders are examples. The attitudes and disposition of the body that are correlates of the depressed state are also familiar to the people around the depressive. The depressive is responded to by others as if he is engaged seriously with a weighty task. For example, the depressive is likely to get "points" for effort rather than performance. This sort of response reinforces the depressive character's armor. We will consider the effects of the depressive character on others in more detail below. At present, I would like to emphasize that the depressive and sadomasochistic character is trapped in a vicious cycle. He acts to produce a depressive state that is a prop to his sense of self and elicits responses from others that maintain the cycle.

As stated above, dynamic psychiatry is predicated on the belief that blindly repetitive behavior that is part of a vicious cycle constitutes an unsatisfactory compromise formation. The compromise formation is more usefully considered as advertising a more primary problem in living. I believe that the depressive and sadomasochistic character armor does indeed constitute such a compromise formation. Furthermore, the elucidation of the more primary problems in living that underlie the depressive and sadomasochistic compromise is crucial to the making of a diagnosis that will support psychotherapy. Although, in general, the more tenaciously the depressive clings to the depressive and sadomasochistic cycle, the more primary the problem in living. It does not follow that therapy will be necessary more or less difficult. As will be more clear later, it takes two people to work out such problems in dyadic therapy and only one of them is the patient.

> A man in late middle life has been overtly depressed for 15 years. It emerged during the course of his work that he had a bitterly disappointing relationship with his parents and was suspicious of the motives of his loving adoptive family. During an off-again, on-again contact with me and several other therapists, he had attempted suicide three times. After one such attempt he talked about the psychological state he was in immediately prior to the attempt. He described an acute feeling that his life energy was draining out through his legs. he suddenly recalled playing a game as a child. While lying in a particular hammock he would try to "get outside himself" by imagining that he was floating. He would force himself "out of his body" by concentrating that he was leaving himself through his legs. He remembered the game as quite pleasant and felt that he played at it because of "boredom." He was, however, always disappointed by the jolt he experienced as the floating self returned to his body. He was similarly jarred as he imagined how he would be if this child would tell him about such a game. The link between the state just prior to the suicide attempt and the childhood game emerged along with the narcissistic hunger that was underneath both.

The depressive and sadomasochistic compromise advertises a deficiency in the development of a sense of self (7). Such a patient is ambivalent about his identity, that poorly understood experience of self that gives life coherence. In an attempt to resolve ambivalence they compromise and arbitrarily skew their view of self to emphasize badness, shame, doubt, and guilt. This strategy is one that, as we shall presently see, is reinforced by the culture at large, and especially those bid to a career of psychotherapy. I alluded above to the tendency to judge the Depressed and Sadomasochistic Personality on effort rather than performance. Their exquisite use of social conventions and rules of propriety gives people around them the illusion that these people are committed to the tasks they perform. Nothing could be more off the mark. The depressed and sadomasochistic seem unable to want for themselves with any consistency. They seem unable to commit themselves to the goal of satisfying their own needs. Instead of zeroing in on appropriate need satisfaction, they experience *self-doubt* along with the very perception of need. The preceding example points to ambivalence about the self. The patient's projected "ideal self" floated above his "actual self" and the reunion at the end of the game was correlated with jarring dysphoric affect. In adulthood the same game is re-enacted with dread as a primary affect just prior to a suicide act. Our understanding of the development of the self system is woefully inadequate. On the one hand, ambivalence about self-worth is universal. On the other hand, how ambivalence about self becomes a correlate of psychotic regression, neurotic symptom formation, or "character armor" is mostly beyond us. We believe that genetic (biological) endowment, sociocultural matrix of the child's family, and psychological capacity seem to interact as determinants, but we are unable to separate the levels. We can, however, recognize when the ambivalence about self is correlated with *stable* formations, e.g., neurotic and characterological "structures," in contrast to *unstable* psychotic and "borderline" formations. It is important to remember that we recognize many things that we don't fully understand. One of these is that character formations *are* durable correlates of ambivalence about self. We *can* discriminate the stable from the unstable formation and such recognition is independent of how tenaciously the patient persists in repetitive behavior, and how early in development a fault occurs. Trusting what we can recognize permits curiosity about areas of ignorance to be diverted to work with individual patients as therapy is permitted to spontaneously unfold. Let us turn from the relation of the manifest behavior and the underlying narcissistic development fault to the interaction between these patients and clinicians.

The clinician at first contact experiences both a desire to rescue and repair this apparently miserable soul and a curiously unsettling feeling that the patient's predictions of doom for the therapy are correct. He feels simultaneously attracted to the role of therapist and threatened by the probability of failure. This double-edged feeling will be characteristic of the subsequent therapeutic work and needs to be understood. The therapist's feelings contain data about the patient, data very much in line with the characterological defense against a fault in the development of the patient's self system. The therapist feels the challenge to do something about the patient's depressive and sadomasochistic life-style. He "knows better" but the misery of the patient seduces him into an unaccustomed desire to actively intervene. At the same time the therapist feels that his ordinary work habit, his familiar "work ego," is being undermined. The conflict in the therapist is related to the patient's conflict. The therapist is re-enacting within himself a conflict between the esteem (self-esteem) he has for his accustomed role as therapist (to wait until he can act with wisdom and understanding) and doing something to "help" (prescribing, advising). Hasty resolution of the therapist's conflict is to be avoided if therapeutic work is to be done. It is the depressive and sadomasochistic defense that is seducing the therapist and not an empathic view of the "whole patient." If the therapist doesn't base his response on the whole patient, that is an accurate appraisal of both the characterological defense *and* the narcissistic fault, he will provide the patient with nothing new. The only clue to the narcissistic fault may be the conflict induced in him as described above.

Contemplating the totality of the Depressive and Sadomasochistic Personality may be difficult for a therapist who is less than heroic. If a therapist can observe himself he may be aware of a desire to rid himself of the burden this patient represents. He may be aware of anger and guilt that follow such wishing. He may seriously begin to doubt his professional competence. All of the affects, anxiety, shame, anger, guilt, doubt, are data about the patient, data that must be included in a prescriptive diagnosis. How the patient may infect the therapist with his conflict follows.

If one listens very carefully to the patient's story (history, anamnesis) as it unfolds, one will discover that the patient is not talking about his misery, not relating a story; he is inflicting himself upon his therapist (4). For example, no paragraph ends without a sigh until the therapist, too, begins to sigh. The patient then both sighs and hunches his shoulders at the end of each paragraph, until the therapist, too, is both sighing and hunching. When the patient automatically notes that the therapist has added a response from out of the therapist's own repertoire, for example, the therapist is frowning between paragraphs more and more, the patient becomes silent. If the therapist has been unaware of the seduction as the important communication, that is, he hasn't been listening with "the third breast," he may be quite jarred and perplexed by the silence. For the unwary therapist, the silence represents a vacuum into which the conflicts about his competence mentioned above surge. The conflicts represent a second chance for the unwary therapist, another opportunity to find the key to the patient's underlying problem inside himself. I have written as if these patients present no problem to the sophisticated therapist. That is not so. A therapist who is so wary and canny that he cannot be trapped by depressive and sadomasochistic characters would probably be selling used cars. The trap set by the patient for the therapist, as he inflicts his self on the therapist, is the only way it can be communicated, given the current state of general knowledge. That the therapist's doubt and feelings of disillusion truly belong to the patient can only be appreciated after the fact. It is incumbent on the therapist, if he is to be of much use to the patient, to accustom himself to attributing such feelings in himself to patients (10). When such "decoding" happens, even more quickly, the therapist can and should feel that he is becoming more effectively empathic.

The life-style of the patient has been such that he has come to expect rejection and a feeling of loneliness that is made vivid by the presence of others. It is important to distinguish between the feelings of loneliness that relate to "real" interpersonal distance, and the feelings of people that carry the diagnosis we are considering here. The depressive and sadomasochistic character experiences dysphoric affect that is actually made more vivid by the "actual" company of others. His character armor includes an automatic, nonverbal, and potent skill in inflicting his feeling state on others. He is unaware of what he is doing to elicit painful feeling in the other; he is only aware of the consequences—rejection.

> A patient was talking quietly about himself. I was reflecting my concern that he was masking or keeping some feelings from me. Hurt by this familiar accusation, the patient experienced anxiety, and a tension in his legs. He hunched over and the tension in his legs disappeared. I felt and restrained an urge to hunch forward in my chair and felt a familiar token depressive feeling in my own legs. I reported this to the patient and he didn't believe it. I hunched forward and the tension left my legs. He reported that the feelings had returned to him. For him the feeling was not unpleasant but for me the feeling was disagreeable.

The patient in the above example uses depressive feelings as a device to control anxiety. He has learned the automatic and nonverbal behaviors that are correlated with depressive affect and these are incorporated into the structure of his self system. For the patient they are security operations in the sense that by dint of such strategies anxiety is managed (11). Those around him, however, catch the depressive message that the patient automatically sends. The depressive state is projected into the other person. Characterological projection seems to differ from the defensive use of projection in neurotic and psychotic disorders. Characterological projection seems more actual and concrete. The "sender" makes use of channels that are both out of awareness and common elements in ordinary social communication. These elements are acted rather than thought, or felt. They are ordinary behaviors rather than ego-alien attitudes (thoughts, feelings, wishes, dreads, etc.). They are part of the manifest identify and the communicative heritage of all people. (The "conning" of the psychopath makes similar use of the same channels.) For the character disorder the anxiety correlated with the fault in the development of the self system is linked to the repetitive behavior manifest on the surface. The behavior both advertises the fault and, by eliciting rejection as the depressive state is concretely projected onto others, perpetuates it.

The making of a characterological diagnosis is difficult because the diagnostician must enter into concrete interaction. As can be inferred from the example and discussion, half of the diagnostic process is "in the diagnostician." Moreover, the riddance wishes, shame and doubt of professional competence, guilt, and retaliation experienced by the diagnostician are data about the patient. The patient has not told the therapist of his dread of success. The very thing he wants most, he fears most. The dread of success relates to the patient's unconscious fear that he will be robbed of his depressive character armor. The more he is effectively in tune with the patient's character armor, the less likely is the diagnostician to be trapped. As the diagnostician resists offering the patient hastily contrived prescriptions for living, the patient will feel anxious and withdraw. The diagnostician is challenging the automatic use of depressive and antidepressive strategies common in the culture and used by the patient to manage anxiety. The underlying anxiety related to the patient's ambivalence about self breaks through. The patient may, as in the following example, threaten to withdraw from treatment as the anxiety appears.

> The sadomasochistic defense of a young woman, which included distressing psychomatic symptoms, was both becoming increasingly clear and not being gratified. She felt that she was going insane and wanted to be admitted to a hospital. When told that I would continue to see her as usual even in the hospital, she declined. She said, "If I can't be rid of you, what good would it do?"

The patient in the above example is responding "adversely" to an "effective" perception of her defenses. Such "negative reactions" occur earlier in the course of relationships with "character disorders" and represent management problems. In the therapy of the more treatable disorders, defenses that are more neurotic may be challenged after a therapeutic alliance has been well established. In a therapeutic relationship that deals with characterological processes the negative reactions intrude even into the diagnostic phases of the relationship. During the diagnostic process the therapeutic dyad is still reducing estrangement, and trust has not become durable.

The curiosity that underlies the collaborative alliance between the therapist and the more easily treatable patient seems absent in the therapy of the sadomasochistic and depressed character. In depressive and sadomasochistic patients an active curiosity about the self is rarely possible in those areas relevant to the narcissistic fault (2). Indeed, an active sustained attitude of curiosity toward an area central to the self seems to make the diagnosis suspect. The depressive and sadomasochistic attitude seems to turn active curiosity into passive confusion and perplexity. I have found that a focus on the patient's bewilderment represents a useful hook upon which to hang the cloak of collaboration. The patient's bewilderment about how things get the way they do may help to bridge the diagnostic and therapeutic processes.

If, however, the patient's confusion can be brought to the center stage of therapy, the patient will attempt to trap the therapist into a quick resolution of the confusion. He will begin asking the therapist "why" questions, seeking replies that are globally corrective. Once again the therapist's mettle is tested and once again attention could usefully be directed to the therapist's self-in-response-to-the-patient. As we shall see later there is a similarity in the family constellation that leads to both a career of service and the use of depressive and sadomasochistic armor as a narcissistic defense. Because of such similarity the therapist may be prone to counteridentify and to be unable to extract information from his involvement early in the therapy. He may also miss the intrusion into the opening phases of therapy of management problems typical of middle phases when collaborative trust has been consolidated. Similarity in dynamics, in other words, leads the therapist to feel prematurely that he knows the patient. He cannot substantiate such knowledge, for it does not come from data about the patient, but emerges automatically from within himself. A tendency to want to give in to urgent requests for quick resolution of the patient's confusion as well as to offer a "cure" for a long-standing perverse way of life might alert the therapist to "counteridentification."

The therapist will not, of course, be able to satisfy the patient's request for a quick cure. He may feel the pull to gratify the patient for reasons other than counteridentification. As mentioned above, these patients are skilled in using the nonverbal channels to inflict depressive affect and participation in the nonverbal message exchange is much more easily done than said or consciously controlled. The use of the couch in psychoanalysis minimizes the visual channels available to nonverbal exchange but doesn't eliminate them. The patient demands that the therapist prove the utility of therapy by using his suffering as blackmail. The dilemma for the therapist is to choose a therapeutic response. A therapeutic response is one that both includes the ordinary cultural response and simultaneously transcends it. For example, in depressive and sadomasochistic transactions the dilemma would be to respond to the miserable patient rather than the misery of the patient.

> A young woman complained that her life had been singularly unhappy. She spoke repetitively of a series of unhappy relationships with a monotony that filled me with pessimism. Instead of focusing on her "unhappiness," I reflected the monotony of her account of her life back to her. She readily agreed and then

said that she had been expelled from a rather sheltered environment. I asked her how this came about. She began talking in a remarkably different way, going into very interesting interpersonal detail. As her story gathered momentum she realized that she had never permitted herself to be listened to and we ended the consultation on an optimistic note. Her future course with another therapist was anything but monotonous.

In the above example the following occurred. The patient filled me with pessimism by dint of a monotonous anamnesis. She was inflicting her misery and I caught it. By attending to the goings on inside myself I was able to realize that I was being drawn into responding to the monotony. With some luck my reflecting the monotony to her addressed "the miserable patient." Reflecting the pessimism, as I did outside awareness in the very first clinical example, would have been responding to the "misery of the patient." The common cultural response is to respond to the misery by either becoming sweetly sympathetic or rejecting. The therapeutic response (rare in the culture at large) includes and transcends the common cultural response. The pseudoclassic response of silence is more often than not perceived by patients as rejection. Silence and avoiding an overt response is not therapeutic, for the patient unconsciously "knows" that the "pseudoclassic stance" is based on ambivalence in the therapist. He will similarly recognize a saccharine offer of help, for the patient has encountered that in the culture at large as well. He knows that which is too easily tendered as proof of his worth can just as easily be turned into self-doubt, for the need of proof paradoxically demonstrates that he seems unself-worthy to the therapist.

> I was filled with impotent anger as a patient reported how a night terror of one of his children intruded on a sadomasochistic battle between himself and his wife. The couple's lack of compassion in simply telling the child to go back to his room seemed extraordinary and I was drawn into an identification with the child. It was unfortunate that the struggle with my own rage and anxiety distracted me from using what I had learned for the patient's benefit. Had I had my wits about me, I would have realized the utility for the patient of my identification with the child. The patient's dilemma was identical with that of his child. He truly wanted to find a better way to relate to his wife. The sadomasochistic defense against the threat of feeling as rejectible as his child actually was, could have been pointed out. It wasn't because I was unable to extract information from within myself by dint of my anxiety.

The depressed and sadomasochistic character's demands of the therapist for a quick cure can be understood as a bid for self-esteem. They would trap the therapist into a process identical with their internal substitution of conscience and convention, sadistic attack and masochistic depression for genuine self-worth and the actual company of others. The therapist is perceived as having a more powerful convention and a more effective conscience. The therapist who deigns to treat such people is vulnerable, for he comes from the same culture. The therapist's vulnerability to countertransference problems in the treatment of depressive and sadomasochistic characters is noteworthy. It is common to find depression in a mother underlying the decision to become a therapist (10). The search to validate the self of the therapist-to-be, which began in a vain attempt to be a mother's antidepressant, continues in the need-to-cure. Such a need-to-cure has dire implications in the therapy of these disorders. The therapist with a need-to-cure and a patient with a need-to-fail establish one of the most stable and enduring and unchanging pairs in the civilized world.

There are troubles in the therapy of these patients that feel like countertransference problems in the restricted meaning of the term, but seem more usefully considered responses to the patient's transference. The effective memory bank for maintaining these perverse and painful ways of life include repetitive nonverbal, preconscious communication with significant others. The disorder is "only half in the patient" and even that half includes "introjects" of important others from the patient's past life. These patients are skilled in using their contemporaries in the "service" of perpetuating the disorder. They trap the other into using ordinary conventions and rules to inflict pain.

> A patient and her husband went to buy a washing machine. The salesman showed them several models in a medium price range. Of those they narrowed down their choice to two. One had an automatic dispenser; the other didn't. The difference between the models was 10 dollars, a sum the patient and her husband could well afford." She said, "I have been running up and down stairs for 8 years, I can do it for 8 more." The salesman was taken aback, and the husband got angry at the patient's "sacrificial act."

The misery elicited by the defensive strategems of these patients is contagious because the messages are made of the cloth of everyday experience. The therapist who has a conventional attitude toward psychological suffering is vulnerable to the patient's demands. This vulnerability of the therapist is a prerequisite of the utility of therapy. If the patient is to bridge the gap between that which he learns and works through in the therapy, there must be certain commonalities in the therapist and significant others outside the consulting room. No matter how thoroughly a therapist understands himself, such understanding is enlarged as a result of each psychotherapeutic journey. A therapist should pay therapeutic attention to both his patient and himself during the course of his work with his patients. This is especially true of the therapy of depressive and sadomasochistic characters. The dysphoric affect induced in the therapist by the patient's demands for a "quickcure" and for "self-esteem" and "self-confidence" needs both therapeutic attention and understanding. As the therapist pays useful attention to the operations of his self-in-response-to-the-patient he will be able to tolerate delay in responding to the patient. The delay will be of therapeutic value for the patient, for the therapist will be able to offer a more useful set of responses. On his part, the patient will experience the utility of gratification postponed.

Theory and technique come together in the consulting room as therapists use what they know to further understand the "goings on" inside themselves and their patients and the interactive dynamic that "is asking for gratification." The therapist has a need to know what he is denying the patient before it is withheld. The dysphoric affect induced in others by the patient could be understood as an archaic request for limits in an area of "spoiled development." In areas of faulty development of the self, the limits on greed are inappropriate to that phase (6). The patient relies on more primitive strategies to manage in the "area of the fault." Patently fraudulent requests and pseudosacrifices are examples of such perverse attempts to set limits on greed.

Ordinary limits result from a child-parent interaction directed at providing the child with mastery of phase-specific skills. At each moment the child experiences a regressive pull to earlier phases and a progressive push toward maturation (5). The effective parent provides a context that simultaneously favors progression toward mastery and recognizes the regressive trends. If the parent achieves an empathic blend of coddling and disciplining (1), both aspects of the child's experience of self are validated. The child becomes able to feel and validate his needs and delay gratification for longer periods. During periods of delay the child becomes able to keep optimistic contact with the parent. In such a context the child simultaneously separates from more childish forms and joins the adult world by learning how to describe his needs in more individual ways. Of course, ordinary development includes miscarriages on intent, e.g., as the child feels that he is being punished for precocious or regressive behavior. A parent is only able to achieve a consistent empathic blend of coddling and discipline over the long haul because he has succeeded in mastering the inexorable "phasic challenges" in his own development.

Because child development is never complete, every family experiences each phase of its children's development as both an opportunity and danger. There is the opportunity that the more adult members will further their own mastery of phasic needs as a spinoff of participation (3). There is the danger that regressive trends in the more adult family members will lead to a failure on the part of the child along with a regression in the more adult family members. The more faulty is the development of an adult, the more likely it is that the adult will experience participation as a parent in his child's development as dangerous, and the more likely may a developmental fault be repeated across generations.

The parent with a development fault has difficulty communicating in the area of the fault. Transactions in the area of the fault become contaminated with a here and now tentativity and pessimism that is transferred from his childhood. The parent's real life includes adaptive and defensive adjustments to sequester the fault and may also include moderate accomplishment in areas outside the fault. He may suppress and deny major components of needs. He may learn to communicate needs in the area of the fault in such a way that he experiences a repetitive rejection that justifies his pessimism. His fantasy life may include grandiosity and idealization; he may expect to magically achieve the power to satisfy needs in the area of the fault, and/or he may idealize others who seem to be able to negotiate his area. His envy of idealized others in this area does not motivate him to success. Rather, he uses the envy to further validate his tentativity and pessimism about himself. His fantasy life is a closely guarded secret and is used to maintain the belief that he is somehow different from other people.

The adjustment he makes toward others in the area of the fault is undermined by his children. Children differ from other object relations in that they are included inside a parent's narcissistic boundaries. The long familiar adaptive and defensive devices are short-circuited by the intrusion upon the parent of the phasic needs of his children. The parent's ambivalence and threat in the area of a development fault impair his performance as a parent. Whether in or out of awareness, the impairment aggravates the problem. His impairment is manifest "in process" as lack in recognition of his children's phasic need, a lack of the capacity to teach the skills appropriate to advertise the need, the skills to satisfy needs, and of an inability to suffer delays, should needs reach awareness.

The multileveled defects in the parent's capacity constitute a pathogenic matrix for the formation of depressive and sadomasochistic character disturbances. There are multiple reasons for a parent to become unavailable to a child in any given developmental period. Examples are: bereavement, unemployment, illness, and the advent of another child.

The effect of a parent's unavailability on the development of children depends on the quality of the ensuing dynamic "feedback system." One may consider two classes of dynamic feedback systems. One class is deviation counteracting and the other is deviation amplifying (8). The deviation-counteracting process tends toward homeostatic equilibrium. The deviation-amplifying process moves progressively away from equilibrium. Should a parent recognize that his unavailability to his child is temporary and caused by factors that he may potentially master, the effect of his child's development may not be "permanent," for the feedback in the family may tend toward equilibrium. Should a parent become neurotically defensive about his unavailability, the effect on the child may be traumatic, indeed. This unavailability may lead to a (deviation-amplifying) spiraling vicious cycle. In such a circumstance the unavailability may affect his child's development in the same way as a parental developmental fault.

In all cases the child will experience the parent's unavailability as a process. By that it is meant that the content of phasic needs, e.g., for trust, for autonomy, and for initiative, are repetitively experienced in the dynamic context of the parent's unavailability. For example, 3-year-old sons normally seek adoration from their mothers. The adoration is in part sought to validate the child's felt mastery of increasingly complex social situations. The mother who was deprived of such adoration from her father when she was 3 will be unable to effectively respond to her son. From repeated attempts and rebuffs, the character of the son becomes skewed toward a "developmental fault," not unlike that of his mother. The list of alternatives open to him, e.g., to seek adoration from father, to postpone and seek adoration from other audiences, should not distract us from what he also must deny: namely, that the developmental fault of his mother has a pathogenic effect on his attitude toward himself in relation to others. To the extent that he can value anything, he will need to value his mother. He would therefore rather devalue himself (his self system) in the experientially immediate context of his burgeoning mastery. Moreover, never having experienced what life would be like with a mother without such a fault, he is unable to use his felt need for adoration to detect his mother's fault. This constructed example points to a process that is both within and without the son, within and without the mother, and between them.

Because the need to value the mostly unavailable parent must lead to a corresponding devaluation of self, goals may become need frustration rather than need satisfaction. Any particular need in the child may in this way become primarily and structurally linked to disappointment. The disappointment may be experienced in the "self," the depressed and masochistic outcome, or in the other, the sadistic outcome. In the usual case, participants are more linked than separate and both suffer the disappointment internally from sadistic and masochistic behavior. The pathogenesis of depressive and sadomasochistic character seems best related to a "developmental field" in which the above process is repetitively experienced.

The dynamics of treatment become understandable as a re-enactment in the therapy of the process of child-parent interaction. Depressive and sadomasochistic process includes first a (structuralized) ingrained devaluation of the core of the self. Second, at the surface the process becomes manifest as depressive, sadistic, or masochistic behavior. Third, involvement of the other in the devaluation is intrinsic to the process, inasmuch as the devaluation of self is designed to distract attention from the unavailability of the parent-therapist. The patient will therefore challenge the therapist devaluation of self, therapist, and therapy. He may also defensively idealize self, therapist, and therapy.

Character disorders almost by definition have behavior patterns that are determined at the core of the self system and at the interpersonal surface. The link between the core of the self system and surface manifestations differs from that which obtains in neurotic and psychotic processes. In both neurotic and some psychotic processes the link between symptom and the core of the self is experienced as distressing. Practically, the means that the link between symptom and self is both perceived and a source of motivation for getting rid of the symptom. In character disorders the link between the core of self and the surface strategies is not perceived. The person is as likely to want to get rid of "self" as a character trait. The latter is all the more important in dealing with depressive and sadomasochistic characters. Distress is part and parcel of their patterned behavior and so patients feel and seem motivated to try to change. However, they also confuse the self with these surface manifestations. This link between self and manifest character trait is a potent source of resistance to therapeutic modification (id-resistance).

The alien quality of a neurotic symptom may permit the patient to assume a therapeutic attitude. A therapeutic attitude toward the self-in-relation-to-symptom is more easily recognized than understood. One gains the clinically useful idea that a therapeutic attitude includes a capacity for symbolism. Given such a capacity the patient can attempt to explore a range of experience-near processes by freely descriptive association. Less threatening pathogenic processes can be explored first. The resulting utility serves to reinforce trust in the attitude and consolidate the alliance with the therapist. Language, thought, and psychic reality are experienced by both patient and therapist as part of an integrated communication system. When the transference neurosis, the shared reliving of neurotic development process, intrudes on this kind of dyad, the relationship has been prepared to both withstand the stress and use the experience.

The character disorder does not seem to be able to trust the shift from the raw data of experience to free descriptive association in the area of his developmental fault. For reasons more apparent than truly understood, he confuses the data of experience with self. Free descriptive association threatens depersonalization. At the same time, of course, he cannot help exhibiting disordered behavior within the consulting room and inflicting himself on his therapist.

The therapist, however, does have a capacity for symbolism. In the therapy of character disorders, the therapeutic attitude is at first mostly "in the therapist." His capacity for the symbolic permits him a more tolerant view of what can only be raw experience for the patient in the area of his fault. For example, this more tolerant view may permit the therapist to respond to the miserable patient in contrast to the misery of the patient. The therapist may only gradually introduce the patient to the utility of free descriptive association in the area of the fault. The therapy of character disorders is more taxing, first, because the recapitulation of the faulty child-parent interaction is enacted in the consulting room from the start; second, because the therapist must from the beginning treat himself-in-response-to-the patient as well as the patient; and third, because of the "id-resistance" he can only gradually model for the patient a therapeutic attitude.

Therapeutic intervention in character disorders seems to shed light on the process of counteridentification. Knowing by counteridentification bears certain similarities to the manifest behavior of the character disorder. Both are automatic and ego-syntonic. Both use the cloth of acculturation common to others in the service of maintaining interpersonal processes. Fortunately, it is possible for a therapist, with effort, to route through awareness that which is gained by counteridentification. The results are self-reinforcing, for the therapist learns much about himself that is of considerable utility.

It seems interesting to speculate about culture and character formation. For example, if the script for the depressive and sadomasochistic character is more likely to be of Jewish authorship, one could ask, "Is it to a patient's advantage to have a therapist from a similar subculture?" The answer would seem to hinge on the initial benefit to the patient of the familiarity of the therapist and the possible future cost to the patient of the undermining of the work by counteridentification.

I have discussed the process of treating depressive and sadomasochistic characters. I have attempted to use clinical examples to illustrate and clarify. I may have not given "diagnostic precision" its due. I take it for granted that constitutional predispositions to manic-depressive disease that are amenable to pharmacotherapy will be recognized and treated. In any case, the dynamics of treatment from the patient's point of view may not be different from those outlined. The same can be said of psychotherapeutic intervention in the lives of people that are primarily neurotic. There is no major problem in living that is not linked at some level to depressive and sadomasochistic despair about the self. Clear qualitative distinctions between processes labeled as reactive, psychotic, endogenous, and characterological are made most securely after the need for drawing the distinctions has passed. The important summary statement about a patient is that statement which will permit a wise, firm, and tolerant response to his total life dilemma. Therapists who continue to develop personal theories of technique will more likely find therapeutic responses.

It may be useful to refer to others those patients toward whom tolerance and optimism are not forthcoming. In those instances where a referral can't be made, it is sometimes helpful to place the patient in group of family therapy. Some people are so oblivious to their own behavior and attitudes that more vigorous feedback than a therapist can usually provide is necessary. For them group therapy or conjunctive group and individual therapy may be preferred. Other patients may be too anxious to benefit from information provided in group settings and may need preparation and conjoint individual and group settings.

REFERENCES

1. Aries, P. Centuries of Childhood. Alfred A. Knopf, New York, 1962.
2. Balint, M. The Basic Fault. Tavistock Publications, London, 1968.
3. Benedek. T. Parenthood as a developmental phase: A contribution to the libido theory. J. Am. Psychoanal. Assoc., 7:389–416, 1959.
4. Bion, W. R. Attention and Memory. Basic Books, New York, 1971.
5. Freud, A. *Normality and Pathology in Childhood.* International Universities Press, New York, 1965.
6. Klein, M. *Envy and Gratitude.* Basic Books, New York, 1957.
7. Kohut, H. *The Analysis of the Self.* International University Press, New York, 1971.
8. Maruyama, M. The second cybernetics: Deviation and amplifying mutual causal processes. Am. Scientist, 51:164–179, 1963.
9. Mettler, F. The structural basis of the self. Ann. N. Y. Acad. Sci., 96:687–724, 1962.
10. Olinick, S. On empathy and regression in the service of the other. Br. J. Med. Psychol., 42: 41–49, 1969.
11. Sullivan, H. S. *The Interpersonal Theory of Psychiatry.* W. W. Norton, New York, 1953.
12. Wolff, C. T., Hofer, M. A., and Mason, J. W. Relationship between psychological defenses and mean urinary 17-hydroxycorticosteroid excretion rates. II. Methodologic and theoretical considerations. Psychosom. Med., 25:592–609, 1964.

14

ADDICTIVE PERSONALITIES

Leon Wurmser, M.D.

The Personality of the Compulsive Drug User

The vast majority of "drug abusers," as defined by law and public opinion, are emotionally healthy, stable, or at least not more disturbed individuals than the total population. If we turn to the relatively small group of compulsive drug abusers, or "addicts," we find not just the commonly described "psychopaths" or "passive-dependent" personalities, but nearly the whole range of psychopathology of personality disorders and symptoms. Therefore, we have to start out with a more precise definition of drug abuse and a basic distinction of types of "drug abuse" and then proceed to a far more careful and critical approach to the problems of personality structure and etiology.

Some Basic Distinctions

The usual definition of drug abuse is based simply on sociolegal criteria, e.g., by Jaffe "the use, usually by self-administration, of any drug in a manner that deviates from the approved medical or social patterns within a given culture." Jaffe narrows this wide notion down by focusing on those "drugs that produce changes in mood and behavior" (37).

Similarly, in the book *The Treatment of Drug Abuse: Programs, Problems, Prospects*, edited by Glasscote et al. (25), the term drug abuse is applied "to illegal, non-medical use of a limited number of substances, most of them drugs, which have properties of altering the mental state in ways that are considered by social norms and defined by statute to be inappropriate, undesirable, harmful, threatening, or, at minimum, culture alien" (25). It is obvious that this definition has a strong connotation of moral judgment and is based on specific ethical values.

For the following, I suggest a narrower definition: drug abuse should be called the *use of any mind-altering drug for the purpose of inner change* if it leads to any *transient or long-range interference with social, cognitive, or motor functioning or with physical health*, regardless of the legal standing of the drug.

Here the judgment is based on impaired functioning and thus on an observable medical criterion, vague though it might still be.

However, for our purposes here, even such a delimitation of our task is unsatisfactory because of its breadth. We would like to exclude all those occasional or irregular drug abusers in whom the impairment was transient. This latter group comprising all the experimenters and occasional users of illicit drugs has to be studied separately; it appears a particularly heterogeneous conglomerate of personalities. Instead, we narrow our scope still further by studying only drug abusers who fall unquestionably in the group of "compulsive drug abuse" (38). Glasscote et al. stressed the importance of this factor, too: "By contrast (to the term psychological dependence), compulsion is a more specific term that connotes one of the greatest obstacles in successfully treating people who have abused drugs. Compulsivity can be manifest in practically any aspect of behavior. One may feel compelled to step on every crack in the sidewalk and suffer great distress if for any reason he cannot. Compulsivity is believed to commonly underlie any number of widespread behavior problems, such as overeating, heavy use of alcohol, gambling, and so on. It seems certain that some portion of those who use illegal drugs do so out of compulsion. The significance is this: compulsions are notably resistant to presently known methods of treatment; the long-term success rate is low, the relapse rate is high" (25).

A Phenomenological Approach

The importance of the personality for the development of compulsive drug use has been well known, but barely studied. A very interesting observation may serve as opener: Patients treated with opiates during physical illness may become pharmacologically addicted, but most of them do not show any propensity after withdrawal to return to drug use. They do not develop psychological dependency. The same held true for melancholics who, in the past, at a time when other antidepressants were not yet known, were often treated with an opium solution, but according to available information, never developed narcotics addiction.

There is no pathology typical for all compulsive drug users (or for all narcotics addicts alone). One finds all forms of psychopathy and of neurosis, and also some psychotics among them. Usually, they are bored people, dissatisfied with themselves and with society, often very markedly depressed and anxious. Their conscience is inconsistent, in some regards too harsh and rigid, in others indulgent and easily seduced. It is archaic and easily projected to the outside.

The reliability and honesty of these patients is therefore often (though by no means always!) poor. Superficially, this is the consequence of their need to conceal their habit; mostly, however, it reflects certain aspects of their deeper pathology to be studied later on. As a matter of fact, most of the narcotics addicts at least have had a criminal record already as youngsters, years before they even started taking drugs (see below). Indeed, as mentioned before, it may happen that a notorious criminal rather improves socially under the moderating influence of narcotics. Also, severe chronic anxiety states and incapacitating depressions may actually improve once the person becomes addicted.

Beyond these generalities little is described in the literature. Kolb writes: "The present-day addict combines a number of traits which add up to his being an immature, hedonistic, socially inadequate personality" (43). More in detail: "Emotional disorders affected 86% of the addicts, of whom 13% were criminal psychopaths, 13.5% psychoneurotics, 21.5% inebriates, and 38% hedonistic, unstable types" (43). He describes these types more in detail (43); we forgo here further quotes, however, since the later studies appear to me to have superseded Kolb's concepts and classification which essentially go back to 1925.

Ausubel (1) defends, I believe rightly, the crucial relevance of personality factors as disposition for compulsive drug use (especially narcotics addiction) against the one-sided sociological-physiological theory of Lindesmith (54). He distinguishes between "primary addiction, in which opiates have specific adjustive value for particular personality defects; symptomatic addiction, in which the use of opiates has no particular adjustive value and is only an incidental symptom of behavior disorder; and reactive addiction in which drug use is a transitory developmental phenomenon in essentially normal individuals influenced by distorted peer group norms" (1).

His first group coincides with the type we are concerned with, the compulsive user. "Two sub-groups may be delineated: (a) the inadequate personality and (b) anxiety and reactive depression states." The vast majority belong to the subgroup of the "inadequate psychopath": "He is passive, dependent, unreliable, and unwilling to postpone immediate gratification of pleasurable impulses. He demonstrates no desire to persevere in the face of environmental difficulties, or to accept responsibilities which he finds distasteful ... " (1). "Psychiatric history and examination and a battery of psychological tests reveal the following picture of adolescent heroin addicts treated at Bellevue Hospital: motivational inertia, lack of motivation at work and in school, low frustration and anxiety tolerance, inability to concentrate effort, constriction of interests; passive, dependent, and narcissistic personality trends; abnormally strong attachment to mother; superficial and easily disrupted interpersonal relationships; superficial social maturity; tendency toward withdrawal, regressive, and fantasy adjustive techniques" (1).

He goes on: "Representative clinical studies of adult drug addicts yield essentially the same results. 55% of 1,036 drug addicts at the U.S. PHS Hospital were classified as manifesting 'psychopathic diathesis', a diagnostic category roughly equivalent to inadequate personality ... Lambert diagnosed 58% of 318 adult addicts at Bellevue Hospital as inadequate, emotionally unstable, or nomadic personalities ... " (1). Causative patterns do not appear to lie in early disruptions, but in middle childhood and preadolescence, described by Ausubel as an extremely overprotective, or an extremely underdominating, or extremely overdominating parent (1). Psychoneurotic personalities who use drugs to cope with depression and anxiety are, according to Ausubel, rare (in Lexington, e.g., 6%) (1).

More detailed and sophisticated studies started appearing in the 1960s. What J. H. Jaffe wrote in 1965 (37) is a good, still acceptable summary: "Older views that compulsive users of opiates or alcohol were morally weak persons who simply over-indulged themselves have been largely replaced by the realization that such individuals are emotionally disturbed. It is also felt that the emotional disturbance would have manifested itself even in the absence of drug use, and that the use of drugs may be an attempt to cope with this disturbance. The nature of the emotional disturbance predisposing to such compulsive drug use is not clear. Formal clinical psychiatric diagnoses have placed opiate users and alcoholics in a number of seemingly distinct classifications (e.g., schizophrenias, character disorders, psychoneurosis, etc.). It has been suggested that individuals with widely differing problems use pharmacological agents for different reasons. Thus, the neurotic may use a drug to relieve anxiety (negative euphoria), the psychopath to get a thrill (positive euphoria), and the psychotic to alleviate depression or to suppress delusions."

There is, however, "a growing tendency to see in compulsive drug users a constellation of common characteristics that cuts across the diversity of clinical diagnoses and that may be thought of as the 'addict' or 'alcoholic' personality. Thus, alcoholics are often schizoid, depressed, dependent, hostile, and sexually immature.... Although most narcotic addicts show a constellation of common features similar to that seen in alcoholics, they also exhibit striking differences. Alcoholics tend to solve conflicts about aggression, dependency, and sexuality by 'acting out' in a 'pseudomasculine' fashion; narcotic addicts prefer to handle such anxieties and conflicts passively, by avoidance rather than by aggressive acts.... Wikler and Rasor (80) have suggested that, regardless of conventional personality classifications, narcotics addicts are individuals in whom the chief sources of anxiety are related to pain, sexuality, and the expression of aggression. Opiates seem to suppress the sources of these anxieties, thus permitting the user of narcotics to make a passive adaptation to his inner tensions. Alcohol and barbiturates, by contrast, reduce the inhibition of drives and often aggravate the basic conflicts.... Over the past few years, there has been an increasing awareness that, whether the drug is an opiate, a barbiturate, alcohol or amphetamine, the psychological disturbance in the compulsive user is both profound and extensive. A considerable number of such persons are thought to be overtly or incipiently schizophrenic. However, it is also clear that there are many more people who exhibit the alcoholic or addict personality than there are addicts or alcoholics.... We do not know what factors permit such individuals to adjust without drugs" (37).

A number of inquiries with tests have been undertaken. They shed light from a different angle on what we try to study. St. A. Sola and W. F. Wieland (72) reported elevated D and Pd scales in the MMPI, indicating the presence of depression and psychopathic deviancy. The authors used the Zung Self-Rating Depression Scale, the Beck Depression Inventory, and the 35 Symptom Check List, and tested 196 patients on methadone maintenance. The previous findings of depression were borne out in those self-rating tests, and this "despite the fact that they are in treatment with methadone and counseling" (72).

"The Beck Depression Inventory revealed that irritability was the predominant factor, followed by disorders of appetite, weight, and sleep, and performance difficulties.... These findings present objective evidence that opiate dependent patients under treatment in a methadone program tend to continue to experience dysphoria. It is more severe than normals but less severe than neurotics or psychotics. Furthermore, the nature of the dysphoria differs qualitatively from neurotics and psychotics in that opiate addicts experience more irritability, performance difficulties, and negative outlook as the important constituent factors of their depressions whereas neurotics and psychotics tend to experience a predominance of deeper depressive mood" (72). The motivation to use heroin was related to these feelings of dysphoria, worries, nervousness, depression, coping with anger, relating to other people, and self-blame.

Heller and Mordkoff (32) compare the MMPI findings in narcotics addicts with those in nonaddicted, multihabituated adolescents. They postulate two general types of "drug abusing personalities." The first, associated with heroin addiction, seems to show "a psychopathic type of personality with little evidence of overt reports of anxiety, guilt, insecurity, or depression, and dominating anti-social tendencies." The other set of studies, probably of less severe forms of multiple drug abuse, "seems to indicate a personality marked by anti-social tendencies but also evidencing overt signs of the anxiety and depression lacking in the first type" (32).

Interestingly, another recent MMPI study (33) finds no correlation of MMPI findings of various types of drug abusers with "drugs of choice." The wide range of pathology is again reflected in a large series of MMPI studies presented by Monroe et al. (56). In newly referred voluntary patients characterological disorders (psychopathic deviate and hypomania), emotional disturbances (neurotic triad), and thinking disturbances (paranoia, psychasthenia, and schizophrenia scales) are fairly evenly balanced whereas the previous admissions in Lexington show a preponderance of the character disorder scales.

On the other side, a New York team reported in 1967 (9) that they succeeded in selecting a 57-item "heroin scale" (He) from the MMPI with an accuracy of 75% for adults and 67% for adolescent addicts. In the latter category, "false positives" turned out to have some predictive valence: a number of non-using test-positive adolescents were seen to have turned to heroin 1 year later.

Independent from the MMPI, Haertzen and Panton (29) developed an Addiction Research Center Inventory (ARCI) with 550 structured questions, containing a scale of 74 items permitting the differentiation of "psychopathic" from "non-psychopathic" groups of patients. According to this scale "criminals and addicts were most socially deviant, alcoholics were intermediate, and normal subjects were the least deviant" (29).

Schooff et al. (71) compare the MMPI profiles of black inner city addicts with those of suburban heroin addicts. In the former group, the major elevation is on the Pd scale (psychopathic deviate), reflecting alienation from social groups, dissatisfaction with and bitterness toward parents, and a dysphoric and resentful subjective state; in the latter there is the same Pd peak, but in addition the so-called neurotic constellation (hypochondriasis (Hs), depression (D), and hysteria (hy). Both groups show also Sc-elevation, indicating feelings of alienation, social isolation, and idiosyncratic, unrealistic thinking. On the basis of the MMPI, Rorschach, TAT, and clinical findings, the authors delineate two groups of heroin addicts who are psychologically quite different: "The suburban addicts can be described as more verbal individuals, who experience greater feelings of anxiety, futility, and hopelessness. They experience alienation from accepted social conventions, and anger towards their parents and peers ... these individuals use heroin to alleviate their anxiety and to avoid reality. The inner city group, in contrast, appear to be less neurotic and to experience minimal anxiety. These individuals can be described as impulsive, using little mediation between the initiation of a thought and its transference into action, relying minimally upon an internalized set of standards, living in the here-and-now, having more unrealistic self-concepts and using denial as a major means of coping. In short, this group appears to be less mature and to rely upon others for limit setting and directions in everyday living." A very important, albeit tentative, conclusion is drawn by these authors: for addicts falling "into the neurotic classification, heroin usage may represent a symptomatic expression of individual psychodynamic conflict and an attempt to alleviate subjective distress or to 'act out' in relation to parents and other significant emotional figures. In contrast, for those addicts falling into the 'character disorder' classification, heroin usage may be more closely related to sociopsychological environmental factors than to individual psychodynamic conflict, in that these latter subjects evidence fewer signs of internal psychological struggle." They emphasize that there is not a complete congruence between neurotic and suburban versus character disorder and inner city, but a higher respective incidence. The last conclusion, of course, pertains to the clinical, not the social groups.

According to the newest, not yet published, highly sophisticated and comparative studies, the Yale Research group of Rounsaville et al. found that 56% of their narcotics addicts show chronic affect lability and chronic intermittent depression. "Nearly 90% had longstanding personality pathology or longstanding difficulty in the regulation of dysphoric affect" (Research Report, NIDA Contract 271-77-3410). Even more dramatic is the finding of current diagnoses: 71% suffered from a current "affective illness" (various depressive disorders). A broad range of diagnostic instruments of high reliability was used; equally the numbers were large (711). (Among evaluation measures used SADS-L, DSM III, SCL-90, RDC, Beck, Social Adjustment Scales Self Report (SAS-SR), Maudsley Personality Inventory, WAIS, Global Assessment Scale, Addiction Severity Index (ASI), Levinge and Bellak tests). A smaller group of 72 addicts was evaluated for neuropsychological impairment: "Overall impairment was moderate to severe in 51% of opiate addicts, mild in 29% and absent in 20%." Moreover "the significant relationship between poor school performance and childhood hyperactivity and neuropsychological impairment supports the proposition that this dysfunctioning preceded drug use for some" (l.c.).

Similar findings were reported by Grant et al. in 1978 (27): in 151 poly drug users the Halstead Reitan Neuropsychological Battery showed deficits in 37% 2 to 3 weeks after entering treatment and in 34% at 3-month follow-up (8% and 4% for nonpatients). No differentiation as to preexistence of such impairment was possible.

In another, current study (NIDA Research Contract 271-77-3431) again the prevalence of depressive disorders was noted: In various groups of compulsive drug users the percentage hovered between 70% and 80%, anxiety disorders between 5% and 15% (DSM Axis I). In Axis II (Personality Disorders), "antisocial" was vastly prevalent (41%), with a few schizotypal, schizoid and paranoid (13%), narcissistic and "mixed B" (10%) (Treece et al., report of February 1980).

Personality Disturbances from a Psychodynamic Point of View

There are still relatively few comprehensive attempts to describe the personalities of narcotics addicts from a dynamic point of view.

Rado attributes the proneness to addiction to a presumably genetically rooted predisposition to retain an archaic "more powerful primordial, omnipotent self than is the case with the vast majority of the members of society." Due to this predisposition, "narcotic pleasure elicits a response of narcotic grandeur." It is this grandiose conception of the self which makes the craving for the drug uncontrollable (63).

Very typical are omnipotence, grandiosity, and magical thinking, as M. Nyswander writes; they are revealed by conscious daydreams. "Mistrust bordering on paranoid projection is frequently encountered. An inability to relate other than in a narcissistic fashion is best illustrated by the addict's frequent belief that he is so uniquely interesting that he should be paid by the treating psychiatrist" (58). In a later publication, however, she repudiates this view; describing her methadone program she states: "We have seen no sign of a fundamental psychological defect or of a pleasure seeking personality" (59).

Hoffman describes (in terms very reminiscent of Rado's early papers) as most striking clinical finding in the psychoanalytic psychotherapy with drug addicts an "abysmally low self-esteem" (34). "The addict without his drug suffers from a 'tense depression' which is then relieved by a pharmacogenic elation. This pharmacogenic elation is characterized by two essential points: (a) It is brought about by the ego itself, at will, and therefore gives the addict an omnipotent sense of control over his mood. (b) It resembles and is patterned on what Rado called the 'alimentary orgasm' . . . if the addict is indeed fleeing a depressive state, he needs a euphoric agent which will act as long as possible. Sexual intercourse is too brief a depression-free interval for him; thus, he needs a long-acting euphoriant which he finds in opium— acting long enough to gratify his wish for the 'alimentary orgasm.' . . . When an unfortunate event occurs, they tend to develop an immediate sense of depression, since they always attribute the event to their own basic unworthiness. If they are to defend against this feeling by a show of hostility, they must really do this with a vengeance. Therefore, their hostility is of necessity quite strong. This frightens them, in many cases, and therefore they look for a good 'out.' Heroin provides the ideal answer, for it depresses the hostility and raises the crumpled self-esteem at the same time."

Very little has been described beyond these general, partly outdated descriptions. In the following, we will proceed step by step into areas which have been explored but little.

Among the first really modern, good, extensive, conceptually satisfactory studies of the personalities of compulsive drug users I select particularly the work of Chein et al., *The Road to H* (11); the psychoanalytic book by H. Krystal and H. A. Raskin, *Drug Dependence: Aspects of Ego Functions* (47); the brief essay by H. Wieder and E. H. Kaplan, Drug Use in Adolescents:

Psychodynamic Meaning and Pharmacogenic Effect (79) (and their more popularly written book, *Drugs Don't Take People, People Take Drugs*) (40).

In regard to causation, Chein et al. (11) state that, at the inception of their studies, they did not ask (as they came to later) "how much drug-taking behavior would not take place were it not for the challenge of the risk; the attractiveness of the forbidden; the glamour of defying authority; the power of self-destructive needs given a socially validated channel of expression; the drawing power of an illicit subsociety to lonely individuals alienated from the main stream and the lure of its ability to confer a sense of belonging, interdependence of fate, and common purpose to individuals who would otherwise feel themselves to be standing alone in a hostile world; and the inducements to drug use motivated by vast profits made possible by the very effectiveness of the law enforcement agencies and the operation of the economic law of supply and demand. We did not, then, have any notion that the most dangerous consequences of addiction to the individual were a direct outcome of the existence and enforcement of the law" (11).

On the road into narcotics use, the historical antecedents are relevant: "Already by the eighth grade, about a fifth of the boys in highly deprived areas give evidence of having acquired what we have characterized as a 'delinquent' orientation to life. This orientation consists of moods of pessimism, unhappiness, a sense of futility, mistrust, negativism, defiance, and a manipulative and 'devil-may-care' attitude on the way to get something out of life" (11).

Farther back, the signals of alarm are up in regard to their family life: "Relations between parents are far from ideal, as evidenced by separation, divorce, overt hostility, or lack of warmth. In almost half the cases, there was no father and no other adult male in the household during a significant portion of the boy's early childhood. As children, they tended to be overindulged or harshly frustrated. The parents were often unclear about the standards of behavior they wanted their sons to adhere to and tended to be inconsistent in their application of disciplining measures. Their ambitions for their sons were typically unrealistically low, but in other instances, they were unrealistically high.... The evidence indicates that all addicts suffer from deep-rooted, major personality disorders. Although psychiatric diagnoses are apt to vary, a particular set of symptoms seems to be common to most juvenile addicts. They are not able to enter prolonged, close, friendly relations with either peers or adults; they have difficulties in assuming a masculine role; they are frequently overcome by a sense of futility, expectation of failure, and general depression; they are easily frustrated and made anxious; and they find both frustration and anxiety intolerable. To such individuals, heroin is functional; it offers relief from strain and makes it easy for them to deny and to avoid facing their deep-seated personal problems.

Contrary to common belief, the drug does not contribute rich, positive pleasures; it merely offers relief from misery" (11).

"Heroin is a tranquillizer—perhaps the most effective tranquillizer known—but it comes in expensive doses" (11). And, "The addiction of the adolescents we have studied was adaptive, functional, and dynamic" (11).

If we narrow these crucial findings down to the personality characteristics, we read again that in terms of clinical psychiatry "there is no single type or syndrome of maladjustment specific to the adolescent opiate addict" (11). In 52 tested adolescent addicts, about half of the patients belonged to character disorders, in the case of women of the sadomasochistic, the angry, aggressive, or the "cool" psychopathic type, in the case of men more of the oral dependent or of the "pseudopsychopathic" delinquent type, the latter compensating for their wishes for passivity and dependency by their boisterous, "dangerous" exterior (11). About one-fourth of the 52 were described as borderline schizophrenics, about one-sixth were overt schizophrenics, and the few remaining ones "inadequate personalities" (with particularly striking paucity of interests and goals and an impoverishment of thinking and emotional expression) (11). Narcissistic disturbances, expressed by lowered self-esteem, dysphoria, and depression, often covered by a facade of strength and cunning, are typical (11). Consequently, suicide is a serious hazard (11), though no numbers are given.

Fitting to this picture is the very ambivalent relationship to their mothers—clinging dependent and mutually destructive—a relationship where the mother appears as pathogenic as the child pathological (11).

In the 1969 issue of *The Psychoanalytic Study of the Child*, two connected papers, one by Dora Hartmann, the other by Herbert Wieder and Eugene H. Kaplan, were presented. Hartmann stressed mainly the defense aspect of drug use ("the wish to avoid painful affects (depression)") and "the need to replace a lost object" (31). The personalities of the compulsively drug-using adolescents were seen as mostly "orally fixated (or regressed)," whereas the occasional drug users used the symptom just as a form of transient rebellious acting out.

Structurally the compulsive users were either inhibited ("very passive") in regard to aggression or at times had uncontrolled outbursts of aggression. They showed crumblings of superego and ego functions under the drug's influence. Most had been *depressed* prior to drug use and "felt less depressed when on drugs" (31).

In Wieder and Kaplan's outstanding essay, we find a penetrating study of the psychodynamic substrate and meaning of drug use within the texture of the whole development (79).

The authors open the presentation of their own concepts with the statement that "chronic drug use, which we believe always occurs as a consequence of ego pathology, serves in a circular fashion to add to this pathology through an induced but unconsciously sought ego regression" (79). Again, they see the dominant conscious motive for drug use not in the seeking of "kicks," but in "the wish to produce pharmacologically a reduction in distress that the individual cannot achieve by his own psychic efforts" (79). But they go a crucial step farther: "we believe that different drugs produce different regressive states that resemble specific phases of early childhood development. The user harbors wishes or tendencies for a particular regressive conflict solution, which the pharmacology of a particular drug may facilitate; the repeated experiences of 'satisfaction' establish preference for the specific drug" (79). Their crucial summarizing statements as they refer to personality organizations are the following: "The more urgent the need for continuing pharmacogenic effects, the more severe is the pathology. Borderline and psychotic patients rely on drugs in this way to shore up and supply controls and gratifications which adequate structuralization provides unaided. Drugs act as an energic modifier and redistributor, and as a structural prosthesis.... When an individual finds an agent that chemically facilitates his pre-existing, preferential mode of conflict solution, it becomes his drug of choice. The drug induces a regressive state, but the drug taker supplies the regressive tendencies.... Those who persist in taking drugs are persons who have suffered significant regressive disorganization and faulty structuralization in early childhood, that is, prior to taking drugs in adolescence" (79).

The book *Drug Dependence: Aspects of Ego Functions* by H. Krystal and H. A. Raskin presents another discussion of the personality structure of compulsive drug users (47). The authors state that the etiology of drug use "resides in the psychological structure and functioning of the human being, rather than in the pharmacological effect of the drug," that "the drug is not the problem but is an attempt at a self-help that fails," and that "drug dependence represented a manifestation of ego function, a mode of adaptation, perhaps the sole adjustive mechanism to living problems the person has available to himself at the moment ... " (47). They direct the focus of their exploration on three areas of drug-personality interaction: affect, object representation, and modification of consciousness.

In regard to the first item, they write: " ... in many drug dependent persons we find an affect combining depression and anxiety, a disturbance in which the de-differentiation of anxiety and depression takes place or a state in which the differentiation was never successfully accomplished ... the affect seemed to approximate the infantile 'total' and somatic distress pattern rather than a clear-cut adult affect pattern" (47). This "total," archaic affect precursor shows another aspect of its primitivization, besides the already mentioned resomatization, namely "deverbalization" (47). Because of the overwhelming, "traumatic" nature of affects in such persons, "drugs are used to avoid impending psychic trauma in circumstances which would not be potentially traumatic to other people" (47). The drug serves either to raise the stimulus threshold (e.g., with opiates) or to evoke alternate stimuli to ward off threatening perceptions (e.g., amphetamines): "This is a selective 'numbing' and blocking" (47). They again refer to drug use as a "defense against affects" (47). Again they stress the specificity of drug effect for the relief sought.

Krystal's and Raskin's thoughts about the aspects of the object relation (the ambivalence, especially the combination of intense oral dependency and inordinate guilt) are fascinating elaborations of the earlier mentioned concepts (cf. especially Chein and Rado): "In some drug dependent individuals we witness the twin phenomena of the craving for reunion and the need for separation." By substantiating a "thing" for a person, "he denies the disappointment and rage towards his depriving object-representation, declaring instead that it was not the real article. Once he finds the drug, he has the 'perfect' substitute, one that he can control, repeatedly introject, and that eliminates the danger of the object. It is a concrete, easily controlled source of gratification, which takes the place of human love objects, and is unconsciously experienced as the transsubstantiation of the original love object" (47). And, "We view drug dependence, with Dorsey, as an instance of extreme form of transference" (47).

Lastly, they describe the alteration of consciousness, especially disorientation and dissociation, as major defenses: "as a block against confrontation or for carrying out a dangerous impulse" (47), e.g., " . . . the hyper-attention to the minimal stimuli acts as a distraction and protection against painful affects and threatening ideas" (47). The latter is true mainly for psychedelics and stimulants. In short: "Their way of dealing with problems could be conceptualized as their manipulating their sensory, perceptive, and interpretive functions, instead of dealing with the real sources of their unpleasant affects by problem resolution or adaptive changes" (47). Very interesting are the following implications: " . . . the person given to drug abuse hypercathects the perceptory system. In fact, the drug user seems to have a fear of ideas and words, and seeks a regression to pre-verbal, hallucinatory experiences, such as visual, auditory, or tactile ones. . . . However, the drug user is interested in the modification of his consciousness primarily as a method of modifying his affective states (47).

A few additional recent studies that have some bearing on our topic should be briefly mentioned before we turn to a more detailed direct examination of the personality problems, as they have been explored by this author.

Khantzian, e.g., emphasizes "how addicts (take) advantage of the antiaggression action of opiates in the service of drive defense" and stresses "the disorganizing influence of aggression on ego functions in individuals whose ego stability was already subject to dysfunction and impairment as a result of developmental arrest or repression" (unpublished manuscript).

Moreover he and Krystal, in a number of studies, see a peculiar "self-disregard," based on "impairments of a generic or global ego function that I have chosen to designate as 'self-care and self-regulation'" (42). Similarly, Krystal: " ... in drug dependent individuals it is the 'walling-off' of the maternal object-representation, and within it self-helping and comforting modes, which is the specific disturbance. Thereby, the alcoholic loses his capacity to take care of himself, to attend to his needs, to 'baby' or nurse himself when tired, ill or hurt narcissistically" (46). He also refers to the deep and regressive ambivalence: " ... while the drug-dependent yearns for the union with his maternal love object (representation), he also dreads it. He really can't stand it either way. Schizophrenic patients and some borderline individuals yearn for union with their love object (representation) and once they achieve it (in fantasy) they cling to it passionately, giving up conscious registration of all contacts with whatever might spoil it. Drug-dependent individuals are very busy getting the drug, but can feel themselves reunited with the idealized love object only rarely for short periods of time, and only at moments when they are virtually totally anesthetized ... it may be said that they are addicted to the process of taking and losing the drug rather than to having it" (40). Their affect tolerance is severely impaired, due to "massive childhood psychic trauma"; they are afraid of their feelings and need to block them (46). Especially intense rage against the maternal love object is deeply repressed, leading to the rigid "walling off" of its representation and an idealization of the mother figure. Thus he "manages (in his fantasy) to protect the love object from his fantasized destructive powers" (46). Woollcott (78a) sees as common "basic fault" in addict personalities: "a) Incomplete, faulty separation-individuation, and b) a particular intense conflict around symbiotic striving which I would call a fusion-individuation conflict." Specifically, then, "the drugged state will be found to represent an affect-dominated nucleus of primitive pleasurable experiences of merger or bliss, which are linked with affect-memory clusters of an extremely fearful and pathological kind, specific to the particular patient."

Compulsion, Equivalence of Symptoms, and Life-Style

We turn now in more detail to the problem we have been encountering up to now, the problem of inner compulsion which cannot be broken by external force or persuasion.

Drug abuse, except in experimenters, has this quality of an irresistible urge. This aspect of compulsiveness is the central operational criterion of emotional disorder: the more an action or a feeling, an attitude or a thought shows this aspect of rigid, stereotyped, irresistible, and insatiable compulsion, the more we have to view it as psychologically sick. The hallmark is the feeling: "I cannot help but—" regardless of the consequences. In other words, it is not social usefulness or acceptability which marks a piece of behavior as healthy but the sense of freedom, of inner choice, the absence of inner drivenness and urgency; R. Waelder (77) and Kubie (48) deserve particular credit for having emphasized this point (86).

This point has several implications. One is that the really difficult task in treating drug abusers is by no means the physical dependency, but the emotional need to use a drug, any drug, to find relief. I have not seen as yet any drug abuser in the real sense who was not an emotionally deeply disturbed person. If we get a feel for their life histories and the histories of their families, we are not fooled into believing that it is the drug which has caused the emotional disturbance. Only secondarily we encounter the devastations caused by the drugs themselves. This, by the way, also explains why the pusher is of little importance; he is only the profiteer, not the causative agent.

A further implication is that there is a kind of equivalency between various symptoms. If we succeed in suppressing one symptom like drug abuse, we are soon likely to encounter another, perhaps equally destructive one—a suicidal depression or violence. This became poignantly clear to me when I worked for a number of years in programs of compulsory abstinence. The few patients successful with that method very often resorted either to alcohol or to acts of violence, even homicide, once they were abstinent for a long period of time. I came to wonder whether the narcotics addiction in these instances was not an attempt at self-cure, and indeed whether *our* cure was not worse than the illness we tried to treat. To add some color to the theoretical discussion and particularly in order to illustrate as vividly as possibly this last point, I excerpt two case studies written at the end of the first 1½ years of the program of compulsory abstinence (Baltimore Narcotics Clinic, 1964—1965). These were our few "successful" cases at that time (December 31, 1965).

> **Case 1.** This very heavy set white man, 24 years old at the beginning of the program, cannot be considered a real drug addict, although he was sentenced to 1½ years for possession of narcotics, burglary, and larceny. The patient is the second of three children. No one in the family allegedly had gotten into any conflict with the law. The patient's parents are well and live together. His father is strong willed and dominant, his mother is soft hearted, although somewhat nagging toward father and pleading for sympathy by various physical complaints. Patient was bedwetting until he was 11 years of age and started with sexual relations at the age of 13. The patient completed a 10th grade education, spent 4 years in the Navy, and got an honorable discharge there. He worked inconsistently in various positions as a truck driver, sheet metal worker, construction laborer, and promotion worker. During his military service, he was attacked by a robber and severely injured. He had to stay 7 months in a military hospital. He has no marked aftereffects from the shot wounds.
>
> By friends he was introduced to the intake of barbiturates and, about 3 or 4

months later, to the use of morphine. Two weeks after starting with the use of the opiates he was picked up by the police. The drug was in no manifest connection with his injury. This patient has had no positive specimens since joining the clinic. He looked down with disdain on the "junkies" and was in turn considered by the others as an alcoholic, not as a drug addict.

He emphasized that he had no urge to take drugs and that he satisfied his desire by excessive food and alcohol intake and by a rapid turnover of sexual relations. Besides that, he has an almost insatiable craving to travel; he says he has driven to New York or Philadelphia just to have breakfast and then returned home. He wishes to be free, to be able to travel and not to work, and he was afraid that one day he would drop everything, take off, and go too far—especially after a disappointment. He loves engines and likes to race cars and boats; it is really not the speed, but the power of the motor he likes. He liked either to dominate the group sessions by an argument or a feigned story—or then to remove himself from the discussion by his scorn and distaste of the rest of the group members and by his anger at his forced participation. He stayed completely drug-free and was discharged from our program 393 days after his admission when his time of parole expired.

Although he professed at the end to have gained quite a bit of insight into his personality and the reasons for his conflicts with society, it was felt that he had replaced the urge to take drugs (opiates and barbiturates) by quite comparable cravings for food, alcohol, sexuality, and travel. He felt unable to contain these or gain really founded insight into his attitude of oral omnipotence and the ensuing feelings of helpless fright and ruthless rage. Not able to renounce, he merely shifted the symptom to another type of insatiability.

Case 2. This is a tall, usually quite neglected looking, beardy and haggard, white man, age 36; because of his apprehensiveness and trembling, he was called by the name "Shaky." He started taking drugs after his wife had left him about 4 years prior to his conviction and had soon become dependent upon them. He was sentenced in 1963 to 2 years; he had been a seller of narcotics. The father, a minister, is described as very harsh. He would "get carried away with temper." This was the only unpleasant thing about him. The patient says: "I loved him. He was not unjust" yet adds that he was punished by being beaten with a belt until he was about 15 years of age. Mother was nagging and semi-illiterate. The parents were divorced when the patient was 22 (1950). The patient, youngest of three children, completed an eighth grade education. He had frequently changing sexual relationships since age 16. After 20 months in the Army, where he was honorably discharged, he went in 1949 to work on the railroad as a trainman; he was a very hard worker, frequently working one shift on and one off. About his wife, whom he married in 1951, he says: "I had her on a pedestal. I had a guilt complex. She was perfect; everything had to be my fault." He bought her a house and practically lived on the railroad to earn money to support his family.

When the marriage broke up after 7 years, he stopped working, started drinking, and soon was introduced by a girlfriend to the use of opiates. He financed the habit mainly by transporting and selling drugs. During his stay in the program, he got increasingly depressed, talked about suicide, and used narcotics in the first months not infrequently, though still sporadically; he had to be warned several times that he would be returned to jail if he did not stop taking drugs. While he took narcotics less and less often, his depression became so marked that he was put on Elavil. His depression was mainly motivated by the loss of his wife and his son—to a minor part also to the monotonousness of the lowly jobs open to him now. He felt everyone disliked him. About 8 months after his admission to the program, he stopped violating the rules of the clinic; he came in quite regularly and did not show any positive urine specimens anymore. Often, however, he came unkempt, disheveled, unshaved, and obviously inebriated to the meetings. He admitted freely that he could stay away from drugs only when he took to alcohol and, as he added, the day when he left our program (he stayed in it for 545 days), also to marijuana: "How did you think I was able to stay away from drugs? I have to have some escape." And he said: "The threat has been a help more than anything else—I wish I still had it." He indicates he probably will return to drugs once he is off the program.

The impression is that this extremely passive, orally dependent man has exchanged the gratification by opiates with that by alcohol and hashish. He suffers from a severe neurotic depression which had become manifest by the break of the apparently symbiotic relationship with his former wife, a symbiosis which he now has to re-establish with the drug experience.

The conclusions we can draw from these cases of patients in the program of compulsory abstinence are briefly the following.

Only a very few addicts stay off narcotics altogether; at least sporadically, drug use can be discovered; there are obvious correlations with times of inner and external tension bringing about these periods of decompensation.

The conflicts underlying these tensions are of some individual specificity and thus cannot be reliably generalized. These conflicts are usually quite archaic in nature and consist of primitive wishes for omnipotence, total dependency, and passive gratification.

There are also feelings of deep despair and self-devaluation, emptiness, and rage, if these frustrations cannot be covered and denied.

When the narcotics exit is closed, other forms of no less pathological substitute-gratification and substitute-denial are sought. Most frequently, the patients resort to excessive use of alcohol; in fact, it was a general impression that the more a patient was able to switch to another type of addicting substance, particularly alcohol, or addictive activity, the more successfully he coped with the problem of opiate addiction. Other substitute gratifications used in addition to alcohol were marijuana, barbiturates, promiscuous sexuality, and excessive food intake.

In several patients, the aggressiveness, based mainly on *intense oral rage*, tends to become overwhelming and threatening once the drug use is suppressed. Many patients had big difficulties containing their potentially dangerous explosivity and violence.

In surprisingly many patients we encountered depressive episodes which became so serious that an antidepressant (Elavil) had to be given—usually without convincing results.

All patients state that it was mainly the fear of discovery and reinstitutionalization which kept them from returning to the use of opiates; they basically detested the vilifying, humiliating, and physically harmful effects of alcohol, but saw it as a necessary evil as long as they had no other legal way of gratifying their cravings. Only a rare patient felt that he was really cured from drug addiction. Most assumed that they would eventually return to the occasional use of narcotics, although they abhorred the social consequences of drug use.

If we want to explore the etiology of compulsive drug use in more detail, we would have to distinguish various layers of causative specificity. We would see how the drug enters in a time of crisis as an adventitious, contingent agent, just precipitating the outer manifestations of the inner illness which we can call the "addictive search." We also can only touch on the role of decompensation, played by "narcissistic crises." These concepts are presented in other papers of the author (81, 82, 84–86). In this context, we can merely examine in a summary form some of the personality factors predisposing to the "addictive search." This will be followed by several more specific subchapters, devoted to an analysis of the leading anxieties, the leading defenses and protective systems, and to a more comprehensive summing up formulation. It will be followed up by an outline of some family characteristics.

Predisposition to the "Addictive Search"

The Defect of Affect Defense. We have to start off with what I believe to be the most important concept in a dynamic understanding of drug use: all compulsive drug use can be considered *an attempt at self-treatment*; more specifically, the importance of the drug effect in the inner life of these patients can perhaps be best explained as an artificial or surrogate defense (denial, cf. below) against overwhelming affects. It appears that there exists some specificity in the choice of the drug for this purpose.

In the past, the satisfying, wish-fulfilling aspects of the drug effects have been emphasized. To put this in a catch phrase: drug use was mainly seen as an expensive search for a cheap pleasure. This certainly holds true for the popular and unreflective concept of why people take drugs. Earlier analytic theoreticians (14, 26) followed this lead, except that they saw in drug use, as in other symptoms, the satisfaction of unconscious wishes.

In other psychological studies of drug abuse, the focus was on the symbolic (again mainly wish-fulfilling) meaning of drug intake as such (as oral supplies, illusory penis, or its self-destructive, self-punitive aspects) with little regard for the psychodynamic impact of the pharmacological effects themselves. I do not deny the importance of the wish-fulfilling aspects, but I believe we might be more specific about the obverse side of the same coin, namely, of drug use as a defense.

Certainly the view that drug use is an escape has also been popularly held, but again only in regard to intolerable external situations. The concept of the need for drugs as a defense against intolerable internal factors—and more specifically affects—has been described little.

It was Homer about 2800 years ago who sang about Helena having "drugged the wine with an herb that overcomes grief and anger and lets forget everything bad" (36). Freud (20) described narcotics as a means of coping with pain and disillusionment. Glover was explicit in regard to "drug addiction" (referring to cocaine, paraldehyde, and presumably also to opiate addictions): "its defensive function is to control sadistic charges, which, though less violent than those associated with paranoia, are more severe than the sadistic charges met with in obsessional formations" (26). And, "Drug addiction acts as a protection against psychotic reaction in states of regression" (26). In turn, he saw in unconscious homosexual fantasy systems "a restitutive or defensive system ... acting as a protection against anxieties of the addiction type" (26).

Rado named this aspect "narcotic riddance" and opposed it to what he called "narcotic pleasure" and to "narcotic intoxication" (a climactic sense of triumphant success) (63). Fenichel writes in regard to some cases: " ... the addiction can be looked upon as a last means to avoid a depressive breakdown ... " (14). Hartmann points out that the conscious motivation for the use of drugs was in most cases "the wish to avoid painful affects (depression), alleviate symptoms, or a combination of these factors" (31).

Wieder and Kaplan describe the drug of choice as "acting as a psychodynamic-pharmacogenic 'corrective' or 'prosthesis'" (79). Thus they write: "Chronic drug use, which we believe always occurs as a consequence of ego pathology, serves in a circular fashion to add to this pathology through an induced but unconsciously sought ego regression. The dominant conscious motive for drug use is not the seeking of 'kicks', but the wish to produce pharmacologically a reduction in distress that the individual cannot achieve by his own psychic efforts" (79).

The notion of defense against affects is a well-known analytic concept and has been elaborated by Jones, Anna Freud, Fenichel, and Rapaport. Jones described the stratification of affects in his 1929 paper "Fear, Guilt and Hate" (39), and mentioned how the hate-sadism reaction can be recognized as a defense or protest against inhibition and guilt (39); he also "called attention to the various layers of secondary defense that covered the three attitudes of fear, hate and guilt, and pointed out that the defenses themselves constituted a sort of return of the repressed" (39). Fenichel wrote a paper in 1934 under the expressive title "Defense Against Anxiety, Particularly by Libidinization" (15). Anna Freud (17) and Rapaport (67) have discussed more in detail the concept of defense against affect.

We can be more precise and describe how different drugs have differing effects on specific affects.

Narcotics and barbiturates apparently calm intense feelings of rage, shame, and loneliness. These three affects are usually derivatives of pervasive conflicts about the limitations of life: most prominently we encounter rage and shame as a reaction to the massive disappointment and disillusionment in regard to their own grandeur; less obtrusively we find an intolerable sense of loneliness and hurt, a longing for a symbiotic bond with a need-fulfilling, powerful other person who would give in to all demands.

All 16 patients seen in intensive psychotherapy while on methadone maintenance described feelings of loneliness, emptiness, and depression, of meaninglessness and pervasive boredom preceding drug use and following withdrawal. However, more specifically, in everyone very intense feelings of murderous rage and vengefulness, or of profound shame, embarrassment, and almost paranoid shyness, or of hurt, rejection, and abandonment were discovered during psychotherapy. Regularly these feelings of rage, shame, and hurt were reduced as soon as they were on methadone. In a few of them, they disappeared altogether; in some they still occurred occasionally, but had a less overwhelming quality. Some of them stated simply that the drug made them feel normal and relaxed—implying that they felt those pervasive feeling states to be abnormal, sick, intolerable. Others said it helped them "not to think of the depression." Several stated that they felt bored, but that they preferred this over the overwhelming feelings before (82).

It was obvious that in none of these patients the underlying inner problems were resolved, but that the dampening of the mood disorder brought about by methadone was experienced as a great relief. Both the resulting boredom and the insufficient relief from the underlying conflicts led several of them to occasional or habitual use of other drugs while on methadone, mainly alcohol or stimulants.

Psychedelic drugs counteract potently the emotional state of emptiness, boredom, and meaninglessness. The drug-induced illusion that the self is mystically boundless and grandiose and that the world becomes endowed with unlimited meaning seems to be a direct antidote to the pervasive sense of disillusionment in the ideal other person. It artificially recreates ideals and values when they have been irreparably shattered inside and outside. It is important that this artificial ideal formation has a peculiarly passive-receptive ring, most like the identification with a hero in a movie or on TV. Indeed, there seems to be a remarkable similarity between the psychedelic experience and the turning on and tuning in to TV; several patients actually compare it with an inner movie (79).

Amphetamines and cocaine have superficially much in common with what we just described. They also eliminate boredom and emptiness (79). However, these more or less conscious affects appear mostly to be caused by repression of feelings of rage and shame whereas, in the previous group, these moods are induced by the collapse of ideals. Accordingly, these stimulants provide a sense of aggressive mastery, control, invincibility, and grandeur, whereas the psychedelics impart a sense of passive merger through the senses.

However, there is more to it: the amphetamine effect serves as a defense against massive depression or general feelings of unworth and weakness. In the few cases of compulsive amphetamine abuse which I was able to treat in intensive psychotherapy, the long-term abstinence was accompanied by intense, self-directed aggression, in some by suicidal rage and despair, in others by lethargy and self-degradation. Thus, amphetamine abuse can, at least in some patients, be called an artificial normalizing or even manic defense against the underlying affect of depression.

From this most cursory and tentative survey, we recognize the central role of narcissistic conflicts in all types of compulsive drug use. The choice of a specific drug of preference—often found only after long shopping around—is specifically related to the affects engendered by these conflicts; when the inner structures fail as defenses, the pharmacogenic effect has to serve this purpose of inner barrier. If we suppress this attempt at self-treatment without massive support to the ego of the patient, we force him into often more serious forms of decompensation: violent, even homicidal rage in the narcotics addict, severe suicidal depression in the amphetamine user, a careless apathetic drifting in the psychedelics user (86).

Faulty Ideal Formation. Another aspect, implicit in some of what I have already described, is the superego pathology, the lack of meaning-giving, life-determining, life-guiding values and ideals, or, in their personified form, all-powerful myths. The affects just described usually emerge during or following a crisis where such central values, ideals, and myths have been shattered or when the need for such an ideal has become particularly prominent, its absence or unreliability particularly painful. Here the family pathology enters. Parents who did not provide a minimum of consistency, of reliability, of trustworthiness, of responsiveness to the child, especially during his crises of growing up, are not usable as inner beacons, but as targets of rebellious rage and disdain. Parents who vacillate between temper tantrums and indulgence, who allow themselves a living out of most primitive demands, parents who are more interested in their political or professional careers and their clubs and travels than in the needs of their children to have them available, parents who are absent for economic reasons and cannot impart that important combination of love and of firmness, of sympathy and of discipline, of tolerance, and of structure, of forgiveness and of consistency—all these parents, unless replaced in their crucial functions by capable nannies, make it terribly hard for their children to accept them as secure models for conscience and ego ideal, to internalize them and to build them up as inner guardians against transgressions.

The "high," the relief and pleasure sought with help of the drug, is a surrogate ideal, a substitute value, a chemical mythology, which normally would be supplied by the internal sense of meaning, goal-directedness, and valuation. A deeper look into this particular aspect will be provided below. The next aspect is the least secure and most presumptive one; yet, it may prove to be easier to observe and even quantify than the other elements (86).

Hyposymbolization. I refer to the frequent observation of a general degradation, contraction, or rudimental development of the processes of symbolization and with that, of the fantasy life. This curtailed ability or massive defect to symbolize pertains particularly to the patient's inner life, his emotions, his self-references: one example for this is the inability of most of these patients to articulate feelings. Many, if not all, relevant affects are translated into somatic complaints, e.g., about craving and physical discomfort or into social accusations: "it's all society's fault." They remain preverbal as affects. The same constriction seems to hold true for the entire fantasy life (4, 79). It is just this lacuna—whether it is a conflict-induced scotoma, or a genuine deficiency—which makes psychotherapy so particularly difficult and frustrating. After all, psychotherapy employs precisely the verbal band out of the spectrum of symbolic processes as its instrument. Tentatively, we might dub this defect "hyposymbolization," and it is, I believe, identical with what Peter Blos described as "concretization" (4). (We would speculate that the television, with its nonsymbolic overload, fosters, though not causes, this disorder.)

The drug is utilized, not to substitute for the lacking symbolization proper, but to remove that discomfort which is now perceived not as an affect, but as an untoward somatic or outer reality: it alters body image and world image into a less unpleasant or more meaningful one. In other words, it modifies (though does not remove) the projection (86).

Archaic Object Dependency. Up to now, we have examined the psychodynamic role of the various pharmacological effects of these drugs. There is a further dynamic implication which is very important and far better known than these three: "Among the unconscious motivations (in addition to oral gratification and passive identification with a parent), the need to replace a lost object seemed to play a very important role" (31). Many patients talk about their drug and the paraphernalia and circumstances surrounding it, with a loving tenderness as if it were a love partner. Obviously, it is the object character of the drug which assumes a central motivating power in this regard, less its pharmacological character (79). Actually, the very word "drug dependency" reminds us of what we are dealing with, namely, an *archaic passive dependency* on a hugely inflated object. The single-minded devotedness, the frenzy of the chase after the beloved—the incorporative greed, the masturbatory and orgastic aspects of the use, the mixture of ecstatic idealization and deprecation vis-à-vis the drug ("star dust," "blue heavens," "white lady" versus "shit," "scag" (79); they refer to "oral ambivalence") and all point to the dependency on a narcissistically perceived object. Much of this reminds us of fetishism. Dynamic similarities and dissimilarities of these two syndromes need to be worked out: Do we find a similar split of the ego in addictive illness as in the one described in fetishism? Glover implicitly raised this question already in 1932: " . . . in the transition between paranoidal systems and a normal reaction to reality, drug addiction (and later on fetishism) represent not only continuations of the anxiety within a contracted range, but the beginnings of an expanding reassurance system" (26). He calls fetishism the companion problem of addiction (86).

Self-destructiveness. Very well known is the self-destructive, self-punitive aspect of drug abuse (26). In some cases, we may observe the direct equivalency of drug use with suicide. If we take the first away, the second may become the menace. Drug abuse in itself can often (not always) be considered a tamed and protracted suicidal attempt, though we have to be cautious not to fall into the pitfall of the teleological fallacy (post hoc, propter hoc), In line with the other aspect of superego pathology described above where the faulty ideal formation was underlined, we may now add the important role of archaic forms of shame and guilt—as reflected, e.g., in much of the vindictive measures in Synanon and other therapeutic communities (as well as in most of our legislation). There is no question that very primitive and global fears of humiliation and revenge play a dominant role in the social interaction of these patients, and they are usually not only the consequence of society's reaction, but part of the patient's makeup to begin with (see below, 86).

Regressive Gratification. This aim of drug use has been studied most extensively. Our previous emphasis, especially on the notion of the artificial affect defense, has been used to counterbalance the historical emphasis on this aspect. Both are obviously two sides of the same coin. Fenichel, e.g., summarizes these findings very well in stating that "addicts" use the pharmacological effects "to satisfy the archaic oral longing which is sexual longing, a need for security, and a need for the maintenance of self-esteem simultaneously. . . . During the drug elation, erotic and narcissistic satisfactions visibly coincide again" (14). Also, "Erogenously, the leading zones are the oral zone and the skin; self-esteem, even existence, are dependent on getting food and warmth" (14).

Among all the forms of regressive gratifications attained with the help of the drug the increase in self-esteem, the re-creation of a regressive narcissistic state of self-satisfaction is the most consistent one. This is particularly relevant when we see this aim of drug use as an integral part of the narcissistic crisis which very often marks the onset of compulsive drug use. To this we turn now (86).

Narcissistic Crisis. The specific cause is the acute mobilization of the underlying conflicts and with that of those affects which cannot be coped with.

Such a mobilization quite typically occurs at first during adolescence, rarely earlier, not too often later. Often the relapse from abstinence into drug use, again, is regularly marked by the recurrence of such a narcissistic crisis which in turn often is triggered by an external event setting in motion the juggernaut of pervasive anxieties, rages, and narcissistic demands.

By definition, a "narcissistic crisis" would have to entail a particularly intense disappointment in others, in oneself, or in both, so intense because of the exaggerated hopes and so malignant because of its history, reaching back to very early times.

Precipitating external events of such a crisis can typically be found in family crises coinciding with the maturational crisis of adolescence.

Thus, this crisis is the point in time where the conflicts and defects converge with a particular external situation and with the availability of the seeming means of solution: the drug (86).

The Etiological Equation. It appears very likely that it is the convergence at least of some, if not all, of the first six elements: the massive defect of affect defense, the defect in value formation, the hyposymbolization, the desperate search for an object substitute, the intensely self-destructive qualities, and the search for regressive gratification—together with the intensity of the underlying narcissistic conflicts—which forms the predispositional constellation for "addictive illness" in general, for compulsive drug use in particular. Although it appears to me that the most specific of these predispositional factors are the needs for affect defense and the compelling wish for regressive gratification, only further research, including predictive studies, can elucidate the relative relevance of these six factors.

The specific cause is the mobilization of the underlying narcissistic conflict in what we call the narcissistic crisis.

The precipitating cause is the advent of the drug on stage, functioning only like the crucial though irrelevant messenger in the antique tragedy, a hapless catalyst.

In the following a more careful in depth probing of the personalities of compulsive substance abusers is attempted as it emerged in the experience of this author in the past 5 years (86, 87).

Defense Analysis of Drug-dependent Personalities

Commonly, "defense analysis" includes or even stresses the study of anxiety situations above the defenses proper. In the following I suggest, however, to separate "anxiety analysis" from "defense analysis" proper; in other words: the motive for defense is sharply distinguished from the nature of the defense itself.

The leading preconscious anxieties in the drug-free state are: (a) anxiety about overwhelming affects, of affective storms (44, 45, 47), and of drives in general; (b) claustrophobia; and (c) shame anxiety. They are disguised derivatives of deeper, more or less unconscious anxieties: very severe castration anxiety, terror about self both in separation and in merger, and the characteristic fears involving scopophilia and what is commonly, though inexactly, called exhibitionism.

The major defense mechanisms employed to cope with these feelings are: denial, reversal, affect mobilization, and externalization.

The result of this constellation is the need for a specific protection system, whether in form of drugs, or of symbiotic love bonds, of groups and cults, or the transference. Motives for defenses, detailed defense mechanisms, and countercathexis in form of countervailing protective systems lead to a peculiar form of conflict solution that is characteristic for toxicomania—different from neurosis, psychosis, and sociopathy.

A. Motive for Defense

While it appears that affects very generally need to be suppressed, since they are of such regressive nature (global, deverbalized, resomatized), as H. Krystal (44, 45, 47) has presented in such a thorough and convincing way, detailed observation discovers that all these overwhelming feelings (and not only negative ones) are signaled by milder forms of anxiety or cut short by intense flooding with it. Instead of the underlying affect there is just an unpleasant sense of inner tension, restlessness, uneasiness, and unhappiness, followed and yet increased by more and more focused thoughts about drugs, craving for them, and impulsive or planned search for them.

Besides *anxiety about such intense feelings* (often multilayered anxiety at that), we very often encounter a second affect as direct motive for defense—the feeling of emotional pain, injury, loss, woundedness (or vulnerability)—in short a *depressive affect*. Instead of grieving the drug is taken.

To return to anxiety as motive for defenses, we not only encounter controlled anxiety warning against uncontrolled "flooding" forms of terror and panic, but all the fears of most other intense emotions: of rage, of love, of excitement, of disillusionment, of boredom and emptiness, and, particularly importantly, of feeling guilty and ashamed. Occasionally it may also be anxiety about any drive manifestation—of libidinous and particularly of aggressive nature in the sense of what A. Freud described as "the ego's primary antagonism to instinct (17)." There is, with this, indubitable evidence for this anxiety about "bursting" with uncontrollable impulses, mostly rage—so much so that, e.g., Khantzian sees in narcotics addiction a specific coping strategy with aggression (42). On this level, the fact and nature of the anxiety are relatively easily accessible to scrutiny, more preconscious than unconscious. In a sense this anxiety itself functions also as a defense against the other affects and the drives, that, of course, are unconscious. Not only my own experience, but also the generally observed prominence of depression in recent studies of narcotics addicts (Treece et al. and Rounsaville et al., cf. above) supports Brenner's contention that the affect of depression is just as much a motive for defense as is anxiety.

It also appears to me more and more persuasive to narrow down the specificity of many of these affects that are most importantly denied with the help of drugs: I think they are either those that directly connote superego condemnation (guilt, shame), loss of superego approval (sense of unworth, sadness, emptiness), loss of ideals (disappointments, disillusionment, meaninglessness), or then affects and drives that would lead to such condemnation, especially aggression (Khantzian, see below).

The following two anxieties, claustrophobia and shame anxiety, are really only special cases, albeit particularly prominent ones, of what has just been described as the broader, vaguer, though milder anxiety, covering more specific, more sharply delimited, but usually much more intense anxieties. I found these two in most cases quite prominently once I started looking for them.

In a considerable number of cases I have been struck by the prevalence of *claustrophobia*, the fear of being closed in, trapped, captured. The patients feel stifled by limitations of any kind: closeness and commitments, obligations and expectations, restraints and constraints. Restlessly, they try to burst out from them. Certainly anxiety by itself already has such a quality of narrowness and confinement, almost physiologically; yet, if we look at the concomitant compelling need, also to *seek*, not only to avoid claustra, it appears to me that far more specific meanings reside in this symptom. On the one side it represents both the wish and fear for merger, union, fusion, and the opposite wish and fear to be separate, isolated, individuated. On the other the claustrum is a concrete symbol for all those superego limitations that so centrally need to be repudiated. Careful study of addicts reveals that most already showed an infantile neurosis with strongly phobic features, usually of the claustrophobic type, or phobic systems.

Claustrophobia in particular clearly reflects (as presented elsewhere and following up on suggestions by Fenichel and Rangell) intense terror about uncontrollable "bursting" drives (archaic sexual and, even more importantly, aggressive overstimulation caused by the very severe traumatization discoverable in most cases). It seems to be what I called the "primary phobia" dealing with Jones' "aphanisis" (39).

In line with the predominance of narcissistic concerns and vulnerability, *shame anxiety*, as one particular expression of the conflict with the superego, is particularly prominent. It is the fear of being *exposed*, seen, watched, or heard as weak and a failure, as not living up to an image that one wishes to have of oneself. With the strongly grandiose self-image, coupled with exaggerated expectations of what others could and should do, there is a continued fear of (and proneness to) massive disappointments, to "narcissistic crises."

Quite concretely it refers to losing control—whether in form of bed-wetting or loss of social poise, of being ridiculed, rejected, or of giving in to affects and wishes of any kind. The underlying drive conflicts about what is commonly called "voyeurism" and "exhibitionism"—or, more appropriately, of "scopophilia" and "delophilia" (the wish to express, manifest, show and reveal oneself)—and their centrality, neglected up to now, for the study of narcissism have to be bypassed in this short outline. Yet again it will be noted that shame is once more centrally evoked by conflicts between ego and superego.

Now to the defenses proper.

B. Defense Analysis

Denial. *Drug use is lastly only a pharmacologically reinforced denial*: at least implied before in the paragraphs about "defect of affect defense," drug use props up the specific defense of denial, i.e., an attempt to get rid of feelings and thus of undesirable inner and outer reality. Denial can be defined as "a failure to fully appreciate the significance or implications of what is perceived" (75); it is a defense making the emotional significance of a perception (including that of a memory) unconscious. It is as if to state: "I don't want to feel the way I do and I resort to external means to shut out any inner perception of such feelings—although I never fully succeed with this."

Not only are the painful feelings quite generally denied, but also so is the awareness of inner conflict: "There is really nothing wrong with me. I take drugs only to have some fun, to feel relaxed and to enjoy the company of my friends," is a frequently encountered statement. Yet, such disclaimer is only momentarily successful and is quickly followed by the admission: "You are right, I do not feel well. There is something wrong with me." The feelings denied are perceived, repudiated, and yet again acknowledged. This denial is inherently accompanied by the split in the ego, described by Freud (23): On the one hand "he rejects reality and refuses to accept any prohibition; on the other hand, in the same breath he recognizes the danger of reality ... this success is achieved at the price of a rift in the ego which never heals ... The two contrary reactions to the conflict persist as the centre-point of a splitting of the ego." He described it in regard to depersonalization (21) and to fetishism (19), but mostly in these terms (22): "Their behavior is therefore simultaneously expressing two contrary premises. On the one hand they are disavowing the fact of their perception—the fact that they saw no penis in the female genitals; and on the other hand they are recognizing the fact that females have no penis and are drawing the correct conclusions from it. The two attitudes persist side by side throughout their lives without influencing each other. Here is what may rightly be called a splitting of the ego" (22).

What is thus both perceived and not perceived—in wild back and forth vacillation—is *not* presence or absence of the penis, as in fetishism, but the presence of a more or less extensive province of emotions and impulses that reminds them of a severe trauma (separation being one, early overexposure to violence and sexuality a second, shame conflicts a third, castration a fourth).

In contrast to this sharp definition, what is currently so often described as "splitting" is really the defense by denial combined with the *countervailing fantasy of idealization* (functioning as countercathexis). All of what has been drawn into the phobic system is avoided as dangerous and bad, while all of what has become part of a reassurance system protecting against these dangers is sought out and idealized as all good and great. Such contradictory ("split") self and object images are very unstable, and easily flip-flop. These *countervailing idealizing*, i.e., *narcissistic fantasies* are a typical phenomenon accompanying denial.

Also such extensive denial is always accompanied by much displacement, a spreading out and generalizing of what is avoided or sought. A typical example is the "withdrawal" reaction and craving in patients who are not physically addicted. Many addicts have noted that whenever they are anxious or angry, or when they return into the former drug associated situation, they go into "acute withdrawal"; the absence of the drug becomes equated with any acute anxiety. This occasionally occurs after many years of abstinence (e.g., return from jail to the hometown). The longing for relief and the anxieties have been displaced from the original crisis to the city, the entire environment, and even to paraphernalia and injection rituals. The ensuing trembling and yawning are microconversions based on these displacements—all phenomena so thoroughly familiar to us from the psychopathology of everyday life and from dream analysis.

One consequence of pervasive denial is *depersonalization* in its multiple variants. An entire side of the person (the dirty, the angry, the exhibitionistic self) may be detached, unreal, unfelt, not quite part of inner life. Feelings of tenderness and quiet or expressed caring are shunned as unbecoming, as shameful loss of control (equated with bed-wetting or loss of bowel control), and need to be turned off and covered over by a stony mask of rigid "manly" self control—only to break through in sudden spells of weeping and overwhelming sadness or anxiety.

Quite often the patient feels "split" into the compliant, kind, yet false self, and the nasty, cruel, vengeful, spiteful self—an inner dissociation temporarily effaced with the help particularly of barbiturates and alcohol.

With the massivity of affects mobilized and their often very regressed nature, denial may also become very massive: more and more affects need to be blocked out and frozen, and their expression hidden behind a mask of wooden rigidity. Affect denial thus seems a precursor to pervasive shame.

Reversal. A number of drive reversals are generally of much greater significance as defenses than the literature indicates: turning active into passive, turning passive into active, and turning against the self. The latter is very important in depressions and the first in masochistic characters. However, it appears to me more and more persuasive to see in the defense of *turning passive into active* a cardinal type of defense in severe psychopathology—particularly in compulsive drug users and other forms of severe character neuroses ("borderline," much as repression is in the more typical neurotics).

Just as it is a main theme of his life that the patient suffers and fears disappointment and helplessness, he does everything in his power first to enlist help, but then to turn the tables and to prove the therapist helpless and defeated. Thus he wants to inflict the same helplessness, defeatedness, and humiliation on others—his familiy, the therapist, the treatment of the penal system—that he has suffered himself. He wants to defeat *them*, because he feels defeated; he wants to make *them* feel helpless, weak, and ashamed, because so does he; he tries to scare them, because he is so scared. He tries to corner them and box them in, because he feels so confined, limited, and wishes to break out. In a concrete example, a patient makes her therapist feel completely in the dark and helplessly groping, unable to understand what is happening and what to do—reflecting how she herself had been feeling vis-à-vis a mother who repeatedly abandoned her and eventually killed herself. She keeps everyone around guessing, just as she had been helplessly lost ("ratlos").

As will be seen later, the majority of compulsive drug users were massively traumatized, severely emotionally and physically abused as children. The archaic defense of drive and affect reversal is pervasively used from very early on to master these often panphasic traumata.

The next two defenses are very closely related to this second one.

Affect Mobilization and Affect Freezing. I mentioned earlier how anxiety itself tends to function not only as a motive for defense—the well-known case—but, as I suspect more and more, as a kind of defense itself. Anxieties of many kinds—again prominently the ones already described, like shame anxiety and phobic anxieties—serve as clamorous screen affects against deeper, unconscious ones. Shame anxiety especially may defend against severe castration anxiety and fear of masochistic excitement. These recurrent, fairly stereotypical affect mobilizations cannot easily be subsumed under the better known concepts of reversal of affects and of affect regression. These defensively used affect storms—not just of anxiety, but also of rage, of hectic, frenetic excitement, and especially of severe depression—appear to be a way station, an in between stage to externalization, the fourth defense.

As mentioned, both in recurrent affect mobilization and in more global affect regression, pervasive denial in form of *"global affect freezing"* is employed. May this not underlie much of what we now designate as alexithymia?

Externalization. This defense is just as much a counterpart to denial, as was described by Waelder for projection. In it "the whole internal battleground is changed into an external one" (18); put the same in different words: externalization is the defensive effort *to resort to external action in order to support the denial of inner conflict.* That means an internal conflict is changed back into the external one, e.g., ridicule, rejection, and punishment are provoked (not just suspected) from the outside world—a very frequent form, by no means restricted to compulsive drug users. Or: Limit setting is invited and demanded from the therapist, but then fought against. Or: Oral and narcissistic "supplies" are quite concretely requested and sought from spouses and friends; their limitation is responded to with envy and rage. Much of the "acting out," the "impulsiveness," is such a defensive use of action, an action with the aim of taking magical omnipotent control over the uncontrollable, of risking the ultimate threats (separation, humiliation, castration, dismemberment), yet—counterphobically—proves that these terrors are unfounded, that fate can be propitiated and forced to protect. It may be action by gambling, motorcycle jumping, and racing; it may be by lying, manipulating, cheating; it may be by violence and revenge; it may be just by any exciting action. Or it may be by drugs: "I have the power, with help of this magical substance, to master the unbearable."

The all-permeating tension and restlessness is broken by such externalization which, especially if forbidden and dangerous, is an attempt to get rid of the almost somatic uneasiness and pressure, and is experienced as primitive "discharge," a breaking out of being trapped with this undifferentiated, but deeply frightening tension within.

All defensive externalization is dehumanizing. The action, not the needs, qualities, properties of the persons "used," is relevant. However, what is the true nature of this defense by externalization? Waelder (78) pointed to the *isomorphism* of defense and the return of what has been defended against in the symptom: specifically, what has been disclaimed (denied) would return now as claim and assertion, though in disguised form. Is this applicable to externalization too? The claim is bluntly: "I have the right to feel good." What is disclaimed is: "I have no such right; in the contrary I should feel profoundly ashamed or guilty for seeking any gratification, since it always comes down to total merger or to total power or to total fulfillment what I crave for." Since the denial specifically concerns the recognition of limitations, boundaries, and confinement set by outer reality and, more importantly, by the superego, the breaking through in the symptom of what has been disclaimed takes on the form: "I bring about new confinement and restrictions. I need both outer assurance and protection—the 'good' superego—and outer punishment in form of injury, condemnation, and particularly humiliation—the 'bad' superego." The form of externalization specific for drug abusers thus reclaims the disclaimed superego, both as one that sanctions the violation of all boundaries and as one that punishes such transgression. Just like denial has a characteristic Janus quality, being always accompanied by partial acknowledgement, so externalization shows a double quality—bringing about by action both protection and condemnation.

Lastly, though, I gain the increasing impression that this entire defense by externalization is really but a subspecies of turning passive into active, not a separate mechanism at all.

C. Protection System

By now it has become amply evident that as the outcome of the use mainly of denial and of externalization we find the overriding need of a quite specific "countercathectic" system set up to protect solidly and concretely against the overwhelming general and more phobically focused anxieties. Simply put: the system of phobic fears is now opposed by a *protective system* in the form of protective figures and protective fantasies. I use as prototype a well-known vignette given by Anna Freud (17) of the boy who used the tamed lion as his protector. The phobically feared animal—the substitute for the hated and feared father—had become his protector: " ... he simply denied a painful fact and in his lion fantasy turned it into a pleasurable opposite." Since we already know now that the major defenses are mainly directed against superego functions and superego anxieties, the protective system serves to a good part as a superego substitute in its many facets. It has also been noted how the superego mostly appears in the concrete form of claustra that need to be burst and escaped from (the anthropomorphized formulation, reflecting the prevalent concretization, be forgiven). The fear of the superego and of external figures representing archaic forerunners of it recurs in the claustrophobia and other forms of anxiety.

The drug now is part and parcel of such a protection system; it is *equally compulsively sought, as a phobic object may be compulsively avoided*. It is the photographic negative of a phobia—just like the tamed lion is the negative of what Anna Freud called the "Angsttier," the phobically feared animal. (There may be fascinating parallels to sexual perversions: again it appears that the perverse act is not primarily dictated by the goal of pleasure, but by that of protection against otherwise overwhelming anxiety.)

To be yet more exact: Such a countervailing fantasy of a protective object, that has been split off from the hated and frightening anxiety object but shares in the power of the latter, is the direct counterpart to the phobia. It is in this novel sense that we may now correlate more convincingly the addictions to phobic neuroses.

While the phobic neurotic compulsively *avoids* the condensed and projected symbol for his anxiety on the outside, the toxicomanic equally compulsively *seeks* the condensed and projected symbol of protection against uncontrollable, overwhelming affects, again on the outside. Its protective efficacy is proven by the introduction of the magically powerful means from the outside and the ensuing mobilization with its help of a transient and, lastly, spurious counterforce.

In both instances, addictions and phobias, the therapy can only succeed if this countervailing protective fantasy is reexperienced in the transference. This aspect of transference is in my experience much more resistant to recognition and working through than the negative transference.

The drug effect itself is a type of counterphobic fantasy that validates the attempted and hoped for protection against the phobic fears, a protective countervailing fantasy against the main anxieties, and with that also against the major phobias: "I am strong, not vulnerable" (with stimulants); "I am blissful, not enraged" (for narcotics and other sedative drugs); "I am trustful, not disillusioned" (with psychedelics); "I am accepted, approved, and belonging, not isolated and guilty" (with alcohol) (86).

As mentioned the therapist has to replace the drug as an object to depend upon, as again Anna Freud proposed—but the intensity of anxiety and anger becomes so great that we lose very many patients precisely then. I have not yet found a generally applicable method of how to make this transition safer. However, it appears to me that a consistent attention from the beginning on to the twin problems of claustrophia, and the fear of feeling guilty or ashamed as mobilized in the therapy and witnessed in countless situations of current and past life, may reduce the likelihood of this flight from therapy.

D. The Question of "Ego Splits"—the Sense of Discontinuity

There is a lot of talk today about "splitting" and fragmentation." It is my experience that the prevalence of archaic conflicts, with their radical forms of anxiety and defenses, mostly of the reversal type described, leads *phenomenologically* to a remarkable discontinuity of the inner sense of self as well as to outward manifestation of "split" and "multiple" personalities, of sudden flip-flops, and of that radical unreliability that is so difficult to take in these and many other severely ill patients. One moment they give honest pledges, make grand plans, engage in ambitious, often idealistic enterprises, show love and affection, considerateness, and caring—the next moment all promises are angrily broken, the plans forsaken, the commitments forgotten, and anger, contempt, and arrogance rule supreme (86).

That is, as pondered in connection with denial, not a defense, but an "ego defect," a functional disparity and contradictoriness that, by the way, affects not solely the ego, but also no less the superego ("superego splits"). In the latter, ideals and loyalties are suddenly replaced by opposite ones, inner prohibitions suddenly betrayed under the onslaught of desire and dread.

Again, by deploying the protective system, the effort is made to ward off this bewildering discontinuity and fragmentation and to cover it over, not because of any specific narcissistic supplies or of any counteraction to a supposed defense by splitting, but by temporary elimination of the pervasive and globally threatening anxiety and related affective storms, certainly much more observably so than if we resorted to the notion of "structural deficits."

Thus, as remarked, this protective person or protective system is a reexternalized version of the archaic superego, one set up to guarantee and assure power, continuity, and mastery for an ego that is faced by traumatic anxiety and depression. It is set up to oppose another version of the archaic superego, a harshly condemning, also easily externalized authority, that operates almost exclusively with shame rather than with guilt, one that has become the repository of the severe traumatization.

E. The Structural Specificity of Conflict Solutions

What has been observed up to now leads to the following fascinating conclusion about the crucial conflicts in various categories of disease.

In psychoneurosis the ego sides more with the superego and reality against the id. In psychosis the ego allies itself more with the id *and* the superego against reality. In what Rangell (65, 66) called the "syndrome of the compromise of integrity," and, more generally, in so called sociopathy and similar deviations the ego joins up more with the id against the superego, but not against reality. Finally, and for us most importantly, in compulsive drug abuse, the ego sides more with the id against the superego, but also markedly against reality, as far as it has superego quality. (The difference with the "compromise of integrity" may therefore be mostly quantitative). In all these four types, conflicts and attempted conflict solutions usually are only partial, not total, and may coexist.

The anxieties and depressive affects described straddle therefore the borders both towards superego and outside world, and the defenses are directed not only against these affects of anxiety and depression, but also against the admonishing, observing, condemning functions and some, but not all, ideal-positing sides of the superego and against the perception of the outside world, mostly in so far as outer reality again shares superego qualities (especially "limitations"—the "guilt" and "shame boundaries"—cf. ref. 86). When Waelder writes in regard to psychosis: "Emancipated from reality, the ego creates for itself a new world which is set up in accordance with the desires of the id (78)", this may actually be more true for drug abuse than for psychosis (though in a particularly time-limited way), since the claims of the superego are usually retained and even particularly prominent and exaggerated in psychosis, but are specifically repudiated on a broad front during the states of acute intoxication. To be even more precise: Ultimately, it is still the terror of the id (and I believe mostly rage, engendered by severe early helplessness) that underlies the conflict. However, the toxicomanic gangs up with broad segments of the id (mostly its libidinous drives) and choses the superego as its main enemy that can be, at least momentarily, vanquished by denial.

As in psychosis the defense by *denial* is central, and so is the process of "splitting the ego," but in contrast to psychosis it is not projection, turning active into passive, and dissociation (decomposition, disjunction, fragmentation), but especially externalization and turning passive into active that dominate. Psychosis and neurosis are mainly autoplastic; drug abuse and "sociopathy" are mostly alloplastic. Generalized affect regression and probably also the mobilization of screen affects is shared by both. So is the defense by concretization, not specifically discussed here.

Especially whereas decomposition generally rules in psychosis, condensation prevails in the core of conflict in drug abuse. Easy displacement is common to both. When Waelder suggests "that paranoid ideas are as much the results of unsuccessful denial, as psychoneurotic symptoms have long been known to be results of unsuccessful repression" (78), it seems to me that the same statement could be made about toxicomanics. It is the ensuing defenses that make the difference, mostly the focus of them on action instead of on perception and cognition of the outer world (with that the stress on alloplastic alteration) and the role of condensation in symptom formation instead of decomposition. Most of all it is, however, the target of denial (and of the other defenses) that varies: In psychosis it is mostly external reality and the instinctual drives that are denied, while in drug abuse, it is mostly one group of affects, namely, those reflecting (self) condemnation, superego censure, and ideal formation.

As in all denial there are fantasies to support it (as countercathexis)—in psychosis as part of the delusion, in drug abuse as the described protective system. This fantasy has to counteract specifically the central anxiety and thus to prop up the denial. The split in the ego between denial and acknowledgement, the ultimate failure of denial, is far more pronounced in these patients than in the "syndrome of the compromise of integrity." It is a much more radical "rift in the ego" and hence a far more encompassing attempt to restore a new, though very flawed, "integration" with pharmacological means (what Kohut called "the false way to the self").

To return once more to the issue of isomorphism of symptom and defense mechanism that Waelder postulates ("if the defense was denial, the return of the disclaimed has the form of a claim") (78). May it again be *not* the fact itself of disclaimer versus claim that separates paranoid psychosis from drug abuse but rather *what* is primarily disclaimed? May it be that in toxicomania it is the narcissism vested in the ideal that is denied, but then returns as the narcissistic gratification reclaimed in the drug-induced intoxication whereas in the paranoid psychosis it is, according to Freud and Waelder, the homosexual wishes, according to my experiences, the wishes for union, mostly by perceptual and expressive means? Specifically, as to the former (drug abuse) it can be stated: "I am as good, as grand, as full, rich and strong—as my wishes bid me to feel because I am protected, not what my inner judge commands me to live up to (i.e., as purified image of myself)." In other words: "I am close to an ideal state because I am protected and am one with the protector and thus have eliminated the voice of my conscience and of every limit setting authority."

Yet another return of the disclaimed (besides that of the "ideal"): punishment is invited by provocative action, externally, after having been denied within, now usually accepted and submitted to in fact. The protector thus changes back into "the monkey on my back"—into the confining, enslaving, imprisoning master. The superego, denied, reasserts its claims—smotheringly, chokingly, paralyzingly—and often fatally.

These formulations are similar to the ones adduced for the manic state. Although drug-induced intoxication is indeed often very similar to such a state, this is not the case in all instances. One difference is of course the very brief, very time-limited character of this merger with a regressive ideal; the other, I believe, may be in the split between denial (as supported by this countervailing fantasy) and acknowledgement—a split absent in mania, but usually present in the drug state. Neither of these two answers though is quite satisfactory. Perhaps the explanation is the following: In toxicomania the defense by denial specifically against the superego continues, while—in a partial return of the denied—a defensive merger with a regressive portion of the superego ("the ideal self") is attempted. In a manic psychosis, however, this defense against the superego (i.e., superego-related affects) is abolished, but, instead, is massively deployed against outside reality.

The just-given description would then appear to be akin to that of depersonalization? Not really—since in the latter the ego squarely sides with the observing superego, denying the instinctual side, while of course in drug abuse the ego sides with the instinctual, mostly the regressive narcissistic side, denying the claims of the superego.

Still a question: Is not it perhaps precisely the denial of the superego-induced affects that is ultimately accountable for the strange flip-flop phenomena, the peculiar switches from one extreme to the other, the utter emotional unreliability since the superego is known to act as a mood and affect "stabilizer" (Jacobson)? If it is temporarily and recurrently made "inoperative," life in all, behavior and attitudes in particular, take on an especially disruptive, chaotic quality.

Yet another sequel: Several leading explorers of this area have recently stressed the deficit in the self-caring function in these patients (42, 46). I believe what is referred to is again the protective, assuring, approving side of the superego that falls victim to the general regression and splintering of this structure caused by the major defensive effort directed against it.

In short we are prompted to follow Rangell's suggestion: "I have long felt that after several decades now, in which an expansion of ego psychology has supplemented what had previously been known of the instinctual life, that the time will come next for an equally concerted effort towards understanding in depth the functioning of the superego" (64).

Family Dynamics

No comprehensive study of the really *specific* features (dynamic, attentional, communicational) of the families of various types of compulsive drug users exist as yet, in contrast to what Lidz and coworkers (52, 53) and Wynne and Singer (88) have done for schizophrenia. What we now know *does not appear specific enough.*

The best studies to date are those of Stanton and his group (73, 74) based on the incisive work of Boszormenyi-Nagy and Spark (5). They see the drug addict's life in antithesis. On the overt side he breaks all the rules and commitments (described by me above as part of the claustrophobia) in order to show his independence and forceful breaking away from home; however, whatever he does he ultimately attains the reverse: a cementing of his dependency on the family and a saving of the family cohesion. Were he to forsake his career of addiction, he would risk the dissolution of the family. Even his death may be a sacrificial move to keep the family together. In turn, the family needs him as the scapegoat, the attacking of which holds them together. "He is a loyal son who denies himself and rescues his family ... He is a savior" (73). "Not only did the addict fear separation from the family, but the family felt likewise toward him ... this was an interdependent process in which his failure served a protective function of maintaining family closeness" (73).

I have little question now that this is generally true—but perhaps too generally so—all neurotics and psychotics show similar hidden loyalty conflicts in their family systems. It may be granted, though, that there is in these families an excessive emphasis on such covert dependency and loyalty, while the front of the stage is ruled by treason and breach of faith.

It seems to me that we can discern four types of families, marked by massive traumatization, deception, intrusiveness, and inconsistency, respectively. Corresponding to the traumatic intensity of anxiety, including the phobic core, we should expect at least in many patients *severe and real external traumatization*. We find this in many, but not all cases. I present a few examples.

Case 3. Danny, a case described by Dr. Anderson, is a polydrug user, alcoholic, and homosexual in his 20's: "The mother was extremely overprotective and intrusive with Danny, always interested in his every activity. She insisted on absolute obedience, and when he failed to do exactly as she wanted, she administered harsh physical punishment such as beatings with a belt and putting his head underwater. Punishments were for such things as being a few minutes late for a meal or not practicing his piano lessons. Additionally, Danny was invited into his parents' bed when frightened at night, and he recalls they always slept in the nude."

Case 4. "My mother tried to kill herself when she was pregnant with me. I was always taught that sex is a bad thing. She now keeps me all the time at home and locks me up ... she said if I did not shape up—with sex or drugs—she would shoot me and herself. She slit up my clothes, so that I cannot leave the house ... " Her father tried to rape her. "My mother threatened to kill him ... they always yelled at each other. He used to whip us with a belt. If he tried again to sleep with me I'd kill him with a butcher knife ... The mother has already bought three burial plots."

All this was confirmed to me by the mother. The girl, a barbiturate and narcotics addict, soon thereafter killed herself by overdose.

Case 5. "When I was 12 or 13, I stole some money from my father and gave it to friends. When it was discovered, my father beat me up with a stick and made me eat a pack of cigarettes. My mother is just crazy. She steals and sells furniture and pictures of my stepfather. They scream all the time at each other. She is either raving about a person or feels persecuted."

Again I found external corroboration for much of this.

Case 6. "... many fistfights between mother and father, grandfather and father. When I was about 5, my father tried to kill himself with iodine. He told me what he had done ... " Later, when the parents were separated, the mother had a coterie of boyfriends: "I slept in mother's bed and was often awakened by her intercourse (with a lover)—with me in the same bed. Often she left me alone in the 2nd floor apartment to go out with one of her lovers. I remember how once they slammed the door and locked me in. I climbed out of the window and jumped onto the roof of the car, so they would not leave me alone. They brought me back, gave me a beating and left me at home anyway."

Let me stress again that this has not been the case in all instances of compulsive drug use. I see severe *parental violence* and *intense exposure to sexual activities* as a frequent, but not as a regular, etiological family factor in compulsive drug use. Yet at least I would like to single it out as one prominent group: that of traumatization by family violence, brutality, and overt continued involvement of the child in sexual activities, including sexual abuse and incest.

Based on the extent of profound anxiety I would, however, postulate that other more subtle, more veiled forms of traumatization would have to have occurred in many other addicts—unmanageable *over-stimulation of aggression and libido*; yet, I do not know yet where exactly to look for it, without once again unduly stretching the concept of trauma. I am also quite certain that such traumatization would have originated in early childhood, but would not have remained confined to it.

In a second group *intrusiveness* is the prominent feature. It is in much similar to what has been described for families of schizophrenics and results in the same curious mixture of pseudoidentity and pervasive shame in the children. If anything, the abuse of the child for the parents' grandiose expectation and the disregard for his age-appropriate needs is often even more pronounced, more crass than in the families of schizophrenics. This includes the crossing of intergenerational boundaries, the parentification of the child, and the sexualization of the parent-child relationship. I am puzzled though: Why then this symptom choice and not schizophrenia? May it have a much lesser impact on the cognitive and linguistic functions in the transactions? I hope further studies of shared focal attention and communication may give us here some clues.

It needs to be emphasized how much such intrusive running of the lives of the children, this exploiting and "busybody" behavior, evokes both rage and shame in the child. The *intrusive family* breeds a child that is, though manifestly compliant, secretly, then overtly rebellious, and profoundly shame prone. There is nothing he feels proud and confident of. Everywhere he senses impending put downs and humiliation. Some neurotics with strong phobic and paranoid inclinations show milder forms of this correlation; severer versions are found among many compulsive drug users of various types. Why this prevalence of shame in the child? The steady intrusions into the emotional and physical intimacy leave him exposed, not in control over his most private concerns. He has to assume a mask-like pseudoidentity in order to shield the nucleus of something very much his own from the possessive overbearing invasions—*a refuge of privacy protected by the walls of shame*. The "drug therapy" of shame is then a method of choice—as one form of affect defense. Not only does the drug dampen the shame anxiety, but it safeguards by yet an additional curtain the real self while simultaneously guarding the dependency on the parent.

The next group is almost a counterpart to the second one—here it is not intrusiveness, but *secretiveness* and unavailability on the parents' part. It is *they* who live out their shame, hiding a family humiliation behind a sham existence. They live their *"life lie"* behind a facade of propriety and respectability—the false life described by Ibsen with the highest mastery in play after play, a life of masquerade and secret mongering.

Case 7. A young female barbiturate and narcotics addict was not informed, e.g., when her older brother had to get married; she was 9 years old at the time. She found out when the rest of the family came home from church in festive clothes. It was a screen memory for much else that had remained hidden from her—veiled by a thick muffling curtain of decorum and religious piety. Some of the demons hiding behind those curtains were cold self-centeredness of the mother, weakness and sexual seductiveness on the side of the father, and the noticeable deep marital discord and mutual undermining.

As with the intrusive family, the secretive family promotes a profound depersonalization, a pervasive sense of unrealness and lack of authenticity: this estrangement is recreated or combatted by various drugs (barbiturates and narcotics deepening it, amphetamine and cocaine piercing the veil, psychedelics variably doing both).

A fourth type is represented by a family of utter *inconsistency and unreliability*. It is again any narcissitic whim which dictates what should be real, what should be right and proper. Today's sin is tomorrow's merit. Mother's reward is father's penalty. "Take but degree away, untune that string, and hark what discord follows! Each thing meets in mere oppugnancy." ("Troilus and Cressida"). No law and no hierarchical structure holds: "the rude son should strike his father dead." In a number of the cases in my book this was nearly literally true. The *dissolution of hierarchy* and with that, of stable superego structures is, to some extent, present in all compulsive drug users and may well be one of the most specific family hallmarks, but we are probably entitled to single out a fourth group where such a dissolution of boundaries and limitations is particularly remarkable, where just everything goes, where the law of the day is lawlessness. Much more study of this would be needed. Characteristically, such patients do not stay in treatment and come perhaps at best to a first interview; therefore they have been quite insufficiently studied.

Looking back I believe we can discern these four major types of families predisposing somewhat selectively to drug use without yet distinguishing more precisely what type of drug abuse may correspond to which kind of family. I do not think we can distinguish these types too sharply; much overlapping occurs. Still there may be some heuristic value in starting more systematic and controllable research with such clinical types.

In addition these family types exemplify some of the central dynamic features of the individual patients: defective affect defense and externalization ("traumatizing families"), ego and superego splits, the flip-flop syndrome ("inconsistent, antihierarchical, anarchical families"), denial and prevalence of shame ("deceptive and secretive families"), separation anxiety, clinging demandingness and possessiveness ("intrusive families"). Since we see in most cases these types combined, it may be legitimate to talk about a *tetrad of family characteristics in compulsive drug use of aggressive and sexual overstimulation, inconsistency, deceptiveness, and intrusiveness.*

The Long-range Effects of Drugs on the Personality

An interesting observation was stated already decades ago: in general, people are predisposed to use that drug which in the long run increases their inherent weakness. The opiate, barbiturate, and analgesic addict is basically passive-dependent. He has a sucking kind of demandingness, with his aggressions turned mostly against himself. He is a rather weak, soft-spoken, passive personality. This attitude is increased by his addiction. The alcohol, amphetamine, and cocaine addict is usually inclined to turn his aggressions outward, and to live out his sexual impulses in a "pseudomasculine" fashion. Again, this increases in the course of abuse and addiction.

If we turn now more in detail to the long-term effects of various types of drug use on the personalities, we find the following.

The personality of the cocaine and amphetamine user can be recognized from the agitation and restlessness, the driven, flighty, uncontrolled, irritable behavior, the tangential, jumpy, often fragmented way of talking, the straw-fire type of rage. Tremulousness, insomnia, and loss of appetite are typical. The inclination to paranoid reactions, including homicidal and suicidal outbursts, is well known.

The long-range effect on the personality of the intensive user of psychedelic drugs (LSD, hashish, marijuana, psilocybin) consists in characteristic disturbances in focal attention, either in the direction of fragmentation or of diffuseness and of the so-called "amotivational syndrome" (55). These observations can be summarized in the following six points (3, 6, 8, 35, 41, 86).

1. The patient very frequently loses the thread of thinking and has to ask the therapist time and again what he is talking about. Equally, he has to repeat to himself quietly the question or comment made by the therapist. It is as if he had not quite heard or understood what is said to him. He himself may feel that his thinking is "spaced out" and discontinuous.

2. Partly due to this lack of intellectual continuity, more importantly due to the massive denial of disappointment and rage, psychotherapy remains shallow. No clarification or interpretation is retained; no comment sinks in.

3. There is often a state of emptiness in the patient, where he has just nothing on his mind. In contrast to the usual opinion, the expressiveness is vastly reduced. The vocabulary is remarkably lacking in richness and vividness. This poverty of associations and ideas is perhaps the most striking impression.

4. Most comments are tangential and rambling, amorphous, vague, often interrupted by long and empty silence.

5. No limitations of reality are accepted; the undiluted pleasure principle is upheld. Rage is quick at hand ("straw-fire rage") if a demand is not met; and denial interferes with cognition.

6. Lethargy, a dull, bored, empty state, prevails, and interest in work and social activities is replaced by a retreat into a dreamy, wordless, "mystical" state.

On the basis of these six points, it appears rather difficult to carry out any meaningful psychotherapy as long as the patient is using hallucinogens. These effects are usually reversible, once the intensive drug use is discontinued.

The personality of the barbiturate and phenacetin user has been described as "entkernt," as losing the "core of personality," as shiftless, drifting, shallow, empty, unreliable, mendacious. Whether the clinical description is correct and, if so, irreversible is unknown to me.

To turn to personality and life history of the narcotics addict, three very important aspects of the prolonged abuse of, or addiction to, narcotics have to be mentioned: one is the self-confirming nature of the "cop out," of the relief effect of the drug; the other is the meaning in life that the "hustling," the chase after the illegal drug, provides; the third is the social spiraling down or being stuck.

Analysts and psychotherapists are familiar with the first phenomenon: how a symptom, once developed, acquires a self-perpetuating and spreading momentum. It becomes the favorite way of dealing with tension and anxiety, with external pressure and frustration; it extends its use as response, becomes more and more generalized and unspecific, automatic and rigid, and difficult to be overruled from inside or outside. We may call this phenomenon, which was particularly prominent in the schizophrenic patients I saw in psychotherapy, in an only partially applicable metaphor, the "avalanche effect" (this metaphor leaves out the continuous dynamic nature of this process). A "personality" who has developed the elaborate system of drug search, drug intake, and drug reaction as a means of coping with life's demands and limits needs this system as an indispensable part of functioning. If this crutch is pulled away, it is replaced by its closest resemblance—always, as earlier stated, an external, manageable, controllable means of dealing with internal conflict and crisis: either an ingredient of the situation itself, e.g., the needle, even if the drug is unavailable ("needle habit"), or another drug with closely resembling effect—e.g., sedatives for narcotics and vice versa, or at least the hustling, "copping," "fencing" (cf. 11).

This brings us to the second effect on personality and life-style. Preble and Casey described this effect masterfully in their paper, Taking Care of Business—the Heroin User's Life on the Street (61). They write: "For them ... the quest for heroin is the quest for a meaningful life, not an escape from life. And the meaning does not lie, primarily, in the effects of the drug on their minds and bodies; it lies in the gratification of accomplishing a series of challenging, exciting tasks, every day of the week.... Their behavior is anything but an escape from life. They are actively engaged in meaningful activities and relationships seven days a week. The brief moments of euphoria after each administration of a small amount of heroin constitute a small fraction of their daily lives. The rest of the time they are aggressively pursuing a career that is exacting, challenging, adventurous, and rewarding. They are always on the move and must be alert, flexible, and resourceful ... " (61).

Third, not dissimilar to the inner life and the family reality of all the other politically and legally more acceptable "winners" (which Ibsen portrayed more skillfully than most modern writers), the obverse side of the life history of most drug-dependent persons shows a social degradation, an emotional and social spiraling down; they are caught in a web of exploitation and cruel relationships. No other skills were developed than those useful for conning and surviving on the street. They have no abilities corresponding to their intellectual potential; socially acceptable work is tedious, boring, and of little financial reward compared with the role in the huge pyramid of buying and selling of drugs and stolen goods. Most addicts eventually become "employees" in this huge enterprise of black marketing and are enmeshed in its entangling net of loyalties, honor code, frightful retribution, glorious remuneration, and social prestige. The invidious lampooning of the "welfare Cadillac" and its unjustified political use against the welfare system points to clinical cases I have seen myself.

So often and so long as the considerable risks do not outweigh the gains, how difficult is it to give up a daily income of many hundreds of dollars for an unskilled job, if not for being outright unemployed!

Obviously, the answer to this problem would be the elimination of the black market.

Treatment

Without going into the technicalities of treatment of the drug addict, I mention several modalities of therapy which relate to the issue of the personality of the addict.

Therapeutic Communities. Therapeutic communities patterned after Synanon and Daytop operate with intensive appeals to group solidarity and shame. This modality is open just for highly motivated patients and seems effective only as long as the patient spends most of his time within the community. Quite obviously, this method gratifies the archaic dependency needs and the equally primitive demands of the conscience of the typical addict, and successfully replaces one dependency with another (70). The ideology and almost religious fervency is directed against all drugs, including methadone. In Daytop Village (Staten Island, New York), an intensive prolonged program combating narcissistic withdrawal and encouraging pride and group cooperation is being employed (7, 24).

Narcotics Antagonists. Antagonists (like cyclazocine, naloxone, naltrexone) have so far shown little practical, though much philosophical, promise and theoretical appeal to believers in conditioning theory (10, 28, 68). They are applicable only with highly motivated patients, show many side effects in the effective dosage, and are very expensive (50). The results so far are disappointing (30).

Perhaps the most important cause for disappointment strikes at the root of antagonist treatment: since narcotics are used as drugs of self-treatment, the simple drug-enforced abstinence does little to the immediate antecedent cause, the affects (and other dynamic aspects) underlying the symptom. Thus, it is not surprising that not very many patients seek this essentially external control. Hammond (30) rightly suggests their usefulness as preventive drugs for casual heroin users, or in combination with a therapeutic community, or as a prophylactic in high drug risk areas during a crisis. I might add that its use in combination with compulsory abstinence with frequent urine surveillance and close parole supervision, and as an adjunct to intensive individual or group psychotherapy, might prove to be more beneficial than its use as the major therapeutic agent.

Compulsory Abstinence. In the last 20 years, it has become more and more obvious that one essential element of treatment is compulsory supervision after discharge from prison or hospital unless the patients voluntarily sought treatment, as in a methadone maintenance program. Without any systematic follow-up therapy, the success rate is minimal. It was observed that more than 90% of patients discharged from the Federal Hospital in Lexington, Kentucky (during the period from 1952 to 1955 in the New York City area), became re-addicted, most of them within the first 6 months (57). Not unexpectedly, the prognosis after jail sentence is not any better than after prolonged hospitalization (76).

In contrast, if the patient was put on parole after release, 67% stayed abstinent in the community for a year or more (76). Similarly, "92% of California physician addicts who were subjected to a long and strict period of probation, were known to be abstinent for at least two years" (76), whereas the relapse rate after voluntary hospitalization is over 90%. Vaillant writes that 90% of his parole successes had relapsed after other forms of treatment, 80% after hospitalization, and 60% after long or short imprisonment. The essential difference lies in the close supervision by the parole officer, with his close affiliation with the police.

That compulsory supervision is effective to a certain degree makes sense also from a psychodynamic point of view. Patients with acting out of delinquent behavior of many kinds have "minimal internalization and inadequate superego control" and often demand external controls (2). The question is how this substitute superego can be made more enduring (49-51) and gradually internalized. We do not know how. A grave danger inherent in these supervisory manipulations should not be overlooked: the risk is that these external controls take on the same archaically punitive character as the patient's own fears, and thus in the long run intensify the underlying conflicts. I refer in particular to punitive measures which lower even more the already very vulnerable and shaky self-esteem. In contrast, measures which heighten self-reliance and responsibility (and certainly supervision can be used for this purpose, too) are much more helpful and appropriate than restrictive authoritarian interventions.

How can this supervision be made more reliable? If the parole method is combined with a stringent urine control with the help of thin layer chromatography or newer, less expensive methods, compulsory supervision is much tighter. The success rate in such a very strict parole program is only about 20%. Another 20% abscond. The rest are back in jail (49). The result rate with this modality is so much lower (20 to 30%) than in a methadone maintenance program (70 to 90%), and the costs are considerably higher (about $3,000 per patient per year), that we cannot wax enthusiastic about this form of treatment. In my personal experience a new variant of this modality is proving a very valuable adjunct and precondition for intensive psychotherapy and even psychoanalysis: *civil commitment* to the state's drug abuse agency in lieu of parole or probation. This measure gives an added, although necessarily coercive, incentive to choose exploratory and other forms of psychotherapy, instead of the guilt relief with drugs.

Methadone Maintenance Programs. Methadone, first used for this purpose in 1959 in Vancouver, B. C. (60), was introduced on a large scale and with remarkable courage by Vincent Dole and Marie Nyswander (12, 13). Its main effects are a vast reduction of the craving for narcotics used and, in appropriate doses, a full "blocking" effect against other narcotics. (This latter is due to the pharmacological tolerance). Methadone is a narcotic but, due to its protracted effect, is much more practical than heroin: it has to be taken only once in 24 hours and withdrawal is slower and milder. Moreover, it does not need to be injected.

Nobody should be fooled, though, about the fact that what we recommend with methadone use is a partial legalization of narcotics addiction, as the lesser of two evils. The use of the long-acting narcotic methadone, on a long-term or indefinite basis (maintenance), has a double rationale: the main one is that it reduces and in many addicts eventually stills the hunger for relief, the "craving" to get "high," and thus allows the patient to work out most of his more important problems; the second one is that it establishes cross-tolerance against other narcotics (rendering them ineffectual), thus making the illicit use of narcotics a waste of time and money as well as fully preventing overdoses from them. However, in my experience, the first effect was the crucial one: the overwhelming affects which had driven the patient into criminality and illegal drug use are sufficiently calmed to make it possible for the staff of a well-run treatment program to assist the patient in disentangling some of his most injurious attitudes ("the entitlement"), in finding a more satisfying profession or job or more helpful skills, and in overcoming the stigmata of a long, devastating (and often rewarding!) career in criminality. To achieve this, the drug is by far not enough: the program has to have a stable inner structure, combining firmness and discipline with respect, emotional support, and honesty vis-à-vis the individual patient. This includes intensive, often daily counseling, assistance in court and for vocational retraining, and often tutoring, home visits, and additional medical and psychiatric treatment when needed. Moreover, only if the drug is given daily under tight supervision, mostly in the clinic, and in a dose of around 80 mg, is the risk of diversion to the black market practically averted while the optimal drug effect is sustained. Thus, methadone is an indispensable part of a comprehensive treatment strategy, not a drug effective as a curative agent in and by itself. In a good program, the results, even with acceptance of bad risk patients, in regard to social rehabilitation and emotional recompensation, are somewhere between 60 and 90%, a far higher rate than with other treatment methods (16, 86).

The side effects, occasional decrease in libido, constipation, and transient drowsiness, are transient and minimal if compared with the discomfort and health disasters of untreated addiction. Why methadone and not heroin or morphine? Because it has a slow and protracted action, and it is far more practical and less interfering.

The methadone controversy boils down to the question of whether to accept indefinite, though medically supervised, addiction to a narcotic, accompanied by social and emotional stability, without any but slight side effects, and at decreasing costs to patient and society, or to hold out for a now only rarely effective, drastic, or radical cure involving total abstinence while the vast majority of addicts are hounded as criminals. It appears that for the individual and society methadone maintenance is the lesser of two evils by far: not for all narcotics addicts, but for a majority now; not as a cure, but as a supportive kind of treatment and part of a more comprehensive treatment plan; not as a means of detracting from deeper problems, but as an instrument to make the solution of some of these other problems possible. (For a more detailed description of the structure in a methadone maintenance program, cf. ref. 16).

Psychotherapeutic Approaches. In my personal experience, intensive, analytically oriented psychotherapy can be very helpful, especially with multihabituated adolescents. It can be combined, e.g., with methadone maintenance, once the patient has become medically and socially stabilized. However, practical, especially economic factors will make this method always a rare commodity—at least as long as psychiatry (and in particular, its core, psychotherapy on a psychoanalytic basis) remains the Cinderella as compared with its powerful sisters: somatic medicine and social sciences (83, 86).

To be sure, a solution of the underlying character difficulties appears very difficult. Unfortunately, very little has been done in the form of psychoanalysis or psychoanalytically oriented psychotherapy.

The focus of insight-oriented but not very intensive, reconstructive psychotherapy, is on clarification of the main elements which had been covered by denial or remained inarticulate: (a) the grandiose self-image and the general demandingness and unwillingness to stand frustration; (b) the low self-esteem and sense of emptiness; and (c) the resentment and rage. Clarification of these elements—although not reaching really unconscious levels—can be quite helpful. Particular note should be given that in better motivated or less severely ill drug-abusing patients, "focal," nonintensive, short- or long-term psychotherapy has led, in my personal experience, to remarkably many and surprising successes. While the time investment was relatively small, the honing in on the cardinal anxieties and major conflicts leading up to them proved to be a particularly cost-efficient, effective method. The problem is: Why does this method succeed in some, while in others this and much more thorough treatment fails? In effect a potent outer protective system substitutes for the drug in that function. Alcoholics Anonymous and other similar "ideal-giving" groups have often yielded striking results in many forms of substance abuse, not just in alcoholism.

The psychotherapeutic techniques used most frequently fall, however, into the category of "repressive inspirational" methods (15), where the defenses are increased and where group solidarity and dependence upon an authority figure are fostered and used as main therapeutic agent. Examples are supportive individual or group therapy (2).

Generally, it can be stated that if any psychotherapy or psychoanalysis wants to have any chance, it usually has to be coupled either with a surveillance in regard to the return to drugs carried out in the form of verification of abstinence, or in a residential facility, or with supportive treatment in the form of methadone maintenance, or at least with ample counseling or group therapeutic help in addition—although exceptions may occur where intensive psychotherapy alone may help.

To sum up, the core of the problem of compulsive drug use does not lie in the drug, but in the personality of the user. The etiological question is complex, the disorder profound; no cure or simple answer is known, but there are many, though difficult and complicated methods of treatment which can improve the illness and, very often indeed, bring about at least a partial or full social rehabilitation.

REFERENCES

1. Ausubel, D. P. *Drug Addiction: Physiological, Psychological, and Sociological Aspects,* pp. 1, 42–44, and 47. Random House, New York, 1958.
2. Beres, D. Superego and depression. In: *Psychoanalysis—A General Psychology,* Essays in Honor of Heinz Hartmann, R. M. Lowenstein, L. M. Newman, M. Schur, and A. J. Sonit (Eds.), p. 490. International Universities Press, New York, 1966.
3. Blacker, K. H., Jones, R. T., Stone, G. C., and Pfefferbaum, D. Chronic users of LSD: The "Acid Heads." Am. J. Psychiatry, 125:341–351, 1968.
4. Blos, P. Adolescent concretization: A contribution to the theory of delinquency. In: *Currents in Psychoanalysis,* I. M. Marcus (Ed.), pp. 66–88. International Universities Press, New York, 1971.
5. Boszormenyi-Nagy, I., and Spark, G. M. *Invisible Loyalties.* Harper & Row, Hagerstown, Md., 1974.
6. Carey, J. T. *The College Drug Scene.* Prentice-Hall, Englewood Cliffs, N. J., 1968.
7. Casriel, D., and Deitch, D. New success in permanent cure of narcotic addicts. Phys. Panorama, 4:5–12, 1966.
8. Casswell, S., and Marks, D. F. Cannabis and temporal disintegration in experienced and naive subjects. Science, 179:803–805, 1973.
9. Cavior, N., Kurtzberg, R. L., and Lipton, D. S. The development and validation of a heroin addict scale with the M.M.P.I. Int. J. Addict., 2:129–137, 1967.

10. Chappel, J. N., Senay, E., and Jaffe, J. H. Cyclazocine in a multi-modality treatment program: Comparative results. Int. J. Addict., 6:509–523, 1971.
11. Chein, I., Gerard, D. L., Lee, R. S., and Rosenfeld, E. *The Road to H. Narcotics, Delinquency, and Social Policy,* pp. 6, 7, 12, 14, 64, 194, 196, 202, 209, 210, 212–216, 310, 311, 356, 388, 389. Basic Books, New York, 1964.
12. Dole, V. P., Nyswander, M. E., and Warner, A. Successful treatment of 750 criminal addicts. J. A. M. A., 206:2708–2711, 1968.
13. Einstein, S. (Ed.). *Methadone Maintenance,* pp. 376–378. Marcel Dekker, New York, 1971.
14. Fenichel, O. *The Psychoanalytic Theory of Neurosis,* pp. 49, 380. Norton, New York, 1945.
15. Fenichel, O. *Collected Papers,* Vol. II, Chap. 27–28, Norton, New York, 1954.
16. Flowers, E., Weldon, C., and Wurmser, L. Methadone, discipline and revenge. Presented at 5th National Methadone Conference, Washington, D. C., 1973.
17. Freud, A. *The Writings of Anna Freud,* Vol. II, pp. 31–34. International Universities Press, New York, 1971.
18. Freud, A. Normality and Pathology in Childhood: Assessments of Development, In: *The Writings of Anna Freud,* Vol. VI, p. 223. International Universities Press, New York, 1965.
19. Freud, S. *Fetishism,* standard edition XXI, pp. 147–157. Hogarth Press, London, 1927.
20. Freud, S. *Civilization and Its Discontents,* standard edition XXI, p. 75. Hogarth Press, London, 1971.
21. Freud, S. *A Disturbance of Memory on the Acropolis,* standard edition, XXII, pp. 237–248, 1936.
22. Freud, S. *An Outline of Psychoanalysis,* standard edition, Vol. XXIII, pp. 139–207, 1940.
23. Freud, S. *Splitting of the Ego in the Process of Defense,* standard edition, XXIII, pp. 271–278, 1940.
24. Glaser, F. B. Gaudenzia, Incorporated: historical and theoretical background of a self-help addiction treatment program. Int. J. Addict., 6:615–616, 1971.
25. Glasscote, R. M., Sussex, J. N., Jaffe, J. H., Ball, J., and Brill, L. The Treatment of Drug Abuse. Programs, Problems, Prospects, pp. 3, 4, 12. Joint Information Service, American Psychiatric Association and National Association for Mental Health, Washington, D. C., 1972.
26. Glover, E. On the Early Development of the Mind, Chaps. 5 and 12, pp. 202, 203, 206–208, 211. International Universities Press, New York, 1970.
27. Grant, I., Adams, K. M., Carlin, A. S., et al. Organic impairment in polydrug users: Risk factors. Am. J. Psychiatry, 135:178–184, 1978.
28. Grupp, St. E. Drug user's attitudes toward the nalline test. Int. J. Addict., 5:661–674, 1970.
29. Haertzen, C. A., and Panton, J. H. Development of a "psychopathic" scale for the Addiction Research Center Inventory, ARCI. Int. J. Addict., 2:115–127, 1967.
30. Hammond, A. L. Narcotic antagonists: New methods to treat heroin addiction. Science, 173:503–506, 1971.
31. Hartmann, D. A study of drug-taking adolescents. In: *Psychoanalytic Study of the Child,* R. S. Eissler, A. Freud, H. Hartmann, S. Lustman, and M. Kris (Eds.), Vol. 24, pp. 384–398. International Universities Press, New York, 1969.
32. Heller, M. E., and Mordkoff, A. M. Personality attributes of the young, non-addicted drug abuser. Int. J. Addict., 7:65–72, 1972.
33. Henriques, E., Arsenian, J., Cutter, H., and Samaraweera, A. B. Personality characteristics and drug of choice. Int. J. Addict., 7:73–76, 1972.
34. Hoffman, M. Drug addiction and hypersexuality: Related models of mastery. Compr. Psychiatry, 5:264–266, 1964.
35. Hollister, L. E. Marihuana in man: Three years later. Science, 172:21–29, 1971.
36. Homer. *Odyssey,* Book IV, pp. 219–226.
37. Jaffe, J. H. Drug addiction and drug abuse. In: The Pharmacological Basis of Therapeutics, L. S. Goodman and A. Gilman (Eds.), Ch. 16, pp. 285–287, Macmillan, New York, 1965.
38. Jaffe, J. H. Pharmacological approaches to the treatment of compulsive opiate use: Their rationale and current status. In: *Drugs and the Brain,* P. Black (Ed.), p. 352. Johns Hopkins Press, Baltimore, 1969.
39. Jones, E. *Papers on Psychoanalysis,* Chap. 14, pp. 316, 318. Beacon Press, Boston, 1967.

40. Kaplan, E. H., and Wieder, H. *Drugs Don't Take People, People Take Drugs,* p. 9. Lyle Stuart-Secancus, New York, 1974.
41. Keeler, M. H., Reifler, C. B., and Liptzin, M. B. Spontaneous recurrence of marihuana effect. Am. J. Psychiatry, 125:384–390, 1968.
42. Khantzian, E. J. The ego, the self, and opiate addictions: Theoretical and treatment considerations. In: *Psychodynamics of Drug Dependence,* NIDA Research Monograph, Vol. 12, pp. 101–117. Washington, D. C., U. S. Government Printing Office, 1977.
43. Kolb, L. *Drug Addiction. A Medical Problem,* pp. 5, 6, 39–49. Charles C Thomas, Springfield, Ill., 1962.
44. Krystal, H. The genetic development of affects and affect regression. Ann. Psychoanal., 2: 93–126, 1974.
45. Krystal, H. Affect tolerance. Ann. Psychoanal., 3:179–219, 1975.
46. Krystal, H. Self- and object-representation in alcoholism and other drug dependencies: Implications for therapy. In: *Psychodynamics of Drug Dependence,* NIDA Research Monograph, Vol. 12, pp. 88–100. Washington, D. C., 1977.
47. Krystal, H., and Raskin, H. A. *Drug Dependence. Aspects of Ego Functions,* pp. 10–12, 20, 22, 31, 34, 70–71, 73, 79, 83, 93–95. Wayne State University Press, Detroit, 1970.
48. Kubie, L. S. The fundamental nature of the distinction between normality and neurosis. Psychoanal. Q., 23:167–204, 1954.
49. Kurland, A. A., Kerman, F., Wurmser, L., and Kokoski, R. Intermittent patterns of narcotic usage. In: *Drug Abuse: Social and Psychopharmacological Aspects,* J. O. Cole and J. R. Wittenborn (Eds.), pp. 129–145. Charles C Thomas, Springfield, Ill., 1969.
50. Kurland, A. A., Krantz, J. C., Henderson, J. M., and Kerman, F. Naloxone and the narcotic abuser: A low dose maintenance program. Int. J. Addict., 8:127–142, 1973.
51. Kurland, A. A., Wurmser, L., Kerman, F., and Kokoski, R. The deterrent effect of daily urine analysis for opiates in a narcotic out-patient facility: A two and one-half year study. Reported to Committee on Problems of Drug Dependence, National Academy of Sciences, Lexington, Ky., 1967.
52. Lidz, T., Fleck, S. and Cornelison, A. *Schizophrenia and the Family.* International Universities Press, New York, 1965.
53. Lidz, T. Egocentric cognitive regression and the family setting of schizophrenic disorders. Ch. 49. In: *The Native of Schizophrenia,* L. Wynne, et al. (Eds.), pp. 526–533. Wiley, New York, 1978.
54. Lindesmith, A. R. *Addiction and Opiates.* Aldine, Chicago, 1968.
55. McGlothlin, W. H., and West, L. J. The marihuana problem: An overview. Am. J. Psychiatry, 125:370–378, 1968.
56. Monroe, J. J., Ross, W. F., and Berzins, J. I. The decline of the addict as "psychopath": Implications for community care. Int. J. Addict., 2:129–137, 1967.
57. Narcotic Drug Addiction. Mental Health Monograph No. 2. U.S. Department of Health, Education and Welfare, P.H.S. 1021. U.S. Government Printing Office, Washington, D.C.
58. Nyswander, M. Drug addictions. In: *American Handbook of Psychiatry,* S. Arieti (Ed.), Ch. 30, p. 618. Basic Books, New York, 1959.
59. Nyswander, M. The methadone treatment of heroin addiction. Hosp. Pract., April, p. 33, 1967.
60. Paulus, I., and Halliday, R. Rehabilitation and the narcotics addict. Can. Med. Assoc. J., 96:655–659, 1967.
61. Preble, E., and Casey, J. J. Taking care of business—the heroin user's life on the street. Int. J. Addict., 4:1–24, 1969.
62. Rado, S. The psychoanalysis of pharmacothymia (drug addiction). Psychoanal. Q., 2:1–23, 1933.
63. Rado, S. Fighting narcotic bondage and other forms of narcotic disorders. Compr. Psychiatry, 4:160–167, 1963.
64. Rangell, L. Aggression, oedipus, and historical perspective. Int. J. Psychoanal., 53:3–11, 1972.
65. Rangell, L. A psychoanalytic perspective leading currently to the syndrome of the compromise of integrity. Int. J. Psychoanal., 55:3–12, 1974.

66. Rangell, L. Lessons from Watergate: A derivative for psychoanalysis. Psychoanal. Q., 45: 37–61, 1976.
67. Rapaport, D. On the psychoanalytic theory of affects. In: *Collected Papers,* M. M. Gill (Ed.), Ch. 41, pp. 476–512. Basic Books, New York, 1967.
68. Resnick, R. B., Fink, M., and Friedman, A. M. A cyclazocine typology in opiate dependence. Am. J. Psychiatry, 126:1256–1260, 1970.
69. Rounsaville, B. J., Weissman, M. M. et al. Detecting depressive disorders in drug abusers. J. Affect Dis., 1:255–267, 1979.
70. Samuels, G. Where junkies learn to hang tough. New York Times, p. 31, May 9, 1965.
71. Schooff, K. G., Ebner, E., Lowy, D. G., and Hersch, R. G. Inner city and suburban drug users: A comparison. Presented at Annual Meeting, American Psychiatric Association, Honolulu, 1973.
72. Sola, St. A., and Wieland, W. F. The psychopathology of narcotic dependent individuals. Some objective considerations. Personal communication.
73. Stanton, D. M. The Addict as Savior: Heroin, Death, and the Family. Fam. Proc., 16:191–197, 1977.
74. Stanton, D. M., Todd, T. C., et al. Heroin addiction as a family phenomenon: A new conceptual model. Am. J. Drug. Alcohol Abuse, 5:125–150, 1978.
75. Trunnell, E. E., and Holt, W. E. The concept of denial or disavowal. J. Am. Psychoanal. Assoc., 22:769–784, 1974.
76. Vaillant, G. E., and Rasor, R. W. The role of compulsory supervision in the treatment of addiction. Fed. Probation, 1–7, 1966.
77. Waelder, R. The problem of freedom in psychoanalysis and the problem of reality testing. Int. J. Psychoanal., 17, 1936.
78. Waelder, R. The structure of paranoid ideas: A critical survey of various theories. In: *Psychoanalysis: Observation, Theory, Application,* pp. 207–228. International Universities Press, New York, 1976.
79. Wieder, H., and Kaplan, E. H. Drug use in adolescents: Psychodynamic meaning and pharmacogenic effect. Psychoanal. Stud. Child, 24:399–431, 1969.
80. Wikler, A., and Rasor, R. W. Psychiatric aspects of drug addiction. Am. J. Med., 14:566–570, 1953 (cited by Jaffe (30)).
81. Wurmser, L. Drug abuse: Nemesis of psychiatry. Am. Scholar, 41:393–407, 1972.
82. Wurmser, L. Methadone and the craving for narcotics: Observations of patients on methadone maintenance in psychotherapy. In: *Proceedings, 4th National Conference on Methadone Treatment,* pp. 525–528, 1972.
83. Wurmser, L. Author's reply. Int. J. Psychiatry, 10:117–128, 1972.
84. Wurmser, L. Psychosocial aspects of compulsive drug use and the role of the physician. M. State Med. J., 190, 1973.
85. Wurmser, L. Psychoanalytic considerations of the etiology of compulsive drug use. J. Am. Psychoanal. Assoc., 22:820–843, 1974.
86. Wurmser, L. *The Hidden Dimension.* Jason Aronson, New York, 1978.
87. Phobic Core in the Addictions and the Paranoid Process. Int. J. Psychoanal. Psychol., 8: 311–337, 1980.
88. Wynne, L. C., Singer, M. T. Thought disorder and family relations of schizophrenics. Arch. Gen. Psychiatry 9:191–198, 199–206 (1963); 12:187–212 (1965).

15

PARAPHILIAS AND PERSONALITY DISORDERS

Chester W. Schmidt, Jr., M.D., Jon K. Meyer, M.D., and Jane Lucas, R.N.

Introduction

In the recent past, individuals who engaged in Paraphilias were despised and feared because they were considered immoral degenerate criminals by both health professionals and the public. A review of the subject of Paraphilias in current psychiatric textbooks does much to dispel the notions of immorality, constitutional degeneracy, and criminality. The same textbooks, however, call attention to the characterological problems of Paraphiliacs. The American Psychiatric Association Diagnostic and Statistical Manual of Mental Disorders III lists Paraphilias among Psycho-Sexual Disorders, a change which is in marked contrast to previous diagnostic ordering. Paraphilias or sexually deviant behaviors had always been listed in the category of personality disorders. Separating the two diagnostic entities is in concert with the authors' stated position that individuals who engage routinely in sexually deviant behaviors are heterogenous with regard to their character structure and manifest personality trait disturbances or personality disorders in a markedly varied degree. The authors will develop their conceptions about the relationship between paraphilias and personality disorders through a review of case material and then discuss treatment strategies based upon those conceptions.

Before beginning, it is necessary to make several additional statements about past and present attitudes towards individuals who engage in paraphilias. For centuries the cultural milieu associated with the Judaeo-Christian religious traditions required religious and civil sanctions against sexual behaviors other than coitus between husband and wife. Socially deviate sexual practices were considered heretical or criminal acts. If an individual was convicted of performing such acts, severe religious and civil penalties were imposed. It is not surprising that people accused of homosexuality, pedophilia, fetishism, exhibitionism, sodomy, etc., were labeled "perverts," a term which connotes moral wrongdoing.

Many leading 19th Century psychiatrists considered persons who performed "perverted sexual acts" to be suffering from a degeneracy caused by hereditary factors. These investigators later modified their opinions about the congenital predisposition of sexual deviations by including environmental conditions as possible progenitors of the aberrant behaviors.

Freud's Three Essays on the Theory of Sexuality (5) revolutionized traditional theories of sexuality and provided new means of understanding aberrant sexual behavior. The insights from his writing had little in common with the earlier views of constitutional degeneracy, but viewed the behavior as an arrest of psychosexual development, free from moral taint. In 1935 (11) he wrote to the mother of a homosexual son, "Homosexuality is assuredly no advantage, but it is nothing to be ashamed of, no vice, no degradation, it cannot be classified as an illness, we consider it to be a variation of the sexual function produced by a certain arrest of sexual development."

Despite the humane and scientific views of Freud and others, deviant behaviors are still stigmatizing. The public tends to react to deviant behavior with anger and rejection. Psychiatrists and other professionals, in the absence of adequately controlled studies, correlate paraphilia with a set of disorders carrying their own stigma—mental retardation, organic brain syndrome, and/or antisocial personality disorders. At the present time there is little data to support these correlations. Correlations of Paraphilias with other specific psychiatric or demographic variables is tenuous.

With regard to organic brain syndromes, Blumer (2) has reviewed the literature for cases of sexual aberrations related to brain and particularly to temporal lobe dysfunction. He suggests there is good evidence for an occasional close relationship between transvestite behavior and temporal lobe disorders. Fetishism and fetishism-transvestism may also occur and homosexual behavior is occasionally found. Hyper or hyposexuality associated with temporal lobe disorders occur more frequently than any of the Paraphilias mentioned.

The criminality of those who perform paraphilias is examined carefully by Gebhard et al. (8). They found in their studies that sexual offenders had fewer juvenile records and the offenses committed were generally less serious than a comparison prison group. Half to two-fifths of the total convictions of the sexual offender group were for nonsexual crimes. However, up to one half of these crimes within subgroups of sexual offenders were for vagrancy or disorderly conduct. Crimes against the person were significantly numerous only for several subgroups of sexual offenders who used force against children, minors, or adults. Other sex offenders were considered nonviolent. Finally, there was no data to indicate a progression from minor to serious offenses. There was a pronounced tendency for the sex offender to repeat the type of offense rather exactly.

In the experience of the authors, sexual deviates present with a variety of character and neurotic disorders of varying severity. Furthermore, there does not appear to be any direct relationship between the type of severity of the character disorder and the frequency or pervasiveness of manifest deviant behavior.

Definitions

A number of terms used in the chapter have varying definitions in the literature. Because the usage of the terms is essential to understanding the content of the chapter, the following definitions are offered.

Personality (Character) Structure

> "The character represents the specific way of being an individual, an expression of his total past." (18) "The character consists of a chronic alteration of the ego which one might describe as a rigidity. It is the basis of becoming chronic of a person's characteristic mode of reaction. Its meaning is the protection of the ego against external and internal dangers." (19) As Freud pointed out in *The Ego and the Id* (6) the basis of character formation, in the sense of the particular structure of the ego, is through the process of identification with important individuals in the child's very early history.

Personality Traits and Personality Disorders

> *Personality traits* are enduring patterns relating to perceiving and thinking about the environment and oneself, and are exhibited in a wide range of important social and personal contexts. When *personality traits* become inflexible and maladaptive and cause either significant impairment in social or occupational functioning or subjective distress, they then constitute a *Personality Disorder*. The manifestations of Personality Disorders are generally recognizable by adolescence or earlier, and continue throughout adult life, sometimes becoming less obvious in middle or old age.

Paraphilias

> Aberrant sexual activity; expression of the sexual instinct in practices which are socially prohibited or unacceptable, or biologically undesirable.

Homosexuality

> Homosexuality is no longer considered by the American Psychiatric Association as a Psychiatric Disorder. The DSM III does make provision for a category of Ego-dystonic Homosexuality which is defined basically as a sustained pattern of homosexual arousal which significantly interferes with desired heterosexual relationships. It is the authors' view that homosexual behavior may not be a

psychiatric disorder but it remains a sexual activity which is deviant. As such it legitimately can be discussed with other paraphilias as an individual, either male or female, who is motivated in adult life by a definite preferential erotic attraction to members of the same sex, and who usually, but not necessarily, engages in overt sexual relations with them (14). The term "homosexual' has been applied to a broad variety of behavior, conscious intent, and unconscious motivation, as reflected by the qualifiers "overt" "covert," "latent," "weekend," etc. The spectrum of behaviors and fantasy was illustrated by Kinsey and his coworkers (12, 13), who established, for both sexes, a heterosexual-homosexual rating scale reflecting the shades of overt and covert responsivity. Behaviors and fantasies ran from the exclusively heterosexual through individuals balanced between heterosexual and homosexual contacts and responses ("bi-sexual individuals"), to the totally homosexual fantasy and activity. The sexual practices that result in orgastic release in a bisexual or homosexual population may include any of the practices utilized by adults in their sexual activities. In other words, homosexuals may also be fetishistic, sadomasochistic, etc.

Fetishism

The relatively exclusive displacement of erotic interest and satisfaction to an object or a body part other than those usually associated with genital sexuality. Common fetishes are for feet, shoes, and female garments—particularly worn or soiled ones. The fetish replaces the substitutes for the love object, and although coitus may occur, arousal and gratification is at least partially dependent upon the presence of the fetish in reality or fantasy. This is primarily a male deviation. Orgastic release may be achieved by any of the practices utilized by adults in their sexual activities.

Transvestism

A condition characterized by recurrent and persistent cross-dressing by a heterosexual male. Female clothes are used as a preferred, although not exclusive, source of erotic arousal, with erotic satisfaction usually being accomplished through masturbation or coitus while cross-dressed. Transvestism, in the sense of fetishistic cross-dressing, is a condition limited to heterosexual males, whereas both sexes will cross-dress for reasons other than direct erotic arousal or gratification.

Zoophilia

Sexual excitement is produced by the act or fantasy of engaging in sexual activity with animals repeatedly and as a preferred mode of sexual expression.

Pedophilia

A condition in which adults characteristically or compulsively involve children or immature sexual partners who are at least 10 years younger than themselves in sexual activity. The sexual behaviors that result in orgastic release may be heterosexual or homosexual and may include any of the practices utilized by adults in their sexual activities. In a majority of cases, however, the pedophile is concerned with mutual masturbation or fondling, rather than coitus.

Exhibitionism

The display of the genital organs for the purpose of sexual gratification. This deviation is predominantly a male deviation. The object to whom the display is made is usually a young and/or innocent-appearing female. Her shock or surprise is an important factor in the degree of erotic arousal and subsequent gratification through masturbation. The act of exposure is final, with no further sexual activity sought from the victim. There are socially acceptable forms of male and female exhibitionism. These acts, however, are at the beginning of an extended series of behaviors designed to ultimately bring about coital release. For the exhibitionist, the exhibiting behavior is part of an abbreviated series of behaviors, almost an end in itself, and certainly close to ultimate point of release.

Voyeurism

Sexual stimulation and gratification is obtained primarily from looking at the sexual organs, or observing the sexual activities of others. Further sexual contact does not occur between the voyeur and his victim. Orgastic release is usually achieved by masturbating during, or just following, the period of observation.

Sexual Masochism

Masochistic individuals on a preferred or exclusive basis intentionally participate in activities in which they are physically harmed or threatened in order to experience sexual arousal. The spectrum of masochistic activities ranges from being physically beaten to being subtly humiliated. Orgastic release may occur through any of the means used by adults in sexual activity.

Sexual Sadism

Sadism is a condition in which sexual arousal and release is dependent upon inflicting pain or suffering. Some individuals repeatedly and intentionally select nonconsenting partners while others select consenting partners. The range of sadistic behavior runs from physically aggressive, even murderous behavior to subtle psychological humiliation. Orgastic release may occur through any of the means used by adults in sexual activity.

Other Paraphilias

This is a residual category for numerous described conditions such as Coprophilia (feces), Urophilia (Urine), and Necrophilia (corpses). A modern condition of interest is Telephone Scatologia. The individual in a preferred or exclusive manner is sexually aroused by uttering swear words with sexual connotations or offering sexual opportunities described in exceptionally lewd terms over the telephone to unknown victims. Orgastic release is usually achieved by masturbation during the act of calling, or upon completion of the call. Sexual arousal is heightened by the shocked response of the victim, especially if the victim stays on the line and engages in a dialogue.

Gender Identity Disorders

Although no longer listed in DSM III with sexually deviant behaviors, the authors believe that Transsexualism should be discussed along with the Paraphilias. Individuals exhibiting this disorder will manifest the following: Persistent sense of discomfort and inappropriateness about one's anatomic sex; persistent wish to be rid of one's own genitals and to live as a member of the other sex; choice of sex partner of the same sex but opposite gender; periodic or constant use of cross-gender hormones; periodic or constant cross dressing and periodic or constant attempts to live and function in the cross-gender role (4). Sexual activities include all of the usual adult sexual behaviors; however, some transsexuals avoid having their genitals touched or viewed, even to the point of compromising erotic satisfaction.

The Etiology of Paraphilias

Any discussion of the etiology of Paraphilias must take into consideration both psychodynamic-familial-cultural factors and physiology, particularly hormonal physiology. The effect of dynamic and psychologically genetic factors is well known. The biological substrata upon which these factors operate, however, is also worthy of mention.

There are two primary periods of hormonal effect in sexual life. The less well known but earlier period of hormonal influence occurs during fetal life. In the male fetus, under the influence of testosterone and an additional postulated inhibiting substance, the anlage of female internal reproductive structures is caused to regress, whereas the male anlage are fostered. This process eventually leads to development of the male internal reproductive apparatus. Testosterone also has an effect on the external genitalia, modifying it from the fetally indeterminant state to the male situation. The basic principle of hormonal influence in fetal life is that androgen masculinizes. In the absence of androgen, the female structures will proliferate both internally and externally while the male anlage will regress.

In addition to the effect on reproductive structures there are also profound hormonal effects on the mammalian central nervous system. These effects are mediated by the presence or absence of normal levels of testosterone. In abnormal situations, the presence of an excess of testosterone or estrogen will also have an influence. The basic pattern of sexual functioning of the hypothalamus, and through it the pituitary, is "female" or cyclic. This is represented by the female pattern of ovulation on a monthly basis. When testosterone is present, the hypothalamic mechanism is set in "male" or acyclic pattern, thus, the male pattern of continuous responsivity and production of spermatozoa. The hypothalamus exercises its control through the cyclic or noncyclic release of gonadal stimulating hormones from the pituitary.

At the same time as the establishment of cyclic or acyclic sexuality there seem to be established in the human, as well as animals, certain levels of aggressivity. For example, in girls with the adrenogenital syndrome, in which there has been an excess of testosterone analogs during the late fetal life, there seems to be more manifest activity and aggressivity than in the usual female, most often without any sense of gender dysphoria. Rodent studies have indicated that judiciously applied hormones during certain critical periods in fetal life have profound effects on the sexual *behavior* of the animals in adult life, with males exhibiting lordosis and other posturing (an invitation to be mounted) usually typical of female rodents. While similar direct correlations between hormonal environment in fetal life and sexual behavior have not been observed in humans, it seems likely that the same basic effects apply for humans as for other mammalian species, but are simply overshadowed by the human capacity for socialization and diversion of drives.

Recently, just as with the study of the adrenogenital girls, work has been reported in adolescent male children of diabetic mothers who had received large dosages of estrogens to prevent fetal wastage (22). These adolescent males apparently showed more passive and "effeminate" behavior than control groups but without a sense of gender dysphoria. Thus, while fetal hormonal experience in humans seems to set the cyclic versus acyclic sexual pattern and to contribute to the level of tomboyishness or effeminacy in children and adolescents, there is as yet no clear-cut correlation between this type of exposure and adolescence or adult homosexuality or gender identity disorders. Such animal work and "experiments of nature" in humans, however, offer intriguing neurophysiological possibilities for understanding some aspects of later deviant behavior (7, 17).

A second phase of importance in the development of sexuality is the critical period for the development of "core gender identity," i.e., the basic sense of masculinity or femininity in the individual. The critical period for core gender identity differentiation seems to be between the neonatal period and age 2 to 3½. The seminal work has been done with intersex children with genital defects in which sex assignment or sex reassignment has been necessary. In these cases, sex reassignment before age 2 produced no adverse psychological results, whereas thereafter and certainly after age 3½, the psychological capacity of the child to re-adapt to the new sex was markedly diminished (10). There is some evidence that certain types of disordered mother-child relationships during this period of life may result in failure of adequate gender identity development (20).

Concurrent with the period of critical gender identity development is the unfolding of the component sexual instincts as described originally by Freud (5). These component instincts are the oral, anal, and phallic. The oral refers to incorporative modes of behavior through the mucous membrane surfaces of the mouth, the earliest expression of sexuality in the broad sense. The anal phase relates to the expulsive or retentive behavior related to the mucous membranes of the anal orifice. The obviously sexual derivatives of these earlier drives are seen in such behavior as pre-emptive fellatio or cunnilingus and anal intercourse.

The emergence of genital or phallic sexuality occurs first at the age of 5 or 6 at the oedipal period during which, in oversimplified terms, there is a competitive relationship with father and a loving sexualized relationship with the mother. Depending upon the vicissitudes and complexities of drive strength and relationship with the parents, these oedipal relationships may be resolved or may provide a serious stumbling block. If the resolution of the Oedipus Complex is too difficult, there may be regression to previous levels, such as the oral or the anal, with subsequent oral or anal adult characters. These regressive compromises limit genital sexuality either in a neurotic or in a perverse manner. It is worth noting that certain component drives are stronger in some individuals than in others and/or may yield more gratification in certain individuals than in others. Because of this excessive strength or excessive gratification at a particular developmental level, a fixation point may be established which will serve as a point to which regression occurs if there is unusual frustration at the phallic stage.

It should be noted that genital primacy is attained through the successful negotiation of the oedipal phase in the circumstances of a relative lack of fixation points.

The chronologically later but best known of the two periods of hormonal activity begins in adolescence. At that time, under central nervous system influence, gonadal secretion of hormones undergoes an upsurge to adult levels. With this comes the development of secondary sexual characteristics, genital capability, and the capacity for procreation. Quite frequently, the possibility for perverse behavior which has been laid down in childhood becomes manifest in adolescence under the influence of heightened libidinal drives. The first psychiatric or medical contact with the individual showing perverse forms of behavior may come in adolescence.

In adolescence, as was mentioned previously, there is the emergence of sexual behavior under the impetus of hormonal release. At that point there may again be regression to fixation points representing inadequately resolved previous developmental stages. One of the great issues of adolescence and maturity is the gradual development of a capacity for intimacy, an area in which most sexually deviant individuals have great difficulty.

Paraphilias as a Part of Personality Disorders

Psychodynamic, familial-cultural, and physiologic factors not only contribute to the development of sexual behaviors (normal and deviant) but also to the totality of each person's character or personality structure. The sharing of etiologic factors plus the recognition that behavior is in some manner determined by character structure, suggests a close relationship between sexual behaviors and character structure. However, what is the nature of the relationship? Are Paraphilias the result of deficiencies in the development of the character structure? If so, what are the deficiencies? Are Paraphilias associated with certain types of personality disorders? Is Paraphilia always associated with character pathology? Do individuals with more manifest sexually deviant behavior have more severe character pathology? Answers to these questions might clarify the relationship being examined. To this end we now turn to the case material.

Paraphilia Associated with Mild Character Pathology

Mr. P. is a 31-year-old white married male, who presented with the chief complaint of, "I get into these homosexual situations and don't know why." A year and a half prior to his self-referral he had periodically allowed himself to be picked up on the street or in public bathrooms by homosexuals. At times he would allow fellatio to be performed in the public bathrooms. He felt compelled to seek out these contacts, but found them to be only partially gratifying. He was frightened and guilty after they were completed. The patient is a writer who has received both local and national recognition. He has been married for 2 years and has one child. He is the youngest of five children. His parents had never been separated, although there is a history of much family fighting about the father's alcoholism. The patient describes a close relationship to his mother. He remembers being terrified of his father. The older brother introduced the patient to homosexual experiences when he (the patient) was 13 years of age. These experiences are remembered as pleasurable but also guilt provoking. During high school the patient dated socially prestigious girls, but did not develop any crushes or any lasting relationships. While in college he had two satisfying homosexual relations but continued to date girls and enjoyed heterosexual kissing and petting. During his courtship and shortly after marriage he stopped all homosexual activity. He stated he enjoys coitus with his wife. He believes that she is orgasmic and he described a fairly rich and varied sexual relationship with her.

Mr. P came for treatment with symptoms of anxiety and depression related to his homosexual behavior. His personality structure contained elements of passive-agressive and compulsive features. His homosexual experiences were physically gratifying and often were used by him to relieve tension or anxiety. Despite the initial symptoms, the deviant sexual behavior and the character pathology (passive-aggressive and compulsive traits) he had accomplished a great deal vocationally and had demonstrated his capacity for developing and maintaining relationships.

Mr. T was a 16-year-old white male when first seen in this clinic with his parents, at his own request. His presenting complaint was a wish to pursue an evaluation which would ultimately lead to sex reassignment surgery when he reached the age of 21. He is the middle of three children, the two siblings being females. Both parents are college educated and his father is a successful businessman. His earliest remembrances are of his interest in playing with girls and girls' toys. He was identified by his peers as being effeminate and was teased. He was unhappy both at school and in social situations because of the teasing. He has a close relationship with his mother and sisters, but feared his father. He remembers at the age of 4 being thrown against the wall by his father, and a year later being hit on the head with a piece of lumber by his father. Cross-dressing began at the age of 11, when he began to feel that he wanted to be a girl. Despite his social difficulties he did well in school academically, excelled in the arts, and was a high school varsity swimmer.

Following the first evaluation the patient was told to keep in touch with the clinic and return for re-evaluation at the age of 21. Over the next 5 years he graduated from high school and attended college for 2 years. During this time he had several psychiatric contacts for both evaluation and treatment. While at college he had a prolonged relationship with a popular male athlete. He took a great deal of pleasure in controlling and manipulating his partner. He was repulsed by his own genitals and did not particularly enjoy sexual contact with his partner. He states he did so merely to maintain their relationship and satisfy his partner. He continued to occasionally cross-dress in college and was assisted by his sisters and mother. He did well at college, but dropped out in preparation for the psychiatric evaluaton on his 21st birthday, which he hoped would lead to sex-reassignment surgery.

The case of Mr. T. most dramatically illustrates the association of a person completely invested in sexually deviant behavior, yet demonstrating competence in many other areas of his life. On the basis of his history of relationships and his behavior in therapy, Mr. T. was thought to have a histrionic personality. He never demonstrated or complained of anxiety or depression.

Mr. L. was a 27-year-old white single male who was referred by his probation officer with a history of two recent arrests for exposing himself. The patient gave the history of being the sixth of seven children born to a lower middle class family. He describes his mother's and father's relationship as distant. His mother ruled the family with an iron fist, and he felt both a sense of closeness and dependency on her. He recalls almost never making his own decisions. He was pushed by his mother into the priesthood, following graduation from high school. During his training as a priest he graduated with a degree in philosophy and was given his first assignment. He had experimented with masturbation while he was in high school, but because of his strong religious convictions, discontinued this practice entirely. On beginning the work assignment he began experimenting with masturbation again. Because of his inability to control the frequency of masturbation and his sense that it was not a sinful act, he began to re-examine his vocation. He finally decided to leave the priesthood and obtained a preferred draft status by working as a nurse's aide. As soon as he left the priesthood, masturbation accompanied by fantasies of women became a daily experience. Once while masturbating near a window in his apartment, he thought that several passing girls might have observed him. This thought was very stimulating. He then made definite attempts to be observed on subsequent occasions. He experienced a great sense of sexual excitement and gratification. From this point on he engaged in frequent episodes of exposing himself, accompanied by masturbation. These experiences moved from his apartment to his car. Eventually he was reported and arrested. His first charge was dismissed, but within a month's time he was again arrested, leading to a conviction and a period of probation. The patient had no history of heterosexual experiences or homosexual experiences.

Mr. L. might best be described as a dependent personality who experienced a delayed adolescence. Leaving the priesthood appeared to be the equivalent of separating from mother. His sexual experimentation was initially masturbation, but later included females in a passive yet hostile manner through his exhibitionism. By history he had moderately good relationships with peers and family, and had done well scholastically.

Paraphilias Associated with Moderately Severe Character Pathology

Miss A. is a 41-year-old unmarried female who was self-referred. Her chief complaint was "I want to be changed into a man so I can marry my girl friend." The patient stated she was in love with a woman who is a nun. The nun was willing to leave the order, provided they could be married. This would, of course, only be possible should Miss A. obtain sex reassignment surgery. Miss A. was herself a nun, but left the order following a disciplinary action which was, in part, the result of alleged homosexual activity. For the past 20 years she has been a teacher in a small private school, establishing an excellent reputation as a teacher and as an administrator. The relationship with the girl friend has been of 1½ years' duration. Before this relationship she had lived with the headmistress of her school. Their relationship was stormy, with frequent fights and disagreements. Miss A. had never had any heterosexual experiences, save for some kissing and petting when she was in high school. These experiences are not remembered as enjoyable. Miss A. was the third of four children born to a poor rural family. She describes her father as a hard-working, warm, outgoing individual. Her mother is described as a cold, strict disciplinarian. She remembers being a tomboy during her adolescence. She attended an all girl high school and college. She had a series of crushes on teachers and her first homosexual experience, during her mid-adolescence, was with a teacher. She then had several homosexual experiences with peers. On entering the convent she refrained from any homosexual activity. Several years after taking her vows she was engaged in a series of homosexual relationships which in part led to her leaving the order. She gave no history of cross-dressing or of using male hormones. She has always thought of herself as a woman, but now is investigating the possibility of sex reassignment surgery in order to resolve several of the problems posed by her current relationship.

The personality characteristic most striking about Miss A. was her compulsiveness. In many ways she had used this trait to her advantage in her vocation. She would "lock-on" to a target or goal and move ahead with all speed. Although her sexual experiences were exclusively homosexual and in conflict with her own rigid religious system, she rarely suffered guilt or depression. She had at least two prolonged relationships of some substance or depth. The sexual part of these relationships was not entirely satisfactory because Miss A. tended to use sex to control the relationships and because of the continuing religious conflict.

Mr. R. was an attractive, bright, wealthy young businessman who was self-referred with the chief complaint of "My wife and I are having sexual difficulties." He had been married for approximately 2 years. Almost immediately following the marriage he found himself becoming sexually disinterested in his wife. This led to a series of arguments during which his wife found out that the patient frequently exposed himself and made obscene phone calls. The patient's father was in his fifties when the patient was born and was a multimillionaire. His mother, some 20 years younger than her husband, was a beautiful, outgoing woman with whom the patient had a close relationship until she remarried following the patient's father's death. The patient was 13 years old at the time of his father's death. The stepfather had three children and the patient suddenly became part of a larger family. His close relationship with his mother was intruded upon by the new father and half-siblings. He felt depressed and isolated from the members of his family. In spite of this he did well at school, had friends, and participated in some social activities. At the age of 13 he exposed himself for the first time to two little girls in the neighborhood. He experienced a sense of forbidden pleasure and from that time on continued to expose himself to younger girls in reasonably safe situations. As these activities continued he began to place himself in more precarious situations, taking more and more risks of being caught. In addition, he began making obscene phone calls when he was a freshman in college. When making the calls he would masturbate and fantasize about heterosexual intercourse. All the while the patient continued to do well in his school work and was moderately successful in social activities. He joined a fraternity and dated. During his senior year he met a girl with whom he quickly developed a regular sexual relationship. They were married shortly after his graduation. He has maintained a responsible business position for 8 years. He superficially gets along well with his colleagues, but has no close friends at the present time. He spends a great deal of time fantasizing about sexual relationships with young girls. He is also obsessed about money, his inheritance, and the management of money on the stock market. At the time of evaluation there had been no legal entanglements secondary to his deviant behavior.

By history Mr. R. gave the impression of having had a number of good relationships within his family life and with his peers as he grew up. However, shortly after beginning treatment it became apparent that he had never shared any of his inner thoughts or feelings with anyone. He displayed fairly marked schizoid and compulsive traits. There was little evidence of anxiety or depression. The character pathology helped to make understandable the marked deviant behavior of this functional attractive individual.

Mr. A. is a 44-year-old, white, married male, who was brought to consultation by his wife, with the chief complaint of "we are having a great deal of difficulty organizing our sexual life." Over the past 5 years of their marriage the patient and his wife had developed a series of rituals for performing their sexual activities. The patient obtains pornographic literature that describes many different kinds of sexual scenes. The wife designs and handsews costumes to match the scenes described in the pornographic material. The patient and his wife then act out these scenes, at times posing individually, or as a couple, before a polaroid camera with a timing device. The pictures are developed and then viewed, being used as a stimulus for the patient in order to maintain his erection and bring him to orgasm. Orgasm may be reached by masturbation or by coitus. In addition to this behavior, the patient masturbates almost daily with the use of pornographic material. The patient is one of four children raised in a semirural area. His mother is described as having been very nervous and preoccupied with multiple physical complaints. The father had a number of hospitalizations for a schizophrenic illness. One older sister has also had psychiatric treatment for psychotic episodes. The patient has always considered himself brilliant and intellectually "better than most people." He has never finished anything that he has started, including school, or vocational development. He has held many jobs over the years. He frequently changes jobs because of problems created by his suspicious and paranoid behavior. He married at the age of 38 and his wife, a teacher, is 2 years his senior. They have two young children. He described his early adolescent experiences as very successful, dating many girls, and having intercourse "with a respectable percentage of them." He is proud of having been considered a "stud." His reason for marriage was the recognition that time was passing by and if he did not do something he would be too old to marry and have a family.

During the unsuccessful treatment attempt with Mr. and Mrs. A., Mr. A.'s paranoid view of the world became a major obstacle to treatment. In addition, although he was currently working as a mental health counselor, he could see little reason for altering his sexual practices. Mr. A. never displayed evidence of a thought disorder or symptoms of anxiety or depression. In his sexual relationship with his wife he was totally committed to obtaining his own gratification with little awareness of his wife's needs.

Paraphilias Associated with Severe Character Pathology

Mr. M. was a 17-year-old white single male referred by a habilitation center for adolescents because of a 3-year history of pedophilia. The patient had been apprehended several times by the police, and finally at the age of 15 was sent to a center for adolescents with emotional problems. His sexual attempts were directed towards both younger boys and younger girls. At the time of his visit to our clinic he was receiving training as a janitor at the center. The deviant sexual behavior continued during his stay at the school, despite rigid limit-setting and counseling by the staff at the center. Although there had been no change in his pedophilic behavior, he had made some progress in the area of socialization and development of job skills. Psychological testing during his stay at the Center revealed that he had a full scale IQ of 77. The patient was the oldest of two children. When the patient was 4 years of age his father developed a psychiatric illness which has continued up to the present time. The illness required several hospitalizations. The mother of the patient recalls periods of sexual precociousness starting at the time of her husband's illness and continuing throughout the patient's childhood. The patient describes his father as punitive, angry, anxious, and restless. The mother was thought by the staff of the center to be passive-aggressive, controlling, and undermining the patient's treatment situaton. The parents stated the patient had difficulty with other children, beginning in nursery school. His sister has made only a marginal adjustment, and a cousin has also recently been sent to the same habilitation center for sexual acting out and incorrigible behavior. The nature of his sexual behavior is that he approaches younger children and attempts to undress them and then lay on top of them. While on top he does thrusting movements which usually lead to his ejaculating. He has not attempted to penetrate little girls or to perform anal intercourse on boys. He makes no attempts to hide his behavior and does nothing to protect himself from the consequences of the behavior. In addition, he has a history of masturbating, sometimes two or three times a day. Fantasies are of sexual contact with either young boys or young girls.

Mr. M. was diagnosed as a borderline mental retardate and an inadequate personality (DSM III stresses specific behavior patterns rather than functional impairment so that the term "inadequate" has been deleted as a formal term. It can still be used as a qualifier for Atypical, Mixed, or Other Personality Disorders). The development of pedophilic behavior in this individual appears to have been the result of poor internal and external constraints on Mr. M's desire for sexual gratification. The pattern of deviant behavior was well established before he was sent to the habilitation center and treatment attempts at the center were often undermined by the parents.

Mrs. C. is a twice-divorced, 40-year-old black female, who is self-referred for "feelings of depression." The patient has recently broken up with a woman with whom she has been living in a homosexual relationship for approximately 6 months. She gives a history of having been raised in a chaotic family situation, marked by bitter parental fighting, separations of the parents, and heavy drinking by the parents. During her adolescence she did a lot of running around without any attempts at control by her mother. She had her first experience with intercourse at the age of 15 and from that point on has been very promiscuous in her sexual relationships. She married at the age of 17. The marriage lasted 2 years and produced one child. As the marriage was breaking up, and under the stress of financial hardship, the patient began prostituting herself and was arrested twice for prostitution. She began drinking heavily at the age of 20 and has continued to do so up to the present time. She married for the second time at the age of 25 and was deserted by her husband after 6 months. In addition to the two arrests for prostitution she has one arrest for drunken driving, one arrest for being drunk and disorderly, and one arrest for a drug charge. At the age of 23 she had her first homosexual experience and found it pleasurable. Up until recently she has had an occasional homosexual experience when the opportunity presented itself, but has also continued to have heterosexual relationships and occasional return to prostitution. For the 6 months she lived with the woman she found herself quite satisfied sexually and emotionally, and is now distraught over having lost the girl friend. The reason for their separation was principally a financial one, insofar as the girl friend had found a man who could support her in a better fashion than her living situation with the patient. In her discussion of her sexual responses she indicated that she was only occasionally orgasmic during heterosexual experiences. She states she was more often orgasmic in her homosexual experiences than in the heterosexual experiences, but, even so, the impression is she was not particularly responsive to her partner or to her partner's needs.

Mrs. C. had led a relatively chaotic existence which included a moderate amount of criminal activity. She had never committed any crimes of aggression against others. Her history of sexual experimentation and opportunism without any evidence of investment in the other person fit with her severe characterologic pathology of an Antisocial Type.

Mr. B. is a 33-year-old, twice-divorced man who was interviewed while being incarcerated for alleged kidnapping, rape, and assault. The patient had a record of many arrests and convictions for robbery and drug charges. During a prolonged drinking bout he decided to abduct a neighborhood woman and held the woman several days, during which time he continued to drink and take barbiturates. He forced the woman to have intercourse with him while they were observed by his girl friend. Over the next 2 days he became increasingly physically assaultive, cutting her on the breasts and burning her on the buttocks with a cigarette. He forced her to perform fellatio on himself with his girl friend watching, and tried to entice the girl friend to be physically abusive towards the prisoner. When he decided to end the ordeal he beat the woman severely, inflicting severe damage upon her. There was no earlier history of physically assaultive behavior, or history of sadomasochistic behavior. He preferred heterosexual relationships, and, in fact, had had many sexual experiences with many different women. He reported episodes of impotence when drinking or when using various drugs. He was uncertain as to whether either his two wives or his girl friend were orgasmic. His current girl friend is several years older than he is and he describes their relationship as her being more motherly towards him than being a girl friend. He denies any homosexual experiences, despite many opportunities for such experiences. He is the oldest of three children born to a poor rural family. His mother deserted the family when he was 3 years of age and his father left when he was 4 years of age. He and one sister were placed in a series of foster homes and orphanages. At the age of 16 he escaped from an orphanage and came to an East Coast city where he heard his father was located. He found his father, lived with him for several months, and then struck out on his own. He served a short time in one of the armed services, but was given a dishonorable discharge following a series of court-martials for insubordination and heavy drinking.

The dangerous criminal behavior of Mr. B. was a constant throughout his adolescent and adult life. The sexually deviant behavior was a single episode of near homocidal sadomasochism. By history it is easy to feel that the potential for such behavior was there, just waiting for the proper circumstances for it to become manifest. Nevertheless, the case illustrated the episodic occurrence of sexually deviant behavior in an individual with a severe antisocial personality disorder.

The case studies provide data for the purpose of answering some of the questions raised and for furthering our understanding of the relationship of sexually deviant behavior to personality disorder. First, it is clear that there are several different personality traits and disorders represented in the series of cases. The types include antisocial, passive-agressive, paranoid, compulsive, schizoid, and histrionic disorders. Criminality as a feature of the antisocial personality is present in two cases (Mr. B. and Mrs. C.) but noticeably absent in the remainder of the cases. Mental retardation is also present in one case (Mr. M.) but the intelligence of all the other patients is average or above average. Thus it is apparent that sexually deviant behavior is performed by individuals of varied personality types.

The second observation is that the severity of the personality disorders (or character pathology) varies from one case to the next. For example, compare Mr. P.'s assets, ego strengths, and functional competence to those of Mr. B. A second obvious comparison is between Mr. L. and Mr. M. In both instances all four of the patients engage in sexually deviant behavior but there are significant differences between the character pathology of Mr. P. and Mr. L., as compared to that of Mr. B and Mr. M. The difference in severity of character pathology between Mr. T. and that of Miss A. or Mr. R. is noticeable and important, but not as dramatic as in the former comparisons.

A third observation available from the case material is the recognition that the frequency of sexually deviant acts is not a function of the severity of character pathology. Two of the three patients with mild degrees of character pathology experienced periods of time during which they frequently engaged in deviant acts. The third patient, Mr. T., was totally invested in his deviance as a way of life. Two patients with the most severe personality disorders (Mr. B. and Mrs. C.) probably have the lowest frequency of sexually deviant behavior. All three of the patients with moderately severe character pathology participated in deviant behaviors frequently.

The last observation is that the patients with very different personalities appear to use their deviant behaviors for a similar purpose. With several exceptions (Miss A. and Mr. T.) the goal of the behavior is sexual gratification with little or no commitment to, or psychological investment in, a partner. The most direct illustrations of this point are the exhibitionistic behaviors of Mr. R. and Mr. L., who obtain their sexual gratification without physical contact with, or even knowing, their victim-partner. Mr. M. had no concept of relatedness to the young children he used, and Mr. P. wished for no further contact with the men who picked him up. Mr. A. used his wife to act out his fantasies with no regard for her needs. In the case of the two possible exceptions to these uses of deviant behavior (Miss A. and Mr. T.) neither patient reported particular enjoyment of their sexual experiences but appeared to use sex in order to control the partner. Thus, if the deviant behavior is not used to obtain gratification without intimacy with a partner, it may be used to control or manipulate a partner. Certainly the same conditions can exist in nondeviant, heterosexual behaviors, but in that instance, and in deviant behaviors, the characterologic deficit appears to be an avoidance of, or inability to form, intimate mutual relationships.

In summary, it appears that all the sexually deviant patients presented had some degree of personality disorder, at least in the sexual sphere of interpersonal relationships. The degree of sexual deviancy was not a function of the severity of the personality disorder and the Paraphilias were not associated with any one particular type of personality disorder.

Treatment of Paraphilias

The psychiatric treatment of Paraphilias is complicated by the relationship of the deviance to character structure. The behavior is often ego-syntonic so that sexual deviates often come to treatment with little psychologic pain or discomfort. Anxiety and/or depression may be associated with the fear of being discovered, arrested, or punished, but once those dangers have passed the uncomfortable affects disappear. Thus the deviant patient's motivation for treatment, based upon psychic pain, is absent or limited. Individual psychotherapy, which relies heavily on the patient's motivation, has not fulfilled the expectations of therapists in the treatment of Paraphilias and has led to use of group therapy, married couple therapy, and family therapy as alternatives to individual treatment. In addition to the talking therapies, hormonal treatment, surgical castration, sex reassignment, and behavior therapies are also available. The purpose of the discussion that follows is not to promote one treatment modality or another, but rather to bring the new methods to the awareness of physicians and encourage a flexible approach to the treatment of sexual deviations.

As we have attempted to demonstrate, all individuals who display Paraphilias are not the same characterologically. The degree of sexual deviance (frequency of acts, psychological investment) is not a function of the severity of the personality disorder, and the Paraphilias are associated with various types of personality disorders. The therapeutic implications of these observations are of great importance. First, evaluation of patients should include some notion of a rating scale for the degree of deviance (conceivably similar to the Kinsey scale for homosexuality), as well as a rating scale for the degree of personality disorder. Identification, separation, and evaluation of these two components of the individual's personality and behavioral repetoire will eventually become part of the diagnostic formulation. (The diagnostic formulation is a concise statement of the patient's stresses, symptoms, dynamics, assets, and liabilities). If these two components are not evaluated separately there is a tendency to consider individuals with Paraphilias as characterologically a homogeneous group, which leads to inaccurate diagnostic formulations and ultimately to inappropriate treatment plans.

Inherent in the formulation is the concept of therapeutic leverage. Therapeutic leverage is the means by which the therapist and the patient utilize the symptoms and/or circumstances which bring the patient to treatment for the purpose of initiating and continuing treatment. Leverage is not exactly equivalent to "motivation," although motivation can be utilized as leverage. For example, if a patient presents with symptoms of anxiety and depression related to his deviant behavior, the psychic discomfort motivates the patient to seek relief. The psychic discomfort is the lever for initiating patient-therapist contact and facilitating their initial efforts of relieving the patient. If, however, the patient is brought to the clinic by a probation officer and has no "motivation" for treatment, the probationary status of the patient may be used by the patient-therapist-probation officer system to begin therapy. The evaluation of leverage points in each patient's life situation or symptom complex is a critical element in the designing of therapeutic plans for the treatment of sexual deviants, for, as previously mentioned, many deviant patients are not "motivated" by psychic discomfort. The therapist must be flexible and search for a means of inducting patients into therapy and holding on to them long enough to be of assistance. In fact, the development of leverage might be the most important element in therapeutic planning because, if the patient does not begin treatment, or does not stay in therapy, then nothing can be accomplished.

Individual Psychotherapy

Mr. L., presented in the previous section, was referred to the clinic by his probation officer for exhibitionism. Initially he was angry and uncooperative. During the evaluation it was recognized that Mr. L. respected his probation officer and reacted to him as a figure of authority. The probation officer strongly supported the need for treatment, which, combined with the patient's relationship with the probation officer, became the leverage for initiating treatment. Once Mr. L. had begun treatment, his curiosity and intellectual nature was intrigued by the therapeutic process. He evolved into a cooperative, hard working patient. He gained initial control over his exhibitionistic behavior by substituting concealed masturbation in public places for the exhibitionism. Finally he was able to give up this behavior as well. He began dating and had his first heterosexual experiences. A 6-month follow-up revealed Mr. L. has remained free of exhibitionism.

Although the individual treatment program was established on a once-a-week basis for 20 consecutive visits, all the elements of individual therapy were experienced by the patient. Evaluation had revealed the patient to be a passive-dependent individual, with many ego strengths and assets. He appeared to be making steps toward independence from his family and in doing so was working through problems usually associated with late adolescence. The clinical judgment that he had the capacity to respond to individual treatment was verified by his hard work and the successful outcome. The key points in the case identified during the evaluation were the probation officer's supportive role for inducing the patient to begin treatment and the judgment that the patient had the capacity to work in individual therapy.

Hormonal Treatment

Evaluation may indicate psychotherapy is not the treatment of choice. Mr. M. presented with pedophilic behavior, borderline intelligence, and an inadequate personality. He had received several counseling experiences with no success in controling the behavior. His limited intelligence and impulsive behavior did not seem amenable to psychotherapy. Recently Money[16] has reported developments in experimental techniques for the hormonal control of hyperaggressive states associated with sexual abuse and hypersexual states without concomitant aggressivity. The cases described were of individuals who expose themselves, masturbate, or make inappropriate sexual approaches to adults or children on a frequency seemingly related to heightened drive levels. Often there were frequent contacts with police and other social agencies. In Europe antiandrogens such as cyproterone acetate and methylestrenolone had been used in the control of sex offenders. Neither of these drugs have been released for research purposes in the United States and an alternative drug, medroxyprogesterone acetate (Provera R, Upjohn) as injectible Depo-Provera R, has received several limited clinical trials. Depo-Provera R effects a fall in the level of plasma testosterone with accompanying reduction in libido and potency, without feminizing effects such as breast development. There may be some weight gain during the treatment. These effects appear reversible with the cessation of the drug. Effective dosage, in the sense of substantially lowered plasma testosterone levels, has been 300 to 400 mg i.m. every 10 days. In certain cases this regimen has been accompanied by a decrease in socially and sexually deviant behavior, without recurrence of the behavior after tapering and cessation of injections. Mr. M. was considered a candidate for treatment with Depo-Provera R and was begun on the drug. It was arranged that his family doctor was to administer the medication. He was begun on the regimen and his sexual activities decreased. He was placed in a job and was doing well until he stopped going to his physician for injections. The pedophilic behavior immediately reappeared and he was apprehended for child molesting a month after discontinuing injections. He returned to the clinic for reevaluation. Drug treatment was resumed on a regular basis and the patient's sexual impulses and behavior decreased. Six months later he was reported as doing well, with no recurrence of the pedophilic behavior. At the time of his reevaluation it was decided to add brief psychotherapy sessions to the regimen, for the purpose of helping him maintain his drug regimen. In this case, evaluation revealed there was little in the way of therapeutic leverage. The patient was not capable of engaging in psychotherapy as the sole means of controlling behavior. His parents had been known to undermine earlier treatment efforts. The injection of the hormone, in fact, became the leverage by which treatment could be implemented. Following his discontinuance of the medication it became apparent that his parents could not be counted upon for even maintaining the drug schedule, and psychotherapy on a brief, intermittent basis was added to the regimen in order to assist the patient's maintenance on the drug schedule.

The rationale for suppressing androgens for the purpose of controlling sexual activity related to heightened drive levels comes from the awareness that sexual drive or libido is affected by androgen levels. The effects of castration of men have long been known to modify sex drive. Castration as a treatment for sex offenders was introduced in West European countries towards the end of the last century. Several states in the United States experimented with this method of treatment for a short period of time. Bremer (3) reviewed the literature and reports a generally favorable therapeutic outcome for a follow-up study of 244 castrated sex offenders.

Stürup (21) more recently reports on the satisfying results of voluntary castration as part of the treatment of the sexual offender. Whether by surgical or chemical means, it appears certain sexual deviants will benefit from a lowering of their androgen levels with the result of control of behavior that causes them and their victims grievous harm.

Sex Reassignment

Mr. T., presented in the previous section, was a biologic male who requested sex reassignment surgery at the age of 16. When he returned to the clinic at the age of 21 for reevaluation, he had been taking hormone treatments for 1 year. There was some breast development, softening of the curves of his body, and lessening of his musculature. He had entirely lost his beard and was speaking in a falsetto voice. For one year he had passed as a female sucessfully, finishing school and working. Further psychiatric, psychological, and endocrinologic evaluations were completed. Mr. T. underwent a series of surgical procedures which included removal of his testes and penis, the surgical creation of a vagina, using remnants of the scrotal sac, and augmentation mammoplasty. Follow-up visits of 6 and twelve months revealed the patient to be physically, emotionally, and socially well. The patient was engaged to be married, was working, and felt comfortable in her social role and relationships. She felt that surgery had enabled her to become at last a whole and happy person. Between the first evaluation at the age of 16 and the second evaluation at the age of 21, several attempts at psychotherapy were made by the patient (and his family). Two therapists, either overtly or covertly, tried to talk Mr. T. out of his plans for sex reassignment. During this period Mr. T. was depressed, fearful that he would not reach his goal. A third therapist did not attempt to change Mr. T.'s plans, but, instead, offered support while Mr. T. worked out a number of details enroute to the final evaluation. Mr. T. stabilized his life situation and prepared himself for initiating hormone treatment and passing as a female.

Issues of surgical sex reassignment present profound ethical and medical problems, since normal sexual and reproductive organs are irreversibly sacrificed and hormonal environment modified in the absence of life-threatening disease or demonstrable physical pathology, in order to correct a profound disharmony between psychological orientation and anatomy and physiology. The assumption inherent in this procedure is that extreme gender dysphoria is immutable through any of the known therapeutic techniques.

Initial psychiatric evaluations and psychotherapy, where possible, are clearly essential. Psychotherapy should be recommended from an exploratory, rather than curative, point of view, in order to help the patient clarify his current situation and his drives in the cross-gender direction. There have been unfortunate results from sex reassignment surgery, and it is in the patient's own best interest to explore his motivation, both overt and covert, prior to reaching a final decision. Psychotherapy presented to the patient from the point of view that "this will cure you" only runs head first into his most firmly held and highly defended convictions resulting in *a priori* rejection of therapy. In the few appropriate individuals, as determined by initial psychiatric contact and exploratory psychotherapy, the individual must live and work at least a year in the desired gender role, the point being that fantasies of benefits to be derived from cross-gender living often do not meet the test of reality. If such an outcome is to occur, it is better that the individual know prior to taking an irreversible surgical step.

While living and working in the cross-gender role there must be a concurrent period of at least 1 year during which the individual receives appropriate cross-sexual hormones. In this way the individual may experience the physiologic consequences of altered hormonal status prior to surgical ablation of the gonads. In the male, for example, exogenous female hormones would result in chemical castration, with a resultant decrease of sexual drive and sexual potency. In the female on exogenous male hormones, there would be increased sexual drive, increased growth of body hair, and perhaps partial or total baldness.

Only after these have been taken should the patient be *considered* for sex reassignment surgery. The best means of accomplishing the final evaluation is through a panel, under the direction of a psychiatrist, representing the psychiatric, psychological, gynecological, urological, and surgical disciplines which will be necessary for the patient's ultimate reassignment and rehabilitation. It should also be understood that, since there are permanent and potentially deleterious consequences to the individual, and since the long-term outcome of such procedures is still unknown, any such panel should become involved in this work only where a major component of their activity is research and follow-up.

The surgical treatment itself, in the male, consists of castration and penectomy, while preserving the scrotal tissue and the skin of the penis, the utilization of the scrotal skin to form labia, the dissection of a pocket posterior to the truncated corpus spongiosum as a vaginal cavity, and lining that vaginal cavity with the skin of the penis as well as with split thickness skin grafts. Thus relative genital approximation of the desired gender role is achieved, as well as the capacity for sexual relations "per vaginum."

In the female, to be reassigned as a male, the usual procedure consists of careful breast amputation, with reimplantation of the nipples to simulate the male chest, and removal of the uterus and ovaries. A variety of phalloplastic techniques are available, most of which are sufficient to construct only a partially sensitive, nonerectile phallus. The clitoris remains in place and serves as the primary focus of sexual satisfaction.

For references on many of the surgical and rehabilitative aspects of sex reassignment surgery, see Green and Money (9) and Edgerton and Meyer (4). For comments on sexual adaptation among sex reassignees, see Meyer (15).

Behavior Therapy

Even when the patient appears to be well motivated, individual psychotherapy may not be successful in controlling deviant behavior. In such instances behavior therapy may be a useful alternative.

The following case report (1) is that of a 33-year-old transvestite, married for 4 years, with a 2-year-old son. The patient's motivation for seeking treatment was fear that his son would discover his behavior, his concern about his wife's attitude towards his behavior, and fear of arrest while cross-dressing. The patient had been engaged in individual psychotherapy for 6 years before being referred for behavior therapy. His history of cross-dressing dated to the age of 4 when he started wearing his mother's shoes and thereafter he dressed secretly in his mother's and sister's underwear. His first orgasm, while cross-dressed, occurred at the age of 12 and he remembers the experience as very pleasurable. Cross-dressing continued in secret at frequent intervals from ages 12 to 18. Erotic pleasure was derived from observing his image in the mirror and feeling the female clothes next to his skin. Black shoes and stockings produced the greatest sexual stimulation. He was unable to cross-dress during a 2-year tour in the armed forces, and during that time developed a duodenal ulcer. He married at the age of 29 and found more pleasure during intercourse while cross-dressed, but abandoned this practice because of his wife's objections.

The treatment selected was Faradic aversion conditioning. The patient was seen on a daily basis from 9 a.m. till late afternoon for 6 days. Treatment sessions were 30-minute intervals, each consisting of five trials of dressing and undressing in female attire. Four hundred trials were given in 6 days; there was a break of 2 days between the fourth and fifth treatment days. The trials included unpleasant electric shock while actually dressed in female clothes and repeated shock while undressing. He was positively reinforced by absence of shock for escape from, and avoidance of, female clothing. A 6-month follow-up revealed there was no recurrence of the transvestite behavior. In addition, the patient reported an improved relationship with his wife and a decrease in his overall state of anxiety. He reported testicular pain and sexual tension relieved by intercourse with his wife and by masturbation. The patient's motivation was good, and despite this, individual psychotherapy was not helpful in controlling the cross-dressing. The extent of the patient's motivation is manifested by his willingness to undergo a treatment method which involved minor-to-moderate amounts of pain. In this instance the patient's motivation provided considerable leverage for finding a treatment modality which eventually was successful.

Married Couple Therapy

Married couple therapy may provide therapeutic leverage when a marriage is valued by both members of the couple, and when deviant behaviors by one or both threaten to end the marriage. Mr. H. was a 41-year-old male who was brought to the clinic by his wife with the statement that she felt he had a sexual problem. History revealed that Mr. H. was engaging in multiple heterosexual liaisons, homosexual liaisons, group sexual experiences, and, more recently, sexual relationships with a total family unit, consisting of the mother, the father, and two adolescent daughters. Intercourse with his wife had diminished to zero during the 6 months prior to coming for evaluation. The patient was not anxious about his behavior and appeared to be acting out his problems sexually rather than dealing with them on a cognitive level. His willingness to come to the clinic was the direct result of his desire to preserve his marriage. His wife, at the time of their arrival at the clinic, was threatening to leave him. Mr. H. was thought to have a severe passive-aggressive character disorder, and his wife a hysterical character disorder, bordering at times on psychosis. Married couple therapy was elected as the treatment modality and the first goal selected was that of increasing the couple's ability to verbally communicate with one another. As treatment progressed the couple's preoccupation with sexual behaviors decreased as they began to focus on other problems in their relationship. They resumed their sexual relationships which included intravaginal, oral, and anal sex. The patient's wife was satisfied to limit sexual contacts to twice monthly. The patient did not consider this sufficient and continued to masturbate regularly with fantasies of relationships with other women and with men. They continued in therapy for 4 months, on a once-a-week basis. As communication improved the patient and his wife were able to work out compromise agreements on many of the day-to-day issues that cropped up in the family life situation. With the improvement of verbal communication, Mr. H's sexual demands decreased slightly, and the patient's wife increased her demands, so that they reached a compromise in their sexual relationship. At the end of treatment they were having intercourse on a frequency of approximately once a week; the patient continued to masturbate but found it possible to eliminate his need for extramarital sexual experiences.

Psychoanalysis

Psychoanalysis and psychoanalytically oriented individual therapy also have a place in the treatment of sexual deviations in those instances where the individual is well motivated and is subject to a sense of discomfort regarding the sexual deviations. Once into treatment the sexual deviations are in some sense the mirror image of their neurotic difficulties. Freud commented in *The Three Essays on the Theory of Sexuality* that the neuroses are the "negative" of the perversions. Impulses towards the whole variety of perverse sexual activities will gradually emerge from regression during the analysis of the neurotic individual. What is manifest in the perversions, therefore, is unconscious in the neurosis. To some extent this condition is reversed in the analysis of sexual deviations. As the analysis proceeds, historial determinants, fantasies, affects, and other symptomatology will gradually emerge, whereas in the neurotic individual aspects of sick sexuality have been repressed and been allowed only to appear as compromise formations, thereby interfering with the richness and capacity for enjoyment of sexual experience. In the sexually deviant individual genital sexuality has been subverted or "dammed up," forcing the sexual drive to flow into collateral channels. Very often there is a severe prohibition against the expression of genital sexuality which will gradually emerge from repression during the course of treatment.

Psychotropic Drugs

Psychotropic drugs are used in the treatment of Paraphilias principally for alleviating anxiety, depression, or symptoms of psychotic illnesses. In those instances when individuals with Paraphilias are manifesting symptoms of mental illnesses, psychotropic drugs should be prescribed in the usual manner.

Summary

Current knowledge has dispelled an earlier association of immorality, constitutional degeneracy, and criminality with Paraphilias. Although the nature of the relationship between sexual deviancy and character structure is far from completely understood, it appears the totality of the personality and sexual behaviors are formed by the complex interaction of psychodynamic, familial-cultural, and physiological factors. On a psychodynamic-behavioral level, case material suggests that all individuals exhibiting paraphilias have some degree of character pathology, most usually in the area of their capacity for intimate mutual relationships. However, the degree of character pathology varies considerably from patient to patient, the degree of deviancy is not a function of the degree of character pathology, and sexual deviation is not associated with any one particular type of personality disorder. The implications of these findings for treatment are very important. First, Paraphilias should not be considered as a characterologically homogeneous group. Secondly, it is necessary for accurate diagnostic formulations to scale the degree of deviancy as well as the degree of personality disorder. The various therapeutic modalities currently available, provide the therapist and patient the means by which they can optimistically treat the vexing problem of Paraphilias.

REFERENCES

1. Blakemore, C. B., Thorpe, J. G., Barker, J. C., Conway, C. G., and Lavin, N. I. *Behavior Therapy Research and Therapy.* Vol. 1, pp. 29–34. Permagon Press Ltd., England, 1963.
2. Blumer, D. *Transsexualism and Sex Reassignment,* R. Green and J. Money (Eds.), pp. 213–219. Johns Hopkins Press, Baltimore, 1969.
3. Bremer, J. *Assexualization.* MacMillan Co., New York, 1959.
4. Edgerton, M. T., and Meyer, J. K. Surgical and Psychiatric Aspects of Transsexualism. In: *Plastic and Reconstructive Surgery of the Genital Area,* C. Horton (Ed.). Little, Brown & Co., Boston, in press, 1980.
5. Freud, S. *Three Essays on the Theory of Sexuality.* Standard Edition, Vol.7 pp. 123–245. Hogarth, London, 1953.
6. Freud, S. *The Ego and the Id.* Standard Edition, Vol.19, pp. 12–59. Hogarth, London, 1961.
7. Gadpaille, W. Research into the physiology of maleness and femaleness; its contributions to the etiology and psychodynamics of homosexuality. Arch. Gen. Psychiatry, 26:193–206, 1972.
8. Gebhard, P., Gagnon, J., Pomeroy, W., and Christenson, C. *Sex Offenders,* pp. 693–732. Harper & Row, New York, 1965.
9. Green, R., and Money, J. *Transsexualism and Sex Reassignment.* Johns Hopkins Press, Baltimore, 1969.
10. Hampson, J. L., and Hampson, J. G. The Autogenesis of Sexual Behavior in Man. *Sex and Internal Secretions,* W. C. Young (Ed.), Vol. II, Ed. 3, pp. 1401–1432. Williams & Wilkins, Baltimore, 1971.
11. Jones, E. *The Life and Work of Sigmund Freud—The Last Phase 1919–1939,* Vol. 3. Basic Books, New York, 1957.
12. Kinsey, A., Pomeroy, W., and Martin, C. *Sexual Behavior in the Human Male.* W. B. Saunders, Philadelphia, 1948.
13. Kinsey, A., Pomeroy, W., Martin C., and Gebhard, P. *Sexual Behavior in the Human Female.* W. B. Saunders, Philadelphia, 1953.
14. Marmor, J. Introduction. In: *Sexual Inversion,* J. Marmor (Ed.), pp. 1–26. Basic Books, New York, 1965.
15. Meyer, J. K. Sex after transsexual surgery. Med. Aspects Hum. Sexuality, 7:204, 1973.
16. Money, J. The therapeutic use of an androgen-depleting hormone. In: *Treatment of the Sex Offender,* H. Resnik and M. Wolfgang (Eds.). Little, Brown & Co., Boston, 1972.
17. Money, J., and Ehrhardt, A. Fetal hormones and the brain: Effect on sexual dimorphism of behavior. A review. Arch. Sexual Behav. 1:241–262, 1971.

18. Reich, W. On the technique of character-analysis. In: *Character Analysis*, p. 44. Orgone Institute Press Inc., 1949.
19. Reich, W. The characterological mastery of the infantile sexual conflict. In: *Character Analysis*, p. 145. Orgone Institute Press Inc., 1949.
20. Stoller, R. *Sex and Gender*. Science House, New York, 1968.
21. Stürup, G. *Treating the "Untreatable"*. Introduction. The Johns Hopkins Press, Baltimore 1968.
22. Yalom, I., and Fisk, N. Prenatal Hormonal Administration in Humans as an Etiologic Factor for Gender Problems. Presented by Dr. Fisk at the Interdisciplinary Symposium on Transsexualism, Stanford University School of Medicine, Palo Alto, California Feb. 2–4, 1973.

16

PERSONALITY DISORDERS AND ADOLESCENCE

Richard C. Marohn, M.D.

Introduction: Overview of Adolescent Development

The uniqueness of adolescence as a distinct developmental phase is ignored in many circles. There is a tendency throughout psychiatry, in the academic sphere, in institutional and clinic work, and in public policy, to group childhood and adolescence together as an area of focus. At the other end of the spectrum, when many adult or general psychiatrists talk about the adolescents they treat, they are frequently referring to 18, 19, and 20 year olds, and many case reports of adolescent treatment are treatments of young adults.

Being in this kind of controversial, in-between position is not new to the adolescent, or apparently is not foreign to an understanding of his psychology and psychopathology. DSM III repeats this erroneous emphasis by lumping together many disturbances as disturbances of childhood and/or adolescence. This runs contrary to the increasing emphasis in recent years on adolescence as a separate developmental phase and to the recognition that treating the adolescent patient depends on unique training with this age group, well differentiated from work with children or adults.

This misplaced focus may, in part, result from Freud's viewing adolescence as a recapitulation of childhood, specifically, the oedipal conflict and oedipal resolution (16). We are all aware of epigenesis, and we all recognize that what happens early affects significantly what happens later on. Yet, no such bias burdens an understanding of adulthood or later life, which are not viewed simply as a recapitulation of childhood or adolescence. Perhaps a sharp distinction is drawn between childhood and adolescence, and adulthood, in the practice of psychiatry and certainly in DSM III, because character formation and consolidation occurs in late adolescence; the person before character consolidation is different from the person afterwards, just as the preoedipal child is different from the postoedipal. Yet, despite the fact that the preadolescent is quite different from the adolescent, the tendency to group the latter with the former prevails.

There are, of course, biases about adolescence, because its conflicts and struggles are so frequently painful to so many people. In the treatment of adult patients, adolescent memories and experiences often do not emerge, even though struggles for autonomy and independence, relationships to authority and parents, difficulties integrating sexuality into the personality, and failures to structuralize and develop a well-functioning character pervade the treatment of adult patients. Many general psychiatrists do not recognize the significance of adolescence, and such blindness is aided and abetted by the strong emphasis in psychoanalytic and psychodynamic theory on childhood, particularly preoedipal and oedipal issues. Anna Freud (14) observed this paucity of thinking about adolescence, and a noteworthy example is that in a companion article in that 1958 volume of the *Psychoanalytic Study of the Child*, Eissler (11) attempted to describe how one would treat an adolescent, but noted that since neither he nor others seemed to have had worthy experience, he had to develop a hypothetical case to demonstrate his recommendations about technique. We seem to have progressed beyond that point.

However, let us return to some of the first dynamic statements about adolescence and review how thought about adolescent development has evolved. Freud (16) emphasized the importance of integrating genital urges into the personality; while emphasizing adolescence as a recapitulation of the oedipus, he noted that the libidinal drives were now genitalized and intensified so that the incest barrier would not permit simple repression of fantasies and wishes, as in the oedipal child; now sexual impulses had to be displaced onto peers. This gave way to Anna Freud's (13, 14) emphasis on ego development in adolescence and the psychological modalities of separating from the parents of childhood. Thus, a second major task of adolescence has emerged, psychological separation, and this focus led to further considerations about adolescent object relations and adolescence as a "second individuation phase" (8). Adolescence is "second" because, of course, how the earlier "hatching" is accomplished does affect all later development. Yet, the move here is of a monumental nature, and this "second" phase involves not just separation from the parents, but also individuation in an extremely important sense—structuralization of the personality. Still later, Blos' emphasis has shifted from an ego desperately trying to keep ahead of strong drive pressure (7) to the maturation of ego, superego, and ego ideal as processes in themselves (9).

That adolescence is the developmental phase in which the primary objects become dangerous is important to recognize. That most adolescents are depressed simply because of needing to grieve the primary attachments is also well accepted. That separation involves to and fro movement, mood swings, and unpredictability is known by therapists and parents alike. That assessing normality and diagnosing psychopathology in adolescence are complex tasks is recognized by most professionals.

Recent developments in the psychology of the self and understanding the narcissistic line of development have enriched our appreciation of adolescent development. Adolescence is a significant period when primitive narcissistic structures are transformed and, hopefully, mature; grandiosity is resurgent and idealization is frequently rampant. Both these occurrences are important aspects of personality formation in adolescence and go hand in hand with the psychological separation process. Losing the parental self-object support causes fears of fragmentation, and peers are readily sought, not only for their incestuous relief, but also for many important psychological functions. So, the separation process involves not simply shifts in libidinal ties but in narcissistic bonding as well (24). Similarly, negativism in an adolescent may be an important part of this developmental process and may be an indication that a narcissistic bond exists, rather than is absent. How primitive narcissistic structures are modified to energize the personality with ambition, goals, and ideals, to measure the person's accomplishments, and to be experienced as a sense of worth are all important adolescent transformations.

Charting these trends is important to an understanding of the adolescent, and any assessment of his personality must take into account various lines of development: libidinal, aggressive, ego, superego, ego ideal, narcissistic, object relations, etc.

Adolescent Development, Character Formation, and the Genesis of Personality Disorders

Just as the superego is heir to the oedipal complex, so too is the personality and the character structure heir to the closure of adolescence. Blos (7) notes that late adolescence is characterized by a period of quiescence and a considerable decrease in experimentation. Earlier, the adolescent has been beset by increases in instinctual tension and has responded to these pressures by experimenting with and developing various and new ways of coping. Such coping mechanisms are applied to the tasks of integrating genitality into the personality structure as well as of achieving psychological separation from the parents of childhood. Increasingly, as one shifts to peer relationships to replace the self-object functions of parents, various narcissistic and libidinal claims and wishes are frustrated. If these frustrations are tolerable and can be mastered, they may be reintegrated into the personality as functions which the adolescent now performs for himself. Just as Freud (17) had noted earlier (in *Mourning and Melancholia,* 1917) that identification will replace object choice after a loss, so too studying the importance of frustration and limit-setting in childrearing has demonstrated that the development of psychic structure emerges not from gratification, but from appropriately dosed frustration. The functions that peers, same sex and opposite sex, provide for the adolescent are eventually replaced by small accretions of psychic structure. The adolescent gradually begins performing certain important functions for himself, as in minute ways relationships fail him. Hopefully, he learns how to modulate and channel his urges, to calm and soothe himself, to regulate his self-esteem, to judge his performance realistically, to plan ways of fulfilling his ambitions, and to revere and respect important people without being swept away in crushes. The multiple infatuations of the fickle adolescent eventually give way to a capacity for intimacy (12) which can derive only from a relatively intact and cohesive personality that has suffered the threats of adolescent fragmentation, integrated genital urges as parts of the self rather than as foreign temptations, begun to be regulated by his own ideals and values rather than those of parents or society, and experienced himself as someone with a continuous past and prospective future. The interpersonal experiences of adolescence provide rich opportunities for the maturation and growth of psychological skills (28), but the kinds of experiences that many adolescents have reflect, rather than cause, the internal shifts and growths that are occurring.

The resolution of the oedipal conflict in psychoanalytic theory is spotlighted as a crucial time in the development of the superego. Identifications with the parent of the opposite sex replace the love relationship of the hoped-for oedipal victory and account for the content of the superego value system. The process, however, whereby the superego applies such judgments to the self reflects more the relationship with the parent of the same sex, which is usually tinged with aggressive or competitive qualities. The aggression and hostility that a child may feel towards the parent of the same sex is projected onto that parent and reexperienced as threats from the outside; these eventually are subsumed into the superego, which may beset the personality with benign acceptance and tolerance or with punitive and devastating self-criticism.

Yet, there is more to the character than the oedipal superego, or for that matter, the ego skills developed during the latency of childhood. Crucial and monumental maturational steps are achieved in the adolescent separation process and the integration of genitality into the personality. Whether the adolescent is capable of responding to affectionate bonding to the parents dictates whether or not all affectionate feelings need to be denied, or covered over by a layer of hostility, or experienced in later relationships with peers, intimates, and children. Whether an adolescent is capable of separating at all or needs to maintain some sense of infantile omnipotence by withdrawal into the self or by a regression to a preadolescent infantile level of development are questions of great import in determining how crippled or well-functioning an adult he will be. Must he cling to his spouse, or to his job, or to his religion, or to his political beliefs as a child to a parent? Does he see genitality as a feeling from within, or as something provoked by a temptation from the outside, or as something for which he must condemn other people? Is he easily led or influenced by fads or demigods, or can he sail onward, steered by the rudder of his own convictions and ideals? Is he capable of intimacy, or must he push others away because affectionate feelings within have never been integrated into his psychological world? Are his ambitions and goals realizable, or do they serve as nagging reminders of failures, or, conversely, unrealistic tokens of self-perfection? These are the questions to be answered in assessing the nature of adolescent character formation, and it is these kinds of psychological experiences and maturational steps which so meaningfully influence the emergence of the adult personality. More than the defensive maneuvers used to deal with oedipal fantasies, how genitality is integrated into the personality and how a psychological separation from the parents is achieved truly determine the adult outcome. When such maturational steps cannot be taken, or when the adolescent falters, "prolonged adolescence" (6) is the outgrowth. Later, adult psychiatrists and psychoanalysts may not recognize these as unresolved adolescent problems, but as expectable adult conflicts and deficiencies. Perhaps these kinds of prolonged adolescent struggles are so prevalent among so many of us that we cannot recognize them as typically adolescent. Perhaps Freud's recognition that sexuality is universally conflictual causes us to deny the importance of adolescence where sexuality blooms in its full strength, insisting on its recognition and demanding its integration. How the adolescent masters these challenges as well as integrates resurgent narcissism, motivational, yet needing to be tamed, determines the nature of the adolescent, and, before too long, adult personality.

It is from this matrix that personality disorders emerge. Because the personality is not completely established until the close of adolescence, it is contradictory to speak of adolescent personality disorders. The very presence of a personality disorder in an adolescent suggests a premature closure of adolescence or a failure to experience adolescent experimentation and maturation. Yet, we can speak of some fairly well-established behavioral patterns among adolescents which could be called personality disorders. Delinquent adolescents typically show such patterning. In our own work (25, 27) four parameters of nonpsychotic adolescent delinquent behavior were demonstrated: impulsive, narcissistic, depressed borderline, and empty borderline. This work demonstrates the possibility of understanding, rather than simply describing, deviant adolescent behavior and shows that pervasive behavior patterns and psychodynamic formulations can be inferred, from which generalizations about assessment and treatment can be made.

Freud (16) had observed that certain behavioral problems were the reverse of the psychoneuroses in that the neurotic conflict is externalized via an alloplastic solution, and the problem becomes one not of internal pain or disabling symptom, but rather of conflict with the real world or some attempt to change the real world or an external relationship. Frequently, internal tension is discharged through behavior that is delinquent or criminal. Aichorn (1) was impressed by Freud's ideas, and in his work with Viennese delinquents attempted to understand their delinquent behavior as an expression of unfulfilled wishes. He tried to gratify these wishes, believing that this would lead to the establishment of a transference neurosis which could then be analyzed. He noted, however, that a certain kind of delinquent established a different kind of relationship, a narcissistic relationship, in which the therapist or staff member was not experienced as separate or distinct from the adolescent, but rather as part of himself and a reflection of his own goals and ideals. Alexander and Staub (2) observed that certain criminals were expressing behaviorally their internal sense of guilt, hoping to be caught and punished for a psychological crime they had committed. Friedlander (17a), building on Freud's and Aichorn's contributions, postulated that delinquent adolescents needed to be converted into neurotics by blocking the avenues for instinctual discharge and attempting to reinternalize a previously externalized internal conflict. Anna Freud (15) viewed delinquency as a failure of the socialization process, a concept that we see reechoed today in DSM III, that is, that the child failed to internalize controls and limits which were applied externally by parents and other authority figures. However, she also noted that some adolescents in the process of separating from their parents and in the process of attaching onto peer groups in their community are frequently presented with only one option, delinquent gangs, and hence become delinquent because of the involuntary cathexis of criminal types in the neighborhood. This formulation is questionable because group formation and group loyalty also reflect something of the internal psychological world of the adolescent. If structure development occurred passively and simply reflected the kinds of identifications available to the teenager, then we could not explain upright people emerging from delinquent subcultures. Yet, we know that character formation and ego growth in adolescence are also active, initiating, and seeking, and not simple reflections of the family or the environment.

Johnson and Szurek (19) described a number of delinquent children who were responding to and gratifying the unconsciously held delinquent urges of their seemingly upright parents, and Bird (5) described the predicament of the delinquent child who consistently responds to the unconscious communications of his parents and others while developing no capacity to cope with his own internal urges.

Glover (18) described two kinds of delinquents, the functional, who is responding to the surges of adolescent maturation and experiences a temporary psychic imbalance, and the structural, who shows significant psychopathology both before and after adolescence and whose delinquency truly represents psychopathology of a persistent nature. Baittle and Kobrin (4) utilized these formulations in their assessment of delinquent gangs, in which they demonstrated a close correlation between psychoanalytic and sociological explanations.

In sum, personality disorders may develop along any and all of the lines of development and may, in a general sense, reflect either unresolved or unresolvable conflicts or serious psychological deficiencies. To tease out the important causative factors and to differentiate the presenting picture as clinical psychopathology, as distinct from normal variations of development, is indeed a challenge to the clinician.

The Adolescent Personality Disorders of DSM III

Adult personality disorders are to be noted on Axis II, according to the classification system of DSM III; thus, they represent substrata of adult pathology which underlie more obvious and more florid presenting symptomatology. In terms of DSM III, disorders that are classified on Axis I and Axis II are both considered "mental disorders." The fact that comparable personality disorders in adolescents are coded on Axis I, rather than on Axis II as in adults, reminds us that much of the core psychopathology of adolescence presents as behavioral problems rather than as traditional psychiatric symptomatology (23).

The relationship between personality disorders and personality traits needs to be clarified. According to DSM III, "Personality *traits* are enduring patterns of perceiving, relating to, and thinking about the environment and oneself, and are exhibited in a wide range of important social and personal contexts. It is only when *personality traits* are inflexible and maladaptive and cause either significant impairment in social or occupational functioning or subjective distress that they constitute *Personality Disorders*. The manifestations of Personality Disorders are generally recognizable by adolescence or earlier and continue throughout most of adult life, though they often become less obvious in middle or old age" (3). It is important to recognize that in the context of DSM III, a personality disorder may cause "subjective distress"; or, traditionally, a personality disorder represents a character constellation that seeks for alloplastic solutions to internal distress. Hence, the personality disorder traditionally seeks to change the external reality, the environment or interpersonal relationships, rather than to experience internal pain. It is only when external behavior is blocked that the personality disorder is subjectively distressed. Quite obviously, the less flexible and adaptive personality traits are, the more likely internal distress will develop, but a personality disorder is rarely diagnosed on the basis of internal distress and is more commonly on the basis of external malfunctioning.

The *conduct disorder* of adolescence is to be diagnosed when a "repetitive and persistent pattern of conduct in which either the basic rights of others or major age-appropriate societal norms or rules are violated" (3). Because a certain amount of delinquent behavior is seen in any sample of modal adolescents (26a), we must distinguish ordinary adolescent pranks from deviant behavior that has become engrained. This is a distinction, too, that one must make between experimenting with drugs and habitually using drugs. When a pattern has emerged, the clinician must be concerned about a conduct disorder. Of course, his clinical judgment is still tested when confronted with questions like: Are two runaways a pattern? Three? What about cutting class three days in a row? Or on three different occasions? It is not only the pattern and the repetitiveness which would cause one to diagnose a conduct disorder, but also the clinician's awareness that the adolescent has become fixated and certain developmental steps are not being accomplished smoothly. Thus, for example, if an adolescent needs marijuana to accomplish certain expectable psychological tasks, like socializing with peers, one must diagnose a disorder rather than an adjustment phase.

Now the kind of unacceptable conduct which an adolescent might show can be specified along two parameters: undersocialized or socialized, aggressive or nonaggressive. This leads then to the four subtypes of undersocialized aggressive, undersocialized nonaggressive, socialized aggressive, and socialized nonaggressive. An undersocialized adolescent is one who has not learned to tame and sublimate certain basic drives and urges and, as a result, to establish bonds and relationships with others; he is extremely egocentric and uses others for his own needs, according to DSM III. On the other hand, the socialized adolescent has developed social attachments, at least to some people, and is capable of bonding and loyalties. Unfortunately, as Kohut (20) has demonstrated, these distinctions are superficial and simplistic. A social relationship is not necessarily characterized by object love, but may be narcissistic in nature; a person with few relationships is not necessarily primitively narcissistic but may be capable of intense "love." It is important to remember that bonding may be either libidinal or narcissistic in nature (24). It is the representation of the relationship in the adolescent's psyche that is crucial, and this is particularly important in understanding delinquents and conduct disorders (22).

The *aggressive adolescent* is one who, through either physical violence or other kinds of assertive behavior, infringes actively upon the rights of other people, whereas the nonaggressive adolescent tends to violate rules and mores or misbehaves by default, rather than by asserting himself physically. Any adolescent whose presenting difficulties are delinquency as it would be defined, for example, by a juvenile court would be classified as one of the conduct disorders; if he were capable of loyalties to the norms of a peer group, such as a gang, which in the past caused him to be viewed as an antisocial personality, he would now earn for himself the label "socialized." The deviant asocial loner who ascribes to the norms of no peer group would be viewed as the undersocialized adolescent, and this would ultimately have to be distinguished from the avoidant disorder; the undersocialized, however, would present with significant mischief and delinquent behavior, in contrast to a simply withdrawing adolescent. Isolated and individual acts of antisocial behavior do not call for a diagnosis of conduct disorder, but rather should be seen as adolescent antisocial behavior because no repetitive and persistent pattern exists. Some oppositional adolescents will disobey and fight authority but still maintain respect for the basic rights of others and show a major commitment to age-appropriate social norms.

The *avoidant disorder* of adolescence is characterized by a pattern of shrinking from contact with others which interferes with peer relationships, family relationships, and social, school, and vocational functioning (3). Such adolescents may cling to their parents or to their homes and may appear excessively timid and shy. The hallmark of the avoidant personality disorder is the tendency to avoid contact with strangers or new relationships which distinguish it from the adolescent with separation anxiety, where the primary focus is on not leaving the home or the parents, and from a socially reticent child who will eventually warm up to contact with others. The overanxious adolescent experiences anxiety in most situations, certainly not limited to stranger contact. The schizoid adolescent shows little desire for contact with anyone, including those in the home. The problem is more appropriately an adjustment disorder rather than an avoidant disorder when the adolescent withdraws because of a clear-cut precipitant.

The *schizoid disorder* of adolescence (3) is characterized by a disability in forming social relationships. Adolescents with this problem rarely have a close friend of a similar age, but do not appear to be depressed by such isolation and show little desire for social involvement. They are inept and unskilled in social situations and have little interest in peer relationships, group activities, clubs, and the like. On the other hand, avoidant adolescents are interested in social participation, but are inhibited by contact with strangers. Schizophrenic adolescents have marked impairment of reality testing in contrast, and the adolescent with a conduct disorder presents predominantly with antisocial behavior.

The *oppositional disorder* of adolescence (3) presents with a pattern of disobedient, negativistic, and provocative behavior towards people in authority; yet, there is no violation of the basic rights of others or age-appropriate social mores. Frequently, the oppositional attitude and rebellion are directed at parents and teachers and, from a psychodynamic point of view, may reflect an adolescent who needs to use negativism in order to defend against positive affectionate ties to the parents, from whom he is trying to separate. In contrast, the adolescent with a conduct disorder violates the basic rights of others and social norms. In schizophrenia and other pervasive mental disorders, though there may be negativistic and oppositional behavior, contact with reality is severely impaired, and functioning is impaired in many sectors of the personality.

The *identity disorder* of adolescence (3) refers to severe personal distress which the adolescent experiences when he is unable to experience a prevailing and acceptable sense of himself. He is uncertain about many issues such as goals in life, vocational choice, choice of friends, sexual identity, value systems, and the like, and such preoccupations are not phases of experimentation, but last for a more extended period of time, persist in a state of chronic confusion, and lead eventually to social, academic, and occupational disability. Normal adolescent experimentation and turmoil is usually not accompanied by severe stress or functional impairment, and although schizophrenics and other more severely disturbed adolescents may also show identity confusion, these diagnoses are based on more pervasive disturbances in personality functioning.

Each of these diagnoses of a personality disorder in adolescence implies that, though a pattern exists, it is not yet well-entrenched or likely to persist throughout adult life. However, each of these so-called adolescent personality disorders has its adult counterpart, and according to the guidelines of DSM III, once the person has reached the age of 18, a more appropriate adult diagnosis should be used (3).

The undersocialized aggressive and nonaggressive and the socialized aggressive and nonaggressive conduct disorders of adolescence must be considered true personality disorders when they persist throughout adolescence, and by the age of 18 are to be understood as the antisocial personality disorder of the adult. The avoidant disorder of adolescence, if it persists, is to be understood as the avoidant personality disorder of the adult, as is the schizoid disorder of adolescence to be seen as a forerunner of the adult schizoid. The oppositional adolescent leads to the passive/aggressive personality disorder of the adult. The identity disorder is a truly adolescent personality disorder, beginning in late adolescence and frequently persisting into young adulthood; however, DSM III notes that it may later express itself in a full-blown borderline syndrome, a personality disorder of adulthood. Yet many of these adolescents will emerge as narcissistic personality disorders in the psychodynamic sense (20), though not necessarily as DSM III's narcissistic personality disorder, which is mistakenly limited to blatant, haughty grandiosity.

It is uncommon that adolescents will show enduring personality configurations of such rigidity that they would be considered personality disorders; it is even less likely, if not impossible, that children would show such patterning. Nonetheless, the failure of DSM III to make this distinction again implies a bias to compartmentalize childhood and adolescence together, the sole exception being the identity disorder. "Conduct disorders" conveys a sense of fleeting symptomatic behavior; yet, we know that in some adolescents there is a well-entrenched personality pattern, not at all unlike the psychopathology of the antisocial personality, the narcissistic personality disorder, or the borderline personality disorder. While it is true that character formation results from the maturational changes of late adolescence, "disorder" by its very definition implies a disturbance in normal development, and "adolescent personality disorder" refers to the stunting and restriction of personality growth. These would be important distinctions then to make in assessing an adolescent: whether the clinical picture is simply comparable to symptomatic behavior of a child, or whether it more accurately reflects an engrained personality pattern, well entrenched in the adolescent, likely to persist into adulthood, and requiring major therapeutic intervention for correction. We do see paranoid, histrionic, narcissistic, antisocial, borderline, dependent, and compulsive adolescents; they present us with personality structures, rather than symptomatic or transient experiments at coping. They are likely to persist as personality disorders into adulthood and should not be viewed simply as a reflection of childhood psychopathology. Rather, they represent a failure of the adolescent maturational process, indeed, a premature closure of adolescence.

Our own research supports some of these conceptualizations (25, 27). For example, though we attempted to describe fairly typical caricatures of each of the four dimensions of adolescent delinquency—impulsive, narcissistic, depressed borderline, and empty borderline—most of our subjects were not typical exclusively of any of the four factors, but showed various mixtures of each of the motivations. Consequently, one might say that most of the delinquents we studied were not fixated on a particular path of development, but rather were experimenting with various psychological pathways. At follow-up, it may very well be that these adolescents prove to be the most healthy in terms of their later structural development. Yet, there were some who, though not necessarily the most impulsive or the most narcissistic or whatever, were *exclusively* so; such an orientation may represent a significant stunting of personality growth and inhibit adult functioning. These are the adolescent personality disorders that must be recognized and attended to therapeutically.

Treatment Considerations

The hallmark of a personality disorder is creating a disturbance in the external world in order to preserve the psyche from experiencing internal distress. Many adolescents achieve this through disagreeable behavior or conduct. The adolescent attempts to deal with his internal conflict or heal his psychological deficit by turning to the outside world, either to discharge tension or guilt, to achieve gratification of a neurotic conflict, or to utilize someone or some experience in the environment to complete the self, to soothe, and to calm the self.

Approaching the adolescent with this kind of conceptualization implies that behavior has meaning and can be understood psychodynamically. From this it flows that proper assessment will lead to formulating and implementing a psychodynamically oriented treatment program (26). Many such adolescents can be treated only in an institutional hospital setting, particularly when they are not capable of sustaining themselves in a treatment alliance or facing the throes of an intense transference without a supportive environment (10). If the adolescent has resources that he can call on in the family or in his peer relationships, he may be a suitable candidate for outpatient therapy. However, often it is necessary to provide him an environment that will teach him that there is, indeed, an internal psychological world, that affect can be distinguished and identified, that his behavior has meaning, and that he behaves as a result of his internal experiences. The child care or hospital staff perform extremely important preliminary and supportive functions in helping the adolescent engage in meaningful insight-oriented psychotherapy. However, such environmental work need not be limited to the aggressive delinquent or behaviorally disordered adolescent. Often, a withdrawn, a schizoid, or an oppositional teenager needs the same kind of reality engagement that the delinquent requires in order to begin experiencing the flexibility of coping mechanisms and the experience of internal distress. The adolescent with an identity disorder, however, seems to be more likely a candidate for outpatient treatment, as he will so desperately utilize the therapist to support him in his search for internal meaning. Yet, the sicker adolescent with an identity disorder or that adolescent approaching more of a borderline constellation will require a residential or hospital setting in order to support him in the important and stressful work of psychotherapy.

Negativism and hostile feelings are common occurrences in the treatment of any adolescent, especially adolescents who show their psychopathology predominantly through their behavior. Not only may they resent interferences with their now traditional personality patterns, but hostility may be their defense par excellence or their focal psychopathology. To misinterpret adolescent rebellion, defiance, hostility, and negativism as the absence of a therapeutic alliance, or as the absence of bonding, or as an indication that the adolescent is beyond hope, are serious errors. In many instances, such negativism is indeed the manifestation of an intense transference, a transference of disillusionment, or of rage at the failure of the therapist to respond to transference wishes, or of defenses against the emergence of a strong blossoming, idealizing transference. Such negativism accounts for the unpopularity of many adolescent patients and the failure of some psychiatrists to treat behavioral disorders among teenagers. It is a common occurrence that as a child grows older, he is increasingly shunted away from the mental health field into the correctional field (21), partly because of his increase in size and therefore the concomitant danger of treating him, but also because of the failure of the mental health professional to recognize that the adolescent behavior disorder is an outgrowth of the symptomatic behavior of children. From this point of view, it may be helpful to categorize together childhood and adolescent disturbances and to differentiate the conduct disorder of the adolescent from the personality disorder of the adult; these kinds of distinctions DSM III makes sharply. Yet, descriptive categorizations will never substitute for more thoughtful assessments and understanding of the underlying roots of psychopathology.

It is from this latter vantage point that we must approach the behavior disorder and the personality disorder of the adolescent. He acts because, in a sense, he cannot react—he cannot feel—he must behave. It may be because his very personality style is one of immediate discharge, as in the impulsive. It may be because he needs to control the other in the environment or immediately discharge any feeling of omnipotent rage over that environment, as in the narcissistic. It may be that feelings of depression and sadness are denied by assaulting the environment. Or it may be that feelings of emptiness are replaced by frantic activity. So, although the words "socialized," "unsocialized," and "aggressive" may tell us something about the behavior, they are classifications that do not necessarily help us plan treatment. For example, "The *Undersocialized* types are characterized by a failure to establish a normal degree of affection, empathy, or bond with others. Peer relationships are generally lacking, although the youngster may have superficial relationships with other youngsters. Characteristically the child does not extend himself or herself for others unless there is an obvious immediate advantage. Egocentrism is shown by readiness to manipulate others for favors without any effort to reciprocate. There is generally a lack of concern for the feelings, wishes, and well-being of others, as shown by callous behavior. Appropriate feelings of guilt or remorse are generally absent. Such a child may readily inform on his or her companion and try to place blame on them" (3). This description is amazingly similar to the description of narcissism when equated with selfishness. The crux of this description is the implication that the undersocialized adolescent does not bond with others; rather, in many instances, the bond is characterized not by object love, but by narcissistic features. In fact, the psychiatrist may miss the point if he looks only at the external features of the interpersonal relationships and believes that bonds exist or don't exist when an adolescent has many contacts or no contacts. The important factor to be assessed in planning treatment is whether the nature of that bonding involves a sense of separation and individuation and whether or not that bonding is characterized by narcissistic features or not. Many socialized adolescents relate, but experience their peers as extensions of themselves and their own goals and ambitions. They seem to be concerned about the needs of others, but these are learned behaviors rather than true empathy. A classificatory system that does not take into account these kinds of distinctions fails an important purpose, namely, that one diagnoses in order to prescribe. However, before one can prescribe adequately, one must recognize the uniqueness of adolescent development and adolescent psychopathology.

REFERENCES

1. Aichorn, A. *Wayward Youth.* Viking Press, New York, 1935.
2. Alexander, F., and Staub, H. *The Criminal, the Judge and the Public: A Psychological Analysis.* Collier Books, New York, 1956.
3. American Psychiatric Association, *Diagnostic and Statistical Manual of Mental Disorders* (DSM-III), Ed. 3, pp. 45, 54, 60, 63, 65, 305, and 314. Washington, D. C., 1980.
4. Baittle, B., and Kobrin, S. On the relationship of a characterological type of delinquent to the milieu. Psychiatry, 27:6–16, 1964.
5. Bird, B. A Specific Peculiarity of Acting Out. J. Am. Psychoanal. Assoc. 5:630–647, 1957.
6. Blos, P. Prolonged adolescence: The formulation of a syndrome and its therapeutic implication. Am. J. Orthopsychiatry, 24:733–742, 1954.
7. Blos, P. *On Adolescence.* Free Press, New York, 1962.
8. Blos, P. The second individuation process of adolescence. Psychoanal. Study Child, 22:162–186, 1967.
9. Blos, P. The Function of the Ego Ideal in Adolescence. Psychoanal. Study Child, 27:93–97, 1972.
10. Easson, W. M. *The Severely Disturbed Adolescent.* International Universities Press, New York, 1969.
11. Eissler, K. R. Notes on problems of technique in the psychoanalytic treatment of adolescents. Psychoanal. Study Child, 13:223–254, 1958.
12. Erikson, E. H. *Childhood and Society,* Ed. 2. W. W. Norton & Co., New York, 1963.
13. Freud, A. *The Ego and the Mechanisms of Defense.* International Universities Press, Inc, New York, 1946.
14. Freud, A. Adolescence. Psychoanal. Study Child, 13:255–278, 1958.
15. Freud, A. *Normality and Pathology in Childhood: Assessment of Development.* International Universities Press, Inc., New York, 1965.
16. Freud, S. *Three Essays on the Theory of Sexuality.* J. Strachey (Ed.), Standard Edition, Vol. 7. The Hogarth Press, London, 1958.
17. Freud, S. *Mourning and Melancholia.* J. Strachey (Ed.), Standard Edition, Vol. 14, The Hogarth Press, London, 1958.
17a. Friedlander, K. *The Psycho-Analytical Approach to Juvenile Delinquency: Theory, Case Studies, Treatment.* International Universities Press, New York, 1960
18. Glover, E. *The Roots of Crime. Selected Papers on Psychoanalysis,* Vol. II. International Universities Press, New York, 1960.
19. Johnson, A. M., and Szurek, S. A. The genesis of antisocial acting out in children and adults. Psychoanal. Q., 21:323–343, 1952.
20. Kohut, H. *The Analysis of the Self.* International Universities Press, Inc., New York, 1971.
21. Lewis, D. O., and Shanok, S. S. The use of a correctional setting for follow-up care of psychiatrically disturbed adolescents. Am. J. Psychiatry, 137:953–955, 1980.
22. Marohn, R. C. The 'juvenile imposter': Some thoughts on narcissism and the delinquent. Adolescent Psychiatry, 5:186–212, 1977.
23. Marohn, R. C. A psychiatric overview of juvenile delinquency. Adolescent Psychiatry, 7:425–432, 1979.
24. Marohn, R. C. Adolescent rebellion and the task of separation. Adolescent Psychiatry, 8:173–183, 1980.
25. Marohn, R. C., Offer, D., Ostrov, E., and Trujillo, J. Four psychodynamic types of hospitalized juvenile delinquents. Adolescent Psychiatry, 7:466–483,
26. Marohn, R. C., Dalle-Molle, D., McCarter, E., and Linn, D. *Juvenile Delinquents—Psychodynamic Assessment and Hospital Treatment.* Brunner Mazel, New York, 1980.
26a. Offer, D., and Offer J. B. *From Teenage to Young Manhood: A Psychological Study.* Basic Books, New York, 1975.
27. Offer, D., Marohn, R. C., and Ostrov, E. *The Psychological World of the Juvenile Delinquent.* Basic Books, New York, 1979.
28. Wolf, E. S., Gedo, J. E., and Terman, D. M. On the adolescent process as a transformation of the self. J. Youth Adolescence, 1:254–272.

17

PERSONALITY DISORDERS AND THE ELDERLY

Kenneth Solomon, M.D.

Older individuals are more likely to demonstrate evidence of acute or chronic psychopathology than are individuals in any other stage of life. Indeed, Post (68) suggests that 20–30% of the elderly have evidence of psychiatric disorders. Old age is a time of major stress, including physical disease, social losses, and changed or diminished roles, stresses that accumulate within the individual over time. Frequently, these stresses occur practically simultaneously, adding an additional burden to the strained psychic defense mechanisms and coping abilities of the older individuals. Because of this, older people make up a large percentage of admissions and long term stay patients in state hospitals and other institutions. Approximately 5% of the elderly are institutionalized because of psychopathologic or behavioral difficulties.

The two most common psychopathologic syndromes in the elderly are depression and dementia. The incidence of depression in the elderly has been estimated to be between 20% and 68%, with most estimates between 30% and 40% (2). What this means is that approximately one third of individuals over the age of 65 will suffer from at least one episode of depression severe enough to inhibit functioning at some time in their remaining years. In addition, approximately 2% to 3% of the elderly age 65 have signs and symptoms of dementia, the incidence of which rises to approximately 20% by age 80 (45). Many patients with dementia have secondary affective and behavioral disturbances that complicate the ability of family and society to care for these individuals.

Personality disorders in the elderly are much less common. These are disorders that involve lifelong maladaptive patterns of behavior. Thus, they do not develop in old age, although they may first become manifest during that time of life. They frequently become manifest either because the maladaptive behavioral patterns themselves have become exaggerated, the social network has become unable to cope with behavioral patterns that have been the standard for the individual for many years, or because of the onset of another psychopathologic syndrome that highlights the presence of an underlying chronic personality disorder. As the syndromic behaviors associated with personality disorders remain relatively fixed over time, the emergence of the personality disorder thus represents a change in the older individual's biological status, a major psychosocial stress response, or a change in the capacity of the network to compensate for and cope with the individual behavioral disturbances. Sometimes, the underlying behavioral disturbances would be tolerated and even considered within the realm of normal behavior when the person was younger. In others, the behavioral difficulties have been manifested in younger age, but did not lead to psychiatric referral for many reasons, including resistance of the client, resistance of the network, or because of the therapeutic pessimism or nihilism that led to a misbelief that psychiatric intervention would not be useful.

This chapter will review personality disorders in the elderly. It will examine a typology of this group of disorders and look at the course and prognosis of these disorders as people age. Issues of assessment and differential diagnosis of personality disorders in the elderly will be discussed. Epidemiologic aspects of personality disorders in the elderly will be briefly noted. The majority of the chapter will examine stress and coping in the elderly and why individuals manifest these disorders for the first time in old age, followed by techniques of and problems with intervention in these disorders in the elderly.

Typology and Clinical Course

Personality disorders may be broadly divided into two types. These disorders may be grouped around the parameters of cognitive style and affective and behavioral impulsivity and lability. Each of these disorders have different courses throughout the life cycle and lead to different clinical presentations in older people. The description and dynamics of these disorders are described in other chapters of this book and will not be repeated here. Older persons who display these disorders have similar semeiologic and psychodynamic pictures, although the behavioral and affective components of the disorders are generally less intense than in the younger individual.

The labile types include those personality disorders in which affective and behavioral lability are most prominent. The cognitive style of these individuals is impulsive and present-oriented. Their cognitive experience is global and impressionistic (77). Regression is commonly seen, as are other primitive neurotic defenses and symptoms. Interpersonal relationships are short-lived, but intense, with an almost paradoxical shallowness to them. Basic needs, as defined by Maslow (54), are frequently expressed in raw form and satisfaction of these needs are paramount drives for the individual. The satisfaction of esteem needs are frequently swallowed up in the Maelström of libidinal expression. These personality disorders include the borderline personality disorder and other severe narcissistic disorders, including the narcissistic personality disorder, dependent personality disorder, histrionic personality disorder, and the antisocial personality disorder.

The stable personality types are personality disorders that are characterized by an over-control of impulsivity and affect. There is a narrowing of subjective experience and an emphasis on datum and fact, rather than affective experience (77). Projection and social withdrawal are common defenses. These individuals attempt to structure and control their environment to avoid the expression of affect. Basic needs are frequently repressed and esteem needs are frequently satisfied by material accomplishment. Included in this group would be the paranoid, compulsive, schizoid, and schizotypal personality disorders.

It has been suggested for two millenia that impulsive individuals seem to get better as they age (11). Thus, the prognosis for the person with a labile personality disorder is fairly good. For example, individuals rarely commit violent crimes for the first time in life after age forty (71), although nonviolent crimes may be relatively common in elderly men (99). The abuse of illegal drugs rarely begins after that age, although exceptions are known. It has been suggested that individuals with labile personality disorders may show behavioral improvement because of a decrease in libidinal energy associated with the aging process (what Ciompi calls "libido involution") (12). Aggressive impulses in men are particularly diminished in intensity, as noted by Gutmann and co-workers (33), thus diminishing the need for the maladaptive defenses that keep these impulses in check. In addition, as part of a process that takes many years, even the immature or maladaptive ego learns coping mechanisms that minimize the negative consequences of maladaption. For example, an extremely dependent individual may find someone who will tolerate his/her dependency, and marry for the first time in his/her 40's, 50's, or even later. Women in particular become more androgynous (33), and this has been clearly associated with improved adaptability and coping in younger men and women (4) and older women (10, 28, 38, 104). In others, the channeling of conflicts over dependency, anger, or trust may be subsumed under a superficial veneer of good ego functioning. The person's network also learns ways of avoiding certain triggers to the psychopathologic behavior, leading to a diminution and perhaps a relative extinction of those behaviors. Furthermore, superego development may occur belatedly, and the negative consequences of the maladaptive behaviors may be integrated into the personality so that they are less likely to occur.

Older people with labile personality disorders are most likely to evince symptoms that either emphasize behavioral dependency and conflicts about dependency or suggest an overinvestment of libidinal energy in the individual's body. As aggressive impulsions diminish in intensity, the regressive and immature ego faces major conflicts over dependency. This may come to the fore in older age when individuals may become widowed or otherwise alone (such as through the illness of a spouse), and lose the person upon whom they have been dependent. Any loss for the psychologically healthy older person stirs up dynamic issues related to nurturance and oral needs, conflicts which are exacerbated in the individual who has major conflicts over dependency. These become the major dynamic issues in older people who have had preexistent narcissistic disorders, and much of their behaviors are aimed at satisfying these basic narcissistic needs and resolving the conflicts. In some, libidinal energy becomes overinvested in the person's body, with the subsequent development of hypochondriacal symptoms. Other narcissistic, somatically invested older men and women may become a caricature of youth as they attempt to dress and look youthful in a way that is clearly inappropriate. The repetitious losses of objects upon whom they had become dependent more frequently leads to depressive symptomatology of a type different from that seen in the stable type of personality disorder. With the stable type, anger and fear are the dynamic hallmarks, as will be discussed below. The depression seen in the labile type are more likely characterized by an existential sense of loss (33) as well as fear, with the minimal expression of anger and guilt.

The stable disorders tend to remain stable or get somewhat worse as individuals age. Symptoms of rigidity and suspiciousness tend to worsen. For example, compulsive individuals, when faced with the stresses of aging, tend to become more rigid and more demanding of others. They expend much psychic energy further controlling the expression of affect and minimizing the subjective experience of anger. Paranoid individuals become more suspicious and may rightfully fault society or their network for the wrongs that have been done to them. These individuals frequently have been somewhat guarded and aloof when younger, although not to the degree as to constitute a psychopathological disorder. Schizoid and schizotypal individuals become more eccentric and more socially withdrawn and anxious as they age, utilizing the defenses of withdrawal that they had used when younger.

Stable personality types are particularly prone to the development of secondary psychopathology when the stresses overwhelm their coping abilities and sense of mastery. Obsessive-compulsive individuals are particularly prone to develop depression in old age. They have attempted to be in control of all aspects of their life when younger and turn their energies to a massive attempt to repress their uncomfortable affect of anger. When faced with overwhelming stress, especially loss, or repeatedly faced with the fact that they cannot control their environment, or perhaps even their destiny, the anger is partially released, but its discharge is blocked by other obsessive defenses. This anger is then turned against the self with the subsequent development of depressive symptomatology. Paranoid individuals become more blatantly paranoid and frequently experience delusions and hallucinations. The latter is more likely to occur if there is the presence of either an underlying organic disease of the brain, or as noted by Kay and associates (46), demonstrable visual and/or hearing deficits that lead to a state of relative sensory deprivation that further contribute to the psychotic manifestations. Schizoid individuals, when faced with the stresses of older age, are likely to become lonelier, and when faced with increasing anxiety over the need to interact with others because of real dependency needs, may become paralyzed by their anxiety; they may subsequently develop either depressive or psychotic episodes.

Most older people with personality disorders come to therapy not because of the personality disturbance, but because of secondary problems. One possible problem is the presence of an underlying brain disease such as Alzheimer's Disease or multi-infarct dementia. Because of the underlying brain disease, coping skills further diminish and the maladaptive personality traits become exaggerated, leading to the need for intervention. A 79-year-old woman had always resisted efforts of others to get her socially involved. She was very dependent upon her late husband and would only follow his dictates. However, each attempt by him to get her to do anything in her life was preceded by cajoling, arguments, stubbornness, and obstinacy on her part. Over a three year period, she developed symptoms of memory loss, confusion, disorientation, perseveration, and apraxias and the probable diagnosis of Alzheimer's dementia was entertained. Also during this period of time, she became progressively more stubborn and obstinate and actively refused to participate in many family/social activities or change aspects of her lifestyle. With further evaluation, a diagnosis of an underlying passive-aggressive personality was also made, along with the impression that, because of the lack of ego controls and behavioral controls occasioned by her brain disease, the negative personality traits associated with this personality disorder became more paramount, and she became more difficult for the family to handle.

A second reason why older people with personality disorders come to therapy is because the social network is unable to manage and cope with the behavior. A 77-year-old man was referred to therapy because he was hostile, belligerent, and manipulative with his third wife. He had a long history of antisocial behavior, including a prison term for the murder of a previous wife. He had a lifelong history of frequent fighting, rule breaking, arrests, and an inability to hold jobs or maintain marital or other romantic relationships. He had beaten his present wife, who was forty years his junior, on many occasions without her complaining. She was hospitalized for a hysterectomy and upon discharge from the hospital found that she no longer had the mental or physical energy to tolerate his beatings; she therefore requested an evaluation and intervention. The man's diagnosis was antisocial personality disorder.

The third major reason for referral of older people with personality disorders is because of the onset of another psychiatric disturbance, usually depression or paraphrenia. A 78-year-old woman was admitted to the hospital with persecutory auditory hallucinations, paranoid delusions, nihilistic delusions, anorexia, insomnia, loss of interest in activities, suicidal ideation, and marked agitation. She was diagnosed as having psychotic depression and treated appropriately, with amelioration of her symptomatology. Premorbidly, she was a stubborn woman who paid attention to minute details and rule following. She cleaned her house daily until it was spotless and became upset if something were moved out of place. She was always punctual, her personal appearance was immaculate, and she demanded perfection of herself, her children, and her grandchildren. Following the onset of severe diabetic retinopathy and a hearing deficit, she began to withdraw, and gradually began to evince the psychotic and depressed symptoms that led to intervention. Following treatment of her major disorder, psychotherapy was aimed at modifying her underlying obsessive-compulsive personality.

It has been reported by many authors that depressive and psychotic symptoms are the end result of personality disorders in the elderly (16, 39, 67, 99). For example, Post (67) noted that of his sample of depressed elderly, 50–75% had premorbid "longstanding interpersonal difficulties," 32.4–50% had premorbid sexual maladjustment, 23.5–44.4% had premorbid obsessive-compulsive traits, and 38.2–55.6% had a premorbid "inadequate personality." Dias Cordeiro (16) noted the following premorbid personality types in his sample of elderly patients who developed late-life psychoses: introverted (23%), obsessional (12%), chronic depressive (11%), and hysterical (2%).

Why the elderly with personality disorders are so prone to developing major psychopathology in old age relates, in large part, to the characteristic way in which the elderly cope with stress. The basis for this dynamic scheme was first elucidated by Goldfarb (29, 31) to explain psychiatric symptoms in demented elderly. I will expand upon Goldfarb's pioneering work, as I believe that it has validity for all elderly having to cope with stress. The progression of dynamic events is quite consistent in each elderly individual, and in large part, is related to their lifelong abilities and modes of coping with stress.

The takeoff point are the stressors themselves. These stressors, which may be biological, psychological, or social, cause subjective stress in the older person. As this stress is experienced by the older person, it leads to a sense of diminished mastery over his/her environment. This sense of diminished mastery is both over the internal biopsychological environment as well as the external environment. This diminished mastery may not be objectively observable, but it is the internal distress and perceptions that are important in setting off the following sequences of events. Difficulties with mastery lead to increased feelings of helplessness and ambivalence about dependency needs. These feelings of helplessness may be reinforced by the attitudes and behaviors of the person who aids the older person (82, 84). Feelings of helplessness lead, in turn, to the affective experience of fear or anger. Whether the person feels fear or anger or a mixture of the two is dependent upon how the person has responded to stress throughout his/her life. The basic stress response does not change with increasing age. Thus, the person who primarily responds to stress with fear when younger will experience fear and anxiety when stressed in old age. Similarly, the person who primarily responds with anger will primarily experience that affect. In addition, as most of the traumatic stressors involve loss, the affect of loss and sadness also becomes an important component in this dynamic sequence. These losses are both real losses and symbolic losses (101), as well as major narcissistic injuries and existential blows (33). They clearly stimulate major affective responses in the individual.

If the person has a life history of adequate coping mechanisms to deal with these stressors, and if the individual's current biopsychosocial situation is blessed with resources that allow him/her to be able to use these strengths, he/she will, after a few days at most, begin to bring these resources into play and start appropriate problem solving with only transitory, if any, symptomatology. However, if the person has inadequate coping mechanisms, he/she develops symptoms of psychopathology. These symptoms are based, in part, on his/her idiosyncratic experiences of fear, anger, or loss, as part of the dynamic sequence noted above, as well as his/her previous symptoms when stressed in the past. For example, if the experience is primarily one of loss, depressive symptomatology with a dynamic sense of an existential loss and a phenomenologic picture of retardation and vegetative disturbances will be paramount. If a person primarily experiences fear, he/she will report much anxiety and panic. If a person primarily experiences anger, physical or verbal abuse might be the symptomatic result. A mixture of fear or anger with a predominance of the latter might lead to paranoid symptomatology, or a mixture of fear and anger with the predominance of the former might lead to hypochondriacal or anxious symptomatology. This affective mixture may also lead to an agitated depression.

Inadequate coping mechanisms in the elderly may develop via three dynamic mechanisms. In one process, the intensity of the stress or stressors is so severe, and often recurrent or chronic, as to overwhelm the individual's previously excellent coping skills. This is frequently seen in many elderly who quickly experience one severe stress after another, at times when they are most vulnerable; they then develop psychopathologic symptomatology because their strained defenses are already overtaxed. A 72-year-old man requested help for depression, with anorexia, insomnia, social withdrawal, tearfulness, self-deprecation, anxiety, difficulty with concentrating, and suicidal ideation. In the ten years prior to entering therapy, his business of 35 years burned to the ground, his first wife died, he and his second wife separated twice, all three of his children divorced, several of his close friends died, his mother died, and a son's business went bankrupt. The straw that broke this camel's back was when his job was terminated because his employer became bankrupt. Although this is an extreme case, it is important to remember that the most severe stressors, such as death of a spouse, retirement, and illness, are most likely to occur in the elderly (37).

A second major cause of inadequate coping mechanisms is the presence of brain disease which limits the functional capabilities of the ego to bring into play the individual's previously adequate coping skills and defense mechanisms. An example of this was given above.

The third group of individuals are those who never had adequate coping skills. A previously present but partially submerged personality disorder or longstanding neurotic conflict may then come into the foreground at this time in life. For example, a person who loses his/her spouse may suddenly face the fact that his/her dependency needs are being unmet, which may, in turn, lead to clinical symptomatology. An example is that of a 71-year-old man who came requesting therapy because of compulsive utterances. His premorbid history was consistent with an obsessive-compulsive personality. It was not until retirement, however, that his symptoms began. In reconstructing his history, he was a "workaholic" who harbored much resentment and anger towards his wife, some of which was based on reality, some of which was neurotic. When he retired, he suddenly found that he was no longer able to avoid interacting with his wife to the degree that he had previously. However, he was characterologically unable to express his anger, leading to the development of the neurotic symptoms of compulsive utterances. When seeking therapy for that, the underlying personality disorder quickly became evident and became the major focus of therapy.

As is well known, there are many crises that affect the elderly. In order to explicate the process by which these crises exacerbate personality disorders, I will discuss special problems that affect older men (89–91). This is not to deny the analogous problems of women, and the reader may easily see some of the dynamic similarities, as well as differences, between men and women facing these problems. By discussing these stressors in depth, I hope to elucidate some of the dynamic conflicts brought to the fore in all men, conflicts that are exacerbated in older men with personality disorders.

One of the primary issues facing the older man in American society is that of retirement. The effects of retirement on the older man vary depending upon the nature of the bond to work, the importance of work and breadwinner roles to the individual, the voluntariness of the retirement, and the depth of economic and psychological preparation for retirement (25). Social class also plays a role in choice of and adjustment to retirement, as blue collar workers are more likely to welcome retirement than are white collar workers.

In turn, white collar workers are more likely to welcome retirement than are professionals. Indeed, blue collar workers frequently ask for an early retirement as it helps them get away from boring, repetitive work that has been non-stimulating for an extended period of time (78). Retirement is less likely to cause psychological difficulties for the man who chooses retirement and has made adequate provision for financial, physical, and emotional health during the retirement years. These men have developed interests and activities that are meaningful to them and serve as multivariate sources of pleasure and meaning in their retirement years. Good health and adequate income, important concomitants of life satisfaction (63), allow these men to enjoy their meaningful pursuits.

However, men currently entering their 60s and 70s have been raised with a catechismic inculcation of the American Protestant work ethic. As I have previously noted (92), the work role is a major source of man's identity, for men define themselves and their status in society by their level and sophistication of productivity. The occupational role is intimately associated with the breadwinner role and a need to be the sole provider for the financial health and welfare of the family (49) as well as the man's insatiable pursuit of success; this makes the activities of work all the more important. In addition, many men's social contacts involve the work arena, and although these contacts have a certain structure that inhibits the development of intimacy between men, they may be the most supportive and intimate relationships with other men (and perhaps women) that the retiring man has. Thus, retirement may lead to an aura of uselessness and rolelessness which may be a harbinger of future psychopathology. The retiree loses contact with most of his social network and loses status in the eyes of society (and frequently his peers and family). Diminished income leads to real problems. And the retired man loses a major, if not the major, source of self-esteem he has.

The older man who has given up work roles also has to face new issues of intimacy with his spouse as well as with his peers and children in a way that he never had to deal with before. He is suddenly home with his wife seven days a week, 24 hours a day. He has more time to spend with friends, children, grandchildren, and frequently, parents. If relationships are not to become boring and stultifying, the man must risk further intimacy with these people, a risk that involves developing new patterns of interpersonal behavior and a willingness to risk vulnerability with others. These are changes that are extremely threatening to many men.

The use of leisure time also becomes a major issue. Appropriate use of leisure time demands the ability to relax, something difficult for a man who has spent a lifetime involved with work. The more emotionally involved with work the individual has become, the more difficult it is to change a behavior pattern that emphasizes activity, aggression, and competition. It is not uncommon for men with the Type A personality (48), which is a caricature of the traditional masculine role, to suffer a myocardial infarction following retirement, rather than while in the work arena.

The loss of role and the inability to find substitute roles that reinforce one's sense of masculinity as defined by society leads to a sense of diminished mastery over the environment and a subsequent sense of helplessness, as noted above. The loss of identity becomes both a narcissistic injury and an existential loss, which also contributes to the development of depression. The stress of retirement also frequently unmasks other neurotic conflicts and symptoms.

A second major issue for the older man is widowerhood. Widowerhood, although less common than widowhood, has been very poorly studied. Widowerhood throws the man into a major crisis over and above the emotional crisis and narcissistic loss that occurs with loss of a person with whom he may have been intimate for over 50 years. The widower, having been socialized in the dimension of masculinity called "No Sissy Stuff" (15, 92) or avoidance of all that society defines as feminine, must now adopt new feminine role behaviors. For example, he must do the laundry, cook, shop, and clean the house, roles for which he has been psychologically and behaviorally ill-prepared. The loss of spouse makes great demands on the affective interchange of the older man who may be called upon to cry and grieve, to be expressive, and to share feelings that he may not even know how to label.

Because of the sex differential in survival, the widower may suddenly find himself the object of attention by many other women. This leads to interpersonal strains that he may be ill-equipped for, as he may not have related in an intimate way with other women for over 50 years. There may be actual sexual demands or he may fear sexual demands, which may lead to secondary problems, such as social withdrawal or sexual dysfunctions; these may be felt to reflect negatively upon his masculinity. As men are ambivalently dependent upon a mothering figure, the sudden thrust into widowerhood, a situation without such a figure, leads to ambivalent expressions of dependency needs, often in the form of psychopathological syndromes. The overwhelming nature of these various tasks, never before encountered by the man at a time of crisis, coupled with demands that he be "unmasculine," may lead to a prevailing sense of helplessness, or even frank depression in older men.

The many diseases and their associated disabilities that the elderly face are a threat to the man's sense of invulnerability. This is the third problem that is special to older men, as the elderly become acutely and chronically ill more frequently than do younger persons. These diseases may be caused in part by the life-style of men (35, 60, 90-92) and may force men to question their role behaviors, which is extremely threatening. These and other diseases may lead to a chronic loss of functioning and may drastically change men's life-style. For example, amputation for circulatory difficulties may make a man wheelchair-bound with subsequent increases in real dependency that may be defended against. The presence of chronic aches and pains may be a constant reminder of a threat to the older man's invulnerability and may lead to inappropriate expressions of anger. The threat to invulnerability from all diseases may lead to a counterphobic refusal to follow through with medical procedures of either a diagnostic or therapeutic nature.

Two particular devastating diseases affecting older men are Alzheimer's Disease and multi-infarct dementia. The dementias have an equal incidence in both sexes but are twice as common in men aged 65–70 than in women that age (45). Its major effect on men is the effect on the person's sense of mastery. The progressive memory loss, disorientation, apraxias, aphasias, agnosias, and inability to function as well as in the premorbid state may be particularly frustrating for the man who sees himself as active, competent, invulnerable, and omnipotent. The difficulty coping with these symptoms becomes manifested in secondary depression or behavioral disturbances.

Older men are less likely to use health facilities than older women (60). This may not be because they are less ill but because they are less willing to admit that they may have an illness. In part, this is because of the difficulty men have accepting the sick role. The sick role has several dimensions which run directly counter to the traditional masculine role. The sick role means that the man must give up power and control and adopt dependency-inducing behavior (64, 100). The sick role may lead to helplessness and subsequent demoralization (82, 84). The sick role involves passivity and a willingness to express discomfort and pain. All these are particularly difficult for men to do.

The fourth issue, very intimately related to the previous three, is that of rolelessness. As the older man gives up institutionalized roles, roles defined by clear behavioral expectations and defined status in society, he must adopt informal or tenuous roles or lapse into a state of rolelessness. Tenuous roles, in which the associated status is clear but role expectations are not, may be clearly deviant, and although they give some secondary gain to the individual, they do so at major interpersonal cost (73). Other tenuous roles (e.g., honorific titles such as Chairman Emeritus of the Board) may lead to certain status-associated behaviors in certain arenas, but the true hollowness of such situations may be evident to the man who then sees himself as useless. Informal roles (in which the behavioral expectations are clearly defined but the associated status is not), such as "kibbitzer" or "neighborhood chauffeur," require assent on the part of others in the environment for the individual to take on these roles, for the behaviors are defined by the informal social systems and the primary groups with which the individual interacts. Many informal roles may mean taking on various feminine role behaviors, for they may mean being expressive or being put more into the company of other men in a way that may increase intimacy with them. However, many men fail to adopt meaningful, self-perpetuating informal roles and fall into a state of rolelessness.

I have previously suggested that rolelessness is a cause of psychopathology through the intervention of stereotyping the older person, the power differential in society at large, a psychological contingency set that leads to helplessness, and the development of alienation (82, 84, 88). The type of roles dictated by society make it very clear to the older individual that the stereotype of uselessness holds true, and they are indeed useless members of society. Rolelessness leads to feelings of alienation and anomie. A loss of self-esteem accompanies the self-blame that occurs with the acceptance of the stereotype. Furthermore, rolelessness directly leads to a sense of helplessness through a loss of control of one's life, which is then further reinforced by the stereotypes that society has for the older individuals. This loss of social role also becomes a major narcissistic injury that stimulates major feelings of loss, subsequent mourning, and depression.

The sexuality of older men, the fifth issue, has been studied in depth from the psychologic point of view. Masters and Johnson (55) have clearly noted that sexual potency remains present throughout life and that older men are capable of continued sexual activity. Approximately 16% of men over age 65 label themselves as "very sexually active" (34) and about 70% of 68-year-old men have regular sexual activity (66). There are some physiologic changes that occur with age (55) and many older men make use of these changes in sexual functioning in a positive way.

But the older man who has placed heavy emphasis on the external manifestations of his sexuality may have difficulty adapting to these changes. The older man who is unwilling or unknowledgeable in the changes in his sexuality may become anxious over the loss of extremely hard erection. This may lead to secondary impotence or premature ejaculations because of a need to perform (56). The physical changes may lead to satyrism or Don Juanism in an attempt to recreate a sexuality stereotypically associated with youth, which also increases performance anxiety and is therefore more likely to lead to further problems with sexual performance.

Another problem with the sexuality of older men is the belief that many older men have that once procreation is done, men should not be sexually active, a belief frequently supported by the spouse. This belief is further reinforced by the societal stereotype of the older person as asexual (83, 85, 96). This may lead to ambivalence with subsequent guilt or inappropriate behaviors when sexual urges develop.

Thus, it can be seen how the aging process is a major stressor for the psychologically well-adjusted older man (and woman). These stresses easily become a trigger for the breakdown of already tenuous defenses in the older person with a personality disorder, leading to the development of severe secondary psychopathology. Or, these stressors may lead to the expression of maladaptive behavioral responses as an attempt to cope with severe problems of daily living.

Epidemiology

The personality disorders are the least common of the psychiatric disturbances of the elderly. In the United States, in 1969, there were slightly more than 3000 patients over the age of 65 who were admitted to psychiatric facilities (inpatient and outpatient) with diagnoses of personality disorders (Table 17.1) (69). Less than 0.5% of the elderly patients who were inpatients in psychiatric hospitals in 1969 had a primary diagnosis of a personality disorder (69). Similarly, inpatients with personality disorders only constituted about 5% of the elderly discharged from psychiatric facilities (69). In a British study (61), only 6% of geriatric patients in the community had a diagnosis of a personality disorder. A cross-national study (17) of diagnosis on first admission of elderly patients to psychiatric hospitals revealed that diagnoses of alcoholism or personality disorder (lumped together in this study) accounted for 10.9% of the geropsychiatric patients in England and Wales (1966), 11.7% in the United States (1967), and 28.7% in Canada (1969). Thus, one can say that although individuals with these disorders may be relatively common in the community, elderly patients with personality disorders rarely come to the attention of the mental health delivery system for these maladaptive behaviors.

Differential Diagnosis

The two major concerns in the differential diagnosis of personality disorders in the elderly are the differential diagnosis among the different psychiatric disorders as well as the need to differentiate organic medical diseases from psychiatric dysfunctions. In order to do either, there is always a need for behavioral specificity and a detailed history. It is important to note the

TABLE 17.1
*Admissions of Elderly Patients with Personality Disorders (1969)**

State/County mental hospitals	310	9.8%
Private mental hospitals	144	4.5%
General hospital psychiatric inpatient units	949	29.9%
Outpatient psychiatric services	1377	43.3%
Community mental health centers	397	12.5%
Total	3177	(100.0%)

* Adapted from R. W. Redick et al. (69).

exact behaviors that are being evidenced by the patient, for inaccurate descriptions may easily lead to inaccurate diagnosis. For example, a 79-year-old man was described by nursing staff as refusing to eat. He was thus labeled as being hostile and passive-aggressive. On observation, however, it was noted that he could not recognize what was put in front of him as food and demonstrated a severe motor apraxia so that he was unable to coordinate the movements necessary for feeding. This observation was the first step in the eventual diagnosis of Alzheimer's Disease, rather than a personality disorder.

It is important to know exactly what is meant by any psychiatric jargon utilized, as terminology is frequently misused by mental health professionals (80). It is inadequate to accept oversimplified behavioral descriptions. It is important to note, for example, whether the person is obstinate, stubborn, or just dawdles. It is important to ask that patient what he or she is experiencing when demonstrating the given behaviors. For example, what may be labeled as dawdling may be motor weakness or evidence of a cerebellar dysfunction. What is labeled as confusion might be a passive-aggressive refusal to cooperate with the examiner. What is labeled as disorientation may also be a conscious refusal to cooperate. What is labeled as circumstantiality and rambling may be an obsessive attention to detail. Thus, in each case, clear behavioral descriptions of the behavior in question is vitally necessary.

Furthermore, a detailed life history is required in the evaluation of personality disorders. The personality disorders are lifelong maladaptive patterns. Thus, if a person evidences what is in reality a major personality change, one is more likely to be dealing with an acute organic process, either neurological or systemic, than with a psychiatric disturbance. Careful history is necessary to determine if the behavior is an exaggeration of preexisting personality or behavioral patterns, or truly new behavior.

A 78-year-old woman was referred to the Neurology Service for evaluation of sudden behavioral change. She was described as suddenly becoming paranoid and with well-systematized persecutory delusions. When further history was obtained, it was discovered that she had repeated psychiatric hospitalizations for paranoid episodes since her 20s, and had spent a total of nearly 40 years in hospitals, a fact that she kept hidden from the examining physicians (and which the family was ashamed to mention), although she had been asked if she had a previous psychiatric history. A diagnosis of chronic paranoid schizophrenia was made.

A 65-year-old woman was referred for evaluation of belligerent behavior, anger, hostility, and paranoid delusions of her husband's unfaithfulness. Careful history revealed a woman who had been well functioning for many years, was extremely extroverted and trusting, and rarely showed anger in an inappropriate way. Her symptomatology developed over a 1-year period. Evaluation revealed a nonfunctioning thyroid, which, when treated, led to complete reversal of her psychotic symptomatology. Thus, in this case, the absence of the syndrome in question in the person's premorbid personality led to the suspicion and subsequent diagnosis of an organic disease.

An 86-year-old woman was referred by a nursing home because of her violent behavior. A careful history revealed that whenever she did not get her way and have her dependency needs met, she responded by throwing a temper tantrum. Throughout life, she would frequently either scratch or physically mutilate herself or physically attack those around her. This had been her response to stress since she was in her adolescence. The diagnosis of a personality disorder was made and she was treated with environmental manipulation and behavioral modification, rather than with antipsychotic medication.

A major factor that plays into the misdiagnosis of personality disorders of the elderly is the stereotyping that is done of older people. The stereotype of older people in our society has been repeatedly shown to be held quite strongly by health and mental health professionals. This has been supported by numerous studies of health workers and caregivers in general (1, 36, 54, 59, 97), mental health workers (59, 72), medical students (94–95), interns and residents (94), nurses (51–52, 59, 103), nursing students (42, 47, 70), dental students (3, 19), social workers (21), social work students (21), attorneys (21), law students (21), occupational therapy students (58), and psychiatrists (14, 24).

The stereotype has 13 major components to it, which can be summarized as follows (96):

1. Old people are conservative, old-fashioned and rigid.
2. Old people have limited activities and interests.
3. Physical deterioration is inevitable in older people.
4. Older people are poor.
5. Older people have various negative personality traits such as demandingness, obnoxiousness, gullibility, dependency, etc.; or, conversely, older people have positive personality traits, e.g., they are kind to children, generous, etc.
6. Old people are dirty.
7. Mental deterioration is inevitable.
8. Old people interfere in the lives of others.
9. Older people are repudiated by their families and disengage from society.
10. Older people are asexual.
11. They're in the best period of their lives; or, they are in the worst period of their lives.
12. They are pessimistic about the future.
13. They are insecure and helpless.

Adherence to the stereotype may easily contribute to misdiagnosis. For example, if dependency is felt to be a personality trait of the normal elderly, then the dependency needs of a patient may not be identified as being pathological or part of an underlying personality disorder. If older people are felt to be rigid, diagnoses of compulsive disorders may be dismissed. If older people are seen as unattractive patients (26, 44, 50), then adequate evaluations become less likely.

In addition, stereotyping, as I have previously noted (82, 84), is a major factor in the development of pathological dependency in the older person by virtue of the creation of learned helplessness (53, 76). A person's (actor's) attempts to meet his/her needs elicit behavioral responses from a member of the social network. If this person (operant) responds appropriately to the actor, response-outcome is consistent with both response and with need satisfaction, thus reinforcing the actor's behavioral response to the need in an interpersonal context. However, if response-outcome is either nonexistent or inappropriate, the actor's responses to needs diminishes, leading to a sense of helplessness in the actor. The helplessness then leads to the "giving up-given up" syndrome noted by Engel (18), along with the development of apathy and a dependency upon the environment for satisfaction of needs. As helplessness is a particularly frequent phenomenon in health situations, as it is part of both the sick role and the power differential between healer and patient (64, 100), it may be misdiagnosed as pathological on the part of the patient when, in reality, it is a common behavioral response to the stereotyping done by the health professional. Thus, what is labeled as pathologic may actually be a mislabel for therapist-induced behavior.

Furthermore, if the older person is stereotyped as being unable to grow, rigid, dependent, and unable to care for himself/herself, the therapist will not identify the potential therapeutic strengths in the patient. The therapist is then more likely to accept the inadequate coping mechanisms associated with the maladaptive personality patterns as normal and not intervene with the appropriate psychotherapeutic approach that would aid the individual's overall functioning and modify a lifelong personality disorder.

Differential diagnosis between the personality disorders and medical disease is also particularly important. Certain medical diseases are more likely to cause these behavioral syndromes than are others. As common medical illnesses may have uncommon clinical presentations in the elderly (20), a high degree of diagnostic sophistication is necessary and a high degree of suspicion is frequently necessary to rule out the medical disease.

The primary differential diagnosis relates to the presence or absence of brain disease. The acute onset of brain disease, such as a cerebral vascular accident, infarcted tumor, or head trauma, may lead to either a major personality change in the individual or a major and sudden exacerbation of the underlying personality disorder. Indeed, this may occur, for example, in frontal lobe disease, in the absence of classical organic signs or symptoms, such as memory disturbance, disorientation, etc. Frequently in this situation, apraxias are misdiagnosed as passive-aggressive behavior and frontal lobe neglect is misdiagnosed as depression. A full neurologic evaluation is obviously important to rule out the presence or absence of brain disease.

Thyroid disease, as noted in the case above, may also mimic many personality disorders. This is true for both hyper- and hypothyroidism, neither of which may present with classical symptoms of thyroid disease. As noted in the case above, there was evidence of weight loss, in spite of her hypothyroidism, but none of the other signs and symptoms associated with hypothyroid disease in the elderly; her reflexes were normal, she did not have cold intolerance, her speech was normal, etc. It was only a high index of suspicion that this type of clinical picture may be the only clues to the presence of thyroid disease that led to the diagnosis.

Other endocrine diseases, especially adrenocortical or parathyroid disease (27) may also lead to a confusing picture in which personality disorders or changes may be the presenting symptomatology. This may also be true for milder forms of malnutrition or other medical diseases. Indeed, personality changes may be the sole hint that the patient may have physical, rather than psychiatric, problems. A 79-year-old man with a severe passive-aggressive personality disorder became somewhat less combative and demanding in the nursing home than he usually was. The nurses suspected that there was something physically wrong, although his vital signs were normal, he did not look physically ill, and he did not complain of any difficulties. Medical evaluation revealed evidence of right middle lobe pneumonia, which was confirmed by chest X-ray and sputum culture, and treated appropriately.

The other area of differential diagnosis is between the personality disorders and other psychiatric syndromes. For example, major depressive disorders may mask an underlying personality disorder when the vegetative symptoms of the affective disorder are paramount. However, in many older people, the depression may exacerbate the behavioral disturbances, which may lead to a misdiagnosis of a personality disorder as the primary disorder and a lack of treatment of the underlying depression. The interaction between the two disorders must be noted if appropriate interventions are to occur.

Primarily, assessment of the older person requires a thorough evaluation with an accurate history, as I have noted above. The mental status examination, especially its formal parts, must be complete to pick up any hints of any organic process that might be a part of the differential diagnosis. The Mini-Mental State Exam (23) may be a particularly useful tool at this stage of the evaluation. A complete physical examination must be done to rule out the medical causes of behavioral change. I personally recommend that the physical examination be done by the psychiatrist, as he/she is thus best able to integrate the physical findings with the findings found on psychiatric and social evaluation (86). In the interest of discovering treatable causes of behavioral change, the following laboratory evaluation should also be completed: complete blood count, renal function studies (including electrolytes, urinalysis, BUN, and creatinine), liver function tests, thyroid function tests, serology, chest X-ray, and EKG. If organic disease of the brain is suspected, an EEG and CT scan, along with vitamin B12 and folate levels, should also be done to investigate the presence or absence of acute treatable brain disease. Other specific laboratory evaluations, such as spinal fluid serology, radioisotope brain or thyroid scans, blood levels of drugs such as digoxin, diphenylhydantoin, or barbiturates, and other more sophisticated tests may be done, as needed.

In difficult cases, a psychological evaluation may be particularly helpful. The major problem with the psychological evaluation of the elderly is that none of the psychological tests frequently used have been validated for use in the elderly (7, 105). There are many particular problems in giving psychological tests to older people, including issues of face validity, criterion-related validity, internal reliability, the age and aging of the test, patient fatigue, slow reaction time, and sensory deprivation. These and other problems have been recently discussed by Crook (13). Given these problems, psychological evaluations must be cautiously interpreted and their validity should be questioned if the results do not correlate with data received from other examinations.

A social evaluation should also be included in the diagnosis of a personality disorder. It is important to interview close and important members of the person's social network, especially spouses, siblings, and children, for they are able to give the evidence and the history of behavioral and maladaptive disturbances through the life cycle. Because these disturbances are frequently ego-syntonic for the patient, he/she may not be aware of them and therefore may give a history that is inconsistent with a chronic disorder; corroborating history thus becomes necessary. In addition, the social evaluation will seek out evidence of the strengths and weaknesses in the network. For example, one can evaluate if there are family members available who might serve as behavioral "therapist" with guidance and education on the part of the therapist. Is the family psychologically exhausted and unable to function in any supportive or therapeutic role with the patient? Is the person's housing situation or other aspects of activities of daily living such that the intervention with the personality disorder must become secondary as these more pressing reality problems become paramount?

It is only when these evaluations have been completed can one make a diagnosis of a personality disorder in an elderly patient. These evaluations may take several weeks of interviewing and ancillary examinations. But only once this process has been completed can one begin the process of intervention in these disorders.

Intervention

There have been virtually no studies discussing the treatment of personality disorders in the elderly. Schmidt (75) briefly discussed the use of antianxiety agents, but it must be noted that there have been no published data on the use of these or other drugs in the elderly with personality disorders. There are virtually no studies or papers on the psychotherapy of these disorders in the elderly; the notable exception is a lengthy case report by Ross (74), who worked with a 90-year-old man with a paranoid personality disorder. Her modalities primarily consisted of supportive psychotherapy, environmental manipulation, and the involvement of multiple community resources. Thus, most of what follows in the remainder of this chapter is based upon clinical experience.

The first stage in the intervention of the older person with a personality disorder is what I broadly call "crisis intervention." Its aim is to reverse the psychodynamic scheme noted above. At first, there is a direct attack on symptomatology. The major modalities utilized in this first step are either pharmacologic or behavioral. For example, if the person has psychotic symptomatology, notably paranoid delusions or hallucinations, antipsychotic medication is indicated. My recommendations are that the physician utilize whatever antipsychotic medication he/she is familiar with and is not contraindicated by concurrent medical problems. I prefer an intermediate potency (e.g., mesoridazine, loxapine) or a high potency (e.g., haloperidol (87), thiothixene, trifluoperazine) drug to minimize possible sedative and anticholinergic side effects of antipsychotic medication. However, one must be aware that Parkinsonian symptoms and toxic psychoses may be even greater problems in many elderly patients than the previously mentioned side-effects.

The presence of a major depressive disorder with vegetative symptoms is an indication for tricyclic antidepressant medication. I recommend the use of secondary amines (desipramine or nortriptyline) rather than tertiary amines (imipramine or amitriptyline) because of their diminished peripheral anticholinergic (79), sedative (98), and cardiovascular effects (41, 43).

If anxiety is a predominant problem, benzodiazepines can be effective though there is risk of side-effect; it is my belief that nonpharmacologic techniques may be of greater efficacy (81, 93). Relaxation exercises such as those developed by Jacobson (40), Wolpe (102), or those used in childbirth by Lamaze (6) give the patient voluntary control over symptoms of anxiety.

The therapist then works with the underlying affective responses of fear, anger, or loss. The major therapeutic intervention at this stage is ventilation and the major techniques are clarification of the affect (5).

Once the affect has been expressed and labelled, the older person is then given specific behavioral tasks to minimize helplessness. Emotional, social, and daily living needs are identified and the older person is instructed to respond to those needs with appropriate behavioral responses. Whereas previous phases of therapy tend to utilize the dependency and helplessness inherent in the sick role, these processes are minimized at this stage. This is especially important in institutional settings, such as acute psychiatric hospitals. Simultaneously, a resurgence of mastery is encouraged, not only by giving clear-cut behavioral tasks within reach of the patient, but also by emphasizing the person's choice and motivation in seeking therapy. Choice and options in all aspects of life are actively encouraged, in part to move the older person from an external to an internal locus of control, but also to reverse the dynamic process that led to symptoms. Olin (62) notes that responsibility for one's own life is a necessary part of the therapy of persons with borderline personality disorders. A humanistic orientation requires that the therapist expand this focus to the therapy of older people, so that it must be made clear to the elderly patient that he/she is responsible for his/her life and must take that responsibility if therapy is to be successful.

During this phase of therapy, the therapist also makes a direct attack on the particular stressors the individual is responding to. Losses in the realm of daily living needs may require that the therapist advocate for the patient with various social agencies. In addition, the older person should be encouraged to seek out part-time or full-time employment or, if this is physically or emotionally inappropriate, to search for some other meaningful activity. The elderly patient must be encouraged to experiment with new activities, interests, and relationships, so that he/she can define and create for himself/herself a new and meaningful social and existential world.

In the second stage of therapy, or the stage of long-term psychotherapy, the therapist attacks the underlying difficulties the individual has with coping as well as his/her chronic maladaptive responses to stress.

Older people are appropriate candidates for individual psychotherapy. As there is nothing that occurs in the process of normal aging that would preclude the development and maintenance of qualities necessary for successful psychotherapy, certainly psychoanalytic psychotherapy should be considered the modality of choice for the treatment of elderly patients with personality disorders. Indeed, many older people may be treated by psychoanalysis, as noted by Pollack (personal communication), although the majority will more likely benefit from psychoanalytic psychotherapy.

Some technical modifications may become necessary in working with this age group. Because some patients may fatigue easily, it may be wise to limit sessions to 30 minutes rather than the traditional 50 minutes for these patients. Sessions should be scheduled at such times as to maximize the older person's alertness and diurnal and other biologic rhythms, as well as special travel needs. Many elderly rely on public transportation, limit their driving to daylight hours because of limitations in night vision, or avoid nocturnal excursions into or out of high crime areas. Taking the history requires a much longer time because there are more years of experience. History taking should emphasize an assessment of the person's lifelong strengths and how he/she coped with stress (9) so that these techniques may be utilized and reinforced during psychotherapy. As older persons have frequently done many years of self-examination, it may be possible to start psychotherapy at a level of insight that is deeper than with younger clients. In addition, older persons are aware of their limited life span and are more motivated for psychotherapy than are younger persons (50). Because of this, resistances are diminished, which allows for a more rapid identification and working through of major dynamic issues, followed by the willingness on the part of the older person to put these insights and affective changes into their behavioral repertoire. Interpretations thus may be given earlier in therapy and concentration on resistances may be minimized.

Techniques of the Gestalt therapy and transactional analysis may be particularly helpful in working with the older person with a personality disorder. If there is a degree of somatization, identification of the emotional concomitants of the somatization may be translated into verbal affective statements. For example, somatic pain may first be concretized so that the older person is asked what his/her stomach is feeling. He/she is then asked, using a Gestalt technique (65), to translate that into a statement about what he/she is feeling. That statement is then used as a bridge to the identification of the underlying affective state. Once that underlying affective state is identified, then the person's maladaptive responses to it can be further identified in a way consistent with supportive or insight-oriented therapy. Because many older people with unresolved dependency issues behave in a child-like way, various transactional analytic techniques, as well as responses to the individual as an adult and pointing out the child-like ways in which he/she behaves, may be a particularly helpful form of interpersonal insight (57). It is particularly important for the therapist at this stage not to behave in a parental way.

If interpersonal difficulties are a major component of the maladaptive responses, the older person may benefit more from group psychotherapy than individual psychotherapy. Groups of older persons are quite successful in promoting therapeutic changes (30). They tend to work better when the groups are homogeneous and consist only of older people because many older persons have a reluctance to share in a mixed age group, in which they may be the only older person there, thus allowing younger patients to dominate those groups. However, in a geriatric therapy group, this is generally not so. In addition, because older psychiatric patients are more likely to be women, there are frequently not enough men in the group to dominate it, thus allowing for greater intimacy and sharing. The group may be utilized to be supportive, to confront, to suggest specific behavioral modifications, as well as to give insight and feedback on the interpersonal aspects of the individual's personality disorder. Group psychotherapy is particularly helpful in individuals with dependent personality disorders or passive-aggressive personality disorders because the group is frequently unwilling to tolerate the pathologic behavior, thus forcing change in the maladaptive responses to stress with the support and advice of the group. In addition, as there is an element of social isolation in many elderly patients, the group brings to the patient a consistent social network that can be expected to be helpful in times of crisis.

Family or couple psychotherapy may be helpful when interpersonal issues within the family are of major importance. It may consist of a very behaviorally oriented approach in which the family is used as behavioral engineers to modify, with classical reinforcement, extinction, or punishment paradigms, the behaviors of the identified patient. Or, a communications, functional, or structural model may be utilized to help clarify the person's needs and to help the family members or spouse behave in a way that maximizes appropriate response-outcome. In the relatively nonverbal individual living at home with interpersonal difficulties, utilizing a family member or a substitute for a family member, such as a home health aide, as an intervenor, may be an important element in family or behavioral therapy.

In patients with severe dependency needs or those who are schizoid, day hospitalization or attendance at special social groups for the elderly may be helpful. These social groups may involve nonthreatening activities and may allow for the gradual desensitization of the older withdrawn individual to a social network that may be supportive. Day hospitalization may allow the patient to structure his/her life. In the context of nonthreatening recreational activities, plus therapeutically oriented groups and individual sessions, there can be moderate success with a severely disturbed older person with a dependent, schizoid, or schizotypal personality disorder. In addition, ancillary social and rehabilitative services may be necessary and helpful within the context of any of the therapeutic modalities. There may be a need to teach budgeting, shopping, or advocacy skills, especially for the chronically dependent or schizoid individual. Assurance that the older person is receiving appropriate and complete social services such as food stamps, Medicare, etc. may become an important part of developing the therapeutic alliance as well as a way of minimizing some of the social and day-to-day stresses on the patient that would interfere with ongoing therapy.

Transference Issues

Major transference issues develop during the course of any psychotherapy. A particularly important one in working with the elderly is the development of dependency upon the therapist. The therapist is frequently perceived as a consistently caring and nurturing individual who is always helping out and who frequently does so in a concrete way. The older person, especially one with conflicts around dependency needs, may transfer dependency from family or social network to the therapist and may expect the therapist to make all major and minor life decisions for the patient. For example, a 75-year-old woman could not fill a prescription without asking her therapist to decide which pharmacy she should go to. Some therapists, such as Goldfarb (31), encourage the dependency in the hope that the patient will identify with the therapist and incorporate the therapist's superego as his/her own, thus leading to changes in adaptive interpersonal paradigms. Thus, even after termination of therapy, the dependency becomes encouraged so that therapeutic headway may continue. Other therapists, myself included, emphasize growth and autonomy on the part of the older patient and tend to de-emphasize dependency. In therapy with older patients, I prefer to emphasize choice, responsibility, and risk-taking behaviors to try out new interpersonal skills that are necessary to maximize autonomy and independent functioning on the part of the older patient.

Parentification of the therapist is an important form of transference in psychotherapy with the elderly with personality disorders. In many ways, this parentification is no different from the parentification seen in the context of any transference relationship, in which the therapist is seen as if he/she were various significant others in the patient's life. However, because the parents of the older patients are frequently either deceased or ill or dealing with many of the same stresses that the older patient himself/herself is dealing with, parentification brings out many unresolved psychodynamic issues related to loss, separation, and parent/child relations that have been repressed for several generations. Thus, parentification becomes an important part of the therapeutic involvement as it rapidly brings up important dynamic issues that are dealt with by the usual psychotherapeutic modalities of explanation, clarification, questioning, and interpretation (5). Goldfarb (31) emphasizes parentification without interpretation, so that the elderly patient will identify with the therapist to facilitate the incorporation of the therapist's superego. I prefer to interpret it, so as to foster resolution of the conflicts noted immediately above.

On the other hand, however, the client is usually older and frequently quite significantly older than the therapist. He/she may infantilize the therapist and may relate to the therapist either as a child or a grandchild. This also brings up important therapeutic issues, especially issues of control and dependency, for the therapist is seen as if he/she were the patient's own child or grandchild. This may reach extreme degrees of acting out, such as a 73-year-old woman who brought homemade cookies to one session for the therapist, who was in his mid-20s. The next week, she brought a deck of cards and rather than dealing with therapeutic issues, demanded that she teach him how to play gin rummy. This was handled in the context of relating, in fantasy, to the fact that she had no grandchildren of her own and desperately wanted some before she died. She was then able to discuss her anger at her children for not providing her with grandchildren.

Countertransference Issues

Countertransference issues are many in doing psychotherapy with older individuals. As noted above, adherence to stereotypes may lead to an inappropriate denial of the therapeutic growth potential of the older patient as well as the inappropriate reinforcement of dependency and helplessness of the older patient. In addition, working with the older patient may bring up many anxieties and stresses about the therapist's own aging, which leads both to status inconsistency as well as a state of cognitive dissonance (22). A frequent response to these states in dealing with the elderly is to reinforce the stereotypes of older people (83, 85) which then becomes a therapeutic blind spot in working with older patients.

Because of the age differential between therapist and client, the therapist may parentify the patient. This may have important consequences, as the therapist may fear bringing up certain dynamic issues because they are unresolved between him/her and his/her parents. The therapist may not allow himself/herself to experience anger at the patient and therefore, he/she may allow the patient to act out or to continue various forms of maladaptive behavior rather than confronting the effect of the behaviors. The therapist may be overly gentle, or may avoid dealing with issues related to sexuality in the older patient because of countertransference problems.

On the other hand, the therapist may infantilize the older client. The infantilization may take the form of being overly helpful and reinforcing dependency on the part of the client. This may lead to a crisis in therapy as the therapist had to deal with his/her own relationship with his/her children. Infantilization also diminishes the growth potential of therapy as well as leads to a gentleness in therapy that may be inappropriate.

Final issues that the therapist must deal with when doing psychotherapy with older people are the issues of illness and death. Older persons frequently miss sessions because they become acutely ill or have exacerbations of chronic medical illness that may or may not require hospitalization. The vulnerability of the patient, the therapist, and the therapy then becomes an important issue for the therapist to have to work with and leads to many existential questions, such as limits, attitudes, and the meaning of life, which the therapist may not have worked through with himself/herself. Illness interrupts the flow of therapeutic sessions and, if accompanied by brain changes such as delirium, may actually lead to a major therapeutic reversal; it may then take months of therapy to regain premorbid levels of functioning. Medical illness also leads to the prescription of drugs which may adversely interact with either the person's psyche or with psychotropic medications that may be prescribed.

Dying may be an acute or chronic, or even protracted process. In any case, it may lead to the therapist being unable or unwilling to work with the patient during his/her final hours, when the therapist may be most needed.

The therapist may be angry at the patient for leaving and may take out his/her anger by missing or cancelling sessions, being late for sessions, or prematurely terminating therapy. The therapist has to experience and work with his/her own grief over the loss of the patient. The loss is not only that of the individual patient, but also loss and grief as a generic life issue. Because death is a frequent occurrence in the life of the therapist working with the elderly, the therapist must confront his/her own finitude and limits of his/her own life.

Conclusion

This chapter has reviewed many facets of personality disorders and psychiatric interventions with older patients. It is important to remember that older patients are growing individuals capable of major therapeutic movement. They are motivated patients who realize that their limited life span necessitates rapid change, and they are willing to work for this change (50). Even in the presence of brain disease, it is important to remember that there is still functioning brain that is capable of learning, changing, and responding to environmental stimuli. Thus, even some personality disorders that have become manifest for the first time because of brain disease are capable of being significantly modified.

A major benefit in working with older people is the necessity of the therapist to confront his/her own aging (32). This leads to important sources of growth for the therapist, growth that leads to increased self-awareness and an ability to work well with clients of all ages. In gerontologic psychiatry, it is also necessary to be conversant with multiple therapeutic techniques, to be a competent primary care physician, a competent psychotherapist with both individuals, groups, and families, a competent psychopharmacologist, a competent neurologist, and a competent advocate.

REFERENCES

1. Arnhoff, F. N., and Lorge, I. Stereotypes about aging and the aged. School Soc., 88:70–71, 1960.
2. Ban, T. The treatment of depressed geriatric patients. Am. J. Psychother., 32:93–104, 1978.
3. Beck, J. D., Ettinger, R. L., Glenn, R. E., et al. Oral health status: Impact on dental student attitudes toward the aged. Gerontologist, 19:580–584, 1979.
4. Bem, S. L. Sex-role adaptability: One consequence of psychological androgyny. J. Pers. Soc. Psychol., 31:634–643, 1975.
5. Bibring, E. Psychoanalysis and the dynamic psychotherapies. J. Am. Psychoanal. Assoc., 2:745–770, 1954.
6. Bing, E. *Six Practical Lessons for an Easier Childbirth*, pp. 36–52. Bantam, New York, 1969.
7. Boll, T. J. Diagnosing brain impairment. In: *Clinical Diagnosis of Mental Disorders*, B. B. Wolman (Ed.), pp. 601–675. Plenum, New York, 1978.
8. Brennan, S. J., and Moravec, J. D. Assessing multidisciplinary continuing education as it

impacts on knowledge, attitudes and behavior in caring for the elderly. Presented at the 31st Annual Meeting of the Gerontological Society, Dallas, Texas, Nov. 19, 1978.
9. Butler, R. N. Successful aging and the role of life review. J. Am. Geriatrics Soc., 12:529–532, 1974.
10. Cherry, D. L., and Zarit, S. H. Sex-role and age difference in competency, flexibility and affective status of women. Presented at the 31st Annual Meeting of the Gerontological Society, Dallas, Texas, Nov. 18, 1978.
11. Cicero. On old age (44 B.C.). In: *Selected Works*, translated by M. Grant, pp. 213–247. Penguin, Baltimore, 1960.
12. Ciompi, L. C. Follow-up studies on evolution of former neurotics and depressive states in old age. Geriatric Psychiatry, 3:90, 1969.
13. Crook, T. H. Psychometric assessment in the elderly. In: *Psychiatric Symptoms and Cognitive Loss in the Elderly. Evaluation and Assessment Techniques*, A. Raskin, and L. J. Jarvik (Eds.), pp. 207–220. Hemisphere, Washington, 1979.
14. Cyrus-Lutz, C. and Gaitz, C. M. Psychiatrists' attitudes toward the aged and aging. Gerontologist, 12:163–167, 1972.
15. David, D. S., and Brannon, R. The male sex role: Our culture's blueprint of manhood and what it's done for us lately. In: *The Forty-Nine Percent Majority: The Male Sex Role*, D. S. David and R. Brannon (Eds.), pp. 1–45. Addison-Wesley, Reading, Mass. 1976.
16. Dias Cordeiro, J. Les états délirants tardifs. Hérédité, biotype, personnalité pré-morbide. Evolution Psychiatrique, 37:331–347, 1972.
17. Duckworth, G. S., and Ross, H. Diagnostic differences in psychogeriatric patients in Toronto, New York, and London, England. Can. Med. Assoc. J., 112:847–849, 851, 1975.
18. Engel, G. L. A psychological setting of somatic disease: The "giving up-given up" complex. Proc. R. Soc. Med., 60:553–555, 1967.
19. Ettinger, R. L., Beck, J., Kerber, P., et al. Dental student confidence in prosthodontics and attitudes toward the elderly. Presented at the 32nd Annual Meeting of the Gerontological Society, Washington, D. C., Nov. 29, 1979.
20. Exton-Smith A. N., and Overstall, P. W. *Geriatrics*, pp. 17–34. University Park Press, Baltimore, 1979.
21. Farrar, D. R., and Miller, R. H. Professional and age related attitudinal conflicts of social workers and lawyers. Presented at the 32nd Annual Meeting of the Gerontological Society, Washington, D. C., Nov. 28, 1979.
22. Festinger, L. *A Theory of Cognitive Dissonance*. Stanford Press, Stanford, Calif., 1957.
23. Folstein, M. F., Folstein, S. E., and McHugh, P. R. "Mini-Mental State": A practical method for grading the cognitive state of patients for the clinician. J. Psychiatr. Res., 12: 189–198, 1975.
24. Ford, C. V., and Sbordone, R. J. Attitudes of psychiatrists toward elderly patients. Am. J. Psychiatry, 137:571–575, 1980.
25. Friedmann, E. A., and Orbach, H. L. Adjustment to retirement. In: *American Handbook of Psychiatry*, Ed. 2, Vol. I, pp. 609–645. S. Arieti (Ed.) Basic Books, New York, 1974.
26. Garfinkel, R. The reluctant therapist 1975. Gerontologist, 15:136–137, 1975.
27. Gatewood, J. W., Organ, C. H. Jr., and Mead, B. T. Mental changes associated with hyperparathyroidism. Am. J. Psychiatry, 132:129–132, 1975.
28. Gillett, N., Levitt, M., and Antonucci, T. The relationship between masculinity, femininity and social competence in three generations of women. Presented at the 30th Annual Meeting of the Gerontological Society, San Francisco, Calif., Nov. 20, 1977.
29. Goldfarb, A. I. Clinical perspectives. In: *Aging in Modern Society*, Psychiatric Research Reports, No. 23, A. Simon and L. J. Epstein (Eds.), pp. 170–178. American Psychiatric Association, Washington, 1968.
30. Goldfarb, A. I. Group therapy with the old and aged. In: *Comprehensive Group Therapy*, H. I. Kaplan, and B. J. Sadock, pp. 623–642. Williams & Wilkins, Baltimore, 1971.
31. Goldfarb, A. I. Minor maladjustments of the aged. In: *American Handbook of Psychiatry*, Ed. 2, Vol. III, S. Arieti and E. B. Brody (Eds.), pp. 820–860. Basic Books, New York, 1974.
32. Guth, R., and Kershaw, A. Family groups—Do they really work in geriatrics? Presented

at the 17th Annual Scientific Day Program, Sheppard and Enoch Pratt Hospital, Towson, Md., June 7, 1980.
33. Gutmann, D., Grunes, J., and Griffin, B. The clinical psychology of later life: Developmental paradigms. Presented at the 32nd Annual Meeting of the Gerontological Society, Washington, D. C., Nov. 29, 1979.
34. Harris, L. *The Myth and Reality of Aging in America*, pp. 145–154. Washington, National Council on the Aging, 1976.
35. Harrison, J. Warning: The male sex role may be dangerous to your health. J. Soc. Issues, 34:65–86, 1978.
36. Hickey, T., Rakowski, W., Hultsch, D. F., et al. Attitudes toward aging as a function of inservice training and practitioner age. J. Gerontol., 31:681–686, 1976.
37. Holmes, T. H., and Rahe, R. H. The social readjustment rating scale. J. Psychosom. Res., 11:213–218, 1967.
38. Hubbard, R. W., Santos, J. F., and Farrow, B. J. Age differences in sex role diffusion. A study of middle aged and older adult married couples. Presented at the 32nd Annual Meeting of the Gerontological Society, Washington, D. C., Nov. 29, 1979.
39. Isaacs, A. D. Geriatric psychiatry. Practitioner, 210:86–95, 1973.
40. Jacobson, E. Progressive Relaxation. University of Chicago Press, Chicago, 1938.
41. Jefferson, J. W. A review of the cardiovascular effects and toxicity of tricyclic antidepressants. Psychosom. Med., 37:160–179, 1975.
42. Johnson, D. M., and Wilhite, M. J. Changes in nursing students' stereotypic attitudes toward old people. Nurs. Res., 25:430–432, 1976.
43. Kantor, S. J., Glassman, A. H., Bigger, J. J. Jr., et al. The cardiac effects of therapeutic plasma concentrations of imipramine. Am. J. Psychiatry, 135:534–538, 1978.
44. Kastenbaum, R. The reluctant therapist. Geriatrics, 18:296–301, 1963.
45. Kay, D. W. K. The epidemiology and identification of brain deficit in the elderly. In: *Cognitive and Emotional Disturbances in the Elderly*, C. Eisdorfer and R. O. Friedel (Eds.), pp. 11–26. Chicago, Year Book Medical Publishers, Chicago, 1977.
46. Kay, D. W. K., Cooper, A. F., Garside, R. F., et al. The differentiation of paranoid from affective psychoses by patients' premorbid characteristics. Br. J. Psychiatry, 129:207–215, 1976.
47. Kayser, J. S., and Minningerode, F. A. Increasing nursing students' interest in working with aged patients. Nurs. Res., 24:23–26, 1975.
48. Kimball, C. P. Psychological aspects of cardiovascular disease. In: *American Handbook of Psychiatry*, Ed. 2, Vol. IV, M F. Reiser (Ed.), pp. 609–617. Basic Books, New York, 1975.
49. Lein, L. Male participation in home life: Impact of social supports and breadwinner responsibility on the allocation of tasks. Fam. Coordinator, 28:489–495, 1979.
50. LeShan, L., and LeShan, E. Psychiatry and the patient with a limited life span. Psychiatry, 24:318–323, 1961.
51. McConnell, S. R. The effects of organizational context on service providers' attitudes toward old people. Presented at the 30th Annual Meeting of the Gerontological Society, San Francisco, Calif., Nov. 20, 1977.
52. McGuinness, A. F., and Knox, S. J. Attitudes to psychogeriatric nursing. Nurs. Times 64 (Suppl.):127–128, 1968.
53. Maier, S. F., and Seligman, M. E. P. Learned helplessness: Theory and evidence. J. Exp. Psychol. Gen., 105:3–46, 1976.
54. Maslow, A. H. *The Farther Reaches of Human Nature*. Viking, New York, 1971.
55. Masters, W. H., and Johnson, V. E. *Human Sexual Response*, pp. 223–270. Little, Brown, Boston, 1966.
56. Masters, W. H., and Johnson, V. E. *Human Sexual Inadequacy*, pp. 57–60. Little, Brown, Boston, 1970.
57. Maxwell, J., and Falzett, B. OK Childing and Parenting. Transactional Institute of El Paso, El Paso, 1974.
58. Mills, J. Attitudes of undergraduate students concerning geriatric patients. Am. J. Occup. Ther., 26:200–203, 1972.
59. Montgomery, D., and Wilkinson, A. Intervention in the organizational environment: Correcting the mismatch between staff attitudes and agencies' activities. Presented at

the 31st Annual Meeting of the Gerontological Society, Dallas, Texas, Nov. 20, 1978.
60. Nathanson, C. A. Sex roles as variables in preventive health behavior. J. Commun. Health, 3:142–155, 1977.
61. Nunn, C., Bergmann, K., Britton, P. G., et al. Intelligence and neurosis in old age. Br. J. Psychiatry, 124:446–452, 1974.
62. Olin, H. S. Psychotherapy of the chronically suicidal patient. Am. J. Psychother., 30:570–575, 1976.
63. Palmore, E. Predictors of successful aging. Gerontologist, 19:427–431, 1979.
64. Parsons, T. *The Social System.* pp. 428–473, Free Press, New York, 1951.
65. Perls, F. *Gestalt Therapy Verbatim.* Real People Press, Lafayette, Calif., 1969.
66. Pfeiffer, E. Sexuality in the aging individual. J. Am. Geriatr. Soc., 22:481–484, 1974.
67. Post, F. The management and nature of depressive illness in late life: A follow-through study. Br. J. Psychiatry, 121:393–404, 1972.
68. Post, F. Psychological aspects of geriatrics. Postgrad. Med. J., 44:307–318, 1968.
69. Redick, R. W., Kramer, M., and Taube, C. A. Epidemiology of mental illness and utilization of psychiatric facilities among older persons. In: *Mental Illness in Later Life*, E. W. Busse and E. Pfeiffer (Eds.), pp. 199–231. American Psychiatric Association, Washington, 1973.
70. Robb, S. S. Attitudes and intentions of baccalaureate nursing students toward the elderly. Nurs. Res., 28:43–50, 1979.
71. Robins, L. N. *Deviant Children Grown Up.* Williams & Wilkins, Baltimore, 1967.
72. Romaniuk, M., Hoyer, F. W., and Romaniuk, J. Helpless self-attitudes of the elderly: The effect of patronizing statements. Presented at the 30th Annual Meeting of the Gerontological Society, San Francisco, Calif., Nov. 20, 1977.
73. Rosow, I. Status and role change through the life span. In: *Handbook of Aging and the Social Sciences*, R. H. Binstock and E. Shanas (Eds.), pp. 457–482. Van Nostrand Reinhold, New York, 1976.
74. Ross, F. Social work treatment of a paranoid personality in a geriatric institution. J. Geriatr. Psychiatry, 6:204–235, 1973.
75. Schmidt, C. W. Jr. Psychiatric problems of the aged. J. Am. Geriatr. Soc., 22:355–359, 1974.
76. Seligman, M. E. P. *Helplessness.* W. H. Freeman, San Francisco, 1975.
77. Shapiro, D. *Neurotic Styles.* Basic Books, New York, 1965.
78. Sheppard, H. L. Work and retirement. In: *Handbook of Aging and the Social Sciences*, R. M. Binstock and E. Shanas (Eds.), pp. 286–309. Van Nostrand Reinhold, New York, 1976.
79. Snyder, S. H., and Yamamura, H. I. Antidepressants and the muscarine acetylcholine receptor. Arch. Gen. Psychiatry, 34:236–239, 1977.
80. Solomon, K. An objection to the use of the term "acting-out." Hosp. Commun. Psychiatry, 27:733, 1976.
81. Solomon, K. Benzodiazepines and neurotic anxiety. Critique. N. Y. State J. Med., 76:2156–2164, 1976.
82. Solomon, K. Social antecedents of learned helplessness in the health care setting. Presented at the 31st Annual Meeting of the Gerontological Society, Dallas, Texas, Nov. 19, 1978.
83. Solomon, K. The development of sterotypes of the elderly: Toward a unified hypothesis. Presented at the 31st Annual Meeting of the Gerontological Society, Dallas, Texas, Nov. 19, 1978.
84. Solomon, K. Social antecedents of learned helplessness of the elderly in the health care settings. In: *Sociological Research Symposium Proceedings (IX)*, E. P. Lewis, L. D. Nelson, D. H. Scully, et al. (Eds.), pp. 188–192. Virginia Commonwealth University, Richmond, 1979.
85. Solomon, K. The development of stereotypes of the elderly: Toward a unified hypothesis. In: *Sociological Research Symposium Proceedings (IX)*, E. P. Lewis, L. D. Nelson, D. H. Scully, et al. (Eds.), pp. 172–177. Virginia Commonwealth University, Richmond, 1979.
86. Solomon, K. The geropsychiatrist and the delivery of mental health services in the community. Presented at the 32nd Annual Meeting of the Gerontological Society, Washington, D. C., Nov. 26, 1979.
87. Solomon, K. Haloperidol and the geriatric patient: Practical considerations. In: *Haloperidol*

Update: 1958–1980, F. J. Ayd, Jr. (Ed.), pp. 155–173. Ayd Medical Communications. Baltimore, 1980.
88. Solomon, K. The depressed patient: Social antecedents of psychopathology in the elderly. J. Am. Geriatr. Soc., in press.
89. Solomon, K. Psychosocial crises of older men. Presented at the 133rd Annual Meeting of the American Psychiatric Association, San Francisco, Calif., May 7, 1980.
90. Solomon, K. The masculine gender role and its implications for the life expectancy of older men. Presented at the 1980 Conference on Prolongation of the Life Span, Mountain Lake, Va., June 30, 1980.
91. Solomon, K. The older man. In *Men in Transition: Changing Male Roles, Theory and Therapy,* K. Solomon and N. B. Levy (Eds.). Plenum, New York, in press.
92. Solomon, K. The masculine gender role: Description. In: *Men in Transition: Changing Male Roles, Theory and Therapy.* K. Solomon and N. B. Levy (Eds.). Plenum, New York, in press.
93. Solomon, K., and Hart, R. Pitfalls and prospects in clinical research on antianxiety drugs: Benzodiazepines and placebo—A research review. J. Clin. Psychiatry, 39:823–831, 1978.
94. Solomon, K., and Vickers, R. Attitudes of health workers toward old people. J. Am. Geriatr. Soc., 27:186–191, 1979.
95. Spence, D. J., Feigenbaum, E. M., Fitzgerald, F., et al. Medical students attitudes toward the geriatric patient. J. Am. Geriatr. Soc., 16:976–983, 1968.
96. Tuckman, J., and Lorge, I. Attitudes toward old people. J. Soc. Psychol., 37:249–260, 1953.
97. Tuckman, J., and Lorge, I. Attitude toward aging of individuals with experiences with the aged. J. Gen. Psychol., 92:199–204, 1958.
98. U'Prichard, D. C., Greenberg, D. A., Sheehan, P. P., et al. Tricyclic antidepressants: Therapeutic properties and affinity for α-noradrenergic receptor biding sites in the brain. Science, 199:197–198, 1978.
99. Weiss, J. A. M. The natural history of antisocial attitudes. What happens to psychopaths? J. Geriatr. Psychiatry, 6:236–242, 1973.
100. Wilson, R. N. *The Sociology of Health: An Introduction,* pp. 13–32. Random House, New York, 1970.
101. Wolff, C. T. Loss, grief, and mourning in adults. In: *Understanding Human Behavior in Health and Illness,* R. C. Simons and H. Pardes (Eds.), pp. 378–386. Williams & Wilkins, Baltimore, 1977.
102. Wolpe, J. *The Practice of Behavior Therapy,* pp. 100–107. Pergamon Press, New York, 1969.
103. York, J., Fergus, E., and Calsyn, R. The implications of staff attitudes for a nursing home mental health training program. Presented at the 28th Annual Meeting of the Gerontological Society, Louisville, Ky., Oct. 28, 1975.
104. Zaks, P. M., Karuza, J. Jr., Domurath, K. L., et al. Sex role orientation across the adult life span. Presented at the 32nd Annual Meeting of the Gerontological Society, Washington, D. C., Nov. 29, 1979.
105. Zubin, J. Failures of the Rorschach technique. J. Proj. Techn., 18:303–315, 1954.

18

PSYCHODYNAMIC ASPECTS OF PERSONALITY DISORDERS

Louis A. Leaff, M.D.

Mode of Presentation

The practicing psychiatrist often finds himself poorly prepared, in terms of his own personality structure, his life's experience, his sociocultural background, his medical training, and his residency training in psychiatry for a particular type of patient, most frequently encountered in the military practice of psychiatry, the prisons, and court and police referrals to local mental health centers or private practitioners. The structured institutions of our society, be they business or public organizations, depending on their rigidity and their authoritarianism, lend themselves to the manipulation of such individuals. I refer here to that group of patients characterized under the rubric of character or personality disorders.

The passage of time brings changes in our nomenclature and possibly, but less clearly so, advances in our understanding. In any case, the individuals referred to were known as the passive-aggressive, emotionally unstable, sociopathic, impulse-ridden, or explosive personalities. With the new DSM III, the groupings have been reformed and called histrionic, narcissistic, antisocial, borderline, avoidant, dependent, compulsive, passive-aggressive and, finally, atypical, mixed, or other personality disorder. The schizoid, schizotypal, and paranoid personalities, I believe, should be considered as a separate category. These individuals are more closely related dynamically and genetically to the schizophrenic disorders and appear to suffer more profoundly disturbed ego defects and object relationships. The schizoid group has been broken into two parts, schizotypal and the schizoid, in an attempt to separate those individuals with "only" defects in their capacities to form social relationships and those individuals whose eccentricities of communication and behavior suggest a relationship with individuals either having or predisposed to chronic schizophrenia. The avoidant personality disorder refers to isolated, seclusive, withdrawn individuals with a defect in the capacity to form social relationships but who do not demonstrate eccentricities of communication, behavior, or thought patterns reportedly characteristic of the schizotypal personality disturbances. The paranoid personality remains, as in the past, with pervasive and long-standing suspiciousness and mistrust. The formal addition of the borderline personality category permits us to officially acknowledge what we have known for some time, i.e., that an individual may demonstrate features of almost any of the diagnostic categories, including the personality disturbances, and may have an underlying personality structure sufficiently fluid and unstable, a predisposition to severe regression with primary process thinking, and sufficiently unstable reality testing that the diagnosis of borderline personality is most appropriate.

Although descriptively placed under different diagnostic labels, e.g., dependent, passive-aggressive, etc., such individuals have more similarities than differences, the manifestations of one personality type blending to a greater or lesser degree with another and the diagnosis being made by the most predominant characterological or behavioral manifestation at the time of evaluation. There is a high family prevalence of antisocial reactions, but no strong evidence to demonstrate that this is gene related, as was once thought to be the case. As shown by Robins study, the best predictors of antisocial reactions in adults are the frequency, severity, and variety of antisocial symptoms of these same patients as children (18).

The extent of the inwardly and outwardly directed destructiveness, the poor impulse control, and the transparent, occasionally desperate manipulations of the environment frequently lead us to believe that we are dealing with someone who is "sicker" than "just another character disorder." Indeed we may suspect such individuals to be latent schizophrenics, and indeed careful evaluation must be conducted so that the differentiation from the borderline personality or schizophrenic syndrome is not missed. Psychological testing, however, for the personality-disordered individual fails to reveal evidence of thought disorder or defective reality testing. Clinical observation reveals the ubiquitous presence of such findings as poor impulse control, a suspicious untrusting orientation toward the world, manipulativeness, disturbed interpersonal interrelationships, high levels of subjective discontent including anxiety and depression, as well as poor self-image. Such individuals present for a variety of reasons, including apparent "classic" neurotic symptomatology. Usually, however, poor work performance, the desire to escape or avoid an unpleasant situation, the desire to extract an undeserved gain, organizational manipulation, etc., brings such individuals into conflict with society. At times symptomatic anxiety, depression, poor or erratic work performance, repeated aggressive behavior, disturbing impulses, or evaluation for legal competency brings them to the attention of the psychiatrist, either because of conflict with or within societal institutions or because they themselves are suffering distress. Even when the complaints are of an apparently neurotic nature, evaluation usually reveals them to be directly related in the individual's mind to a variety of external conditions which he has been unsuccessful in altering. Although the subjective experience of anxiety or depression is dystonic to the patient, the characterologic difficulties which bring him into conflict with the external world are ego syntonic, and the motivation of the patient is not for treatment of the self, psychological insight, or characterologic change, but for environmental manipulation or change, the extraction of something from the environment, and the immediate relief of internal distress. Feelings, both good and bad, are seen as a reflection of environmental difficulties rather than the products of intrapsychic conflict, and solutions are sought in the real world rather than in the self.

Childhood Patterns—"The Typical Story"

The childhood histories of these patients are characteristic in their general outline. Almost uniformly they come from grossly disturbed family settings. In contrast to the covert, long-standing "subtle sicknesses" which are found in the history of neurotics and some schizophrenic and borderline personalities, the severe character disorder comes from a home which had obvious disruption. For example, parents were separated or divorced; there was overbrutality from the father towards the children; one or both parents were alcoholics; there were frequent moves or job changes; and the parents fought openly and left for varying periods of time. Recollections of childhood neuropathic patterns are not usually remarkable, with the exception that acting out and socially disruptive behaviors began early. Subjective unhappiness as a youngster is a frequent recollection. Hostility was expressed in subtle and not so subtle ways towards the parents, for example, the child who, apparently without conscious awareness, micturated during the night in such a way as to soil parental property and evoke a punitive response.

Adolescence characteristically ushered in the onset of the antisocial and disruptive behaviors. The peer groups chosen by the patient for identification were the "actor-outers" and the "obstructionists." Repeated disciplinary difficulties with school authorities, expulsion, truancy, poor motivation, failures, late hours, frequent fights, reckless driving, drinking, and encounters with the police are the usual story. Alcohol and drug abuse in today's culture is almost ubiquitous. Repeated failures occurred in meeting societal expectations—school, job, and stable family responsibility. Open conflict in adolescence erupts and intensifies between the child and parents as the failures, legal entanglements, lack of employment, irresponsibility, and antisocial behaviors are laid at the feet of the parents by the community. The child sees the parents as controlling, suppressive, and interfering. After some parental expectation has not been met (e.g., failure in a job or at college), or after repeated failure and frustration at getting along in society and in the parental home, a desperate effort is made to get away from conflict with the parents, and the adolescent enlists in the military, precipitously leaves to be married, or in some other fashion extricates himself from the parental household. Occasionally, the choice of enlistment in the military or prison is offered to the individual by the court. The adolescent chooses the former only to find the inconsistent and intolerable authority of the parents replaced by the even more intolerable authority of the military, or the structure and expectations of a job or marital relationship. After leaving home, the sought for relief is not found as the individual finds himself in other structured situations. Conflict with authority seems inevitably to arise, and the complaint is heard, "It's just like home, only worse. I need freedom. I can't stand being caged in. I can't stand people messing over me all the time." In the military, for example, repeated disciplinary difficulties ensue, following a brief "honeymoon" which may occur after enlistment. Thus, with disciplinary action pending, with high levels of subjective discomfort, and frequently after a "suicide attempt," a characterologically disturbed individual becomes a psychiatric patient. Similar series of events occur in civilian practice as such individuals are "sentenced" to therapy by judges, probation officers, or enforced referral by employers or schools. Whether in an inpatient setting or in group or individual outpatient psychotherapy, however, very shortly complaints are heard of the intolerability of the therapeutic setting, and the patient becomes provocative, acts out, and plays one individual against another. The expectations of having been saved from one intolerable situation are, characteristically, resolved for the individual, only to find himself in another "intolerable situation," this time psychotherapy, characterized by structure and some sort of implied or real authority.

Dynamic Aspects

In deviant children growing up, Robins found that the age of onset of antisocial behavior patterns was before 15 years and usually before 12 (18). In general, certain childhood antisocial symptoms reliably predicted adult antisocial reaction. These included theft, incorrigibility (extreme disobedience), school truancy, running away from home overnight, having associates with bad reputations, staying out late, physical aggression, poor employment record, impulsiveness, reckless and irresponsible behavior, nocturnal enuresis, lack of guilt, and pathologic lying. It is of importance, as will become clearer later as we discuss ego functioning and general dynamic aspects, that in Robins' study there were significant nonantisocial symptoms in the same group. These symptoms include: enuresis, sleepwalking, sleeptalking, irritability, nail biting, poor eating, oversensitiveness, being withdrawn and seclusive, odd ideas, unhappiness, depression, tics, and fears.

In working with severely personality-disordered patients the psychiatrist comes to recognize that in contrast with the neurotic, whose symptomatology results primarily from intrapsychic conflict, the diagnostic psychopathology of the character disorder results from rigid, syntonic personality traits and patterns. Underlying these defensive, relatively nonadaptive personality patterns, however, are a variety of defective or infantile ego functions which have precluded autonomy and mature identity. Developmental failures have resulted in such ego deficiencies as poor impulse control, defective object relations, intolerance of affect, unstable identifications, and superego lacunae.

The characterologically disordered patient does not regress to psychosis, as does the borderline patient. However, just as the neurotic may be considered to suffer from impaired reality testing in circumscribed areas (e.g., the phobic), the characterologically disordered patient also suffers from distortions of reality testing in the sense that they are colored by his own intense needs and distorted by his own internal conflicts. He is not, however, with the possible exception of extreme affective storm, out of contact with reality in the same sense as the psychotic. However, because of primary developmental deficiencies and relatively fixed ego syntonic character traits, modified treatment programs are required. Interpretation, defense analysis, or conflict resolution cannot be expected to be successful unless the opportunity for ego growth (maturation, support, education, stable identification, repair of the defect) is also provided. Identification with the therapist is a gradual but essential part of such growth and maturation. Experience with a consistent compassionate individual whose primary purpose is to understand and yet who is also firm is essential. Conversion of long-standing syntonic personality patterns into dystonic alien modes is accomplished by repeated confrontations with the pathological nature, rigidity, maladaptiveness, and ultimate masochism and self-suffering induced by these patterns. At the same time, alternative coping mechanisms and maneuvers must be presented to the patient along with a stable figure for identification and opportunities for ego growth and maturation.

The ego deficits in the individuals who are categorized in DSM III under the rubric of personality disorders comprise a broad spectrum of type and severity of ego and superego pathology. For example, the histrionic personality may be relatively well compensated at a fairly high level of functioning with productive work and interpersonal relationships. Although affect is frequently intensely expressed, it is possible to form a working alliance which will endure. Even such entities as the narcissistic and borderline personality disorders are frequently sufficiently stable in terms of their defensive patterns, characterologic integrity, and relatedness to the environment, and primitive defenses and primary process thinking are sufficiently modulated so that such individuals are quite suitable candidates for insight-oriented psychotherapy. In fact, intensive one-to-one therapy of such patients may be the only hope of providing enduring characterologic change and concomitant ego growth as compared with the palliative and at times disruptive effects of medication.

With the personality disorders as they are now classified, it is best to undertake an initial assessment of the overall functioning and level of integration of the personality, regardless of the diagnostic label (8), in order to decide which approach is most appropriate for a given patient. For example, a hysterical personality disorder may have primarily oedipal level problems and associated defenses, albeit carrying along more primitive conflicts of an oral nature, whereas another individual with the same diagnostic label and superficial clinical symptoms will have core conflicts centered around issues of a developmentally much earlier time with associated unmodulated impulses and more primitive defenses. The treatment of these two individuals would be quite different. The ego deficits within each of these diagnostic categories may thus represent a spectrum in type and severity of pathology, as it may between different categories. For example, the compulsive individual and the antisocial individual are usually poles apart in terms of superego structure and integration, as well as in terms of ego defenses, modes of adaptation, and object relationships. The treatment implications are quite different. In speaking of the severe or "low level" (8) personality disorder or the so called impulse ridden, impulsive, or explosive personality, whatever other label is applied, we have a somewhat typical picture. The self-image is poor to varying degrees. In spite of apparently successful environmental manipulation, such individuals repeatedly engage in behaviors which eventuate in failure, punishment, or self-destruction. Such is the case because of an inadequately developed and integrated superego which is excessively harsh and rigid in some areas and absent or defective in others, permitting the apparently conflict-free expression of rather primitive impulses and behaviors.

Such individuals use manipulation and "putting something over" as a means of expressing power, maintaining or restoring self-esteem, and expressing anger, contempt, and devaluation (3). Typically, however, the self-image is poor to varying degrees. Their poor self-image, low self-esteem, and disturbed identifications carry them into dangerous, reckless, and destructive situations. Although there may be verbalized a superficially grandiose image of the self, when such individuals are engaged in a therapeutic relationship it soon becomes apparent that the underlying self-representation is of being "bad" or worthless, and is frequently stated in terms of having injured, harmed, or disappointed the important figures in their lives. A not uncommon statement is of being worth more dead (insurance, out of the way, to free the parents or world of the burden and suffering which they induced) than alive to their families. Existing alongside the poor self-images, however, are infantile feelings of entitlement—of having been injured, harmed, deprived, neglected, and hence entitled to recompense. Thus feelings of grandiosity and entitlement frequently coexist with a sense of inner worthlessness. Hand in hand with such feelings of entitlement are omnipotent expectations, both in terms of what can be gotten from the environment and of their own ability to get it. The primitive intensity of the need and the infantile expectations undermine the development of autonomous ego functions, object relationships, adaptive ego mechanisms and, ultimately, sublimatory channels. Aggressive impulses are poorly modulated and integrated into the personality, and aggressive outbursts may be common, either as a characterologic formation or directly when other characterologic defenses fail. Based on early developmental experiences, negative expectations are the rule. Positive feelings, good intentions, and friendly behaviors by others are perceived with suspicion. Such "friendly" relationships are tested, until the hostile, destructive expectations which are feared are elicited from the environment. Object relationships are also defective. Individuals are frequently related to in terms of what they can provide—and what can be gotten out of them. Such essentially narcissistic relationships represent a primitive way of maintaining self-esteem; however, they eventuate in seeing people for what they do and give, rather than for what they are. On the other hand, someone, frequently of the opposite sex, may be selected as a loving object who is maintained as "good," who is idealized, and who is actively clung to in spite of overt abuse and infidelity. For example: "She's the only good thing that ever happened to me. I have to hold onto her no matter what it costs me." Ambivalence has not developed to the degree where positive and negative feelings and attitudes can be combined toward the same object. Consequently, individuals must be experienced as all good or all bad (the defense of splitting). As a result of such a defensive posture, attitudes toward the same object may shift rapidly without apparent subjective contradiction or may be steadfastly clung to in spite of the dictates of external reality.

The severely personality-disordered patient demonstrates nonspecific manifestations of ego weakness which are most readily conceptualized in the terminology of Kernberg, namely (a) lack of anxiety tolerance, (b) lack of impulse control, and (c) lack of developed subliminatory channels. The presence of specific ego deficits, viz., of some degree of lack of differentiation of self- and object images, the blurring of ego boundaries, the presence of primary process thinking, and the periodic loss of reality testing under stress must be evaluated and diagnostic determination made, i.e., whether one is dealing with an individual whose primary problem is characterologic or one whose difficulties should properly be considered in the diagnostic area of borderline personality organization. Both diagnoses may coexist, depending on the level of integration of the personality organization. In Kernberg's formulation (8) he divides character disorders into "high level" and "low level" organizations. Essentially the differentiation is according to the degree to which repressive mechanisms or splitting mechanisms predominate. In Kernberg's schema, many infantile personalities, most narcissistic personalities, and almost all clear-cut antisocial personalities fall into the category of borderline personality organization. Kernberg views the hysterical personality as a middle range actually reaching into the typical borderline field and the narcissistic personality as a typical low level character disorder. In terms of descriptive psychopathology, the lower and some middle level character disorders would correspond to our conceptualization of the severe personality disorder and would include individuals whose character pathology is severe, represented by chaotic and impulse-ridden characterologic structures, in contrast to the classic reaction formation types of character structure and the milder "avoidance trait" characters. If the ego and its defenses are primitive, its habitual character will be primitive as well.

Initially, character traits were classified in terms of the original impulses, i.e., perpetuations of the original impulse, sublimations of them, or reactions against them. Reactive character traits, which were considered pathologic, were divided into avoidance (phobic) and reaction formations. Later Fenichel (5) and Reich (17) provided a classification of character types according to reactive type, character defenses against anxiety, narcissistic character, anal character traits, oral character traits, phallic character traits, and character defenses against the superego. The reactive type resulted in a personality which seemed contradictory to the original drive, e.g., passivity as a defense against underlying rage. Character defenses against anxiety could include almost any characterologic formation including counter-phobic attitudes, identification with the aggressor, turning passivity into activity, etc. Narcissistic characters are in conflict over early oral impulses and fears. Such individuals attempt to enhance self-esteem and recapture early omnipotence through idealization and devaluation. Those with the so-called anal character traits are in fear of the expression of uncontrolled affects or impulses. In the obsessive-compulsive personality, traits of resistance and obedience coexist, e.g., neatness and compliance with underlying stubborness and negativism representing the struggle within the superego. Oral characters are dependent on external sources of narcissistic gratification in order to maintain self-esteem. Such sources are necessary for a sense of omnipotent protection and comfort. Phallic character disorders described by Reich (17) are individuals who are vain, insensitive, and daredevilish, compensating for both castration fears and narcissistic need on an oral level. Masochistic personalities, moral masochists, the fate neuroses, and individuals who are criminals because of an unconscious sense of guilt reflect character defenses against the superego. The antisocial personality demonstrates not only weakness of conscience and other superego defects but also defects in terms of ego integration as well (14).

Because of the defects in the ego integration in any of the categories of the severe personality disorder, repression may not be the major mechanism of defense or when it is operative may not be as effective as it is in the neurotic because of an inadequately structuralized ego. In contrast to the borderline, however, the ego defects in personality disorders, whatever their nosologic category, have defensive elements which provide identity and stability, which prevent the ego from undergoing psychotic regression, and which are at least partially effective in compromising internal and external demands. Albeit rigid, hypertrophied, or defective, they enable the individual to maintain contact with his reality.

Everyone has a personality structure which must enter into a treatment relationship. The neurotic, with a reasonably stable and adaptive character structure, gives evidence of a reasonably well-integrated ego and superego, of a greater proportion of conflict-free ego function and structure, and of the predominance of oedipal level conflicts. The sexual conflicts of the so called "good" hysterical personality (20) represent much more genital than pregenital conflicts. As stated previously, however, the characterologic picture of the hysterical personality, or any personality disorder, may be present, and the core conflicts may be of a more primitive infantile nature, i.e., pregenital with, for example, oral needs and defenses predominating (albeit colored by and coexisting with later higher level defenses and personality traits). In the less integrated version of a given personality-disordered patient, there is a reduced capacity for stable object relationships, a relative lack of repression, and the existence of primitive aggression and sexuality. Infantile needs show through and the need for a child like "orality" or "dependency" of a more demanding aggressive kind than that seen in the patient with a better developed or more stable ego structure also shows through. Such early, primitive fixations and conflicts will be reflected in the history, e.g., nature of object relationships, work history, developmental history, love relationships, etc., and it is imperative that formulation be established both according to the descriptive diagnosis in terms of DSM III, but equally important in terms of the dynamics of the personality structure itself, in order to make possible a treatment approach which will not end in frustration and/or disaster for patient and therapist.

The at times seemingly extreme narcissism and the subtle and at times dramatic masochism of the severe characterologically disturbed patient present problems in treating, as well as understanding, such patients. Kernberg (10) and Kohut (12) have provided us not only with descriptive refinement as regards the narcissistic personality but also a framework, albeit respectively different, for understanding and invaluable approaches and technical refinements to treatment techniques. Although there is overlap, Kernberg and Kohut may well be addressing different patient groups (19).

Kernberg addresses the similarity of the defensive organization with narcissistic personalities and borderline conditions (10), i.e., a predominance of splitting resulting in clinical symptoms of grandiosity, clinically coexisting with feelings of inferiority. The splitting mechanisms are maintained by primitive defenses of projection, projective identification, idealization, and devaluation. Oral conflicts, oral aggression, and pregenital needs override, although they may be condensed with genital manifestations. According to Kernberg the distinction between a narcissistic personality structure and the borderline relates to a specific primitive structuralized intrapsychic relationship, namely, a pathologic grandiose self, condensed with the real self, the ideal self, and the ideal object (11). The idealized self is manifested by fantasies and self-images of greatness, power, magnificence, beauty, etc., compensating for severe early (oral) deprivation, rage, and envy. The idealized object is manifested clinically by the fantasies of all-giving, all-nurturing, totally loving parental objects. Kernberg adopts Kohut's term "grandiose self" to express this pathologic self structure (it must be kept in mind that narcissistic personalities, as well as other personality classifications, may function on a borderline level wherein the narcissistic defenses do not provide sufficiently to maintain a stable ego integration). The disagreement between Kohut and Kernberg revolves around whether the origin of the grandiose self reflects fixation at an archaic although normal stage of development of the primitive self (Kohut), or whether the pathologic structure described above is quite different from normal infantile narcissism. Kohut concentrates on developmental difficulties and arrests and what he considers to be a separate line of narcissistic development and stresses the difference between this category and character neuroses in which regressive compensatory narcissistic or grandiose defenses are employed against conflicts involving parental objects. Although the descriptive clinical picture of narcissistic personality such as provided by Kernberg and Kohut seemingly are the same or similar, they may actually be talking about different patient groups on a deeper level (19). Again we have confirmation of the need for greater precision or subdivision within the category of personality disorder as discussed above, as there will be important implications in terms of treatment technique.

Kernberg describes patients who demonstrate narcissistic defenses against disturbances in early parental relationships. Kohut concentrates on developmental difficulties and arrests and what he considers to be a separate line of narcissistic development (12). These patients evidence object relationships, called by Kohut self-object, in which other persons exist principally to serve some purpose of the self, either to reflect its greatness, perform some function, or supply something needed for the perfection of the self. Such individuals show wide swings in their self-esteem based on seemingly minor provocation and complain of a sense of emptiness and lack of direction. There may be disturbances in their sense of self, their sense of time, space, or even somatic continuity leading to somatic complaints. The treatment techniques and strategies are quite divergent. Kohut aims at the establishment of a full narcissistic transference, what he calls the "mirror transference," which reflects the patient's grandiose self. He feels that this transference development permits the completion of a normal process that has been arrested and permits a growth from primitive to mature narcissism. Kernberg strongly opposes the noninterpretation of the patient's grandiosity with the implication of its underlying envy and rage. He believes that such an approach hinders the working through of the pathologic grandiose self (10). Probably Kernberg's sharpest criticism of Kohut lies in the latter's relating narcissistic manifestations to libidinal conflicts and disregarding aggression. In Kernberg's view both the positive as well as the negative transference must be addressed. Some feel, however, that Kernberg is addressing a fundamentally different population of cold, aloof, paranoid-schizoid individuals with great amounts of projected rage.

In working with severely characterologically disturbed individuals it seems that both issues must be addressed and both processes may occur perhaps simultaneously; namely, underlying primitive aggression and rage as well as disappointment in early parental objects, inner frustration, and emptiness. Devaluation and grandiosity manifested in the transference as well as in actual behavior must be addressed. At the same time, however, in addition to conflict resolution it seems likely that there is a process of structure building, ego growth, superego growth and maturation, defense modification and growth, and to some degree repair of structural deficits wherein identification with the empathic therapist goes hand in hand with interpretation, understanding, and affect integration. This would be a "corrective growth experience" in the best sense of the term.

The at times seemingly extreme narcissism and the subtle and at times dramatic masochism of the severe characterologically disturbed patient present problems in treating, as well as understanding, such patients.

Perhaps in terms of their narcissistic aspects, certain severe personality-disordered patients remind us of the classically described sociopath. Without apparent guilt, they control, exploit, and manipulate. Superego reactions do occur; however, because of the unintegrated and uneven development, the superego may be unusually harsh and masochistically color an entire life. In terms of their narcissistic development, such individuals may be "charmers" with a great need for attention (often passed off on themselves as love) from others. They may, however, be manipulators whose interest is primarily again in terms of their own needs and the maintenance of their own narcissistic integrity. Empathy does not truly exist and life without a steady input of narcissistic supplies (exciting activity which may gain attention, admiration, etc.) results in feelings of inner emptiness, loneliness, isolation (often described subjectively as depression), grandiose fantasizing, somatic symptomatology or preoccupation, disturbances in sense of time or person, or feelings of panic. In spite of their extreme need for external supplies, such patients are in conflict. Their earlier experience with the harsh, inconsistent, and/or depriving figures of their childhood has colored their subsequent expectations of the world, so that they are unable to truly trust and depend, and they view others with suspicion, distrust, envy, and greed.

The depressive-masochistic pattern varies from the mild to severe personality-disordered patients. For example, the masochistic traits may represent an acting out of unconscious guilt over oedipal conflicts essentially reflecting a well-structured superego. In the severe personality disorder, however, there is sexualization of masochistic needs and poor control of aggression. The superego may not be well-differentiated, and there may be a relative inability to experience guilt in some areas while the superego may be overly rigid, harsh, and punitive in other sectors with subsequent masochistic and self-destructive acting out. Preoedipal conflicts predominate in these patients with the result that there is primitive fusion and defusion of aggressive and sexual impulses. In other words, the extreme aggression arising from early conflicts and deprivations colors subsequent triangular (oedipal) and postoedipal development, contaminating and aggressivizing both the structure of the ego as well as interpersonal relationships.

In order to differentiate psychotic, borderline, and neurotic patients, one must look at the state of the ego. Psychotics have a severe lack of ego development with mostly undifferentiated self and object images and a concomitant lack of development of ego boundaries. Borderline patients have a better integrated ego than psychotics, with differentiation between self and object images to a major extent, and with a development of firm ego boundaries in all but areas of close interpersonal involvement; they present, typically, the syndrome of identity diffusion. Neurotic patients present a strong ego, with complete separation between self and object images, and concomitant delimitation of the ego boundaries. Because of the history of extreme frustrations and intense aggression during the early lives of our severely personality-disordered patients, excessive pregenital aggression tends to be projected and cause a paranoid distortion of the early parental images. In both sexes, excessive development of pregenital aggression tends to induce a premature development of oedipal strivings, and as a consequence, a particular pathological condensation between pregenital and genital aims under the overriding influence of aggressive needs (11). A common outcome is the presence of several of the pathological compromise formations, which give rise to a typical persistence of polymorphous, perverse sexual traits. All of these pathologic solutions are unsuccessful attempts to deal with the aggressiveness of genital trends and the general infiltration of all instinctual needs by aggression.

In spite of the obvious overlapping and shared characteristics of the borderline personality, as described by various authors, and the severely disabled personality disorder, this differentiation depends, I believe, for practical purposes, on the ability of the individual to maintain a rather stable delineation between self and object and to identify demands of reality, although he may not, for one reason or another, be able to adapt to them or cope with them. Such a distinction may at times appear to be hairsplitting; however, it is a frequent occurrence for the psychiatrist to be called on to give testamentary evaluation of the ability of a particular patient to distinguish external reality, e.g., whether or not the patient is or was psychotic in a particular situation.

The severely personality-disordered patient has had to deal with premature object relationships of an extremely libidinized and aggressive nature. This leads to the persistence of early introjects and the reliance on such primitive defensive operations as splitting, projection, and denial. The all-good or all-bad introjects subvert superego development, tending toward the formation of an excessively harsh superego on the one hand, and overly idealized ego ideal images on the other. Because of the disturbance in superego integration and a primitive ego defensive structure, there may result projection of the demanding and prohibiting aspects of superego. The normal ego-integrating pressures of the superego are inconsistent or absent as well as the capacity of the ego to experience guilt or perhaps a subjectively different quality to that experience. The devaluation of significant parental images prevents the internalization of some of the most important sources of ego as well as superego formation and interferes with the internalization of realistic demands from parental images as well as the internalization of stable regulation of self-esteem, the basic capacities for trust and relationships uncontaminated by rage, fear, mistrust, guilt, suspicion, suspiciousness, and devaluation. There is a shallowness to the emotional reactions of the severely characterologically disturbed patients, as well as an incapacity to form deep interpersonal relationships. The defective superego development and the relative lack of ego integration and maturation also prevent these patients from recognizing or identifying with the more mature and differentiated aspects of other people's personalities. Such fixation on archaic object relationships and the intense rage involved precludes the smooth flow of subsequent personality development, whether viewed from the side of the drives, from the aspect of self-worth (narcissism), from relationships with others (object relations), or from rigidity of personality patterns (personality disorders). Superficially, they may appear quite "sociable" but their relationships are severely infiltrated with aggression. There is either overt or covert exploitiveness, demandingness, and manipulation of others without consideration of the other individual's needs. There is the need to manipulate others, corresponding to the defensive needs to keep control over the environment in order to prevent more primitive paranoid fears connected with the projection of aggressive self and object images from coming to the surface.

The presence of contradictory introjections and identifications gives, at times, an almost "as if" quality to these patients. All of this represents what Erikson has called "identity diffusion"; namely, the lack of an integrated self-concept and an integrated and stable concept of total objects in relationship with self (16). Such a tendency to reenact partial identifications which may be nearly dissociated is not seen in the less severe character pathology or the neurotic patient, and is a direct consequence of the act of splitting of those introjections and identifications whose synthesis normally would bring about a stable ego identity.

On psychological testing, such patients may demonstrate disturbances of sexual identity and a lack of the usual predominance of heterosexual genital strivings over the polymorphous drives. What appears as a chaotic combination of the preoedipal and oedipal strivings may be a reflection of pathologic condensation. All of these pathological solutions are unsuccessful attempts to deal with the aggressiveness of genital trends and the general infiltration of all instinctual needs by aggression. There tends to be present an identity diffusion. This diffusion, however, has earlier and more complex sources than a simple lack of differentiation of any particular sexual definition but is a combination of several strong fixations of pregenital origin.

The character disorder frequently presents with symptoms of an apparently neurotic nature. The question often arises as to whether he is feigning the symptoms to avoid some unpleasant consequence or is indeed a "neurotic." Particularly striking may be the transiency of the symptomatology which evaporates when the particular environmental crisis is over. The lifestyle of the character-disordered patient is not like that of the neurotic. The neurotic has internalized his infantile conflicts and achieved an internal, but pathological resolution through symptom formation. The severely character disordered patient has not sufficiently introjected or identified with his infantile objects to create a stable intrapsychic sense of self and others. Conflict is dealt with by externalizing one aspect of the struggle and fighting the battle with the environment. For example, feelings of guilt are dealt with in terms of having been wronged by someone. Conflict has not been sufficiently internalized to consider the problem neurotic in the usual sense of the term. Such individuals have survived by becoming adapted to the inconsistent, hostile, rejecting world of their childhood. That adaptation, however, was at the price of a rigidity of ego-integrative and adaptive functions, fixations at primitive defensive levels, and subsequent developmental distortions.

The literature on the severely disturbed characterological patient tends to be scattered and marked by generalizations as to the origins of the problems. For example, some authors focus primarily on superego pathology, others on faulty identifications and introjections of childhood, some on a narcissism and similarities with the borderline, and still others on the descriptive clinical picture without attempted explanations of differing constellations of symptom patterns. The at time close approximation of the personality-disordered patient to that of the schizophrenic is made by several authors. Clinically, I believe the determination must be made on the dynamic evaluation of each patient. It is quite possible that heredity may predispose an individual to pathologic difficulty, e.g., unusually high or low stimulus barriers, level of autonomic reactivity, generalization of stimuli, and general quality and availability of other inborn autonomous ego functions, so that the infant may have greater difficulty extracting its needs from a less than optimum expectable environment. The characterological patterns which we observe in the adult have definite hierarchical and structural relationships and derivations from the primitive instinctualized relationships of childhood. Structure is used in the sense of an organized relationship among the functions and agencies of the mind which develops over time and achieves stability. Psychic structures exist on a continuum of complexity from simple perception, feeling, or cognition, to highly complex adaptive characterologic organizations which are relatively fixed and autonomous. Characterological groupings are not in themselves pathological. Although at times maladaptive, they may be viewed as maintaining the ego organization in a constructive sense. In considering the pathogenicity of defensive and characterological patterns, one must consider inappropriateness, chronology, weakness, or strength in relation to the drives; generalization; inappropriateness in regard to reality situation; severe disturbance of object relations; the combination and entanglement of defense mechanisms with instinctual gratification; superego demands and their defenses leading to masochism; or lack of superego demand resulting in impulsive action (15). Of great importance in respect to the pathogenicity of defenses are their pervasive involvement and relationship with character, object relations, and drive derivatives. Such relationships must be understood in the developmental contextual significance of each individual before adaptive and pathological aspects of characterological patterns can be understood.

It may well be that generalization in terms of pinpointing an exact stage in the development of the ego where a developmental "turning point" for the future sociopath, impulse ridden character, etc., occurs may not be possible. It appears clinically that the severity of the ego pathology of such individuals and, hence, their closeness or remoteness from the schizophrenic disorders, depends on the severity of the trauma, the earliness of occurrence, and inborn perceptual and adaptive capacities. Clinically, pathology may be traced along the lines of development of internalized object relations. The differentiation from the borderline personality who may present with various characterologic manifestations as an attempt to maintain internal stability must be made. The characterologically disordered patient, although he may be chaotic, reckless, and impulsive, does not regress to psychosis as does the borderline patient, nor does he lose the ability to distinguish external and internal realties (14). The characterologically disordered patient also experiences distortions of reality testing to the extent that his perceptions are colored by his own needs and distorted by his own internal conflicts during times of stress, anxiety, or conflict. According to Kernberg (11) the borderline patient is characterized by the splitting of the self representation. The narcissistic patient does not do this but is able to maintain a differentiation of self and object images, i.e., a stable ego boundary because of the pathologic internal structures in the form of a grandiose self, devalued image of self and others, intense oral sadism, and nonintegrated sadistic forerunners. Devaluation of aggressive, depriving, or sadistic parents results in impaired superego structure in terms of values, value systems, and ego ideal.

The behavioral and descriptive manifestations of the various personality disorders may be identical; however, the underlying level of personality integration, defensive organization, and potential for growth may vary widely. Hence, it is essential that not only a careful descriptive but dynamic and structural assessment of the individual's particular ego strengths and weaknesses be made. For example, with the antisocial personality we may have an individual who is essentially neurotic and a "criminal out of a sense of guilt," another individual whose underlying personality structure is essentially narcissistic and whose antisocial exploits give him a sense of well-being and aliveness, and a third individual who may be demonstrating the breakthrough of primitive and unmodulated impulses in a borderline or psychotic personality structure. The treatment implications for each of these individuals would be quite different.

Children with severe deprivation in the very first months of life may develop a superficial, nonpsychotic adaptation to reality. They may be quite skilled in the manipulation of interpersonal relations. In the less fortunate individual, whether because of weaknesses of inborn capacities, insufficient stimulation and gratification, or some combination of these, the establishment of basic trust and differentiation of self and object is tenuous at best, and autistic psychosis or extremely strong predisposition to later psychotic regression occurs (9, 16).

From the 6th to 8th month, the infant recognizes the mother and searches for her. From 6 months to approximately 1½ years, the idealization of the mother as the all-good object is used defensively against the "all-bad" mother of frustration. The development of this mechanism of splitting and separation of polar opposites (good self-good object image; bad self-bad object image), along with the mechanism of projection, becomes part of normal development. The relationship with the good object may thus be maintained in the face of frustration and inconsistency, protecting the self from otherwise possibly overwhelming love and hatred. The persistence of splitting, however, as a central defensive mechanism along with the complementary use of projection are found in borderline patients and many patients with severe characterological problems, particularly those with an intolerance of affect. The stimulation of an intense affect, e.g., anger, challenges a defensive structure which has already failed to neutralize or sublimate a great amount of early aggression, except through the defensive dissociation and splitting of self and object images. This defensive organization attempts to separate love and hate with subsequent projection. This same defensive constellation in the case of psychoses is a protection against fear of engulfment and annihilation (10, 16). Kernberg believes that these particular pathological internalized object relations determine the borderline personality organization. He also includes several types of severe character pathology, e.g., impulse neuroses, addictions, narcissistic personalities, and some infantile and most antisocial personalities as using predominantly this defensive organization.

Manifestations of ego weakness bring about the persistence of primitive emotions with lack of impulse control. Contradictory self and object images, defective superego integration and control, superego lacunae and corruptability, inability to integrate good and bad self object representations, inability to integrate, neutralize, or successfully sublimate sexual or aggressive impulses except through rigid characterological patterns, and a paucity of adaptive mechanisms lead to a rigid, narrow, relatively fixed variety of behavioral patterns, available to deal with the environment or the self. The result under stress is the increasing use of available patterns in what is frequently an inappropriate, maladaptive, or self-destructive manner. With the complete breakdown of such rigid characterological patterns, regression to projection, rage, and impulsive action with attack on the environment or the self may occur.

Although the severely character-disordered patient may have a strong tendency to splitting and rigid nonflexible characterological adaptive patterns, this is a matter of degree. Development is an uneven matter and, although one or another may predominate, generally genital and oedipal conflicts may be found coexisting side by side with pregenital conflicts. The former tend to produce patterns which, although constricting, do not tend to as seriously impair social functioning. The point is that in the treatment of the seriously disturbed characterologic patient, neurotic conflicts (hysterical, obsessive-compulsive, depressive, etc.) will also be found and will have to be dealt with. These healthier aspects of functioning not only increase the patient's adaptive capacities in a relative sense, but also make possible a degree of therapeutic alliance and self-observation which must occur if therapy is to become possible and the more primitive characterological and defensive structures modified.

Depression is a frequent complaint and often the subjective factor which propels the patient with severe characterological problems into the psychiatrist's office. It is, therefore, of some importance to elucidate the dynamic issues involved in the understanding of this depression, for its recognition and successful handling may greatly enhance the chances of establishing rapport and a therapeutic alliance. The classic concept of the depressive constellation relates to the loss of an object of great narcissistic importance. The ambivalent emotions, particularly aggression, become directed against the internalized object through the agency of the superego. The emotions involved are of loss, guilt, and low self-esteem. The importance of the early introjected objects has been stressed in the preceding discussion of the development and dynamic understanding of the severely characterologically disturbed patient. These introjected objects, particularly the mother, play an essential role in determining the defensive and adaptive structure of the individual. An extremely important component of the developing psychic organization is the affects, i.e., the complex internal "feeling states" which relate both to immediate stimulating factors and their intrapsychic representations, integrated and evaluated along lines of past experience. This affective evaluation occurs along many vectors simultaneously, e.g., danger, trauma, safety, pleasure-unpleasure, self-esteem, guilt, shame, etc., and is the ongoing unconscious perception of an affect signal which evaluates the state of the ego and the self. Defensive operations set in motion by affect signals are ultimately designed to maintain the affective state of well-being and safety (13). The feeling states associated with early introjects (good self-bad self) are the polar foci around which psychic structure organizes. Subsequent self-representations are superimposed on the earlier identifications and primitive self-images.

Characterologic patients may present with a clearly depressed mood and low self-esteem but without evidence of clear-cut or recent object loss. To some extent, these "depressions" can be explained on the basis of negative self-representations, poorly integrated and often sadistic superego components, and a relative paucity of stable adaptive mechanisms necessary to establish rewarding and empathic object relationships.

Such "depressions," somatic symptomatology, and dissociations in terms of time, space, and body must also be understood in terms of the narcissistic fixations of such patients. Frustration and lack of gratification are met not only with rage and action-oriented behavior patterns, but also with feelings of impotence, helplessness, and emptiness often described as depression. Such reactions may become apparent when mechanisms of grandiosity and devaluation break down or undermine the treatment. In addition, good feelings are often related to the continual input of narcissistic supplies from the environment. Interference with these supplies, whether in terms of a complete restriction of the characterologic patterns or a decrease in the narcissistic return for whatever reason, leads to feelings of emptiness, loneliness, and depression. Such reactions thus must inevitably arise in the course of psychotherapeutic treatment. The lack of rewarding introjects makes impossible or tenuous at best the stable internal maintenance of self-esteem. The depressions frequently seen differ in that the loss involved does not depend on threat of abandonment by the object, but from the individual's own wish to give up the object. The wish to separate is perceived intrapsychically as an expression of hostile and destructive impulses toward the object. The result may be the clinical picture of rage, with impulsive attempts to break away, alternating with the seemingly contradictory picture of masochistic submission and depression. The self-concept is that of worthlessness, weakness, and helplessness. Idealization, grandiosity, and devaluation may be seen defensively. During acting out episodes, suicide is a real danger. This type of depression in the characterologically disordered patient is characterized by being a function of the continued relationship rather than its loss. Actual separation is unconsciously equated with destruction of the object. The special nature of this mechanism stems from early separation-individuation. On the most primitive level, the individual must masochistically submit to and be engulfed by the object, or at a higher level, be an appendage to the object in order preserve it. The rage engendered and the narcissistic devaluation are directed against the self in order to preserve the object, and the affects experienced are of shame, inferiority, and depression (1).

Another mechanism in the depressions of the patients with severe characterological problems involves an attempt to get rid of a "bad" introject. Certain identifications are experienced as outside the self, whether in the ego or superego. When these labile introjects are involved in a depressive process, the clinical manifestation may be a wish to get rid of the bad part. The clinical picture is of depression with rage, projection, and displacement of the introject. As the introject is projected and experienced more as part of the object, the affect of depression becomes less. For example, a scape-goat may be attacked but also cannot be abandoned. The unacceptable impulses of the attacker are projected onto the victim. Often the relationship is libidinized. The mechanism is one of displacement of a part of the self which causes guilt and self-criticism and which would be assaulted by the superego.

Treatment Implications

The treatment of such individuals will depend not only upon the particular diagnostic category in terms of their descriptive personality disorder, but also more importantly on the level of personality integration and organization. Certain of the categories, e.g., histrionic, compulsive, passive aggressive, etc., may contain individuals whose level of personality organization varies from the neurotic to the borderline or psychotic. Other categories, e.g., the borderline, schizoid, schizotypal, etc., will contain individuals much less varied in terms of their level of developmental and structural advancement and will contain individuals pretty much of the same organization. In treating the usual severe characterologically disordered individual, e.g., the antisocial personality, the passive aggressive, etc., my experience has been that they are more interested in escaping momentary frustration and discomfort, or in complaining about the environment, than they are in looking at the total pattern of their lives, the part they play in their own difficulties, or their inability to inhibit impulses. Cases which have had a favorable outcome are those which have either been in a hospital setting for long periods of time or who have been able to remain in outpatient psychotherapy for extended periods. In such instances, the stability of the setting and consistency of approach were of paramount importance. The therapist removed himself from the position of omnipotent decision making and presented himself as a relatively benign but powerful individual who was available when needed. He was not overrun by the patient's omnipotent, narcissistic demands, nor was he destroyed by the patient's aggressive impulses. On the other hand he was (libidinal consistency) available when the patient needed him. Questions of trustworthiness, reliability, and integrity must be of paramount importance to the therapist, and manipulation by the therapist is not part of the therapeutic game. Needless to say, such therapeutic endeavors are extremely demanding on the therapist, and treatment of such patients is a difficult and tedious process. It is frequently necessary, particularly in the early phase of therapy, to let the patient set the tempo and degree of intimacy of the interviews, although insistence on regular appointments is essential. Consistency and limit setting are equally as important as benignness, availability, and good intentions. When each demand of the patient was met with yielding or bending of the rules, as with demanding, angry, overtly hostile patients in an attempt to keep them from "exploding," the result was greater loss of control, even more demanding behavior, more action, and less meaningful interaction. It was found to be most helpful when these individuals whose lives had been marked by hostile rebellion against authority became able to assume positions of authority and assume some responsibility, whether within a hospital structure or in their daily lives outside of therapy. It then became possible for them to begin to internalize the conflicts they had been fighting with the environment, and establish some sort of meaningful identification with a stable authority figure, with subsequent ameliorization of primitive ego and superego introjects. Much has been written about the treatment of the borderline and more recently about the narcissistic personality disorders. Suffice it to say that treatment modalities may range from psychoanalysis to psychotherapy of either an insight-oriented or structured supportive nature. Treatment, particularly with the borderline, could also require the use of institutionalization as well as medication. In terms of the narcissistic personality disorder, as described previously, depending on one's theoretical orientation, there is recognition of underlying aggression and pathologic structure formation (Kernberg) or fixation at a very early stage of libidinal development (Kohut). The treatment implications at this point are vast. In the former, interpretation and confrontation with the underlying grandiosity and aggression are present; in the latter the acceptance of the patient's grandiosity with the establishment of a narcissistic transference (the mirror transference reflecting the activation of the grandiose self) is present, with the implication that this transference development completes a normal process which had been arrested. While these authors may be addressing somewhat different groups of patients, e.g., Kernberg the cold, aloof, grandiose, paranoid patient and Kohut the empty, depressed, dissociated, as if patient, we are in an area of expanding theoretical and clinical development, the full implications for treatment of which have yet to be determined.

As indicated by Giovacchini, the treatment of patients suffering from severe characterological pathology often confronts the therapist with disruptive countertransference reactions (6). Most frequently these responses in the therapist may be related to overt provocativeness or repeated acting out behaviors by the patient. Other countertransference difficulty may arise, however, relating to more subtle issues, e.g., the patient's repeated use of externalization, overt or covert attack, or seduction of the therapist's values, or stimulation of the therapist's own unconscious fantasies and impulses so that an unspoken and unnoticed collusion may go on within therapy itself. Vicarious gratification may be obtained by the therapist through the patient's acting out behaviors. The opposite may also occur wherein the therapist is so threatened by his own instinctual processes, which are stimulated by the patient, that he unconsciously causes the patient to leave, or becomes rigid, dogmatic, and moralistic. Another and frequent possibility is that the therapist is confronted by the patient's direct or implied aggressive tendencies. Such aggression may mobilize fear in the therapist and withdrawal, or he may respond with undue "permissiveness," e.g., conscious or unconscious sanction of aggressive or destructive behaviors or bending of rules and regulations so as to avoid confrontation with the explosive patient. Any of these situations reflect countertransference difficulties with the therapist and must be recognized and dealt with if the patient is to be helped. Not every therapist can work with all varieties of severely or even moderately disturbed patients. It is incumbent on the therapist to recognize his own limitations and select his patients accordingly or to deal with the particular aspects of his own personality which are producing difficulties within the treatment situation.

REFERENCES

1. Asch, S. S. Depression: Three Clinical Variations, In: *Psychoanalytic Study of the Child*, R. S. Eissler, A. Freud, H. Hartman, S. Lustman, and M. Kriss (eds.), Vol. 21, pp. 150–171. International Universities Press, New York, 1966.

2. Boyer, B., and Giovacchini, P. *Psychoanalytic Treatment of Characterological and Schizophrenic Disorders.* Science House, New York, 1967.
3. Bursten, B. *The Manipulator.* Yale University Press, New Haven, 1973.
4. Cleckley, H. M. *The Mask of Sanity.* C. V. Mosby Co., St. Louis, 1964.
5. Fenichel, O. *The Psychoanalytic Theory of Neurosis.* W. W. Norton & Co., Inc., New York, 1945.
6. Giovacchini, P. L. Technical Difficulties in Treating Some Characterologic Disorders; Countertransference Problems." Int. J. Psychoanal. Psychother., 1:112–128, 1972.
7. Giovacchini, P. L. *Treatment of primitive mental states.* Jason Aronson, New York, 1979.
8. Kernberg, O. A psychoanalytic classification of character pathology. J. Am. Psychoanal. Assoc., 18:800–822, 1970.
9. Kernberg, O. Early ego integration and object relations. Ann. N. Y. Acad. Sci. 193:233–247, 1972.
10. Kernberg, O. Contrasting viewpoints regarding the nature and psychoanalytic treatment of narcissistic personalities: A preliminary communication. J. Am. Psychoanal. Assoc., 1974.
11. Kernberg, O. *Borderline Conditions and Pathologic Narcissism.* Jason Aronson, New York, 1975.
12. Kohut, H. *The Analysis of the Self.* International Universities Press, New York, 1971.
13. Leaff, L. A. Affect vs. feeling: On the concept of structuralized affect. J. Am. Psychoanal. Assoc., 19:780–786, 1971.
14. Leaff, L. A. The antisocial personality psychodynamic implications. In: *The Psychopath: A Comprehensive Study of Antisocial Disorders and Behaviors*, William Reid (Ed.). Brunner/Mazel, New York, 1978.
15. Lowenstein, R. M. Defensive organizations and autonomous ego functions. J. Am. Psychoanal. Assoc., 15:795–809, 1967.
16. Mahler, M. S. On human symbiosis and vicissitudes of individuation. In: *Infantile Psychosis,* Vol. 1, International Universities Press, New York, 1968.
17. Reich, W. *Character Analysis.* Noonday Press, New York, 1949.
18. Robins, L. *Deviant Children Grown Up: A Sociological and Psychiatric Study of Sociopathic Personality.* Williams & Wilkins Co., Baltimore, 1966.
19. Schwartz, L. Narcissistic personality disorders: A clinical discussion. J. Am. Psychoanal. Assoc., 22:292–306, 1974.
20. Zetzel, E. The So Called Good Hysteric. Int. J. Psychoanal., 49:256–260, 1968.

19

SOCIOCULTURAL DETERMINANTS OF PERSONALITY PATHOLOGY

Joel S. Albert, M.D.

This chapter discusses certain sociocultural aspects of the pathogenesis, diagnosis, and treatment of character pathology. The central thesis presented is that sociocultural factors do have significant effects in determining character pathology. It is also suggested that the recent increase in incidence and prevalence of character pathology may be traced to an increasingly anomic American society.

Cultural anthropologists, social psychologists, and psychiatrists have made it increasingly clear that the manner in which a child is reared in a society has a lasting and significant influence on his personality. Abraham Kardiner (23, 24) observed that where children are quite regularly cared for in a specified manner by a given culture, all or most ot them are likely to develop a similar "basic personality." For example, when a child is consistently frustrated in goal attainment and asked to renounce pleasure strivings, a sense of sin with belief in the possibility of atonement and redemption by a savior may develop. In his book *The Psychological Frontiers of Society*, Kardiner (24) makes a list of key situations which have been found to influence personality formation. He believes that techniques of child care are probably of primary importance, but that they do not determine the whole life cycle. He uses the study of primitive culture to illustrate this. For example, the infant in Alor is adequately fed by primitive standards, but the society expects women to do much work and requires that the mother absent herself from the child except for brief periods in the morning and evening. Neither the father nor siblings take responsibility for rearing. Thus, the child does not experience a significant mothering agent; consequently, the "basic personality" of the Alorese is mostly distrustful, suspicious, procrastinating, lacking in initiative, noncooperative with one another, quick to anger, and amenable to casual reconciliation. Benedict (6) and Mead (28) have made similar observations in other cultures and subcultures.

Erik Erikson (15), in *Childhood and Society*, noted that the actual contemporary incidence of "character problems" was increasing. He pointed to the possibility of a changed American society to account for this. As did Kardiner, he greatly emphasized the importance of the early years. He described the epigenetic principles of the "seven stages of man" and the particular psychosocial reality in which the ego develops and functions. The relation between society, community, family, and individual is one of mutual regulation and interdependence. He strongly emphasized the theory of object relations and explored the significance of various roles and identities within different collective bodies.

Talcott Parsons (33, 34) examined the significance of internalization of value patterns in the structuring of personality. In his article, "Social Structure and Personality," Parsons articulated the function of pre-oedipal and oedipal social interaction in personality development. His analysis is based on a "theory of action"—behavior as a system which is broken down into four major subdivisions which he calls the behavioral organism, the personality, the social system, and the culture system. Parsons believes that the structure of personality is derived mostly from social systems and culture through socialization.

At all stages of the socialization process, the essential concept is that of role. In examining the oral stage of psychosexual development, Parsons emphasized the mother-child social interaction. He described the mother as the overwhelmingly powerful object, controlling the time of feeding and other acts of care; the child develops an attachment to the mother in which her responses to his needs become organized into a motivational system. Therefore, even the neonate is becoming integrated into the social system. The infant is faced with two cognitive dilemmas. First is the problem of "understanding" the conditions on which his instinctual gratifications and frustrations depend. The second is his organizing and conceptualizing external input (cues) to produce action or means to improve his chances of generalized gratification. Thus, the child is able to internalize successful modes of coping when he is presented with a clear set of sanctions, expectations, and obstacles by the mother. When there is no such clarity in the object situation, a constriction of behavioral responses ensues. Such a construction is an early sociocultural determinant of character pathology.

The individual developing a personality disorder seems able to achieve ends only by a limited or constricted repertoire of means. Early frustration in achieving ends or goal attainment, without being offered alternative ends or alternative means, leads to character pathology. It fosters a personality which seeks immediate attainment of ends without proper evaluation of conditions such as societal norms (laws, social conduct, etc.) and uses destruction and/or avoidance of obstacles. To reiterate Parsons essential point, "This system of internal control over the child's own instinctual or impulse system has become established through a generalized pattern of sanctions imposed by the mother, so that the child learns to respond, not simply to proffered rewards, but to intentions, and thereby learns to 'conform' to her wishes or expectations" (35). Identification is a process by which the child learns a role complementary to his mother.

Parsons describes the major task of the pre-oedipal period as development of the capacity for object choice. He sees this capacity as the foundation of motivation and essential to learning basic performance patterns. During this stage, the ego is further differentiated and able to assume the role of "autonomous initiative." This ability is thought to be impaired in individuals with personality disorders. During the oedipal period, the family becomes the "object with which the child identifies, and through this becomes a full-fledged member of that family . . . the superego, then, is primarily the higher-order normative pattern governing the behavior of different members in their different roles in the family as a system" (35). As familial patterns and roles become internalized, the child uses them in the extrafamilial world without reference to the pre-oedipal sanction system.

Various authors have attempted to explain personality pathology and deviant behavior on the basis of abnormal superego development. In 1921 and 1922, Sigmund Freud (18, 19) developed the concept of superego formation through identification with social objects. He saw the normal process as involving the internalization of the values and norms of society. As such, the superego becomes an agency of the personality system and the basis of articulation with the social system in later life.

Four types of personality defects have been postulated to account for certain character pathology. Some workers (2) consider personality disorders as a character neurosis, that is, that character disorder is the acting out of internalized neurotic conflict. They postulate that early social experiences of harsh punishment and frustration of goal attainment produce an overly strict superego. These individuals perform or admit to deviant acts so that the punishment they receive will relieve their neurotic guilt. A second group of workers (20) have formulated the concept of deficient superego formation resulting from the fact that the family did not provide the necessary external structure, morals, and values for the child to internalize. Friedlander hypothesizes this as the basic defect in the Antisocial Personality disorder. These individuals suffer no guilt from deviant action and are unable to learn from their past mistakes.

Adelaide Johnson's (22) theory of "superego lacunae" cites unconscious permissive familial interaction as leading to areas of confused normative responses during the process of goal achievement. The parents may encourage the child to act out some of their own sociaolien, ambivalent wishes. An example of this might be a teenage girl from a "respectable" family who becomes overtly promiscuous. A fourth group of workers have described the development of the superego in a period of anomie. This will be described in greater detail in the next section of this chapter. Briefly, it is a period in which norms are regarded as inconsequential compared to the achievement of success. The value placed on internalization of normative elements is little compared to the value placed on goal attainment.

Certain cultures demonstrate "basic personalities" which we would label as personality disorders.

Gregory Bateson and Margaret Mead, in their book *Balinese Character: A Photographic Analysis*, describe a personality similar to that of the "schizoid" personality. The Balinese mother indulges the child during the first 2 or 3 years of his life while he is nursing, but then she withdraws this attention and purposefully chides the child. The child develops strong envy of his younger siblings which he cannot express in familial interaction; consequently he becomes aloof.

Hopi parents similarly indulge their children and try to avoid frustrating and punishing them; however, they threaten them with a supernatural being, Kachinas, which will come and beat them if they are not obedient. If the child misbehaves, the parents act as if they are protecting the child, when in fact they have asked others to come in disguise and whip the child. When these children learn the truth, they are deeply disillusioned. Such disillusionment of others fosters a suspiciousness and vigilance of people and their motives, akin to a "paranoid" personality.

Personality disorders are characterized by patterns of observable behavior which develop early in an individual's life, are consistent with his self-image and life-style, and produce a persistent, usually life-long constriction of his adaptive responses. The concepts of role and strain are necessary to understanding social diagnosis. Role is defined by repeated performances, interactions, expressions of sentiments, and attempts by one person to influence another. Role inflexibility is a characteristic of character pathology, i.e., a basic inability to reverse roles or to empathize. Persons diagnosed as personality disorders are particularly intolerant of externally generated strain. Psychological strain often leads to an increase in deviant behavior. The healthy personality is able to tolerate psychological strain and make successful attempts at alternate forms of adaptation. He is able to find the means to deal with new obstacles, conditions, or object loss. The person with personality pathology withstands psychological strain poorly. Restorative efforts are geared toward consummation or immediate goal attainment, thereby reducing the distinction between means and ends. These restorative efforts are often regressive in nature and result in deviant and sometimes criminal acts. Such psychological strain may take many forms—role ambiguity, role conflict, etc.

> An example of role conflict leading to criminal behavior is a 20-year-old black male incarcerated for car theft and breach of parole. He stole a car and purposefully violated traffic laws until he was arrested. At the time of arrest, he was an "A" student in college. His past history was replete with delinquent and criminal acts, usually involving car theft. He expressed a feeling of being torn apart, being part of two different worlds—"the street" and "the white middle-class 'success' world." He wondered if his real father whom he had never seen was white, and he had wishes to search for him. He was searching for a meaning to his existence. In social terms, this youth was experiencing a state of anomie. Both roles, that of a serious student in college and that of "big man in the

street" have in common the Machiavellian value system: "the ends justify the means." In order to become part of a collective body and develop significant object relationships, he needs to accept certain normative elements and values. As he begins to understand this, he experiences a sense of "anomie" (normlessness)—he can't "get it together." This man has been diagnosed as a personality disorder. In this case, we can see how psychological strain imposes integrative difficulty in the form of confusion between means and ends resulting in maladapted, deviant behavior.

Robert Merton (30), in his text *Social Theory and Social Structure*, emphasized that the initial response to social system strain is often deviant and disintegrative behavior. He categorizes such behavior in the following ways: evasion of norms, compulsive conformity, ritualism, automatism, rebellion, and withdrawal. The study of deviance has had a major impact upon social systems theory and is helpful in diagnosing true personality pathology. Merton, Cohen (30, 32), and others have explored the relationship of cultural system (goals and norms) and social system (opportunities, or access to means) with deviance. Merton attempts to discover how some social structures exert definite pressure upon certain persons in the society to engage in nonconforming rather than conforming conduct. He defines two polar types of deviant culture. The first occurs when cultural emphasis is placed upon certain goals without regard to institutionally prescribed means (little concern is paid to institutional norms). The second polar type of deviant culture is where activities originally conceived as instrumental are transmitted into self-contained practices, lacking further objectives. The original purposes are forgotten and close adherence to institutionally prescribed conduct becomes a matter of ritual. In this system, sheer conformity becomes overvalued and often becomes an end in itself. The central question in the first polar type is, "Which of the available procedures is most efficient in netting culturally approved value?" The most efficient procedure to achieve "success" becomes the preferred behavior whether it is legitimate or not. As such a process continues, a society becomes increasingly unstable and develops what Durkheim (11) termed anomie (normlessness). Merton considers contemporary American culture to approximate this model. This might help account for the increased incidence and prevalence of personality disorders. As the American society becomes deinstitutionalized and literally demoralized, external controls and sanctions, whether in the family or community, will become more difficult to internalize. As was previously noted, this is a core defect in personality pathology. Merton's types of deviance may be correlated with types of personality disorders—"ritualism" and obsessive-compulsive type; "retreatism" and addictive, schizoid, and asthenic types; "rebellion" and paranoid, explosive, and antisocial types. Thus, Merton states, "the social structure produces a strain toward anomie and deviant behavior. The pressure of such a social order is upon outdoing one's competitors" (31). Deviant behavior also arises in collectives as in delinquent subgroups and this should be differentiated from true personality disorder. This diagnostic category is 308.5 in DSM II. This diagnostic category is 312.23 Conduct disorder, socialized, aggressive in DSM III (4): individuals with this condition have acquired the values, behavior, and skills of a delinquent peer group or gang to whom they are loyal and with whom they characteristically steal, skip school, and stay out late at night. They display a "repetitive and persistent pattern of aggressive conduct in which the rights of others are violated and evidence social attachments to other members of the group."

Albert Cohen (8) examines strain as "the degree of disjunction between goals and means, or of sufficiency of means to the attainment of goals." He extends Merton's theory by asking. "What strain does deviance on the part of others create for the virtuous?" (8). He contends that one can become more successful by comparing himself with the morally weak. "Since others' weaknesses set off the jewel of one's own virtue, and one's claim to virtue is at the core of his public identity, one may actually develop a stake in the existence of deviant others, and be threatened should they pretend to moral excellence" (8). Hence, Cohen raises two crucial points in the diagnostic process—first, social compliance, and second, the dangers of a self-fulfilling prophecy in a labeling process. Further, examination of the opportunity structure is essential to our understanding of the differential diagnosis of character pathology. Of essential significance will be the differential diagnosis of deviant behavior with and without personality pathology.

Theoretically, society attempts to classify, control, and correct deviant behavior; however, all deviant behavior, of course, is not a byproduct of personality pathology. In this section, I shall examine ways in which society deals with deviance and shall point to possible social "diagnostic tests" to differentiate deviant behavior based on personality pathology from other types.

William Goode (21) cites two methods by which society attempts to deal with deviance. First, there is the structuring of the immediate social situation by clarifying and making explicit societal or group norms, means, ends, and the hierarchy of role expectations. Second, he cites the use of social controls such as police, press, prison, etc., to handle deviance once it has already occurred. Cohen further explores these methods in terms of the opportunities or access to means made available to the deviant by his society. He defines four situations in these terms: opening up legitimate opportunities; closing down legitimate opportunities; opening up illegitimate opportunities; closing down illegitimate opportunities.

We can now examine how these constructs may help us differentiate the DSM III Personality Disorders from those conditions not attributable to a mental disorder. DSM III V Codes for Conditions not attributable to a mental disorder that are a focus of attention or treatment are reproduced below.

V65.20	Malingering
V62.89	Borderline intellectual functioning
V71.01A	Adult antisocial behavior
V71.02	Childhood or adolescent antisocial behavior
V62.30	Academic problem
V62.20	Occupational problem
V62.82	Uncomplicated bereavement
V15.81	Noncompliance with medical treatment
V62.89	Phase of life problem or other life circumstance problem
V61.10	Marital problem
V61.20	Parent-child problem
V61.80	Other specified family circumstance
V62.81	Other interpersonal problem

Using Cohen's construct, we can hypothesize that deviant persons without personality pathology (V Group of DSM III) will do well when "legitimate opportunities are opened up." Their deviant behavior will no longer be adaptive. The following situations will illustrate this premise. Individuals experiencing marital maladjustment may be given financial means to accomplish divorce or divorce laws may be changed to facilitate divorce. Immigrants experiencing social maladjustment, culture shock, or feelings of uprootedness may be given courses to help them learn about the new culture. Associations might be developed with people who have successfully negotiated the same cultural transition. White collar workers forced into blue collar jobs may experience occupational maladjustment. They might benefit from an increased job market. Someone running a numbers racket (antisocial behavior) might abandon such illegal endeavors if employment with a somewhat comparable income in a legitimate enterprise is made readily available. Such social engineering techniques would not provide effective treatment for true personality pathology. Deviant patterns in personality pathology are based upon a continuous state of psychological strain originating in infancy and already internalized. Such pathology would require at least two other modalities for effective management and treatment. First, there must be a "closing off of illegitimate opportunities" by various social controls. For example, Daytop, Inc., a treatment facility for addiction, sets up a clear set of limits, sanctions, goals, and values for its clients. Any deviance from the rules is countered by swift, usually effective punishment. Second is the setting up of facilities for milieu therapy and psychotherapy (13).

Personality pathology must also be differentiated from Phase of Life Problem (DSM III). These are disorders usually occurring at specific points within the human life cycle in reaction to an overwhelming environmental stress. This stress precipitates severe psychological strain. With the removal of the noxious situation, the person without personality disturbance will be able to readapt in a healthy manner.

Kittrie offers a caution in his recent book, *The Right to Be Different* (chapter entitled "Deviance and Enforced Therapy) (25). He states that in its quest for social order in dealing with the deviant, society acts in a parental role (parens patriae)—"seeking not to punish but to change or socialize the nonconformist through treatment or therapy." He examines such issues as compulsory institutionalization, involuntary commitment, delinquency, and psychopathy. He feels that the individual is often coerced into treatment with no safeguards for his personal interest. Szasz (40), in describing the same hazards to individual liberty, fears that true "substitution of health values for moral and political values will be used to justify coercion where it was not previously tolerated or where it should no longer be permitted in our social order."

The studies on "national character" (17, 29) lend further input to the assessment of a basic personality profile. Kluckhohn (26) defined "national character" as "those modalities of behavior and of view of the world and experience in it that are found or claimed to be characteristic of a specified national or ethnic population at a particular period of time." Kluckhohn spends great energy attempting to elucidate such a "national character" of the Russians living in the area he calls Great Russia. He points to a type of historical drama as the Russian "national character" appears to be changing under the Soviet value system. The themes of conflict which are most apparent are: (1) warm, expressive expansiveness versus formality, control, and orderliness; (2) personal loyalty, sincerity, and responsiveness versus distrust and conspiratorial mentality; (3) strong identification with the face-to-face groups of which the individual is a member versus a single tolerated loyalty; (4) being versus doing, or dependent passivity versus ceaseless instrumental "conscious activity."

Spiegel (39), in his book *Transactions*, uses the family as his major focus but much emphasis is placed on the individual. He criticizes concepts such as "national character" as follows: "But in spite of the new insights provided by the concepts, most of them have had a limited usefulness in the analysis of the relationships between the psychological and cultural processes. For the most part, the difficulties in them arise from an absence of a systematic theory of cultural variation and the consequent tendency to rely too heavily upon mere empirical generalizations." He describes four problems as those common to all human groups: (1) What is the relation of man to nature? *Man-nature orientation*; (2) What is the temporal focus of human life? *Time orientation*; (3) What is the modality of human activity? *Activity orientation*; (4) What is the modality of man's relationship to other men? *Relationship orientation*. With this theoretical approach, Spiegel is able to describe differences between different cultural family patterns and de facto differences in individual personality profiles. An example of this is his description of the value orientations of Italian-Americans which are characteristic of their native culture. He notes that Italian families tend to prefer a "subjugation to nature" solution to the man-nature problem. Thus, man is seen as weak and helpless, and this becomes a central component of his personality profile. When faced with stress the fatalistic expression: "What can I do?" is often a solution. In terms of time orientation, the Italians prefer the present. The third category is that of a preferred mode of activity. Here, Spiegel asserts, Italians prefer the being solution. "Success and achievements aren't nearly so important as expressing one's moods, feelings, and desires." In the fourth value orientation, the relational one. Italians prefer the "collateral solution." They live in large families, in close proximity to other relatives, and a strong sentiment is placed against movement away from the family.

Clinicians faced with the task of evaluating personality pathology are often frustrated in their attempts to explain sociocultural determinants to fellow physicians. An example of this is the Puerto Rican woman who is screaming loudly while in the labor room on a general hospital maternity unit. A psychiatric emergency consultation is requested and upon psychiatric examination it is discovered that it is a custom of this woman's subculture to scream loudly in order to deliver a strong baby. Likewise, it is often difficult to explain such sociocultural factors to the court system. For example, Tony M. was a 29-year-old Italian male who had immigrated to the United States approximately 6 months prior to his examination. The psychiatric examination was requested by the court following the killing of his wife and her paramour. He claimed that when he found his wife in bed with another man it was his right and, in fact, responsibility to kill them. He stated that where he came from this was no crime. The court did not agree, and Tony is serving a sentence for manslaughter at the present time.

REFERENCES

1. Abrahamsen, D. *Who Are the Guilty?* Rinehart, New York, 1952.
2. Alexander, F., and Staub, H. *The Criminal, the Judge and the Public.* Free Press of Glencoe, Ill., Chicago, 1956.
3. Allport, G. *The Nature of Prejudice.* Doubleday Anchor, New York, 1958.
4. American Psychiatric Association. Diagnostic and Statistical Manual of Mental Disorders, Ed. 3. American Psychiatric Association, Washington, D. C., 1980.
5. Becker, H. *Outsiders: Studies in the Sociology of Deviance.* Free Press, Glencoe, Ill., Chicago, 1963.
6. Benedict, R. *The Chrysanthemum and the Sword.* Houghton-Mifflin Co., Boston, 1934.
7. Cloward, R., and Ohlin, L. The differentiation of delinquent subcultures. In: *Delinquency, Crime and Social Process.* D. Cressey and D. Ward (eds.). Harper & Row, New York, 1969.
8. Cohen, A. The sociology of the deviant act: anomie theory and behind. In: *Delinquency, Crime and Social Process.* D. Cressey and D. Ward (Eds.). Harper & Row, New York, 1969.
9. Comer, J. *Beyond Black and White,* pp. 723–724. Quadrangle Books, Inc., New York, 1972.
10. Dubin, R. Deviant behavior and social structure. Am. Sociol. Rev., 24:147–164, 1959.
11. Durkheim, E. *Suicide.* Free Press of Glencoe, Ill., Chicago, 1951 (1895).
12. Eaton, J., and Weil, R. *Culture and Mental Disorders.* Free Press, Glencoe, Ill., Chicago, 1955.

13. Edelson, M. *Sociotherapy and Psychotherapy.* University of Chicago Press, Chicago, 1970.
14. Erikson, E. *Insight and Responsibility.* W. W. Norton, New York, 1964.
15. Erikson, E. Childhood and Society. W. W. Norton, New York, 1964.
16. Feldman, D. Psychoanalysis and crime. In: *Delinquency, Crime and Social Process*, D. Cressey and D. Ward (Eds.). Harper & Row, New York, 1969.
17. Forker, M. The analysis of national character. In: *Personality and Social Systems*, N. Smelser and W. Smelser (Eds.). John Wiley & Sons, New York, 1963.
18. Freud, S. Group psychology and the analysis of the ego. In: *The Complete Psychological Works of Sigmund Freud*, standard edition, Vol. 18. Hogarth Press, London, 1921.
19. Freud, S. The ego and the id. In: *The Complete Psychological Works of Sigmund Freud*, standard edition, Vol. 19. Hogarth Press, London, 1923.
20. Friedlander, K. Latent delinquency and ego development. In: *Searchlights on Delinquency*, K. Eissler (Ed.). International Universities Press, New York, 1949.
21. Goode, W. A theory of role strain. Am. Sociol. Rev., 25:483–496, 1960.
22. Johnson, A. M. Sanctions for superego lacunae of adolescents. In: *Searchlights on Delinquency*, K. Eissler (Ed.). International Universities Press, New York, 1949.
23. Kardiner, A. *The Individual and His Society.* Columbia University Press, New York, 1939.
24. Kardiner, A. *The Psychological Frontiers of Society.* Columbia University Press, New York, 1945.
25. Kittrie, N. *The Right to Be Different.* Johns Hopkins Press, Baltimore, 1971.
26. Kluckhohn, C. *Culture and Behavior.* Free Press, New York, 1962.
27. Lidz, T. *The Person.* Basic Books, New York, 1968.
28. Mead, M. *Growth and Culture; A Photographic Study of Balinese Childhood.* Putnam, New York, 1951.
29. Mead, M. National character. In: *Anthropology Today*, A. L. Kroeker (Ed.). University of Chicago Press, Chicago, 1953.
30. Merton, R. *Social Theory and Social Structure.* Free Press, Glencoe, Ill., 1957.
31. Merton, R. Social structure and anomie. In: *Delinquency, Crime and Social Process*, D. Cressey and D. Ward (Eds.), p. 281. Harper & Row, New York, 1969.
32. Merton, R., and Nisket, R. *Contemporary Social Problems.* Harcourt, Brace & World, New York, 1961.
33. Parsons, T. *The Structure of Social Action.* Free Press, New York, 1937.
34. Parsons, T. *Social Structure and Personality.* Free Press, New York, 1964.
35. Parsons, T. The interpenetration of two levels—social structure and the development of personality. In: *Personality and Social Systems*, N. Smelser and W. Smelser (Eds.), pp. 39 and 45. John Wiley & Sons, New York, 1967.
36. Schur, E. *Crimes without Victims: Deviant Behavior and Public Policy.* Prentice-Hall, Englewood Cliffs, N. J., 1965.
37. Shoham, S. *Crime and Social Deviation.* H. Reguey Co., Chicago, 1966.
38. Smelser, N., and Smelser, W. *Personality and Social Systems.* John Wiley & Sons, New York, 1967.
39. Spiegel, J. *Transactions.* Science House, New York, 1971.
40. Szasz, T. *Law, Liberty and Psychiatry*, p. 4. Macmillan, New York, 1963.
41. Tyler, E. *Primitive Culture.* Brentano, New York, 1924.

20

THE PROBLEM OF IMPULSIVITY IN PERSONALITY DISTURBANCES

Russell R. Monroe, M.D.

Introduction

The psychiatric literature still lacks a careful phenomenological and psychodynamic discrimination between neurotic behavior, impulsive behavior, and characterological disorders. Statements that the perversions are the inverse of neurosis and that impulse disorders reflect the "alloplastic readiness to act" are descriptive rather than explanatory. Dynamic considerations most useful to the psychotherapist describe the impulsive neurotic as one whose impulsive act is rebellion against an overly strict infantile superego, while the impulsive character is an individual whose instinctual urges are not controlled because of weak or underdeveloped superego mechanisms. The present author feels that confusion in this area has been perpetuated through a failure to identify a unique syndrome usually characterized by impulsive acts, which he has labeled episodic behavioral disorders (6).

The episodic behavioral disorders are defined as any precipitously appearing maladaptive behavior, usually intermittent and recurrent, which interrupts the life-style or the life flow of the individual. The disordered behavior, then, is a discontinuity in terms of the space-time relationships. There is a sudden change in personality or life-style as compared with the "before" and the "after" patterns of behavior. In turn, these episodic behavioral disorders can be either episodic disinhibitions of action or episodic inhibitions of action (6). It is the episodic disinhibition of actions, particularly episodic dyscontrol, which will be the subject of this chapter.

Episodic dyscontrol, as a subgroup of episodic behavioral disorders (Fig. 20.1), is defined as an abrupt single act or short series of acts with a common intention carried through to completion with at least partial relief of tension or, at most, an immediate gratification of a specific need. As a subclass of the episodic behavioral disorders, it also has the characteristic of a precipitous, maladaptive interruption in the life-style or the life flow of the individual. In the literature, such labels as "acting on impulse," "impulse neurosis," "irresistible impulse," or "acting out" have been utilized to describe such behavior. The current international classification (ICD-8)

PERSONALITY DISORDERS

```
                    "DISORDERED BEHAVIOR"
                     (Maladaptive Behavior)
                              |
         ┌────────────────────┴────────────────────┐
"Non-episodic Behavior Disorders"      EPISODIC BEHAVIORAL DISORDERS
  (Usual Diagnostic Categories)          ("Precipitous interruptions in
                                          "Life style" or "Life flow")
                                                    |
                                    ┌───────────────┴───────────────┐
                            "Episodic Disinhibition"        "Episodic Inhibition"
                                 (of action)                     (of action)
                                                          (e.g., Narcolepsy, catalepsy,
                                                           akinetic mutism, periodic
                                                           catatonia, petit mal status, etc)
                    ┌────────────────┴────────────────┐
              EPISODIC DYSCONTROL                EPISODIC REACTION
         I. Primary Dyscontrol              (Intermittent, Periodic, or Remitting
            A. SEIZURE DYSCONTROL                    Complex Disorders)
               (e.g., seizure)                I. Psychotic
            B. INSTINCT DYSCONTROL               A. Schizophrenic
               (e.g., "acting on impulse")       B. Brain Syndrome
        II. Secondary Dyscontrol                 C. Depression
            A. IMPULSE DYSCONTROL            II. SOCIOPATHIC
               (e.g., "irresistible impulse") III. NEUROTIC
            B. ACTING OUT                    IV. PSYCHOPHYSIOLOGICAL
```

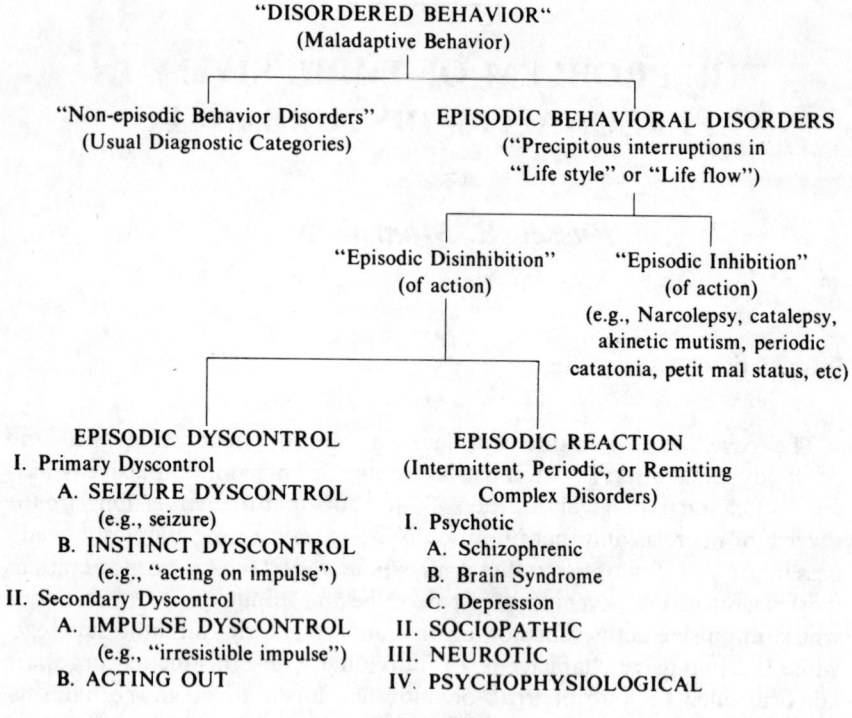

Figure 20.1

indicates almost no specific diagnostic categories which would apply to this particular group, with the possible exception of the diagnosis "explosive personality." For a detailed description of the other subgroups of the episodic behavioral disorders—that is, episodic inhibitions of behavior and episodic reactions—one is referred elsewhere (6).

It suffices for our present purpose to indicate that the one common feature of all episodic behavioral disorders is this precipitous interruption in the lifestyle of the individual.

Dyscontrol acts usually represent an impulsive expression of primitive fear-rage affects, and hence are socially or self-destructive. For this reason, such individuals often come to the attention of law enforcement agencies or courts; hence such individuals should be clearly differentiated from the more common sociopathic offenders. Likewise, an individual manifesting episodic dyscontrol may demonstrate relatively normal, adaptive behavior between dyscontrol acts, but as likely as not these acts may be superimposed on chronic neurotic, psychotic, or character disturbances. A rational therapeutic regimen may then have to contend with two thrusts, namely, treatment of the episodic dyscontrol, as well as treatment of the persistent underlying psychopathology.

Finally, the precipitous onset, short duration, and accompanying confusion during dyscontrol acts suggest that in many such individuals there is an underlying ictal phenomenon representing neurological deficits. All of these factors have important prognostic and therapeutic implications. To identify such important factors, a careful phenomenological, psychodynamic, and neurophysiological analysis is required.

Phenomenological and Psychodynamic Analysis of Episodic Dyscontrol

In looking at dyscontrol acts, one should establish the specificity of the drives or urges behind the act, the coordination and complexity of the motor behavior during the act, and the appropriateness of the motives or goals of the act. The dyscontrol act is characterized, as Shapiro notes, by the feeling, "I just did it, I don't know why." It is an experience of having executed a significant action "without a clear and complete sense of motivation, decision or sustained wish, so that it does not feel completely deliberate or fully intended" (8). Despite this spontaneity and lack of reflection, such actions are occasionally adaptive and may represent the unique contribution of the genius or the man of action. However, more often the abrupt precipitous acts are based on primitive emotions of fear, rage, or sensuous feelings without concern for the effect on the immediate environment or the long-term consequences to the actor or society and are either self- or socially destructive. These acts are disinhibitions of behavior (in the motor sense) and are often sadistic or bizarre crimes, suicidal attempts, or aggressive or sexual acting out.

These spontaneous or impulsive acts are described as representing a "short circuit" between the stimulus and response. This demands, if only briefly, an analysis of the delay between the stimulus and the act which characterizes most socialized human behavior. The short circuit between the stimulus and the act resulting in precipitous behavior implies that the behavior is not corrected by reflection on past experiences or anticipation of future consequences. It is precisely for this reason that the act is usually self-destructive or self-defeating for the individual, or appears antisocial to the onlooker. We can identify two facets to this delay between the stimulus and the response. The first I would designate as reflective delay (often referred to in the psychoanalytic literature as "thought as trial action"), which is the time necessary for establishing the uniqueness or familiarity of the stimulus by associative connections with past experiences, the time necessary to contemplate alternative courses of action, and the time necessary to project into the future and predict the outcome of alternative actions. The second facet is choice delay, which is possibly only following this reflective delay. The choice delay is a decision to postpone immediate action or gratification for long-term rewards, that is, "biding one's time." This choice delay is absent in the extractive sociopathic individual who gives in to his urges, seeking immediate gratification, consequences be "damned," even though he may have made a careful appraisal of the situation and has a good realization of the possible long-term consequences of his action.

Although the sociopathic individual has often been labeled an "actor-outer," he would not here fit our definition of episodic dyscontrol, which means a disturbance in the reflective delay to the extent that it is either absent or severely distorted. On the other hand, we would limit the concept of sociopathic individuals to those who make the choice of giving in to their impulses without delay, the long-term disastrous consequences notwithstanding.

The disturbance in reflective delay characteristic of episodic dyscontrol depends upon a complex interaction among affects, hindsight and foresight, reason, perceptual discrimination, and appropriate generalization. If there is a significant deficiency or inappropriate domination by any one of these mechanisms, the whole process may fail, resulting in a total absence of reflective delay leading to what I have called primary dyscontrol. In such instances, there is an immediate reaction to an environmental stimulus with a seeking of need gratification without even the concept that there is an alternative possibility involving delay. This is the true "short circuit" between stimulus and response characteristic of primary dyscontrol. Figure 20.2 summarizes the phenomenological and psychodynamic differentiation between primary dyscontrol and secondary dyscontrol. Primary dyscontrol is further divided into two subgroups, seizure and instinct dyscontrol. The paradigm of seizure dyscontrol is the postictal confusional state, behavior characterized by intense, indiscriminate affects, chaotic and uncoordinated motor patterns, and an indiscriminate selection of the object acted upon, often the person closest at hand. There is little specific need gratification, although there is usually a reduction in tension. Such dyscontrol behavior can occur without a prior ictal phenomenon and in fact on rare occasions may not even be a reflection of central nervous system instability.

On the other hand, instinct dyscontrol is characterized by affects that are clearly differentiated and more effectively gratified. Although the motor pattern is lacking in subtlety it is none the less efficient and coordinated. In this case, the object acted upon has at least simple associative links with past experiences. In both instinct and seizure dyscontrol, the behavior is characterized by an explosive immediate response to an environmental stimulus which represents a true "short circuit" between stimulus and action.

In secondary dyscontrol there is either conscious or unconscious premeditation between the true stimulus and the act; hence, there is a delay between the stimulus and the act. The reflection, which precedes action, reveals an ambivalent vacillating attitude regarding the choice to either succumb to or restrain the impulse (Fig. 20.2). By and large, individuals

EPISODIC DYSCONTROL

	PRIMARY DYSCONTROL		SECONDARY DYSCONTROL		
	Seizure	Instinct	Impulse	Acting Out	
Phenomenological Differentiation	←—— No Delay Between Stimulus and Response ——→		←—— Delay Between Stimulus and Response ——→		Phenomenological Differentiation
	←——Uninhibited Action——→		←—Transition—→←—Inhibited Action—→		
	←—Uncoordinated Act—→←—Transition—→		←—Sophisticated Coordinated Act—→		
Psychodynamic Differentiation	←—Tension relief—→	←—Direct Need Gratification—→		←—Indirect Gratification—→	Psychodynamic Differentiation
	←——Inhibited Reflection——→		←——Excessive Reflection——→		
	←—Inhibited Intention—→	←—Transition—→	←—Conscious Intention—→	←—Unconscious Intention—→	

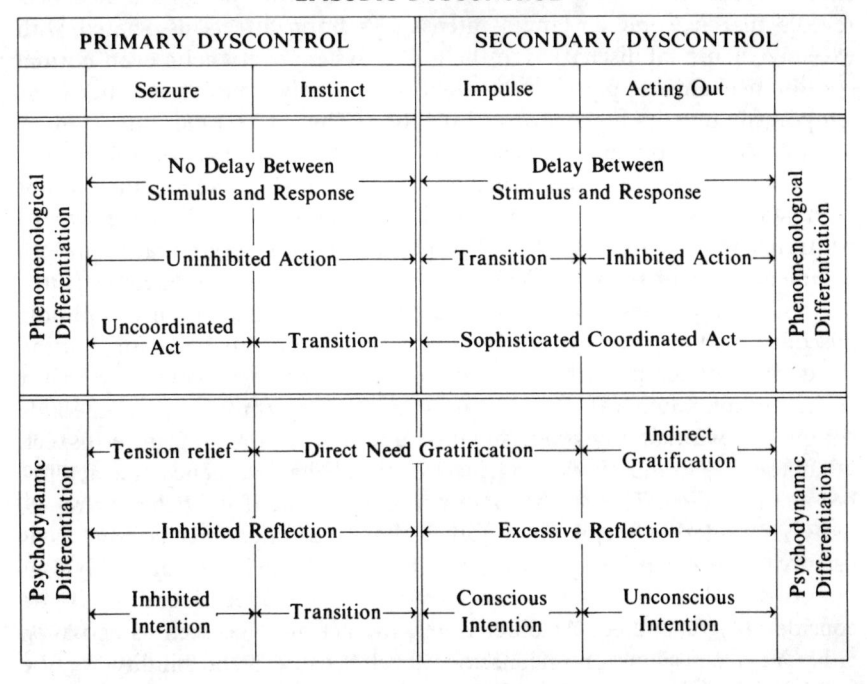

Figure 20.2

showing secondary dyscontrol are, in their general life-style, overly inhibited and at some level aware of the true, even though neurotic, intentions of their action. The act itself is more likely to represent a rebellion against an overly strict and inhibiting conscience mechanism, or a devious substitute gratification of forbidden unacceptable impulses. As an example, one can think of the explosive act in the overly controlled obsessive character or the hysterical analysand's acting out within the transference neurosis. Figure 20.2 summarizes the phenomenological and psychodynamic differences between the two subgroups of secondary dyscontrol, that is, impulse dyscontrol and acting out. The primary differentiation, as elaborated below, is the conscious intention in impulse dyscontrol, with considerable wavering and doubt an example of the excessive reflection which accompanies secondary dyscontrol, but in the case of acting out this reflection is at an unconscious level.

A simplified dynamic statement often applied to impulsive behavior or what we have designated as episodic dyscontrol is that "urges overwhelm controls." This has operational value only if we can determine where an individual falls between the extremes of excessively strong urges overwhelming normal control mechanisms on one hand, and normal urges uncontrolled by weak or deficient inhibitory mechanisms on the other. The traditional psychiatric viewpoint stresses weak control mechanisms. However, careful clinical evaluation, now supported by growing neurophysiological evidence, reveals that in some instances intense dysphoric affects associated with excessive neuronal discharges in the limbic system overwhelm even normal control mechanisms, particularly when the brain dysfunction in other ways temporarily impairs higher cortical function. Thus, it becomes important to identify the group where intense urges overwhelm normal control mechanisms or transiently impair cortical control. The goal in therapy, then, is not so much to develop stronger inhibitory mechanisms, but in some way to neutralize the intense dysphoria. It is particularly this group that requires a complementary pharmacological regimen in one's psychotherapeutic efforts.

Another important dynamic consideration in the evaluation of episodic dyscontrol is the patient's retrospective evaluation of his behavior. During the dyscontrol act itself, the behavior could be called ego-syntonic in that it is an abrupt, often explosively quick act carried through to immediate completion without any procrastination and doubt. However, in retrospect, often the actor himself is chagrined by his behavior, hence the act has become ego-alien. This seems to be particularly true if the behavior represents an underlying epileptoid rather than motivated mechanism, as is usually the case in primary dyscontrol. Of course, if the individual recognizes in retrospect that the act is ego-alien, psychotherapeutic endeavors are considerably facilitated. At other times, the act must be seen as ego-alien either at a conscious or unconscious level because responsibility for the behavior is defensively denied. In such instances, one finds associated amnesia, projection, or rationalization, so one can assume that the behavior is recognized as unacceptable (secondary dyscontrol). Of course, such defensive maneuvers on the part of the patient complicate psychotherapy. It is questionable whether any individual manifesting true episodic dyscontrol as here defined ever commits acts that are truly ego-syntonic, both at the time the act is committed and also in retrospect. This would much more likely occur in the true sociopath. In this last instance, appropriate therapeutic motivation is difficult to develop except in an institutional setting.

Finally, one must consider the intentions of any dyscontrol behavior. As already described, in acting out, the intention is thoroughly disguised, usually representing the symbolic fulfillment of a forbidden impulse. On the other hand, in impulse dyscontrol and instinct dyscontrol the true intention is either directly expressed or only superficially disguised and rationalized. As a simple example of this, one could consider the adolescent boy living in a fatherless family and in the throes of an oedipal renunciation who kills his mother's lover, usually on some superficial pretense. In seizural dyscontrol, that is, the most primitive level of episodic dyscontrol, the act is so diffuse and uncoordinated that it becomes relatively ineffective. Some patients seem to have the capacity to shift dyscontrol acts from instinct or impulse dyscontrol into this more primitive behavior which discharges tension but does not lead to more specific (but unacceptable) need gratification. This is one explanation for the frequently reported clinical observation that with an increase in seizures there is a decrease in other dyscontrol acts. A related defensive maneuver is that the episodic dyscontrol is an episodic inhibition of action. It then protects the individual from the self-destructive consequences of the disinhibited dyscontrol acts, even though the former offers neither need gratification nor release of tension.

The discrete affect most frequently identified with a dyscontrol act is rage resulting in homicidal behavior, probably because such behavior reaches the newspaper headlines and has severe social consequences. However, much of this episodic aggression occurs within the family. Unless there are homicidal consequences this behavior seldom reaches the attention of law enforcement agencies. What is not recognized is that these aggressive impulses can be turned upon oneself instead of the environment. No statistics are available as to how many suicides are manifestations of episodic dyscontrol, but if one is alert to this possibility it would seem to be quite frequent. If the dyscontrol act is at a higher level, that is, secondary dyscontrol, the intentions of the homicidal-suicidal impulses may be sufficiently disguised so as not to be readily recognized by observers. Thus, it has been proposed by Ervin et al. that many serious automobile accidents represent dyscontrol, homicidal, or suicidal intentions (3).

The affects associated with dyscontrol behavior as already mentioned are intense. They usually represent discrete fear and rage, but at other times mixtures of the two with sometimes profound depression. All of these add up to periodic intense dysphoria from which the patient is compelled to seek immediate relief, often through self-medication. The most common example of this is relief through alcohol; as a central nervous system inhibitor, it leaves the individual even more susceptible to dyscontrol behavior. Thus, most of the disorders now labeled as pathological intoxication would fit our definition of episodic dyscontrol. Those individuals who deal with the compulsive drug abuser have likewise observed that a number of such individuals report that they control aggressive impulses through their use of drugs. Hence, a significant number of individuals manifesting episodic dyscontrol might be found in our drug or alcohol clinics.

It has been repeatedly observed that dyscontrol behavior seems almost phase-specific for the adolescent (1). Such behavior represents the complex interaction between the affective turmoil, identity crisis, and undeveloped anticipatory mechanisms characteristic of this age group. Nevertheless, it is important to look carefully at the impulsive adolescent from a phenomenological point of view. Again, a significant number represent a rather specific episodic dyscontrol related to neurological dysfunction. This may represent a neurophysiological maturational lag identifiable with careful neurological and electroencephalographic techniques. As such an identification has specific prognostic and therapeutic implications, this becomes an important consideration for the clinician.

Brain Dysfunction and Dyscontrol Behavior

It is an obvious clinical observation that patients with organic brain syndromes frequently manifest dyscontrol behavior, particularly primary dyscontrol. However, looking at the data from the reverse perspective, individuals with episodic dyscontrol are as likely to reveal significant pathology in areas such as schizophrenic thought disorders or hysterical mechanisms as they are to have organic signs (6). Similarly, children presumed to have minimal brain dysfunction on the basis of hyperkinetic behavior and "soft" neurological signs may also show impulsive, aggressive behavior. It is not clear how many aggressive children would fall in this minimal brain dysfunction-hyperkinetic classification. Also, it has been proposed that episodic dyscontrol is associated with psychomotor or temporal lobe epilepsy.

The data are controversial and have been recently summarized by Monroe. He questions whether such dyscontrol behavior is associated with a specific form of epilepsy, that is, psychomotor epilepsy, or just associated with epilepsy in general. In fact, there is clinical evidence that recurrent seizures may protect the individual from dyscontrol behavior. The inverse relationship between classic seizures of the grand mal and petit mal types, simple automatisms, and more complex dyscontrol behavior has been frequently reported in the literature (6). The controversy extends to the correlation of the abnormal electroencephalogram and episodic dyscontrol. A review of the literature suggests that dyscontrol behavior associated with an altered level of awareness, a primitive uncoordinated behavioral response, and an undifferentiated affective state is most likely to have abnormal EEG's and sometimes typical epileptic seizures. Although epileptoid mechanisms are not a sufficient cause for aggressive behavior and not even a necessary factor for such behavior, at a statistical level there seems to be a correlation between EEG abnormalities and at least primary dyscontrol. However, even in typical epilepsy the routine clinical EEG is often negative so that the EEG cannot be used as a specific test for an epileptoid mechanism (6).

Another possibility is that a maturational lag in the development of the nervous system with its concomitant delay in development of reflective and choice delay is responsible for a persistence of impulsive behavior that is characteristic of many young children or adolescents into adulthood. It has been proposed that this delay is reflected in EEG abnormalities by a persistence of slow theta activity (7) or by paroxysmal high amplitude theta activity. This maturational lag has been offered as a partial explanation for the so-called "phase-specific" impulsivity of the adolescent by Monroe (6).

Studies with chronically implanted subcortical electrodes reveal the reason for the current clinical confusion regarding the correlations between clinical and electroencephalographic data with dyscontrol behavior. It has been shown in a limited but intensively studied group of subjects that storms of electrical activity can occur in the subcortical areas without reflection on the cortex, let alone scalp EEG recordings (4). Simultaneously recording from these subcortical areas and careful clinical observation reveal several findings. First, there is a good correlation between mounting dysphoric affects resulting in explosive primitive fearful and/or aggressive action and ictal subcortical recordings. These develop without reflection onto scalp EEGs and without obvious neurological signs. Careful testing during the prodromal period or during the act itself would probably reveal impaired intellectual functioning, minor disorientation, and confusion and failure in the usual anticipatory-inhibitory mechanisms. These are all characteristics of primary dyscontrol (5). It is still not clear, however, whether this dyscontrol behavior is only associated with a focal epileptic status, a circumscribed or partial epilepsy, or whether such behavior is also correlated with pre-ictal, postictal, or interictal EEG patterns. This would be an important differentiation because of its therapeutic implication. For instance, Monroe proposes that much of episodic behavior is correlated with circumscribed ictal phenomena and, therefore, should be responsive to antiepileptic medication, even though the patients otherwise do not present themselves with typical epilepsy (6). It is for this reason that Monroe proposes that any episodic dyscontrol or episodic reaction, no matter how diverse the symptoms—whether this is fearful, aggressive, or sexual acting out or varying psychophysiological disturbances of a transitory nature with a precipitous onset and remission—should be seriously considered as representing to some degree an epileptoid phenomenon.

Second, the question arises as to whether such an ictal phenomenon can persist for a significant period of time or is limited to a transitory response terminated quickly because of a neuronal exhaustion. Monroe proposes that just as one sees prolonged petit mal states so there can be prolonged ictal responses. They last not only for hours and days but weeks and months, the ictal possibility suggested by the precipitous onset and remission. In such instances, one can see an epileptoid episodic reaction characterized by prolonged psychotic, neurotic, or psychophysiological reaction, which because of its ictal nature responds to anticonvulsant medication.

Differential Diagnosis between Neuropathophysiological and Motivational Factors

It would appear from interplay between psychodynamic and neurophysiological mechanisms behind dyscontrol behavior that man's capacity to respond appropriately to environmental demands depends on two factors: (a) the individual's endowment, that is, the functional integrity of the equipment he possesses; and (b) the appropriateness and extent of his learned behavior. It is difficult to evaluate how much of his maladaptive behavior is due to "faulty equipment" and how much is due to "faulty learning." A patient seldom falls at one or the other of these extremes, his maladaptive behavior, then, being the sum of some mixture of faulty equipment and faulty learning. Nevertheless, it is important for the clinician to evaluate the extent to which each deficit contributes to the patient's behavior in order that he can make an accurate prognosis and establish appropriate therapeutic goals.

Unfortunately, there is no reliable laboratory procedure to measure the neurophysiological or the psychological deficit. As far as the former is concerned, not even the clinical EEG is a reliable instrument. The routine scalp EEG is no absolute measure of whether epileptoid or maturational phenomena play a significant role in the episodic dyscontrol.

An electroencephalographic technique which would significantly reduce the possibility of false negatives without an excessive increase in the false positives would be ideal. Monroe proposes that a combination of activation techniques utilizing sleep, hyperventilation, and specific drug activation (he proposes alpha-chloralose activation) would reduce the false negatives not only in typical epileptic patients but in the larger group of episodic behavioral disorders. Although he states that the possibility of false positives would approach 20%, he believes that the false negatives would be less than 5%.

The positive activation induced by alpha-chloralose or other drugs represents two types of electroencephalographic responses. The first pattern is "specific" and characterized by a focal appearance of spikes and/or slow waves or typical generalized patterns of centrencephalic epilepsy. If this pattern should occur in the base line recording, it is augmented by the activation procedure. The second activation pattern is "aspecific" characterized by high amplitude paroxysmal slow waves (3 to 7 per second). These are generalized and bilaterally synchronous, occasionally with intermixed hypersynchronous wave forms in the same distribution. Such patterns usually appear first in the frontal regions and maintain maximal amplitude in the same area. The incidence of such patterns in patients with uncomplicated epilepsy is high, and Monroe suggests that it is equally high in patients showing episodic dyscontrol (6).

However, it must be mentioned that dyscontrol patients who show either the activated "aspecific" pattern or specific abnormalities or combinations of the two usually have a clear-cut history of a psychologically traumatic past. This underlines the fact that excessive neuronal discharges are not a sufficient cause of episodic behavior. For instance, careful psychiatric histories of dyscontrol patients usually reveal that these individuals have been subjected to intense overstimulation during the first several years of their life, that is, they have been exposed to extreme aggression by parents, siblings, or other significant adults in the environment or exposed to severe panic reactions or persistent sensual, often overtly sexual, stimulation (6). Thus, a conservative generalization would be that if a person for whatever reason is destined to become neurotic, psychotic, or sociopathic, he will likely manifest this as an episodic disorder if there is an associated epileptoid mechanism (or perhaps it is better to consider this a maturational lag) within the central nervous system. Unfortunately, this underlying epileptoid or maturational deficit can only be demonstrated by special EEG techniques. The important clinical consideration is that if such deficits can be demonstrated, anticonvulsant medication will significantly facilitate an effective therapeutic regimen (6).

Certain phenomenological characteristics give us further clues regarding whether the predominant mechanism is epileptoid-maturational or motivated learned behavior. The epileptoid-maturational mechanisms are probable if the dyscontrol acts are primitive and diffuse (primary dyscontrol), the eliciting situation neutral or ambiguous, and the secondary gains slight or absent. Although such statements have common sense obviousness, coming to such conclusions on the basis of the clinical data can be surprisingly difficult. Another distinguishing characteristic between epileptoid and motivated episodic dyscontrol is the disparity between the complexity of behavior during dyscontrol acts and the behavior between episodes. If the disparity between the two is great, one should consider an epileptoid mechanism. For example, if a sophisticated intelligent man has episodic dyscontrol, which is a seizural or an instinctual act (primary dyscontrol), then one should assume that there is an epileptoid element, particularly if there is a stereotyped repetitive quality to the dyscontrol act. On the other hand, this would not necessarily be true of similar dyscontrol acts in a patient who was a mental defective showing organic perseveration and obsessive-compulsive traits. In this instance, despite the basic organic deficit the behavior might well be a motivated or learned response.

Other criteria at the phenomenological level for differentiating between the epileptoid or motivated episodic dyscontrol are the following. If there is a clouding of sensorium during the episodic act, it is most likely epileptoid. Unfortunately, it is usually impossible to evaluate the clouding during the dyscontrol act itself, so we are forced to rely on a history of amnesia to determine the likelihood of such clouding. Contrary to the usual supposition, it is the epileptoid patient who is more likely to have partial recall for the episode (except during a grand mal seizure or simple automatism). Surprisingly, it is also the epileptoid patient who is more willing to accept responsibility for his behavior. Although he feels his behavior is driven, he is perplexed by both the quality and intensity of the act. He is willing to be confronted with his behavior in the hope of exorcising the "foreign body." He sees his act as truly ego-alien and usually begs for help to prevent him from committing such acts in the future. On the other hand, in motivated dyscontrol behavior, the so-called hysterical patient often has complete amnesia for the episodic behavior because he recognizes, at least unconsciously, the unacceptable intentions of his act. He is anxious to deny responsibility for the action, saying simply, "If I did it I didn't know what I was doing."

Examples of Episodic Dyscontrol and Severe Character Disorders

Impulsive Dyscontrol and Drug-dependent Behavior

This is a 28-year-old male who was admitted to the hospital because of habituation to amphetamine and secobarbital. Three months previously he had been admitted to the medical service for a bleeding gastric ulcer treated by gastrectomy. Because of this, as well as his drug habituation, he had been unable to work for the preceding 4 months.

As a youngster this patient had phobias, tics, as well as other evidence of tension, such as hyperactivity and nail biting. Following his parents' divorce when he was 8 years old, he was sent to a boarding school where he was chronically depressed and repeatedly ran away from school. During preparatory school and college, he was disliked by both peers and teachers because they saw him as a "con artist." Because of superior intelligence he completed his college education and successfully entered the military service only to be discharged 6 weeks later because of gastric ulcers. Following this, and with more bravado than expertise, he became a producer of promotional films. For a short time he was highly successful, but his insecurity forced him to play the role of the "big shot," buying sport cars, living in fancy apartments, and saving no money from his relatively high salary because of his taste for "expensive" women. It was at this time he first began using stimulants, his behavior becoming so disorganized that he lost his job. It was necessary to hospitalize him and he went through toxic withdrawal symptoms. His occupational and social career for the next 5 years went steadily downhill with decreasing periods of employment, interspersed by returning home to his family when unemployed. At such times he was depressed, dependent, and repeatedly habituated to amphetamines and barbiturates. After either enforced or spontaneous withdrawal from the drugs, he would find a job on his own initiative, do exceptionally fine work, and then through a series of impulsive acts would lose his job. These acts were thinly disguised attempts to establish himself as the favorite son of one of the chief executives. Through his overt obsequiousness he would alienate himself from his peers and antagonize his supervisors. As his interpersonal relationships deteriorated, he would become frantic, playing off one faction against another, knifing people behind their backs, until everybody was completely fed up.

Psychological evaluation revealed a passive-dependent individual with strong unsatisfied dependent needs, as well as insensitivity to the needs of others. His self-concept was one of unworthiness with no clearly established patterns of values or objectives. There were perverse sexual preoccupations and a poor sexual identification. He ignored major problems to lose himself in obsessive concerns. The tests revealed a number of oral sadistic fantasies and suggested a potentiality to act out his sexual tensions impulsively.

His dyscontrol behavior was diagnosed as impulse dyscontrol. The act followed a period of considerable wavering and doubt regarding whether he should give in to the impulse with obsessive ritualistic attempts to restrain his behavior. The impulse dyscontrol was of three distinct types. The least destructive was in the sexual area. This behavior occurred only when his wife left town. For several nights after her departure he would be aware of mounting tension and the need to "have" a woman. He would resist this impulse by pacing the floor and taking frequent cold showers, but finally would impulsively dash out of the house, trembling and perspiring, to look for a prostitute. When one was obtained he was almost instantaneously orgastic, but the tension release was transitory, lasting only a matter of minutes or at best hours.

The second type of impulse dyscontrol occurred at work. When he was excluded from a business conference, he would become restless, pace the floor, and lock himself in his office so that he would not commit what he recognized was likely to be an indiscretion. Finally, unable to stand it any longer, he would rush out of the office to listen at the door, look through the key hole, or climb up the wall to peer through the transom, even though he recognized the childish, self-defeating nature of this behavior.

A third type of impulse dyscontrol would occur when he was visiting friends or relatives. He would look in the medicine closet and, if he found barbiturates or sedatives, he would phobically slam the medicine cabinet door and run from the bathroom. However, he would return to the bathroom repeatedly during the evening, always open the door, and "peek" at the drugs until finally on one of his trips he would grab the medicine bottle, pour out a handful of capsules or tablets, and gulp them down.

Physical and neurological examinations at the time of his current hospitalization were within normal range, as was the resting EEG record. However, after special activation with alpha-chloralose there appeared bilateral paroxysmal bursts of 3 to 5 per second activity predominantly in the anterior quadrants.

As will be mentioned in the section on treatment, even though this man probably would have responded to anticonvulsant medication insofar as it would have reduced the impulse dyscontrol, it was decided because of his propensity for drug abuse that a medical regimen was contraindicated. He did respond well, however, to psychoanalytic therapy, which ran a prolonged and stormy 4-year course. However, for the last several years of analysis and 12 months without therapy, he has been performing exceptionally well in an executive capacity in a small corporation. His wife reports that he is much more affectionate and considerate at home, relates better to his children, and seems to be utilizing the insight he gained in therapy.

Impulse Dyscontrol Superimposed on a Schizoid-paranoid Personality

This was a 33-year-old unmarried female who was incarcerated because she had driven her car up over the curb to run down and kill her estranged boyfriend outside of the used car lot where he worked. This boyfriend first sold her the car, then seduced her, then lived with and realistically exploited her for 5 months. Only when she ran out of money did he desert her. Three months prior to this act the patient, having seen her boyfriend leaving the car lot, had the impulse to run him down. (She had had a similar impulse regarding another boyfriend who jilted her several years before.) During the intervening months she would often go to church to pray to God that he would not let her do this.

She even went to the extreme of trading cars with her brother, hoping that this might prevent her homicidal impulses. The day of the act, she first went to the used car lot and, not seeing her boyfriend, drove on to a nearby gas station, at the same time fantasizing that upon her return he would have left, or that perhaps instead of killing him she would fall out of the car and run over herself. However, upon her return he was standing on the sidewalk and the event occurred. She said as she sat in the car which was resting on his body, "Mac, ask God to forgive you," and "75% of all men should be dead because of what they do to women." During the mental status examination, she repeated such statements as "It is God's will that Mac die," and "He was so miserable that he wanted to die." As far as is known, that is the only serious impulsive act she committed.

This patient was by far the youngest of four girls born to an impoverished, laboring class family, being reared as a contemporary of a male nephew who was the idol of her mother's eye. The family commented about her domineering attitude, extreme temper tantrums, and tendency to "cuss," even during her earliest years. She was possessive of her belongings and seemed jealous of her siblings, particularly her nephew. During adolescence, she was preoccupied with her physical development, being unhappy because her breasts did not develop as did those of other girls. She had few friends, but was possessive and jealous of the ones she did have. She was restless and nervous; these symptoms were aggravated when she developed tuberculosis which required a year's institutionalization. Although continuously employed afterward as a clerk secretary, she frequently changed jobs and moved to distant parts of the world. She always left her employment because of imagined persecution by her fellow workers, although apparently this did not extend to her superiors. She preferred social isolation, seldom dated, and when visiting her family would almost immediately become irritated and hostile, leaving after a few hours' visit. She had numerous hypochondriacal complaints associated with her genital system, which required frequent pelvic examinations. She had infrequent and painful coital experiences and was particularly disgusted regarding sexuality because of the "sexual perversions demanded of me." She had one overt psychotic break where she wrote pages of typewritten charges against the Navy, Veterans Administration, Atomic Energy Commission, Civil Service Commission, and Federal Bureau of Investigation, listing all the wrongs that were perpetuated against her. These writings were at best rambling and circumstantial, usually reflecting such loose thought processes that it was impossible to make sense of them. One report ended with the statement " ... and because of the information and facts contained in all of the foregoing pages I am definitely suffering from anthropophobia—fear of human society. . . . God please have mercy on those who have hurt me so. . . . Amen. . . . Signed Miss_____, Citizen U.S.A."

In both of these patients the chronic psychopathology demanded as much of the therapeutic "thrust" as did the dyscontrol behavior. However, therapy demanded consideration of both, and neither the episodic dyscontrol nor the chronic disorder could have been successfully treated without consideration of the other.

DSM III and Episodic Dyscontrol

The term "Dyscontrol," although frequently utilized as an informal diagnostic label, was not an official diagnostic term in DSM II nor is it utilized in DSM III. In DSM III, however, the concept of the Dyscontrol Syndrome was utilized as the diagnostic criteria for the syndrome "Disorders of Impulsive Control Not Elsewhere Classified", particularly 312.34 Intermittent Explosive Disorder. The diagnostic criteria can be seen in Appendix B. It will be noted that this syndrome as defined fits the criteria of Episodic Dyscontrol, particularly Primary Dyscontrol, and was based on published accounts of the Dyscontrol Syndrome. The other syndromes under "Disorders of Impulsive Control" (pathological gambling, kleptomania, and pyromania), as defined in DSM III meet the criteria of the Dyscontrol Syndrome, more particularly Secondary Dyscontrol, in that all of these syndromes are characterized by the elements of prodromal increase in "tension"; limited premeditation; temporary resistance to act; gratification of a need or at least release of tension following the act; ego-syntonic element of the act itself; as well as self-reproach or regret following the act.

However, the Dyscontrol Syndrome as described in this chapter encompasses the whole range of possible impulsive acts, including particularly those where the goal is not only an aggressive act but also "flight" behavior or orgasmic release. If such acts have other characteristics of the Dyscontrol Syndrome, they should be classified under the category "Disorders of Impulse Control" 312.39 "Other Impulse Control Disorders", and then labeled specifically regarding the goal of the act. This would be preferable to looking elsewhere in the DSM III categories for an appropriate diagnosis, as this procedure will give us information regarding the prevalence of the Dyscontrol Syndrome. For example, Other Impulse Control Disorder (flight reaction) would be preferable to the diagnosis of 300.01 Panic Disorder. Published data on this Primary Dyscontrol Syndrome reflecting limbic hypersynchrony reveal that electrical stimulation of the limbic area often elicits not only an explosive rage reaction but also explosive panic reaction as described in the diagnostic criteria listed in DSM-III 300.01 Panic Disorder (see Appendix A).

The further advantage of postulating a common etiologic mechanism, namely, limbic dysfunction, to these two disorders (e.g., intermittent explosive disorder and panic disorder) is that one can look for a possible common pharmacologic regimen for behavior that otherwise is quite disparate.

The Dyscontrol Syndrome by definition is intermittent, episodic, or recurrent. This is indicated in DSM III for the diagnosis of both Intermittent Explosive Disorder and Panic Disorder. One of the diagnostic criteria is that the individual has had at least three attacks. Of course, there is always a first attack and so under DSM III one would utilize Isolated Explosive Disorder 312.35 for the first attack (and presumably the second attack). If the individual subsequently develops other attacks, then, the diagnosis could be changed to 312.34, The Intermittent Explosive Disorder. This allows us to collect data on the prevalence of a single explosive disorder which may have quite a different etiologic mechanism. It is unfortunate that the further differentiation of the "other" category under Impulse Dyscontrol does not allow for this differentiation between a single episode and a recurrent episode as it does for the explosive disorder.

The impulse disorders in DSM III are quite rightly designated as Axis I Diagnoses because no matter how ego-syntonic the behavior is during the act itself, in retrospect both the individual and his associates see the act as ego-alien, something quite out of character for the individual actor and out of context for the situation. Thus, the act meets the criteria for a symptom. However, in one subgroup of the Dyscontrol Syndrome "Acting Out" this ego-alien quality is minimized or denied through psychological defense mechanism. The most common defense mechanism is amnesia, and under DSM III the diagnosis of a Dissociative Disorder, either 300.12 Psychogenic Amnesia or 300.13 Psychogenic Fugue is the only possibility, although the diagnostic criteria for these disorders are quite inappropriate for the Dyscontrol Syndrome. Furthermore, defenses other than amnesia may be utilized to minimize the regret or remorse regarding the dyscontrol act. One of the common characteristics of acting out is repression in some form. Thus, acting out was defined elsewhere " . . . the act is so patently inappropriate to the situation and so out of character for the actor, one can only conclude the act is determined by unconscious motives as an attempt to resolve repressed conflicts." As DSM III eschews psychodynamic considerations, there are no psychodynamic terms. Therefore, I propose that the category for dyscontrol acts with amnesia or those dyscontrol acts which meet the definition of acting out would be classified under 312.39 Other Impulse Disorders with Qualifying Characteristics as (amnesia) or (acting out).

Furthermore, I prefer that the same diagnostic category be utilized for another type of deviant behavior not covered in DSM III. This behavior has been labeled in the psychiatric and particularly in the forensic literature as the "irresistible impulse." In this subgroup of the Dyscontrol Syndrome labeled "Impulse Dyscontrol," the act itself might be quite explosive and often aggressive but is proceeded not only by mounting tension listed as a criteria for Intermittent Explosive Disorder in DSM III but also by a conscious awareness of the specific impending action with the realization of the potential disastrous consequences of the act. This awareness is associated with waivering doubt and indecisiveness regarding the action, often accompanied by elaborate and bizarre attempts to control the impulse, thus, commonly referred to as an "Irresistible Impulse." This, too, then could be listed under 312.39 "Other Impulse Control Disorders" (Irresistible Impulse).

As the official labeling under DSM III for Dyscontrol Syndrome is limited to Axis I, this discussion could be considered not pertinent for a text on the Personality Disorders. However, the Dyscontrol Syndrome can be carelessly assigned to the Personality Disorder, leading to serious prognostic and therapeutic errors. It is probably true, as Shapiro proposes, there are individuals with an impulsive life-style. He says these individuals see the world as "a series of opportunities, temptations, frustrations, sensuous experiences, and fragmented impressions." There is no distinct category for such individuals under DSM III. In all likelihood they will be, if males, classified as "antisocial personalities" and if female as "histrionic personalities." I pointed out, elsewhere, that if one is to develop moral values, it demands a continuity and stability which is lacking in the world view of the impulsive personality, hence, they are at high risk for acting in an extractive criminal manner or developing the "flexible" superego characteristic of the histrionic personality. In DSM III these personality disorders are clustered with two other diagnostic possibilities, that is, the narcissistic and the borderline patients, all four personality types being described as "dramatic, emotional, or erratic." It is important to remember that the Dyscontrol Syndrome, by definition, describes deviant behavior as an interruption in the life-style or the life flow of that individual. Stated another way, the impulsive acts are not only out of context for the situation but also out of character for the individual involved. The dyscontrol patient does not manifest persisting deviant behavior but episodic or intermittent behavior. This intermittent behavior is usually a surprise to both the individual who has committed the impulsive act as well as to close associates who know the individual well, thus, they do not fulfill the criteria for the diagnoses of the personality disorders. This differential becomes crucial when one considers that the Dyscontrol Syndrome has a good prognosis with psychopharmacologic and/or psychotherapeutic intervention while the Personality Disorders, with their relatively poor prognosis, often suggest a therapeutic nihilism which is decidedly unwarranted for the Dyscontrol Syndrome. An analogous situation exists in the diagnosis of childhood disorders where careful differentiation should be made between the attention deficit disorders with or without hyperactivity and conduct disorders. For those centers trying to develop differential criteria for the impulsive life-style versus the dyscontrol syndrome as well as personality diagnoses of the histrionic, narcissistic, antisocial, and borderline, it would be well to utilize the diagnosis 301.89 Other or Mixed Personality Disorders and qualify this with the statement, Impulsive Life-Style.

Treatment

The impulsive acting out patient, whether he has associated underlying persistent character disorders or not, presents an unusually difficult therapeutic problem. Some of these difficulties are the following.
1. Although these individuals may be seriously dangerous both to themselves and to society during their dyscontrol action, they may have long periods of normalcy or quiescence. This makes it difficult to insist upon long-term hospitalization for the protection of either the patient or society. The episodic symptoms abate often within a few days after hospitalization,

but on the other hand may recur again immediately upon discharge, even following months of intensive milieu therapy within the hospital. Likewise, if the dyscontrol act has resulted in conviction with imprisonment, such individuals contribute more than their fair share of recidivism following their release.

2. Outpatient therapy is complicated by the tendency of these patients to terminate therapy precipitously as a dyscontrol act. At other times, they use the threat of dyscontrol behavior to manipulate their therapist.

3. Dyscontrol patients with episodic physiological reactions or abnormal EEGs are likely to have multiple physicians, hence often multiple, conflicting therapeutic regimens. A corollary is that a therapeutic program may require combined pharmacological and re-educational (psychotherapeutic) techniques. This complicates the delegation of responsibility for improvement to several responsible physicians.

4. In those individuals where an epileptoid or maturational mechanism is thought to be significant, it is usually desirable to prescribe medication. At the same time, medication alone is seldom sufficient without a relatively intensive re-educational program to teach the patient how to avoid precipitating stimuli, exert inhibitory control through "thought as trial action," and modify his need gratification. The fact that the patient is also receiving medication dilutes his sense of responsibility for behavioral change.

5. These patients tend to misuse drugs. Either they try to control dysphoric moods by indiscriminate drug use with subsequent habituation to drugs, or alcohol, or in confused states they may not remember to take prescribed medication or forget that they have taken it, hence take excessive medication. This problem is further complicated by the fact that toxic symptoms of drug overdose and the episodic symptoms themselves are often quite similar. Differentiating between a patient with too much or too little medication cannot be easily done.

On the positive side, patients with episodic dyscontrol, even where the dyscontrol is superimposed on a severe character disorder, often see their dyscontrol acts as ego-alien in retrospect. They can, during intervals between dyscontrol acts, evaluate their behavior with realistic concern. In this sense, there is the "split in the ego" which is so necessary for any re-educational insight psychotherapy.

The first prerequisite for an adequate therapeutic regimen is to determine the extent to which epileptoid factors contribute to the disordered behavior. If this is significant, then anticonvulsants or the minor tranquilizers, which elevate convulsive threshold, should be used, keeping in mind several limitations. Anticonvulsants are not universally effective even in typical epilepsy, and sometimes one will work when another fails. Also, there is little range between an effective therapeutic dose and dose levels which lead to toxic or at least disagreeable side effects. The therapeutic effectiveness of a medical regimen can often be increased without increasing the side effects by combining several synergistically acting drugs. For example, one can combine one or more of the standard anticonvulsants with phenobarbital or one of the benzodiazepines (Librium, Valium, Serax). The usual procedure is to establish epileptoid mechanisms definitively on the basis of amelioration of symptoms through such a medical regimen. However, all too often dose levels are too small or a combination of medications is not explored before such a regimen is discontinued. The doctor concludes that failure to respond to anticonvulsants indicates the absence of epileptoid mechanisms, whereas it more likely reflects an inadequate drug trial.

If the medical control of dyscontrol acts results in an exacerbation of the chronic, underlying psychopathology, close scrutiny usually reveals that inadequate attention has been given to the re-educational, psychotherapeutic program. For instance, the importance of the secondary gains of dyscontrol behavior has been overlooked, or no opportunity has been provided for the realistic expression of affects and the gratification of basic needs.

If at all possible, phenothiazines or other major tranquilizers should be avoided in the treatment of these patients as they often aggravate dyscontrol acts, particularly if the phenothiazines are administered at low doses. Should the chronic, underlying psychopathology demand such treatment, then the medical regimen should include, in addition, anticonvulsants and/or benzodiazepines. It has been reported that in some instances phenothiazines are useful in the control of the episodic behavioral disorders. If such is the case, they should be given at high doses, and low-dosage maintenance regimens should be avoided. Likewise, when the depressive symptoms are of an episodic nature, patients will respond to the benzodiazepines or anticonvulsants, whereas they may be aggravated by usual antidepressant regimens. The fact that such complicated pharmacological combinations may be necessary indicates that the ideal pharmacological agent has not been found (6).

There are a few generalizations that can be made regarding psychotherapeutic re-educational therapy. The first is that the therapist must be willing to take chances because if he is overly concerned about his patient's dyscontrol acts, the patient will consciously or unconsciously utilize his dyscontrol behavior to manipulate the therapist. A second generalization is that the therapist must anticipate possible future dyscontrol acts and make preparatory plans which are discussed with the patient for handling such behavior. Goals are to intercept the dyscontrol acts before they occur or to minimize the disastrous consequences of these acts. This may require the aid of responsible family members, peers, or cooperating professionals. A third is that during quiescent periods between episodic behavior, the therapist should relentlessly confront the patient with his dyscontrol acts. He should analyze not only precipitating environmental situations, but also disguised motivation and inappropriate need gratification. The fourth generalization is that the therapist must be willing to combine drug and re-educational (psychotherapeutic) techniques on one hand, but on the other he must be prepared to withhold all medication, if the patient will not follow carefully the prescribed drug regimen. This is particularly true in those patients who are prone to develop a psychological dependency upon drugs. Fifth, it is desirable that the therapist be flexible as far as the therapeutic setting itself is concerned. Minor dyscontrol acts which are likely to occur in his office can be microscopically scrutinized by the patient and therapist together. In patients who tend to deny through amnesia or to project responsibility for dyscontrol behavior onto the environment, conjoint sessions with patient and significant peers are often necessary to confront the patient with his dyscontrol behavior. He otherwise hides such behavior from the therapist or defensively rationalizes. However, this flexibility does not apply to the frequence, time, or setting of the therapeutic session. A schedule should be rigidly adhered to if the therapist is to resist secondary gains from dyscontrol acts through manipulation. Finally, it is desirable to have one clinician responsible for the total medical management. As it is seldom possible to find a clinician with equal expertise in the medical, neurological, and psychiatric areas, the primary physician is forced to utilize consultants. However, it should be arranged so that he will interpret the consultant's findings to the patient and dispense any recommended medications himself. All of these generalizations regarding the treatment of the impulsive, acting out individual have been discussed in greater detail elsewhere (6).

Dyscontrol patients whose episodic behavior is superimposed on a persisting, sociopathic character disorder often justify dyscontrol acts with superficial rationalization. The net effect is that both their chronic deviation from the norm, as well as their episodic dyscontrol, are truly ego-syntonic, even in retrospect. It is these individuals who need a 24-hour control of their environment with immediate inescapable punishment for failures in socialized behavior and equally immediate and appropriate rewards for successes. This is the only possibility for developing the frustrations and anxieties necessary to instill an appropriate motivation for behavioral change (2). However, this disciplined environment rarely, if ever, can be supervised by the individual who is also responsible for any re-educational, insight therapy. It is in precisely this situation where clear-cut separation between the "ward administrator" or the custodial personnel on one hand and the therapist on the other should be maintained. Such an environment must prevent the self-defeating action of the termination or avoidance of effective therapeutic sessions. During these sessions, even though one may be utilizing a combined drug/psychotherapeutic regimen, it must be clearly understood that the sole responsibility for the patient's behavior lies with the patient himself, no matter what neurophysiological deficits there may be or how capricious the external environment.

Occasionally, dyscontrol behavior is a single episode or a rare event representing an explosive rebellion against an overly strict conscience which otherwise severely inhibits a patient's behavior. A somewhat related phenomenon is the acting out or impulsivity that the inhibited neurotic may demonstrate as a sign of his "improvement" in the course of psychotherapy. This is particularly true in those neurotics who tend to inhibit action when action otherwise would be appropriate. As they learn to act, the first stage may be inappropriate, impulsive action. In both instances, it is important to understand the dyscontrol act by focusing first on why the patient committed himself to action at this particular time and place. With such a focus, associational connections with past experiences and inappropriate consequences of the act usually become obvious. Again, details of the psychotherapeutic techniques for treating the episodic behavioral disorders have been reported by the author elsewhere (6).

A long-term follow-up suggests that, contrary to the usually expressed pessimism regarding therapy with dyscontrol patients, they do respond well to an appropriate regimen which identifies both the neurophysiological and psychodynamic concomitants of their symptomatic behavior. Despite the turmoil of the treatment process, some of the most gratifying therapeutic successes, for both the patient and the therapist, occur with this group. To mention briefly a few examples: A top executive who was incapacitated for many years, drank heavily, completely neglected his family, and whimpered childishly for help in the therapeutic setting is now abstinent and authoritatively assuming his role as head of the household, as well as functioning successfully in his executive position. A mother whose fugue states were so prolonged and irresponsible that she lost her husband, as well as control of her children, became utterly dependent on elderly parents. With the aid of therapy, she ultimately completed her interrupted professional training, is now gainfully employed, and has resumed responsibility for her children. Another woman whose life was so totally chaotic that she too was forced to give up caring for her children and was divorced by her husband is now working in a highly competitive professional position, at the same time caring for her children, household, and new spouse. A man who could function only at a menial clerical level because of his impulsiveness and frequent habituation to drugs now successfully manages his own successful business. These results are typical of many patients with episodic behavioral disorders who have been treated intensively utilizing both pharmacological and psychotherapeutic techniques.

REFERENCES

1. Abt, L. E., and Weissman, S. *Acting Out; Theoretical and Clinical Aspects.* Grune & Stratton, New York, 1965.
2. Boslow, H. M. Administrative structure and therapeutic climate. Prison J., 46:23, 1966.
3. Ervin, F., Epstein, A. W., and King, H. E. Behavior of epileptic and nonepileptic patients with temporal spikes. A. M. A. Arch. Neurol. Psychiatry, 74:488, 1955.
4. Heath, R. G. Correlations of electrical recordings from cortical and subcortical regions of the brain with abnormal behavior in human subjects. Confin. Neurol., 18:306, 1957.

5. Heath, R. G., Mickle, W. A., and Monroe, R. R. Characteristic recording from various specific subcortical nuclear masses in the brains of psychiatric and non-psychiatric patients. Trans. Am. Neurol. Assoc., 80:17, 1955.
6. Monroe, R. R. *Episodic Behavioral Disorders*, p. 20. Harvard University Press, Cambridge, 1970.
7. Pond, D. A. The development of normal rhythms. In *Electroencephalography*, D. Hill and G. Parr (Eds.). Macmillan Co., New York, 1963.
8. Shapiro, D. *Neurotic Styles*. Basic Books, New York, 1965.

21

PSYCHOLOGICAL TESTING OF THE SEVERE PERSONALITY DISORDERS

Francis L. Carney, Ph.D.

Over the years the role of the clinical psychologist on the mental health team has been expanded and become diversified (4), but there are two areas in which his training sets him uniquely apart from other team members: research and testing. The need for research is patently obvious, and in this role the psychologist generally works in close cooperation with members of other disciplines. The need for testing is not quite so obvious, and what psychological testing can and cannot accomplish is not necessarily too well understood by other disciplines, and this leads to polar extremes in attitudes toward testing. On the one hand there is the attitude that testing is a complete waste of time, and on the other the attitude that testing will supply all the answers. Neither attitude is valid. It is best to conceive of any psychological test as *a sample of behavior obtained under controlled conditions.* There is nothing that will be revealed by psychological testing that will not be revealed in the clinical interview and through observation of the patient over a period of time. Psychological testing is at best a shortcut, the creation of conditions under which particular behaviors will occur rather than waiting for them to occur spontaneously in time.

At what point then can psychological testing be of most value to the psychiatrist? First, when he does not have the opportunity to observe the patient over time as, for example, where a court orders an examination and report within 30 days or less. He may be asked not only to make a diagnosis but also to predict how the patient will behave at some point in the future. In many of these cases the diagnosis and the dynamics are relatively clear-cut, and psychological testing under these conditions would be superfluous. However, the psychiatrist might well run into a situation where he knows the patient is paranoid, but he can't determine if the condition is that of a paranoid personality or a paranoid psychosis; a psychological examination might help resolve the question. Or a psychiatrist might be sure the patient is suffering from a personality disorder, but he isn't sure how dangerous the person is; again psychological testing might help. There is probably only one situation in which psychological testing is absolutely required—usually by law—and that is in determining I.Q. for purposes of assessing criminal responsibility or commitment to a hospital for the mentally retarded.

Second, psychological testing may be valuable at the beginning of therapy. The psychologist can usually answer such questions as: Will the patient profit most by a male or female therapist? Is a dynamic therapy indicated or might a supportive casework approach be best? Is the patient likely to be a management problem in the institution? What is the patient's potential for suicidal (homicidal) acting out? What direction should efforts at vocational rehabilitation take? What problems in therapy can be anticipated? These sample questions do not exhaust the possibilities, but, in general, the more specific the questions the more likely the psychologist can provide the answer.

Third, psychological testing can be valuable during the course of treatment or toward the end of treatment, especially if earlier test protocols are available for comparison. During the course of treatment the psychiatrist has ample opportunity to observe behavioral change, but he can't always be sure that there has been dynamic change as well. This might be of no more than academic interest in the treatment of most neurotic and psychotic conditions, but in the treatment of the severe personality disorders it is of crucial importance. The personality-disordered individual is generally forced into treatment, and he has no motivation to make basic changes; his desire is to "play the therapy game" and to convince others by his behavior that he no longer needs treatment and/or incarceration (6). Psychological testing can tap these dynamics of personality which would indicate if real change has taken place.

Having indicated the value of psychological testing in these broad terms, now let us focus a little more specifically on the tests and how they are used.

Psychological Tests

There are literally hundreds of tests listed in Buros' Mental Measurement Yearbooks (5) (which, incidentally, discuss in great detail the tests I will mention briefly), and only a few of these are used routinely in the clinical situation. Those most used are the Wechsler Adult Intelligence Scale (WAIS), the Rorschach ink blot, the Bender Gestalt, and the House-Tree-Person (HTP), and these four will form the basis of the discussion below. Other frequently used tests such as the Minnesota Multiphasic Personality Inventory (MMPI) and the Thematic Apperception Test (TAT) tend to have limited validity with the personality disorders, though they are excellent tests, especially when used with intellectually bright adults.

The WAIS (4). This test of intelligence is made up of eleven subtests which provide three scores: a Verbal IQ, which taps such functions as reasoning and judgment; a Performance IQ, which gives some indication of perceptual-motor abilities and dexterity; and a Full Scale IQ, which gives an indication of the individual's overall intellectual potential. Though this is specifically a test of intellectual functioning, certain other diagnostic information can also be derived from it.

In the normal individual one can expect the scores on all eleven subtests to be relatively equal, with no more than a point or two spread. When the score of one of these subtests is especially deviant, the clinician asks why. For example, in neurosis it is not unusual to see especially low scores on those subtests which most require attention and concentration, an indication of the debilitating effect of anxiety. Antisocial personalities may get unusually high scores on subtests which measure degree of social awareness, reflecting the fact that the antisocial individual is often shrewdly in touch with the world around him, one reason why his manipulations can be so successful. Sometimes the patterns of subtest scores are completely erratic, and this is characteristic of psychosis in which the thought processes of the individual are erratic and unpredictable.

One can also make inferences from the relationship of the verbal and performance IQs. In the normal individual one doesn't expect more than a 10-point spread. When the Verbal IQ is significantly higher than the performance, this may mean that the individual is unusually introspective and reflective, a thinker rather than a doer, and when the Performance IQ is significantly higher, this may be an indication of a person who solves problems by doing, one who has an acting-out potential. (A low Performance IQ may also be an indication of some perceptual-motor impairment and thus a sign of organicity). Schizophrenics characteristically do better on the verbal section of the WAIS; the score tells us when a person is introspective but it tells us nothing about the quality of his introspections. Antisocial personalities characteristically do better on the performance subtests, an indication of their general action orientation and unreflective life-style.

Every test provides a sample of behavior and no one test is apt to be *the* diagnostic instrument. The WAIS gives us a measure of intelligence, but along the way it also gives us some idea of other personality functions.

The Bender Gestalt (3). This test was originally designed just as a test for organicity, but over the years it has evolved into an instrument for assessing personality. It consists of nine geometric designs printed on cards which are presented to the patient one at a time; the patient is provided with pencil and paper and he is asked simply to reproduce the designs. The reproductions of organics contain characteristic flaws which indicate a need for neurological study and which invalidate this test for further use. In the absence of organicity the Bender may be used as a personality test.

Just how it is used depends upon the psychodynamic orientation of the examiner. For example, psychologists well versed in psychoanalytic theory are apt to make many interpretations based on the relationship of angular figures to curved figures, angles connoting masculinity and curves connoting femininity. While this kind of interpretation may seem a little esoteric, experientially we see certain kinds of drawing over and over again. One figure is a circle touched by one point of a diamond. Rapists frequently have the point thrusting through the circle while men who are afraid of women (or women who are afraid of men) keep a clear separation between the diamond and the circle. Another figure is two rectangular shapes of equal size which intersect with one another at an angle; homosexuals tend to draw the rectangles side by side while passive and dependent men tend to make one rectangle significantly smaller than the other.

Probably the most valid interpretations come from pure behavioral observation. The patient has a blank piece of paper in front of him and he knows he will have to draw a series of designs. How does he handle the task? Some patients start at the upper left hand corner of the paper and proceed in a logical and orderly manner along the top or the side of the paper, an indication of a logical and orderly approach to problem-solving. Others put their drawings any which way on the paper, a schizophrenic trait but not exclusively so. Some patients automatically number their drawings, and this may be an indication of obsessive-compulsive qualities; even more compulsive is the patient who draws a box around his drawings, and the most compulsive of all is the patient who draws the box first and forces the drawing into it. How much space does the patient use? The highly repressed, the depressive, the inadequate and insecure individual will crowd all his drawings into one tiny area of the paper; the expansive, extroverted and aggressive individual will fill a page or two; the manic will use a separate piece of paper for every drawing. The more anxious the individual, the more the line quality of the drawings will be faint or sketchy; the more angry and hostile the individual, the more the lines will be firm and dark.

These are only a few of the interpretations that can be made, and they are usually made in conjunction with psychodynamic interpretations of the individual figures. A good deal of information can be gleaned from this one test, but the test itself is so innocuous that most patients approach it with confidence. With the personality disorders it can be the one test that provides the most information. People with this kind of problem tend to fake or malinger so it is not unusual for them to put forth no effort on the WAIS, to reject the majority of Rorschach cards, and to produce little more than scribbles on the HTP. It is difficult to malinger with the Bender except by absolutely refusing to draw the figures, and while even the psychologically naive patient may have some idea as to how those other tests are interpreted, even the test-wise antisocial personality is ordinarily unaware of the wealth of information contained in those innocent little circles, dots, and squares.

The HTP (8). This test is fairly simple to administer; the patient is provided with a pencil and a sheet of paper for each drawing, and he is instructed first to draw a house, then a tree, then a person, and finally a person of the opposite sex (opposite from the sex of the person first drawn). As with the Bender, many inferences can be drawn from such things as line quality and placement of the drawing on the paper, but in this test psychodynamic interpretations play an increased role.

The house may be a projection of how the patient feels about his own home and family; it can be bright and alive or cold and remote. Windows and doors suggest how the patient may relate to his environment; the psychotic may not supply a door or his door may have no door knob; the paranoid may have windows heavily draped or shuttered. The chimney, as an appendage to something, is often considered to be a penis-equivalent; male adolescents and adult sex offenders often pay particular attention to their drawing of the chimney. Treatment of the roof area gives some indication of fantasy life while treatment of the base area gives some indication of security.

The tree is thought to tap the patient's relatively deep and unconscious feelings about himself. Unhappy, depressed individuals will draw stark, barren, naked trees; euphoric and narcissistic patients will clothe their trees with leaves, birds, fruit; histrionic people may draw more exotic trees like swaying palms or decorated Christmas trees. Children and adolescents frequently show a scar on the trunk of the tree which is thought to be related to some particular trauma in their life, and the closer it is placed to the base line, the earlier in life it occurred. Roots that clutch show a need for security; trees that bend suggest a person who feels at the mercy of forces outside of himself. The personality disorders tend to produce a "keyhole" tree, just white space surrounded by a line; this may suggest a real inner emptiness or it may suggest malingering.

The drawing of the person gets at more conscious feelings about the self. Males are expected to draw their own sex first; failure to do so suggests some problems in sexual identity. The comparative size and general quality of the male and female drawings suggests how the person feels about his own sex and the opposite sex. The age of the person drawn suggests the emotional age of the patient. Adolescents, narcissists, and homosexuals tend to draw young, athletic men; histrionic individuals tend to draw sexy males and females; immature and inadequate men and women draw pictures of children and teenagers; psychotics draw curiously distorted and sexless figures. Every feature of the drawing is also subject to interpretation; in psychosomatic illness the neck may be extremely long, suggesting the unconscious separation of psyche and soma; paranoids tend to pay particular attention to eyes and ears; hands in the pockets suggest people who have guilts over manipulative activity, such as masturbation; absence of hands or feet suggest people who feel they can do nothing and go nowhere; the treatment of bottoms and pockets is interpreted in terms of security; neckties are phallic symbols; and what the person is wearing and doing also suggest interpretations along many different lines.

The Rorschach (1, 2, 10). This certainly is the most sophisticated and most widely used of all psychodiagnostic tests. It can be used and interpreted in such a myriad of ways that in these pages I can give just the briefest hint of its capabilities. Essentially, there are 10 cards, each with a different inkblot, handed to the patient one at a time. The patient is instructed to report what he "sees" or what the inkblot reminds him of. The examiner then conducts an inquiry in order to understand the patient's response more fully.

What the patient sees is rarely so important as how he sees it. A content analysis has validity, but to stop there is to miss the most salient features of the test. What the patient does with form—that is, whether it is possible to see what he says he sees—is a measure of intellectual control. When form quality is grossly impaired, the intellectual controls of the patient are grossly impaired, and he is probably psychotic. When intellectual control is good but rigid, the patient is overcontrolled and highly repressed. Patients dominated by emotions tend in the direction of hysteria.

The movement response (M) is particularly important. Human beings doing something is a good response and tends to be a measure of the person's integrative and creative ability. The normal adult will give two or three M's and bright normals will give many more. However, as with any factor in the Rorschach there must be a balance with other factors, and when the M response is unusually high for a given patient it can be interpreted as mania or flight of ideas. Animal movement responses (FM) are healthy and normal for children; an excess of FM in an adult record suggests immaturity. The movement of inanimate objects (m) is healthy for very young children; in adults it must be considered a sign of regression and an indication that the patient may be at the mercy of very primitive urges.

Shading responses—using black and white as if they were colors—tell us something about anxiety. If in a record only one or two shading responses occur, where they occur may tell us what the patient is anxious about. A record with many shading responses is not unusual in neurosis. Treating the inkblot as if it had a tactual quality—"a furry animal," or "hard, sharp granite"—is typical of people who are very careful and wary in their interaction with the environment, such as both neurotics and paranoids. A vista response such as "There's a man way off in the distance, and he's walking towards me," occurs where the patient is trying to keep distance between himself and the anxiety-provoking stimulus. (That particular response, incidentally, was given by a young man who was in a homosexual panic).

There are so many factors to be considered in the interpretation of the Rorschach. How long does it take to respond? Depressives take forever while the callous antisocial personalities respond without thinking. How many responses in the record? Normal is about 20, the personality disorders give 10 or less, and a manic record can go into the hundreds. What does turning the cards mean or rejection of one or more of the cards? Anxiety, negativism, or passive-resistive—any of these, depending on other factors. In a sense the

Rorschach is the one test no patient can "beat." The experienced examiner can get just as much from what the patient doesn't see as from what he does see, and the patient can say no word or make any gesture that is not subject to interpretation.

The Differential Diagnosis (12, 14)

Differential diagnosis by psychological testing is like other diagnostic procedures: one starts by eliminating what the condition isn't and from what is left over one goes on to determine what the condition is. Severe psychotic conditions can be eliminated fairly quickly because in severe psychosis there is a pattern of deterioration that permeates all test results. Anxiety is the hallmark of neurosis, and test protocols which give little evidence of anxiety are not produced by neurotics. In fact, the classic psychotic and neurotic conditions are so easy to spot clinically that psychological testing really is not necessary. Psychiatrists tend to refer for differential diagnosis when they themselves are not quite sure, and these cases usually are not easy ones for the psychologist either.

One of the most frequent tasks given to the psychologist is to distinguish between a paranoid psychosis and other paranoid conditions when the behavior of the patient is clearly paranoid but when there is no history of personality deterioration. Instances might be a man who has been arrested many times for assaulting or threatening his wife whom he accuses of all kinds of misbehavior, but he has never been assaultive toward anyone else; or the woman who is having a running battle with one particular neighbor but no one else. In either case the reality testing of the patient might be impaired; either might be in the first stages of a severe illness, or either might never be any more "sick" than they are at the moment. The test protocols of such patients tend to abound with paranoid projection but they tend also to show good reality testing and firm if overly rigid intellectual controls. However, there is one indication of deterioration—loss of control and loss of distance—that is very subtle and that can be seen in *how* the patient responds to the Rorschach and which can be labeled "ideas of reference." Following are examples, the pathological content in italics: "It looks like a bat. *I saw a bat like that last year.*" "These remind me of drawing that *I saw in a book once.*" "That's a fur coat. *It looks like the one I bought my wife a few years ago.*" In more deteriorated patients the responses might be something like this: "It looks like a bat. *I was at Carlsbad Caverns a few years ago and there were a lot of bats there.*" "These remind me of drawings. *When my son was in college he'd bring home books that had drawings in them like that.*" "That's a fur coat. *I'm against fur coats—killing all those animals just so some woman can prance and show off.*"

Is that enough to distinguish with certainty between psychosis and non-psychosis? Maybe. It is always the total test picture that makes the difference and not just one factor, but when there is one glaring example of pathology in an otherwise unexceptional record, the psychologist must explain it: it didn't occur by chance. Which leads to another question: When is a psychosis not a psychosis? There are two possible answers: When it is a dissociative disorder or when it is drug-induced.

The protocols of the dissociative disorders are replete with psychotic manifestations: WAIS subtest scores are thoroughly erratic, drawings are placed helter-skelter on the paper, and reality testing is barely adequate. However, where a psychotic will dash off a drawing of a dehumanized person, the dissociative may take painstaking time and attention with it; psychotic productions are bleak and empty while dissociative productions may be overelaborated; and there is a qualititative difference even in their poor form responses on the Rorschach. For example, both the following are poor form responses to Card IX. The psychotic: "The inside of somebody. Somebody has been torn apart and those are his insides." And the dissociative: "Human anatomy. Kidneys, lungs, vertebrae. Like an anatomical drawing."

The psychedelic drugs do strange things to people. The experience of the "trip" has been likened to psychotic thought, and even when the trip is over, vestiges of psychotic thought remain. The forensic psychiatrist, unfortunately, will see too many youngsters who "tripped" and never came back, but there are times when he will want to know just how far the patient has gone and just how much health remains. In general, on testing, an acute psychotic reaction looks like an acute psychotic reaction whether functional or drug-induced, and, in general, the test protocol of someone who has taken LSD is never completely normal again. One can gain an estimate of the amount of intellectual control the patient has, but there are always pockets—big or small—of unusual thinking. It is as if patients who have "tripped" do see the world in a different way, and their ability to survive in normal society depends on some interrelationship between the amount of control and the degree of unusual thought.

For many conditions anxiety becomes a major determining factor, and it is important to distinguish between *objective anxiety* and *neurotic anxiety*. Objective anxiety is fear and apprehension which has a basis in some real, tangible situation. Neurotic anxiety is largely unconscious and apparently has little relationship to objective reality. The majority of patients with a personality disorder will show some signs of objective anxiety but little indication of neurotic anxiety.

In the forensic setting one can readily understand why even antisocial personalities may be apprehensive in that they are usually being examined as a part of some criminal proceeding which may well determine if they are to be free or be incarcerated. Objective anxiety may take the form of being unable to do one's best on the WAIS, inability to concentrate on certain of the subtests, sketchiness and poor line quality on drawings, and nervous turning of the Rorschach cards. These signs are not unusual with any of the personality disorders but neither do they occur with such frequency they can be expected. Signs of neurotic anxiety are such things as heavy shading of any or all of the HTP drawings, and any of the shading, tactual, and vista responses on the Rorschach. The more an individual is clearly neurotic, the more these signs of neurotic anxiety will occur. If signs of neurotic anxiety are accompanied by wild flights of imagination and emotional liability, we may be seeing a dissociative or somatiform disorder; if accompanied by overmeticulous Bender drawings and a concern with small details of the Rorschach inkblots, we probably have an obsessive-compulsive disorder; and if the drawings have a stark, desolate quality and the Rorschach content is either morbid or trite, we probably have a depressive disorder.

On testing, the personality disorders are characterized by rigid, overintellectualized control; Rorschach responses are dominated by good form and there is little use made of movement, color, or shading. These patients are relatively negativistic and uninvolved in testing: drawings are sloppy and hurriedly dashed off; Rorschach responses are unreflective and one or more cards may be rejected; no effort goes into the intelligence test, and wild guessing at answers is common. Malingering is a possibility, and a patient may draw a stick figure for a person and reject all the Rorschach cards. In short, these patients tend to give us as little as they can, so the little they do give takes on particular diagnostic significance.

For example, a patient rejects only one Rorschach card. If he rejected several of them, one would suspect malingering but why only one out of the ten? And which card? Card II is related to feelings of aggression and passivity; Card IV is related to feelings about authority figures; Card VI is called the sex card; Card VII has to do with feelings about women. Therefore, is the card rejected related to some conflict the patient is refusing to face?

We don't expect signs of neurotic anxiety. Therefore, what does it mean if the patient draws a heavily shaded chimney on his house? We don't expect color and movement responses. What does it mean if to Card II he responds, "Two men fighting and blood flying all over the place." What does it mean if he numbers his Bender drawings, if he draws a naked man, or if he draws a decorated Christmas tree? All the personality disorders may start off the same way but each patient then adds something special, something which makes him unique and which points the way toward the differential diagnosis. This, ultimately, involves the interrelationship of so many factors that we cannot take the time here to show how one distinguishes between the antisocial personality and the passive-aggressive personality, and so on. Rather, let us look at behavioral characteristics. Whatever the diagnosis, can we predict such things as dangerousness and response to treatment?

Prediction of Behavior

It is important to remember that the most dangerous patients are not necessarily those who are behaviorally most aggressive; in fact, the ability to express hostility verbally may even be a sign of health (13). For that matter, the commission of a particularly violent offense is not in itself the best evidence that the patient is likely to act out violently again. Consider the following illustrations.

Case Example 1. Peter is a 16-year-old "hippie" type with long flowing hair whose attitude toward adults is one of condescending superiority. He was rejected by his parents from birth and his early childhood was a nightmare of abuse and neglect. At the age of 12 he ran away from home, and in the course of his wanderings he was befriended by a Mr. J who took the boy into his home and then began using him homosexually. Peter ran away again and this time was picked up by the juvenile authorities. Peter refused to go home, and rather than go to an institution he asked to be placed in Mr. J's custody. The court went along with this, even though Mr. J's reputation was none too savory and even though he was having domestic problems of his own. Also in the home was Mr. J's daughter, a girl the same age as Peter. In the course of the next three years Mr. J became even more disturbed; while he had a passion for Peter, he became even more abusive to his wife and daughter. Peter suffered Mr. J's attention while he fell in love with the girl. Mrs. J eventually ran off with another man, leaving her husband and the two teenagers in a very peculiar *ménage-à-trois*. Mr. J then became so abusive toward his daughter that Peter could stand it no longer, and coldly and premeditatively, he shot and killed the man. Peter was sent to a State Psychiatric Hospital for evaluation. On psychiatric examination both his attitude and history clearly labeled him a sociopath. But on psychological examination he proved to be anything but a sociopath. In fact, considering his life history, the degree of mental health in the youngster was astounding. For one thing, even though his education had been interrupted many times, he had an IQ of 115, bright normal range, with every indication that his potential was higher still. In spite of his homosexual activity, he clearly identified as a male, and in spite of his disastrous interpersonal experiences he clearly had the capacity and desire to relate positively and warmly to others. His cold facade was just that—a defense, and beneath this defense there was a warm, creative, striving young man just aching for positive growth experiences and the opportunity to be *somebody*. On the basis of the psychological it was possible to predict that the youngster was not dangerous and that imprisonment would be the most ego-destructive of "treatments." While psychotherapy was not contraindicated, it also seemed that this youngster would make significant progress with little more than placement in a good home and a warm, friendly, and supportive case work approach. For the record, he was diagnosed "adjustment reaction of adolescence."

Case Example 2. Billy is another 16-year-old, a slightly built boy with short blond hair, blue eyes, and a baby face. He was born and raised in an upper-middle class suburb, and there is no history of unusual family problems. Billy was always a quiet and withdrawn boy, a child who was never a problem to any adult. His behavior in school was excellent and his grades above average;

however, he was described as a loner, and he never voluntarily participated in any group activity. At puberty he became even more withdrawn, and he assiduously avoided the company of girls. At age 16—"because I was curious"—he started breaking into the homes of neighbors. The first time he did nothing more than look around. The second time—and the third and the fourth—he looked specifically for women's jewelry, which he stole, and he then proceeded to tear the house apart, breaking everything breakable and then slashing at mattresses and cushions with his pocketknife. In the fifth house he was still looking for jewelry when sounds outside alerted him to the fact that the lady of the house was returning. Though he had every opportunity to run away, he instead went to the basement where he found a hammer, and then carried the hammer back up to the bedroom where he waited for the woman. As soon as she entered he hit her over the head—then hit her several more times. Finally, to make sure, he strangled her. After he was apprehended he was examined as to "competency to stand trial," and he was found to be sane and competent with a diagnosis of "schizoid personality." After he was convicted he was sent to Patuxent Institution for further evaluation and possible treatment. One criteria for commitment to Patuxent is dangerousness. Clinically, this boy is a classic schizoid: cold, aloof, and withdrawn, curled into a tight little world of his own but still able to adequately test reality and function in society if only in his muted, low key way. He looks harmless; in fact, he looks pathetic. But he has killed once, and what is the likelihood that he will kill again? From the clinical history alone one can judge only on the basis of past behavior, but the test results say with a resounding "Yes! He will probably kill again." The test results aren't especially dramatic. It would be nice if the Rorschach gave us some insights into his fantasy life but it doesn't, because, at this point in time the boy is still too closely guarded and the Rorschach reflects mainly his repression and intellectualization. The HTP continues to reflect the barren, cold world in which the boy lives, but here we get the first indication of his warped sexuality: his drawing of a male is a very pleasant and prepubertal boy; the woman he draws is large and menacing, her face distorted, ugly, evil. However, it is the Bender which gives the clue to his control. The tight, withdrawn schizoid should produce Bender drawings that are tightly confined to one area of the paper. This boy explodes outward, his Bender drawings occupying all the space on both sides of two full sheets. With this as the primary clue we now spot psychodynamic indications of a barely controlled acting-out potential with aggressivity directed primarily toward women.

Billy was committed to Patuxent and he is now in treatment.

Note: Seven years have passed since these boys were first examined, and this is what happened to them. Peter, in spite of the hospital's recommendation against it, was sent to prison, and later he was admitted to Patuxent Institution. However, though Patuxent is the most humane of prisons, and though the boy was in psychotherapy, Patuxent is still a prison, and the prediction that Peter's ego controls would break came true. He is still in Patuxent and still in treatment, but he is now psychotic. Billy, on the other hand, had the ability to wall himself off from the destructive forces within the prison environment so that, in a sense, the prison atmosphere never touched him. Luckily, he also grabbed on to his therapist as to a lifesaver, and with this one human relationship as a start, he was able to resolve many of his interpersonal conflicts, and to get his feelings under control. Eventually, he was moved to outpatient status, and at this writing he has been in the community for nearly 3 years. He is in college, pursuing a career in a laboratory science which requires minimal human contact.

These two cases are extremes, and the more common situation is the assessment of a violence potential in paranoid personalities and passive-aggressive personalities. In every case the best indication is the relative way the patient handles color and movement on the Rorschach plus the degree of control indicated on the projective drawings. This is not to discount the content of Rorschach responses: there is certainly a qualitative difference between these two responses to Card II: (a) "Bears, fighting and tearing at each other; bleeding." (b) "Teddy bears kissing." As always, it is the total constellation of test factors and their relationship to one another which makes prediction possible.

In addition to the violence potential it is often important to predict the potential for sexual acting-out, especially in the assessment of pedophiles. (In the assessment of rapists, violence rather than sexuality is the big factor.) The typical pedophile is a passive-aggressive type or a dependent personality, and in either case emotional immaturity is the outstanding personality characteristic. His defenses usually include rigid intellectualization and an absolute absence of anxiety. Thus, any indication of neurotic anxiety becomes a sign of health and provides a clue to behavioral functioning. Thus, in two recent cases both patients gave Rorschach responses that were ladden with animal movement (immaturity) and content such as "pretty flowers" and "clowns" (passivity) which gave no indication of a violence potential nor of a potential for growth and insight. Both patients produced orderly Benders which gave more evidence of their intellectual control than of their individual psychodynamics. Patient 1, who molested prepubertal girls, drew male and female figures, both of which were under age 10; his drawings of the house and tree were unexceptional. Patient 2, who molested teenage boys, drew as a male figure a rather handsome and idealized teenage boy, and the female was an older, rather stern looking woman; he produced a tree which was heavily shaded and which had prominent roots which clutched at the ground line; the house was more shaded still, heavily reinforced by double lines, and the treatment of the doors and windows suggested that they were barred. With this information one could predict that both, if set free, would continue their pedophiliac activities because both were heavily defended and neither of them had the slightest remorse, guilt, or understanding about themselves or their behavior. One could also predict that Patient 1 would be the most difficult to treat because there wasn't a single crack in his defensive structure, but Patient 2 was threatened, and he found it necessary to reinforce every barrier that he had erected to prevent both anxiety and meaningful interactions with others. One could predict that

Patient 2 would put up the most initial resistance to therapy but that his defenses were highly vulnerable, and that Patient 1 might enter therapy passively and that months and years later he might be just as passive and invulnerable as on his first day.

The assessment of other paraphiliacs—transvestism, fetishism, voyeurism, exhibitionism—presents a multitude of problems because there is no such thing as a typical profile for any of these deviations. There is a marked distinction between the deviate patient who voluntarily seeks help for his problem and the patient who is referred after one or more arrests. (One may also assume that there are many such deviates living in society who never see a psychiatrist for any reason, and their personality patterns would be different still.) The deviate who seeks help generally produces a fairly neurotic record; the deviate who is arrested tends in the antisocial direction; in either case the deviation is symptomatic of a more pervasive disorder. Among neurotic deviates one tends to find more than usual indications of a repetition compulsion; among antisocial deviates one finds a more than usual degree of depression. In either case the self-concept is markedly distorted and the patient is intrapunitive, and perhaps the most important dynamic is the felt need for punishment. One can predict that neurotic deviates will respond quickly to therapy and—if the law is involved—no more than probation plus treatment should be necessary. Antisocial deviates will need a lot of treatment before they begin to respond, and in the meantime they will continue to act out. However, most of the time these patients are more a nuisance than a danger to society and their incarceration serves no great purpose; in fact, most often incarceration deprives them of treatment so that on release they start their deviant behavior again. Both the court and the psychiatrist face a philosophical problem here—the needs of the individual versus the rights of society—and there is no easy solution.

In the discussion thus far the treatability of the patient has been linked to the prediction of his acting-out potential, and this isn't accidental. In general, the more ego we have to deal with and the more manifest the anxiety, the greater the treatment potential and the less the potential for acting-out. Therefore, when we come to the true antisocial personality with his huge deficit of both ego and anxiety, we are ordinarily correct in predicting that he will continue to act-out and that incarceration will serve his needs best, that is, unless there is some specialized treatment institution available as there is now in several states (7, 11). Given that the "untreatable" antisocial personality is forced into treatment, how can we assess his progress? That will be the subject of the following section.

Predicting Progress in Therapy

The Patuxent Institution in Maryland has been relatively successful in treating the personality disorders. They have been treated in other settings too, and wherever treated, their general pattern is to "play the therapy game" and "con" the therapist into believing that there has been improvement. Patuxent is so organized that a patient is likely to be tested two or more times during the course of his treatment, and these comparative test results are able to tell us when a patient is "conning," when he is involved, and whether or not he continues to be a danger to society.

The most important determinant in assessing therapeutic progress is how anxiety is handled, and here we must be ever more careful to distinguish between objective and neurotic anxiety. For example, it is not unusual for these men to make steady increases in their IQ score; this is most apt to indicate that they have become comfortable in the institution and in the testing situation and so are intellectually less hindered by "nervousness" in the situation. Improved IQ is not in itself indication of positive personality change. In fact, one would be more optimistic about a patient who, after a series of steadily improving IQ scores, was to fall back, a finding that would suggest that situational anxiety was no longer operating and that neurotic anxiety was. In every way, patients who do play the therapy game can be expected to display more intellectual control on subsequent testings; this is surely not a sign of real improvement in the intellectually overcontrolling antisocial personality.

So one looks for the various signs of anxiety, and while their appearance suggests that therapy is taking hold, they do not suggest that therapy is over. For example, there was a bland antisocial personality who, after 5 years of therapy, produced a Rorschach made up almost entirely of shading and color responses; from intellectual overcontrol he had moved to the extreme of intellectual undercontrol or, to put it another way, he was now at the mercy of his chaotic emotions. Another patient, a rapist, eventually gave evidence that he was upset and guilty about his aggressive sexuality, but he gave evidence, too, that he was just as hostile as ever to women and that his impulse control was still sadly deficient. Thus, neurotic anxiety is mainly a sign that the patient is working in therapy.

Indications that therapy has been successful or that the patient is no longer dangerous vary widely and are intimately connected with the original test results. However, there are some general test findings which suggest that the patient feels better about himself and more able to cope with problems in a nondestructive way. We find little evidence of resistance on any of the tests, an indication that the patient is willing to share with the examiner both the best and the worst of himself. Anxiety is still present but counterbalanced by other factors—such as the healthy M response on the Rorschach—which suggests that the patient is both coping and creatively striving. Both judgment and reasoning become improved, and there is an absence of those factors which indicate primitive impulsivity. There are indications of a newfound ability to establish trusting interpersonal relationships and an active reaching out for people. No one pretends that the basic characterological problems have been resolved; what we see at the end is a man who now has the tools to solve problems and the ability to use them.

Conclusion

The psychological testing of the severe personality disorders does not differ significantly from the testing of any other group; the difference lies in the results. There are significant clusterings of factors which do differentiate these disorders from other psychiatric disorders, and there are specific combinations of factors which do permit the psychologist to predict such things as the potential for acting-out, the direction acting-out might take, suitability for treatment, and the best possible form of treatment. Testing can uncover in a relatively brief period of time hidden personality dynamics that might take the busy clinician months to spot. Testing is a clinical tool; what it will accomplish for the clinician will depend on how wisely it is used.

REFERENCES

1. Allen, R. M. *Elements of Rorschach Interpretation.* International Universities Press, Inc., New York, 1954.
2. Beck, S. J. *Rorschach's Test: III. Advances in Interpretation.* Grune & Stratton, New York, 1952.
3. Bender, L. *A Visual Motor Gestalt Test and Its Clinical Use.* The American Orthopsychiatric Association, New York, 1938.
4. Brodsky, S. L. (Ed.) *Psychologists in the Criminal Justice System.* American Association of Correctional Psychologists, University of Alabama, 1972.
5. Buros, O. K. *The Sixth Mental Measurements Yearbook.* The Gryphon Press, Highland Park, N. J., 1965.
6. Carney, F. L. Some recurring therapeutic issues in group psychotherapy with criminal patients. Am. J. Psychother., 26:34–41, 1972.
7. Goldfarb, R. L., and Singer, L. R. Maryland's defective delinquency law and the Patuxent Institution. Bull. Menninger Clin., 34:223–235, 1970.
8. Hammer, E. F. *The Clinical Application of Projective Drawings.* Charles C Thomas, Springfield, Ill., 1958.
9. Hodges, E. F. Crime prevention by the indeterminate sentence law, Am. J. Psychiatry, 128: 292–295, 1971.
10. Klopfer, B., Ainsworth, M. D., Klopfer, W. G., and Holt, B. R. *Developments in the Rorschach Technique. I. Technique and Theory.* World Book Company, New York, 1954.
11. Kozol, H. L., Boucher, R. J., and Garafalo, R. F. The diagnosis and treatment of dangerousness. Crime Delinquency, 18:371–392, 1972.
12. Rapaport, D., Gill, M. M., and Schafer, R. *Diagnostic Psychological Testing.* International Universities Press, Inc., New York, 1968.
13. Sadoff, R. L., Roether, H. A., and Peters, J. J. Clinical measure of enforced group psychotherapy. Am. J. Psychiatry, 128:224–227, 1971.
14. Schafer, R. *The Clinical Application of Psychological Tests.* International Universities Press, Inc., New York, 1948.
15. Wechsler, D. *The Measurement and Appraisal of Adult Intelligence,* Ed. 4. The Williams & Wilkins Co., Baltimore, 1958.

22

THERAPEUTIC COMMUNITY AND MILIEU THERAPY OF PERSONALITY DISORDERS

Mayer C. Liebman, M.D., and Douglas A. Hedlund, M.D.

Therapeutic community is a term which describes a total approach to the treatment of a person within his environment (milieu). All experiences within that environment should be beneficial to the recovery of that person. The most frequent experiences are between the person and the staff and among people in the group setting; these latter may be patients, clients, inmates, or students, depending on the illness, problem, charge, or goals. These exchanges between and among people become therapeutic at several different interpersonal and social levels: on a one-to-one dyadic basis, within various small group situations, and throughout the overall social setting itself. The task, then, of the therapeutic community is to facilitate a better understanding of the person and professional staff of the person's inner feelings and conflicts, of his interpersonal relationships, and of his appropriate social role.

The term "milieu therapy" is often used interchangeably with "therapeutic community." The authors have chosen to use the latter term, "therapeutic community," because the efficacy of the therapeutic process described is centered in the social or group (community) processes, not in the milieu program per se. While most residential treatment settings such as hospitals, prisons, and schools have some scheduled daily therapeutic activity operating within the ward milieu, e.g., work therapy, recreational therapy, group therapy, the therapeutic community concept encompasses more than the sum of such milieu activities, according to Kraft (55).

Therapeutic communities are characterized by certain values and treatment methods (55). Some of these values and methods include focusing on communications, enhancing opportunities for living-learning, and the sharing of some responsibilities by both patient and staff. Communications—verbal and nonverbal, conscious and unconscious—between patient and staff, patient and patient, staff and staff—are scrutinized closely and carefully. From staff's and patients' observations about such communication the patient should begin to understand his thoughts and feelings and his behavior as a derivative of his interpersonal relationships (81). Also the staff can learn about their reaction to the patient's behavior and how their attitudes can affect the milieu and the person (7). The day-to-day activities and setting of the milieu should encourage the learning of new and appropriate ways to relate to people and to behave in different social situations. This, in turn, will enhance feelings of self-worth and experimentation with different, more fulfilling relationships and activities (90). The community must permit the person to experiment with various modes of behavior, some of which may engender both negative and positive responses from the group. However, in turn, both the person and the group can share in the growth-promoting learning-living experience. The sharing of responsibilities with patients for certain individual and group activities will also help enhance self-growth and maturity. However, the cooperation of many different levels of administrative responsibility is necessary if this is to be meaningful and constructive (89). Ultimately, staff permits patients to participate in decision making and to share directly some responsibility for realistic issues. Without the community, this sharing is a difficult and dangerous process, especially for persons with severe personality and other related disorders, where limit setting is vital to the treatment. Either a pseudodelegation of responsibility or a renunciation of ultimate responsibility by the appointed staff authority will ultimately undermine the therapeutic process.

Application of Therapeutic Community to Personality and Other Related Disorders

While personality and other related disorders are characterized primarily by deeply ingrained maladaptive patterns of behavior (5), persons with such disorders also have abnormalities in their thinking and emotional life. The authors believe that people suffering the symptoms of the diverse personality disorders (5), as well as of the substance use disorders and some psychosexual disorders, share large areas of underlying severe psychopathology, the treatment of which requires close supervision. Within a structured setting the therapeutic community operates to help the patient become aware of and understand his aberrant behavior and emotional problems, and then develop more functional and appropriate ways to cope with them. This setting may operate either part-time, as in a day hospital or halfway house, or full-time, as in a hospital, a residence, a jail, or a school. Most therapeutic community programs for severe personality disorders treat the patient for an average of 6 months, though some programs have been developed for acute short term care (40).

History and Development of Therapeutic Community Concept in the Treatment of the Mentally Ill

The concept of therapeutic community includes both the old (and rare) humane treatment tradition and the application of recent therapeutic techniques to the ward situation. With few exceptions, the mentally ill have historically been grouped with criminals, indigents, or sinners and retardates, and their treatment has been minimal. In the 8th century, Baghdad and Damascus under the influence of Islam built asylums which were specifically designed to help the recovery of "the insane" (67). Similar approaches appeared in Europe in the late 18th century. Chiarugi in Florence, Italy, Tuke in York, England (72), and Pinel (112) in France expressed the growing concern for more humane care for the mentally ill. Tuke's "moral treatment" approach, which emphasized "kindness and firmness" to the individual patient, was especially important and was transplanted to the United States in the early and middle 19th century under the leadership of Dorothea Dix. While this enlightened institutional care was mostly for patients with schizophrenic and affective disorders rather than personality disorders, the humanistic roots must be recognized as important to the therapeutic community. In addition, the therapeutic community also utilizes recent psychotherapeutic techniques developed since the late 19th and early 20th centuries. Beginning with the classic psychoanalytical model—that behavior results from intrapsychic, unconscious conflict, which is ameliorated with intensive individual treatment—the psychotherapeutic process has been expanded to include treatment of small groups, families, and finally, the group milieu as a social process. More recently, behavioral modification methods have been incorporated. The therapeutic process will continue to evolve with the discovery of new somatic techniques, with the application of certain learning theory techniques, and with the better understanding of individual and group dynamics.

Recent History of Therapeutic Communities

The first inpatient setting structured on psychoanalytic principles was developed by Schimmel (85). He closely followed the individual classic analytic model within the framework of a 24-hour supervised setting. There were rather strict rules about patients having contact with the outside world, and a concern that behavior be controlled in accordance with the expectations of the "milieu" and "community." Harry Stack Sullivan (94, 95) directed a six-bed research ward at the Sheppard and Enoch Pratt Hospital in Towson, Maryland, from 1922 to 1929. His patients were young schizophrenics. He extensively utilized psychiatric aides in motivating and rehabilitating patients. While his treatment approach was originally based on classic psychoanalytic concepts, he was the first investigator to articulate the thesis that mental illness was a problem of interpersonal relationships within a social and cultural environment. The Menninger family, father and sons, began their hospital and clinic in the late 1920s (66). By the 1930s, it was of sufficient size to develop an active hospital program, which treated primarily schizophrenics and severe character disorders. Their milieu program was based on classic psychoanalytic theory. Following a careful evaluation, the physician-therapist, in conjunction with the nursing and supporting therapy staff, would prescribe an individual program for each patient, focused on activities which would enable the patient to uncover and resolve an unconscious conflict in a gratifying and socially acceptable manner. Program activities, in turn, had goals, such as affording an outlet for aggression, encouraging advantageous identifications, permitting atonement for guilt, affording a means of obtaining love, encouraging the acting out of fantasy, and offering the opportunity for creativity.

Maxwell Jones (49) began his work in England in 1943 on an effort syndrome-cardiac neurosis ward, in collaboration with an eminent cardiologist, Paul Wood. He noted the beneficial effects of teaching the patients as a group about cardiac physiology, so as to change their attitudes about their physical symptoms and signs. After World War II, he developed a ward program for returning prisoners of war and utilized some ideas from his previous experience with cardiac-neurosis patients. These included the use of group interaction and support by nursing personnel and their assistants as part of a continuous treatment process. Patients' behavior was closely scrutinized so as to facilitate this process. In addition, the hospital community was seen as a paradigm for the outside community, and the unit began utilizing resources in the outside community for job placements and social activity. In 1947 he began the development of the Industrial Neurosis Unit at Belmont, England. Most of these patients had severe personality disorders which impaired their ability to work, and treatment was directed toward getting them back to work. Jones described in detail the "changed" roles and relationships of the nurse, the doctor, and the patient. The nurse was seen as the major authority, a social implementer, and a therapist. The physician prescribed medication and discipline when necessary and also encouraged socialization. He was responsible for administration. The patient was seen as needing to cooperate and participate in all activities. The major modalities of therapy were psychotherapy and group therapy. Intrapsychic conflicts and dynamics were not approached, though the model of the family relationship was used quite extensively. Jones was the first clinician to use the term "therapeutic community."

In 1931, Dr. Dexter Bullard (18) assumed directorship of a small psychiatric hospital in Rockville, Maryland, founded by his father. He redesigned its treatment program and employed intensive analytically oriented psychotherapy as the major treatment modality. In one early paper, he discussed his program in terms of staff attitudes and problems. For him the hospital was a "place to be sick as needed" and the staff was expected to be tolerant of regressive and aggressive behavior for long periods of time. With the exposure of his psychopathology, and its causes, the patient would develop more socially acceptable forms of behavior. Bullard was greatly influenced by Sullivan, and he focused more on staff attitudes toward patients' problems and interpersonal communication, in contrast to the Menningers, who emphasized more individual patient treatment programs to modify the patient's attitude. During the 1940s, the administrative structure of Dr. Bullard's hospital changed. Responsibility for the patient became "split" between an administrator who coordinated nursing personnel and a psychiatrist-therapist who did individual psychotherapy. From 1947 to 1952, Dr. A. Stanton, a psychiatrist, and Dr. M. Schwartz, a sociologist, studied a 15-bed disturbed women's ward (91). Their professional perspective was interpersonal-sociological, and their research also included the entire hospital structure as it related to the specific women's ward activities and the interactions between staff and patient. They described both "formal" administrative-organizational relationships and certain "informal" covert relationships which often conflicted with or ignored each other. These relationships were factors in such problem situations as "special cases," pathological excitement heightened by hidden staff agreement, incontinence, and breakdown of morale. Communication and the distribution of power, as the two major modes of enhancing the operation and integration of the institution, were meticulously examined. As an example, the authors chose an incident in which a patient became psychotic and destroyed some of her clothing. With great care, they scrutinized the incidents which precipitated her destructive behavior—the communication between her and different staff, disagreement among different staff, and the enforcement of "certain" hospital rules.

Other workers have described their work with children and adolescents using the concept of a therapeutic community as a treatment modality (15, 78). August Aichorn (1) was especially important because he incorporated classic psychoanalytic concepts to delinquent boys within an institutional setting. Moreover, Aichorn was an educator. Increasingly, nonhospital settings have been utilized in the treatment of such disorders as antisocial behavior, alcohol addiction, and drug dependence, which the authors believe all relate to the same kinds of basic psychopathology underlying severe personality disorder. While the historical narrative focused on the group and social pressures in the therapeutic community, the authors believe that individual psychotherapy should be available as part of the overall treatment program. The authors see no inherent contradiction or conflict between the sociotherapy of the therapeutic community and the psychotherapy of the individual person. To the contrary, in many situations, both "therapies" are seen as essential and are generally complementary in patients with personality disorders.

The Intermediate and Long-term Psychiatric Hospital as a Treatment Approach

The treatment program at the Sheppard and Enoch Pratt Hospital is used as an example of a milieu approach to the therapy of personality disorders.

In the historical development of the treatment program at the hospital, the psychoanalytic model became the basis of the treatment philosophy, and long-term individual psychotherapy was seen as the major treatment modality. Whether there was, in fact, one major treatment modality was a question yet to be seriously considered. This continued through the period when psychoactive drugs became more widely used, and it survived the euphoria of the early community mental health center "movement," during which some saw hospitalization as merely a necessary evil. In the mid-1960s, there was a major change in the patient population at Sheppard. Schizophrenia and serious affective illnesses had previously been the major focus of the treatment efforts, but now more people were being admitted whose problems tended to be expressed less directly through their thoughts or feelings, but more through their behavior. The new challenge was the treatment of personality disorders, and many of those afflicted were adolescents and young adults. For a time, the "acting out," drug-using adolescents dominated the hospital culture. This led to some collaboration by staff members out of idealization of youth and envy (44). The staff, at first, used the term "adjustment reaction" when referring to the acting out patients. This represented an effort to avoid stigmatizing young patients by using "malignant" diagnostic terms in a fluid situation where accuracy was difficult to achieve. This became a problem in that the term was an understatement of the scope of the patients' intrapsychic and behavioral problems. That is, the term became a euphemism and obscured the fact that the hospital had to deal with increasing numbers of people with serious personality disorders. The question of major changes in treatment philosophy had to be raised, because many questioned the hospital's usefulness for these patients. There was, for a time, a sense of hopelessness shared by staff and patients, e.g., various staff members spoke of a "critical mass" phenomenon, suggesting that when the hospital exceeded a certain percentage of acting out-type patients, the whole program would be unworkable. The hopelessness on the part of patients often was expressed by their running away—to the larger society which, itself, during that period, was in turmoil.

The basic idea of long-term individualized treatment with attention to the genetic and dynamic aspects of maladaptive behavior has been retained, but changes had to be made. The patients were now to remain on the same "autonomous" unit throughout their stay, rather than going from "disturbed" to intermediate to predischarge halls. One of many important reasons for this was that those patients with personality disorders often would quickly find their way to the less structured predischarge halls without staying anywhere long enough to get to know one group of people—this was often a recapitulation of their life history. In preparation for this change, each therapist's patients were assigned to a single service to facilitate (using daily team meetings) the therapist's knowing what his patients' total daily experiences were like. This meant that therapists now shared more of the responsibility for making "administrative" decisions. One effect of this was to diminish the therapist-administrator split. This avoided the illusion of an impartial and benevolent therapist and a demanding, frustrating administrator, and proved useful in starting the patients on the task of dealing with their neurotic (parent-centered) ambivalence about all forms of authority. Because more patients were dealing with their conflicts by actions that were directed at staff members and other patients (rather than some internal process that resulted in their becoming, for example, depressed or disorganized), the staff had to develop the means for clarifying and identifying interpersonal and group processes. Intensive group therapy became more widely used, the use of family therapy was increased, and the role of hall administrator was enlarged to include the task of making explicit (e.g., by comments in hall meetings) the social forces operating in the entire group of patients and staff, i.e., the hall and hospital community. At first, an attempt was made to use an unstructured group therapy-type format in the hall meetings. This turned out to be unworkable. The hall meetings evolved into fairly well-structured problem-solving sessions, led by the hall administrator, a nurse or, in some cases, a patient chairman. However, intensive group therapy did become a major treatment modality, supported by the availability in the residency training program, of additional supervision and training in group therapy techniques. The book *The Theory and Practice of Group Psychotherapy* (111) by Yalom became a major training resource. Group dynamics, as a "new" theoretical model or basis of treatment philosophy, became, for a time, a training department obsession. The most frequently cited paper in the residency training program was *The Therapeutic Community* by Alan Kraft (55), and the entire staff was struggling with the question of whether the hospital as a whole or any unit was a therapeutic community or whether the hospital remained an old traditional hospital dominated by physicians and thereby, by definition, not a therapeutic community.

In examining the treatment program that now exists, one can isolate four essential therapeutic elements. They were seen over many years to be useful in the hospital treatment of schizophrenics and other severe illnesses and, with very important changes in emphasis, are essential in setting up a program that has as its ambitious goal the curative treatment of severe personality disorders: (a) acceptance—the milieu should allow some regression and a recapitulation of maladaptive behavior; (b) control—the milieu should provide enough control to allow the emergence of the feelings that underlie the maladaptive behavior; (c) support—the milieu should provide enough support to enable the patients to endure the emergence of those underlying feelings—to do so long enough to make sense out of them and find another way to get their needs met without using the maladaptive behavior patterns; (d) learning—the milieu should offer the means whereby patients and staff can learn about their characteristic ways of behaving, thinking, and feeling and, possibly, more adaptive alternatives; in short, a setting that is accepting, reasonably controlling, supportive over a significant period of time, and one that offers the means for learning a better way to cope with the problems that led to hospitalization.

Acceptance refers mainly to that early phase of hospital treatment when the staff members necessarily present themselves as real objects for the patient. That is, less of the therapeutic task is thrust back onto the patient. The staff members are there to be useful in concrete and humane ways. This parallels the therapist's initial task of obtaining a history and answering questions or fears the patient may have about his new environment. (One does not facilitate development of a therapeutic alliance by offering obscure, speculative, or interpretative comments.) What often happens is that the patient will, in response, begin demonstrating and recapitulating his own symptomatic patterns of relatedness with all staff members and with other patients. Part of acceptance is tolerating enough of this symptomatic recapitulation to find out what it is like. Finding out what it means comes later. It is not unusual for patients to demonstrate again the initial symptomatic pattern just prior to discharge. At that point, both the patient and staff need to be accepting.

Control refers to stopping or altering the behavioral representations of inner conflicts. In some cases, this begins immediately, e.g., a drug-addicted patient is hospitalized and thus is prevented from continuing to use drugs, or a sexually "promiscuous" patient is hospitalized and expected to remain temporarily celibate. More often, control involves the other patients' and entire staff's confronting the patient with his maladaptive behavior and expecting him to look at and consider changing it. In this sense, it follows a period of acceptance. Thus, acceptance and control are not as contradictory as they seem, although in a hospitalized patient, it is difficult to define acting out, since one is prepared to deal with a patient's entire behavior (101).

Support means providing respect, honest feedback, and empathetic acknowledgment of the patient's troubled circumstances or painful feeling-states. It refers to all aspects of ego-building, including enhancing reality testing, enhancing self-esteem, and relieving overwhelming anxiety (chemically, physically, or by psychological means).

Learning includes the patient's use of the more formal and structured therapies, individual psychotherapy, group psychotherapy, occupational therapy, and the various activities therapies (art, dance, work), bibliotherapy, and others. These would have the goal of insight in the traditional sense or some limited range of increased self-knowledge, experientially and intellectually acquired. It would certainly include the school. Learning would also include the multiple and varied opportunities for interpersonal learning one acquires by being a part of a small cohesive community—i.e., the hospital-wide therapeutic community and a living unit that necessarily is a part of it. It should be noted that of the four elements, learning is perhaps the most important and is the one that cannot be given by the staff to a passive patient-recipient.

The physical setting at the hospital is comfortable and humane. The patients live in several large Victorian buildings that are comfortably furnished. They have the high ceilinged "airy" rooms that the founder specified—he had observed the dank, cramped almshouses of his day and felt such factors as space and lighting had to be considered if one were to have a curative facility. The grounds are spacious and attractive. The design of the buildings is not altogether practical—there are lots of nooks and crannies—but, to many, this contributes to their charm and effectiveness. Discharged patients have often remarked about the physical design when reporting on what they felt were "curative" factors—such comments as "the buildings and grounds give you a sense of privacy and enhanced life space...." In addition to spaciousness, the physical setting has a secure look. The outside walls are 18 inches thick. The doors to each unit can be locked. The windows have safety screens. There are seclusion rooms on all units.

The staff includes the usual range of psychiatric hospital personnel: nurses, nurses' aides, occupational therapists, and those trained in art, dance, and related forms of activity therapy. There are psychologists working in a number of capacities (psychotherapy, research, hall administration). There are staff psychiatrists working as psychotherapists, administrators, and in training. There are psychiatric residents engaged in direct patient care as the major part of their training. There are students of nursing and social work engaged in a measured amount of patient care. There are social workers engaged in traditional casework and engaged in family intervention of various types. There is a high school with a standard but essentially academic curriculum. It is made clear to all that the school offers an educational opportunity, not "special" training by therapy-oriented teachers.

Most staff members wear ordinary clothes, rather than uniforms. They are encouraged to be accessible, accepting, respectful, empathetic, and kind, yet they are often called upon to be firm, in the interest of setting limits. They are also trained in the use of cold wet sheet packs for controlling severe agitation (52). Yet there exist no dicta against the use of major tranquilizers for control of severe anxiety or dyscontrol. These seeming paradoxes require no apology; the setting is designed to treat severely ill patients and therefore is equipped to tolerate a degree of regressive or uncontrolled behavior. It is also equipped to prevent dangerously destructive behavior. The alternative is to exclude many patients who could not manage themselves in an "open" setting. It is useful to expect responsible behavior from patients, but if rigid preconditions for staying in the hospital are set up (such as no running away, no fighting, no breaking of property), the hospital ends up automatically rejecting a lot of patients and is left with a well-screened, exclusive group of patients that will not include many with severe personality disorders. The physical arrangements on all patient units (halls) are the same; that is, there are no open units or "disturbed halls." All halls are "autonomous" in that they have a variety of "levels of responsibility"—on a given hall, some patients are very disturbed and others are ready to return to the community. The patients are not segregated by age, except for units designed for 11- to 15-year-old adolescents. Most halls have 20 beds, with one to four beds per room. Most are coed units. Two or three adjoining halls make up a single service. There is no segregation by diagnostic category, except for a 20-bed alcoholism unit.

The patients are expected to be up by 7:30 a.m. Typically, from 8:15 to 8:55, there is a hall meeting—all patients are expected to be there. This hall meeting is the major opportunity for contact between the hall administrator and the patients (the hall administrator is usually a psychiatric resident). Hall nurses, social workers, and environmental therapists attend, and sometimes senior staff physicians. The hall meeting is informal but fairly well structured. It sometimes resembles a town meeting, where shared problems are rationally discussed, or it may be dominated by one argumentative patient with a highly personal grievance. The patients may elect a hall chairman and run a highly organized meeting. However, the hall administrator is sometimes left with the responsibility for generating participation. Problems involving the group as a community are often discussed and sometimes solved, e.g., room changes, locking or unlocking of doors, and the execution and planning of group projects, such as dances or trips. The problems may be more complex, such as the development of patient or staff cliques, drug traffic, hospital romances, suicide threats, impending discharges, staff vacations, etc. At times, the problems to be solved may be the behavior of one disturbed patient or a single disturbing act on the part of one patient. At times, one patient's personal problems may be brought up in the hall meeting for the purpose of clarification. These personal crises are usually not solved in the hall meetings but the distress they cause can be acknowledged there—the distress in the individual and its effect on the group.

At 9:00 a.m., the hall administrators and the nurses, occupational therapists, teachers, social workers, psychologists, psychiatric aides—the treatment team on the service (two or three halls)—meet with the chief of service (an experienced staff psychiatrist) to review the events of the previous day. The therapists who have patients on the service are present to gather information about their total behavior. Decisions requiring treatment team collaboration are made based on information reviewed and exchanged in these service conferences. On some services, a brief hall staff meeting precedes the service conference. For most of the rest of the day, the majority of the patients are away from the hall, engaged in a variety or pursuits: school, occupational therapy, recreational therapy, work therapy, individual therapy, group therapy, or outside jobs. The degree of supervision or freedom of movement that the patients have depends on their "responsibility level." That is, every patient is given an appropriate range of responsibility (it used to be called "permission level," but that term is now avoided as if an anachronism from feudal times) based on his or her total performance. The decision for designating this level is made by the treatment team after a review of all pertinent information, including the stated wish of the patient and the views or observations of the other patients of the hall community.

As one looks at the range of events in the patient's day, one can see the impossibility of isolating a single major treatment modality. Including recreation, school, work therapy, hall community experience, patient activities councils (a clearly limited form of patient government), group and individual psychotherapy, occupational and other activity therapy, and building design in a concept of total therapeutic effort is not just an egalitarian gesture—it is a statement describing the way the task of treatment gets done. One staff person, of whatever discipline or technique, cannot provide all of the elements needed in a total therapeutic effort, whether defined as acceptance, support, control, and learning or in some other terms. This has to be understood and felt to be a reality by everyone in the hospital if the patient is to experience the hospital as a therapeutic community.

There is an effort made, from the day of admission, to evaluate the patient's specific needs and design a treatment program to meet them. The following case history and treatment synopsis is presented to demonstrate this effort to individualize treatment within the hospital as a therapeutic community.

> R. L. was 17½ years old on admission. He had a 3-year history of extensive illicit drug use—mostly mescaline and LSD. He had been expelled from three private schools for truancy, fighting, poor academic performance, and using and pushing drugs. His parents had divorced when he was 12 years old, after several years of bitter fighting. Part of the stated "family history" obtained from the mother was that the birth of the patient had ruined the marriage. The mother also described with considerable enthusiasm in front of the patient that the father was a "queer." The admission was precipitated when the patient was arrested for selling drugs. On admission, the patient was calm, flippant, and negativistic. He made it clear that he was not a "voluntary" patient.
>
> After a 2-week evaluation, including the obtaining of a social and medical history, close observation by the nursing staff, and an evaluation of his interests and skills by the environmental therapy staff, the treatment team met to determine a specific treatment plan. Generally, it was felt that he would need enough controls and structuring of his daily life to help him control impulses and enough support and acceptance to enable him to deal with the feelings beneath his maladaptive behavior. It was decided that he would attend the high

school. He would engage in the recreational and O.T. activities of his choice. The rationale here is that, with some exceptions, there are insufficient data to predict the usefulness of specific forms of activity therapy. Letting him choose offers him an opportunity to express something about his own needs and interests. It turned out that he became quite interested in sculpture and ceramics, and eventually assisted in teaching others. He was placed in intensive group therapy which met 3 hours a week. Family therapy was indicated—a series of exploratory family interviews was arranged. This turned out to be very productive from the point of view of the staff's obtaining important information, but was so painful for both the patient and his mother that they said they had to stop. Thereafter, the mother was seen regularly by a social worker, in an effort to provide support and clarify financial questions. This helped to remove an inappropriate and impossible burden from the patient, i.e., the task of being her only social and emotional resource. The treatment team later recommended that the mother obtain psychotherapy for herself.

Acceptance in his case involved tolerating his setting himself up as everybody's therapist. He did this on the hall and in group therapy. This served, for a time, to keep his own feelings well hidden—including the feelings he had about his inevitable failure at this impossible job.

Control, in his case, included preventing him access to drugs, keeping him in school, and keeping him out of fights. He was offered close nursing supervision and was kept on a low responsibility level for a significant period of time. He complained constantly about his lack of freedom—but not very convincingly.

Support, in his case, took some doing. He was characteristically negativistic, e.g., in a stormy family therapy session, he became silent, then cried bitterly yet quietly for several minutes. His doctor (group therapist) offered him a Kleenex. He said, "That's the first useful thing done for me since I came here—thanks."

He learned, from many sources, a lot about his characteristic mistrustfulness of adults, his need to control ("therapize") his peers, and his previously unrecognized need for reasonably reliable people with whom he could work out his loneliness and self-hatred. To survive, he had had to assume, at one time, that nobody could be relied upon—but this way of dealing with others had outlived its usefulness.

In group therapy and in his relationships on the hall, he got much feedback from other patients and staff that went something like this: "We resent your sitting back at a safe distance and telling us what's wrong with us." He gradually discovered that what people really wanted from him was for him to be more accessible. After the painful family therapy session described above, he was able to tell the group how angry and hurt he felt. He also disclosed suicidal fantasies. The group responded by acknowledging his painful circumstances and showing genuine concern, as did the patients and staff on the hall with whom the information about the suicidal fantasies was shared. After several similar experiences in the group and on the hall, he gradually learned that openly expressing needfulness does not necessarily lead to abandonment.

In his school experiences, he learned about his conflicts about achievement. He was very bright, which he knew, but he tended to either do very poor work or engage in superhuman efforts: in biology class, he wrote a 90-page book entitled "Human Biology." His teacher offered the opinion that a short paper on a more limited topic would have been more appropriate. He was enraged but was able to express this feeling in group therapy sessions.

In dealing with the hall community, he at first saw his hall administrator as harshly punitive. In contrast, he at first saw his group therapist as totally benevolent. They both worked as members of the treatment team and shared responsibility for making "administrative" decisions. The patient refused, for months, to give up his distorted view of these two people who had become important to him in his daily life. Very slowly, through daily contact with the hall staff and other patients, and by engaging in heated arguments in hall meetings, he gave up the fantasy of the "all-bad" authoritarian hall administrator, as well as the fantasy of the "all-giving" group therapist. This came about, in part, through his learning that the group therapist was making demands on him—demands that he accept some responsibility for what happened to him, e.g., his responsibility level. This learning opportunity was enhanced by the fact that the hall administrator and group therapist did, in fact, have real disagreements concerning his treatment, but were able to work them out. In doing so, they asked that the patient contribute to the solution. This kind of cooperation required frequent sharing of information by all members of the treatment team.

R. L. did well in this treatment program and was able to abandon much of his antisocial behavior. He became less self-absorbed and more sensitive to the impact his actions and words had on those around him. He was more capable of delaying impulsive actions and examining the underlying feelings and thoughts. His capacity for sustained productive work was remarkably increased. He was pleased by the changes he saw in himself and, in the month prior to discharge, he was able to reflect on those elements of the hospital experience that had helped bring about the changes:

"When I came here, I right away figured something had to change. This was a new kind of place—once inside that gatehouse entrance and all the trees and space—it sort of made me feel I had gotten off my treadmill and was in for a new kind of living. Not that I liked it—I mean, getting up early and those horseshit questions on hall meetings and all—but it was like being completely *immersed* in a new, different, and freaky world, but one that had a consistent and solid feel to it. It's not a dream world here, but it's sort of a different *culture* almost—and you get caught up in it, like you're swimming in it. At times, I'd say it was just a lot of head games and tricks and promises, but I never quite believed that. The people here don't have the same ax to grind as parents or boarding schools do. They do tell you things like 'Think about that experience and try to make some sense out of what you are feeling,' and they do get mad if you won't do it, but then it occurs to you that they don't really want something from you—they want you to want something from yourself. Anyway, I'm leaving soon and I feel like the same person, but I'm moving at a safer speed, from a different starting point."

This account of his "immersion" in a new culture with different rules and values, a different "starting point," and less binding expectations provides a description of something very difficult to define—the impact of the total milieu as experienced by the patient.

R. L. left the hospital after a full year of treatment. He had responded well. After discharge, he went to college in California. A 1-year follow-up report indicated that he was doing well.

The Hospital, the Community, and the "Outside World"

The hospital opened an outpatient department in the early 1960s as a first step toward developing a major commitment to the mental health needs of the surrounding community—Baltimore and northern Baltimore County. In the past decade, the hospital has developed a wide variety of other direct care services, such as a crisis intervention clinic, a day treatment center, a comprehensive drug abuse program, and the psychiatric component of the college health service on two nearby campuses. Consultative services to a variety of local institutions and agencies in the adjacent, relatively affluent suburban locale and the inner city ghetto also evolved from this commitment. This changing relationship of the hospital to the "outside world" has altered the character of the inpatients' experience in a number of fairly subtle ways. This is illustrated by the following comments made by a 17-year-old inpatient to her therapist:

> "I was walking alone near the road over by the tennis courts. I guess I was worrying about the prospect of being discharged 4 months from now, but I was actually thinking about what the staff would think about my walking alone—would they say I was being seclusive—would they question my readiness to leave or question my 'unescorted' responsibility level? I then started to worry about the fact that these concerns are so tied to this place—who cares what the staff thinks?—I've got to make some plans—I'm going to go to college in months, and no one there is going to give a damn where I walk or if I'm alone. Anyway, just then, as I was about to cross the road, I saw a car coming. He was going fairly fast, so I stopped to wait, but then he signaled that he was going to turn into the parking lot before he got to where I was. It sounds stupid, but I was thrilled about his obvious assumption that I knew about traffic rules and the meaning of his little blinking signal light. I suddenly realized that I wasn't in some cloister. I was in a place where the roads have two-way traffic and were connected to busy streets and freeways. I then began to think about the fact that, last week, I went to the high school in town to take college boards with people who live around here and that my roommate here goes to graduate school classes at Johns Hopkins at night and that people from town attend the hospital school. I began to realize that I've been to more museums and concerts since coming here than I ever did before. I was telling all this to that guy—he's scared, too—that guy I met who was on methadone in the drug clinic here—he's in the day treatment program now, and we started talking at the hospital tennis tournament—anyway, he said I shouldn't worry too much. He reminded me that those vocational interest tests I took showed my plan to go into anthropology is pretty realistic, in terms of what I'm interested in—You see what I mean?"

If a hospital-based treatment program is to be useful, it must provide something that the patients can take with them and ought to give patients a sense that they have somewhere to go—a "somewhere" that is not necessarily a hostile place (46). This requires that the hospital demonstrate that it views the "outside world" as a potentially useful resource, rather than a dangerous place that was and remains the source of the patients' problems. The way the hospital views the community and the outside world will be picked up by patients. A hospital program can be set up as a "world apart," wherein little is given to the community in terms of specific services and little is expected in terms of using the community resources. This certainly could convey a suspicious view of the world as a hostile place and could harm the patient's chances of making a successful postdischarge adjustment. This does not mean that the patient should not be expected to seek to change the situation he was in prior to hospitalization. It does mean that adjustment to a hospital setting should not be an end in itself.

Failures, Limitations, and the Need for Other Approaches

The hospital tries to offer a comprehensive treatment program. Patients are not refused admission on the basis of their symptoms or problems, e.g., violence-prone people, those with addictions, those facing criminal charges, and people with organic brain damage, senility, or seemingly "incurable" psychoses are not excluded. This policy requires liberal use of "outside" consultants and cooperation with community agencies. However, the hospital, at times, faces the dilemma of trying to help a patient who presents a major threat to the well-being of other patients, the staff, or the buildings. The clearest example is the patient who sets fires. There is no automatic exclusion of such patients, but they may well be asked to leave because of the special vulnerability of this hospital—some of the buildings are over 100 years old. In recent years, some patients who have repeatedly been involved in distributing illicit drugs have been asked to leave. These examples represent special threats to the hospital. A different problem is those patients who may be sent to other facilities because the hospital fails to meet their special needs. For example, a patient whose need for physical controls is extreme and persistent may well need a facility that can comfortably offer more "security," such as a "security hospital," where specially trained personnel and a specially designed physical setting are available. Some patients with alcoholism or other addictions may well need a program that offers the "consciousness-raising" and peer support aspects of specialized separate facilities. For some people, asking them to view themselves as needing psychiatric care is just too threatening.

Nonhospital Settings as a Treatment Approach for Personality and Other Nonpsychotic Disorders

Antisocial Personality disorders and Psychosexual disorders are discussed together because the total setting and treatment situation are often the same. Most persons in treatment for such disorders have been referred by the court and have usually been committed to a penal or mental institution or a similar type of outpatient program. The APA Diagnostic and Statistical Manual (first edition) (4) had included these two disorders within the same diagnostic category until 1968 (5). The close relationship between the two severe disorders has been recognized by some legislators. For example, Kozol et al. noted that some state and local laws restrict "dangerous criminal behavior" to "sex offenders" (54). However, in over half the legal jurisdictions in the country which have specific laws about the dangerous offender, it refers to someone who is an "actual danger to society" or "a menace" to the safety of others (54).

In 1963, Guttmacher wrote that it is "far sounder psychiatrically to include the really serious sex offenders among the general group of dangerous offenders than to isolate them in a separate category ... for the disposition and treatment of the dangerous sex offenders need not differ radically from that of the more general group" (42). Most of the treatment efforts prior to the mid-1960s included individual intensive psychoanalytic psychotherapy (3, 13, 57), counseling, or group psychotherapy. The McCords, in their book, *The Psychopath* (62), written in 1965, mentioned only one therapeutic community to treat the antisocial person, and this was the live-in residence program at the Wiltwyck School for early adolescent delinquent boys from New York City. While group therapy had been utilized on an outpatient (58, 76) and inpatient (48) basis, few therapeutic community programs had developed and been identified as such. This was, in part, due to the fact that most offenders were in penal institutions with legal restraints, which made the development of a therapeutic community more difficult than it might have been perhaps in a mental hospital for offenders. However, some progress has been made. A study published in 1968 (84) identified 153 institutions that evaluate and/or treat offenders for mental illness, including sexual deviations. These institutions included 116 public mental hospitals, 22 state and federal correctional institutions or prison hospital departments, and 15 other facilities, such as general hospitals, mental health centers, and state security medical facilities. The major treatment modalities and the percentage of facilities using such modalities for "most or all" offenders were as follows: recreational therapy (68%), psychotropic drugs (65%), religious guidance (45%), occupational therapy (43%), group psychotherapy (36%), and individual psychotherapy (29%). Of the 153 institutions surveyed, only two were described as having therapeutic community-type programs. However, the correctional system is clearly increasing its application of mental health treatment to offenders with severe personality and other nonpsychotic disorders (59).

Antisocial Personality

In 1966, 51 inmates were admitted to an experimental therapeutic community at Clinton Prison, Dannemora, New York. The unit was established under the sponsorship of the governor of New York and was designed with the help of Dr. B. Cormier, director of the Forensic Psychiatry Clinic of

McGill University. Its mission was to develop the methods for rehabilitating the persistent offender and predicting postrelease behavior, and to conduct research and training in the field of correction. The resident staff included not only psychiatrists, psychologists, and social workers, but correctional officers as part of the treatment team. Inmates were usually of average or high intelligence and had 6 to 18 months left to serve prior to going before the parole board. Most men were over 25 years of age and had a persistent history of criminal offenses and imprisonment. Men with records of alcoholism, mental disorder, or drug addiction were not accepted. Fink et al. (30) described the program as organized on the basis of a team approach, "with all members, professional staff, officers and inmates" participating in and sharing responsibility. While there were few rules on the unit, thus allowing the prisoner to act out, he gradually became anxious as he tried to utilize his habitual adaptation styles in the new situations. Other inmates and staff would point out to him what he was doing and how others responded. When he tried to leave the program and return to jail, other inmates exercised group pressure to keep him in the program by criticizing his rationalizations for leaving and by supporting his progress and wish for recovery. The values of the group became "rehabilitative," permitting the prisoner to learn to conform sufficiently so as to tolerate the values of the outside authoritative society. The daily interchanges between staff and inmates at various group meetings forced him "to relate in a new way to professional staff and officers." Gradually, his attitudes and values changed as he thought about the future in a more realistic way. Consequently, "his behavior changes as he develops a new concept of self."

Throughout the therapeutic rehabilitative process, the offender and the program itself have been evaluated. Several positive changes occurred. The treatment cohort, as compared with the control group, showed improvement with both ego strength and superego strength. Testing of object relationships indicated a greater trusting of and sensitivity to others and their needs. "Of particular significance was the change from the poorly-integrated, vague self-concept toward a better image of oneself" and "more positive attitude regarding a sense of purpose." Finally, there was a general reduction in the level of tension, feeling of frustration, and depression. The amount of recidivism of the treated offender was lower than the control.

A somewhat similar type of program has been operating at Patuxent Institution in Jessup, Maryland, for over 20 years. While controversial and castigated by civil libertarians for its indeterminate sentencing and by some psychiatrists for its limited treatment program, Patuxent has made an effort to treat the incorrigible sociopath. The inmate must be referred by the court to Patuxent as a "defective delinquent" for such criminal behavior as aggressive and sexual crimes and repeated arrests and convictions. The usual treatment modalities are group, occupational, and recreational therapy. The average offender who is finally discharged remains 4½ years. Discharge is, in part, based on a graduated system of four "tiers," through which the offender progresses as he demonstrates that he can handle more responsibility and assume more privileges. At the highest tier, there is patient government, where offenders make many of the rules. Patuxent reports recidivism rates of less than 50% (63, 84).

Unlike these two previously mentioned inpatient institution-type programs, the Probationed Offenders Rehabilitation and Teaching Program (PORT) of Olmstead County, Minnesota, is based, oriented, supported, and directed by the community (102). It is a private, nonprofit corporation whose board of directors includes two district court judges, an attorney, a local banker, and a psychiatrist, the PORT program director, one PORT client (patient), and one PORT resident-volunteer (aide). The corporation leased a building on the grounds of the Rochester State Hospital campus and hired a director from the administrative staff of the State Department of Corrections.

The residents of the program range in age from 13 to 32 years old, and their offenses include repeated running away from home, arson, and burglary. The offender is referred to PORT by the district, municipal, or juvenile courts. The client must spend a 2-week probationary period, during which time both the client and PORT staff decide whether participation in the program would be beneficial to the client. The PORT decision is made by a screening committee composed of clients, resident volunteers, the director, the probation officer, a local businessman, and a psychiatrist.

The program itself has three paid staff, a director, an assistant director, and a secretary. In addition, there are 10 to 12 resident volunteers, mostly local college students, who are reimbursed with room and board. These resident volunteers take responsibility on the evenings and weekends for supervision and encouraging therapeutic interaction. Clients themselves who demonstrate responsible behavior may also advance to the client-volunteer level. If the client, PORT, and the court agree, the court places the offender in probation to PORT or sentences him and stops the execution of sentence, with the stipulation that he enter the PORT program.

When the offender-client enters the program, he is assigned to a resident-volunteer as "a peer model in a mirror image fashion." A daily activities program is developed and the client either works or goes to school: "The core of the PORT program is group process and the pressure it exerts on each member." The clients meet as a group three times weekly with the assistant director and once a week with all the resident-volunteer staff. Extra meetings occur when crises arise so as to have the entire client-volunteer group decide how best to control deviant behavior.

It was suggested that "internal controls" develop due to peer group pressure. In fact, the total group—clients and staff—determine the amount of "freedom" each client may have along a scale rated 0 to 5. At the lower end of the scale for new clients, only minimal activity is permitted outside the building. At the higher end of the scale, home visits and overnight and weekend visits are permitted. Following discharge to the "outside" community, they return to the PORT building for group meetings as long as needed.

Aside from the community group experience, other factors contribute to the rehabilitation program. The probation officer maintains regular contact with clients to help with such matters as buying a car, renting an apartment, etc. A psychotherapist is available at the local mental health clinic and provides individual treatment when requested. Also, the client is expected to pay all or part of his room and board at the residence, and the parents of school age youngsters do likewise.

The results so far reveal that there has been a decrease in commitment to prison by the courts. Of 10 clients discharged (in 1971), six were considered "successfully rehabilitated," with four others sent to institutions with expectations that three will be readmitted to PORT eventually.

Several other workers have published a report of their efforts using group and individual psychotherapy. At the Walpole, Massachusetts, Correctional Institute (19), a recent study reported on 115 subjects which had received group therapy for more than 25 weeks. When compared with a nontherapy sample, the recidivism rate was 53%, as compared to 68%.

Therapeutic community-oriented type successful programs have also been developed in Europe, e.g., Stürup (92, 93).

In another study (48) from California, 257 offenders treated for at least a year with individual and group therapy between 1958 and 1962 were compared with a similar group who did not have individual and group therapy; the 1-year follow-up showed a significant improvement in those with individual treatment. However, this difference disappeared over a 4-year period.

Psychosexual Disorders

The center for the Diagnosis and Treatment of Dangerous Persons in Bridgewater, Massachusetts, was established in 1959 to diagnose and treat "dangerous sex offenders for an indefinite period of time." A study (54) of 592 male convicted offenders evaluated over a 10-year period was published recently. Most were sentenced for sex crimes, but sometimes the convictions were for murder, manslaughter, and assault. Of the 592 offenders, 304 were judged "not dangerous" and not kept at the Center. Of these, 8.6% later committed crimes. Of the 257 who were kept for treatment, 82 were discharged by the Center and 49 were discharged on their own petition or by the court. Of the latter (incompletely treated offenders), 34% committed crimes, as against 6.1% who completed treatment. The treatment consists of individual and group psychotherapy.

A similar program for sexual offenders is in operation at the Washington State Hospital, Fort Steelaium, Washington (84). The 55-bed unit has a treatment program "based on the assumption that deviant sexual behavior is learned...." The total therapeutic program is directed toward overt behavior. "The group members live and work together in fairly close proximity and can readily focus their attention on their ways of reacting both in and out of the group, and they exert social group pressure to control one another's behavior. The group represents the values of society." The program uses intensive group therapy, industrial assignment, and a total life approach, and awards privileges and responsibilities as they are earned. Data from 1965–1966 reveal that of 152 people in the program, 129 were released, with a recidivism rate of 9%.

Schwitzgebel (86) has described the behavior modification treatment of antisocial and sexual offenders. Peters and his group have studied the effect of group psychotherapy for sexual offenders on probation (75, 76, 79). The observations of these workers are useful in understanding the dynamics and behavior of the offender within the group situation.

Substance Use Disorder

Alcohol Dependency

Though physicians have been treating for centuries the medical complications of alcoholics, most general care and responsibility for alcoholics throughout history has been assumed primarily by lay religious groups, courts, and the police and, more recently, the social agencies (20). Aside from individual physicians occasionally concerned with alcoholism, it was not until 1956 that the American Medical Association's Council on Mental Health proposed a resolution that ... "the profession in general recognizes the syndrome on alcoholism which justifiably should have the attention of physicians" (113). The medical profession has been primarily concerned with the treatment of the acute toxic stage and the chronic physical disease which occurred later in the process, though there has been an increased awareness and involvement with family and social complications (8) during the last decade. Professionals in psychiatry, psychology, and sociology have come to recognize alcoholism as a complicated illness, requiring multidisciplinary collaboration. Society, through private and public programs, has likewise recognized the serious nature of alcoholism by giving greater grant support for basic scientific and clinical research (65) and development of clinical programs (21).

The first organized group to offer a consistently reliable sobriety program successful for some alcoholics was Alcoholics Anonymous. Alcoholics Anonymous (2) began in 1935 in Akron, Ohio, when a broker and a physician, both "recovered" alcoholics, avidly worked to help other alcoholics brought into local hospitals' emergency rooms. These men were able to induce some other alcoholics to maintain themselves from becoming intoxicated. Spiritual-religious ideals permeated their motivation to help each other and themselves. These ideals have been embodied within the AA "twelve traditions" and "twelve steps" which guide the organization and individual members. The Akron group soon spread to New York City, and then, in the early 1940s, throughout the United States to aid the uncontrollable alcoholic. They have broadened their services to include programs for the spouses and children of the alcoholics.

Psychiatry has been associated with the treatment of alcoholism at least since 1864, when the New York State Inebriate Asylum opened in Binghamton, New York (20). However, little intensive long-term care specifically for the alcoholic was available until the 1940s and early 1950s when, at that time, individual and group psychotherapy were offered on an inpatient and outpatient basis. By the late 1950s and early 1960s, psychotropic drugs for the symptomatic relief of anxiety and depression and the aversive drug Antabuse were added to the chemical armamentarium. In addition, the more total, comprehensive 24-hour program was developed, and included the concept of the therapeutic community for the first time (86). With the gradual application of therapeutic community to the inpatient and outpatient programs for alcoholics, clinicians began to recognize and respond to the similarities and differences between the complex problems of alcoholics and other psychiatric patients. It was clear that many group experiences during the day could be valuable in helping the alcoholic learn new roles. Likewise, it was useful to staff and alcoholic patients to observe the relationship between the alcoholic's problems and his use of alcohol. Many alcoholics refuse to recognize and admit that there is an alcohol problem. This denial impedes progress, for recovery cannot occur unless the patient becomes aware of his problem and the necessity of changing his attitude and behavior about drinking (6). The staff and other patients in a therapeutic community can help such a resistant patient become more aware of his actions and denials; yet, too often, staff will either become "too rigid" or "overidentify" with the patient and treat the alcohol problem rather than the personality problem (32). This problem of working with alcoholics extends to professionals as well as nonprofessionals. Thus, careful selection and training of staff in interpersonal relations is very important, especially when many staff come from different professional backgrounds. While staff training and competence are vital to any treatment program, this is more so in alcoholism for several reasons. First, the causes, courses, and sequelae of the disease are so protean. Second, the alcoholic, even more than the drug addict or sociopath or severe personality disorder patient, is more likely to have a wife and family. A relatively well-paying job and other community responsibilities are all threatened by alcoholism. Thus, there is a greater need for a multiple discipline team approach. Yet a study of 500 halfway houses (70) which treated either psychiatric patients or alcoholic-psychiatric patients or only alcoholic patients revealed that the programs for alcoholics were the least professionally staffed. About 29% of their workers were volunteers, and there were three nonprofessionals for every professional, which is relatively high. Social workers who traditionally do most of the coordination and family therapy in such programs are 64% of the total professionals. Over 70% of the nonprofessionals are recovered alcoholics in 12% of the programs. Also, many of these programs were church or private corporations, sponsored with an orientation in one or another direction such as toward work of socialization rather than a comprehensive approach. Some such programs did have loose affiliations with hospitals and outpatient psychiatric clinics.

Because of financial constraints, despite the limited contributions of many local communities, most programs choose to focus their resources on the broadest of patient needs. For example, in one publicly sponsored low budget program, many lower socioeconomic alcoholic patients had severe physical illnesses and somatic complaints, which were best evaluated and treated within an integrated psychiatric-medical program (45). In such a therapeutic community whose staff size was sorely limited, the daily activity program was well structured. Role responsibilities for patients and staff were more clearly defined, with the latter being " models of identification." Many group activities were structured about a didactic teaching approach to the problems of alcoholism. These low budget programs extensively utilized community resources such as vocational rehabilitation and employment services, and AA members either consulted within the treatment setting itself or were available at outside community programs to be visited by the patient. Another outpatient-oriented program had frequent community group meetings which focused on "re-educating" the alcoholic about his problem and its myriad physical, psychological, and social manifestations. In addition, individual and psychotherapeutic sessions often involved family members, when appropriate (17).

Despite the association of illicit drug use with youth, younger persons have been increasingly identified with alcohol abuse. In part, this is related to the problems of drug dependency and the cross-tolerance between alcohol, barbiturates, amphetamines, and narcotics as psychic depressants or stimulants. One alcoholism program has actively integrated drug-dependent patients within their therapeutic community originally designed for alcohol patients, with some successful results in rehabilitation (27).

Eagleville Hospital and Rehabilitation Center in Eagleville, Pennsylvania, began its program for "skid row" type alcoholics in July 1966. Prior to its opening, several staff members had visited Daytop Village on Staten Island, New York, a therapeutic community for drug addicts. They were so impressed with Daytop's staff morale, confrontatory group therapy technique, and apparent therapeutic successes that they encouraged their colleagues to visit Daytop and to develop their own alcoholism program along with a similar therapeutic community approach, which they did. Soon afterward, they developed another ward program oriented toward behavior modification. A research study conducted in 1968 after approximately 18 months of operation demonstrated that the overall hospital program had a moderate degree of success, with 20 of 43 former male patients chosen for the study either partially or completely rehabilitated. However, the staff also discovered that 22% of their alcoholic men had drug problems other than alcoholism. Average duration of the nonalcoholic drug problem was 4 to 6 years and included the addictive drugs, both narcotic and nonnarcotic, amphetamines, hallucinogens, and tranquilizers. An overwhelming majority of the men thought that drug problems were similar to and as serious as alcoholism, and that the Eagleville type of therapy could benefit both drug and alcohol addiction. More patients specifically with drug problems were soon admitted so that by 1971 55% of the patients were alcoholic and 45% were drug addicts. On admission, these patients are mixed without regard to their addictive problem. The overall program at Eagleville, however, has shifted in emphasis since its inception. Many posthospital and community-type programs have been developed to assist the inpatient in returning and remaining in the community. These programs include day hospitals, an emergency-crisis intervention service, consultative and training programs to police and parole officers, and street worker-type community organizations.

Drug Dependence

Addictive drugs have been used for thousands of years with varying degrees of personal and social abuse. However, by the early 20th century, narcotics addiction had become such a serious concern to so many countries that several international congresses were convened to ask for international cooperation and control. The United States Congress in 1914 established strict laws controlling narcotics importation, manufacture, and use by physicians. Soon afterward, outpatient detoxification clinics were established, but apparently failed, and were closed in 1921 and 1922. Federal treatment hospitals were established in 1935 at Lexington, Kentucky (for men), and a few beds were allocated at Fort Worth Public Health Service Hospital in Texas several years later (for women). Some psychiatric and a few general hospitals did detoxification for narcotics and other addicting drugs, but most treatment until the 1960s was oriented toward medical treatment of acute intoxification or withdrawal (104–105). As with other personality-like disorders, the treatment psychiatry offered included individual and group psychotherapy for drug dependence. In the late 1950s psychoactive drugs were added to the treatment armamentarium to help relieve symptoms of withdrawal, anxiety, and depression. The results of treatment programs in terms of patients remaining drug-free, especially with narcotics addicts, was very discouraging, although evaluation of the data was quite difficult (71). The major problem of treatment has been that drug dependence is a very complex process which involves the interdependence of sociological (108), personality (77), pharmacological (28), and learning factors (56, 107).

Despite the combined medical, psychiatric, and legal approaches to addiction, it is perhaps surprising (or understandable) that the first program which seemed to help some narcotics addicts recover and maintain themselves drug-free was a self-help group called "Synanon" (109–110). In January 1958, Charles Dederich began holding "free association" discussion groups in his small apartment with friends from Alcoholics Anonymous, of which he was a member. Gradually, narcotics addicts joined the discussion group, and soon the number had increased from about 15 to 35 people. Dederich noticed that some of the addicts were using progressively less drugs, and he attributed it to the intensive "free association" group meetings, which permitted a strong "father-type attachment" to him and an enormous "catharsis" of the intense rage within the addict. The group soon rented a storefront clubhouse in April 1958. In September 1958, the drug addicts left the AA group because of "subliminal mutual disrespect" and disdain for the other group's life-style. The Synanon members now met in study groups, as well as in their intensive therapy-type "synanons." By October 1958, the Synanon Foundation was incorporated, and Dederich was asked to speak to a group of Southern California parole officers. In his talk, he described the "more or less autocratic family structure" which was helpful for the addict to control his usually impulsive and rebellious behavior. The Synanon member was expected to take all orders, regardless of his feelings, and talk about these feelings in a synanon, later called a "game." Each game is composed of different people at each session, so that no synanon is the same. Games meet three times weekly, with 10 to 15 people. A game is organized by a synanist, an addict who has arrested his symptoms and is experienced in the Synanon process. The senior synanist is expected to serve as a "role model." The games vary in form and context. The synanist generally chooses a "balanced" group and sets the tone intuitively. Some focus on a "haircut," where more experienced members "take apart" a new person by pointing out his unacceptable infantile behavior, attitudes, and ideas. Such games with newer members are usually loud and raucous. A game with more experienced members is more controlled, though, as with all synanons, confrontation and the "search for truth" are the guidelines. No member is ever allowed drugs or alcohol of any kind in the House or elsewhere. A permissive attitude within the environment with regard to verbalizing anger and resentment is encouraged, with the expectation that assigned tasks be completed, no matter how menial. A feeling of "caring" while "criticizing" is inherent in all synanon confrontations, and there is enormous commitment to the group and its ideals of "self-help" and "actualization." As Synanon has crystallized into an identifiable community, specific administrative structures relating to the outside community have developed, such as a Saturday night "open house event" and business enterprises to help the organization become self-supporting.

The central feature of the program is the game, which not only provides "therapy" in the sense of catharsis, insight, awareness about self and relating to others, and control of emotions, but also helps maintain the interpersonal relationships and social interactions of the Synanon organization as it matures and expands. Within the Synanon community, any member may rise to a more responsible position in the hierarchy. This promotion is intended to raise the person's self-esteem and encourage him to continue progressing.

Despite many branch chapters of Synanon, it still regards itself as a self-contained, ex-drug addict community within a larger geopolitical community and will maintain its members indefinitely.

In the late 1970's Synanon came under criticism because some of its leaders were brought to court and tried for criminal activity.

Still their programs have helped many persons and have been useful as one approach in utilizing the therapeutic community for treating personality disorders.

Other therapeutic communities designed to combat drug addiction along treatment lines similar to Synanon usually have their ultimate goal as returning "graduates" back into the general community at large.

Odyssey House (25) was founded by a psychiatrist-lawyer, Dr. Judianne Densen-Gerber, in 1965 in New York City. It is an in-residence program which demands total commitment from the person who wishes to be relieved of his narcotic addiction. The milieu therapy is described as "all-involving," as the addict needs constant observation and reinforcement if he is to change long-established negative behavior patterns.

The Odyssey program is divided into three phases: a motivation, a treatment, and a re-entry phase. In the first phase, the patient "must demonstrate he has some understanding of the concept of a therapeutic community and commitment to abide by it while in residential therapy." This includes accepting the doctor-patient relationship, looking into himself, and accepting the authority and discipline of the community. The second phase of the treatment focuses on the "here and now" of behavioral relationships and attitudes. All activities are carried out in groups and later examined and evaluated in group therapy. This constant attention and involvement by staff and patients in all activities results in a minimum of dissimulation and manipulation, which is such a pervasive trait of the addict. The peer system of ex-addicts as staff minimizes distortion of "authority figures" and, as such, rebellion.

The re-entry phase occurs in steps and levels where the ex-addict increasingly accepts responsibility outside the residence. These responsibilities refer to a clear understanding of his relationship with his family, achievement of a high school diploma or its equivalency, and a self-supporting job outside the field of drug addiction (except for 10%). In the latter states, when "neurotic" symptoms begin to emerge, individual psychotherapy is encouraged. The problem of re-entry back into the community is probably the most difficult one, and may account in part for the higher recovery rates claimed by Synanon, which maintains its members within its own Synanon community. Mayer and others (61) have also noted that the re-entry problems from the therapeutic community to the "outside world" include difficulties with rule consistency, violence, prohibitions, group activity focus, total commitment to and involvement in program and community, and minimal staff-patient differentiation in responsibility for their lives and their community life. Most therapeutic community programs report a greater than 50% drug-free population when a member completes his prescribed treatment regimen (24).

Theoretical Considerations

While initially it makes "sense" that people living in a community can help each other feel better (or worse), think more rationally (or irrationally), and behave more appropriately (or inappropriately) in a particular situation or the community at large, it is not clear how this happens. More specifically, how does the therapeutic community affect the individual person with personality (behavioral) disorders, and how does that individual person in turn affect the total community? An understanding of the therapeutic process would enable the hospital and nonhospital administrative and clinical staff to implement and utilize better the therapeutic community within their own environments for their patients and clients. In order to study such a process, the assumption is made that man and his society are inextricable parts of each other and of the whole human system. The life experience of man as a person reflects both an individual aspect and a societal aspect. Conversely, a society's experiences reflect both the individual's efforts, as well as the efforts of the societal group. Man and society cannot exist apart or separately to the extent that a human being reared from infancy completely in isolation from all other human contacts can barely survive at best (88), and a society must by definition have more than one person to be a society.

For heuristic purposes, the individual person and society are each studied as separate systems with certain general assumptions made about the effects of one on the other. For example, classic psychoanalysts have intensively studied the intrapsychic mental functioning of the individual person and assumed until recently (106) the basic premise that "ego" development includes and is facilitated by "adaptation" to the environment (43). Conversely, social scientists have studied intergroup and intragroup behavior and assumed that there are certain basic "biological givens" (96) and personality-psychological systems operating (73). Some writers, such as Cooley (22), have stated that the person's actions are the "precipitates" of society's dictates, while others have seen the social process in terms of personal actions and intrapsychic dynamic processes (37). We believe that Talcott Parsons' (73) General Theory of Action Systems is a useful model for understanding the complex processes and relationships which occur within the community and the individual person. Parsons theorizes that to understand action as a system itself requires that three separate and distinct, though interdependent, subsystems be considered—a social system, a personality system, and a cultural system. He notes that while they may have corresponding homologs, conceptually they are always in balance with each other and influence a particular activity. Various authors have discussed the theoretical aspects of the therapeutic community from different perspectives. Cummings and Cummings (23) use the structural theory concept of the "ego" as originally proposed by Freud (38), but in their discussion modify the concept for their purposes to include ideas from other workers, such as Hartmann, Mead, Erickson, and Federn. As the Cummingses were writing primarily about their work in schizophrenia, which is often defined as an illness characterized by a severe "ego defect," an "ego model" is quite useful. Artiss (7), in his studies with young male schizophrenics at Walter Reed Army Hospital, used communications theory on explaining how the therapeutic community helps the patient. Stanton and Schwartz (91) utilized the psychosocial model to comprehend the therapeutic processes of a ward at Chestnut Lodge and the total institution itself. Stainbrook (89) borrowed T. R. Sarbin's sociopsychological role theory model. According to Sarbin, "self-qualities" and "role-expectations" develop together within a growing child, and "interpenetrate and interrelate so that the roles are internalized within the self." Sarbin describes the social behavior as an action system which arrives out of this self-role interplay (83).

We believe it is useful to discuss the therapeutic community from a theoretical framework of object relations. Clearly, most programs for people with behavioral disorders have been designed toward focusing on group activity and how people relate to each other. More recently, this has come to include modifying aberrant behavior with certain techniques from learning theory (68). In order to understand theoretically how this therapeutic concept has an effect on the psychopathology of personality disorders, we propose to explore three general psychological approaches with reference to aspects of object relationships. It is understood that while these approaches are independent, they overlap in their scope, and none can describe adequately exactly what is happening in the therapeutic community. The first approach is the psychosocial (interpersonal) model, and has been described by scientists from several disciplines. Psychiatrists include Sullivan (96), Edelson

(29), and Horney (80). Psychologists following from gestalt psychology and the functionalism of James culminated in the field theory of Lewin (26) and his disciples. Sociologists G. H. Mead (64), Cooley (22), and Talcott Parsons (73) have also studied such intra- and intergroup processes. The second approach is the personality (intrapsychic) model, as first conceptualized by Sigmund Freud (34) and later modified by his followers, Anna Freud (33), Heinz Hartmann (43), and Edith Jacobson (47). Heinz Kohut (53) and Otto Kernberg (50) have also contributed to an understanding of self and object within the classic psychoanalytic framework. Harry Gunthrup (41) has described other self and object theories developed by nonclassic psychoanalysts. The third theoretical approach is behavior modification or learning theory (11, 14) derived from Watson's behaviorism, Skinner's operant conditioning (87), and the Russian physiologist Pavlov (74).

The Psychosocial (Interpersonal) Model

The concepts of both Sullivan and Horney were considered as a theoretical framework for understanding the effect of therapeutic community from the psychosocial (interpersonal) perspective. Both psychiatrists went beyond their classic psychoanalytic backgrounds to study personality from the interpersonal and societal perspectives, respectively.

Sullivan (82, 100), in his work with obsessive-compulsive and schizophrenic patients, postulated a self-system (self-dynamism) which grew out of cultural restraints by the parents on biological satisfactions, e.g., food and sex. Basic anxiety arises when these needs are not met and when the need for parental and cultural security is not met. This self-system is a part of the personality and develops in relation to interpersonal experiences and needs (satisfaction, security). The self-system contains the personification of earlier childhood interpersonal experiences in the self form of "the good me," "the bad me," and the dissociated "not me" and in the object form of the "good mother" and the "bad mother." The mobilization of "bad me" and "not me" for self and "bad mother" for objects results in nonhealthy behavior. Treatment for Sullivan focused only on investigating the patient's anxieties within the interpersonal context. The patient's neurotic (and psychotic) defense against the anxiety was studied by the participant-observer therapist and the patient, in order to learn how to adapt better to other individuals and the social situation through a more expanded realistic self-system.

Horney (80), in her work with neurotics, developed a holistic view of personality in which the individual person is functioning within a social situation. The total personality (self) is composed of many "attributes" which include biological-social needs, behavioral traits, feelings and attitudes toward others and self, self-evaluation concepts, social values, expectations, inhibitions, etc. These individual characteristic attributes change constantly and interact dynamically with each other within the social framework. Self (nee, personality) is conceptualized as: (a) the actual self (the sum total of an individual's experiences, (b) the real self ("a central inner face common to all but unique for each individual"), and (c) the idealized self (a neurotic self-concept). Horney focused in treatment on self-realization systems of the here and now experience, based on certain childhood experiences and how such attitudes and feelings affect oneself and one's relationship to society.

While the self-concepts of Sullivan and Horney are helpful in understanding the therapeutic community from the object relation perspective, the dynamics of the group process and its effect on the individual person and the community are more germane.

The psychosocial (interpersonal) model, chosen to explain the therapeutic community as a treatment modality, focuses on group processes. The model is taken from the writings of Marshall Edelson (29) and Talcott Parsons (73). This group dynamics model focuses primarily on ward-size groups, but it is applicable to the whole hospital and the extramural community at large. The group is defined as composed of interdependent members, parts, or objects which function together under the influence of shared values, beliefs, and ideas of normal behavior. The extent to which the members or objects are committed to these shared values determines the action and behavior of the group and distinguishes the social aspects from the individual aspects of the members and group itself. These social values partially influence both how the group as an "object" itself relates to another "object" group, and how the members within a group relate to each other as objects or members within the same group. Relationships between any members in the group will affect the behavior of each and every other member as a social phenomenon of the group. At the same time every group member has certain individual (personality) aspects and values which influence behavior apart from the social aspect. According to Parsons' general theory of action, the interaction among these social, cultural, and personality systems is constant and complementary and determines the relationship between members of the same group and between different groups.

The group carries out specific actions and functions in order to maintain itself and pursue certain goals. Edelson has delineated four functions of the group as a system. These four group (subsystem) functions are interrelated and interdependent, yet they compete functionally with each other internally within the group. In order to understand how the therapeutic community group is functional, one must understand these specific group functions. For example, at any one time the group as a whole can carry out only one major function while the other three functions continue to complement and compete differently, depending on the "major function." The first major function of the group is "adaptation" to a particular situation. Adaptive functions include orienting and educating the group as to a problem situation, mobilizing resources, making certain cognitive decisions about the most effective and rational action to take toward an already agreed upon role. Communication is important to effecting the function. It is assumed that when the group is functioning in an adaptive manner, certain decisions have already been made. For example, a community meeting which is planning how best to organize a trip to a ball game is in an adaptive phase. That is, an adapting group is preparing to take certain action outside of its own group system, e.g., deciding when to leave and when to return to the hospital based on curfew, etc. The second function is the actual "consummating" of a goal itself. Group functioning at this stage includes decision making and goal setting, and in such discussions the group might decide certain values and standards, e.g., whether the group activities should be expressive, supportive, or insightful. For example, making the decision (a) to go to a ball game, and (b) to which ball game is a consummating group function. This function is similar to the adaptive function in terms of the group going outside of its own system, e.g., leaving the hospital, but these functions differ as the consummating function is actually achieving a specific goal or fulfilling a need rather than preparing for one. The third function is the "integration" of the group members within itself. The group attempts to have its members identify more closely with group values and to re-establish certain group norms and values, allows members sufficient latitude and freedom to speak out on differences in goals and values, and tries to induce dissidents to reidentify with the group as a whole. For example, the group discussed above may have recognized that there were staff-patient differences. The discussion of these differences in order to improve group harmony and solidarity and the group decision to go to a ball game together with staff and patients may have integrating function. This function is different from adaptation and consummation as it affects the group within itself, rather than going outside of its system. Still, it is similar to consummation as it is achieving or effecting an action. The fourth function is "motivation" of the group and its members. Such functions could include improving the internal condition of the group, discussing the behavior patterns within the group, discussing new ideas, formulating new thoughts, and relieving the tensions of the group itself. As with the integrating function, the motivating function occurs within the particular community, rather than going outside of it. But like the adaptive function, it is a potentiating and preparing rather than achieving function. For example, the group may discuss that while there is the (integrating) value of every member going to the ball game together, the group may also agree that some persons may appreciate the group more (i.e., be motivated) if there is no excessive group pressure forcing each member to attend the ball game. The teenager who was once judged "withdrawn" because he wanted to "read" rather than "rap" with other members on the hall is an example of how community values and group functioning attempt to influence individual members' behavior.

These four functions all go on at the same time within the group as the group moves from one activity to the other. Its members carry out an adaptive function at times to fulfill certain agreed upon goals. The group also maintains itself by integrating its members and motivating them to agree to certain discussed goals and values, which, in turn, can integrate, adapt, etc. These values, beliefs, moral codes, expressive symbols, and knowledge as part of the cultural system regulate the actions of the group as a whole and the relationship of the individual members to each other to the extent that the individual person has internalized or identified with this particular culture and is willing to submit himself to them. Many patients with severe personality disorders are particularly dysfunctional in their interpersonal relationships and within society as a whole. Of course, it is precisely at this group level that the "social therapist" utilizes the resources of the therapeutic community. His knowledge of the above dynamics and his awareness of the values and importance of group processes in regulating group behavior are essential.

The treatment programs for alcoholics and drug addicts very clearly depend upon the integrating and motivating functions of the group. Alcoholics Anonymous and many church-sponsored alcoholism programs have a religious, philosophical creed as part of their membership. The therapeutic communities for drug addicts, i.e., Synanon, Odyssey House, and Phoenix House, are even more strict and demanding of their members. As one counselor was heard to say to a recalcitrant addict, "Do you want to give our program a bad name? Do you want to join us in trying to build a better tomorrow? I'd love to go out and get 'high,' but I know how this would reflect on our program. Will you commit yourself to us?"

Personality (Intrapsychic) Model

We have chosen to discuss the personality (intrapsychic) object relations model and the development of the personality structure using the classic psychoanalytic "object relations" ego model. Freud originally described the ego as a "dominant mass of ideas" which perceived, remembered, and controlled both motor activity and certain conscious and unconscious functions in order to manage anxiety which had been converted from "dammed-up sexual energy" (35–36). This ego was also responsible for discerning and pursuing reality as against permitting pleasurable wishes to tyrannize the individual's activities (97). Next Freud used ego to describe "the self" (98) as opposed to an object. This particular ego or self was developed gradually through identifications with the object choices by relinquishing rather than having the self maintain the object apart from itself (99). In this case, the ego formation developed as "the graveyard of the abandoned object relations," which included identifications with former objects. Last, Freud developed the tripartite model with ego, superego, and id (38). The ego organization here was described by its functions and efforts to maintain contact with inner and outer reality as well as mediating and controlling id and superego pressure. Gedo and Goldberg (39) have thoughtfully conceptualized an overall model of the mind which integrates these three ego models and the topographical model (conscious-unconscious) and then applied these models to clinical situations and developed an appropriate nosology. These authors suggest that the object relations ego model is much more germane to patients with severe personality disorders than the tripartite model because such patients haven't solved self-object differentiation. The treatment of these patients usually requires that the therapist serve as a more real object to the patient. This is contrasted with the neurotic patient whose treatment requires, in the analytic setting, that the therapist be neutral and equidistant from the patient's id, ego, and superego.

The personality (intrapsychic) model is based on clinical research (47), child analysis and observations between mother and child (60), and psychoanalytic reconstructions in adults (51). The infant regulates and controls his biological drives and impulses through physical and emotional reactions and interactions, first with his mother and then with others in his environment. Initially, the infant cannot perceive the difference between himself, whose needs push to be fulfilled, and his mother, the satisfier of needs and fulfiller of wishes. The "self" and "object" are one. As the child grows and matures, he becomes better able to perceive something external to him and to discern who and what the external word is. He develops a sense of "me" (self) as opposed to the "other" (object) as he gradually separates himself from his mother. At first, these perceptions–fixations differentiate in a fanciful, fantastic manner. Earliest feelings about self and object are felt as "all good" for the "me" internal world and "all bad" for the "not me" painful, unpleasant external world. Some external objects bring pleasure and are incorporated as part of "me"; conversely, certain internal states are unpleasant and are expelled as part of the "other." As the child continues to grow and mature, he differentiates more and more the external object from his own inner self and the introjections and projections are no longer based on the pleasure principle, but are more related to appropriated feelings and ideas associated with the inner (self) and outer (object) worlds. Gradually, within the mental world of the child, many more specific different representations of self and objects develop. The "other" becomes a more realistic "good" but sometimes "bad" whole object, which is usually the mother, and thus establishes an object constancy upon which other relationships develop. Similarly, a whole "good" but sometimes "bad" self emerges out of the many identifications and becomes a realistic self-identity. At first, they are primitive fantasied identifications, but they gradually change and are superseded or coalesced into more mature identifications. These identifications also include certain social roles and expectations accompanying self and object representation. It is presumed that some primitive fantasy types of representations of self and objects remain. Ego and superego maturation have occurred as part of and in conjunction with the growth and differentiation of self and object representations and, likewise, the development of the ego and superego functions of the structural model enhance development of the self and object concepts. As the child develops a more stable sense of self, his ego becomes better integrated and functioning, thus enabling the child to control his impulses better and fulfill his capabilities to get his needs more autonomously from the outside world. While he has become more independent of his parents to meet his needs and control his impulses externally, he had "internalized" their psychic representation in his superego with all the prohibitions and expectations of society and family. Other primitive fantasies have become internalized as representations of oneself and objects, not necessarily parents. Some of these develop into "ideal self" and "ideal object" representation. These nuclei of ideal self and ideal object representations finally "coalesce" to become the "ego ideal," a part of the superego. Intrapsychically, the superego is associated with primitive parental prohibitions which become "formed" about the oedipal period (4 to 7 years old) and include both guilt feelings and aggressive impulses. The ego ideal continues to be more "flexible" until the 20s and is associated with identifications, identity, and the feeling of shame.

In patients with mild neurotic character disorders of neuroses, the conflicts are between the structured ego, superego, id, and external reality, and the ego identity itself is fairly well integrated. Symptoms and defense are more "alien" to the person's ego-reality. People with personality disorders have conflicts often "within" the specific structures themselves, and their psychiatric problems are with ego functioning and ego and superego integration. For such people, character traits (69) are more "syntonic" and "symptomatic" with the patient's ego-reality, and the patient is more comfortable with his behavior than the neurotic patient. In addition, there is less stable ego identity and object representation, and so such patients regress more quickly to a primitive multiple self and object representation when in treatment. Kernberg (51) notes that such regressions to the primitive self and object representation do occur in more stable persons in the classic analytic situation, but much more slowly, and the transference focus is usually on parental objects at the oedipal level rather than at the primitive multiple object level. However, even more mature people in group situations which have a vague task or role definition experience a rapid regression to the multiple primitive object representation. Kernberg suggests that "role enactment" in the family situation and in interpersonal relations protects most stable people from such regressions but with an unstructured group situation, the primitive fantasies occur. When there is regression to this more primitive fantasy level, the ego defenses also become more primitive in terms of projection, splitting, denial, and primitive idealization. Behavior is that of the personality disorder. He suggests that sufficient unstructured group situations occur in the therapeutic community to encourage the eruption of these primitive fantasies and allow the staff to help the patient and group to recognize, understand, and control them. These fantasies may also be utilized in individual treatment where symptom complaints at first may be comparatively rare with respect to such experiences in the community itself. Kernberg also suggests that analytically oriented group psychotherapy may also be useful in treating such severe disorders. Later, intensive intrapsychic investigation may also be useful in such treatment. The therapeutic community then allows for better treatment of the symptoms in severe personality disorders by the identification and control of such pathological behavior and its relationship to feelings and thoughts which arise out of unstructured group-interpersonal situations. The group and individual therapies allow for understanding and alteration of object relationship so as to help the patient learn new ways to adapt to the external world.

Thus, in terms of the object-relations model, self and object representations intrapsychically have their counterparts in the self and objects of the interpersonal external world. Edelson (29) has described how the object relationship models of a psychosocial (interpersonal) group system is related to the personality (intrapsychic) system. Utilizing the structural model (ego, id, superego) of classic analysis, he noted that the superego and ego ideal reflect parental and social demands and expectations (37–38) and thus cultural values of the social system become internalized within the personality (intrapsychic) system.

However, it may be more useful to describe how the individual and group symptomatology overlap clinically. The relationship between social and personality aspects of behavior for the severe personality disorder patient will be noted, first within the social-group context, and then from within the personality context. For example, the (social) withdrawal of a person from the group and its particular values is characteristic of the Schizoid Personality. The fulfilling and conforming to the normal values in an active and rigid, yet spiritless, manner is characteristic of a Depressive or Obsessive Personality. The rebelling against responsibilities and expectations of the group is characteristic of the Antisocial Personality.

Thus, the areas of expertise of the therapist responsible for social behavior include similarities to, as well as differences from, the areas of expertise of the therapist responsible for individual personal behavior. A social therapist must be aware of both social-group and individual personal deviations within the functioning framework of the therapeutic community. He must understand how the person's pathological behavior is affected by the community and how each person affects the group and its members. The individual therapist must be aware of the therapeutic community activities and its effects on the patient, and vice versa.

The psychiatric hospital functions as a large therapeutic community group, with many smaller therapeutic communities and other activities, with the same four subsystem functions (adaptive, consummating, integrating, and motivating) operating as with the smaller ward-size therapeutic community groups which collectively make up the hospital community. The ward therapeutic community thus is a member of an object within the overall hospital therapeutic community and, as such, it should be in agreement with the hospital values and carry out its goals. No ward therapeutic community can function successfully if it does not have the support of the overall hospital administration. It cannot function alone. Similarly, the hospital itself cannot carry out its functions successfully if its values are not shared by the subgroups which provide care at the patient level. Edelson discusses some of the "values" which a hospital and ward therapeutic community might share. They could include a preference for active involvement with other patients and staff, an effort to develop a set of priorities and a willingness to delay certain immediate gratifications, a preference for exploring one's thoughts and feelings, albeit a painful and slow process, an effort to understand oneself, and an effort to increase one's adaptational effectiveness.

Learning Model

The authors have generally conceptualized the efficacy of the therapeutic community in terms of object relations from personality-intrapsychic and social-interpersonal theoretical perspectives. The learning theory perspective must also be considered because it is increasingly being used as a therapeutic tool (16) and because it focuses on the changing social-interpersonal behavior per se, and is thus germane to the treatment of severe personality and other related nonpsychotic disorders. Bachrach (11) states that "learning is a change in behavior that results from practice with learning represented as the intervening process or variable which links organismic states before and after a change in behavior occurs." The treatment focus in learning theory is on the specific aberrant behavior and the specific situations, emotional difficulties, and other symptoms related to the behavior (68). Behavior therapy seeks to modify the behavior and attitudes themselves, using specific techniques in contrast to investigating and focusing on unconscious, intrapsychic, and interpersonal social conflicts and resultant defensive symptoms behavior, as characterized by the other psychological approaches. For example, in alcoholism and certain sexual deviations, the specific behavior to be changed is discussed and understood in terms of situational causes and associated emotional and cognitive concomitants. Behavior modification techniques applied were aversive conditioning methods such as disulfiram or mild electric shock. The behavioral therapist would not find it necessary to explore internal conflicts and early childhood experiences and defenses related to the dysfunctional behavior. An exploration of the interpersonal relationships would be in terms of how the aberrant behavior is "reinforced" by the other person or group members. For example, if a person exhibited himself, the therapist would try to analyze specific details surrounding, preceding, and following the exhibitionistic experience as to setting, time, feeling, and attitude. The therapist, having discovered the stimuli conditions, would develop a program to "learn" new responses, reactions of victims, etc. Thus, applied learning theory helps the patient "unlearn" dysfunctional behavior and "re-learn" appropriate behavior. To many behaviorists, the person is not seen as a "patient" with a medical-psychiatric problem, but as a poorly or incorrectly educated person who has learned to cope with interpersonal situations inappropriately. He must be taught new methods and kinds of behavior.

Operant conditioning as developed by B. F. Skinner has been applied increasingly to patients with severe psychiatric and personality symptoms (103). In contrast to the classic conditioning situation of Pavlov, where an unconditioned stimulus is associated with a conditioned stimulus and its response (e.g., bell—food—salivation), operant conditioning occurs in a rather free situation. Thus, the client's own voluntary stimuli and responses are studied so as to learn how best to change the behavior. Bandura (12) lists three "systems" which regulate and control learning. The most studied and utilized treatment technique in social settings is the feedback processes based upon reinforcement consequences. In behavior therapy, the emphasis is first on identifying clearly the specific behavior to be modified, knowing when it occurred and what factors cause it to persist. Next, a set of treatment conditions is selected and a schedule of retraining is arranged using certain learning techniques. These techniques either modify the relationship between the responses and the situations in which they occur or the relationship between the responses and the consequences to which the behavior eventually leads (103). The extent of this relationship within the learning model is still being studied. However, whether one is trying to modify behavior through manipulating either the antecedent or consequences of the environment, the patient and therapist are involved in an object relationship. This relationship itself may be used by the therapist purposely or unknowingly in operant conditioning as positive reinforcement of the newly learned behavior. For example (9), two chronic schizophrenic female patients had problems with eating. One refused to go to eat and the other refused to leave, except under duress. They were both encouraged with candy to behave more appropriately. Staff and patient reactions were both used as rewards of approval within the therapeutic community. This attention and approval, plus the food reinforcement, helped maintain their behavioral gains. Other important techniques include "role identifications" by patients of staff members and aversive control, e.g., punishment, extinction, and counterconditioning methods. These methods have been used in state hospitals, penal institutions, and educational settings (4) with some success.

REFERENCES

1. Aichorn, A. *Wayward Youth.* Viking Press, New York, 1935.
2. Alcoholics Anonymous. *Alcoholics Anonymous World Service, Inc.* Cornwall Publishing Co., Cornwall, N. Y., 1955.
3. Alexander, F., and Healy, W. *Roots of Crime.* A. A. Knopf, New York, 1935.
4. American Psychiatric Association. Diagnostic and Statistical Manual of Mental Disorders, Ed. 1. American Psychiatric Association, Washington, D. C., 1952.
5. American Psychiatric Association. Diagnostic and Statistical Manual of Mental Disorders, Ed. 2. American Psychiatric Association, Washington, D. C., 1968.
6. Armstrong, J. D. The therapeutic community in the treatment of alcoholism. In: *Alcoholism Behavioral Research, Therapeutic Approaches*, R. Fox (Ed.), p. 164. Springer Publishing Co., New York, 1967.
7. Artiss, K. *Milieu Therapy in Schizophrenia.* Grune & Stratton, New York, 1962.
8. Aspects of Alcoholism, Vol. 12. J. Lippincott Co., Philadelphia, 1963–1966.
9. Ayllon, T. Intensive treatment of psychotic behavior by stimuli satiation and food reinforcement. In: *Case Studies in Behavior Modification*, L. Ullman and L. Krasner (Eds.), p. 77. Holt, Rinehart, & Winston, Inc., New York, 1966.
10. Ayllon, T., and Azrin, N. *The Token Economy.* Appleton-Century-Crofts, New York, 1968.
11. Bachrach, A. Learning. In: *Comprehensive Textbook of Psychiatry*, A. Freedman and H. Kaplan (Eds.), p. 166. Williams & Wilkins Co., Baltimore, 1967.
12. Bandura, A. *Principles of Behavior Modification.* Holt, Rinehart, & Winston, Inc., New York, 1969.
13. Beiber, I. Homosexuality—A Psychoanalytic Study. Basic Books, New York, 1962.
14. Bergin, S., and Lambert, W. Stimulus-response theory in contemporary social psychology. In: *The Handbook of Social Psychology*, Ed. 2, G. Linzy and E. Aronson (Eds.), p. 488. Addison-Wesley Publishing Co., Reading, Mass., 1968.
15. Bettelheim, B. *Love Is Not Enough.* Free Press, Glencoe, Ill., 1950.
16. Brady, J. D. Behavior therapy and American psychiatry. J. Natl. Assoc. Priv. Psychiatr. Hosp., 4:27, 1972.
17. Brunner, O. M. A three-dimensional approach to the treatment of alcoholism. In: *Alcoholism Behavioral Research, Therapeutic Approaches*, R. Fox (Ed.), p. 152. Springer Publishing Co., New York, 1967.
18. Bullard, D. M. The organization of psychoanalytic procedure in the hospital. J. Nerv. Ment. Dis., 9:697–703, 1940.
19. Carney, F. Evaluation of psychotherapy in a maximum security prison. Semin. Psychiatry, 3:363–375, 1971.
20. Chavetz, M. Alcoholism. In: *Comprehensive Textbook of Psychiatry*, A. Freedman and H. Kaplan (Eds.), p. 1011. Williams & Wilkins Co., Baltimore, 1967.
21. Chavetz, M., Blane, H., and Hill, M. *Frontiers of Alcoholism.* Science House, New York, 1970.
22. Cooley, C. H. *Human Nature and the Social Order.* Schocken Books, New York, 1964.
23. Cummings, J., and Cummings, E. *Ego and Milieu.* Atherton Press, New York, 1963.
24. Delong, H. S., and Rosenthal, N. Phoenix House. J. A. M. A., 22:8686, 1972.
25. Densen-Gerber, J., and Spears, R. Therapeutic communities—the Odyssey House concept. N. Y. Univ. Q., 28:2, 1972.
26. Deutsch, M. Field theory in sociopsychology. In: *The Handbook of Social Psychology*, Ed. 2, G. Linzy and E. Aronson (Eds.), p. 488. Addison-Wesley Publishing Co., Reading, Mass., 1968.

27. Eagleville Hospital and Rehabilitation Center. Reports of the Medical Director, July 1 to December 31, 1967; January 1, 1968, to June 30, 1968; July 1, 1968, to December 31, 1968; January 1 to December 31, 1969; January 1 to December 31, 1970; January to December 31, 1971; Progress Report, 1971-1972. Eagleville, Penna.
28. Eddy, N. P. Chemopharmacologic approach to the addiction problem. In: *Narcotics*, D. Wilner and G. Casselbaum (Eds.), p. 67. McGraw-Hill Book Co., New York, 1965.
29. Edelson, M. *Sociotherapy and Psychotherapy*. University of Chicago Press, Chicago, 1970.
30. Fink, L., Denby, M., and Morgan, J. P. Psychiatry's new role in correction. Am. J. Psychiatry, 126:542, 1969.
31. Forzis, L. Proceedings of the resource conference on problems of alcohol and alcoholism. Q. J. Stud. Alcohol, 20:415-672, 1959.
32. Fox, V. Difficulties encountered in maintaining a therapeutic community. In: *Alcoholism Behavioral Research, Therapeutic Approaches*, R. Fox (Ed.), p. 164. Springer Publishing Co., New York, 1967.
33. Freud, A. *Ego and the Mechanism of Defense*. International Universities Press, New York, 1946.
34. Freud, S. *Standard Edition of the Complete Psychological Works of Sigmund Freud*, translated and edited by J. Strachey, Vols. 1-23. Hogarth Press, London, 1955.
35. Freud, S. Studies in hysteria. In: *Standard Edition of the Complete Psychological Works of Sigmund Freud*, translated and edited by J. Strachey, Vol. 3. Hogarth Press, London, 1955.
36. Freud, S. The interpretation of dreams. In: *Standard Edition of the Complete Psychological Works of Sigmund Freud*, translated and edited by J. Strachey, Vols. 4 and 5, pp. 1 and 339. Hogarth Press, London, 1955.
37. Freud, S. Group psychology and the analysis of the ego. In: *Standard Edition of the Complete Psychological Works of Sigmund Freud*, translated and edited by J. Strachey, Vol. 18, p. 69. Hogarth Press, London, 1955.
38. Freud, S. The ego and the id. In: *Standard Edition of the Complete Psychological Works of Sigmund Freud*, translated and edited by J. Strachey, Vol. 19, p. 3. Hogarth Press, London, 1955.
39. Gedo, J., and Goldberg, A. *Models of the Mind*. University of Chicago Press, Chicago, 1973.
40. Gottlieb, B., and Digiodomenico, P. Modifications of a therapeutic community on a brief stay ward. Hosp. Community Psychiatry, 22:23, 1971.
41. Gunthrup, H. *Psychoanalytic Theory—A Therapy in the Self*. Basic Books, New York, 1971.
42. Guttmacher, M. S. Dangerous offenders. Crime Delinquency, 9:83, 1963.
43. Hartmann, H. *Ego Psychology and the Problem of Adaptation*, p. 32. University Press, New York, 1958.
44. Hedlund, D. The sweet-and-sour bird of youth-cult. J. Natl. Assoc. Priv. Psychiatr. Hosp., 4:5-8, 1972.
45. Henderson, C. B. Mechanisms of a therapeutic community for alcoholics. In: *Alcoholism Behavioral Research, Therapeutic Approaches*, R. Fox (Ed.), p. 175. Springer Publishing Co., New York, 1967.
46. Henderson, J. The doing character. Adolescence, 7:309-326, 1972.
47. Jacobson, E. *The Self and the Object World*. University Press, New York, 1964.
48. Jeev, C. C., Clanon, M. L., and Maltack, A. L. The effectiveness of group psychotherapy in a correctional institution. Am. J. Psychiatry, 129:602, 1972.
49. Jones, M. The Therapeutic Community—A New Treatment in Psychiatry. Basic Books, New York, 1953.
50. Kernberg, O. New developments in psychoanalytic objects relations theory. Presented at Annual Meeting of the American Psychiatric Association, Washington, D. C., April 1971.
51. Kernberg, O. Psychoanalytic object relations, group process and administration. In: *Chicago Institute of Psychoanalysis*, Vol. 1. Quadrangle Books, New York, 1973.
52. Kilgalen, R. Hydrotherapy, is it all washed up? J. Psychiatr. Nurs., 10:3-6, 1972.
53. Kohut, H. *The Analysis of the Self*. International Universities Press, New York, 1971.

54. Kozol, H., Boucher, R., and Garafola, R. The diagnosis and treatment of dangerousness. Crime Delinquency, 18:371, 1972.
55. Kraft, A. M. The therapeutic community. In: *American Handbook of Psychiatry*, S. Arieti (Ed.), p. 542. Basic Books, New York, 1966.
56. Lindesmith, L. *Addiction and Opiates.* Aldine Publication Co., Chicago, 1968.
57. Lindner, R. *Rebel Without a Cause, The Psychoanalysis of a Criminal Psychopath.* Grune & Stratton, New York, 1958.
58. Lion, J. R., and Bach-Y-Rita, G. Group therapy wtith violent outpatients. Int. J. Group Psychother., 20:185, 1970.
59. Luke, I., Kim, C., and Clanon, T. L. Psychiatric services integrated into the California correctional system. Int. J. Offender Ther., 5:169, 1971.
60. Mahler, M. A study of the separation and individualization process. In: *Psychoanalytic Study of the Child*, Vol. 26, p. 403. Quadrangle Books, New York, 1972.
61. Mayer, J., Semarawara, A., and Myerson, D. A therapeutic framework of drug addiction. Int. J. Soc. Psychiatry, 18:114, 1972.
62. McCord, W., and McCord, J. *The Psychopath.* D. Van Nostrand Co., Princeton, 1966.
63. McDonald, M. C. Maryland's Defective Delinquent Statute, a Progress Report. Patuxent Institution, Jessup, Maryland, 1973.
64. Mead, G. H. *Mind, Self, and Society.* University of Chicago Press, Chicago, 1934.
65. Mello, N., and Mendelson, J. Recent advances in the study of alcoholism—an interdisciplinary symposium, No. 17240143. U. S. Government Printing Office, Washington, D. C., 1971.
66. Menninger, W. C. Psychiatric hospital therapy designed to meet needs. Am. J. Psychiatry, 93:347–360, 1936.
67. Mora, G. History of psychiatry. In: *Comprehensive Textbook of Psychiatry*, A. Freedman and H. Kaplan (Eds.). Williams & Wilkins Co., Baltimore, 1967.
68. Mowrer, O. H. Learning theory and behavior theory. In: *Handbook of Clinical Psychology*, B. B. Wolmar (Ed.), p. 242. McGraw-Hill Book Co., New York, 1965.
69. Nagler, S. Wilhelm Reich. In: *Comprehensive Textbook of Psychiatry*, A. Freedman and H. Kaplan (Eds.), p. 379. Williams & Wilkins Co., Baltimore, 1967.
70. National Institute of Mental Health. Halfway houses service, the mentally ill, and alcoholics, 1969–70. Publication No. HSM 72-9049. U. S. Government Printing Office, Washington, D. C., 1971.
71. O'Donnell, J. A. The relapse rate in narcotic addicts: A critique of follow-up studies. In: *Narcotics*, D. Wilner and G. Casselbaum (Eds.), p. 226. McGraw-Hill Book Co., New York, 1965.
72. Ozarin, L. Moral treatment and the mental hospital. Am. J. Psychiatry, 3:371, 1954–1955.
73. Parsons, T. *The Social System.* Free Press, Glencoe, Ill., 1951.
74. Pavlov, I. *Conditioned Reflexes.* Dover Publications, New York, 1960.
75. Peters, J. J., and Roether, H. Group psychotherapy for probationed sex offenders. Int. Psychiatr. Clin., 8:69, 1972.
76. Peters, J. J., and Sadoff, R. Psychiatric services for sex offenders on probation. Fed. Proc., 35:33, 1971.
77. Rado, S. The psychoanalysis of pharmocothymia, the clinical picture. Psychol. Q., 2:1, 1933.
78. Redl, F., and Wineman, D. *The Aggressive Child.* Free Press, New York, 1959.
79. Roether, H. N., and Peters, J. J. Coherence and hostility in group psychotherapy. Am. J. Psychiatry, 128:1014, 1972.
80. Rubins, J. Karen Horney. In: *Comprehensive Textbook of Psychiatry*, A. Freedman and H. Kaplan (Eds.), p. 327. Williams & Wilkins Co., Baltimore, 1967.
81. Ruesch, J., and Bateson, G. *Communication—The Social Matrix of Psychiatry.* W. W. Norton, New York, 1951.
82. Salzman, L. Harry Stack Sullivan. In: *Comprehensive Textbook of Psychiatry*, A. Freedman and H. Kaplan (Eds.), p. 338. Williams & Wilkins Co., Baltimore, 1967.
83. Sarbin, T., and Allen, V. L. Role theory. In: *The Handbook of Social Psychology*, Ed. 2, G. Linzy and E. Aronson (Eds.), p. 488. Addison and Wesley Publishing Co., Reading, Mass., 1968.

84. Scheidendel, P., and Kanno, C. K. *The Mentally Ill Offender—A Survey of Treatment Progress.* American Psychiatric Association, Washington, D. C., 1968.
85. Schimmel, E. Psychoanalytic treatment in a clinic. Int. J. Psychoanal., 10:70–89, 1929.
86. Schwitzgebel, R. K. Learning theory approach to the treatment of criminal behavior. Serv. Psychiatry, 3:328, 1971.
87. Skinner, B. F. *Cumulative Record.* Appleton-Century-Crofts, New York, 1959.
88. Spitz, R. A., and Wolfe, K. M. Anaclitic depression. In: *Psychoanalytic Study of the Child,* Vol. 2, pp. 313–342. Quadrangle Books, New York, 1946.
89. Stainbrook, E. Society and individual behavior. In: *Handbook of Clinical Psychology,* B. B. Wolman (Ed.), p. 216. McGraw-Hill Book Co., New York, 1965.
90. Stainbrook, E. Milieu therapy—the hospital as a therapeutic community. In: *Comprehensive Textbook of Psychiatry,* A. Freedman and H. Kaplan (Eds.), p. 1296. Williams & Wilkins Co., Baltimore, 1967.
91. Stanton, A., and Schwartz, M. *The Mental Hospital.* Basic Books, New York, 1954.
92. Stürup, G. K. *Treating the "Untreatable."* Johns Hopkins University Press, Baltimore, 1968.
93. Stürup, G. K. Treatment of sexual offenders in Herstedvester, Denmark. Acta Psychiatr. Scand. (Suppl.), 44:204, 1968.
94. Sullivan, H. S. Sociopsychiatric research—its implication for the schizophrenic problem and mental hygiene. Am. J. Psychiatry, 10:977–991, 1931.
95. Sullivan, H. S. The modified psychoanalytic treatment of schizophrenia. Am. J. Psychiatry, 11:519, 1931–1932.
96. Sullivan, H. S. *The Interpersonal Theory of Psychiatry.* W. W. Norton, New York, 1953.
97. Sullivan, H. S. Formulation on two principles of mental functioning. In: *The Interpersonal Theory of Psychiatry,* Vol. XII, p. 213. W. W. Norton, New York, 1953.
98. Sullivan, H. S. On narcissism—an introduction. In: *The Interpersonal Theory of Psychiatry,* Vol. XIV, p. 67. W. W. Norton, New York, 1953.
99. Sullivan, H. S. Group psychology. In: *The Interpersonal Theory of Psychiatry,* Vol. XVIII, p. 67. W. W. Norton, New York, 1953.
100. Sullivan, H. S., and Mullahy, P. Conceptions of psychiatry. The First William Alanson White Memorial Lectures. Harry Stack Sullivan. Williiam Alanson White Psychiatric Foundation, Washington, D. C., 1942.
101. Tarachow, S. *An Introduction to Psychotherapy,* p. 71. International Universities Press, New York, 1973.
102. Tyce, F. A. PORT of Olmstead County, Minnesota. Hosp. Community Psychiatry, 22:74, 1971.
103. Urban, H. B., and Fred, D. H. Behavior therapy. In: *Comprehensive Textbook of Psychiatry,* A. Freedman and H. Kaplan (Eds.), p. 1217. Williams & Wilkins Co., Baltimore, 1967.
104. Victor, M. Opiates. In: *Principles of Internal Medicine,* T. R. Harrison, I. Adams, and J. Bennett (Eds.), p. 755. McGraw-Hill Book Co., New York, 1958.
105. Victor, M., and Adams, R. Barbiturates. In: *Principles of Internal Medicine,* T. R. Harrison, R. Adams, and J. Bennett (Eds.), p. 759. McGraw-Hill Book Co., New York, 1958.
106. Wallerstein, R. The role of reality in psychoanalysis. Presidential address given at Midwinter Meetings of American Psychoanalytic Association, December, 1972. Am. J. Psychoanal., 21:5, 1973.
107. Wikler, A. Conditioning factors and opiate addiction and relapse. In: *Narcotics,* D. Wilner and G. Casselbaum (Eds.), p. 85. McGraw-Hill Book Co., New York, 1965.
108. Wilkins, L. T. Some sociological factors in drug addiction control. In: *Narcotics,* D. Wilner and G. Casselbaum (Eds.), p. 130. McGraw-Hill Book Co., New York, 1965.
109. Yablonsky, L. *Synanon: The Tunnel Back.* Penguin Books, Baltimore, 1967.
110. Yablonsky, L., and Deterich, C. Synanon—an analysis of some of the dimensions of an anti-addict society. In: *Narcotics,* D. Wilner and G. Casselbaum (Eds.), p. 193. McGraw-Hill Book Co., New York, 1965.
111. Yalom, I. *The Theory and Practice of Group Psychotherapy.* Basic Books, New York, 1970.
112. Zilboorg, J. *A History of Medical Psychology,* p. 322. W. W. Norton, New York, 1941.
113. Zwerling, I., and Rosenbaum, M. Alcoholism addiction and personality. In: *American Handbook of Psychiatry,* S. Arieti (Ed.), p. 623. Basic Books, New York, 1959.

23

HOSPITALIZATION FOR PERSONALITY DISORDERS

Katharine V. Kemp, M.D.

In this chapter attention will be focused on factors responsible for hospitalization of patients whose primary diagnosis is a Personality Disorder. Additionally, some thought will be devoted to problems inherent to their treatment in an inpatient setting, as well as therapeutic modalities not necessarily discussed elsewhere. While the bulk of these patients come to the hospital because of behavioral transgressions crossing a threshold intolerable to society, at times quite the opposite is true; some individuals, because of their personality traits and behavioral characteristics, find society intolerable and seek refuge in the hospital.

The personality disorder most often hospitalized is the Antisocial Personality. These individuals arrive via circuitous routes, nearly always associated with some legal infringements. These may be of a violent or nonviolent nature. Admission can be voluntary, or by one of the various involuntary procedures.

First admissions, if voluntary, usually occur reluctantly, at the insistence of family, friends, attorneys, parole officers, or even judges and therapists. The fantasy of those advising hospitalization appears to be one of an inpatient experience providing "the miraculous cure" that will rapidly produce desired behavioral changes. The patients' fantasy is that by accepting help legal authorities will view them in a more benevolent light. Not infrequently, the latter occurs. But these individuals are masters of manipulation and all too often this sets the stage for "the revolving door" phenomenon in which they avoid responsibility for their acts and abuse the hospitals as ready refuges in lieu of legal incarceration.

Within the confines of the hospital, Antisocial Personalities elicit many problems. Staff rarely view them as sick, reacting to their self-generated behavior and deviant social norms with disdain. Since it is well known that the aggressive aspects of their personality disorder can escalate to violence at the slightest provocation, fear is also a countertransference problem. The manipulative aura which nearly always surrounds their admissions can precipitate in staff feelings of distrust accompanied by hopelessness and helplessness. An occasional individual is able to strike a sympathetic cord in beginning therapists or even seasoned clinicians who sense a depressive core which might be responsive to long-term therapy.

Sooner or later these personalities generate within the hospital behavior identical to that which caused their admission. There is repeated defiance of rules and regulations as an ongoing "test" of ward structure. With cunning they indulge in bullying other patients, petty thievery, heterosexual or homosexual acts, or blackmail of patients or staff. They attempt to "rule" the ward, at times with amazing success! Verbal threats of physical harm to patients and staff are made, and physical violence may necessitate seclusion. There are variable staff reactions towards these transgressions. Should the patient evidence appropriate remorse when confronted, it may be interpreted as emerging guilt, evidence of a budding superego. Then staff will allow ongoing hospitalization for amazingly long periods of time. Patients who react in a more calloused and indifferent manner quickly arouse staff anger with resulting prompt discharge, sometimes for relatively minor infractions. Should staff tolerance be surpassed in cases admitted by court order where control of discharge is not staff function, any attempts at therapy usually cease, and staff moves quickly to effect transfer. Should the violent behavior be conceptualized as reflective of an Intermittent Explosive Disorder stemming from an "epileptoid" disease process, possibly responsive to medication, staff tolerance again can be sustained for amazingly long periods of time.

Hospitals agreeing to treat Antisocial Personalities should have staff with special skills, including a unique degree of tolerance. Milieus must be quite intensive. The hospital needs sufficient resources to enable these patients with their surplus energies and exceptional manipulative skills to become almost overinvolved in sports, activity therapies, occupational therapy, vocational goals, and the like. This aspect is discussed in more detail in the chapter on milieu treatment.

The Passive-Aggressive Personality is rarely hospitalized unless obstructionism becomes either so verbally or physically assaultive that it is viewed as dangerous. Admission is usually by involuntary commitment. An associated frank clinical depression may be the precipitant. Should alcoholism be a complication it may be the factor leading to admission. These latter may be voluntary or involuntary. On the ward these people can be extremely manipulative. Passivity generally characterizes their behavior with an affect of pleasant cooperation. Often, staff has difficulty equating admission information obtained from family with behavior the patient displays. Unlike the Antisocial Personality who tests rules and regulations, these individuals test staff cohesiveness. If their desired expectations are not forthcoming, violence can erupt. Both staff and patient become quickly disenchanted. Hospitalization is usually brief.

Paranoid Personalities may be hospitalized when their suspiciousness and argumentativeness becomes so exaggerated that concern is aroused about their dangerousness. Or, it may be merely extremely eccentric behavior that frightens others. At times employees or family are able to coerce these patients to seek voluntary hospitalization. If this fails, involuntary commitment may result.

Staff has difficulty relating to these people. Their chronic mistrust thwarts intimacy and defies formation of therapeutic alliances. This process of fear generating fear permeates the entire ward, which leads to general unrest. Additionally, constant concern about the capacity of these individuals to decompensate into a frank paranoid psychosis further tends to keep staff on edge.

Concerns about decompensation also mark the hospitalization of the Schizotypal Personalities, who display psychotic-like eccentricities in behavior, cognition, and perception. These patients are hospitalized when they either become frankly psychotic or show such psychologically deviant behavior as to warrant involuntary commitment. Within the hospital they are seen as "Schizophrenic" and treated with antipsychotic medication.

Ward problems are encountered when staff or other patients attempt to force interpersonal closeness. At these times verbal outbursts or even physical violence can erupt. Basically, they prefer to withdraw, remaining quiet and seclusive. As such, they can easily "get lost" on a busy ward, with a resultant antitherapeutic hospital experience that fosters overdependence on that protective environment. Hospitalization for these people carries an inherent danger of their learning the value of eccentric behavior as a defense against discharge or a means of obtaining readmission.

These same issues prevail for the Borderline Personality whose admission is most apt to occur after a suicidal gesture or some other impulsive self-destructive behavior. Initially, these patients are conceptualized as having an affective disorder and being depressed, but their shallow object relations is the important diagnostic clue. This "emptiness" with its depressive aspect, somewhat in contrast to the eccentricities of the Schizotypal, hostility of the Antisocial or Paranoid, or obstructionism of the Passive-Aggressive, makes them more acceptable to staff. On the other hand, mood swings of such a stormy nature can occur and evoke a negative countertransference. Thus, all too frequently staff attempts to treat by medicating rather than utilizing the verbal psychotherapies.

Admission of Schizoid, Avoidant, and Dependent Personalities generally results from their inability to continue to function within a social milieu or occupational setting. These types maintain a rather delicate balance of interpersonal relating. Changes in employment status, such as promotion, or even shifts within a corporate structure can lead to intense anxiety. Increasing social withdrawal takes place with subsequent request for hospitalization. On occasion social withdrawal may become so extreme as to require involuntary commitment.

In contrast to the more flamboyant personality disorders these patients remain shy and differential. Their manipulative ability can be every bit as problematic as the Antisocial or Passive-Aggressive Personalities as they attempt to avoid family therapy, group psychotherapies, and other hospital activities. Remaining to themselves, they lead solitary lives, interacting as little as possible with patients or staff. They generate few crises other than frustration as staff attempts to increase their ability to socialize. Staff ultimately view them as not amenable to hospital management. Thus early discharge takes place.

There is one striking feature with therapeutic importance separating the Avoidant Personality from others. The latter are acutely aware of their need for social isolation, yet simultaneously dislike their inability to interrelate comfortably with others. It is not difficult to elicit from them feelings of painful low self-esteem and a strong desire for affection and acceptance. Thus, unlike other personality disorders these people are aware of deviant behavioral traits and have some degree of motivation for change.

The Histrionic Personality Disorders come to the hospital during or after an interpersonal crisis which may or may not involve a self-destructive act. They are easily identified on the ward since they make certain they are the center of attention, monopolizing all group activities. At times they can be quite entertaining. The overactiveness of these patients requires constant staff attention; efforts to subdue their insatiable demands are often met with defeat. In these cases therapeutic skills of a constraining nature are required, quite the opposite of those needed to deal with the Schizoid, Avoidant, or Dependent Personalities.

Often viewed as manic, attempts to control their behavior with medication are ineffective. Various behavior modification paradigms are usually more successful in curbing their lability and making them more congruent with the ward population. The charming nature of their personality, coupled with an essentially negative premorbid history, not infrequently allows them to assume a role of therapist with other patients. At times it seems as though their various manipulative and seductive traps are unending. Staff exhaustion is often present if hospitalization is prolonged.

The Compulsive Personalities are usually admitted when either intrapsychic or external demands make it impossible for them to function in a perfectionistic manner. These personalities are usually high level performance individuals, often "overachievers" who have become both physically and emotionally exhausted. The hospital offers them either a haven for their required "rest" or some milieu in which to dissipate their frantic energies. These individuals often find their way into a general hospital on the medical service rather than to the psychiatric wards. Consequently, they may frequently be seen during hospitalization by mental health professionals in a consultative role rather than as primary therapists.

As can be expected these individuals are prone to respond to the hospital as they have responded to life. That is, they vehemently engage in all ward activities, attempting to inflict their perfectionistic traits on others, becoming extremely demanding in their need to point out many corrections necessary for the ward to run smoothly. Insisting upon unalterable routine and ritual, they elicit negative reactions from staff. Some more highly successful individuals are endowed with leadership skills and become enmeshed in control issues involving ward management. Many of these people are community leaders in arts, politics, and the like who evoke the "V.I.P. Syndrome" in staff. Private hospitals, especially are confronted with this problem. Whether the patient is an actual or self-idealized "V.I.P.," he engages in battle with the therapist as to who is controlling whom, evoking dismay from nursing staff and frustration in management. Both the Histrionic and Compulsive Personalities are often medicated with antianxiety agents, though it is staff members who require counseling and comfort in coping with their treatment.

The Narcissistic Personality usually reaches the hospital because of an interpersonal experience that shatters an exaggerated sense of self-importance and fragile self-esteem. If the sustained "narcissistic blow" is intense enough to precipitate rage, suicidal or homicidal threats or behavior may lead to involuntary commitment. At times they come to the hospital voluntarily, like the Schizoid, Avoidant, and Dependent Personalities, fantasizing the hospital as a magical haven.

If depression is an obvious presenting symptom, staff frequently react with empathy. Should a violent act be attempted or committed, staff may respond with disdain. The inexperienced therapist with little or no forensic training may react with anxiety over possible legal involvement. As with the Antisocial Personality, the patient's response of remorse or indifference may influence staff countertransference. Since these individuals characteristically display a behavioral trait of alternating emotional extremes ("splitting"), staff may experience difficulty with objectivity and become caught up in the "splitting" process. Concern about possible decompensation, a not infrequent event, must be handled. Fear of physical violence further adds to staff discomfort. On the wards there is displayed the basic characterologically disturbed behavior of a lack of feeling and consideration for others and demands for special favors.

A psychiatric inpatient service may well be a useful setting to confront personality disorders with their caricatured styles of coping with life. This requires a ward milieu capable of supportive exposure with much social feedback coming from psychodrama, the various group psychotherapies, and videotape techniques. Compulsive individuals must be shown their compulsivity and need for perfectionism; obstructionism can be demonstrated to the Passive-Aggressive; Histrionic patients may in time come to see the dramatic nature and overreactiveness of their personalities. With the exception of the Avoidant Personality, who already recognizes his shyness as deviant and is somewhat motivated for change, showing other personality disorders their aberrant behavioral traits becomes more difficult. Individuals such as the Schizoid Personality can not easily be made to see that their withdrawal is pathologic. Their life-style has been to avoid social confrontation. Schizotypal and Borderline Personalities may benefit from social feedback techniques, provided they are gentle, supportive, and supervised by a competent clinician. "Encounter group" experiences may be overwhelming for Borderline and Schizoid Personalities, who are the more fragile of these disorders and most capable of psychotic decompensation. Psychodrama may be too unstructured and close to a primary process act. The same may be said for some of the art therapies during which the unconscious is freely interpreted. Paranoid Personalities may learn from videotape confrontation which points out their ongoing suspiciousness and mistrust, as evidenced by body movements such as the constant motion of their eyes. Some of these patients come to understand how they might appear frightening to others. Antisocial Personalities are generally bombarded with confrontations by staff because of repeated transgressions. Unfortunately these confrontations are often unproductive and simply fuel the fires of the antisocial behavior since the life-style is an ongoing struggle with authority.

The role of nurses is crucial to the inpatient management of personality disorders. Physicians see patients for only a few minutes or at most an hour each day, an approach which works well with affective or thought disorder patients who require medication. Personality-disordered patients appear to benefit more from the less threatening, more readily available nursing staff. For much the same reason nursing assistants, activity therapists, or social workers are often more effective in helping these individuals evoke social change than physicians. The most useful therapeutic role for the hospital-based physicians is to point out to the staff characterological traits that require repair and embark on a treatment plan designed to effect same.

On a psychiatric ward, as elsewhere, it is generally presupposed that therapy should be designed to "break down" pathological characterologic defenses and "re-build" the personality. At times it almost seems as though the therapeutic goal assumes Pygmalion proportions. This is highly unrealistic and even destructive since these defenses are crucial for individual functioning and so ingrained as to make change, as equated with eradication, an impossibility. Often it is merely the intensity or degree of the defensive mechanism that is the pathology of the deviant behavior, rather than the defense or behavior itself. Thus therapeutic change is in reality more a process of teaching the patients how to temper responses to society so that their behavior becomes less deviant and self-defeating. Exploration of patients' fantasies regarding the meaning of this "help to change," a statement which clinicians so glibly offer, frequently reveals intense fear of being transformed into an unknown, unrecognizable, unfamiliar person, almost as if therapy kills. It is thus small wonder that resistance to therapy can be intense. Furthermore, the tentative nature of some of these defenses, as seen in the more sensitive personalities like the Schizotypal or Borderline, should warn the clinician of the precarious nature of these patients.

What should be done, then, in a hospital with respect to personality disorders? Obviously, the clinician treads a thin line between "rebuilding" and "upholding" character. One hopes to improve the ability to socialize in those personality disorders who have trouble with socialization, subdue the emotionality of the Histrionic and Narcissistic, quench the aggressiveness of the Antisocial, modify the compulsiveness of the Compulsive, decrease passivity and stabilize a balance between passivity and aggression in the Passive-Aggressive, decrease suspiciousness and increase trust in the Paranoid, decrease impulsivity and improve object relations in the Borderline. Gaining, a realistic degree of self-esteem appears to be a "least common denominator." It is generally recognized that such goals are time consuming and might best be attained in an outpatient setting by intensive psychotherapy. Yet, hospitalization may be necessary following a crisis or to implement a long-term treatment plan.

Within the hospital, there is often a tendency to misuse medication for the treatment of personality disorders. Certain symptoms are targeted for amelioration with antianxiety, antidepressant, antipsychotic, and sedative-hypnotic medication. The use of these drugs in treating personality disorders is discussed in another chapter. There is, however, an issue related to medication that involves compliance and helplessness within patients and staff. Both can see medication as the salvation; ultimately, powerful struggles may ensue over drugs perscribed for control of traits as well as symptoms. Target symptoms may be treatable; there is no medication for a personality disorder, even though staff might well wish for a chemical compound to ameliorate excessive Narcissism, Histrionic expansiveness, Paranoid mistrust, Passive-Aggressive obstructionism, Compulsive perfectionism, Antisocial destruction, Schizotypal eccentricities, empty lability of the Borderline, or pathological shyness of the Schizoid, Avoidant, and Dependent.

Patients themselves ask for medication in specific ways. Thus, the Borderline may want something to fill the void and the Compulsive Personality may seek medication to be ritualistically administered at rigid time intervals on the ward. The Passive-Aggressive may be hostile and resent medication on one level, though being quite demanding of it on another. The Schizoid may look depressed and prefer a pill to group therapy. The Avoidant may want medicine to cure shyness. Antisocial Personalities may make a business of selling drugs on the ward.

Reference has been made to some personality disorders being more fragile than others or more capable of psychotic regression. However, resolution of a psychosis into a personality disturbance is also common. It is a sobering matter to see a severely ill Schizophrenic resolve into a Schizoid Personality and realize that the limits of treatment have been reached. It is equally as sobering to observe a psychotically depressed individual respond to ECT, only to become a moderately severe Compulsive Personality with traits as socially deviant as those which characterized the presenting illness. There lurks, then, just beneath the surface of major affective and thought disorders some characterological disturbances which are often more easily diagnosed than treated. Or perhaps it is the reverse. Deviant characterological traits, while easily recognized, might best be viewed as major defenses against major affective and thought disorders until proven otherwise. As such, the treatment of personality disorders should proceed cautiously.

24

BEHAVIOR THERAPY OF PERSONALITY DISORDERS

Joseph H. Stephens, M.D., and Susan L. Parks, B.A.

The use of behavior therapy in the specific treatment of personality disorders has received only limited attention in the psychiatric literature. On the other hand, a considerable body of research has focused on the deconditioning of anxiety and the development of various behavioral treatments for the neuroses. Extensive reports on the purported alleviation of phobic fears and obsessive-compulsive rituals by behavioral techniques are readily available, and research studies in this area are numerous. Although directly relevant research on the use and efficacy of behavioral treatments of personality disorders is quite sparse, behavioral techniques are increasingly being used in attempts to modify symptoms characteristic of the different personality disorders in patients with other diagnoses.

The behavioral therapist approaches all psychiatric disorders from the premise that maladaptive behavior is learned, and is, therefore, subject to the possibility of unlearning or relearning. Treatment interventions are focused on the specific behavior to be changed and are not concerned with its origins or symbolic meaning. As a result of this theoretical position, it is reasonable to extend research findings from one diagnostic category to another, as long as the behavior being modified is common to both. The personality disorders, as defined by DSM III, will therefore be considered in terms of specific symptomatology or maladaptive behaviors rather than by specific diagnoses.

Techniques of Behavior Therapy

Before considering the strategies to be used in treating the maladaptive behaviors of the personality disorders, the most pertinent behavioral techniques available will be briefly reviewed.

The token economy is widely used in inpatient settings (2). Using this method a patient earns a prespecified number of tokens for appropriately performing designated tasks. These tasks may include taking care of personal hygiene, participating in recreational or work activities, and abstaining from maladaptive, disruptive behaviors. The tokens awarded are usually exchanged for increases in privileges either on or off the ward. At one time, some economies had required the earning and exchange of tokens for a modified system of room and board payments (43). However, such requirements are no longer supported ethically or legally (19, 41). Because it allows a total restructuring of the environment by the administrator, a token economy can occasionally bring about a change in behavior previously thought to be impervious to treatment. Juvenile delinquents are reported to be especially responsive to this approach (4, 13). By their nature, however, token economies are generally restricted to institutional settings.

Contingency management, like a token exchange, requires the performance of a specific behavior for the awarding of a previously agreed upon reward. In a similar but reverse way, the method of extinction withholds reinforcement after the performance of an undesirable behavior. Usually an incompatible response is strengthened simultaneously by directing social attention and other reinforcers away from the unacceptable behavior and toward the alternative action.

Systematic desensitization requires much greater therapist involvement and is used more frequently with outpatients. Here, the construction of a hierarchy of anxiety situations and the teaching of relaxation techniques as described by Wolpe (44) is employed. As the patient is exposed to progressively more threatening levels of the hierarchy, he learns to relax in the presence of the stimuli. Each step is introduced gradually, and whenever distress is evident, the therapist retreats to an earlier, more comfortable level.

Assertiveness training, another behavior technique increasingly used, has been defined as the proper expression of any positive or negative emotion, excepting anxiety, to another individual. The therapist constructs hypothetical situations which will provide the patient with opportunities to replace his maladaptive behavior with more acceptable actions. Frequently, modeling by the therapist will be employed along with role playing, role reversal, and behavioral rehearsal. Sessions usually alternate between modeling and rehearsing with continual feedback and reinforcement from the therapist. Homework assignments may be required to test new skills in the outside environment. Because progress depends upon success, it is considered important for the therapist not to instigate an aggressive act likely to result in unpleasant circumstances (44).

Specific Symptoms of Personality Disorders Amenable to Modification by Behavioral Methods

Choosing from among the behavioral techniques briefly described above necessitates a careful consideration of the specific behaviors to be modified.

Thus, in order to consider possible behavioral treatments of the personality disorders, it is first necessary to discuss the behavioral characteristics of each and determine any common symptoms among the diagnostic categories. On the basis of DSM III definitions, there are 10 different maladaptive behaviors shared by at least two of the eleven possible diagnoses (see Table 24.1). The pattern of social withdrawal is common to the schizoid, schizotypal, and avoidant personalities. A related lack of emotionality can be found in the diagnoses of paranoid, schizoid, schizotypal, and compulsive personalities. Both the histrionic and narcissistic personality display attention-seeking behavior. The avoidant and dependent personalities suffer from a low self-esteem, while the compulsive and borderline find it hard to spend time alone. Manipulative behavior which frequently involves violating the rights of others can be found in borderline, antisocial, passive-aggressive, dependent, and narcissistic individuals. Suicidal attempts are frequent among borderlines and histrionics, and these individuals also exhibit highly excitable responses, as do paranoid persons. Dependent and compulsive personalities are often very indecisive, in contrast to impulsive and aggressive antisocial, borderline, and passive-aggressive individuals.

Possible treatment approaches to some of these shared behavioral problems will be presented here. Also included will be a short consideration of characteristics specific to the paranoid and histrionic personalities. No attempt will be made to discuss treatment interventions for either hysterical symptoms of the conversion type or obsessive-complusive rituals. Although these symptoms often accompany a diagnosis of histrionic or compulsive personality, they would be more appropriately addressed in a discussion focused on the neuroses.

Social Withdrawal and Lack of Emotionality

The lack of effective social contacts is a problem experienced by many individuals with the diagnosis of schizoid, schizotypal, compulsive, or paranoid personalities. Very little has been written on the use of behavioral techniques to combat this pattern of social withdrawal in the personality disorders. However, a growing body of literature is available on social skills training of the hospitalized psychotic patient. Although these patients may be more severely withdrawn, the methods used to bring about a more normal level of social interaction could logically be adapted for use with personality disorders.

Contingency management (operant conditioning) techniques were first applied in an attempt to bring about greater social responsiveness. In a study by King et al. (26), the principle of successive approximations was used to slowly shape the verbal level of chronic schizophrenics. Beginning with a simple lever press which resulted in candy and cigarette rewards and social

TABLE 24.1
Similar Characteristics among the Personality Disorders

	Paranoid	Schizoid	Schizotypal	Histrionic	Narcissistic	Antisocial	Borderline	Avoidant	Dependent	Compulsive	Passive-Aggressive
Social withdrawal	X	X	X					X			
Lack of emotionality		X	X							X	
Attention seeking				X	X						
Low self-esteem								X	X	X	
Trouble being alone					X	X	X		X		X
Manipulative				X			X				
Suicidal							X				
Indecisive				X					X	X	
Excitable	X						X				
Aggressive (impulsive)						X	X				X

approval from the therapist, the patients were guided toward increasingly complex responses. Eventually, tasks requiring communication and cooperation with another patient were introduced. Three control groups were included in the study. One group received occupational therapy, another received verbal therapy which consisted of exploring patients' thoughts and feelings, and the third received no treatment beyond normal ward activities. The results indicated that the operant conditioning training was significantly more effective in bringing about clinical improvement. These patients eventually engaged in more verbal behavior, were less resistant to further therapy, and showed more interest in participating in ward activities.

Schaefer and Martin (35) have also used contingency management techniques but focused their research on efforts to reduce patient apathy as manifested in poor personal hygiene, lack of social interaction, and inadequate job performance on the ward. Chronic schizophrenic patients were reinforced with tokens and verbal praise for behaviors inconsistent with the label "apathetic," such as talking, singing, playing music, and group activities. Specific behaviors reinforced varied from patient to patient, depending upon the individual's level of functioning. A token economy was already in existence on the ward, and tokens were necessary for the procurement of food, permission to watch TV programs, and admission to recreational programs, etc. Control subjects received free tokens on a noncontingent basis. As expected, a significant increase in targeted behaviors occurred for the experimental subjects over the course of the program. Control subjects remained at their pretreatment levels.

The use of tokens to specifically influence the social interaction of one male inpatient with an obsessive-compulsive disorder has been reported by Leitenberg et al. (27). Because it was determined that he preferred leaving the ward, sitting in the hospital lobby and watching TV, it was decided to use the privilege to engage in these activities as reinforcement for obtaining the desired behavior of self-initiated conversation. Tokens earned as a result of each 2 minutes of talking with the nurses could be exchanged for 5 minutes worth of the reinforcing activities. During a base line period when the patient was instructed to talk with the nursing staff as much as possible, his level of interaction was extremely low. With the introduction of reinforcement, a dramatic increase in his social interaction occurred. When a third phase was begun where tokens were given on a noncontingent basis, the desired behavior decreased steadily. Reinstatement of the reinforcement phase resulted in a continued rise in social conversation.

A similar study was carried out by Schierloh and Bernal (36). Self-initiated verbalization was again the targeted behavior, but in this case a patient peer carried out the reinforcement. An extremely withdrawn female paranoid schizophrenic was selected as the subject. Her roommate, also a paranoid schizophrenic, served as the reinforcer. The two patients were asked to participate in discussions of magazine pictures which were videotaped for scoring purposes. After an initial base line period, efforts were made to increase the number of times the subject initiated conversation. Social reinforcers—smiling, laughing, head nods—were provided by the patient peer when the desired behavior occurred. As predicted, initiations of conversation increased. In an extinction phase, the subject's initiations were ignored by her peer and subsequently declined. When social reinforcement was again made contingent on beginning conversations, the behavior was reinstated rapidly.

Social skills involve the ability to perceive subtle cues and require a repertoire of appropriate responses. Conversational skills such as starting, maintaining, and ending a discussion require relatively simple accomplishments. More complicated, however, are the elements of social perceptiveness: listening, clarifying, identifying relevance and timing, recognizing emotions. The training of social skills attempts to fill in deficits in these areas by a positive, educational approach. Bellack and Hersen (8) recommend the construction of a hierarchy of problem situations to enable working from the least to most severe inadequacy. They describe five techinques for the effective use of skills training. First is the imparting of specific and concrete instructions on better ways to handle the problem situation. This is followed by role playing by the patient and therapist. The third step consists of positive feedback in the form of social reinforcement and further attempts at role playing. Modeling may be necessary at this point for more complex responses or more regressed patients. These steps should each be preceded and followed by corrective suggestions and description of relevant details. Directed practice is the fifth step to preserve the learned response. Specific homework assignments with a high probability of success are a necessary step in order to generalize the new response behavior.

Bellack et al. (9) have used these techniques for training social skills in chronically ill patients. A series of interpersonal scenes requiring varying degrees of assertive responses were constructed, after which behaviors such as eye contact, appropriate smiles, rate and duration of speech, and appropriate physical gestures were selected as targets. Treatment effects were significant and were maintained in two cases over an 8- to 10-week follow-up. Responses generalized to untrained but highly similar stimulus presentations, but no conclusions could be made concerning generalization to the natural environmental setting since outside practice exercises were not required.

In a similar study, Hersen and Bellack (20) encouraged the use of self-monitoring and self-reinforcement as a way of facilitating generalization and preservation of the new response. Patients were required to keep simple but specific records of their responses and were trained to provide themselves with reinforcement through positive self-reference statements or earned privileges. Both techniques can be incorporated into the training sessions after they have first been demonstrated by the therapist.

Marzillier et al. (29) have reported one of the few studies of social skills training conducted on socially inadequate patients with a diagnosis of personality disorder. A comparison between the methods of systematic desensitization and social skills training was attempted. Dependent measures of social anxiety, social skills, social activities and contacts, and general clinical improvement were obtained. The treated groups, especially those receiving social skills training, showed more improvement on all measures than most of the controls. However, with the following exceptions, the overall treatment effects were not statistically significant. Social skills training produced a significant change in the patients' social lives, increasing the number of activities and contacts. In general, such training had a therapeutic effect on patients' social lives, but less effect on overall clinical improvement. Systematic desensitization also led to a significant increase in the range of social contacts when compared with untreated controls. However, findings about this group are complicated by a high dropout rate. The final conclusion was that the social skills training was more effective than systematic desensitization. Since socially inadequate patients usually suffer from deficits in social skills, low self-esteem, and poor social perception, focusing on the reduction of social anxiety alone is not likely to be of any direct benefit in these areas.

The use of assertiveness training has also been employed by Bloomfield (11) in an attempt to increase the interpersonal skills of chronic outpatient schizophrenics. The patients involved were overcompliant, submissive, and socially inhibited. In groups of 8 to 10, individual problems were dealt with through identification of the patient's inappropriate withdrawal and behavioral rehearsal of more appropriate responses, including the use of role reversal. Bloomfield emphasizes that precautions must be taken to prepare patients for the possibility that their new assertive behavior may not be well received. A supportive and reinforcing environment is necessary to ensure success.

Alden et al. (1) compared the use of cognitive behavioral modification with assertiveness training to determine which was more effective in bringing about an increase in assertive behavior. Their subjects were not psychiatric patients but normals from the community. The cognitive therapy consisted of focusing on irrational beliefs and negative self-reference statements which were inhibiting assertiveness. New coping strategies were taught to the participants and practiced between group sessions. In the assertiveness training group, assertion techniques were learned through instruction, modeling, rehearsing, and feedback from the group and therapist. Results of the study indicated that both techniques were equally successful, possibly because both methods increased the individual's feelings of competence when placed in circumstances requiring an assertive response.

Aggression and Impulsivity

In sharp contrast to the socially withdrawn and apathetic individuals discussed above are the aggressive and impulsive traits of many antisocial, borderline, and passive-aggressive personalities. In these cases, the behavior therapist must work to modify already existing but maladaptive responses into socially desirable ones rather than simply attempt to elicit social responses. Several relevant studies concerned with delinquent behavior and the behavioral treatment of aggressive-anger responses will be presented.

Burchard and Tyler (12) report a case study of a delinquent with diagnoses ranging from childhood schizophrenia to psychopathic personality. Analysis of his institutional behavior suggested that his antisocial behavior was being inadvertently rewarded by the staff. Contingency management techniques were therefore employed utilizing time-out procedures for unacceptable behaviors and token reinforcement for desired behavior. A gradual decrease in the number of times isolation was required occurred over the course of the study, and the seriousness of the offenses committed decreased.

Recruiting subjects from street corners, Schwitzgebel and Kolb (37) were able to shape the session attendance and arrival time of juvenile delinquents through the use of modest rewards delivered on a variable ratio schedule. Delinquent behavior was slowly counterconditioned through the reinforcement of incompatible behavior. Paid interviews with these subjects were slowly modified through cash bonuses and verbal praise to therapy sessions, and payment was subsequently discontinued. At the 3-year follow-up of 20 subjects, there was a statistically significant decrease in the frequency of arrests and the severity of crimes committed by the former participants when compared to matched-pair controls.

Further work by Schwitzgebel (38) employed the same recruitment methods and operant shaping of arrival times for interviews. Hostile statements by a subject were followed by inattention or disagreement, while positive statements resulted in verbal praise or small rewards. The frequency of positive statements and expressions of concern increased significantly. Hostile statements, however, were not decreased significantly by mild aversive consequences. Schwitzegebal believes "the characteristic impulsivity ascribed to juvenile delinquents is likely influenced or determined by the particular type and schedule of reinforcements in the individual's history." Significant alterations in delinquent speech patterns and promptness in keeping appointments suggests that other maladaptive behavior in such patients may also be amenable to behavior therapy.

Rimm et al. (30) have studied the behavioral treatment of antisocial aggression. Male college students experiencing inappropriate anger while driving were recruited for a study involving systematic desensitization. After construction of a hierarchy of increasing anger, subjects began the next session with deep muscle relaxation. This was immediately followed by the actual desensitization procedure, which continued until the whole hierarchy was completed. Subjective feelings of anger were significantly reduced as a result of the treatment. However, no assessment of actual anger responses was attempted in the natural environment. This study suggests the possibility of using desensitization techniques to lessen the impact of anger-producing situations which have previously led to aggressive acts.

Rimm et al. (32) have used the technique of group assertiveness training with male patients hospitalized primarily for antisocial aggressive behavior. In six 1-hour sessions, they were able to bring about a significantly greater increase in assertiveness when compared to a control group. An informal follow-up investigation revealed that ward staff and relatives reported less hostility and aggression from these patients after the treatment phase was completed.

Nonhospitalized male volunteers with histories of antisocial expression of anger have been similarly treated (31). After 8 hours of group assertiveness training, consisting mostly of behavioral rehearsal, individuals were rated as more assertive and reported less discomfort when presented with a lab situation designed to elicit anger than did a placebo group. No follow-up was attempted in this study.

The use of assertiveness training to combat aggression may seem contradictory at first. However, the goal of assertiveness training is not assertiveness per se, but appropriate assertiveness. Rimm and Masters (33) theorize that individuals often resort to antisocial violence because they are deficient in the verbal skills that would be more effective in expressing their emotions. It is especially important in using this technique to determine exactly what it is that angers the individual, so that particular situations can be dealt with specifically in behavior rehearsal sessions.

Attention Seeking

When attention-seeking behavior becomes continual and increasingly demanding, as is frequently the case with histrionic and narcissistic personalities, behavioral modification has been reported to be an efficacious treatment (6). Since learning theory postulates that undesirable behavior is perpetuated by positive reinforcement, removing social approval and other rewarding consequences from attention-seeking behavior should reduce or even eventually eliminate its occurrence. Thomas (40) believes that resistance to extinction procedures is frequently high because the attention-seeking behavior has been reinforced intermittently for such long periods of time. He recommends that the end of reinforcement be abrupt and total. Replacing the behavior with an incompatible task for which reinforcement is readily provided may facilitate extinction.

Such an approach has been used by Ayllon and Michael (6) to eliminate attention-seeking behavior in hospitalized settings. One patient who continually entered the nurses' station on the ward received a great deal of attention from the nurses, who had to stop their work to bodily evict her from the room. Extinction procedures were initiated and visits to the nurses' station subsequently decreased from a pretreatment average of 16 to 2 visits daily. Similarly, Ayllon and Haughton (5) attempted to reduce constant physical complaints of two hospitalized psychotic patients by behavioral modification. During the treatment phase, all references to physical states were ignored while all other statements were reinforced by staff attention and compliance with requests. This procedure resulted in almost complete elimination of somatic complaints. In the reversal phase, attention was once more given to statements of physical distress, and as expected, these responses rapidly increased. Reinstatement of the treatment phase again brought rapid extinction.

Although these studies are somewhat simplistic and involve only a few patients, the theoretical basis for extinction procedures as a therapeutic intervention for attention-seeking behavior appears sound and merits further investigation.

Suicidal Attempts and Self-Mutilation

Staff manipulation through suicidal attempts or threats and self-mutilation occur frequently in borderline and histrionic patients. Viewing self-mutilative behavior as learned maladaptive responses to anger, two sets of researchers have employed behavioral techniques to teach new, more appropriate responses. Roback et al. (34) have described the treatment of an inpatient with a long history of self-burnings and slashings. Because these incidences of self-mutilation usually followed circumstances which provoked marked anger in the patient, an intervention program was designed to teach the patient more adaptive and appropriate forms of expressing anger. Emotional labeling was undertaken by ward personnel, and the patient was encouraged to notice and define her feelings. Modified assertiveness training was also initiated which included the modeling of various appropriate anger responses. Opportunities for role playing and testing out new behaviors in real ward situations were provided. However, the patient was made aware that *inappropriate* anger responses would be followed by the loss of privileges for 24 hours. During the pretreatment phase lasting 17 days, the patient burned herself six times, contrasted with only once during the treatment program.

Cox and Klinge (14) report a similar approach for another patient engaging in self-burning. The staff was instructed to respond to such episodes with a "matter-of-fact" attitude, and modified assertiveness training was undertaken. Problem social situations were presented during role playing sessions with appropriate responses modeled by the therapist. Newly acquired behavior was then tested in ward situations. When it became apparent that other maladaptive behavior was being used to manipulate the staff and gain attention, social reinforcement for all maladaptive attention-seeking behavior was carefully avoided and was provided only for clearly socially acceptable behavior. Over the course of treatment, self-burnings decreased gradually from 14 during the 2-week base line to 30 over the 18 weeks of treatment. During the last 5 weeks, no incidences were recorded. A 3-month follow-up revealed no recurrence of burnings.

The results of these two studies provide promising though not conclusive evidence for the use of behavioral techniques to combat self-mutilation. Because of the simultaneous involvement of these patients in other treatment interventions, no definitive statements can be made about the efficacy of the behavioral treatments alone.

Paranoid Behavior

Davison (15) has described several behavioral techniques to alleviate paranoid symptoms. One patient preoccupied with "pressure points" above his right eye interpreted his experiences as messages from a spirit attempting to help him make decisions. Cognitive restructuring was carried out by explaining to the patient that unusual phenomena are frequently explained as supernatural when such interpretations are not necessary. After demonstrating to the patient how "pressure points" could arise from severe muscle tension, relaxation training was used to teach him how to ease the distress voluntarily. At the 6-week follow-up, the patient was reported to be greatly improved.

A patient suffering from persecutory delusions was treated by Wickramasekera (42), using a form of desensitization and discrimination training. The patient's difficulty in approaching her son for fear of sexually molesting him was approached by encouraging her to interact with him primarily in situations where no attack could possibly take place. The patient was required to keep a record of her activities and was taught to label her experiences and emotions more accurately.

Kennedy (25) has used reinforcement to decrease the number of delusional statements made by chronic paranoid schizophrenics. Strong positive verbal reinforcement for nonparanoid statements was combined with strong negative verbal reinforcement for paranoid verbalizations. A decrease or disappearance of delusional references occurred in all three cases, with two showing continued improvement at 6-month follow-up.

Similarly, Wincze et al. (43) have employed individualized token reinforcement to reduce delusional speech in seven of nine patients involved. Little generalization to the ward setting was observed. This study required patients to earn tokens exchangeable for necessities as well as luxuries.

Liberman et al. (28) have also used contingency management techniques to increase the amount of nondelusional speech in four patients. Interviews with those patients were terminated as soon as delusional statements appeared. Patients also earned evening sessions with their therapists by responding appropriately during the day sessions. Large increases in the amount of nondelusional speech occurred with only a moderate generalization from day to evening sessions. Little, if any, generalization extended to the wards.

Histrionic Behavior

Specific use of behavioral techniques has been reported by Kass et al. (24) in treating histrionic personalities. They describe the successful use of a multifaceted, group treatment of five women diagnosed as hysterical personalities. Four of the five had been admitted from the emergency room because of suicidal attempts. The patients were assigned to the same large room and were presented with the tasks of: "(1) Specifying each other's maladaptive hysterical behavior, (2) Making up daily schedules for each other, comprised of the kinds of tasks and situations most likely to evoke each individual's maladaptive hysterical behavior, and (3) Providing the environmental consequences designed to promote the waning of these behaviors and their replacement by more adaptive ones." Ward personnel remained in the background but were in charge of making sure reinforcements and definitions were accurately provided. Each patient was required to commit herself to the group and agree with the staff on her specific maladaptive behaviors and the group approach necessary to change them. The program reflected the authors' view that hysteria is manifested by a refusal to participate in adult responsibilities such as schedule keeping requires. Consequently, penalties such as loss of privileges, cosmetics, and cigarettes were assessed only for breaking the schedule and not for exhibiting other hysterical behaviors. Hysterical behavior was extinguished by removing reinforcement from maladaptive behavior and teaching alternative responses.

The specific techniques used included positive and negative feedback, assertiveness training, desensitization, and contingency management. Role playing and psychodrama were both relied upon with sessions videotaped for later self-evaluation. Group meetings and frequency chart recordings monitored the patients' progress. Satisfactory discharge could be acquired by patient request followed by a 2-day trial period during which she had to follow the schedule strictly, draw low frequencies on her behavior charts, and gain approval for discharge from the group and staff meeting.

Each patient's maladaptive behaviors increased, peaked during the program, and subsequently decreased in frequency. All but one were discharged satisfactorily and continued to function well, without the recurrence of symptoms, at 18-month follow-up. The program's success depended partly upon the group setting which allowed for the development of better communication skills. It also prevented the division of staff loyalties and restricted the impact of manipulative behavior. Such activities resulted in the loss of privileges and lack of attention rather than the reinforcing consequences previously attained. Instead of controlling others, the patients learned self-control and assertiveness and were able to express themselves more effectively.

A review of the behavioral treatment of hysterical symptoms by Bird (10) concludes that the behavioral approach is most likely to be effective when the therapist and patient can agree on specific problem behavior and can enumerate specific treatment goals to be dealt with one issue at a time.

Conclusion

The ability of behavior therapy techniques to produce initial changes in behavior in certain patients appears well substantiated. However, no matter how effective such methods may be, the gains realized may be short-lived unless generalization to the natural environment ensues. Numerous studies have documented success in obtaining the desired treatment goals in closed sessions, but report poor generalization of these results to the ward setting itself—much less to the outside community (8, 22). Stokes and Baer (39) have emphasized the need to program generalization into a treatment regimen, rather than assume it will follow. Restructuring a patient's environment may seem desirable at times, but outside of the hospital setting the therapist can realistically exert only a minimum of influence on the natural environment. It is, therefore, highly recommended to train the patient to be his own reinforcer for desirable behavior. Involving the patient in the recording of his own behavior can precede his role of self-regulator (20, 39). Once the patient has acquired the desired response, the therapist can model self-evaluative behavior and reward accurate attempts at self-regulation by the patient. After the patient has become proficient, the task of reinforcing his behavior can be transferred to him alone (7).

The problem of finding effective reinforcers may also plague the behavior therapist. Social reinforcers may be ineffective (23, 44) or even aversive at times (16, 17). Consequently, the selection of reinforcers must be individualized and based upon an observation of what the subjects involved naturally prefer (3, 24).

In order to evaluate the efficacy of behavioral treatments, there is a pressing need for more controlled studies including follow-up data. In an inpatient setting, excluding behavior therapy patients from other ward activities may be unfeasible. However, it is possible to have a control group of patients participating in all activities except the behavioral technique under study. The importance of the use of control groups is highlighted by a study reported by Marzillier et al. (29) revealing that on most measures of social skills, clinical adjustment, and reduction of anxiety, neither the patients treated with systematic desensitization nor those undergoing social skills training improved significantly more than untreated controls. The control group improved during the active treatment phase, even though they were only "on the waiting list" for treatment. The use of patients as their own controls is another method for measuring the efficacy of treatment. This procedure can be executed in a four-phase design consisting of base line measurement, treatment intervention, reversal of treatment gains, and reinstatement of the treatment plan (5, 27, 36).

The need for more long-term follow-up data is self-evident not only to determine the short-term efficacy of treatment methods but also to determine possible generalizations of these specific techniques. In undertaking to present behavioral strategies relevant to the treatment of personality disorders, it has become glaringly obvious that far more research in this area is needed. The majority of the studies referred to in this paper were carried out on hospitalized psychotic patients and must be considered in this light when applied to other types of patients. More controlled research conducted with patients actually diagnosed as personality disorders is urgently needed.

REFERENCES

1. Alden, L., Safran, J., and Weideman, R. A comparison of cognitive and skills training strategies in the treatment of unassertive clients. Behav. Ther., 9:843–846, 1978.
2. APA Task Force on Behavior Therapy. *Behavior Therapy in Psychiatry.* Jason Aronson, New York, 1974.
3. Ayllon, J., and Azrin, N. H. The measurements and reinforcement of behavior of psychotics. J. Exp. Anal. Behav. 8:357–383, 1965.
4. Ayllon, T., and Azrin, N. *The Token Economy: A Motivational System for Therapy and Rehabilitation.* Prentice-Hall, Inc., Englewood Cliffs, N. J., 1968.
5. Ayllon, T., and Haughton, E. Modification of symptomatic verbal behaviour of mental patients. Behav. Res. Ther., 2:87–97, 1964.
6. Ayllon, T., and Michael, J. The psychiatric nurse as a behavioral engineer. J. Exp. Anal. Behav. 2:323–334, 1959.
7. Bandura, A. *Principles of Behavior Modification.* Holt, Rinehart & Winston, New York, 1969.
8. Bellack, A. S., and Hersen, M. Chronic psychiatric patients: Social skills training. In: *Behavior Therapy in the Psychiatric Setting*, M. Hersen and A. S. Bellack (Eds.), Williams & Wilkins Co., Baltimore, 1978.
9. Bellack, A. S., Hersen, M., and Turner, S. M. Generalization effects of social skills training in chronic schizophrenics: An experimental analysis. Behav. Res. Ther., 14:391–398, 1976.
10. Bird, J. The behavioural treatment of hysteria. Br. J. Psychiatry, 134:129–137, 1979.
11. Bloomfield, H. H. Assertive training in an outpatient group of chronic schizophrenics: A preliminary report. Behav. Ther., 4:277–281, 1973.
12. Burchard, J., and Tyler, V., Jr. The modification of delinquent behavior through operant conditioning. Behav. Res. Ther., 2:245–250, 1965.
13. Colman, A. D. *The Planned Environment in Psychiatric Treatment: A Manual for Ward Design.* Charles C Thomas, Springfield, Ill., 1971.
14. Cox, M. D., and Klinge, V. Treatment and management of a case of self-burning. Behav. Res. Ther. 14:382–385, 1976.

15. Davison, G. C. Differential relaxation and cognitive restructuring in therapy with a "paranoid schizophrenic" or "paranoid state." In: *Proceedings of the 74th Annual Convention APA*, pp. 177–178. Washington, D. C., 1966.
16. Gattozzi, R. E. The effect of person on a conditioned emotional response of schizophrenic and normal subjects. Conditional Reflex, 6:181–190, 1971.
17. Gelburd, A. S., and Anker, J. M. Humans as reinforcing stimuli in schizophrenic performance. J. Abnorm. Psychol., 75:195–198, 1970.
18. Goldstein, A. P., Martens, J., Hubben, J., van Belle, H. A., Schaaf, W., Wiersma, H., and Goedhart, A. The use of modeling to increase independent behavior. Behav. Res. Ther., 11:31–42, 1973.
19. Hersen, M. Token economies in institutional settings. J. Nerv. Ment. Dis., 3:206–211, 1976.
20. Hersen, M., and Bellack, A. S. Social skills training for chronic psychiatric patients: Rationale, research findings, and future directions. Comp. Psychiatry, 17:559–580, 1976.
21. Hersen, M. and Bellack, A. S. Chronic psychiatric patients: Individual behavioral approaches. In: *Behavior Therapy in the Psychiatric Setting*, M. Hersen and A. S. Bellack (Eds.), The Williams & Wilkins Co., Baltimore, 1978.
22. Hersen, M., Eisler, R. M., and Miller, P. M. An experimental analysis of generalization in assertive training. Behav. Res. Ther., 12:295–310, 1974.
23. Johns, J. H., and Quay, H. C. The effect of social reward on verbal conditioning in psychopathic and neurotic military offenders. J. Consult. Psychol., 26:217–220, 1962.
24. Kass, D. J., Silvers, F. M., and Abroms, G. M. Behavioral group treatment of hysteria. Arch. Gen. Psychiatry, 26:42–50, 1972.
25. Kennedy, T. Treatment of chronic schizophrenia by behavior therapy: Case reports. Behav. Res. Ther., 2:1–6, 1964.
26. King, G. F., Armitage, S. G., and Tilton, J. R. A therapeutic approach to schizophrenics of extreme pathology: An operant-interpersonal method. J Abnorm. Soc. Psychol., 61:276–286, 1960.
27. Leitenberg, H., Wincze, J. P., Butz, R. A., Callahan, E. J., and Agras, S. W. Comparison of the effects of instructions and reinforcement in the treatment of a neurotic avoidance response: A single case experiment. J. Behav. Ther. Exp. Psychiatry, 1:53–58, 1970.
28. Liberman, R. P., Teigen, J., Patterson, R., and Baker, V. Reducing delusional speech in chronic paranoid schizophrenics. J Appl. Behav. Anal., 6:57–64, 1973.
29. Marzillier, J. S., Lambert, C., and Kellett, J. A controlled evaluation of systematic desensitization and social skills training for socially inadequate psychiatric patients. Behav. Res. Ther., 14:225–238, 1976.
30. Rimm, D. C., DeGroot, J. C., Boord, P., Heiman, J., and Dillow, P. V. Systematic desensitization of an anger response. Behav. Res. Ther., 9:273–280, 1971.
31. Rimm, D. C., Hill, G. A., Brown, N. N., and Stuart, J. E. Group-assertive training in treatment of expression of inappropriate anger. Psychol. Rep. 34:791–798, 1974.
32. Rimm, D. C., Keyson, M., and Hunziker, J. Group assertive training in the treatment of antisocial aggression. Unpublished manuscript, Arizona State University, 1971. Cited in D. C. Rimm and J. C. Masters, *Behavior Therapy: Techniques and Empirical Findings*. Academic Press, New York, 1974.
33. Rimm, D. C., and Masters, J. C. *Behavior Therapy: Techniques and Empirical Findings.* Academic Press, New York, 1974.
34. Roback, H., Frayn, D., Gunby, L., and Tuters, K. A multi-factorial approach to the treatment and ward management of a self-mutilating patient. J. Behav. Ther. Exp. Psychiatry, 3:189–193, 1972.
35. Schaefer, H. H., and Martin, P. L. Behavioral therapy for "apathy" of hospitalized schizophrenics. Psychol. Rep., 19:1147–1158, 1966.
36. Schierloh, V. C., and Bernal, M. E. Operant conditioning of verbal behavior in a withdrawn patient by a patient peer. In: *Approaches to Modifying Patient Behavior*, M. D. LeBow (Ed.), Appleton-Century-Crofts, New York, 1976.
37. Schwitzgebel, R., and Kolb, D. A. Inducing behaviour change in adolescent delinquents. Behav. Res. Ther., 1:297–304, 1964.
38. Schwitzgebel, R. L. Short-term operant conditioning of adolescent offenders on socially relevant variables. J. Abnorm. Psychol., 72:134–142, 1967.

39. Stokes, T. F., and Baer, D. M. An implicit technology of generalization. Ann. Rev. Behav. Ther. Theory Practice, 6:529–557, 1978.
40. Thomas, E. J. Selected sociobehavioral techniques and principles: An approach to interpersonal helping. Soc. Work, 13:12–26, 1968.
41. Wexler, D. B. Token and taboo: Behavior modification, token economies, and the law. *California Law Review*, 61:81–109, 1973. Cited in K. D. O'Leary and G. T. Wilson, *Behavior Therapy: Application and Outcome*. Prentice-Hall, Inc., Englewood Cliffs, N. J., 1975.
42. Wickramasekera, I. The use of some learning theory derived techniques in the treatment of a case of paranoid schizophrenia. Psychotherapy, 4:22–26, 1967.
43. Wincze, J. P., Leitenberg, H., and Agras, W. S. The effects of token reinforcement and feedback on the delusional verbal behavior of chronic paranoid schizophrenics. J. Appl. Behav. Anal., 5:247–262, 1972.
44. Wolpe, J. *The Practice of Behavior Therapy*. Pergamon Press, New York, 1973.

25

FAMILY THERAPY WITH PERSONALITY DISORDERS

Henry T. Harbin, M.D.

The reader of this chapter should be forewarned; he or she is headed into murky theoretical and technical waters. The title itself evokes a number of latent paradoxical issues and unanswered questions. What is the rationale for discussing an interpersonal treatment approach for a problem, i.e., character pathology, that has been defined as and is presumed to be an individual problem? Are there certain functions and structures at the level of family transactions that are isomorphic to the processes inherent in persons with a character disorder? Is it possible to have relevant classification schemes for dyadic and triadic pathology? How reliable and valid is the present individual diagnostic system for character problems from either a phenomenological or psychodynamic view? One way for the author to approach this chapter would be to ignore these conceptual issues and to focus solely on the technical aspects of the interpersonal treatment of individuals who have a Diagnostic and Statistic Manual III personality disorder diagnosis (6). Indeed, this is the usual approach when one writes about marital and family therapy with psychiatric problems that are labeled with a monadic classification system, e.g., how to conduct family therapy with schizophrenics, alcoholics, etc. This is so because there are no complete and final answers to the questions raised above, and the danger of attempting an explanation is further mystification. Yet, the risks seem worthwhile, as the technical interventions with the patient and family are based on the therapists tentative assumptions and preconceptions about these unresolved theoretical issues. The author will attempt some partial conceptual translations between his understanding of the dynamics of character pathology in individuals and interpersonal processes, as there is some potential for increased clarity.

This discussion will center first around the most relevant general issues that are raised when a patient is diagnosed as having a personality disorder and the consequent implications for their families. Key family processes and dynamics will then be presented with a partial focus on how to understand couples and families from a communications and systems perspective. This will then provide the background for the author's treatment suggestions.

Some general technical issues will be reviewed that apply to a therapist when he attempts to treat a couple or family that contains one or more persons with a character disorder, including type of family therapy used most commonly, treatability of character pathology, who to include, whether to focus on symptoms or personality patterns, and relative indications and contraindications. Finally, the author will present treatment suggestions with brief case examples for specific personality disorders emphasizing the antisocial, the dependent, the schizoid, the obsessive, the paranoid, and the histrionic.

Character Disorders: Individual Features

Fixed, ingrained, habitual, and maladaptive patterns of relating to and preceiving self and others are the essential features that constitute a personality disorder. The clinician usually differentiates between character traits and pathology; the latter label is applied when the personality style becomes more extreme and produces some kind of personal or social dysfunction. The person with a personality disorder classically experiences his pathological attitudes and behavior without undue anxiety and often attributes his problems to people or events outside him. This egosynticity or use of alloplastic defenses is generally viewed as a differentiating factor from the neurotic who characteristically has some symptom that is experienced as dystonic and is labelled problematic by the patient himself. The egosyntonic nature of the character pathology is relative in the author's experience, as often the patient has periodic glimpses of himself as having a maladaptive pattern of relating. But most often this awareness is submerged and the patient views himself as symptom free and usually sees the environment, i.e., significant others, as problematic. Often the character-disordered person has some limited insight, e.g. "people tell me that I'm irritated," but this awareness is not accompanied by anxiety. This self-denying and projective style, coupled to the tendency of most character disorders to act out their inner conflicts by manipulating the environment, has crucial implications for the family. Naturally it is the closest relatives who are usually blamed by the person with the character pathology. Family members are the ones usually "acted upon" when the patient "acts out." In fact, many personality-disordered individuals do not come for treatment unless either forced to do so by their family or because their behavior has led to some disruption in their social network causing a temporary confrontation with the pathological aspects of their own behavior.

Many of the defining features of character pathology imply an interpersonal context. Clinicians rarely make this explicit; the "environment" that is most commonly referred to in diagnostic formulations usually means the significant people close to the patient, i.e., the family. How does one understand and classify the "shyness" of the schizoid personality without knowing certain characteristics of the social context, e.g., How shy are the other family members or the peer group? It is possible to diagnose a dependent personality without the patient having someone, most likely a family member, to depend upon? Is it important or relevant to know the characteristics of the "depended upon" persons in making the diagnosis or can the clinician assume that the "environment" upon which the patient leans excessively is a relatively constant, unchanging factor? Clearly this is not the case, but one must make rather arbitrary and often misleading assumptions about the others in the environment when describing a character disorder. A diagnosis of paranoid personality disorder is made when a patient is inappropriately "mistrustful" of other people, often other family members. Is it possible to understand what is inappropriate without understanding and implicitly classifying the social context in which the "mistrust" occurs? One would have to assume the people this paranoid person mistrusts are trustworthy, but again this assumption is based on the clinician having some knowledge about these other people. These issues are raised to demonstrate the rather simple but often ignored fact that our descriptive system is not based in a social vacuum and that if one tries to tease out the social referents implicit in the classification scheme, then we are led towards a focus of the family, the most important and influential social network.

Some responses have now been provided to the questions raised at the beginning of this chapter as to why to focus on the families of character disorders. Even in trying to understand and classify character problems, the clinician must make certain assumptions about the patient's social network, making it impossible to totally separate the two issues. Consequently, one needs to know something about the family of the patient, even to make an accurate diagnosis, which is separate from implementing a treatment plan.

Systems and Communications Principles as Applied to the Family

Systems theory developed as a way to integrate and explain diverse and seemingly separate phenomena, such as the principles regulating chemical reactions in a laboratory and the principles regulating the growth and development of live organisms (3, 11). In this section, the focus will be on how systems theory can be applied to understanding family relationships. Watzlawick et al. (26) give the following definition of an interactional system: "Interactional systems, they should be two or more communicants in the process of or at the level of defining the nature of their relationship." A family system, like any live or open system, has some degree of wholeness, meaning that if one person in a family is changed, the rest of the family members will also be effected by that new input. Further, the family unit has certain properties that are different and more than a sum of the persons in it. Summativity, the opposite of wholeness, would mean that a group of individuals in the family have no effect upon each other and would equal a "heap" in systems terminology. Clinical observations about the concepts of wholeness led to the development of family therapy. Many therapists noted that when schizophrenic patients improved, it seemed to significantly effect the rest of the family, who then behaved differently to the schizophrenic family member. These reactions by the family led some therapists to try to involve the family members themselves in the treatment process.

Morphostasis and Morphogenesis

Homeostasis or morphostasis is the tendency of a system to maintain a certain equilibrium or balance. As any open or live system such as the family is in constant interaction with the environment, there is a continuous interchange of information and energy. Homeostatic family mechanisms help maintain a stable constancy, and many theorists believe that psychiatric symptoms can become a stabilizing force for a family unit. Speer describes morphogenic properties (as opposed to morphostatic properties) as those that allow for growth, change, or development in a family system rather than movement towards a stable equilibrium (25). Wertheim has gone on to subdivide morphostasis into two types: Consensual Morphostasis (Mc) and Forced Morphostasis (Mf) (27). Mc would mean those homeostatic or steady state mechanisms which contribute to a stable balance but are not based on power imbalances in the family and which lead to the development of mutual security and positive self-regard. Mf would also be a type of homeostatic process; however, the type of stability required would not be based upon "genuine, consensual validation by its members. By contrast, forced morphostasis contributes to intra-family and individual alienation and to disturbed or deviant functioning of the system as a whole and of one or more of its subsystems" (27). Wertheim subdivides families into eight different types based on these systemic properties and in a preliminary way attempts to relate these to various kinds of individual psychopathology.

Feedback Mechanisms

The clinician tries to understand what controls and regulates the behavior of individual organisms and how a certain type of psychiatric problem fits into an individual's intrapsychic dynamics. At the family level one also looks for an explanation of how the system is regulated. Does the behavioral pathology of one family member have a regulating function in the family? The study of feedback mechanisms will tell us something about how families (or any other living system) regulate themselves. The mechanisms can be subdivided into two main types, negative and positive. Negative feedback in the family leads towards stability (or increased morphostasis) in the relational balance. This means that the informational output of the family is fed back into the system itself, leading to "decreased output deviation from a set norm or bias ... " (26). Positive feedback is deviation amplifying, meaning that the information that the system receives leads to more change or a loss of equilibrium. Various communications from family members feed information back into the system, either leading towards homeostasis or towards increased change and loss of stability, with possibly the establishment of a new steady state.

Using these concepts, one can try to understand the role that a family member with a character disorder has within the family system. For example, how does an antisocial personality pattern affect the family system and vice versa? The primary question is whether or not the character pathology has become part of a negative feedback loop within the family. When this happens, the family as a unit has become dependent upon the disturbed behavior for the maintenance of stability. The same question can be asked about the function of psychiatric symptoms in producing stability or homeostasis in the individual personality. Has the individual become dependent upon his own aberrant attitudes and behavior as a way of balancing his internal state? With character pathology this is usually what has happened. For example, repetitive antisocial acts become part of a negative feedback loop within the individual's own personality. This can happen in several ways: the antisocial act may serve as a relief of internal tension leading to temporary internal stability or the antisocial actions may evoke a limit-setting response from the environment, e.g., parents, thereby temporarily helping the individual control and stabilize himself.

Linear vs. Circular Causality

Despite the rather long history of the biological sciences and the application of systems theory to understanding human growth and development, most clinicians tend to persist in thinking in terms of linear, single-chain types of causality as an explanation for human behavior. Is the schizotypal personality "caused" by genetic abnormalities? What series of traumatic childhood experiences "caused" a compulsive personality disorder? Are histrionic personality problems in women "caused" by seductive fathers? Many clinicians make rather simple reductionistic analyses of the variables that influence abnormal behavior and from a technical or strategic point of view, this is defensible. However, it often leads to conceptual mystification and eventual therapeutic error when one forgets that the causes of maladaptive behavior are not so easily categorized and isolated. When one views pathological behavior as a part of an interactive family system which is in itself part of a larger community system, the potential for identifying linear types of causality becomes extremely limited.

The concept of equifinality states that the more open the system, the less the results or outcome of that system can be predicted by initial conditions. For the family one has to look at the interactions and the circular feedback loops in order to predict outcomes. Based on these principles an attempt to understand individual character pathology by tracing out the psychological and biological antecedents will bring only partial illumination. One must also analyze the interactional context, looking for the circular processes that "cause" or maintain character pathology. From the systems framework then it would be very difficult to identify what antecedent factors caused character pathology in an individual, and consequently it will be hard to decide on an individual treatment program. If one views psychopathology as one link in an ongoing communicational sequence, then it will be important to identify the characteristics and the self-regulating properties of these sequences. What becomes particularly important for the clinician thinking in this way is to notice what the responses of the family members are to the psychopathological behavior. Is there a pattern? From the communications and family systems conceptual base, the clinician will want to emphasize the behavioral and communicational consequences of a particular symptom rather than the antecedents. For example, what will be most important to determine is how the wife of a paranoid patient responds to the paranoid attitude, rather than searching for how the wife treated the husband prior to the development of his psychopathology. The clinician will be making the assumption that the husband's paranoia and the wife's reaction to it are two parts of an ongoing, mutually influencing system and that neither can be understood in isolation.

Morphostasis and Character Pathology

Some tentative attempts are being made to classify families based on systems properties and some even more tentative attempts are being made to relate these typologies to monadic diagnostic classification systems. Reiss was able to reliably differentiate between three different types of family styles based upon how they related to themselves and their environment (23). The families that contained a deliquent were seen as "distance sensitive," meaning that they viewed other people as irrelevant and unreliable to their concerns. Wertheim in the work referred to earlier did not identify a subtype that would match the character-disordered group (27). However, the use of the term forced morphostasis may provide some helpful links between what happens at the level of the individual with a character problem and at the level of the family. Character pathology in an individual could be viewed as a type of forced morphostasis, meaning that the particular set of attitudes or behavior that is representative of the personality disorder has become a stabilizing, chronic force in the individuals psychological functioning. This is so despite the fact that the character pathology also has an alienating influence upon the individual. Transactional patterns in the family that might be isomorphic with individual character pathology could be seen as a type of forced morphostasis, i.e., needed for homeostasis but having an alienating influence upon the family members. This would refer to the family members incorporating the disordered behavior of the individual and their "responses" to it as a necessary condition for achieving equilibrium, even though it leads to a lack of consensus and imbalance within individual family members. The consequences of this is that the individual's character pathology cannot change without causing considerable disruptions in the family's stability. This view seems to fit in some ways with Schafer's definition of the egosyntonic nature of character for an individual: "I suggest that the concept of egosyntonicity has always referred to those principles of constructing experiences which seem to be beyond effective question by the person who develops and applies them.... They are the person's fundamental grounds of understanding and certainty" (24). Family transactions that might be described as being like that of a character problem have this quality of appearing to be so basic to the stability of the family that there can be no possibility of change or of challenge. The repetitive nature of certain interchanges between a histrionic wife and an obsessive-compulsive husband provide an example. The histrionic wife dramatically escalates her primitive displays of emotion in synchrony with the cold, affectless, intellectual responses of her husband. The wife's explosive behavior seems to escalate in response to the withdrawal of the husband, and vice versa, bringing about a redundant sequence of communication which is necessary for relational balance and stability. When challenged, the wife blames the husband's character pathology as causing her own behavior and the husband sees his wife as responsible for his attitudes. Their dance together seems to be a basic and stabilizing force despite the consequent lack of mutual subjective consensus: a forced morphostasis.

Family Treatment

This section will include a focus both upon marital and family treatment of character disorders. One rarely makes a diagnosis of character pathology prior to mid-adolescence, meaning that the majority of one's patients with these problems will be adults. Many character disorders are married, and the spouse often provides the motivation for treatment. A family approach, meaning a two or three-generation involvement, is indicated primarily in two instances: when the patient is a teenager or young adult or when the diagnosed adult's children need to be incorporated in the treatment. A two-generational focus is most common when a young person has a diagnosis of either schizoid, schizotypal, antisocial, dependent, or borderline.

Symptoms vs. Character

Many character disorders come to the attention of the clinician when they develop a discrete illness or set of symptoms which should be diagnosed separately from the character problem. The Diagnostic and Statistic Manual III allows for this distinction by classifying all personality disorders along axis II. The compulsive person may become depressed but upon alleviation of the depression, the compulsive character problems continue. The paranoid personality disorder may develop a brief psychosis; when this resolves, the paranoid character disorder persists and becomes the focus of the treatment. Not uncommonly, the character disorder enters family therapy when another family member develops a definite psychiatric illness. A number of times the author has evaluated and treated schizophrenics who married spouses with an antisocial personality disorder. In treatment the symptomatic behavior gives the clinician a fulcrum around which he can pull or push for change with character pathology. The patient and family will be more motivated for help when someone is experiencing a definite illness. This situation provides the clinician with the opportunity to either: a) engage the family for a longer-term treatment which could potentially result in character change or b) use the therapeutic work around the symptoms to bring about character changes. In a previous paper, Harbin reported on the treatment of an obsessive-compulsive neurotic, using combined family and behavior therapy (14). This patient, in addition to having neurotic symptoms, also had an obsessive-compulsive personality disorder (under DSM II terminology) or a compulsive disorder under DSM III terminology. The individual and family treatment that was done, while overtly targeted to symptom resolution, also brought about a mild shift in the obsessive-compulsive personality pattern. Interestingly, the successfulness of the behavioral prescription for the neurotic symptom was enhanced by the compulsive personality pattern of the patient in that she was much more diligent and perfectionistic about following through on the task.

Goals of Family Treatment

Any type of psychotherapy that continues past the stage of symptom resolution begins to deal with character traits, if not overt character pathology. In family treatment once the individual symptoms have diminished, the focus usually shifts to chronic, dysfunctional transactional patterns that seem to be necessary for stabilizing the family system. Some couples and families desire this and others do not. Generally, it is best to leave the choice to the family unless: a) the clinician feels that there is a chance for imminent return of the symptom and further follow-up is felt to be necessary or b) a new symptom has developed in another family member. However, once symptomatic resolution, whether by individual or family treatment, is achieved, the clinician must decide with the patient whether to continue with a longer-term focus upon either character pathology of one member or on certain dysfunctional interpersonal patterns. The goals can then become very vague and hard for either the therapist or the family to articulate. A couple with a husband diagnosed as a dependent personality disorder will say that they would like to have more "joy" in their marriage. Parents might state that they want their schizoid son who has recovered from a psychotic episode to be more sociable, warm, and likeable. These are difficult goals to objectify, and the clinician may find himself not knowing whether definite change has occurred after 6 months or even 1 year of treatment. Many clinicians feel that character disorders cannot be treated at all, while others hold this pessimistic view for only some diagnostic subgroups. Certainly it is not reasonable to talk in terms of "curing" a character disorder. More likely a successful outcome will mean a greater subjective sense of confidence and capacity for pleasure in a number of family members. Usually if therapy goes well, the clinician will see a reduction in the social and occupational impairment of the character-disordered individual and the diagnosis may be dropped. For example, the person with a histrionic personality disorder may no longer fit the Diagnostic and Statistic Manual III classification, but the histrionic traits are still present, even though not causing as many problems for the person.

Type of Family and Marital Treatment Recommended

Several authors have summarized the different types of family therapy (7, 9, 18–19). Family and marital psychotherapeutic methods are as diverse as the individual psychotherapies. The author, based upon his own experience and training, recommends an eclectic approach, depending upon the stage of treatment. A strategic/structural family approach is suggested when one or more family members are symptomatic or in acute distress (10, 20). As stated previously, most patients enter psychotherapeutic treatment when they are symptomatic or in a crisis. Naturally there are exceptions to this, such as with sophisticated consumers, e.g., mental health professionals in training who may recognize some maladaptive personality pattern prior to the development of neurotic symptoms. A problem-solving, structural family approach would tend to: a) emphasize the description of a problem (both of a symptomatic type and a character disorder type) in behavioral terms rather than cognitive/affective terms, e.g., the paranoid person's style of relating would not be interpreted as a problem in using projective defense mechanisms (a psychodynamic explanation) but would be seen as a problem because the patient is acting in a secretive manner by withdrawing, thereby leading to a lack of success in forming close relationships; b) use directives rather than interpretations or catharsis as a way of bringing about change, e.g., the borderline patient in marital therapy who has recently experienced a brief psychotic reaction in relation to her husband would not necessarily be encouraged to explore and understand various factors underlying the psychotic episode; instead, the therapist would look for ways to help the patient suppress the experience, hopefully bringing out the normal aspects of the patients perception, and a task may be designed that would change the husband's reaction to the wife's inappropriate behavior; c) look for ways to change the structure of the family organization, which might be maintaining the symptomatic behavior, e.g., the schizoid adolescent who has developed a reactive depression may be involved in a collusive alliance with one parent, thereby skewing the generational boundaries; the initial therapeutic strategy would be to realign the parents in a closer, more stable relationship using the depressive symptomatology of the adolescent as a lever; and d) maintain an initial focus upon the symptom of the identified patient until some changes occur, e.g., the young adult with a dependent personality disorder who has developed a compulsive symptom, thereby prompting the family to seek treatment, would not be immediately delabeled or descapegoated, with the consequent and premature shift to the parents relationship with each other or to their own parents.

Once a symptomatic resolution is reached, the family therapist has to decide whether: a) to terminate treatment or b) to continue with a different stage of therapy. The family that came to treatment for their adolescent or young adult who had a discrete and now resolved psychiatric illness may ask for help with unhappiness in the marriage. The couple that enters treatment because one member had both a personality disorder and a neurotic symptom may want continued therapy with a more nonspecific focus on the character pathology. This next stage of family therapy often requires different skills and techniques by the clinician; the strategic school of therapy becomes less useful here. At this stage the family members usually articulate their goals in terms of the cessation of some internal distress or of changing the behavior patterns of another person in the family. It is difficult to find discrete bits of behavioral communications that one can design a directive for. The focus has become more nonspecific, and what one is attempting to change are certain transactional patterns that, while problematic, do not allow for the identification of a discrete symptom. For example, the husband with a compulsive personality disorder in marital treatment who has recovered from a primary psychiatric illness but along with his wife feels that they are not as happy in their marriage as they could be asks for continued treatment. The therapist notes to himself it is the interaction of the character pathology of the husband and the wife that leads to the subjective distress. The compulsive character pathology of the husband is sufficient to contribute to the distress in the marriage and also seems to contribute to work difficulties due to his overly perfectionistic standards. The therapist will make those personality traits of the husband such as his aloofness, perfectionism, and intellectualism the focus of the marital treatment, but it will become difficult to translate these traits into behavioral "bits." Additionally, due to the persistence and chronicity of these traits, one or two task-oriented directives (either direct or paradoxical) rarely bring about a lasting change. The novelty of a directive is often a major part of its effectiveness; when using directives to change character pathology, the strategic family therapist begins to lose some of his influence and consequently his authority.

Long-term Family Therapy

The therapist needs to be more eclectic once the treatment has moved past the symptomatic stage. He will want to use experiential methods, make interpretations, utilize confrontation, and shift to a more cognitive/affective focus, as well as to occasionally take a directive stance. The core principles that the author has found helpful in treating character disorders on a long-term basis (i.e., past the symptomatic stage) are those of repetition, consistency, and direct and indirect confrontation. When dealing with transactional patterns that are habitual and ingrained, the clinician should repeatedly confront them. Character pathology will present itself in hundreds of ways over a myriad of content issues, but the family's style will remain similar. The patterns need to be identified, labeled, and brought (often forcefully) to the family's attention. In doing this the therapist is combining principles of learning theory and psychodynamic theory. His interventions will hopefully alter the positive and negative reinforcement of character pathology within the family system; his repeated identifications of these patterns for the couple or family bring about increased anxiety and hopefully change. This kind of work can become very tedious to the therapist, but not necessarily so for the family, which is often experiencing considerable tension due to repeated challenges to rigid homeostatic mechanisms.

In conducting long-term intensive family or marital therapy the clinician must maintain a firm therapeutic alliance with each family member. Ivan Nagy describes this process as one of maintaining "multi-directional partiality" (4). A stable therapeutic alliance is necessary to keep the family engaged during the difficult work of changing habitual maladaptive patterns. Even though interpretations of transactional and personal dynamics are utilized, for a variety of reasons, insight into transference issues becomes less useful as a tool for change in long-term family and marital work. First, the primary loyalties and mutual dependence among family members tends to discourage the formation of intense transference reactions. Further, the activity and often non-neutral stance of the family therapist minimize (but don't prevent) the use of primitive projective mechanisms of the family members towards the therapist. However, families and couples will frequently bring their character pathology both at the individual level and as a family unit into the therapeutic context. The therapist will often be reacted to in the same manner as the family members habitually react to each other. The paranoid husband who is suspicious of his wife may become suspicious of the therapist and his wife. The dependent personality-disordered young adult may become (along with his parents) very dependent on the therapist. The schizoid patient will withdraw during the family therapy sessions and treat the therapist as if he were nonexistent and unimportant. The longer and more intense the therapy, the more the pathology will be re-enacted in the office. Naturally this gives the family therapist even more leverage for bringing about change because of the opportunity to understand, clarify, and confront character patterns that: a) are in the here and now and b) involve the therapist personally. Usually the therapist becomes involved around the traditional boundary and control issues of the family treatment, e.g. fees, time, membership, who is to talk when, etc. The parents of a schizoid 22-year-old may collude with the patient to avoid family treatment sessions, thereby re-enacting: a) the son's habitual autistic withdrawing personality trait and b) the parent's ambivalent and inconsistent reaction to the avoidant reactions of their son. The therapist, in confronting the family about who will be involved in the treatment, will be helping the family change their habitual ways of dealing with themselves and the outside world.

Family and Marital Treatment of Specific Diagnostic Groups

The above discussion addresses some of the general issues involved in the family treatment of character disorders. Now some attention will be paid to the various diagnostic subgroups of personality disorders as they are outlined in the Diagnostic and Statistic Manual III. The author will discuss those particular groups that he has had the most experience with. The various diagnostic entities are grouped below based on: a) certain similarities in traits across groups that can be focused on from a therapeutic point of view and b) those that present frequently for therapy. The Diagnostic and Statistic Manual III has clustered some of the personality disorders together, for example, paranoid, schizoid, and schizotypal, because they "appear odd" or "eccentric" (6). However, these are not particularly useful traits to focus on from a therapeutic perspective. What is needed is a way to cluster some of the more common traits into treatment relevant groups.

Schizoid, Schizotypal, Avoidant, Dependent, and Passive-Aggressive. These will be grouped together, as often there are a number of overlapping traits, e.g., many schizoid patients have avoidant and dependent tendencies. In general, persons with any of these diagnoses end up failing at an active, independent, and responsible social and/or vocational role. Persons with these diagnoses usually take the path of withdrawal or acting "in", in general a passive rather than an active type of pathology. Naturally this influences the overall direction of the family treatment. As mentioned earlier in the chapter, if a patient with a dependent or schizoid personality disorder presents with a neurotic or psychotic symptom, this is addressed first in the family treatment. In the author's experience an individual with one of these diagnoses is usually brought in by his parents and is frequently an older adolescent or young adult between the ages of 20 and 35. The major exception to this is the passive/aggressive who may be older and comes to therapy because of some difficulty with his employer.

Case Example A. John was a 29-year-old white male who was diagnosed as having both a schizotypal and a dependent personality disorder. He experienced one clear-cut psychotic episode at age 22 and had been hospitalized for several months. He had been living quietly at home all of his life and had not been hospitalized or had a clear-cut reoccurrence of a psychosis since the age of 22. He was practically dragged into treatment by his parents, who reluctantly agreed to participate in conjoint family therapy. They presented the initial difficulty as John's social withdrawal and failure at working outside the home; there was no particular crisis or new ego-alien symptoms such as hallucinations, delusions, etc. Essentially, John was almost totally dependent upon his parents; while he did some part-time work at home for his father, he did not cook, clean his room, or wash his clothes. He rarely spoke in the therapy sessions unless pressured by the therapist or his parents. A more functional younger sister who had moved out of the home was included periodically.

Problem-solving Interventions. During the first few sessions the therapist began to reformulate the problem of the patient into quantifiable "bits" of behavior. The patient, of course, viewed himself as normal and felt that if his parents quit pressuring him then everything would be okay and he could live at home in peace. The parents described John's problem in vague terms: "If he were more confident then ... ", "If he felt happier ... ", "John needs to be more assertive", "We feel overwhelmed and unhappy when John looks sad", etc. While most family members present their goals for therapy in terms of ending subjective distress this does not mean the therapist should accept this at face value. It is necessary when carrying out a directive type of family treatment to recast the problem into more concrete, accomplishable goals. However, most family members resist this and want to address either their own inner discomfort or the identified patient's hypothesized lack of confidence or unhappiness. In order to engage the family the therapist needs to speak to this resistance of the family to focus on concrete behaviors; one way to do this is to explain that people will improve their self-confidence by working on and solving specific tasks. In this case the therapist began to ask the family what John needed *"to do"* differently in order for them to be happy. They began to talk about his: a) coming out of his room more often; b) talking when guests are over instead of hiding in his room; c) taking a bus to a downtown office which they rented for him in order that he could spend a few hours out of the house each day; d) going out with some friends; e) stopping making inappropriate comments around his mother, e.g., he would sometimes make sexual references about himself or others; and f) learning how to wash his own clothes and cook some meals.

These discussions around reformulating the problem were very therapeutic. The vagueness of the parents definition of John's problem served a protective function; the lack of precision and quantification allowed them to hide their differences of opinion about what was abnormal about John's behavior. They could both agree that John needed more confidence; they had great difficulty in agreeing how many hours John should go to his office to work, when he would be capable of calling up a peer, etc. The discussion provoked their covert dissension but it also allowed them the opportunity to change towards greater consistency in their view and reactions to John's problem. Once the parents began to agree on the specifics, with varying degrees of participation and resistance by John, they began to decide on a system of rewards and punishments for John to accomplish these tasks. They decided that John's room would be locked if he did not stay out of it for a certain number of hours per day, he would be paid extra by his father if he took the bus to the downtown office, his parents would reduce their demands for him to talk to guests if he would cook more meals and do his own laundry, etc.

Structural Reorganization. The therapist used a problem-solving focus to help analyze and change the various subsystems and generational boundaries in the family. It was clear that the mother, father, and son were overly enmeshed; John, however, was more dependent upon his mother (and she on him) than on his father. They were locked into a developmental dilemma that had not changed for years. Father had not been effective in forming a dyadic subsystem with John that would have helped him separate from mother, a developmental task that should have been accomplished when John was a child. John's schizoid and dependent character pathology was conceptualized as being a stabilizing part of the family's structure, and it was thought that a reorganization of the generational hierarchy and the various subsystems would bring about greater morphogenesis (not increased forced morphostasis) that might not incorporate John's pathological behavior as a homeostatic force. Various tasks were suggested that encouraged the father and John to form a separate relationship, with the goal of decreasing the intensity of the mother-child interaction. For instance, father was encouraged to take John to lunch with him to discuss business matters, and mother was given something else to do during this time.

Long-term Therapy. The family treatment lasted more than a year. The outcome was mixed, like that of many cases when the goal is character change. There was no doubt that John decreased his schizotypal and dependent character pathology. He went regularly to the downtown office, he began to cook and wash his own clothes, his grooming habits improved, he would talk more around company, and his inappropriate remarks around mother decreased; in general he was functioning in a more independent and less withdrawn and autistic manner. Yet, in no way could this patient be viewed as "cured," only partially rehabilitated. He was still working for his father at the time therapy ended, even though he had gone back to school part time. He had gone out on the first date of his life, which scared him badly, and the therapist and parents were unable to get him to go again. He had not developed peer relationships, his social life still revolved around his parents, and he had great difficulty in carrying on a conversation with strangers (including the therapist).

The technical interventions went beyond the prescription of directives. Once the various goals and tasks had been articulated, the majority of the work over the year-long therapy was in reinforcing the implementation of these tasks. The therapist had to repeatedly confront and support the parents to confront and support their son as he and they changed. At times the therapy took on an explorative and cathartic flavor, particularly when the therapist tried to set the stage for son and father to develop a separate and distinct subsystem, e.g., the father was encouraged to share some of his personal history and background so that John might identify more closely with his father. The therapist maneuvered the son and father away from a discussion of tasks to focus on more personal issues. The therapist facilitated a more intimate conversation by asking questions of both son and father but directing them to speak to each other. By asking questions that led the father to speak openly and nondefensively about his own struggles for independence in young adulthood, the therapist began to create an atmosphere within which an emotional experience of intimacy might occur.

The rigidity of the son's character pathology was symmetrical to the redundancy of the parent's transactional patterns, i.e., their inability to consistently agree on how to change a problem and act together for implementation. At one point the son refused to return to therapy, and the parents presented themselves in their usual helpless manner. They were instructed to approach John together the next week, for each to tell him of their expectations, and for each to take one arm to escort, not force, him to the therapy session. The parents were successful, and John came after some initial verbal protest; however, the parents were extremely agitated by the effort that it took to confront John in this new way. In fact the father stated that he was afraid that he would have a heart attack if the therapy went on like this (he had recently been examined and was physically well) and that changing his son was not worth the emotional strain on him and his wife. This happened after 10 months of family treatment and the son had made considerable changes (for him) as outlined above. The therapy had been a series of repeated confrontations of the son's character patterns and of the parents' style of dealing with these traits; progress was slow. The father, over the next few sessions, declared his intentions to stop even though his wife wanted to continue. The therapist told them that the therapy would probably be impossible and ineffective if he terminated, but the father stopped anyway. The therapist met a few more times with mother and son, both together and separately but concluded after this trial that no substantial progress would be made without father. The son maintained the new status quo that he and the family had reached but the therapist terminated the therapy stating that he would see them again only if: a) the father would participate or b) a new crisis occurred.

The Paranoid. This personality disorder often ends up in therapy after the resolution of a major mental illness such as paranoid disorder or depression. The author has had the experience that most of these patients are married. Paranoid features such as extreme mistrust, jealousy, hypervigilance, the search for hidden negative meanings, hypersensitivity, lack of sense of humor, etc. often lead to severe marital dysfunction. The nonparanoid spouse not only suffers from the attitudes of the paranoid but also can cause suffering when he or she acts in such a manner as to exacerbate the paranoid condition. The therapist who treats a couple when one spouse has a paranoid personality disorder focuses on the interactional patterns which seem to maintain the psychopathology. Marriage can be seen as a potentially "rehabilitative" relationship for the personality-disordered spouse, as well as a potentially pathogenic relationship. Naturally the goal of the family and marital therapist is to enhance the positive growth of the couple so as to reduce the character pathology for either or both. The author has found that paranoid patients can be treated with marital therapy despite problems that arise around confidentiality and trust issues. The therapist needs to be constantly aware of whether or not he is playing into the suspiciousness of the paranoid spouse, who will be monitoring closely the therapist's behavior. The paranoid patient will often react angrily if he percieves that the therapist is taking sides or, if it is a therapist of the opposite sex, the patient may become jealous of the therapist's relationship with his or her spouse. The marital therapist should always be very clear and open with this type of patient and spouse as to what he is doing and why, so as not to provoke greater mistrust and paranoia. It is not uncommon for the nonparanoid spouse to attempt to form a collusive alliance that excludes the paranoid patient; obviously, this should be blocked. If the therapist has been consistently "trustworthy," he is in a good position to effectively challenge the paranoid spouse's distortions when they involve the therapist.

One of the more common ways that the spouse of a paranoid patient may exacerbate the pathological behavior is to react passively and secretively when accused or criticized. For example, some wives of paranoid husbands will allow themselves to be bullied by the hypercritical, jealous husband; withdrawing, passive behavior by the wife usually has the opposite effect from that intended. The exception to this is when a paranoid person becomes acutely violent: then it may calm the situation for the spouse to withdraw temporarily. Often the husband gets more suspicious and paranoid when the wife is evasive and withdrawn. During marital therapy, once a therapeutic alliance has been established, the therapist can support the wife to challenge the constant mistrust of the husband. After the initial and expected angry reactions of the husband, the paranoia usually decreases. Again the therapist must closely monitor the potential for physical violence; the confrontations should be made when the patient is in good control of his aggression.

Case Example B. A 26-year-old white male was hospitalized for a second time because of an acute paranoid psychosis that involved some bizarre behavior, extreme jealousy, verbal attacks upon his wife, leaving home for an extended period of time without explanation, persecutory delusions that involved his employers and his wife, and the denial of any problem. The patient's 25-year-old wife was included in the conjoint marital treatment at the beginning of the hospitalization. The first stage of the treatment was directed towards keeping the husband in the hospital and focused on the more grossly irrational and irresponsible aspects of his behavior. During the first few days, even though committed involuntarily, the patient eloped. Initially, the wife was put in charge of him; she was told to make it clear that she would have the police bring him back to the hospital if he eloped again and that she viewed certain aspects of his behavior as irrational, e.g., his persecutory delusions and his extreme jealousy. He was also placed on low doses of neuroleptics. Within 2 weeks the acute psychosis had resolved; what remained were many traits typical of a paranoid personality disorder, as well as some features of a dependent personality disorder, e.g., hypersensitivity, secretiveness, pathological jealousy, unemotional and detached attitudes, passivity, and pervasive mistrust. The marital dynamics begin to unfold as the therapy progressed. The wife was somewhat dominating and secretive; she kept her own fears and vulnerability to herself and tended to focus on her husband's insecurities. The husband was somewhat passive; his increased paranoid condition could be partially understood as a maneuver to take a more dominant stance in the marriage vis-à-vis his wife. Of course, by doing this in an irrational manner he was ineffective. The wife was placed in charge of him initially because of his break with reality, even though the therapist was aware this would place the wife in a more dominant position and might evoke from the husband greater insecurity and paranoia. This didn't happen, even though the husband resented her control; instead his paranoia decreased. The explanation for this seems to be that the inconsistent and insecure reactions of the wife to the psychotic thinking and behavior were more anxiety provoking to the husband than her being clearly in charge and there being a stable family structure. Frequently, during the crisis or symptomatic stages of marital and family treatment one encourages a family structure or organization that is not ideal or what one would like to see at the end of therapy. As the problem improves, the therapist pushes for a more "normal" or age-appropriate family organization.

The second stage of treatment began when the psychosis ended and certain long-standing character problems began to be addressed. Mistrust and pathological jealousy on the part of the wife began to emerge, and the therapist was able to understand how the wife's mistrust often led to a worsening of the husband's jealousy. Her guardedness was challenged repeatedly by the therapist, allowing her to become more vulnerable. This had the effect of decreasing the husband's mistrust, as he could see that his wife was insecure at times also. As they began to be more open with each other, some of the patterns begin to change. Naturally, whenever the stresses reached a certain intensity, they would both retreat into their usual patterns of his passivity and paranoid attitudes and her critical and domineering position. After 6 months of outpatient marital treatment the paranoid and dependent personality pathology of the husband had decreased considerably. In fact, even though the therapy is continuing, both husband and wife state their marriage is happier than before the husband's psychotic break.

Antisocial Personality Disorders. There is a voluminous literature concerning the family dynamics and treatment of antisocial persons (2, 8, 21). Much of this work has focused upon delinquent youth and has not always used rigorous diagnostic criteria. Nevertheless many of these studies have included young adults or older adolescents who would be considered antisocial personality disorders under Diagnostic and Statistic Manual III. A number of family problems have been noted in these studies: a family history of antisocial behavior and alcoholism, poor parental communication, inconsistent discipline ranging from extreme permissiveness to child abuse, high incidence of divorce and separation of the parents, etc. A few studies have shown that short term family therapy is an effective treatment of delinquent teenagers (1, 22). This author has found similar problems in the families of young adults diagnosed as antisocial personality disorders. The family itself is often pushed into treatment by the courts, which have become involved because of some action on the part of the patient, e.g., truancy, shoplifting, and violence. Families are frequently not motivated for treatment and of course neither is the patient. Nevertheless the therapist needs to make some attempt to engage the parents of the antisocial personality disorder or a spouse if the patient is married, as usually the family is more motivated than the patient. In the author's experience, an outpatient therapist has almost no chance of engaging the individual in a consistent therapeutic alliance, as the patient usually bolts when difficult and anxiety-provoking issues are faced. The hospital or prison setting is a somewhat different story as the inpatient may be forced into some sort of stable treatment. However, unless one views the institutional experience as a permanent one, the antisocial personality disorder will return to his natural support system, and if no changes have occurred there the likelihood of a recurrent problem is increased. The family needs to be involved at the beginning of the hospital treatment; this phase of therapy often allows the parents a chance to change their characteristic ways of dealing with the patient (13, 15). The author has had most experience with these character problems in a two-generational context, when the patient is an older adolescent or young adult. If the patient is married then the spouse needs to be involved. A major part of any family and marital treatment of antisocial character problems is in helping the family members set limits on the patient. Family members almost always minimize, ignore, or act inconsistently towards the antisocial behavior. As the family tightens its controls, patients will often begin to reduce their pathological behavior, sometimes developing more egodystonic symptoms such as depression. Usually, if not an overwhelming reaction, this is a positive sign, as it means that the patient is beginning to change and may become more self-motivated to stop his destructive behavior.

Case Example C. This case example will contain a composite of a number of families that the author has treated and evaluated, as the techniques are very similiar (12, 15–17). Tom was a 19-year-old white male who was hospitalized psychiatrically for the first time because of increasing temper outbursts, leading to an assault upon his father. He had a long history of poor school performance, truancy, violence, breaking rules at home, drinking excessively, and recent aggressive behavior targeted primarily at inanimate objects such as furniture, windows, etc. The parents were ambivalent about their decision to bring Tom to the hospital, and when he rebelled against the idea after arriving on the ward the parents began to vacillate. The therapist quickly got the parents together and pointed out to them that their son desperately needed limits from both the hospital and the parents; that Tom had had a long history of problems with rules, and that now was the time to change, meaning that they would have to stand up to him. The parents agreed that they would not take Tom home. Further, after the parents had made their decision, the therapist stated that Tom would be involuntarily committed if he refused to sign in; naturally with those alternatives, Tom decided to stay.

This represented a major change for the parents and led to a restructuring of the family hierarchy with the parents being clearly in charge. The therapist had pushed the parents to magnify the pathological aspects of Tom's antisocial behavior and attitudes rather than ignoring and minimizing, as was often the situation in the past. Tom calmed down and began to engage in the treatment program. This beginning therapeutic maneuver set an important precedent for future outpatient therapy. Upon discharge the family was followed in weekly conjoint family sessions, even though Tom felt that he was "cured." It was clear that he was not, as he continued to lie at times, break rules, refuse to work, etc., even though there were no more violent outbursts. These antisocial behaviors became the focus of the outpatient family therapy. Each time during the week that Tom would break a rule, the therapist would make a major issue out of it, thereby pushing the parents to continuously confront Tom. Tom became depressed and withdrawn at times; however he began to look for a job. After approximately 4 months of outpatient treatment Tom wanted to stop, and as he had a stable job, the parents and therapist agreed. Certainly Tom continued to have antisocial traits but the extremes of his disability had abated. The parents, however, were becoming more unhappy; their dissension over how to handle Tom had become more overt, and they began to talk about chronic dissatisfaction with their marriage. The therapist began to meet with the two of them, encouraging a more realistic assessment of their relationship. They were able to confront a number of difficult issues that had been buried for years but were still bothering them; therapy ended with them feeling that they wanted to stay together, even though there were a number of unresolved issues.

The Histrionic and the Compulsive. These two diagnostic entities are grouped together because the clinician often ends up seeing in marital treatment both a histrionic wife and a compulsive husband. Naturally this is not always the case, and the therapist may see a histrionic personality disorder with his or, usually, her family. Likewise a compulsive patient may end up in treatment with his spouse or parents. The family of the histrionic character disorder often becomes involved after some primitive emotional outburst which may have included some threat of self-destructive behavior. A very common situation is a histrionic wife who regresses during a marital separation or divorce. The loss of a stable dependent figure is a major catastrophe and may lead to a variety of reactions, including increased affective displays, aggressive attention-seeking behavior, increased seductiveness and some promiscuity with other men as a way of making the husband jealous, suicide threats, etc. The clinician is in a difficult bind in evaluating these situations for marital treatment, as bringing in the husband may seem like a reward to the wife for her pathological actions. The author recommends evaluating each situation separately, following these general guidelines: 1) If the histrionic wife and her husband are separated but still seeing each other regularly, the husband should be invited in as a part of the evaluation and possible short-term couples treatment with the goal being a) helping the wife to stop her pathological behavior and b) clarifying the future of the marriage and decreasing the acting out of ambivalent intentions. Or 2) If the histrionic wife wants the husband to come in but he is clearly and consistently separated and is moving to a definite divorce, then he can be included for an evaluation session and then possibly a few sessions to help the wife accept this as a permanent situation and to encourage both spouses to make realistic plans for their children.

The compulsive character disorder is commonly urged into treatment by close family members who are angry with the patient's rigidity, procrastination, perfectionism, detached emotional attitudes, and general lack of enjoyment of life. The wife of a compulsive personality disorder may be threatening divorce if the patient doesn't change and sometimes this is the only motivation for treatment. The clinician will want to include any close family members particularly those that are concerned or anxious about the problem. This anxiety of the non-pathological spouse may be the only leverage for treatment and the therapist will try to get the wife to be more effective in dealing with the compulsive personality patterns; hopefully getting the patient to feel more anxious about his own attitudes and behavior.

Case Example D. A 45-year-old man who was very successful at his profession came into family treatment with his 39-year-old wife because of a problem with their teenage daughter. The husband had a number of compulsive personality features, such as an overvaluation of work, undervaluation of interpersonal relationships, inability to express affects, irritability, perfectionism that manifested itself as a hypercritical view of his wife and daughter, and stubborness. The wife was prone to dramatic outbursts of emotion, usually either expressions of anger or depression. She was alternately seductive or detached, and either demanding attention or very dependent on her husband for reassurance. After the daughter terminated therapy the parents decided to work on their "marital unhappiness." As the marriage became the focus the wife expressed that she felt that the couple had severe problems but that she felt hopeless because her husband didn't want to and wasn't able to change. The husband would listen to these tearful declarations by his wife without emotion, stating after she calmed down that he saw nothing wrong with their marriage. The therapist attempted to help the wife be more persistent and clear in the confrontation of her husband rather than to continue the usual pattern of waiting in frustration for months and then blowing up. The husband usually became so anxious when his wife acted out these affective "storms" that he would simply try to ignore her and minimize the content of her communications which, of course, had to do with his compulsive personality traits. She would then calm down and apologize for her temper tantrums, thereby further disqualifying the validity of her comments. These circular and redundant sequences of communication which involved both of these person's personality pathology were re-enacted in almost every session when important issues would surface. The therapist intervened to block these repetitive interchanges. The therapist would encourage the husband to talk about himself and his own family background, looking for conflictive issues that might evoke some genuine emotions. The therapist would control these parts of the session closely in order to prevent the wife from intervening and attacking, thereby shutting off any possibility for the husband to be more vulnerable. However it was crucial for the wife to be present and listening (and the therapist was very much aware of her presence) and to see that it was possible for her husband to be vulnerable and to experience painful affects the same as she. At one point the husband began to tear up when talking about a particularly painful event in his life, and the therapist then urged the wife to act in a supportive manner. It was a novel experience for the wife to see her husband overtly communicate painful emotion, and she temporarily became more accepting.

Later the therapist shifted to the wife and urged her to be more analytical and intellectual about important events in her life, discouraging her tendency to be overly emotional. Synthetic systems interpretations were made to the couple periodically, i.e., their tendency to exaggerate the pathological traits of the other were identified over and over again. The husband was told that his aloof, rigid, perfectionistic style encouraged the dramatic, emotional outbursts of his wife and vice versa; both were attempting to bring out a more desirable aspect of the other's personality, but they were not successful. These brief descriptions of some of this couple's interactions and the therapist's techniques for handling this should give the reader an idea of how certain types of character pathology are handled in marital therapy.

Narcissistic and Borderline Character Disorders. Because the narcissistic personality disorder is a new diagnostic entity there is little written about marital and family treatment methods. Narcissistic conflicts, i.e., under and/or overvaluation of self, are a part of all personality disorders, and some applicable interpersonal therapeutic methods have been addressed in previous case examples. Spouses and other family members suffer greatly from the self-centered stance of the extremely narcissistic person. As with other personality disorders it may be the spouse who pushes the patient into treatment. Some spouses can become quite depressed when living with a person who is constantly manipulating, hypercritical, and rarely genuinely interested in them as a separate person. Many spouses are initially attracted to a person with a narcissistic personality disorder because they appear to be so warm, charming, flattering, and engaging. Later, after the infatuation has disappeared, the narcissistic spouse's unquenchable thirst for attention begins to become a major problem, and marital conflicts escalate. As with all treatment methods for character disorders, marital therapy is difficult due to the rigid nature of the pathology. It may be impossible to engage the narcissistic spouse in therapy, as he or she may feel so little interest in working on something outside of their own self-interests. This is particularly so if the narcissistic person is having an affair, a not uncommon situation.

Many individuals with a borderline personality disorder end up in marital and family therapy. Often there will be 2 or 3 persons with this diagnosis in the same family; any clinician who has attempted psychotherapy with just one borderline patient can imagine how difficult it is with several at the same time. Indeed, in the author's experience, it can be the most difficult to treat couples or families of any kind of diagnostic group, including the schizophrenics and severe affective disorders. This is not to say that these people can't be treated with family therapy; they can. Some borderline patients, however, become so upset in family sessions, due to their intense sensitivity and dependency, that they may have to be seen separately from their family in individual therapy. These families are the ones that seem to become most explosive during treatment or sometimes psychotic for brief periods. They can become so involved in their destructive interchanges that the therapist is virtually ignored; if this happens repetitively then the family members must be seen separately. Part of the difficulty is with the therapist's expectations. Many borderline patients and their families present initially as being very much in control of themselves, as having true insight into their problems, and as being genuinely interested in changing. This "pseudonormal" presentation can often mislead the family therapist into probing too quickly into sensitive issues, or into expecting an unrealistic level of performance or compliance with treatment. This misperception on the therapist's part can quickly lead to very destructive acting out, both within and outside of the family therapy sessions. After this has happened, the therapist usually learns to go much slower and to realize some of the limitations of the patient and family. Extreme dependency or emotional enmeshment seems to be the major theme that is eventually identified in long-term family and marital therapy with borderline personality disorders. The presence and interventions of the family therapist can help many of these patients slowly differentiate themselves from the other family members; yet this can be very painful therapeutic work for the family. These patients can present with a myriad of signs and symptoms, some of which have been addressed in previous sections of this chapter, e.g., paranoid reactions, depression, antisocial behavior, violence, etc. Consequently, a case example will not be given.

Indications and Contraindications

The author purposely included this part of the discussion last. The reader should have a fairly clear idea about the type of family and marital treatment used with character problems, and a discussion of applicability at this time should be more useful.

There are at least 2 issues that need to be addressed: a) What are the indications and contraindications for a specific type of marital or family treatment for certain character disorders, given that there are many different kinds of family therapy? and b) What are the indications and contraindications for family therapy, as opposed to another type of psychotherapy, e.g., individual psychoanalytic psychotherapy? The first issue was discussed earlier in this chapter, i.e., the more symptomatic or disturbed the patient and family, the more directive and supportive the family treatment should be. With some borderline patients an intensive, explorative, insight–oriented family treatment can encourage significant regression and very negative effects. However with the more stable character disorder, a family treatment method that uses experiental techniques that encourages self-awareness and confrontation, or that increases anxiety, is indicated.

At this time there are not enough outcome studies that will allow us to reliably and objectively determine whether to utilize family vs. individual vs. group treatment of character disorders (5). Therefore we must rely on clinical judgement based on experience. One of the problems here is that most clinicians, particularly psychiatrists, have never received any training in family and marital therapy and consequently have little experience in this area. Yet they are often in the position of deciding whether this therapy is indicated or not, unfortunately many will decide that the only useful therapy is the one they are most familiar with. The author has had training and experience with both individual and family treatment approaches for character-disordered patients. He has found that the indications for family treatment are best defined flexibly and pragmatically. If the personality-disordered patient is feeling little anxiety over his problem but the spouse is, then therapy is likely to be more successful if the spouse is included. If the patient has some motivation for treatment and other family members are not interested in participating, then individual therapy is more indicated. If the therapist believes that the patient is stable and mature enough to utilize an insight-oriented therapy and to form a transference neurosis, then long-term psychoanalytic psychotherapy might be best. Often the clinician will need to make his decision after a trial of either individual or family treatment. The author has found that one of the most important indications for a very active, directive type of family treatment is if the personality-disordered patient is acutely symptomatic or in a crisis. The family can provide much more support and can set limits much more effectively than the therapist, and their involvement may often prevent hospitalization or more severe acting out.

There are some relative contraindications to involving the family, particularly when the personality-disordered patient is not in a crisis. With the more paranoid patient, confidentiality issues can become a major resistance to family treatment. The clinician may feel that this is blocking therapeutic progress and that the paranoid person will engage better in individual treatment. With some older adolescents or young adults the issues surrounding differentiation from the parents become a problem in family treatment. The young person usually feels more free to talk without the parents present, and vice versa. If the adolescent is motivated to work in individual treatment (unfortunately, this is often not the case), then the clinician will want to try to engage him in individual therapy. This doesn't mean that family sessions can't be very useful in helping parents and adolescents separate from each other, as these sessions can be very effective with this. The clinician needs to keep in mind that it is never a one-way situation, i.e., only the adolescent needing help separating from his parents. Yet there are limits to family discussions, as many topics are better left for individual therapeutic sessions with the clinician, e.g., sexual conflicts, peer relationships, dreams, fantasies, etc. Another relative difficulty with family treatment is the guilt that is often engendered when the therapist suggests involving the family. Many family members will feel blamed when they are included and wonder why they need to be present if someone else is the problematic one. While this resistance can be handled it still presents another difficulty that can be avoided if one leaves the family out. Again if the patient appears motivated for individual treatment, these aspects of family treatment become an argument against utilizing it. Another relative contraindication is when the character-disordered spouse seems motivated only to manipulate the other family members when they come for family treatment, e.g., the histrionic wife who is using marital therapy to force her separated husband to return to her or the antisocial youth who wants to use the family sessions as a way to attack his parents and make them suffer. If the clinician believes that the family or marital therapy is being utilized for purely destructive purposes, he may decide to see various members individually. In summary, the patient and family will best be served if the clinician has broad training and experience and can avoid making dogmatic and purely arbitrary decisions in regards to what type of therapy is more indicated or not.

REFERENCES

1. Alexander, J., and Parsons, B. Short-term behavioral intervention with delinquent families: Impact on family process and recidivism. J. Abnorm. Psychol., 81:219–225, 1973.
2. Bandura, A., and Walters, R. H. *Adolescent Aggression.* Ronald, New York, 1959.
3. Bertalanffy, L. von. *General Systems Theory.* George Braziller, New York, 1973.
4. Boszormenyi-Nagy, I., and Spark, G. *Invisible Loyalties.* Harper & Row, New York, 1973.
5. De Witt, K. N. The effectiveness of family therapy. Arch. Gen. Psychiatry, 35:549–561, 1978.
6. Diagnostic and Statistical Manual of Mental Disorders, Ed. III. American Psychiatric Association, Washington, D. C., 1980.
7. Feber, A., Mendelsohn, M., and Napier, A. *The Book of Family Therapy.* Jason Aronson, New York, 1972.
8. Glueck, S., and Glueck, E. *Unraveling Juvenile Delinquency.* Harvard University Press, Cambridge, Mass., 1950.
9. Group for the Advancement of Psychiatry. The Field of Family Therapy. Report No. 78. Group for the Advancement of Psychiatry, New York, 1970.
10. Haley, J. *Problem Solving Therapy.* Jossey-Bass, San Francisco, 1976.
11. Hall, A. D., and Fagen, R. E. Definition of system. Gen. Syst. Yearbook, 1:18–28, 1956.
12. Harbin, H. T. Episodic dyscontrol and family dynamics. Am. J. Psychiatry, 134:1113–1116, 1977.
13. Harbin, H. T. Families and hospitals: Collusion or cooperation? Am. J. Psychiatry, 135: 1496–1499, 1978.
14. Harbin, H. T. Cure by ordeal: Treatment of an obsessive-compulsive neurotic. Int. J. Fam. Ther., 1:324–332, 1979.
15. Harbin, H. T. A family oriented psychiatric inpatient unit. Fam. Proc., 18:281–291, 1979.
16. Harbin, H. T. Violent adolescents: Family dynamics and treatment in synopsis of family therapy practice, C. Simpkinson (Ed.). Family Therapy Practice Network, Inc, Baltimore, in press.
17. Harbin, H. T., and Madden, D. Battered parents: A new syndrome. Am. J. Psychiatry, 136: 1288–1291, 1979.
18. Levant, R. F. A classification of the field of family therapy. Am. J. Fam. Ther., 8:3–16, 1980.
19. Madanes, C., and Haley, J. Dimensions of family therapy. J. Nerv. Ment. Dis., 156:89–98, 1977.
20. Minuchin, S. *Families and Family Therapy.* Harvard University Press, Cambridge, Mass., 1974.
21. Minuchin, S., Montalva, B., et al. *Families of the Slums.* Basic Books, New York, 1967.
22. Parsons, B., and Alexander, J. F. Short-term family intervention: A therapy outcome study. J. Consult. Clin. Psychol., 41:195–201, 1973.
23. Reiss, D. Varieties of consensual experiences. III. Contrasts between families of normals, delinquents, and schizophrenics. J. Nerv. Ment. Dis., 152:73–95, 1971.
24. Schafer, R. Character, ego-syntonicity, and character change. Int. J. Psychoanal., 121:880, 1979.
25. Speer, D. C. Family systems: Morphostasis and morphogenesis, or is homeostasis enough? Fam. Proc., 9:259–278, 1970.
26. Watzlawick, P., Beavin, J. H., and Jackson, D. D. *Pragmatics of Human Communication,* p. 121. Norton Inc., New York, 1967.
27. Wertheim, E. S. Family unit therapy and the science and typology of family systems. Fam. Proc., 12:361–367, 1973.

26

PERSONALITY DISORDERS IN PRIVATE PRACTICE

Ellen McDaniel, M.D.

Introduction

We each have our habitual ways of harmonizing our intrapsychic needs with the demands of the external environment. Such long-standing, fairly persistent patterns of coping can be organized along a continuum. Placed at one end, a personality (character) trait is an identifiable, predictable way of behaving in certain circumstances but does not characterize the more global repertoire of conduct. At the other end, a personality type refers to the most predominant style with which one thinks and acts in most situations.

> Mrs. A., a 48-year-old executive secretary, is described by her family and friends as outgoing, charming, given to dramatics, and emotionally overreactive. She has received rapid promotions at work because, in addition to her vivacious personality, she is very meticulous, well-organized, and can relate to business clients in a gracious yet reserved professional manner.

Mrs. A. has an histrionic personality with certain compulsive character traits that are most evident at work.

Such a person may become involved in a situation in which the lifelong patterns of behavior no longer bring harmony, and the person does not have the flexibility to change his usual style to a behavior more adaptive to the new situation. If seen by a professional because of the consequent disharmony, the person would be diagnosed as having a personality disorder.

> Mrs. A. sought psychiatric care when she discovered that her oldest son was a drug addict. After trying unsuccessfully to cajole and manipulate her son to change, she became depressed. When she made a superficial suicide attempt, her husband insisted she seek help.

Basic Concepts of Personality Structure

In evaluating patients seen in private practice, five aspects of their functioning relate specifically to personality structure: areas of internal conflict, defensive organization, self-image, object relationships, and autonomous ego functions.

Each individual grows up with varying intensities of needs, wishes, prohibitions, fears, and pleasures. These motivating forces and conflicts contribute to each person's uniqueness. The particular clustering of defense mechanisms used and the manner in which these are expressed add further to one's individuality. This defensive organization helps bring harmony between the intrapsychic forces and the demands of reality. Self-image, a third aspect of personality structure, refers to one's experience of himself, including one's gender identity, sexual role, body image, ego ideal, and realistic self-appraisal. Object relationships, the fourth aspect, involves the type and quality of feelings and behavior one usually assumes in important interpersonal relationships. Each of these categories of psychological functioning have a conscious, ego-syntonic aspect and an unconscious, ego-dystonic aspect.

Finally, when one speaks of autonomous ego functions, one is referring to those relatively conflict-free, adaptive, growth-promoting areas of activity.

Formulating a Diagnosis

Patients with a primary diagnosis of a personality disorder in private practice commonly present with a chief complaint that suggests affective distress, e.g., "I feel empty." "I've been depressed." "The pressure is getting to me." The distress varies from mild to moderate in intensity. It usually is not totally incapacitating, and has been either insidious in development or experienced as "always there but worse lately." As the initial interview progresses, the affective distress does not appear as the most striking feature of the person's presentation.

Further conversation often reveals that the predominant problem centers around the patient's relationship with someone else, commonly a spouse, lover, parents, or an authority figure in the person's environment. One may wonder why personality disorders develop such difficulties. If we look again at the basic concept of personality structure, we note that the predominant patterns of thought and behavior are experienced as adaptive, protective, and gratifying. In summary, the patterns are ego-syntonic. The person may state that he has been unhappy or bored or lonely all of his life, but he prefers his way of living to any alternative—if, in fact, he could let himself contemplate another possibility. There is a rigid maintenance of the patterns, and such behavior is within the patient's control (regardless of whether the control is conscious or unconscious).

What the person cannot control as completely as his own behavior are the people and events who enter his life. The schizoid personality may do everything within his power to avoid close interpersonal relationships, but a job promotion may force him to deal more intimately with his colleagues. A compulsive personality may be very skillful in establishing boundaries and rules for a marriage, but an unhappy wife still may threaten to discard the whole relationship if more affection is not forthcoming.

The rigidity of the personality disorder and the inability to perceive experiences and feelings (his own as well as others) in a manner different than that which meets his personal needs, creates problems in interpersonal relationships. The person can function very successfully as long as the outside world complements his personality. When that no longer is the case, the lack of flexibility brings distress.

In the initial interview, the evaluator may consider the mental status exam as essentially unremarkable, except for mild to moderate transient affective distress which seems appropriate for the situation. Nonverbal behavior expressed in the relationship to the interviewer gives clues to the patient's personality traits: the seductive pose or the macho aggressiveness of the histrionic, the meticulous dress and careful speech of the compulsive, the lack of spontaneity of the schizoid.

History taking is a significant part of the evaluation. First, one uncovers repetitive patterns of coping and relating in the data that the patient gives about his current situation as well as his growing-up years. Second, typical defense mechanisms, hints of the patient's self-image, intrapsychic conflicts, and difficulties in object relationships will be expressed in the process of communicating the history.

> Mr. B. is neatly dressed in a three-piece business suit. He enters the office, sits straight and stiff in the chair indicated to him, and proceeds to talk about his marital difficulties before any comment is made by therapist. With a monotone voice and composed manner, he describes the history of his marriage, from courtship to the present situation of arguments, separate bedrooms, and threats of divorce.

At this point, one can perceive an orderliness in appearance and thought, an isolation of affect from content, and a need to control the interview by "taking charge" of it.

> When the therapist interrupts the history, which is very detailed, to ask about feelings, Mr. B. becomes momentarily flustered. He comments, "That is a good question but I'd like to postpone answering it till later." Later, in an effort to ease Mr. B's obvious discomfort while hoping to establish emotional contact with him, the therapist makes a comment which empathically reflects what the patient has said (e.g., an attempt to say "I'm listening and understand your feelings"). Mr. B. responds by correcting the therapist. "No, that's not exactly what I meant," and repeats essentially the same material.

One glimpses Mr. B.'s intrapsychic struggles with autonomy and control as reflected in his manner of relating to the interviewer. He eases his anxiety by characteristic defenses used by the compulsive personality: isolation of affect, intellectualization, undoing. Thus early clues of the problems in the marriage are already available. One does not see a predominant disturbance of affect or a thought process disorder, or difficulty with reality testing.

Sometimes well-ingrained patterns of behavior are not evident initially and only unfold during the course of therapy. In long-term therapy this becomes most evident in the transference.

> Mr. B. began analysis. During the first few months he continued to appear controlled emotionally and in his verbalization. Periodically he would very casually and briefly comment on feeling humiliated over some perceived "misbehavior" on his part ("Dropped my cigarette on the boss' carpet. Was that embarrassing!") but give it no more attention. These fragmented remarks next began to appear in the context of the treatment situation. ("Was ashamed about paying the bill later than usual this month"). Not much notice was paid to the comments by either patient or therapist until one day Mr. B. exploded in rage at the therapist for humiliating him. Upon examination, the following understanding was achieved. The patient's narcissistic problems were expressed in the transference by behavior designed to take advantage of the treatment situation (e.g., to not pay). The patient would lose self-esteem upon awareness of his exploitiveness. Provocative rage reactions secondary to the patient's deflated self-esteem as well as expressive of his defensive position ("You are out to exploit me, not the reverse!") had become a predictable part of the relationship.

If Mr. B. had been seen in short-term psychotherapy, these narcissistic difficulties may not have become evident. In long-term insight-oriented therapy, one sees how certain personality traits have developed as defenses against other ones. Mr. B.'s compulsive need to control protected him from the difficulties his narcissistic problems brought, e.g., intense rage.

Typical Personality Types in Private Practice

A few introductory comments are necessary before examining features of the different personality types. As the preceding cases illustrate, no patient is a pure example of any one kind of pathology. A patient may have a primary diagnosis of one personality disorder but have traits of other personality types. The following examples are therefore exaggerated descriptions of the personality disorders, because the complexity of the real situation is ignored to achieve greater clarity.

Private patients are paying patients which means that the population is skewed by predictable socioeconomic factors. The antisocial personality is not a typical private patient. He is more often seen in clinics or in court. Also, since private outpatient therapy is most commonly voluntary, there is a less than predictable representation in the usual private patient population of the paranoid personality, the schizoid personality, the schizotypal personality, and the avoidant personality. These are not individuals who seek help from people, who readily trust others, who tolerate the stress of anything approaching a close relationship. They may pursue less personally threatening avenues when stressed—religion, drugs, clinics where staff turnover is high, meditation, etc. However, in private practice, people diagnosed with other disorders may have a significant component of these traits.

The personality disorders commonly seen in private outpatient practice are the following: compulsive personality, histrionic personality, narcissistic personality, dependent personality, and the borderline personality.

Compulsive Personality

This individual typically presents with a specific complaint and a methodically arranged explanation of events leading up to the present situation. Initially, the interviewer is impressed by the ease with which information is obtained. The patient is articulate and well-prepared for the interview. Several subsequent impressions soon erode the therapist's comfort.

In an effort to be precise and correct, the patient begins to add numerous unnecessary details, each relevant to the story but the total of which makes listening to a train of thought tedious. If the therapist suggests omitting certain material, the patient may temporarily acquiesce but later sabotage the request. Sometime during the interview the therapist realizes that he feels bored. Examination of this countertransference response will link it to the lack of emotional communication from the patient, despite a wealth of concrete facts. The therapist may also perceive that the patient has difficulty tolerating questions about feelings, empathic comments, an unexpected change or interruption in the order of the hour, advice, recommendations, i.e., anything which lessens the patient's control of the situation.

Common defenses used by the compulsive personality include reaction formation, isolation of affect, intellectualization, rationalization, and undoing. Behaviorally, the mechanisms are expressed in personality qualities of rigidity, self-righteousness, moralism, control, indecisiveness, and meticulousness. The person is reserved in his relationships with others (including the therapist).

Predictable transference issues arise from this dynamic constellation. The patient sees the therapist as an authority figure and therefore a person who potentially can deprive the patient of his autonomy. On the other side, the patient's need for a dependable, warm, caretaking figure may lead to an overvaluation of the therapist. The patient struggles with his autonomy-dependency conflicts. This is most evident in long-term therapy. He demands to know "what you must know but won't tell me," while ready to debate any advice or interpretation. He challenges the techniques and theories of the treatment; he questions the therapist's behavior and intentions. He is not uncommonly very punctual or predictably late (e.g., regularly arriving 10 minutes after the hour begins). He pays exactly on schedule or, again, on a regularly irregular basis. Correct clarifications, positive feelings for the therapist, and improvement in outside relationships will not be acknowledged to the therapist until long after the fact. Anger may not be expressed when appropriate (e.g., when the therapist is late or makes a sarcastic comment) but may flash out unexpectedly. Sad events will be conveyed with stoicism; and tender events will be told with difficulty.

Countertransference attitudes often reflect the therapist's response to the patient's desire for control over both feelings and the therapeutic situation. Irritated by the barrage of questions, angered at the indignant accusations of being unscrupulous, bored by the lack of emotional contact, the therapist may unwittingly escalate the power struggle by becoming defensive and/or accusatory. He thus engages in the battle rather than observes it. Another unfortunate outcome may be a premature termination of treatment by a discouraged or hostile therapist. A third type of countertransference feeling can be described more by its absence—a lack of empathy or even awareness of the patient's anxiety, sadness, and dependency wishes. The patient, because of his isolation of affect and his controlled behavior, appears to be functioning at a more comfortable level than is actually the case. Appropriate moments for offering supportive empathic comments can be missed, giving the patient confirmation that he should not trust his feelings to anyone.

In an average private practice, compulsive characters are one of the two most common personality types seen (the other being the histrionic personality). Some of the qualities of this personality type are quite adaptive and conducive to success in our work-oriented, time-conscious culture. The intellectual desire to seek answers to what seems illogical and the drive towards perfection help motivate the compulsive personality to seek traditional treatment. Because of the ability to control regression, the more mature level of defensive organization used, the intelligence and the verbal skills often present, these people are considered good candidates for long-term insight-oriented therapy, including psychoanalysis. However, one must be cautious that the compulsive traits are not hiding more serious pathology, such as paranoid thinking or an incipient psychosis. In those cases, supportive therapy is indicated. Often, compulsive personalities cannot tolerate the idea of a long-term intimate relationship, and although analysis might be thought preferable by the therapist, a more mutually acceptable alternative will have to be made.

Histrionic Personality

The histrionic patient (more often female but not always) comes in during an emotional crisis—"My world is falling apart." "I've had it with marriage."

"You can't imagine what my best friend just did." In contrast to the compulsive personality, this type of patient quickly communicates the affective distress. She may relate in a warm charismatic manner. However, the relevant content will be presented chaotically. The person will take off in one direction but then divert the focus into a sidetrack which becomes another dramatic story. The associations are clear and easy to follow; yet, somehow, the climax or conclusion of the history is not reached. This patient will readily respond to the interviewer's questions or suggestions and forget the point she was making because of her greater interest in pleasing the therapist. The therapist may be easily captivated by the tension, the excitement of the presentation. After a while he realizes a sense of frustration because of the lack of closure. At the end of the first interview, a repetitive pattern of emotionally charged crisis is evident in the patient's life although the exact difficulty which brings her to therapy may remain fuzzy ("Does she want to leave her spouse or is she more upset by her situation at work? Does she see herself as having a problem or is she coming here to get out of home responsibilities?")

Denial, repression, and regression are characteristic defenses used. The patient will describe a minor event in her life and burst into unexplained sobbing. The affect is available but the emotional importance of the event, the associated connections which would clarify its meaning, are not known. Impulsivity is typical; conflict will be expressed in action rather than in intellectual productions (in contrast to the compulsive). Relationships are of paramount importance; moral issues of responsibility are of no unusual concern (they are not unimportant but do not have exaggerated significance). Reality testing is intact but there is greater personal distortion than is true for the compulsive because of a particular defense used, i.e., denial. Another aspect of this character structure is a lesser degree of internal controls. The patient may make her own flexible schedule for payment and time, regardless of what was agreed upon, etc.

The histrionic patient initally and quickly relates to the therapist as a benevolent parental figure. At times there is a strong current of sexual undertones. If the erotic transference predominates, the therapist will need to rapidly and regularly interpret it. If ignored it becomes a powerful resistance to using the relationship in a therapeutic way. Sadly, some therapists deny that this erotic transference is an expression of the patient's problem and a reflection of the treatment situation, and they gratify the transference wish to meet their own needs. If trouble results from this, as it almost always does, the patient is accused of being seductive and histrionic. When the therapist does not gratify the patient's wish to be taken care of, the impulsive and demanding behavior may escalate. The relationship does not have the flavor of a power struggle unless the therapist turns it into one. Rather, it expresses conflicts over dependency wishes which have become sexualized. The patient often seems to be asking for outside controls and nurturance.

Countertransference reactions develop in opposite directions. The demanding dramatic behavior may be irritating to the therapist who wants the patient to be more like him—controlled, predictable, consistent. These qualities of the therapist are very useful to the patient but cannot be extracted from her. The therapist may be so bothered by the exhibitionistic qualities that he will not be able to relate to the underlying depression. He thus may inadvertently increase that patient's sense of abandonment, and she will escalate the very behavior that turns away the therapist.

Conversely, the therapist may either overidentify with the patient or have such difficulty in saying no (e.g., in setting limits) that he offers too much support and direction, thereby continuing the infantilization of the patient. The message is conveyed to the patient that she, in fact, does not have to take responsibility for her behavior; the therapist will control the situation.

The type of treatment recommended depends again on the overall assessment of the patient's strengths, the degree of pathology, and the motivation. The greater the use of denial and regression, the poorer the reality testing and the less suitable the patient is for insight-oriented therapy. Often the patient is motivated for the treatment that aims more at resolving the precipitating crisis. Conjoint therapy, family therapy, or more supportive individual therapy are then in order. When analysis is undertaken one commonly sees the development of compulsive traits in the histrionic structure.

Case History. Mrs. Lloyd, a 26-year-old nurse, phoned the therapist for help one evening. She opened the conversation with, "My friend gave me your name. I'm really upset (starts crying). I don't know what to do about David (silence). I can't stand it anymore (more crying)."

An appointment was made. Mrs. Lloyd canceled it once, then appeared for the second scheduled hour. She was attractive, dressed very stylishly, and used a lot of hand and facial motion in her communications. With much anger and tears, she described her fights with David. The therapist asked various questions about David and tried to obtain some basic background information. Mrs. Lloyd covered her previous marriage, her relationship with her 3-year-old child, and her difficulties with her parents in about 10 minutes. She soon returned to David. An obvious crisis in a current significant relationship was evident but it was hard for the therapist to put this relationship into some perspective—how significant was David? How did he fit into the patient's life? What else was upsetting her? After a 2-week period of frequent phone calls and interviews the patient had calmed down, and the therapist had developed a better picture of Mrs. Lloyd's overall functioning. Long-term insight-oriented therapy was recommended because of the persistence of chronic distress and the evidence of considerable ego strength (Mrs. Lloyd was successful at work and had long-standing close relationships. She was articulate, intelligent, psychologically minded, and motivated by her concern for her child's development).

One of the major accomplishments of her 3-year analysis has been the ability to recognize the aims and objects of her affective storms and to appreciate her own involvement in creating these crises. Her self-esteem and sense of autonomy have developed; her interpersonal relationships have matured. Histrionic traits are still evident in her flair for the dramatic, her moodiness, and her exhibitionistic life-style. These are no longer maladaptive but could best be described as interesting, adding to her attractiveness.

Narcissistic Personality

A blow to the person's self-esteem motivates this individual to seek help: a denial of a promotion, the rejection by a friend, a failure to obtain anticipated support or rewards. The patient may express considerable rage and hurt during the initial interview. The affective discharge is not as labile as the histrionic's presentation, nor is it conveyed in as dramatic a manner. The history may be fairly well-organized and specifically related to the chief complaint, while lacking in the detail and chronological cohesiveness typical of the compulsive. The patient is sensitive to any perceived criticism and will overreact with defensive anger to questions or comments which are misinterpreted as attacks, or he may withdraw. Empathic remarks may be consciously ignored, or pass unrecognized by the patient. Once the person has recouped his self-esteem, he appears as unperturbed, superficially self-confident, and self-righteous.

These patients use primitive defenses which affect their reality testing. Projection, introjection, and denial frequently can be present. These patients may be highly successful professionally but the quality of their interpersonal relationships is seriously impaired. Involvement with others is sought but more to bolster the patient's self-esteem, to gratify some personal fantasy, to reflect the patient's grandiosity. When the other person does not provide that gratification or fulfill the private fantasy, the relationship is terminated—often with much anger and depreciation expressed towards the disappointing person. In general, people are insignificant; they are experienced more as bothersome intrusions than as enjoyable contacts.

In the beginning of the therapeutic relationship, the patient wants the therapist to be the perfect object that has been sought for so long. Finally, someone will give the nurturance, will make up for past humiliations, will help the patient achieve his potentials. When these expectations are not met, the therapist is attacked, degraded, scorned.

Any behavior from the therapist, including deprivation of the expected love and esteem, is interpreted on a very personal level. For example, if the therapist cancels an appointment, one may see a very angry and humiliated patient the next hour who is convinced that the cancellation had to be due to the therapist's boredom with the patient. Failures to fulfill fantasies are perceived as a purposeful rejection, not as a realistic limitation.

Countertransference feelings can be quite intense with this type of patient. An insecure therapist may want to prematurely interpret or end the patient's grandiose expectations because of his own fear of being a disappointment. The temptation to defend oneself against the often skillful depreciation exists. At some point in the therapy, the therapist may feel insignificant to and emotionally detached from the patient. This may seem puzzling because of the personal material and affective discharge so readily revealed to the therapist. This countertransference feeling of estrangement in part reflects the type of relationships formed by narcissistic individuals—ones which are highly personalized, yet in which the "significant other" can be easily replaced by the next available person.

Therapy can be approached in two ways. The narcissistic personality suffers very greatly during the acute loss of self-esteem. In his overall functioning, he sacrifices joy and companionship in his search for retribution. A short-term approach provides support through the period of immediate assault. Long-term insight-oriented therapy provides a chance to reduce the patient's narcissistic vulnerability and increase his sense of self and self-esteem. The patient's motivation and willingness to continue in a therapeutic relationship are two of the determining factors. With the more ill patients, a long-term supportive approach is in order—the therapist can offset narcissistic injuries and provide an objective perspective on the patient's interpersonal difficulties.

> Mr. James, a 35-year-old college teacher, began therapy following a professional slight. A colleague of his—a man about 10 years older—had asked another person in the same department to help him with a research project, thereby bypassing Mr. James. The patient felt that this perceived rejection by his friend would prevent him from attaining the enormous success potentially possible. Furthermore, with this confrontation of not being special to the colleague, Mr. James believed that he was humiliated and alone in the world. His narcissistic rage was so great and expressed so inappropriately (caustic comments spilling out, withdrawal from activities, etc.) that other faculty members suggested he seek help.
>
> A large part of the beginning of therapy was spent in berating this older colleague: "His research is very ordinary, he must be mentally ill, he is a despicable person who achieves success by unscrupulous means, he is uncultured, unfeeling." Finally, after many stormy sessions, the therapist was able to refocus the center of attention away from this colleague's supposed problems and onto Mr. James' life. Time was spent examining what he wanted to do with his own life. Support was given while early developmental and dynamic interpretations were slowly made.
>
> The patient was in therapy 3 years. He achieved a greater intellectual understanding of his difficulties and he was able to structure his life to minimize conflict. His depression was significantly reduced. However, his narcissistic vulnerability persisted. One day during a difficult period in therapy when a lot of anger was felt towards the therapist, the patient decided to terminate. He attended the two sessions following his announcement and left. Follow-up

information on him suggests that he has continued his successful career but remains isolated and lonely, and is considered to be somewhat peculiar socially.

Dependent Personality

A situation which threatens the patient's dependent position in a relationship or institution commonly causes the distress that motivates referral. The threat may be self-initiated, as well as imposed by external circumstances; for example, a wife decides that separation from her husband is most appropriate but becomes symptomatic with the possibility of being on her own. When first seen, the patient commonly will wait for the therapist to initiate the conversation. After an opening statement from the therapist, the patient will present an adequate description of the current situation, and then retreat to silence again. Predictable comments from the patient are, "It would help if you'd ask me some questions so I know what's important to talk about," or "I don't know what to say. I've never seen a psychiatrist before." The therapist makes some encouraging remarks or asks some questions and the cycle begins again.

Histrionic and compulsive defenses are used (repression, denial, regression, isolation of affect, reaction formation); or one may see a mixture of traits common to the schizoid or similar personality types that are typified by a shyness, insecurity in social situations, and a lack of ability to function comfortably yet independently in close relationships.

The therapist becomes another person to rely on for guidance and support. It is not the qualitative presence of these expectations but rather the intensity with which they are sought that makes them problematic. One senses that the patient is behaviorally paralyzed unless someone is pushing her into action. Hours may pass slowly because of the lack of spontaneity, of vivaciousness, in these individuals.

These patients can be very gratifying for some therapists. They are compliant and may respond with much appreciation to short-term support. The therapist may be tempted to infantilize the patient by being unnecessarily active and directive in response to the patient's passivity. Irritation at the patient's passivity by a therapist with low tolerance for the clinging is another common countertransference response.

These patients are not usually good candidates for long-term insight-oriented therapy. The secondary gratification obtained by them can be considerable. Open-ended therapy becomes another support for maintaining the status quo rather than changing it. If the patient does not feel gratified enough in a more insight-oriented treatment (wherein the therapist is less active) she may end treatment by drifting away, e.g., by not showing up for several sessions, rather than assertively deciding to stop. Crisis intervention and short-term supportive therapy are more often in order. Sometimes though, the presenting situation is such that a combination of approaches is necessary.

> Mrs. Richard, a 42-year-old housewife, entered treatment after making a decision to leave her husband. His alcoholism had become so destructive to family life that she felt she had little choice. However, she began dating another man who she described as much like her husband.
> The therapist felt that a supportive approach was necessary to assist her in coming to some resolution about her marriage. In addition, because of clear evidence that the patient was rapidly getting herself into a very similar situation, some explorative work was also in order.
> For months on end, Mrs. Richard would describe her unhappiness and her concern for the childrens' well-being, yet take no steps to initiate change. It was only with a combination of encouragement and confrontation from the therapist that she finally initiated separation procedures. Therapy continued for another year with two goals: to help her make the transition in her marital status, and to better her understanding of the type of relationships she formed.

Borderline Personality

These patients enter treatment in a crisis and remain on and off in a crisis situation throughout much of treatment. Their histories reveal marginal functioning. Often, the financial support of family keeps these people out of legal or other difficulties, as well as pushes them into private psychiatric treatment. The crises are less narrowly the interpersonal disappointments and threats experienced by the narcissistic or histrionic. They are more often personally threatening—a brush with the law, an overdose of drugs. One does not hear a thought process disturbance on initial evaluation but the story is confusing and dramatic in that immediate action seems required. The patient's history not uncommonly reveals a precarious existence, an impaired ability at self-preservation.

These patients most closely resemble the histrionic and the narcissistic personalities. Their defenses can be quite primitive and massive—to the degree that reality testing is significantly impaired. Yet one does not see the delusions, hallucinations, or total loss of contact with the outside world that is seen in psychotics. Sometimes one is amazed at the borderline's ability to continue functioning despite severe setbacks.

Therapy in private is typically long-term and is a combination of supportive and insight-oriented. In clinic situations, the approach is more crisis intervention. Great flexibility is needed in treating these patients—scheduling of hours may vary from week to week, intervention with the patient's social and work worlds may be required, and ancillary modes of treatment can be very helpful.

> Mr. Lee, a 20-year-old unemployed college dropout, gave a history of polydrug abuse, compulsive homosexual escapades, and most recently entangle-

ment with the law over a forged prescription. Over the course of treatment, he was seen in a methadone clinic and participated in group therapy, as well as continued in individual treatment.

During homosexual panics and when his legal problems were at their most stressful point, visits were scheduled sometimes as frequently as 4 to 5 times a week. Otherwise, regular appointments were weekly.

Therapy with Personality Disorders

Therapy can be artificially divided into two types: supportive-suppressive and uncovering-expressive. Goals of the former are: (a) to reduce emotional turmoil during a present-day stress situation, (b) to establish a more realistic objective perspective of oneself and the environment, and (c) to resolve or suppress symptomatic distress. Goals of uncovering therapy are: to increase the ego's ability to handle repressed unconscious conflict situations in order to effect new solutions to old unresolved, or symptomatically and characterologically resolved, conflicts, and to effect far-reaching structural changes in the mental apparatus. Suppressive therapy gratifies dependency needs, supports defenses when necessary, manipulates the patient's environment, and directs the patient towards appropriate action in coping with the current environment. Expressive therapy deprives the patient of advice and gratification and works towards examining and loosening the defensive organization in order to clarify and interpret the unconscious conflicts.

In treating personality disorders, the choice of therapy depends in part on patient factors such as the patient's ability to regress and recover from the regression upon the conclusion of the hour, the patient's tolerance for frustration, the primitiveness or maturity of his defenses, his self-image, reality testing, intelligence, and motivation.

The way the problem is identified, a reflection of both the therapist's orientation and the presenting circumstances, is another factor. Does the therapist consider the problem to be a family in distress and thus recommend family therapy? Is the problem considered instead an individual crisis? Or does the therapist view the difficulty as a manifestation of a characteristic maladaptive response to persistent unconscious conflict?

In short-term therapy, the ego-syntonic personality traits are not really examined to any degree. In insight-oriented therapy, the traits are examined to such an extent that they no longer serve as effectively in providing protection from conflict. The traits become ego-dystonic; the patient appears more distressed for a period of time while conflicts are being uncovered. In all therapy, preservation of the patient's self-esteem is important.

In conclusion, one must consider the need for flexibility. What can clinically appear as a rather stable and mature individual for whom analysis is recommended may turn out to be a much more ill person. The therapist has to be open to changing treatment approaches and goals, and to introducing adjunct therapies.

27

PSYCHOPHARMACOTHERAPY IN THE PERSONALITY DISORDERS OF ADOLESCENCE AND ADULTHOOD

Lino Covi, M.D.

Introduction

Rational pharmacological treatment is an ideal which can be achieved only in proportion to the degree of specificity of the available drugs and to the level of accuracy in diagnostic classifications. In the area of the pharmacological treatment of Personality Disorders, the availability of specific drugs and of accurate diagnoses is far from being a present reality. This situation is in part a reflection of the stage of development of the young science of psychopharmacology which is still struggling to define mechanism of action, and spectrum of effectiveness of the psychotropic drugs. The notorious difficulty in obtaining interrater reliability in the diagnosis of Personality Disorders further illustrates the limitations of our present knowledge.

The third edition of the Diagnostic and Statistical Manual of Mental Disorders of the American Psychiatric Association (DSM III) represents an almost unprecedented effort in magnitude and thoroughness in the difficult endeavor of achieving a scientific nosology. Past diagnostic classifications of Personality Disorders have been very unsatisfactory (48); the new DSM III classification is a step forward of great promise.

The social implications of a pharmacological treatment of Personality Disorders have attracted wide attention in the United States. Call for the discovery of new "pharmacological miracles" in the control of antisocial behavior have been heard from the journalistic, the political, and even the academic professions. In fact, Talcott Parsons (46) saw the efforts of defining socially deviant behavior as psychiatric conditions as a manifestation of the tendency of society to increase its stability by making such deviant behavior as psychiatric conditions as a manifestation of the tendency of society to increase its stability by making such deviant behavior less dangerous through the simple device of calling it "disease." Furthermore, types of deviancies for which the promise can be held out of a pharmacological "cure" are likely to be accepted by society as less stigmatizing than those for which such promise is clearly elusive.

In fact, the achievement of pharmacological "miracles" in Personality Disorders is even less probable than in other psychiatric disorders, such as the Clinical Syndromes; furthermore, a doubt can be legitimately entertained that such a goal should be pursued at all. Powerful pharmacological tools capable of deeply influencing Personality Disorders can be dangerously abused by governments or private parties, resulting in violation of basic individual liberties. The realization of such inherent dangers probably has been the main force which has fueled the pervasive resistance that has developed in the last 10 years to research in this field. Unfortunately, some of the most promising directions for psychopharmacological research in the area of Personality Disorders are actually to be found in the study of the Antisocial Personality, so common among prisoners (13). Such studies have been made all but impossible by a body of legal and administrative doctrines, and present research has to be largely limited to noninstitutionalized subjects who tend to deviate from research protocol more often than individuals with a less defective sense of personal responsibility or better external controls.

The development of psychopharmacology has historically proceeded from the initial discoveries of drugs effective in major psychosis to later contributions to the treatment of known psychotic disorders, and to further development of predictors of effectiveness. Since a similar pattern can reasonably be expected in the development of the pharmacotherapy of Personality Disorders, the more clean-cut disorders should be the most promising area. The Antisocial Personality Disorder seems such an area, but this avenue of progress is almost closed now due to the development of the legal and administrative obstacles already mentioned.

General Conceptual and Clinical Guidelines

As a result of the above-discussed dilemmas, the psychiatric clinician is left with little or no guidance for his use of drugs in Personality Disorders.

While future research may supply more scientifically based guidelines, at the present time some useful principles can still be developed on the basis of clinical experience, as well as of past research conducted with previous diagnostic systems.

Three possible approaches are proposed as helpful in guiding the clinician:

1. A pharmacological approach to emerging psychiatric symptoms in Personality Disorders. In terms of DSM III, this approach consists in treating Axis I Clinical Disorders with careful consideration for the difference in response to drugs in individuals with such combinations of diagnoses. For example, drug treatment of an Anxiety Disorder in an individual presenting also an

Antisocial Personality Disorder would have to allow for special consideration of the higher probability of abuse of a benzodiazepine in such an individual.
2. A pharmacological approach geared to a "profile" of the characteristics of the individual patient classified as a Personality Disorder. In using this approach, a person classified as schizotypal may present an individual profile where ideas of reference or depersonalization dominate the picture, while in a second individual, isolation or aloofness is more predominant. In the first case, an antipsychotic agent may be tried more comfortably, while in the latter case, an antidepressant may have a higher probability of success.
3. A pharmacological approach predicated on a hypothetical "core anomaly" (49) which may imply a continuity in psychopathology between a given Personality Disorder and some Clinical Syndrome. For instance, a Schizotypal Personality Disorder may be assumed to have continuity with Schizophrenia, therefore supplying a rationale for use of antipsychotic agents. If this approach should obtain a higher success rate than other approaches, a possible interesting interpretation of that outcome may be that Personality Disorders are, in fact, chronic mild equivalents of Clinical Syndromes ("formes frustes").

Specific Guidelines

Specific applications of the above-proposed general guidelines are going to be made difficult by the dilemmas inherent in the necessity of translating reports using very different nosological nomenclatures into a DSM III framework. Such translation will be attempted in this section. In order to facilitate this task, the two Personality Disorders described in the DSM III will be grouped into four clusters suggested by the DSM III Manual.

First Cluster: Paranoid, Schizoid, and Schizotypal Personality Disorders

DSM III describes individuals with these disorders as often appearing odd or eccentric. Paranoid and schizotypal individuals presenting an Axis I Clinical Syndrome for which an established pharmacotherapeutic approach is available may be quite reluctant to take the prescribed drugs. These individuals present characteristics of "pervasive, unwarranted suspiciousness and mistrust of people, and expectation of trickery or harm" (18). A struggle to persuade or force them to take prescribed medications may be futile since these individuals may resort to subterfuge such as "cheeking" the pills or capsules.

An important different between paranoid and nonparanoid patients is in their response to phenothiazines. Hollister et al. (27) have shown that schizophrenics classified as paranoid types respond less well than schizophrenics classified as nonparanoid types.

While the report by Klein et al. (34) on the effectiveness of imipramine in "pseudo-neurotic schizophrenics" may indicate that schizotypal and schizoid individuals with depression may respond quite well to tricyclics, Glassman et al. (22) found a lack of response to tricyclic drug therapy in delusional and paranoid patients. These findings point to the probability of a lack of response in Affective Disorders emerging in Paranoid Personalities, as opposed to a possible positive response in Schizotypal and Schizoid Personalities presenting an Affective Disorder. However, individuals with these three types of Personality Disorders, when treated with the most activating antidepressants, such as protriptyline or MAO inhibitors, could, in some cases, present a hyperalert type of reaction similar to that found in amphetamine psychoses (58).

If the present questions of renal toxicity of lithium should be resolved favorably, a good case could be made for the combination of lithium and antipsychotics, or lithium and antidepressants, in view of the experience with patients having many features in common with "population of this type— individuals presenting combination of depression and first cluster type of personality disorders (50). At the present time, however, extreme caution should be exerted because of the evidence of renal damage from lithium in some individuals (3).

The pharmacological treatment of acute symptoms of anxiety in these three Personality Disorders requires careful attention to the phenomenology of such anxiety. If agoraphobic or panic features are present, definite indications for the use of imipramine are present (62). If somatic type of anxiety and tension are present, propanolol could be tried (24). The use of benzodiazepines requires careful monitoring for the development of possible habituation, and their use should be limited to 16 weeks or less (15).

Personality Disorders with pronounced paranoid features manifested as paranoid jealousy have been reported to be responsive to treatment with phenothiazines (44). Detailed descriptions of course of treatment in individual cases of Paranoid Personality Disorders (31) have reported some success with chlorpromazine treatment.

Second Cluster: Histrionic, Narcissistic, Borderline, and Antisocial Personality Disorders

DSM III describes individuals with these disorders as often appearing dramatic, emotional, or erratic.

Histrionic Personality Disorder is the new term for the time honored "Hysterical Personality" (57). These individuals seem to react to precipitants more often with depression than with other neurotic or psychotic symptoms (1). In fact, the combination of depression and "hysteria" is so common that Klein and Davis (33) have described an entity called "Hysteroid Dysphoria": these subjects, almost always women, are reported to react with sudden short-lived depressive symptoms to rejection ("rejection-sensitive dysphoria"). In DSM III terms, these women may be diagnosed as presenting as Affective Disorder and a Histrionic Personality. In a detailed description of a case of "Hysteroid Dysphoria," Klein (31) reports on the failure of a variety of psychotherapeutic and somatic treatments followed by a remarkable and durable response to phenelzine. The same author summarized more recently (32) the response of "Hysteroid Dysphoria" to drugs. He reports the following. a) imipramine often has a negative effect in these patients because of reacting thoughts, somatic distress, feelings of depersonalization, or hypomanic states. b) MAO inhibitors can remarkably reduce vulnerability to dysphoria due to rejection. Phenelzine, 45 to 90 mg daily, is suggested; higher dosages may precipitate insomnia or hypomania. Prolonged treatment and observation of dietary restriction of tyramine containing foodstuff is recommended. c) Nonsedative neuroleptics can be of some use in combination with MAO inhibitors while sedative neuroleptics are poorly tolerated by hysteroid dysphoria. d) Alcohol decreases anticipatory anxiety and bolsters the courage of these patients. Apart from Klein's last observation, it should be noted that barbiturates and benzodiazepines, and diazepam in particular, often have very similar effects to alcohol and may also present similar dangers of abuse and habituation in Histrionic Personality Disorders.

Histrionic Personality Disorders may also be present in individuals presenting schizophrenic symptoms. This type of combination has been described by Klein (32) as a "histeroschizophrenia." He reports that these patients are refractory or respond negatively to psychotropic medication and tend to abuse stimulants and sedatives.

Narcisssistic and Borderline Personality Disorders have much in common and are probably identifiable with the "emotionally unstable personalities" (33). While distinguishable from Cyclothymic Disorders, Narcissistic and Borderline Personality Disorders are often associated with depressive and hypomanic symptoms. Klein et al. (34) have reported good response to both imipramine and chlorpromazine in a sample of patients with "emotionally unstable character disorders." Klein (31) has published two detailed case reports of the treatment course of emotionally unstable character disorders where a combination of imipramine and chlorpromazine was quite successful. Rifkin et al. (52) have studied 21 patients with "emotionally unstable character disorder" and reported excellent results with lithium. In papers more clearly framed in terms of "borderline" diagnosis (7, 32, 42), the higher potency neuroleptics, like the nonaliphatic phenothiazines trifluoperazine and fluphenazine, or the butyrophenone haloperidol, are reported more effective than chlorpromazine. The effects of antidepressants are reported to be diverse and unpredictable, while lithium is said to decrease self-destructive and assaultive behavior (32).

Paykel et al. (47) have reported that women presenting depression and a personality disorder improved less on amitriptyline than women who were psychotically depressed, or depressed and hostile, or depressed and anxious. They describe such "personality disorders" as characterized by higher incidence of disturbed life patterns and social relations, which may be compatible with diagnoses of Histrionic, Narcissistic, or Borderline Personality Disorders. We can, therefore, reasonably expect a somewhat weaker antidepressant response to amitriptyline in these three Personality Disorders, as opposed to that of similarly depressed patients without a Personality Disorder.

The Antisocial Personality Disorder can be considered the prototype of all the Personality Disorders and is the easiest to define. In fact, DSM III has retained the traditional concept of this disorder while further describing the criteria. Further improvement has been achieved by DSM III in the validity of this diagnosis by clarifying the Intermittent Explosive Disorders, an Axis I diagnosis. While absence of generalized impulsiveness or aggressiveness between episodes is necessary for the diagnosis of Intermittent Explosive Disorder, outbursts of aggressiveness and impulsivity are described as common in Antisocial Personality Disorders; a pattern of continuous antisocial behavior is also needed for the diagnosis of Antisocial Personality Disorder.

Most of the literature discussing the pharmacotherapy of aggression is based on the study of Intermittent Explosive Disorders or of aggression in psychotics or epileptics. However, Lion (39) states that "most of the violent patients seen in clinical and forensic settings are patients with severe character disturbances of the explosive antisocial or passive-aggressive types."

Overt depression is probably far from rare in Antisocial Personality Disorder. Interestingly, until recent reports on the effect of lithium and carbamazine, the effect of the antidepressants in Personality Disorder has been paid little or no attention. This lag may indicate that Antisocial Personalities presenting symptoms of depression and eventually treated with antidepressants are usually not seen by clinicians as Antisocial Personalities. Cormier (12) has indicated that "an inability to be depressed is a major feature in persistent criminal offenders." In spite of pilot data (17) giving a promising lead in the direction of confirming Cormier's hypothesis, no systematic studies have been done on this phenomenon.

The beneficial effects of stimulants on aggression, however, have been widely reported (2, 56), and as early as 1944, Korey (36) completed a controlled study of the effects of amphetamines in severe delinquents, reporting improvement in subjective feelings and behavior in half of the boys treated with amphetamines. Eisenberg et al. (20) conducted a controlled study of dextroamphetamine and placebo and no treatment in 42 black delinquent boys between the ages of 11 and 17, residing in a juvenile correctional institution. Statistically significant differences were reported in favor of amphetamines in improving destructive behavior. Several uncontrolled studies (26, 55) report the use of stimulants in adult Personality

Disorders, and Wood et al. (61) published a double-blind study with 11 adults with histories of hyperactivity in childhood and presented diagnosis of either Antisocial Personality Disorder or Generalized Anxiety Disorder. The outcome measures favored methylphenidate over placebo.

Several published case reports of patients whose violent behavior was controlled by lithium were reviewed by Shader et al. (53).

Three controlled studies have been reported of lithium in antisocial individuals. Sheard (54) conducted a single-blind comparison of lithium with placebo in 12 prisoners, selected for aggressive behavior, and showed a decrease in aggressive effect as well as decreased aggressive behavior in favor of lithium. He and his coworkers later conducted a double-blind study (55) in a correctional institution with young delinquents with severe personality disorders who had a mean age of 19 years. Sixty-six subjects completed the study. The decrease in the number of infractions was significantly greater in the lithium group.

Tupin et al. (6) selected and treated a group of prisoners with diagnoses of explosive personality or of "possible schizophrenia" who had been previously treated unsuccessful with phenothiazines and assigned them to lithium. Fifty percent of the subjects showed a substantial decrease in aggressive behavior.

Ballenger and Post (4) reviewed the evidence for the therapeutic effect of carbamazepine, an anticonvulsant with antidepressant effects, and listed several uncontrolled and controlled studies reporting favorable response to carbamazepine in patients with behavioral problems and nonspecific EEG abnormalities. This type of subject showed improvement in: the reduction of aggressiveness; emotional instability; agitation; restlessness; irritability; depression; hyper- and hypoactivity, and difficulties in social adaptation. Tunks and Dermer (59) recommended using blood level measurements to decrease the risks of side effects.

The concept that the Antisocial Personality would be in some way related to epilepsy goes back to the 1870 writings of Cesare Lombroso (41). In recent years, and before carbamazepine, several anticonvulsives have been tried with varied success on this type of individual. Conners et al. (10) compared the effect of diphenylhydantoin (DPH) with methylphenidate and placebo but found no differences. Gottschalk et al. (25) compared the effect of 300 mg of DPH with that of 24 mg a day in 44 antisocial inmates of a mental institution. The Gottschalk-Glazer Content Analysis Method did not reveal a difference between the two groups. Lefkowitz (38) studied 50 boys in a controlled study of DPH and placebo, but no difference between the two groups was revealed. Some borderline indications of superiority of DPH over placebo in decreasing disciplinary infractions were reported by Covi et al. (14) in the same population reported by Gottschalk et al (25). Boelhouwer et al. (5) found that adolescents and young adults who showed antisocial and uncontrollable impulsive behavior, and who had 14 and 15 per second positive spiking on the EEG, benefited more from a combination of DPH and thioridazine than from either of the two drugs alone. Matching subjects who did not have such an EEG problem benefited from DPH alone. Monroe et al. (43) reported benefits from primidone in antisocial prisoners. Itil et al. (28) treated 25 adolescents with aggressive and explosive traits with either a combination of diphenylhydantoin and thioridazine (15 subjects) or with no treatment. Improvement in the EEG correlated with improved behavior, and a decrease in symptomology was reported.

Antisocial individuals are traditionally considered to be "anxiety free" (9); however, anxiety symptoms are very common in antisocial personality disorders. While Gleser et al. (23) reported significant decrease in hysteria and anxiety in a double-blind study with delinquent boys in a single dose of 20 mg. chlordiazepoxide, and Rickels and Downing (51), in a controlled study with benzodiazepines, have shown a decrease in hostility in neurotics: the repeated findings (16, 21) of increased hostility in patients treated with benzodiazepines have to be kept in mind. DiMascio et al. (19) hypothesized that only those patients with a history of lack of impulsive control would show the rage reaction to chlordiazepoxide, which has been reported in the literature. Obviously, Antisocial Personality Disorders should be watched very carefully for abuse and habituation to benzodiazepines. Propanolol (24) should be considered in treating anxiety in this type of Personality Disorder.

Itil and Wadud (29) point out that the only major tranquilizer recommended for use in aggression associated with anxiety disorder is pericyazine, a neuroleptic not licensed in the U. S. Among the available neuroleptics, fluphenazine has been reported to be effective in the treatment of dangerous and aggressive criminals.

The role of androgens in male sexual and nonsexual aggression has been studied for some years (8). A number of antiandrogens has been tried with positive results both in the U.S. and Europe (11).

Third Cluster: Avoidant, Dependent, Compulsive, and Passive-Aggressive Personality Disorders

DSM III describes these individuals as anxious or fearful. These four types of Personality Disorders are frequently associated with Affective Disorders, particular the unipolar recurrent type. Kupfer et al. (37) have reported that 34 depressed patients who had been successfully treated with tricyclic antidepressants showed a much larger prevalence of traits of chronic anxiety and obsessiveness than the group of nonresponders to tricyclic antidepressants.

This group of Personality Disorders also frequently presents phobias.

Klein et al. (35), in a review of antidepressant effects on anxiety, panic, and phobia, concluded that imipramine improved phobic anxiety reaction while chlorpromazine made it worse. MAO inhibitors have been reported by Kelly et al. (30) as effective in phobia; Lipsedge et al. (40) and Mountjoy and Roth (45) conducted controlled studies indicating effectiveness of MAO inhibitors. Zitrin et al. (62) recently reported a study of 75 agoraphobic women where imipramine was significantly superior to placebo therapy in agoraphobia.

The Passive Aggressive Personality Disorders have been reported by Klein et al. (34) to be nonresponsive to either imipramine or chlorpromazine. In his presentation of two case histories of this disorder, Klein (31) stresses the difficulties in treating these individuals; he points out that the utility of drugs in these patients depends entirely upon the manifestation of affective disorders.

This group of Personality Disorders are also obvious candidates for treatment with benzodiazepines. Their response to these drugs cannot be doubted, but it should be borne in mind that after several weeks (15) benzodiazepines tend to lose their effectiveness.

Fourth Cluster: Atypical, Mixed, or Other Personality Disorders

This fourth category is provided as a safety valve for both the clinician and the diagnostic system. The implications of an overuse of this category are clear. If the clinican would find himself with the need of treating a patient classified under this diagnosis, the most sensible approach would be that of a target symptom approach similar to that described in the general outline as hinging on the possibility of identifying a symptom profile for the individual patient.

Conclusion

The clinician, as well as the researcher, should not lose sight of the fact that Personality Disorders are largely defined by an interaction of the individual with society and its values; deviancy is defined according to constantly changing customs and values. While social deviance has existed throughout the ages and across cultures, one should not forget the danger of mistaking visionary pioneering views and behavior for psychopathology. While holding on to this awareness is just as important for the psychotherapist as for the pharmacotherapist, forced or precipitous use of drugs in social deviants would be even more dangerous and would potentially violate the individual's rights and could damage society as a whole.

REFERENCES

1. Alarcon, R., and Covi, L. Hysterical personality and depression. A pathogenetic view. Comp. Psychiatry, 14:121–132, 1973.
2. Allen, R. P. Safer, D., and Covi, L. Effects of psychostimulants on aggression. J. Nerv. Ment. Dis., 160:138–145, 1975.
3. Ayd, F. Lithium and the kidney. Int. Drug Ther. Newsletter, 14:25–28, 1979.
4. Ballenger, J. C., and Post, R. M. Carbamazepine in manic-depressive illness a new treatment. Am. J. Psychiatry, *137:* 782–790, 1980.
5. Boelhouwer, C., Henry, C. E., and Glueck, B. C. Positive spiking. A double-blind control study on its significance in behavior disorders both diagnostically and therapeutically. Am. J. Psychiatry, 125:65–73, 1968.
6. Brinkley, J. R. Haloperidol and other neuroleptics in the treatment of the borderline patient. In: *Haloperidol Update, 1958–1980*, F. J. Ayd (Ed.). Ayd Medical Communications, Baltimore, 1980.
7. Brinkley, J. R., Beitman, B. D., and Friedel, R. D. Low-dose neuroleptic regimens in the treatment of borderline patients. Arch. Gen. Psychiatry, 36:319–326, 1979.
8. Blumer, D., and Migeon, C. Hormone and hormonal agents in the treatment of aggression. J. Nerv. Ment. Dis., 160:127–137, 1975.
9. Cleckly, H.*The Mask of Sanity*. C. V. Mosby Co., St. Louis, 1950.
10. Conners, C. K., Kramer, R., Rothschild, G. H., Schwartz, L., and Stone, A. A treatment of young delinquent boys with diphenylhydantoin sodium and methylphenidate. Arch. Gen. Psychiatry, 24:156–160, 1971.
11. Cooper, A. J., Ismail, A. A., Phanjoo, A. L. and Love, D. L. Antiandrogen (cytoproterone acetate) therapy in deviant hypersexuality. Br. J. Psychiatry, 120:59–63, 1972.
12. Cormier, B. M. Depression and persistent criminality. Can. Psychiatr. Assoc. J., 11:S208–S220, 1966.
13. Covi, L. Problems of clinical psychopharmacology researcy in aggression. Presented at the 120th Annual Meeting of the American Psychiatric Association, Miami, May 11, 1976.
14. Covi, L., Derogatis, L. R., Uhlenhuth, E. H., and Kendel, A. Effects of diphenylhydantoin in violent prisoners. Presented at the 7th Congress of the Collegium Internationale Neuro-Psychopharmacologicum, Prague, August 1970.
15. Covi, L., Lipman, R. S., Pattison, J. H., Derogatis, L. R., and Uhlenhuth, E. H. Length of treatment with anxiolytic-sedatives and response to their sudden withdrawal. Acta Psychiatr. Scand., 49:51–64, 1973.
16. Covi, L., Lipman, R. S., and Smith, V. K. Diazepam induced hostility in depression. Presented at the 130th Annual Meeting of the American Psychiatric Association, Toronto, Canada, May 4, 1977.
17. Covi, L., and Uhlenhuth, E. H. Methodological problems in the pharmacological study of the dangerous antisocial personality. In: *Aggressive Behavior, Proceedings of the Symposium on the Biology of Aggressive Behavior*, Milan, May 1968. Excerpta Medica, Amsterdam, 1969.
18. Diagnostic and Statistical Manual of Mental Disorders (DSM III), Ed. 3. American Psychiatric Association, Washington, D.C., 1980.
19. Di Mascio, A., Shader, R. I., and Harmatz, J. Psychotropic drugs and induced hostility. Psychosomatics, 10:46–47, 1969.
20. Eisenberg, L., Lachman, R., Molling, P. A., Lockner, H., Mizelle, J. D., and Conners, C. K. Psychopharmacologic experiment in a training school for delinquent boys. Methods, problems, findings. Am. J. Orthopsychiatry, 33:431–447, 1963.
21. Gardos, G., DiMascio, A., Salzman, C., and Shader, R. I. Differential actions of chlordiazepoxide and oxazepam on hositility. Arch. Gen. Psychiatry, 18:757–760, 1968.
22. Glassman, A. H., Kantor, S. J., and Shostak, M. Depression delusion, and drug response. Am. J. Psychiatry, 132:716–719, 1975.
23. Gleser, G. C., Gottschalk, L. A., Fox, R., and Lippert, W. Immediate changes in affect with chlordiazepoxide. Arch. Gen. Psychiatry, 13:291–295, 1965.
24. Greenblatt, D. J., and Shader, R. I. Pharmacotherapy of anxiety with benzodiazepines and beta-adrenergic blockers. In: *Psychopharmacology: A Generation of Progress*, M. A. Lipton, A. DiMascio, and K. F. Killam (Eds.). Raven Press, New York, 1978.

25. Gottschalk, L. A., Covi, L. Uliana, R., and Bates, D. E. Effects of diphenylhydantoin on anxiety and hostility in institutionalized prisoners. Comp. Psychiatry, 14:503–511, 1973.
26. Hill, D. Amphetamines in psychopathic states. Br. J. Addiction, 44:50, 1947.
27. Hollister, L. E., Overall, J. E., Kimball, I., and Pokorny, A. Specific indications for different classes of phenothiazines. Arch. Gen. Psychiatry, 30:94–99, 1974.
28. Itil, T. M., Rizzo, A. E., and Shapiro, D. M. Study of behavior and EEG correlation during treatment of disturbed children. Dis. Nerv. Syst., 28:731–736, 1967.
29. Itil, T. M., and Wadud, A. Treatment of human aggression with major tranquilizers, antidepressants, and newer psychotropic drugs. J. Nerv. Ment. Dis., 160:83–99, 1975.
30. Kelly, D., Guirguis, W., Frommer, E., Mitchell-Heggs, N., and Sargent, W. Treatment of phobic states with antidepressants. A retrospective study of 246 patients. Br. J. Psychiatry, 116:387–398, 1970.
31. Klein, D. F. *Psychiatric Case Studies: Treatment, Drugs and Outcome.* Williams & Wilkins Co., Baltimore, 1972.
32. Klein, D. F. Psychopharmacological treatment and delineation of borderline disorders. In: *Borderline Personality Disorders. The Concept, the Syndrome, the Patient,* P. Horticollis (Ed.). International Universities Press, New York, 1977.
33. Klein, D. F., and Davis, J. M. *Diagnosis and Drug Treatment of Psychiatric Disorders.* Williams & Wilkins Co., Baltimore, 1969.
34. Klein, D. F., Honigfeld, G., and Feldman, S. Prediction of drug effect in personality disorders. J. Nerv. Ment. Dis., 156:183–198, 1973.
35. Klein, D. F., Zitrin, C. M., and Woerner, M. *Antidepressants, Anxiety, Panic and Phobia in Psychopharmacology. A Generation of Progress,* M. A. Lipton, A. DiMascio, and K. F. Killam (Eds.), Raven Press, New York, 1978.
36. Korey, S. R. The effect of benzedrine sulphate in the behavior of psychopathic and neurotic juvenile delinquents. Psychiatr. Q., 18:127–137, 1944.
37. Kupfer, D. J., Pickar, D., Himmelbach, J. M., and Detre, T. P. Are there two types of unipolar depression? Arch. Gen. Psychiatry, 32:866–871, 1975.
38. Lefkowitz, M. M. Effects of diphenylhydantoin in disruptive behavior: A study of male delinquents. Arch. Gen. Psychiatry, 20:643–651, 1969.
39. Lion, J. R. Conceptual issues in the use of drugs for the treatment of aggression in man. J. Nerv. Ment. Dis., 160:76–82, 1975.
40. Lipsedge, J. S., Hajjoff, J., Huggins, P., Napier, L., Pearce, J., Pike, D. J., and Rich, M. The management of severe agoraphobia: A comparison of iproniazid and systematic desensitization. Psychopharmacologia, 32:67–80, 1973.
41. Lombroso, C. *L'Uomo Delinquente.* Hoepli, Milano, 1876.
42. Mandell, A. J. Psychoanalysis and psychopharmacology. In: *Modern Psychoanalysis,* J. Marmor (Ed.). Basic Books, Inc., New York, 1968.
43. Monroe, R. R., Paskewitz, D. A., Balis, G. U., Lion, J. R., and Rubin, J. S. Response to anticonvulsant (primidone) medication. In: *Brain Dysfunction in Aggressive Criminals,* R. R. Monroe (Ed.). Lexington Books, Lexington, Mass., 1978.
44. Mooney H. B. Pathologic jealousy and psychochemotherapy. Br. J. Psychiatry, 111:1023–1042, 1965.
45. Mountjoy, C. O., and Roth, M. A double-blind clinical trial of phenelzine in anxiety states, reactive depression and agoraphobia. In: *Neuropsychopharmacology: Proceedings of the IX Congress of the Collegium Internationale Neuro-Psychopharmacologicum,* Paris, 7–12 July, 1974. Amsterdam, Excerpta Medica, 1975.
46. Parsons, T. Illness and the role of the physician. A sociological perspective. Am. J. Orthopsychiatry, 21:452–460, 1951.
47. Paykel, E. S., Prusoff, B. A., Klerman, G. L., Haskell, D., and DiMascio, A. Clinical response to amitriptyline among depressed women. J. Nerv. Ment. Dis., 156:149–165, 1973.
48. Penna, M. Classification of personality disorders. In: *Personality Disorders, Diagnosis and Management,* J. R. Lion (Ed.). Williams & Wilkins Co., Baltimore, 1974.
49. Pichot, P. The dimensions of behavior disorders and the actions of psychotropic drugs. In: *Proceedings of the Leeds Symposium on Behavioral Disorders,* F. A. Jenner (Ed.)May and Baker, Ltd., Danengam, Essex, England, 1965.
50. Prien, R. F., Caffey, E. M., and Klett, C. J. A comparison of lithium carbonate and

chlorpromazine in the treatment of excited schizoaffectives. Arch. Gen. Psychiatry, 27: 182–189, 1972.
51. Rickels, K., and Downing, R. W. Chlordiazepoxide and hostility in anxious outpatients. Am. J. Psychiatry, 131:442–444, 1974.
52. Rifkin, A., Quitkin, F., Carillo, C., and Klein, D. F. Lithium treatment in emotionally unstable character disorders. Arch. Gen. Psychiatry, 27:519–523, 1972.
53. Shader, R. I., Jackson, A., and Dodes, L. M. The antiaggressive effects of lithium in mania. In: *Progress in Psychiatry, Drug Treatment*, D. F. Klein and R. Gittelman-Klein (Eds.). Brunner Mazel, New York, 1975.
54. Sheard, M. H. Effects of lithium in human aggression. Nature, 230:113–114, 1971.
55. Sheard, M. H., Marini, J. L., Bridges, C. I., and Wagner, E. The effect of lithium on impulsive aggressive behavior in man. Am. J. Psychiatry, 133:1409–1413, 1976.
56. Shovron, J. J. Benzedrine in psychopathy and behavior disorders. Br. J. Addict., 44:58, 1947.
57. Spitzer, R. L., Williams, J. B. W., and Skodol, A. E. DSM III: The major achievements and an overview. Am. J. Psychiatry, 137:151–164, 1980.
58. Snyder, S. H. Amphetamine psychosis: A "model" schizophrenia mediated by catecholamines. Am. J. Psychiatry, 130:61–67, 1973.
59. Tunks, E. R., and Dermer, S. W. Carbamazine in the dyscontrol syndrome associated with lymbic system dysfunction. J. Nerv. Ment. Dis., 164:56–63, 1977.
60. Tupin, J. P., Smith, D. B., Clannon, T. L., Kim, L. I., Nugent, A., and Groupe, A. The long-term use of lithium in aggressive prisoners. Comp. Psychiatry, 13:209–214, 1972.
61 Wood, G. R., Reimherr, F. N., Wender, P. H., and Johnson, G. E. Diagnosis and treatment of minimal brain dysfunction in adults. Arch. Gen Psychiatry, 33:1453–1460, 1976.
62. Zitrin, C. M., Klein, D. F., and Woerner, M. G. Treatment of agoraphobia with group exposure in vivo and imipramine. Arch. Gen. Psychiatry, 37:63–72, 1980.

28

PERSONALITY DISORDERS IN THE MILITARY SERVICE*

Robert E. Strange, M.D.

Introduction

" ... Now there can exist no irritating juxtaposition of dissimilar personalities comparable to that which is possible aboard a great warship fully manned and at sea. There, everyday, among all ranks, almost every man comes into more or less of contact with almost every other man. Wholly there to avoid even the sight of an aggravating object one must needs give it Jonah's toss, or jump overboard himself. Imagine how all this might eventually operate on some peculiar human creature the direct reverse of a saint?" (10).

Thus, in his great novel *Billy Budd* did Herman Melville depict the tragic conflicts precipitated by personality disorders aboard a British man-of-war in 1797. He called these disorders "natural depravity," which was consistent with 18th and 19th century views on psychopathy. Today we have different terms but the same problems, as personality disorders continue to be one of the major sources of social, legal, and operational difficulties in military organizations.

In the youthful and predominantly male population of the U.S. Navy and Marine Corps, personality disorders comprise between 56% and 63% of all diagnosed psychiatric ailments (8). The new military psychiatrist who has been trained in programs emphasizing care of psychotic and psychoneurotic patients is frequently dismayed to discover that in his service practice over half of his patients have personality disorders. His past training and experience have ill prepared him for this sudden exposure to large numbers of emotionally immature, unhappy, and impulsive young men who are in conflict with the world around them, as well as with themselves. For many physicians, learning to recognize and manage personality disorders is a major educational reward of their military experience, as it adds a facet of clinical training which is not generally available elsewhere and is most valuable in their future practice.

---

* The opinions expressed herein are those of the author and cannot be construed as reflecting the views of the Navy Department or the naval service at large.

Personality disorder has a high incidence in the military service because of that segment of population which predominantly makes up defense organizations, along with the particular stresses of military life. This is a youthful group, many of which have had adjustment problems even prior to enlistment. Frequently, young men attempt to escape from disciplinary, social, scholastic, and family problems at home by enlistment. Also, correctional and judicial agencies sometimes promote military enlistment as an alternative to civilian legal action for delinquent activities. Consequently, large numbers of youths with poor adjustment histories find their way into the military. In many cases maladjustment continues and may indeed be exacerbated by military life. For others the military environment provides a developmental and rehabilitative milieu which enables them to mature and perfect new coping mechanisms. Attempting to differentiate the potentially successful from the unsuccessful among those who present personality disorders is a difficult but fascinating task for military psychiatrists.

Certain aspects of military life are predictably stressful for those with personality disorders. Military structure, social setting, roles, and activities all can make life difficult for a young man who already has adjustment problems. Adjustment to such a new, different, and sometimes threatening milieu is initially difficult for the most stable person, and for someone already crippled by immature or pathological personality development, the stresses can be intolerable. The organizational structure of the military services is marked by firm and clearly delineated authority patterns, direct assignment of responsibility, strict disciplinary standards, and comparatively rigid standards of conformity. There is isolation from previous sources of support and gratification, particularly in separation from family, along with enforced intimacy of barracks, camp, and shipboard life. In the role of soldier or sailor the young man finds active and/or passive reinforcement for the acting out of aggressive and other conflicts. At a time in late adolescence when his resolution of identity crises and other conflicts is especially important, the symbolic as well as real aspects of military roles and activities may be particularly significant for him.

These intertwined problems of adolescent and military adjustment are obviously much more difficult for those with personality disorders. A young man who enlists in the military because he cannot tolerate the authority of home, school, and community will immediately find himself confronted by another authority system even more direct and pervasive than that which he left. Others, struggling with tenuous masculine identities, problems in aggressive control, dependency, and impulse disorders, will have serious problems in the social setting and activities of the military service. These are the young men with personality disorders who will make up over half of the military psychiatrist's practice.

Military service, however, can be highly beneficial for some young men with personality disorders. For them it can be a genuinely maturing experience. Limit setting by military structure and authority, particularly in its consistency and predictability, may be very helpful to someone who has developed poor controls through inadequate and inconsistent limit setting in his family. Experienced officer and senior enlisted personnel can provide positive parental figures with whom to identify, so that military service will be a supportive and maturing experience for those who are exposed to competent leadership. The opportunity to form satisfying peer relationships and to participate in group and individual pursuit of realistic, positive goals can also be most important in the development of healthy emotional and behavioral patterns. Military activities can furnish and teach constructive outlets for aggressive and other drives, the learning of which will be very helpful in maturation.

Unfortunately, although vast amounts of research time and effort have been expended, there are few specific data to aid in the differentiation of those individuals with personality disorders who will do well in the service from those who will do poorly. Although certain factors such as age, educational level, and previous adjustment problems are helpful in predicting which groups may be successful or what the percentages of likely success may be, there are no figures which will allow exact prediction of individual adjustment. This must remain a delicate and chancy judgment by the psychiatrist, based on a combination of clinical, experimental, and intuitive factors.

Common Syndromes

The Diagnostic and Statistical Manual of Mental Disorders (DSM II) defined personality disorders as "characterized by deeply ingrained maladaptive patterns of behavior ... lifelong patterns, often recognizable by the time of adolescence or earlier" (2). Under this broad definition was classified a heterogeneous collection of syndromes, all of which share a common factor: a stereotyped life-style with patterns of behavior which interfere with successful living in society, and which impair the individual's ability to realize his full potential. The most recent Diagnostic and Statistical Manual of Mental Disorders (DSM III) agrees with this general concept of personality disorder, stating that " ... when personality traits are inflexible and maladaptive and cause either significant impairment in social or occupational functioning or subjective distress ... they constitute Personality Disorders" (3). DSM III, however, classifies personality disorder subtypes in a manner much different from that of the previous diagnostic system, and attempts to increase reliability of diagnoses by the establishment of more specific diagnostic criteria. It is important to note that in DSM III some of the older personality disorder categories have been eliminated, others have been modified, and some persist unchanged. All require more rigor in establishing diagnoses in accordance with the diagnostic criteria. It has been well demonstrated that clinicians have in the past been inconsistent in their differentiation and identification of personality disorder subtypes (11). DSM III makes a commendable effort to provide greater diagnostic order in this group of syndromes, and in the following discussion, DSM III diagnoses are included when they differ from the more traditional nomenclature.

As described above, diagnostic manuals have greatly varied in their classification of personality disorders, since these are clinical and phenomenological diagnoses. There are, however, certain common personality disorder syndromes occurring in the military which will be immediately recognizable to the experienced psychiatrist regardless of which diagnostic nomenclature is utilized. These common syndromes are: (a) Emotionally Unstable Personality (Borderline—DSM III), (b) Passive-Aggressive Personality, (c) Passive-Dependent Personality (Dependent—DSM III), (d) Schizoid Personality (including Schizotypal and Avoidant—DSM III), and (e) Antisocial Personality. Although officially now obsolete, the first edition of the Diagnostic and Statistical Manual of Mental Disorders assigned these classic names which have since continued in common usage (1). These disorders have commonly been referred to as "immaturity reactions" and have been reported as making up as much as 72% of all diagnosed personality disorders in the naval service (5). Schizoid Personality (including Schizotypal and Avoidant—DSM III) was categorized as a "personality pattern disturbance," defined as a "more or less cardinal personality type which can rarely if ever be altered." This group of personality disorders has been known as "pathological personality types" and also includes such diagnoses as Paranoid and Cyclothymic Personalities (Cyclothymia—DSM III). Schizoid Personality (with Schizotypal and Avoidant—DSM III) has been the disorder most often seen in the military service, reportedly accounting for 11% of all personality disorder admissions in the Navy (4). Antisocial Personality was previously categorized as one of the "sociopathic personality disturbances," which were defined as characterizing those who are "ill primarily in terms of society and of conformity and with prevailing cultural milieu" (1). Although this category is somewhat less often seen by the psychiatrist than the previously noted syndromes, its importance is heightened by the severe disturbance that it provokes in the military and social milieu. The following examples, with DSM III diagnoses included, illustrate major features of these common personality disorder syndromes in the military service.

Emotionally Unstable Personality (Borderline Personality Disorder—DSM III). The patient was a 19-year-old, single Airman Recruit, USN, with approximately 9 months of active duty who was admitted to a naval hospital after he reported taking an undetermined number of analgesic medications which had previously been prescribed for headaches. He stated that he had done this because of his despondency after he had been restricted to his base by disciplinary action of the commanding officer following an episode of unauthorized absence. His brief military career had been marked by minor disciplinary actions, repeated sick call visits, and generally inadequate performance of duties. His past history indicated that he had dropped out of school in the 11th grade after many difficulties with his teachers. Although he reported having friends, his friendships had always been marred by his impulsivity and poor emotional control. He had minor difficulties with the police and admitted having used drugs and alcohol throughout adolescence whenever he felt under stress. He had made one previous suicidal gesture prior to his military service when he had taken a mild overdose of drugs during an unhappy romantic affair.

This patient well illustrates the cardinal features of this personality disorder: poor impulse control, excitability, ineffectiveness under stress, widely fluctuating emotions, unpredictable behavior, and unstable interpersonal relationships. After a brief hospitalization, he was returned to his command with the recommendation that he should be administratively separated because of his unsuitability for military service. Frustrated by his constant difficulties, the patient's command was happy to comply with this recommendation.

Passive-Aggressive Personality (Passive-Aggressive Personality Disorder—DSM III). This patient was a 21-year-old, single Seaman, USN, with approximately 1 year of active duty who was admitted to a naval hospital after he took a small overdose of aspirin. He was treated with ipecac and was then retained as an inpatient for evaluation. He reported that he took the aspirin tablets because he was "fed up with the service." He recalled that he had impulsively enlisted in the Navy because he was angry with his father, but he had found that the "Chiefs in the Navy were even worse." In his unit he had been well known for having a "smart mouth," but he had thus far avoided official disciplinary action. Past history indicated that his parents, though living together, were in constant covert conflict. The patient recalled that his father "hassled" him, but that he had learned how to "get around the old man." Although of above average intelligence, he had received barely passing marks in school because of his conflict and "putting down" of the teachers. His peer relationships were gratifying to him, especially since he became a folk hero as a result of his demonstrated talent in manipulating and confounding teachers, police, and other authorities. During his brief hospitalization, the patient was sullen and obstructionistic. He stated repeatedly that "I'll do anything to get out of the Navy." He was unreceptive to any attempts to explore his authority problems. Eventually, he was returned to duty with the diagnosis of Passive-Aggressive Personality and the recommendation that his retention in the Navy should depend upon his performance of duty as evaluated by his command. It was the psychiatrist's opinion that the patient would continue to be a source of difficulty in his unit, but that only in his unit could his capacity for adjustment be accurately judged.

This case demonstrates the classic manner in which conflicts with aggression and authority can be expressed by passive measures such as obstructionism, inefficiency, obstinacy, hostility, manipulation, and covert defiance.

Passive-Dependent Personality (Dependent Personality Disorder—DSM III). This patient was a 20-year-old, single, Airman, USN, with approximately 1½ years of continuous active duty who was admitted to a naval hospital after he had presented himself to a chaplain in an agitated, despondent state. Since leaving home at age 18 when he enlisted in the Navy, the patient had felt lonely and concerned about his parents. He went home at every opportunity to "help them out" although he admitted that the primary reason for his frequent visits home was "to make me feel better." Although he successfully completed boot camp, he was put in constant emotional turmoil by minor reprimands and demands. After boot camp, he was increasingly preoccupied with the impulse to go on unauthorized absence and return home. He was unpopular with his peers because of his need for constant reassurance and support. After a minor accident in which he injured his hand, he was hospitalized for a month, during which time he spoke regularly to a chaplain, and once to a psychiatrist about his "nervousness." On returning to his base, he felt unable to face the future and became agitated and tearful. Seeking authorization to go home, he talked with a chaplain who then referred the patient for psychiatric consultation and hospitalization. Past history indicated that he was the youngest of three children in a highly religious and very close family. He described his mother as "worrying about me a lot," and his relationship with her was very close. He was reported to have been a "nervous" child with much fingernail biting, shyness, and constant desire to stay near his parents. He joined the Navy with his parents' encouragement, in hopes that he might become more independent, but this was unsuccessful. After evaluation by the psychiatrist and discussion with his command, the patient was discharged from the naval service by reason of unsuitability with the diagnosis of Passive-Dependent Personality (Dependent—DSM III).

This patient manifested characteristic features of this syndrome: helplessness, indecisiveness, and a great need to cling to others and establish dependent relationships. It is noteworthy that a young man with this personality disorder will occasionally be able to gratify his dependency needs in the military service and will indeed be initially successful. It may be some years before increased responsibility, need for independent action, or separation from spouse will disturb the symbiotic relationship between the patient and the service, revealing the severe nature of the personality disorder.

Schizoid Personality (Schizoid Personality Disorder—DSM III). This patient was a 21-year-old, single Fireman, USN, with 1 year of naval service who was hospitalized after having turned himself in from unauthorized absence, complaining that he felt "lost." The patient had a long history of social isolation and throughout his childhood the bulk of his time had been spent in lonely daydreaming. He failed two grades in school because of his lack of attentiveness and withdrawal; he finally quit school in the 11th grade. He had no friends and did not date. He enlisted in the Navy because he felt "confused and did not know what I wanted." His adjustment in boot camp had been marginal, and when he was sent to a naval base to await assignment to a ship, he became increasingly apprehensive. He felt "awkward" with other men in the barracks. When he first boarded his ship, a destroyer, he was appalled by the confined intimacy of shipboard life. After several days at sea, he was panic-stricken, and when the ship returned to port he fled, on unauthorized absence. After several days, however, he turned himself in to the Shore Patrol and was then hospitalized for psychiatric evaluation. Following observation in the hospital, during which time the presence of psychosis was considered but ruled out, the patient appeared before a Medical Board which recommended administrative separation by reason of unsuitability due to Schizoid Personality.

His disorder was classicially marked by seclusiveness, aloofness, and inability to tolerate the enforced closeness that is inherent in military, and particularly shipboard, life.

Antisocial Personality (Antisocial Personality Disorder—DSM III). This patient was a 19-year-old, divorced Seaman Recruit, USN, with approximately 1 year and 10 months active service. He was admitted to a naval hospital after he had made a gesture of attempting to hang himself while in disciplinary confinement. During his 22 months of service, the patient had been in continuous disciplinary difficulties because of multiple drug use, thefts, unauthorized absences, and assault. Most recently he had been confined as a consequence of disciplinary action for attempting to sell drugs. He reported having felt angry and despondent, so he tied a shirt around his neck and attached it to a bar. He was subsequently hospitalized for evaluation. His past history revealed almost continuous conflicts with parents, teachers, and police. He fought with his father regularly and was expelled from school in the 9th grade after repeated disobedience and truancy. He had numerous difficulties with the police because of auto theft, curfew violations, alcohol, drugs, and fighting. He had been confined in jail and in juvenile detention centers. He admitted frequent use of drugs and alcohol, starting in early adolescence and progressing in scope, variety, and frequency. He impulsively married at age 18, but within a few months the marriage failed and he was divorced. He entered the Navy at the insistence of a local judge, and while in the Navy his antisocial career continued. Following his suicidal gesture while in confinement, he was briefly hospitalized and the diagnosis of Antisocial Personality was established. It was recommended that he be separated from the service by either administrative or disciplinary action; and after resolution of his legal situation, this was accomplished.

In his continuous legal troubles, lack of loyalties, hedonism, poor judgment, and generally antisocial attitudes, this patient well exemplified the syndrome of Antisocial Personality.

All of the patients noted above were similar in their young age, low military rank, and short length of service. Indeed, this is characteristic of the military psychiatrist's experience with most personality disorders. One study has indicated that the relative incidence of personality disorder is 75% of all diagnosed psychiatric problems in the 17 through 19-year age group of the Navy and and Marine Corps (8). In the 17 to 20-year age group, the overall incidence of personality disorder throughout the Navy and Marine Corps has been reported as 324 per 100,000 men per year (8). It is true that individuals with personality disorder in the military are usually young, over half being 20 years of age or younger. It is also interesting that in the hospitalized cases, slightly less than half are returned to duty after hospitalization (8).

Personality Disorders in Older Personnel

Not all personality disorders in the military service present in young people, however. Indeed, studies have indicated that the overall Navy-Marine Corps incidence rate of personality disorder for servicemen, age 30 and above, may be very similar to the under age 20 group (8). For example, the possibility of someone with Passive-Dependent Personality (Dependent—DSM III) successfully completing some years of service before having difficulty was discussed above. Frequently, these problems in older personnel come to the psychiatrist's attention through alcohol abuse, as is demonstrated by the following case.

> This 32-year-old, married Commissary Steward Second Class, USN, with 13 years of active service was admitted to a naval hospital because of increasingly poor duty performance and several minor automobile accidents associated with excessive drinking. History revealed that he had been experiencing progressive difficulties with his work and marriage for the previous year because of increasing alcohol use. Prior to this, for approximately 10 years, his service career had been excellent. In the past year, however, he had been given increasing responsibility, particularly in the management of a number of other workers. Childhood history indicated parental divorce and much conflict with his stepfather. Although he made satisfactory marks, the patient had been frequently truant and quit school in the 11th grade. In adolescence he had been involved in minor difficulties with the police. He impulsively enlisted in the Navy in order "to get away from my parents." His first 18 months in the Navy had been marred by minor disciplinary actions and marginal performance of duty. At one point, it had been recommended that he should be administratively separated from the service. This recommendation was not followed, however, and the patient came under the leadership of a firm but understanding petty officer, with whom he developed a close relationship. He began to conform, and his performance of duty improved. He eventually re-enlisted and made a career of the Navy. Although he performed his duties quite successfully, his personal life was marked by impulsivity and excesses. This did not create a problem, however, until he was faced with the responsibility of increasing leadership status and authority. There was a resurgence of his youthful behavior patterns, particularly alcohol abuse. The patient was treated in a naval alcohol rehabilitation program under the supervision of a psychiatrist and successfully returned to duty.

Personality disorders are found in all ranks, and the types of syndromes which officers exhibit differ only because of their ages, background, and career patterns. The most common personality disorders among officers are Paranoid, Cyclothymic (Cyclothymic—DSM III), and Obsessive-Compulsive Personalities (Compulsive—DSM III). These are exaggerations and distortions of personality traits which are frequently found in ambitious, conscientious, and upward-striving individuals. The ambition, enthusiasm, and high energy level of an officer may result from the elation of a Cyclothymic Personality (Cyclothymic—DSM III), and may even alternate with periods of worry, pessimism, and low energy. The attention to detail and adherence to standards of conscience which can promote success in organizational management may be part of the rigidity, excessive inhibition, and overconscientiousness of an Obsessive-Compulsive Personality (Compulsive—DSM III). These are both life-styles which may initially contribute to the success of a military officer's career, but as responsibilities and competition increase at higher ranks, these attitudinal and behavioral patterns are diagnosed as personality disorders when they interfere with effective functioning. Sometimes this personality disorder insidiously leads into psychoneurosis. In other cases, the internalization and anxiety of neurosis never occurs, but the rigid life-style itself causes vocational, social, and marital difficulties which bring the officer to the attention of the psychiatrist. Managerial success in the military, as in civilian organizations, is frequently aided by strong self-confidence and belief in one's own ability. Talent for manipulating others and skill in public relations are also valuable assets for success in a competitive system. It is therefore not uncommon to find individuals with grandiose and psychopathic trends in positions of authority. There have been some legendary cases of Paranoid and Psychopathic (Narcissistic or Histrionic—DSM III) Personality disorders in senior personnel, and one of the military psychiatrist's most difficult tasks is the management of such cases when they occur. Usually this patient is a previously competent officer whose conscientiousness, attention to detail, and ambition have been parts of a paranoid pattern of rigidity, hypersensitivity, suspiciousness, grandiosity, and hostility. Eventually, the personality disorder becomes a detriment rather than an asset as duties and responsibilities become more complex. This paranoid senior officer represents an ultimate test of the psychiatrist's skill. The following case example illustrates some of the above points.

> This 38-year-old Commander, USN, was ordered to a naval hospital for psychiatric evaluation because of complaints from both his seniors and juniors about his performance and behavior. History indicated that his 15-year naval career had previously been successful. He had been considered to be quite competent although there had been occasional reports of excessive attention to detail and inflexibility. Because of his conscientiousness and the high standard of performance which he set for himself, he had performed excellently in a number of staff jobs which involved research and administrative paper work, but which did not necessitate final decision making. Approximately a year prior to his psychiatric evaluation, he was assigned command of a ship, with the authority and final responsibility which is an integral part of such a command assignment. After he assumed command, the previous operational efficiency of

the ship began to deteriorate. Gradually, reports accumulated which indicated that he was making excessive demands upon the crew, insisting upon rigid compliance to an excessively severe code of appearance and treating his senior officers and petty officers in a suspicious and untrusting manner. Unofficial complaints from his crew became frequent and the number of disciplinary actions and absences without leave increased on his ship. When the vessel was deployed for combat duty, these problems increased, and his supervisors became aware of his difficulties in maintaining flexibility and making decisions in the uncertainties and confusion of combat operations. Ultimately, he was referred for psychiatric consultation, and his compulsive personality patterns and paranoid trends were apparent to the psychiatrist. History indicated that his recent behavior was a continuation of rigid, compulsive, and suspicious patterns throughout his youth and adulthood. The patient had no insight into these problems and he manifested little anxiety, although he was angry about being relieved of his command and being required to undergo psychiatric examination. Psychotherapy was unsuccessful, as he persisted in externalizing and projecting his problems onto others, complaining bitterly of inefficiency, disloyalty, and general stupidity of those with whom he associated. The patient was eventually returned to duty with a diagnosis of Compulsive Personality, after which he was again given staff assignment rather than command authority.

This case demonstrates the manner in which personality disorder may be unrecognized in some situations, but may become visible and obviously harmful in other circumstances.

Personality Disorder and Psychosis

The most common diagnostic problem encountered in military psychiatry is the differentiation between personality disorder and psychosis. Although in their classic manifestations these conditions can be easily distinguished, in practice the diagnostic dilemma of borderline areas is the topic most often discussed at psychiatric case conferences in military hospitals. There is a notable tendency for even well-trained clinicians to think in a stereotyped and simplistic fashion and assume that these two conditions cannot exist simultaneously, or at different times in one patient. In fact, the patient with a personality disorder may well be, may have been, or will become psychotic, and the psychotic patient frequently has a personality disorder in his premorbid state which is manifested at various times as his psychosis waxes and wanes. DSM III emphasizes this by encouraging the concurrent diagnosis of personality disorder on Axis II when a more acute diagnosis is established on Axis I, and also by designating Borderline Personality Disorder as an official diagnostic entity. It has been recognized that in childhood and adolescence "stormy personalities" are frequently found in those who are preschizophrenic (4). These personalities can be antisocial, aggressive, passive-aggressive, or emotionally unstable and, indeed, may well qualify for a specific personality disorder diagnosis. Due to the late adolescent stage of development in these patients and the stressful conditions of military life, their psychoses are frequently revealed for the first time.

The term pseudopsychopathic schizophrenia has been used to describe this group of patients, so common in the military service, in whom the schizophrenic symptoms are masked by delinquent, antisocial, "acting out" behavior (6). The term originally emphasized sexually deviant behavior in these cases, but through usage, the concept has been expanded to include schizophrenia associated with all types of impulsive and/or sociopathic behavior. Although not an official diagnostic title, pseudopsychopathic schizophrenia is a particularly appropriate and descriptive term characterizing many cases in military psychiatric ward. The following example illustrates such a case.

> This 21-year-old, single Private, USMC, with approximately 3 years of active duty, was admitted to a naval hospital after transfer from disciplinary confinement where he had become increasingly difficult to manage. He had recently become progressively more agitated, assaultive, and unpredictable in his behavior, and he was hospitalized because of the medical officer's concern about his mental state. Past history revealed continuous difficulties with police, teachers, and authorities. His parents were divorced when the patient was quite young; he had been raised by his mother, although they had a distant relationship. He was a poor academic achiever in school, and he eventually dropped out of school in the 11th grade. He was repeatedly involved in criminal activities during adolescence, particularly theft and assault. His peer relationships were marked by extreme sensitivity to others' remarks, along with frequent physical aggression in response to what he felt were slights or derogatory attitudes of others. Because of his delinquent activities, he had spent considerable time in jails and juvenile detention centers. He enlisted in the U.S. Marine Corps because he was unable to find other employment and he looked forward to the aggressive image of being a Marine. His 3 years in the service had been marked by frequent disciplinary actions, impulsive behavior, and many fights. He was initially confined because of assault charges, and while in confinement he was involved in some group aggressive acts that led to charges of riot and an additional sentence. Because of his disciplinary problems, on at least three occasions he had been evaluated psychiatrically, and consistently the diagnosis of Antisocial Personality had been established. At no time had there been evidence of psychosis. He had, in fact, been confined on several occasions prior to the current episode without any evidence of psychotic decompensation. His particularly unmanageable behavior during recent confinement led to hospitalization. During his initial examination in the hospital, he was noted to be angry, sullen, and uncommunicative, but there was no evidence of thought disorder. In repeated evaluations, however, his attending psychiatrist became increasingly suspicious of a borderline psychotic disorder, based upon the patient's blunted affect with tendencies to concreteness and projection. He was hostile to staff personnel and became involved in frequent altercations with both staff and other patients. Ultimately, during one of these incidents when he required restraint, the attending medical officer was surprised to hear the patient speak in a grossly tangential and grandiose manner. An associative defect in thought

process was apparent, as well as a loosely formed but pervasive delusional system, and auditory hallucinations. Treatment with appropriate phenothiazine medication was initiated, and clinical management was modified in a manner consistent with that of other psychotic patients on the ward. Within several weeks his condition improved, he became more cooperative, and evidence of his schizophrenic thought disorder subsided. He continued to demonstrate faulty impulse control, and antisocial behavior persisted, but he was able to adjust to the hospital routine and to make some positive plans for the future. He was ultimately discharged to the care of the Veterans Administration while still continuing on phenothiazine medication.

This case illustrates the need for alert and flexible management of patients with personality disorder, a point that cannot be overemphasized. Such individuals can, and frequently do, have other psychiatric illness which require specific treatment but which can be easily missed in the turmoil created by their behavior disorder.

Suicidal Gestures and Drug Abuse

Most of the cases previously described demonstrate two behavior problems that are particularly related to personality disorder. Self-destructive gestures frequently bring personnel to medical attention, as does the abuse of all types of drugs, including alcohol. When these are symptoms of neurosis or psychosis, the psychiatrist feels some sense of confidence in his therapeutic attempts, but when they are manifestations of personality disorder, as they so often are, he frequently finds his usual treatment methods inadequate.

A suicidal gesture may be defined as an act of self-harm without serious intent to achieve death. Such gestures are comparatively common manifestations of adolescent psychopathology, although also occurring in older individuals, and they are a frequent reason for psychiatric referral in military medical practice. Usually, such a gesture indicates emotional immaturity, often to the degree of personality disorder. The quality and significance of such an act and what it communicates vary according to each individual's psychopathology. The emotionally unstable young man may impulsively leap from a dock into the water after he receives a rejecting letter from his girl friend. The passive-dependent sailor may ingest a number of aspirin tablets when he has to return to his ship after a period of leave at home. The passive-aggressive seaman may angrily but superficially cut his wrist instead of attacking his Chief Petty Officer after being ordered to work detail. The severely schizoid youth may systematically and deeply lacerate his arms in self-contempt and despair with his isolation. Frequently, but not always, there is a conscious intent to achieve some goal by the gesture. Sometimes it is an act of momentary impulse. Sometimes, as in the example of the Schizoid Personality (Avoidant—DSM III) noted above, the act has more malignant meaning, indicating more severe and internalized psychopathology. It is well known that although suicide may not be the intent of these gestures, it may be an accidental result. Also, self-destructive gestures do not rule out the possibility of future serious suicidal intent in the same individual. The suicidal gesture may be a desperate plea for someone developing a serious mental illness as well as an impulsive or manipulative act by someone with personality disorder. It does, therefore, always require serious attention by the clinician.

Drug abuse is a problem for the military services just as it is for society at large. Soldiers, sailors, and marines are predominantly young people; and as such, they have the drug problems of contemporary youth. As drug abuse appears to be related to rebellion, escape, and alienation in modern youth, so it is a common manifestation of personality disorders in the military. For the Passive-Aggressive or Antisocial Personality, drug abuse is a mechanism by which to reject and rebel against the authority structure. For the Emotionally Unstable (Borderline—DSM III) and Passive-Dependent (Dependent—DSM III) Personality, drug abuse may supply some escape from emotional turmoil and some support in times of stress. For the Schizoid Personality (including Schizotypal and Avoidant—DSM III), it may make social isolation intolerable.

The Southeast Asian conflict coupled unusual stress with easy availability of drugs, thereby compounding the problem. Contrary to initial fears, however, there was little evidence to indicate that Vietnam duty turned normal young men into drug addicts. Military experience has indicated that most drug abusers in the services have longstanding problems in social and emotional immaturity (11). It appears that more than half of them used drugs prior to entering the service and many, if not most, have diagnosable personality disorders. Drug rehabilitation centers were set up by all services, and a number of therapeutic approaches have been utilized. It is generally reported that rather than treating drug abuse per se, these centers deal with a heterogeneous collection of personality disorders in late adolescence who happen to have abused drugs as one of the several manifestations of their psychopathology (6).

Alcohol abuse can also be a symptom of personality disorder, especially for the older military population. As in the misuse of any drug, of course, such alcohol abuse is not pathognomonic for personality disorder and may be a manifestation of other problems. Frequently, however, the Passive-Dependent Personality (Dependent—DSM III) may turn to alcohol for solace and support, and the Antisocial Personality may use alcohol as an excuse for his antisocial behavior. Alcohol abuse is a serious problem for any organization because it tends to disable members who have achieved places of leadership and responsibility. In the predominantly male, action-oriented society of the military, alcohol may sometimes be associated with masculinity, and thereby its abuse may be reinforced. Awareness of the problem of alcohol abuse has recently caused all defense organizations to mount active programs of both prevention and treatment.

All the types of behavior described above represent avenues for the acting out and externalization of unconscious conflicts. Such behavior is an attempt to solve psychic problems, but in reality it precipitates more problems for the individual and is therefore ultimately self-destructive. This is especially true in the close-knit structured environment of the military service.

Personality Disorders in Combat

Combat involves multiple and unique stresses, including threats of death and injury, direct responsibility for others' lives, and physical deprivations. Success in this violent environment requires considerable adaptability, and it is not surprising that many young men with personality disorders cannot adjust to these life-threatening and chaotic conditions. Those who have greatest difficulty are those with poor emotional and impulse control. Under fire, these patients frequently develop acute panic or hysterical symptoms resembling those of true combat fatigue. This latter diagnosis is usually reserved for patients who develop a transient situational disturbance in combat without evidence of longstanding adjustment problems. Patients who develop true combat fatigue have histories of satisfactory adaptability and, with treatment and removal from combat, their symptoms rapidly subside. The superficially similar syndrome which occurs in those with personality disorders has been referred to as "pseudocombat fatigue" (13). Historically, these patients reveal impulsivity, poor stress tolerance, and fragile emotional control. Characteristically, they have been in the combat zone less than 6 months and their exposure to combat stress has not been as severe. Their response to the supportive but highly directive, reality-oriented therapeutic techniques of combat psychiatry is distinctive. Because of the longstanding nature of their problems, inadequate motivation, and poor identification with their military group, these patients with personality disorder and pseudocombat fatigue symptoms respond poorly to treatment. Although their superficial anxiety, despondency, and/or somatic complaints seem to improve in a comparatively sheltered noncombat environment, the crucial test is the prospect of return to duty. At this point, their symptoms recur or new ones appear, and the severity of the personality disorder becomes apparent. The following case is typical of the pseudocombat fatigue syndrome in a patient with personality disorder.

> This 22-year-old lance corporal, U.S. Marine Corps, with 2 years of active duty and 4 months of service in the combat zone, was hospitalized aboard a

hospital ship after he "froze" under enemy fire. At the time of admission, he was grossly anxious, tremulous, and agitated. His speech was in explosive bursts, interrupted by periods of preoccupied silence, and he reported only vague memory for his recent combat experience. He was treated with mild sedation, and in 24 hours his symptoms had improved. History could then be obtained, and this indicated longstanding problems with impulse and emotional control which had caused difficulties in social, family, and school relationships. He enlisted in the Marine Corps after impulsively quitting high school, and his 2 years of service had been marked by frequent emotional upheavals, marginal performance of duty, and disciplinary actions for a variety of minor offenses. His initial 2 months of duty in the war zone had been comparatively peaceful. As his unit made more contact with the enemy, however, over the next 2 months, he grew increasingly apprehensive, and this became more severe after he received a minor shrapnel wound. On the night prior to hospitalization, he was involved in a brief but intense firefight, and he "froze" in a state of tremulous dissociation. After evacuation to the hospital ship, his symptoms seemed to improve, although tremulousness and apprehension recurred whenever new casualties arrived or when combat ashore was visible or audible. He demonstrated an acute exacerbation of agitation and tearfulness when confronted with the prospect of possible return to duty, and he was finally evacuated back to the United States with a diagnosis of Emotionally Unstable Personality (Borderline—DSM III).

This patient, although he initially appeared to have a situational syndrome of combat, demonstrated personality disorder by history of poor adaptive patterns and multiple family, scholastic, social, and delinquent problems. It is likely that he would have become a military psychiatric patient even if he had not been exposed to combat stress.

There are, however, some types of personality disorder which adapt well in the combat situation. Because of the unusual opportunity for outlet of aggression and hostility, those with personality disorders in which aggressive, passive-aggressive, and antisocial features predominate can sometimes perform well and obtain considerable gratification from combat. There are general relaxation of authority relationships and more casual attitudes toward nonessentials in a combat environment. This less rigid structure and the opportunity and reinforcement for aggressive behavior may be welcomed by young men with authority and aggressive conflicts. It is not uncommon for them to extend voluntarily their tours of duty in the combat zone because of the realization that their personality problems in that environment are, for the first and only time, assets rather than liabilities. While in the combat zone, these personality disorders are often demonstrated by occasional incidents of misdirected violence, such as fighting and indiscriminate firing of weapons, especially under the influence of alcohol, but there is great tolerance for this occasional acting-out behavior as long as it does not seriously endanger the survival of the group. Otherwise, adjustment problems may appear to be temporarily suspended in this unusual situation, and it is on return to a peaceful home environment that difficulties are again severe.

The more rigid military structure of stateside duty with a "spit and polish" attitude and inflexible authority relationships can be more stressful than combat for these patients, especially since they must re-establish control of aggression. Psychiatrists often see these personality disorder patients after return from combat, and their behavior patterns are typically passive-aggressive and antisocial, as in the cases previously described.

Military Psychiatry and Personality Disorders

For administrative purposes, personality disorder is not regarded by the military services as a disease or, more specifically, as a compensable military disability. Instead, these disorders are considered to be longstanding problems in adjustment, not caused by or related to military service and therefore not compensable per se. When personality disorders render individuals unsuitable for service, however, such disorders provide sufficient grounds for separation from the military by administrative action. Each service has specific administrative policies and directives for effecting the discharge of those young men who cannot adjust. Frequently, psychiatric evaluation reports are the most important factor in implementing these discharge procedures, even though the process is an administrative rather than a medical one.

In his contacts with personality disorders, the military psychiatrist is therefore placed in an important but sometimes ambiguous and difficult position. He is called upon to evaluate these patients, to differentiate their problems from other emotional disorders that may be more amenable to immediate treatment, and to recommend appropriate personnel action. The physician is involved in a complex interplay of clinical, administrative, and legal functions, in addition to being asked to accomplish as much rehabilitation and treatment as possible. He is likely to view all of this with ambivalence at best and angry frustration at worst. Frequently he has been poorly trained in the recognition and management of personality disorders and is uncomfortable with these patients' lack of interest in, or response to, his traditional means of therapy. He may be trapped by his own feelings and inexperience, reacting to the notorious propensity of those with personality disorders to manipulate, stimulate anger, and create chaos. It is of the utmost importance that the doctor maintain his objectivity and not allow his own apprehension, anger, and discomfort to cloud his perception and judgment. Although there are those who may argue that the psychiatrist is wasting his talent and skills on personality disorders, it is the author's opinion that only good psychiatric training and experience can fully develop the clinical acumen and objectivity necessary for optimal recognition, understanding, and management of such disorders.

Throughout the years the military services have made many attempts to treat personality disorders. These have met with varying degrees of success and have sometimes been controversial, but they have been worthwhile. In correctional units and retraining commands there have been well organized and serious efforts to rehabilitate young men with severe maladaptive behavior patterns. In military hospitals there have been, and continue to be, pioneering programs in milieu treatment and therapeutic communities for personality disorders. In recent years the role of the military as a rehabilitative agency has gained increasing emphasis because of social concern for drug and alcohol abuse. Rehabilitation programs at local commands, along with major drug and alcohol rehabilitation centers, are now in vigorous operation in all services. In practice, these drug and alcohol rehabilitation efforts usually are treating personality disorders.

As agencies of society, the miliary services reflect the problems, conflicts, and concerns of society. Personality disorders create problems of great magnitude, both for society at large and its defense organizations. The military services, however, provide a unique opportunity to study these disorders which have always caused such social turmoil, and so much legal and medical controversy.

As Herman Melville wrote of another Navy in another century: " ... 'a depravity according to nature'.... Can it be this phenomenon disowned or not acknowledged, that in some criminal cases puzzles the courts? For this cause have our juries at times not only to endure the prolonged contentions of lawyers with their fees, but also the yet more perplexing strife of the medical experts with theirs?" (10).

REFERENCES

1. American Psychiatric Association. Diagnostic and Statistical Manual of Mental Disorders, Ed. 1. American Psychiatric Association, Washington, D. C., 1952.
2. American Psychiatric Association. Diagnostic and Statistical Manual of Mental Disorders, Ed. 2. American Psychiatric Association, Washington, D. C., 1968.
3. American Psychiatric Association, Diagnostic and Statistical Manual of Mental Disorders, Ed. 3. American Psychiatric Association, Washington, D. C., 1980.
4. Arieti, S. *Interpretation of Schizophrenia*, p. 74. Brunner, New York, 1959.
5. Arthur, R. J. Psychiatric disorders in naval personnel. Milit. Med., 131:354–361, 1966.
6. Drake, A. M., and Kolb, D. Rehabilitation of Drug Abuse Patients in the Naval Service. Report No. 72-12. Navy Medical Neuropsychiatric Research Unit, San Diego, 1972.
7. Dunaif, S. L., and Hoch, P. H. Pseudopsychopathic schizophrenia. In: *Psychiatry and the Law*, P. H. Hock and J. Zubin (Eds.), pp. 169–195. Grune & Stratton, New York, 1955.
8. Gunderson, E. K. E. Epidemiology and Prognosis of Psychiatric Disorders in the Naval Service. Report No. 70-15. Navy Medical Neuropsychiatric Research Unit, San Diego, 1970.
9. Information on Character Disorders. Neuropsychiatry Branch (Code 313), Bureau of Medicine and Surgery, Department of the Navy, Washington, D. C.
10. Melville, H. *Billy Budd, Foretopman* (1924), pp. 33–36. Bantam, New York, 1965.
11. Nail, R. L., and Gunderson, E. K. E. Characteristics of hospitalized drug abuse cases in the naval service. J. Nerv. Ment. Dis., 155:91–98, 1972.
12. Shuckit, M. A., and Gunderson, E. K. E. The clinical characteristics of personality disorder subtypes in naval service. J. Clin. Psychiatry, April 1979.
13. Strange, R. E. Effects of combat stress on hospital ship psychiatric evacuees. In: *The Psychology and Physiology of Stress*, P. Bourne (Ed.), pp. 75–92. Academic Press, New York, 1969.

29

PERSONALITY DISORDERS IN PRISONS

George Bach-y-Rita, M.D.

Prisons are generally thought of as the repository for severe personality disorders. If we exclude deviates, the drug addicts, and the alcoholics, few except those with the diagnosis of Borderline Personality, Antisocial Personality, or Passive-Aggressive Personality are incarcerated for crimes related to their mental disorder. On the other hand, county jails and city jails abound with individuals arrested for nonvictim crimes related to what might be considered a personality disorder such as alcohol or drug abuse.

The concept of the prisoner as a personality disorder has been strongly imbedded in Western thinking since the 19th century. As a result of the attempts to introduce science to criminology and the serious research in personalities which has been carried out with prisoners, this concept has been sustained. Some excellent studies have been made attempting to follow patients over a period of many years in an effort to link or predict those individuals that would develop symptoms of personality disorders and particularly of antisocial personality. The works of Robins (28), the Gluecks (13), Gibbens et al. (10), and Guze (14) are particularly noteworthy. In addition, some of the best articles on the psychopathic personality disorders are to be found in the journals devoted to criminology or in the psychiatric journals devoted to criminal behavior. An excellent review of the syndrome, written some years ago, is that of Maughs (24). The same author had previously written a historical review for the criminology literature which traces the concept of the then-called psychopathic personality back to its origins (23).

Cleckley (5), on the other hand, points out how individuals with the personality disorders are to be found as readily in the general population as in prison.

It often appears as if it is the inept individual or the Antisocial Personality who can still feel some guilt that ends up in the prison. Frequently, it is this underlying guilt which leads a criminal to get caught and eventually convicted.

An example of this is a young man with a long history of burglaries and assaults whom I had an opportunity to see. His past history was consistent with what one might expect of an Antisocial Personality. On examination he appeared with a nonchalant air about him, and had a low frustration tolerance and appeared grossly selfish, irresponsible, and unsocialized. It was clear that he had set himself up to get caught. He described the events leading to his arrest. They occurred when he was feeling "low." He got drunk with a group of cronies and attempted to steal a large safe from a butcher shop while heavily intoxicated. The patient and his friend, weakened by alcohol and laughter, were unable to lift the safe into the back of a truck, and their noise and laughing attracted the attention of neighbors, who called the police. After this conviction, he appeared almost relieved. Underneath the unsocialized, hard, selfish, irresponsible exterior, this patient proved to be a seriously depressed individual. Incarceration restricted his ability to act on his anxieties, and he became an appropriate candidate for therapy.

Diagnostic Problems in the Prison

Within the correctional system the diagnoses personality disorder, Passive-Aggressive Personality, and Antisocial Personality are used very frequently. Often they reflect a pejorative sentiment or are used as a result of a physician's biased social attitudes. They may also result from a communication difficulty between patient and physician. The misuse of the diagnosis of what is in other areas called the psychopath is not unique to the American prison. Craft (6) notes that in Wales whether or not a diagnosis of psychopathy is applied often depends either on chance factors such as whether or not a patient is screened along mental health lines or along penal pathways.

Social class also would often determine the use of the terms personality disorder, Psychopathy, Antisocial Personality, etc. This factor, too, was recognized by Craft. All too often, the lower class "psychopath" gets into repeated conflicts with the law because of his stealing and ends up in prison with a diagnosis of a personality disorder. His upper class counterpart will more likely end up with accolades or a corporate title. This is graphically described by A. Harrington (19). In addition to social class, the type of doctor to which a patient is referred will also greatly influence whether or not he receives a diagnosis of a personality disorder or of psychopathy.

In making the diagnosis of Antisocial Personalities, one of the criteria is that the patient present a pattern of continuous antisocial behavior or that the behavior patterns have brought the individual into repeated conflict with society. A problem arises when the diagnosing physician has to ask whether or not his patient's behavior is in conflict with his own cultural or ethnic subgroup and is adaptive for that population. Frequently the behavior that is adaptive for a social or ethnic subgroup is not adaptive for the greater society. The answer to this question can easily elude the physician if he is unfamiliar with the varieties of subcultures in the prison. The same difficulty holds true when he attempts to define whether or not the individual holds loyalties either to people or to social groups. Here the difficulty arises when the social values of a subgroup are in opposition to the values of the dominant culture. Among the heavily relied upon diagnostic criteria in diagnosing the Antisocial Personality are the observations that the individual failed to accept social norms with respect to lawful behavior or that the individual has a disregard for truth, as indicated by repeated lying. In a prison this can easily be misinterpreted by the physician when a patient does not follow advice, counseling, or recommendations and persists in behavior, often covertly, that brings him into conflict with the authorities. Prior to attempting to use information of this sort, the physician must understand the prison culture and environment so as to learn what is adaptive and what is maladaptive for the patient within his subculture. All too often, acquiescence to the wishes of the authorities or physician would bring the patient into conflict with his peers and be not only maladaptive but self-destructive.

Difficulties also arise when a physician working within a custodial institution attempts to diagnose a Passive-Aggressive Personality. A prison environment, almost by definition, prohibits the expression of overtly aggressive behavior. This often carries over to mean that strongly assertive behavior is viewed with suspicion. The astute inmate quickly learns that certain behavior that might lead to conflict, particularly with custodial personnel, is maladaptive. In addition, physically aggressive behavior that might be observed by custodial personnel and that would surely result in disciplinary action is either avoided or covertly practiced. The inmate is forced to learn new techniques in order to assert himself. With actively aggressive channels closed to him, the prisoner may resort to passive-aggressive behavior.

The passive-aggressive behavior is one of the expressions of the patient's resentment at failure to find gratification in a relationship with an institution on which he is overdependent. This dependency is virtually infantilizing. As a result of this, there is great resentment and little gratification.

The Borderline Personality is another disorder which can and should be identified in the prison. Here is a personality disorder which lends itself more readily to diagnosis than any of the previously mentioned. This disorder is often characterized by gross outbursts of rage, either verbal or physical, which are usually inappropriate. The affective instability with mood shifts is often reflected in repetitive self-damaging acts and, often, identity disturbances (3). The outbursts are clearly maladaptive, and the patient is not likely to engage in this behavior so as to consciously or apparently make his existence easier during his stay in the prison. In addition, since the patient with this diagnosis is generally considered excitable, aggressive, and overresponsive to environmental pressure and is generally unable to control his outbursts, we have additional information which frequently can be gathered by observation rather than by questioning. Differential diagnosis, in this case, is with intermittent explosive disorder. In the intermittent explosive disorder, there is less likelihood of the repetitive, self-destructive, or self-mutilative acts that are more commonly seen in the Borderline Personality. In addition, the outbursts are more circumscribed and usually more violent and followed by genuine regretful self-reproach.

Estimation of the number of patients in a prison with the diagnosis of personality disorder or "psychopathy" is fraught with as much difficulty as is the formulation of the accurate diagnosis. Estimates vary from 5 to 75% (8, 10).

The British concept of the psychopath is similar to the American concept of the Antisocial Personality. Among the criteria used in diagnosing these patients are the observations that the patient is impulsive, aggressive, suspicious, cold hearted, selfish, and tends to be explosive. Gibbens also notes that they are more casual about money and morals than are neurotics. He has observed that they have a higher frequency of suicide attempts as a result of convictions than do neurotics. These patients also tend to have more frequent abnormalities of the electroencephalogram and are unresponsive to treatment. The incidence of personality disorders (psychopathy) in the United States is estimated to lie between 10 and 20% of convicted criminals (22, 27).

Other studies have resulted in an equally wide range of figures for sociopathy, psychopathy, or personality disorders. Guze et al. (16) estimated that sociopathy was present in some 56 to 81% of their population. The same authors (16) also observed that when using consistent criteria the diagnosis of Antisocial Personality in a population of convicted male felons remained consistent over a period of years. They feel that the prisoners generally provide accurate and honest information in the clinical interview. Glueck (12) gives a much lower figure and estimates that approximately 22% of 200 cases of incarcerated offenders were suffering from character disorders.

Other Psychiatric Disorders in the Prison

Prisons, like other institutions where men are gathered, have their share of psychiatrically ill patients. Certain of these tend to be exacerbated by incarceration, and some of these are improved or stabilized by incarceration. The former mental patient often falls victim to the prison environment and develops illness. One type of character disorder that is not helped by the prison environment is the paranoid personality. These patients are frequently seen as uncooperative, isolated, and hostile. They, together with the paranoid schizophrenic, frequently find the isolation of maximum security confinement comforting or consistent with their delusional systems, and so tend to remain in maximum security, where they are freed of the pressures of contact and conflict with their peers. The isolation will frequently stabilize but not improve these patients over long periods of time. Unfortunately, the realities of prison life only substantiate what otherwise would be delusional thinking.

The patient with a gender identity disorder, on the other hand, is frequently if not usually exploited by his fellow inmates.

The absence of normal sexual patterns and heterosexual contacts creates an environment where the homosexual patient becomes a virtual commodity. It is a commentary on the prison environment that the aggressive homosexual, the prisoner who is assaultive or dominant, is not viewed either by his peers or by himself as a homosexual. Only the individual who submits either willingly or under duress is viewed as a homosexual. Under these circumstances the traits of power and dominance are viewed as masculine and the traits of submission or weakness are viewed as feminine. This artificial environment can create serious diagnostic difficulties for the psychiatrist trying to diagnose a personality disorder while relying upon behavior or characteristics that might have developed in a patient after incarceration. For example, since some inmates have spent much of their lives in closed institutions, it often becomes very difficult to distinguish the true homosexual from the adaptive homosexual or the heterophobic.

The more obviously severely ill psychiatric patient is less likely to go to prison. Most states have established institutions for the criminally insane. Patients who are deemed incapable of cooperating with defense counsel, or are too ill to stand trial, are generally sent to institutions for the criminally insane. These institutions are usually run by treatment personnel, rather than by correctional personnel, a factor which tends to increase the possibilities of appropriate treatment.

Etiological Factors in Personality Disorders

Since the concept of psychopathy first came into use, originally under the term moral insanity or moral idiocy, controversy has raged over whether it is the result of an organic deficit, or a moral or learned problem. Grohmann (1819), as quoted by von Krafft-Ebbing (34), was probably the first to associate what he called ethic degeneration and organic causes. It was also he who termed the name congenital moral insanity or moral idiocy. The subject of organicity and criminal psychopathy continues to this date. Murdoch (25) notes that psychopaths and nonpsychopaths differ significantly on EEG measures.

Other authors prefer to view psychopathy as neurotic. This approach is supported by Thorne (32).

Effects of Incarceration on Personality Disorders

Although modern prisons are generally called correctional institutions and are expected by the public to rehabilitate criminals, the unfortunate reality is that they neither rehabilitate the personality disorders nor contribute to resocialization. Although the prisons do protect society from the undesirable personality disorder, this effect is very temporary, and the patient is released with a new array of skills useful in the perpetuation of deviant behavior. If he is resentful towards society when he goes into prison, he is likely to be all the more bitter when he gets out. If there is any alteration in his personality structure, it is more likely to be towards the identification with his now deviant peer group.

Prisons place an enormous load on the personality of even the healthy prisoner. For the already deficient ego structure of the personality disorders, the load is often intolerable. The stresses with which the prisoner is confronted are almost beyond the imagination of those who are unfamiliar with prison environment. Problems with sexual identity have already been mentioned. They are ever present for the confused or marginally adjusted adolescent personality disorders. Moreover, these difficulties are compounded and magnified in the segregated society where contact with the opposite sex is virtually nonexistent. Strong sexual drives, as well as a need for intimacy, force the patients into behavior patterns and gender roles that are totally ego-alien.

Isolation is frequently another dreadful factor which becomes intolerable for the marginally stable personality. The standard procedure in many prisons is that aggressive or assaultive inmates are placed in an isolation cell. Although the isolation is not total, the deprivation continues over a period of days or weeks and, at times, years. The result of this, all too often, is that the patient will become more agitated, disorganized, and belligerent, frequently culminating in delusional and paranoid thinking. This state can be accompanied by visual hallucinations. In addition, the borderline personality disorder, frequently prone to repeated episodes of loss of control, is likely to be housed for years at a time in or under maximum security conditions. The long placement in solitary cells, either for the protection of the inmates or for the protection of others, contributes to the personality disorganization of an already disturbed patient.

The phenomena of hallucinations occur in normal subjects deprived of environmental stimuli (37). In addition, patients who scored high on the Psychopathic Deviant Scale of the Minnesota Multiphasic Personality Inventory were more likely to be intolerant of stimulus deprivation (36). The same author has hypothesized and demonstrated that high sensation seekers will not adapt well to isolation. Since the Antisocial Personality is essentially a stimulus seeker (26), it is understandable that the personality disorder or psychopaths have considerable difficulty under the conditions found in segregation cells.

Although varying degrees of psychopathy are encountered in the prison, the patient with the highest tendency to act impulsively is the more likely candidate to be a source of concern for the institution. In prisons that are adequately staffed, this is also the more likely patient to come to the psychiatrist. This patient is usually either the Borderline Personality or the patient suffering from intermittent explosive behavior.

The Borderline patient in prison will often display the characteristic features of the Antisocial Personality with all the superficial appearance of little surface anxiety and a rationalization for antisocial behavior. Underneath there is often an overwhelming guilt which is bound in the personality structure and often with obsessive symptoms. Beneath the tough exterior there usually lies fear, anxiety, and depression which are manifested by frequent suicide attempts and a very high frequency of self-mutilation. A clinging dependency seems to oscillate with isolation or withdrawal.

The past histories of the patients usually reveal severely disrupted families with parental violence and considerable rejection of the patient. By age 10 they will likely have broken bones and will have suffered concussions (2, 3). The patient is likely to appear schizophrenic when under stress and has been considered outright schizophrenic (15). These patients were at one time labeled pseudoneurotic schizophrenics (7) because of the full-blown psychotic episodes that they can present.

An example of the above is the case of Mr. W., whom I had occasion to interview and observe over a period of time in prison. This patient, at the time I saw him, was 30 years old and had been incarcerated almost all his life, having first been in a youth camp at age 14 for burglary. He first entered the state prison at age 16, and was currently in his third term on a felony conviction. This patient had a family history of a father who had been brutal to him, and both his mother and his sister had histories of psychiatric hospitalization. Violence was part of the family, with his mother being brutally beaten on occasions by his stepfather. He had a relatively positive maternal figure, nonetheless. The patient was a loner as a child and functioned at an average level in school and through much of high school. His five sisters have done well, but his seven brothers all had difficulties with the law. At age 13 he suffered an accident, at which time he states he was electrocuted.

In the prison he had numerous fights and homosexual contacts. He was caught making a knife which he insisted was for defense. He continued to have numerous unpleasant encounters with the correctional officers, and spent long periods of time in solitary cells. He would become severely depressed when locked up, and mutilated his body repeatedly during these episodes. He described feeling greatly relieved after mutilating himself. Physical examination revealed 125 scars as the result of these activities. Electroencephelographic examination revealed bitemporal slowing.

At one point after being transferred to a more secure environment following an altercation, this patient became agitated and was moved out of hearing of his peers so as not to disturb them. His associations became progressively looser, and he began to ramble and to display pressured speech. His anxiety level increased and over a period of days he became extremely agitated. As he became intolerable to other prisoners on the cell block, he was placed at a distance at which he was less and less audible to them. When he set fire to his cell, he was brought before a disciplinary board and as punishment was placed in an isolation cell. While here he became grossly delusional with paranoid delusions. He also began to have visual hallucinations. He became severely depressed and cut his arm. Further questioning revealed that numerous episodes of this sort had occurred in the past. The patient was transferred to a section of the institution for the psychotic inmate, and he quickly improved; three weeks later he was no longer psychotic. As part of an experimental trial, this patient was placed on lithium carbonate, and over a period of months he remained free of any aggressive outbursts.

This case serves as an excellent example of the effects of isolation and stimulus deprivation on a patient with a diagnosis of Borderline Personality disorder.

The Treatment of the Personality Disorders in Prison

The treatment of the personality disorder or the psychopath in prison tends to be a relatively disheartening and only marginally successful task. Psychotherapy in particular is very difficult, and its difficulty is universally recognized. Roosenburg (29) discusses some of the problems and difficulties inherent in treating the psychopath. She also remarks that the world literature on psychotherapy of the psychopath, as she sees it, is not very helpful. Indeed, this is true, because the patients tend to be rather suspicious. This is inevitably the result of the deprivation and the psychopathology of the individual patient, but is also largely due to the use to which psychotherapy is put in correctional institutions. The attitude that the patient takes toward psychiatric treatment often reflects the attitude taken by those in control of the correctional institution. It also reflects the role that the therapist or psychiatrist plays as an employee of the state rather than as a physician friend of the patient. The patients know all too well that the correctional institutions are there to control them, and that the psychiatrist and therapist are likewise employees of the institution and obligated to the institution before the patient. The Antisocial Personality who blames others for his difficulty and has a poorly developed ethical conscience tends to ignore rules or social mores. He has no genuine concern or anxiety related to his antisocial behavior and little desire for change. He generally makes a poor subject for a therapeutic relationship. Probably the most thorough study on this topic was recently conducted by Yochelson and Samenow (35). The authors experienced a great deal of difficulty in the early part of their project treating criminals. They found that the incarcerated offender wanted only release and not change. They also recognized that psychoanalytic probing produces only justification for past behavior and is not utilized by the patient to modulate future behavior.

One of the more successful approaches to the treatment of the personality disorders in prison appears to be the therapeutic community as employed in Holland (20). Although the group deals with offenders in general, their population consists of people sent by the court and deemed only partially responsible for their crimes as a result of mental disorder (30).

Part of these generally pessimistic attitudes toward therapy with personality disorders derives from research that has demonstrated that the effect of psychotherapy with prisoners is at best short lived (21).

The controversies are far from resolved (9, 18).

In individual psychotherapy, unless a patient is engaged in the first interview around critical issues, therapy will fail (1). The most severe problem is that of trust. From the patient's point of view, this is not unrealistic. The patient seeking help does not approach the physician; rather, the physician is sent to the patient by the institution in an effort to help in controlling him. Under these circumstances the patients often appear aloof and distant, if not disdainful, in the first contact with the therapist. They may also appear overly friendly and "con" the therapist. Patients often harbor unreasonable wishes for treatment. They expect that the therapist will gratify primitive desires and make restitution for past deprivations. These magical expectations lead the patient to pose demands on the therapist that are impossible to meet. Given the distorted doctor-patient relationship and the impossible demands placed on the therapist, the foundation is set for a therapeutic failure. Another serious impediment to therapeutic success is the patients' tendency to externalize rather than accept responsibility for their difficulties. This blaming others for their discomfort relieves them of having to take any responsibility or work in therapy. The personality disorder has poor powers of observation and little ability to introspect. When he does look inward, the dependent wishes can be terrifying. They lead to his invoking mechanisms of projection or denial. One of the problems that Adler has encountered is the prisoner who acts out so as to get himself locked up. He thereby interrupts therapy and avoids the intensity of feelings which arise in the dyadic situation.

When the patient does not have his wishes gratified, he tends to respond with the rage which is characteristic of many patients with personality disorders.

Since the past histories of most of the prisoners with a personality disorder reveal a high incidence of early parental loss or of family disruption (2, 3), the prisoner entering into a therapeutic relationship expects that this relationship will also be short lived.

Adler and Shapiro (1) also stress that in therapy the most common reasons for failure are the therapist's failure to define the patient's self-defeating style, the therapist's passivity, his reluctance to use his own ego skills to counteract the patient's defective reality testing, and the failure to give the patient enough support to bear the confrontation with previously avoided conflicts.

The true Passive-Aggressive Personality, unlike the Antisocial Personality, rarely comes to therapy in the prison. Since his behavior does not lead him into open conflict with the institution and his behavior is so frequently emulated by other inmates, it is hardly viewed as abnormal. When these patients are involved in conflicts, they tend to make themselves the apparent victim and so are not punished or forced into treatment.

Summary

Although the personality disorders have been the subject of research for decades, there have been difficulties inherent in all the studies to date. First, the diagnosis is a difficult one to make in those cases that appear on the surface to be healthy. Second, the difficulties encountered in custodial institutions in which a doctor-patient relationship is so distorted make trust an almost impossible situation. Without a thorough overhaul in the system for delivery of diagnosis and treatment to the prisoner, the future for research and treatment in this field remains extremely doubtful.

REFERENCES

1. Adler, G., and Shapiro, L. N. Psychotherapy with prisoners. Curr. Psychiatr. Ther., 99–105, 1969.
2. Bach-y-Rita, G., and Veno, A. Habitual violence: A profile of 62 men. Am. J. Psychiatry, 131:1015–1017, 1974.
3. Bach-y-Rita, G. Habitual violence and self mutilation. Am. J. Psychiatry, 131:1018–1020, 1974.
4. Casy, M. D., Segall, D. R. K., Street, C. E., et al. Sex chromosome abnormalities in two state hospitals for patients requiring special security. Nature (Lond.), 209:641, 1966.
5. Cleckley, H. *The Mask of Sanity.* C. V. Mosby Co., St. Louis, 1964.
6. Craft, M. J. The moral responsibility for Welsh psychopaths. Int. Psychiatry Clin., 5:91, 1967.
7. Dunaij, S., and Hoch, P. H. Pseudopsychopathic schizophrenia. In: *Psychiatry and the Law*, American Psychopathology Association Proceedings, P. H. Hoch and J. Zubin (Eds.), Vol. 43, pp. 169–195. American Psychopathology Association, 1955.

8. East, W. N. *Medical Aspects of Crime.* Churchill, London, 1936.
9. Gendreau, P., and Ross, B. Effective correctional treatment: Bibliography for cynics. Crime Delinquency, 25:463–489, 1979.
10. Gibbens, T. C. N., Briscoe, O., and Dell, S. Psychopathic and neurotic offenders in mental hospitals. Int. Psychiatry Clin., 5:143–151, 1967.
11. Gibbens, T. C. N., Pond, D. A., and Stafford-Clark, D. A follow-up study of criminal psychopaths. J. Ment. Sci., 105:108–115, 1959.
12. Glueck, B. C., Jr. Changing concepts in forensic psychiatry. J. Crim. Law Criminol., 45:123–132, 1954.
13. Glueck, S., and Glueck, E. *Criminal Careers in Retrospect.* Commonwealth Fund, New York, 1943.
14. Guze, S. B. A study of recidivism based upon a follow-up of 217 consecutive criminals. J. Nerv. Ment. Dis., 138:575, 1964.
15. Guze, S. B., and Goodwin, D. W. Diagnostic consistency in antisocial personality. Am. J. Psychiatry, 128:360–361, 1971.
16. Guze, S. B., Goodwin, D. W., and Crane, J. B. Criminality and psychiatric disorders. Arch. Gen. Psychiatry, 20:583–591, 1969.
17. Guze, S. B., Woodruff, R. A., and Clayton, P. J. Psychiatric disorders and criminality. J. A. M. A., 227:641–642, 1974.
18. Hallock, S. L., and Witte, A. D. Is rehabilitation dead? Crime Delinquency, 23:372–382, 1977.
19. Harrington, A. *Psychopaths.* Simon & Schuster, New York, 1972.
20. Jessen, J. L., and Roosenburg, A. M. Treatment results at the Dr. Henri van der Hoeven Kliniek, Utrecht, The Netherlands. Paper presented at the Fifth World Congress of Psychiatry, Mexico City, 1971.
21. Jew, C. C., Clanon, T. L., and Mattocks, A. L. The effectiveness of group psychotherapy in a correctional institution. Am. J. Psychiatry, 129:602–605, 1972.
22. Lindner, R. M. *Stone Walls and Men.* Odyssey Press, New York, 1946.
23. Maughs, S. B. A concept of psychopathy and psychopathic personality: Its evolution and historic development. J. Crim. Psychopathol., 2:329–356, 1941.
24. Maughs, S. B. Psychopathic personality: Review of the literature 1947–54. Arch. Crim. Psychodynam., 1:291–325, 1955.
25. Murdoch, B. D. Electroencephalograms, aggression and emotional maturity in psychopathic and non-psychopathic prisoners. Psychol. Afr., 14:216–231, 1972.
26. Quay, H. Psychopathic personality as pathological stimulation-seeking. Am. J. Psychiatry, 122:180–188, 1965.
27. Rabin, A. I. Psychopathic (sociopathic) personalities. In: Legal and Criminal Psychology, H. Toch (Ed.), pp. 271–293. Rinehart Publishing Co., New York, 1961.
28. Robins, L. N. *Deviant Children Grown Up.* Williams & Wilkins Co., Baltimore, 1966.
29. Roosenburg, A. M. Mental health aspects of the prevention of crime. Submitted to Third United Nations Congress on the Prevention of Crime and the Treatment of Offenders, Stockholm, August 9–18, 1965.
30. Roosenburg, A. M. Presented to the American Psychiatric Association, Miami, 1969.
31. Swank, G. E., and Winer, D. Occurrence of psychiatric disorders in a county jail population. Am. J. Psychiatry, 133:1331–1333, 1976.
32. Thorne, F. C. The etiology of sociopathic reactions. Am. J. Psychother., 13:319–330, 1959.
33. Tupin, J. P., Smith, D. B., Clanon, L., Kim, L. I., Nugent, A., and Groupe, A. The long term use of lithium in aggressive prisoners. Compr. Psychiatry, 14:311–317, 1973.
34. von Krafft-Ebbing, R. *Textbook of Insanity.* F. A. Davis Co., Philadelphia, 1904.
35. Yochelson, S., and Samenow, S. *The Criminal Personality.* Jason Aronson, New York, 1976.
36. Zuckerman, M. Variables affecting deprivation results. In: *Sensory Deprivation: Fifteen Years of Research,* J. P. Zubek (Ed.), pp. 47–84. Appleton-Century-Crofts, New York, 1969.
37. Zuckerman, M. Hallucinations, reported sensations, and images. In: *Sensory Deprivation: Fifteen Years of Research,* J. P. Zubek (Ed.), pp. 85–125. Appleton-Century-Crofts, New York, 1969.

30

PERSONALITY DISORDERS IN THE COURT

Jonas R. Rappeport, M.D.

Introduction

Criminal offenders who are diagnosed as "personality disorders" present a special problem to the criminal courts as well as to the psychiatric profession. Is their criminal activity *substantially* a product of their illness or are they basically criminals who merely happen to suffer from a concurrent illness? Should they be treated, or punished by confinement? (Are they victims of psychiatric forces or are they essentially criminals? Should they be treated as patients or punished as wrongdoers?)

These offenders confuse both the legal and the medical professionals. To the judge, attorney, or probation officer they differ from the usual offender because their offenses seem bizarre or their attitude and actions to the court officers are irrational. Reflecting common sense, the legal profession is saying to itself, "If I acted that way I would consider myself sick. Therefore, this person must be sick. But just how sick is he really?"

The judge tends to use himself and his own life experience as a yardstick of normality whereas the psychiatrist uses his training, professional experience, and the diagnostic manual as well as himself and his own life experience. Do our professional criteria clear the muddy water? DSM III lists personality disorders on Axis II, making a clear distinction from most other types of psychiatric illness. In further defining personality disorders it says, "It is only where personality traits are inflexible and maladaptive and cause either significant impairment in social or occupational functioning or subjective distress that they constitute Personality Disorders" (1). Is this a concept that is easy to grasp? While we hope DSM III will help us, I suspect that many psychiatrists will continue to have difficulty defining personality disorders. Should they then expect judges and correctional officers to understand? The idea that an individual is "sick but not sick" is not easy to appreciate. The psychiatrist may see a patient as possessing a pathology and, therefore, he is sick. This does not mean that he is not legally responsible for his behavior or that he could benefit from psychiatric treatment. Legal "sick" and medically treatable sick are not the same. In attempting our explanation, little good is accomplished in stating that the patient has a confused sexual identity or that his object choice is distorted or that the patient is not psychotic or neurotic but "only has a personality disorder." In fact, we must be careful that we do not use this term in a critical fashion.

Assuming that we have a clear understanding, it is going to be very difficult for us to convey to these lay persons an appreciation of this intriguing group of patients who become involved with the law. The courts consider that the neurotic and psychotic patient belongs to the mental health system while the person with a personality disorder, when he becomes an offender, is generally considered to be the property of the criminal justice system. In attempting to clarify the concept of the personality disorder, I find a very useful method utilizes everyday feelings which the lay person, himself, may have experienced. For instance, in attempting to explain the power and force of sexual drives responsible for sexual offenses I ask my questioner if he would forego his normal heterosexual behavior if it were declared illegal. Most judges or attorneys will admit that they might have difficulty struggling with such an illegal urge. I then point out that the homosexual, exhibitionist, or voyeur has a similar difficulty in conforming his behavior to the requirements of the law. (This does not mean to say that I feel such patients are not legally responsible.) The concept of the Schizoid, Paranoid, Histrionic Personality Disorder can be understood without too much difficulty if described in sufficient detail. In a similar fashion, many people have had tantrums and because of this can equate such personal behavior with the Intermittent Explosive Disorder or Isolated Explosive Disorder (see Appendix B). Those who have unsuccessfully tried to stop smoking may be able to appreciate the difficulties of the alcoholic or addict. An understanding of the Antisocial Personality and of some of the sexual deviations may be more difficult. Each of us who examines such individuals for the courts must develop our own technique of explaining the patient's behavior in an understandable fashion.

The particular demands of the law are such that the judge must make specific clear-cut decisions. As a result, he may insist upon our answering inquiries in as clear and specific a fashion as our profession will allow. Obviously, in the area of personality disorder, we may not be able to present a yes or no answer and, of course, under such circumstances we must describe the disordered personality in "understandable language." (This is no place for psychiatric jargon.) We may feel that the system "demands" more; actually, we are only expected to do our best. The final decisions to be made are legal and not medical decisions.

The Psychiatrist in Court Work

In this chapter, I shall speak of the role of the psychiatrist in dealing with the personality disorder in relation to the criminal justice system. I shall refer to my work as a court psychiatrist and attempt to clarify some of the differences between my specific role in the system and the role of the private practicing or state hospital psychiatrist. I shall not discuss specifics of how those with the various personality disorders become involved with the law since I believe the other chapters in the book will cover such material. I shall, instead, discuss the particular problems such patients cause the mental health professional in his attempt to serve both the patient and the judicial system.

The court psychiatrist does not function in the usual "adversary" role, but, instead, acts as an amicus curiae, or friend of the court (6, 14). Hopefully, he can be free to express his opinions without conscious or unconscious bias related to the defense or prosecution.

The patients the psychiatrist examines for the court are quite different from those usually encountered in private practice. We all, of course, see patients who have a tendency to "act out"; however, the patients seen in reference to the court are individuals who have, in fact, committed offenses for which they have been charged and generally do not come to the psychiatrist in a truly voluntary sense. They are referred to a private psychiatrist by their attorney in order to assist him in the defense of the case or are referred to the court psychiatrist by the judge to assist him in various ways to be described later.

We therefore have a group of patients who do not want help in the usual medical sense, but instead want to limit their criminal responsibility or prevent incarceration. This produces important changes in the manner in which history and symptoms are presented. Because of this, it is imperative that much more information be obtained from sources other than the patient, such as police, attorney, victim, parents, spouse, etc.

The psychiatrist is called upon to render opinions in two distinct situations: before the actual trial has begun and after the trial, but before a sentence is given. Unlike the usual TV portrayal, many judges, after finding the defendant guilty, will hold the disposition in abeyance (sub curia) in order to obtain a probation and/or psychiatric evaluation to better fit the punishment to the criminal and not the crime.

Before the trial begins, there are three areas to be considered—dangerousness of the defendant (to himself or others) relative to his release while awaiting trial, his ability to stand trial, and his criminal responsibility at the time of the crime. After the trial, but before sentencing, the questions of dangerousness and treatability are the important factors.

Pretrial Examination—Ability to Stand Trial

Those suffering with personality disorders are generally found able to stand trial since the criteria or "test" requires a very high level of incapacity. Although this "test" may vary from one jurisdiction to another, it is stated as: "A person is unable to stand trial if 'as a result of a mental disorder' he is unable to understand the nature or the object of the proceedings against him or to assist in his defense" (2). Until the recent work of Thomas and Hess (19), Robey (16), and McGarry et al. (9, 11), there was little in the literature to be used as a guide. The Competency Screening Test and competency assessment instruments designed by Lipsitt and McGarry are excellent "tools" to use as a foundation in evaluating competency (ability to stand trial). Because of our fear of "incarcerating" patients in hospitals for years while awaiting their "recovery" so they might then stand trial, we have adopted a philosophy that says, "A man should be given the benefit of the doubt in the direction of standing trial." When this is applied to those with personality disorders, only the rare individual would be found incompetent (unable) to stand trial. An example is the patient who at first appeared to be a personality disorder, but actually suffered from mental deficiency or another organic condition such as Korsakoff's, epilepsy, etc. Such a condition may be seen in relation to charges of petty larceny or sexual offenses. None of the cases presented below were unable (incompetent) to stand trial.

Criminal Responsibility

Currently, in the United States, most jurisdictions use either the Mc-Naghten test or the American Law Institute's Model Penal Code Test (3). Many authors imply that a person must be psychotic in order to be considered not guilty by reason of insanity, regardless of the test. While this is a "safe" rule, it leads to a "battle of labels" and may easily obscure the patient's singular personality structure. An example of a patient whose criminal responsibility was felt to be related to his diagnosis by several examiners is the case of B. C. (Case 1).

> *Case 1—B. C.* This 23-year-old man was charged with assault with intent to murder following the shooting of the mayor of his town, which he did "in order to gain publicity and fame, having failed at everything he had tried so far in life. He hoped to call attention to himself and the miserable treatment he had received at the hands of his parents, particularly his mother."
> He stalked several important local personalities for several weeks, but did not shoot them for obvious reasons. On some occasions, his view was obstructed and on other occasions, someone else might be hurt by shattering glass, etc. He kept a diary of his "hunt" with the thought that it would be found and published in which case he or his estate would be paid by those who loved his victim. He would then have "the last laugh."
> **The History.** (Numerous reports and interviews with friends, etc., were utilized.) He was raised in a disordered home, the fourth of five children. His mother is defective intellectually and/or a schizophrenic. His father might be described as a Schizoid Personality, although he has worked regularly at a semiskilled job and supported the family. Both parents come from broken

homes with much deprivation in their lives. The patient was his mother's favorite and there is evidence that she "hounded" him constantly and supported his criticisms of others.

The patient was always seen as a quiet, shy young man with few, if any friends. Those who attempted to befriend him were slowly pushed away. In high school, he played third string lacrosse one season and participated minimally in a few school clubs, graduating in the first third of a large class. Following graduation, he tried junior college, on two occasions, but failed both times. He blamed the teachers and the school. In fact, all of his trouble was the fault of others, his parents, teachers, society, etc. He worked two jobs, a truck driver's helper and stock boy, and moved into his own room. Because of his uncooperative behavior in his helper's job, being surly with customers, whistling loudly, etc., he was moved to a less lucrative route. He became angry and felt the dispatcher was unfair to him. He bought a gun and planned to shoot him, but complained to the Human Relations Commission instead. (They found no discrimination.) He thought of committing a robbery, but decided against that.

Shortly thereafter, he met his first girl friend. The romance lasted 2 months, perhaps 10 dates, and then he was rejected. She described him later as odd, demanding, controlling, unfriendly and uncooperative with her other friends, and too serious.

After he failed in his attempts to get her back, he decided to commit suicide. He bought an automatic pistol and planned to go to the center of town and stand on the railing of a bridge with a rope around his neck tied to the bridge. He would then shoot as many people as possible, shoot himself, fall off the bridge, break his neck, and drown.

He prepared for this, writing a farewell note to his former girl friend and writing "killer" across his forehead, covering it with a wool ski cap. Then, he went to a restaurant near the bridge for his final meal. He dined well and was so impressed with the warmth and friendliness of his waitress that he left her an exorbitant tip before progressing to the bridge and preparing for his deadly deed. All was in readiness when who should come by but the waitress. He could not kill her, he couldn't really kill anyone, himself included. He untied the rope, went home, tore up his note, and cried. Shortly thereafter, he decided to kill a well-known figure and attain his fame, believing, of course, that he probably would be killed in the process. He "stalked" various persons for 2 months and finally committed the offense.

My mental status examination read: This man was examined for a total of 8 hours. He is of average build (about 5 feet 8 inches) with black hair and no particularly distinguishing features. His build is stocky. His arms appear short, but not pathologically so. His most frequent facial expression was a smile which varied from a smirk to a laughing smile. He was generally cooperative to the interviews. He was not restless or hyperactive and showed no real anxiety or tension except when pushed or challenged; then he became angry. His general demeanor was one of grandiosity. He spoke well, using average vocabulary spiced with mild profanity when angry. He controlled most of the interviews by going into excessive detail and circumstantiality. At times, he was vague and guarded, particularly when questioned specifically about his early life and parents, or very personal matters. Answers to questions were relevant; however, at times he responded with "I don't know." There was no evidence of confusion or disorganization of thought or evidence of time or space distortion.

His mood was best described as varying between a general carefree happiness, then from seriousness to anger. There was little direct evidence of sadness or depression. Affect was frequently inappropriate to the content. He laughed when speaking of being depressed and of contemplating suicide. He did express anger and annoyance, which seemed excessive, toward his family and others who he felt mistreated him. Outstanding, however, was his apparent light hearted attitude toward the serious charges and his relish in relating the events of the past few months.

There was no evidence of hallucinations, delusions, or ideas of reference, although he is clearly a suspicious person who has never trusted others "because they made fun of him." He spoke of his parents with hate, particularly his mother, who he feels was lazy and "never cared." "The government shouldn't let people like them be parents."

He was "45 when he was born" because he didn't have a happy childhood. He made no friends because he was ashamed to bring them home. He also spoke hatefully or derisively of most of the people in his life, although he did remember some kindnesses and remarked about them. When asked why he didn't kill his mother whom he hated so much he said, "It wasn't worth the effort." He describes his life as miserable, in a manner best described as self-pity. His hostility and negative view of the world are excessive.

His girl friend was the first he made himself. The few other friends he had became friends on their initiative. He felt destroyed when she finally rejected him and wanted to kill himself. He tried and couldn't. He thought of killing her, but "couldn't." He finally decided he would do something by which he could gain notoriety and, thereby, let the world know how he had suffered, particularly in his childhood. He then made plans to carry out a deed which he hoped would produce those desired results. He now feels that he failed in doing the job the way he wanted to. Once again, he feels he has failed as he has done all his life; nevertheless, this is said in a grandiose manner.

At no time did he appear to be trying to make himself look more ill than he was. He was oriented in time, person, and place. There was no evidence of impairment of recent or remote memory or immediate recall. (Psychological testing covers the other usual tests of this part of the exam.)

When asked if he thought he was mentally ill at the time of the alleged crimes, he says, "I hope so." When asked if he thinks he is mentally ill now, he says, "I don't think so." His superficial social judgment shows no impairment; his deeper judgment would seem impaired and controlled by his own feelings with little consideration for the needs or feelings of others. His insight into his personality problems is extremely limited.

Psychological Tests. A thorough battery of psychological tests was performed.* The summary read: Mr. C. presently functions within the bright normal range of intelligence and shows no signs of organic brain damage. He is basically a schizoid person who acts in a very grandiose, self-centered manner. He feels alienated from other people and society in general, and maintains a suspicious, guarded attitude. He is preoccupied with feelings of failure and low self-worth and needs to strongly deny and defend himself against such feelings. He defends himself by using an obsessive concern with detail, immature, sometimes inappropriate attempts at humor, and a general avoidance of people and threatening situations. Problems regarding sex and sexual identity were evident and he has conflicts regarding male authority

---

* Olsson, J. E., Ph.D., Chief Psychologist, Supreme Bench of Baltimore, Baltimore, Maryland.

figures and sexuality in women. Although he has strong antisocial attitudes and feels resentment toward society, he is not considered a typically antisocial, psychopathic individual. While certain test results suggest some disturbance in reality testing, such findings did not indicate severe psychopathology or a psychotic process.

An EEG using alpha-chloralose (13) was performed and reported as follows†: This man's base line record was entirely within normal limits. He received 500 mg of alpha-chloralose, a sedative that is particularly useful in eliciting latent abnormalities in the EEG. After the alpha-chloralose, the record showed no evidence for specific abnormalities such as temporal lobe spikes, focal slowing, or discharges, nor did it show evidence for 6 and 14 per second spikes, which have been associated with aggressive behavior.

It did show nonspecific changes in the form of paroxysmal 5 to 7 per second waves representing a mild activation (2+). It is generally thought that this pattern represents an instability of the central nervous system, but the clinical significance of this factor can only be determined on the basis of other data. For instance, 20% of the population with no history of neurological disorders or psychiatric difficulties shows such a pattern, whereas between 50 and 70% of the people with episodic psychiatric difficulties or impulsivity will show such a pattern.

My full report was summarized as follows: My opinion is that Mr. C. is currently sane and the he is able to understand the proceedings against him and properly assist is his own defense.

He understands and can relate clearly his actions at the time of the alleged offense and understands the alleged injuries of the victim and that he has been charged with having caused them. He has a clear understanding of the seriousness of these charges, the legal defenses to same, and the possible findings of a judge or jury and the resultant acquittal or sentences within the capacity of the average layman. During three of my four interviews, his attorney was present. Mr. C. discussed various issues with him and gave him directions and requests.

It is further my opinion that at the time of the alleged offenses, he was *not* insane or mentally incompetent under the American Law Institute Test. I believe that he suffers from the mental disease, a personality disorder. It appears that he has a Schizoid Personality Disorder with paranoid and antisocial features. However, I believe that on the day of the offense, he *had* substantial capacity both to appreciate the criminality of his conduct and to conform his conduct to the requirements of law.

A schizoid person is one who is shy, overly sensitive, seclusive, avoids close or competitive relationships, and is often eccentric. Such people daydream excessively and use autistic (relating to themselves) thinking, but without the loss of the ability to recognize reality. They may also have difficulty expressing hostility and ordinary aggressive feelings. The paranoid features are seen as hypersensitivity, rigidity, jealousy, unwarranted suspicion, envy, excessive self-importance, and a tendency to blame others and ascribe evil motives to them. The antisocial features, which seem related to the current offense, are seen as self-centeredness, hedonism, lack of loyalty to any group, scheming, and antisocial behavior. It has been difficult to classify this man clearly, a not uncommon problem with psychiatric nosology since he presents a mixture of

---

† Monroe, R. R., Professor of Psychiatry, Institute of Psychiatry and Human Behavior, University of Maryland Medical School, Baltimore, Maryland.

symptoms. Nevertheless, it is clear that there is no major distortion of reality testing. While his capacity to conform his behavior to the requirements of the law might be impaired to a slight extent, I do not feel that this impairment was substantial.

His counsel obtained the services of two outstanding psychiatrists in the community who also conducted extensive evaluations. They obtained the services of an experienced social worker who interviewed B. C.'s parents. Their opinion was that while the patient was competent to stand trial, he was psychotic at the time of the crime (schizophrenic, latent type) and, therefore, lacked substantial capacity to *conform* his behavior to the requirements of the law. The thrust of their argument was that because he was schizophrenic he could not be responsible.

A fourth psychiatrist saw him for the courts and said he found no mental illness.

This tendency to rely on the diagnosis as equal to responsibility constantly causes us trouble. Historically, only the delusional (psychotic) were considered not responsible so that we tend to look upon psychosis as the important factor. Mental illness has, however, encompassed a larger area of abnormal human behavior since McNaghten (1843) and now includes such diseases as the personality disorders, although they generally are not useful as a diagnosis to exculpate.

In U.S. vs Brawner (20), the decision that substituted the American Law Institute test for the Durham test in the District of Columbia, the court said, "Testimony in terms of psychiatric labels (Diagnosis) obscures the fact that a defendant's responsibility does not turn on whether or not the experts have given his condition a name and the status of disease (10). In its attempt to restrict conclusory expert testimony and present basic factual information to the jury, several decisions of the Durham court (10) attempted to define "product" and "mental disease" or defect in broad terms. ". . by discouraging the use of psychiatric labels (Diagnosis) which often served to hide the fact that the experts were providing virtually no information about the defendant's underlying condition."

The ideas expressed above by the District of Columbia Court of Appeals with reference to the jury having as much information as possible are similar to concepts expressed in the commentary associated with the Model Penal Code (12). The law is not primarily interested in whether or not a person is "sick," but only whether or not he can be held responsible for his behavior according to the applicable test. The law has established a high level for the determination of criminal responsibility stating that all people are considered "sane" or responsible unless proven otherwise. Although varying in each state, the degree of proof of insanity required is great and the burden of proving it is upon the defense. In Case 1 (B.C.), the jury felt the defendant was responsible and he was sentenced to prison.

More detailed discussions of the issues involved in determining criminal responsibility may be found in the writing of such authors as Bromberg (4),

Goldstein (5), Sadoff (17a), and Robitscher (17), who have made excellent contributions to our understanding of this subject. The McNaghten test is used in about 30 states and reads as follows: "at the time of the committing of the act, the party accused was laboring under such a defect of reason, from a disease of the mind, as not to know the nature and quality of the act he was doing; or, if he did know it, that he did not know he was doing what was wrong" (17a). It is obvious that those suffering with personality disorders certainly know, in a cognitive sense, that what they are doing is illegal or wrong. In most jurisdictions using McNaghten, it is rare for a person suffering with a personality disorder to be considered not responsible. However, to further complicate matters, some McNaghten jurisdictions have added "irresistable impulse" as an additional test. This reads: "accused is not criminally responsible despite his knowledge of the wrongfulness of the act, if by reason of mental disease or defect there is created in his mind an irresistible impulse to commit the offense. Impulse must be such that the accused is deprived of the power to choose between right and wrong, too adhere to the right or to control the impulse to commit the wrong" (17a).

Case law has made it clear that the law does expect everyone to exert control and is only willing to exculpate by virtue of an irresistible impulse those who *really* couldn't control themselves. This must be an irresistible impulse, not merely an impulse "that wasn't resisted." Irresistible impulse has frequently been equated with the "policeman at the elbow test," i.e., "would he have committed the act if a policeman were literally standing at this elbow?" This test has proven unsatisfactory for many reasons, the least of which is that we know there are patients who will commit an offense only if they would be caught. Unfortunately, this is not the issue. The test applies to a total inability to control behavior or an overwhelming impulse or sudden uncontrollable action.

In general usage, irresistible impulse has not been extended to include the kind of impulse related to compulsive behavior disorders as kleptomania, exhibitionism, or arson. This, of course, raises the question of impulse versus compulsion. A person compelled may be unable to control the impulse.

Those suffering from Intermittent Explosive Disorder and those with evidence of episodic dyscontrol cause concern when considering impulsiveness. To my knowledge, there is little case law on this, a fact which is understandable when we consider that there is also little in the psychiatric literature. In practice, we find that medical testimony relating to "controllability," while not resulting in a finding of not guilty by reason of insanity, may result in a reduction in the degree of the findings, i.e., from first degree murder to second degree or manslaughter.

Case 2–Q.L. Mr. Q. L. was referred by his attorney for a psychiatric evaluation. He had been charged with murder in the first degree. The circumstances of his offense were as follows.

Mr. and Mrs. L. had been separated 3 months before the offense. She took their two children and established an apartment not far from their home. A few months prior to the separation she had obtained a position as executive secretary to the manager of a new business enterprise at an excellent salary. The patient had become suspicious of his wife's relationship with her employers, because of the excellent salary she received as well as various "benefits" such as trips, furniture, etc. Two nights before the current offense he had seen her in a restaurant-night club with one of her employers and had become annoyed and insulted her. Later, that night, he went to her apartment and broke the door down in a rage when she did not answer it. Upon finding her there alone, however, he beat her up and the next day she charged him with assault. She agreed to drop the charges if he would see a psychiatrist because of his vicious temper and inability to control himself as well as his recent excessive drinking. He called a psychiatrist who was unable to see him immediately and set up a future appointment. However, a few nights later, the patient wanted to talk with his wife further to see if they could not accomplish a reconciliation. He went to her apartment, but upon finding that she was not at home and that the stereo was playing, he assumed she was out shopping, which was her usual procedure on that night. He sat around the house for about an hour and a half, drinking more and more, when he decided in disgust to leave, assuming that she had farmed the children out to a baby-sitter and had gone out socially. Before he could leave, however, he heard his wife come in with her boss. He went into the living room and confronted them. At this point, his wife told him to leave immediately and went to call the police. He suddenly noted that the night latch was on the front door; he became enraged and tore the phone out. Words were exchanged and when he could not receive a satisfactory explanation he hit the man with his fists several times, in the stomach and face, knocking him to the floor. His rage and fury seemed to increase and he "decided to give the man something to feel sore about the next day." He proceeded to kick him in the ribs and face in the belief that he would break the man's nose and, perhaps, a few ribs. He then mixed a drink and stood looking at his prostrate victim, noticing the long stylish hair on the man. He got a knife and cut off a "chunk" of the hair knowing that this would then require a haircut. He then waited until the police arrived and admitted what he had done. Unfortunately, the next day the man died, apparently of a subdural hematoma.

The patient is 37 years old. He was born in the United States in a northeastern suburban community not far from an industrial area. His parents fought constantly. His father was stubborn, overbearing, demanding, forthright individual who left the patient's mother when he was 5. The patient's mother remarried three additional times since then, with the patient having extreme difficulty in getting along with any of his stepfathers. He could not get along with his father either and was raised for several years by relatives. Finally, at the age of 16, he attempted to work with his father, but after a year "felt put down" and joined the Army. While there, he was married for the first time. Following a tour of duty he was discharged and attempted to develop a trade, but after several years he ended up as a salesman for a heavy industrial manufacturing company. He had quit school, but got his high school equivalency while in the service. He had no further formal education, but was able to advance himself from a salesman to a manufacturer's representative. At the time of the current offense, he was dealing with purchasing agents from many large corporations and government agencies in the Philadelphia area.

relate the history to his personality development. Another physician testified as to the significance of the EEG findings.

Although charged with second degree murder, the jury returned a verdict of manslaughter. In this case, the medical testimony was probably helpful to the jury in arriving at this conclusion. Such a result is very similar to that achieved in some jurisdictions that utilize the concept of Diminished Capacity (California, Michigan, Pennsylvania, and elsewhere).

Model Penal Code

More jurisdictions are switching from McNaghten to the American Law Institute's Model Penal Code Test. This test is:

1. "A person is not responsible for criminal conduct if, at the time of such conduct as a *result* of *Mental Disease* or *Defect* he lacks *substantial* capacity to either *appreciate* the criminality (wrongfulness) of his conduct, or to *conform* his conduct to the requirements of the law."

2. The terms "mental disease or defect" do not include an abnormality manifested only by repeated criminal or otherwise antisocial conduct (12). (This was the test used in Case 1.)

In reading the discussions of the drafters of the Model Penal Code, most authorities believe that their goal was to liberalize and modernize McNaghten, in view of modern psychiatric developments. By eliminating the moral, right-wrong concept as well as any limits to the concept of cognition alone, they hoped to do this. Further, the conformity part of the test was felt to include some of the irresistible impulse concept. The antisocial caveat was included since the authors felt that without such a limit almost any "criminal" might be included since this diagnosis was used by many to apply to anyone who committed antisocial acts. Additionally, the prognosis for successful psychiatric treatment of the Antisocial Personality was (and still is by many) considered very poor. This elimination of antisocial conduct automatically excludes from consideration many of the personality disorders. In order to overcome this in practice, some examiners "find" other bits of pathology in those with sexual deviations, and some of the compulsive disorders such as kleptomania and arson. The alcoholic and addict, if their behavior is considered primarily antisocial, may also be excluded.

Except in the case of supersedent organic brain damage, it is rare to find a situation in which a patient with a personality disorder would be unable to appreciate substantially the *criminality* of his behavior (unless we consider the patient at one brief moment). However, it might be argued that a Depressed, Paranoid, Schizoid, or Schizotypal may have his capacity to appreciate criminality impaired. The issue is whether or not such impairment is "substantial." Substantial means more than a lot, a great deal, in percentages, certainly over 50%, more likely 70%. Would it not generally require a serious degree of impaired reality testing to meet this high level of impairment? On the other hand, I have seen some personality disorders who I felt met this part of the test, "unable to substantially conform their behavior to the requirements of the law." Important forensically are the words substantial and conform. I have already spoken of substantial. What does conform mean? It means to regulate or control, to follow a known pattern, etc. There is some evidence, as stated, that the authors of this test expected this part to include some of the features of the irresistible impulse test. There are patients who are not psychotic, but who suffer from such severe personality disorders that they lack substantial capacity to conform their behavior under certain circumstances, such as the paranoid or schizoid individual who is taunted or pressured or placed in some other very stressful situation. Such cases are rare and in presenting them we do not have the assuredness that exists in the case of the delusionally psychotic paranoid murder. These are "borderline" or "fence hanging" cases and, as will be seen from my examples, one might readily have given an opposite opinion. (Case 1 is an example.) Nevertheless, I propose that nothing would have been clarified by changing the diagnosis to schizophrenia, latent type, etc. I speak here of such disorders as the Schizoid, Paranoid, Depressive, or Borderline. A look at a few of these might enable the reader to understand the frame of reference that I use. Although these case descriptions are abbreviated, the reader will recognize that ancillary information was utilized in evaluating the patient—police reports, social work interview of relatives, etc. Contrary to the usual "treatment-oriented" private practice, the rule for such evaluations should be, "the more information available the better."

>*Case 3*—S. Z. S. Z., 22 years old, was referred to the court psychiatrist for a pretrial examination because the court had heard divergent psychiatric testimony as to criminal responsibility and wished another opinion. He was charged with first degree murder of a 12-year-old girl. He described the incident as follows. He was alone and reading a book in his candy store when the victim entered and began looking at the candy cases. He claims, then, that within a short but indefinite period of time after this he picked up a hammer and walked over to where she was standing in front of the candy case and struck her one blow with the hammer, whereupon she fell. He then recalls bending over and striking her several subsequent blows with the hammer—the exact number he can't recall. He denies that there was a struggle or that she put up any resistance at any time during this occurrence.
>
>He then dragged her down the aisle between two candy cases, around the front of his counter, through the door into the back room, across the back room to another door leading to a downstairs staircase and propped her against a wall next to the open staircase. He left her and retraced his steps only to hear what he presumed was her body falling down the stairs. He went back, looked down the stairs, and observed her body upside down (i.e., her feet and legs pointed toward the top of the stairs.) He claims that he then went down the

stairs and inserted his finger into her vagina for an indefinite period of time, moved the body, and returned up the stairs. He denies that he engaged in any further sexual experiences with her either before or after this time. He also denies experiencing an erection or engaging in any masturbatory practices at that time. He also denies experiencing any erotic feelings then. He claims to have gone back upstairs, walked into his store through the back door and, upon observing the "blood all over the place, I sort of came to myself and wondered what in the world have I done." He admits that one of his first impulses was to call the police, but claims that he was too frightened to do so. When asked what was he afraid of, he simply said, "the gas chamber."

Mr. Z. claims that during the course of all of this activity, the front door to his store remained unlocked. He stated that the slaying took place at a spot in the store which was clearly visible through a plate glasss window overlooking a section of the main avenue which would be fairly active during that part of the afternoon. After coming upstairs, he locked the door and turned out the lights so that it would appear that he had left the store, "for a shipment or something," and he then proceeded to clean up the blood with a mop, a bucket of hot water and detergent, and a sponge. He believes that it took him anywhere from 15 minutes to 1/2 hour to clean up the blood and he thinks that he cleaned it up to such an extent that it would not be discernible by the ordinary customer. He had blood on his clothing and left the store and went home for a change of clothing. When his mother questioned him about being home at that unusual hour in the afternoon, he told her that he came home to get some papers relative to operating the business; he then went into his room, changed clothes, and left. He returned and opened the store; a helper subsequently came in to help with the afternoon and evening business. Mr. Z. went home for supper as usual, but could not eat, came back to the store and, after closing, disposed of the body. He said about this, "I wanted her to be found. I was scared to death all the time, but I wanted them to find her."

Mr. Z. admits that this version of the occurrence is different from the version which he initially gave to the police. He claims that he gave another version to the police, "to make it seem reasonable; to make it seem like something had happened to account for me doing this, but it got more complicated as I went on so I decided to tell the truth when they were getting ready to give me the lie detector test." He admits that even before this change in his story, he had told the police that he was innocent, but could not keep to that story because he reports a police officer told him, "a lot of innocent men go to the gas chamber and that's enough to break anybody down."

Mr. Z. is an only child who grew up, until 8 with both mother and father. His father died at that time, leaving limited financial resources, whereupon his mother went to work to provide for the family needs. He recalls very little of his relationship with his father. His entire parental orientation centers around his relationship with his mother, whom he admires and idolizes, in one sense, for her dedication for his rearing and the preservation of their home. He has, in many ways, transposed his whole existence up to this time to a life resigned to staying with her and providing for her. He has also come to rely on her for the fulfillment of numerous personal functions. As he says, "I've grown accustomed to three hot meals a day, to having someone prepare clean clothing for me, and to having someone to clean my room. If I left my mother and had to do these things myself, I'd be a slob."

He had severe difficulties in adjusting in school and by 8 was seen by the school counselor regularly for over a year. He was given a "Big Brother," but

Mrs. Z. interfered so much that a relationship could not be established. He was seen by "special services" of the Department of Education at 15, at which time contacts with the mother revealed that Mrs. Z. had definite emotional problems which made it difficult for her to lend understanding to any problems her son might have. The comment of the examiner was "she tends to project blame for his behavior, and ends by saying that it is all the fault of the school." That examination also indicated that, at that time, the patient tended to act out without thinking and to be "not too concerned about reality boundaries," i.e., "he knows that they are there, but ignores them." Even then, it was noted that he had poor relationships with female figures. He gave no evidence, at that time, of having any clear-cut idea or understanding about the adult male authority figure. There was also an indication, at that time, that he may have been suffering from an agitated depression. From then until this current incident there is no history of any further psychiatric, psychological, or social agency intervention in this young man's case. He, himself, denies that there has been need for any. He admits that there were difficulties in the late 1950s and early 1960s, but he, himself attributes these mainly to school adjustment problems. His concern is that he displeased his mother because "she had to always be going down to school for him."

For the past 6 years, Mr. Z. has been dedicating himself to the support of his mother and, over that period of time, he has given the majority of his income to her for her own and household needs, taking out some money only for car payments and a small amount for pocket change for himself. Even as a younger child with a paper route, he recalls making $4.00 a week and giving half of it to his mother. He has an extreme distaste for his mother's disapproval. He admits that he has made many job changes during his relatively brief work history and that whenever these changes came, at a time when his mother thought he was doing well financially, she would express displeasure, and that would lead to arguments between them. He has, occasionally, during the course of some of these arguments, threatened to leave, but has never carried this out.

The Model Penal Code Test was applied to this case. The staff of the state hospital concluded that he was a Schizoid Personality, but that he probably did not suffer from a mental disease or defect at the time of the alleged offense leading him to lack substantial capacity to apppeciate the criminality of his conduct or to conform his conduct to the requirements of the law. The report further said, "the clinical and psychological examinations of Mr. Z. indicate that there are certainly psychodynamic explanations for his behavior, but these dynamic explanations, in my estimation, fall short of adding up to a psychiatric illness syndrome which could prove exculpatory."§

Two psychiatrists hired by his attorney likewise diagnosed him as a Schizoid Personality, but thought that he did lack substantial capacity to conform his behavior to the requirements of the law.

After reviewing all of the material and examining the patient, I reported: "During my examination of Mr. Z. he related his history and the offense in much the same manner in which he related it at the state hospital.

"He is a tall, well developed, well nourished, young man. There is a slight depressive undercurrent to his conversation. However, he is relevant and to the point. He attempts to be friendly and somewhat familiar and shows some emotional feeling. However, it is obvious that his human relationships are

---

§ Clifton T. Perkins State Hospital, Jessup, Maryland.

rather limited and reveal no deep attachment to anyone other than his mother. He describes the offense by saying, 'I don't know what came over me.' There is no evidence of any gross mental illness or psychosis.

"It is my feeling that we are here dealing with a schizoid individual, that is, one who tends to be overly sensitive and seclusive and avoids close or competitive relationships. Added to this are many features of the passive-aggressive personality with severe psychosexual inhibitions.

"It is my feeling that at the time of the crime this young man exploded into a period of what we might call 'temporary insanity.' As a result of this, at the time of the crime he lacked substantial capacity to both appreciate the criminality of his behavior and to conform his behavior to the requirements of the law. I feel that he is capable of understanding the nature and object of the proceedings and assisting in his defense."

I had obtained some additional information which I felt was very important in setting the stage for this crime. These data came separately from both Mr. Z. and his mother.

On the day of the offense, when Mr. Z. left home in the morning, he forgot to take his lunch, which his mother regularly packed for him. She noticed it and called the store, but there was no answer. Finally, around 11 a.m. she took it to the store. He was there; however, she discovered that he had, that morning, met a friend and bought a $900 boat despite her previous objections and his precarious business status. She proceeded to "raise hell" with him and they had a loud argument.

It was my impression that this only added to his internalized rage, which then was redirected to his helpless victim. In essence, he was killing his mother.

Another member of my staff, who examined the patient with me, agreed that the patient was a Schizoid Personality, but in his opinion this condition did not cause him, at the time of the offense, to lack substantial capacity to appreciate the criminality of his conduct or to conform his conduct to the requirements of the law. There was no argument as to his ability to stand trial.

The jury found this man responsible and guilty of first degree murder, but did not recommend for or against death. The judge, who had a reputation for being very harsh, gave him a life sentence in view of the psychiatric testimony, particularly the information about the pathological relationship between Mr. Z. and his mother.

It is important to remember that at the pretrial stage the law isn't interested in Mr. Z.'s treatability or his diagnostic label. The answer to the court's question was dependent on the relationship between his illness and the crime. Because of the nuclear nature of this relationship, it is perfectly understandable that "experts" should frequently disagree. In this case, there was agreement as to diagnosis. We disagreed on how his personality (illness) related to the crime.

How does this case differ from Case 1? While both were Schizoid Personalities, their crimes were different in many important ways. One (Case 3) was impulsive and motivated by unconscious drives without any overt or rational gain.

Case 1 was planned to accomplish a real goal (bring him notoriety) which it, in fact, accomplished. I am aware, of course, of its unconscious motives, etc. Unless we are to say that all offenders are sick and, therefore, not responsible, we must establish some limits and standards. Whether or not we should be involved at all is a separate argument; however, every legal system, so far evolved, has had to develop on the basis of individual responsibility.

Case 4 (below) describes briefly a situation of impulsive behavior in a previously impulsive individual who did not have the explosive quality of Case 2.

> *Case 4—K. J.* This 25-year-old single male was referred by the court with a charge of assault by stabbing. He was referred because at the time of the offense "he seemed out of it," according to the victims. He had stabbed his former girl friend and her current boyfriend. "I didn't realize what I had done and thought it was a dream."
>
> He is the oldest of four and was born and raised in the city. When age 3, he had meningitis with convulsions, following which he was pampered and thereafter became a behavior problem. When he was 7 years old, his parents separated because of incompatibility and his mother remarried 2 years later. He did not get along with his stepfather and went to live with his father. He was described as "nervous." By 11, he was referred for psychiatric care because of his chronic misbehavior in school. He failed several grades and quit while in the 7th grade, at the age of 16. He worked as a laborer and apprentice bricklayer.
>
> As a juvenile, he was in trouble for fighting and some stealing. Since 1965, he has been charged with assault and striking, assault and shooting, possession of a deadly weapon (twice), and unauthorized use, and minor with alcohol (twice).
>
> At the time of the present offense, he was under general medical care as a result of back and shoulder injuries received in an auto accident many months before. He was taking Valium prescribed by that doctor, but denied abusing the drug. Despite his history of aggression, he denied any hostile or aggressive feelings stating, "When someone hurts me, I want to hurt myself."
>
> He had developed a strong relationship with Mary, whom he hoped to marry when she graduated from high school. However, when she graduated she began going with another boy. He threatened and begged for her return, to no avail.
>
> Apparently, the patient decided to make one more desperate appeal to Mary and attempted to call her. He could not get her by telephone, but was told that she had gone to Ocean City. Apparently, he did not believe this report and went to Mary's home to check it out. He said that when he got there no one answered the door, so he went around to the side. He saw Mary and Carl nude on the floor having intercourse. He said, "I was very mad and lost my temper. I broke the window, unlocked the door and went in. Carl jumped up and hit me and knocked me to the floor. Mary was all upset and crying. I grabbed this hunting knife, I think it belonged to Mary's father. I am not sure what happened after that. I am not sure what I really did. I must have thrown the knife down and ran out of the house. I wasn't sure whether it was a dream or if I really stabbed them. Finally, I decided that I must have stabbed them. I went to a friend's home, told him what happened, called my mother, and after talking to her, I turned myself in to the police."

I asked the patient how seriously the two victims were injured. He said both had to be hospitalized and Carl was in the intensive care unit for a while. Apparently, both have recovered satisfactorily. I asked the patient how he felt after being arrested and had a chance to think about the offense. He said, "It all seemed so unreal, my whole life was falling apart."

Psychological testing|| revealed a lot of anxiety with excessive use of denial, low average intelligence, neurotic conflict in the sexual area, and no clear organic damage.

The staff felt this man was able to stand trial and was responsible. Two factors stand out here. With the history of meningitis, etc., is there a possibility of some brain dysfunction? Apparently, no one was impressed with this enough to order an EEG. In a similar vein, no one thought of the behavior as being beyond his control (conform). He was diagnosed as an Antisocial Personality (although I see him as Passive-Aggressive) and was considered very dangerous.

He was found guilty of assault. Is there a substantial difference between this case and Case 2, the man who also beat his wife's boyfriend? This case certainly should have had an EEG. If one had been done and the results were similar to Q. L.'s (Case 2), would you have felt satisfied in recommending probation on the condition that he take Dilantin?

In an area such as this, which deals with much subjective material, some personal bias may influence our opinions and recommendations. Extreme vigilance is required to overcome any such bias. Of particular help in guarding against such bias are: follow-up of your opinions, review of and discussion of particular cases with "partisan colleagues" (the psychiatrist for the other side), evaluation of "treatment" programs (yours as well as others), review of the literature, etc. There is always a tendency to form certain "sets" in our thinking based on unreliable recollections, which have no place in our efforts to be scientific. At the Supreme Bench Medical Service we attempt to overcome these problems by various means. First, we hold staff conferences of selected cases. At these conferences, guests with varying experience participate, as well as residents who help us by presenting a fresh view. If the patient has been seen by a private psychiatrist, he is always invited. In addition, at these conferences, at least one member of the staff usually assumes a "devil's advocate" role in order to stimulate our thinking and avoid any preconceived bias. Second, our administrator randomly reviews reports before they are submitted, and third, each secretary is instructed to consider the quality and reality of recommendations while typing reports.

I hope that I have been able to convey the essence of the pathology in each of the above cases. I am sure that many will disagree with my conclusions. Such disagreement only exemplifies my point, that the person-

---

|| Steinbach, I., M.S., Psychologist, Medical Service, Supreme Bench of Baltimore, Baltimore, Maryland.

ality disorders can present a very difficult and "borderline" decision with reference to criminal responsibility.

Dangerousness

As mentioned before, one of the areas in which the court needs help is to determine dangerousness on at least two different occasions. First is immediately after arrest, when the concern is whether or not to release the person on bond or upon his own recognizance. Recent Supreme Court decisions have made it more or less mandatory to release a large number of arrestees while they are awaiting trial. Second is after a finding of guilt, but before disposition. (There is a third time, after a finding of "not guilty by reason of insanity," which I will not discuss.) Here the court wishes guidances since, if not dangerous, probation might be the answer, but if dangerous, then a maximum sentence will at least protect society for a while.

Are personality disorders dangerous? The arsonist is of particular concern, as is the sex offender, particularly the pedophile. Many jurisdictions still loop upon the exhibitionist, voyeur, fetishist, and obscene phone caller as potentially dangerous, while our experience indicates that these offenders rarely "escalate" (commit more serious crimes), although they do repeat. This group consists primarily of passive and frightened people who are unlikely to repeat while awaiting trial. In fact, I frequently invoke my "6-month rule," i.e., most such defendants are so upset at being arrested that they are deterred from repeating their crimes for at least 6 months. Hopefully, by that period of time, they will have come to trial.

The arsonist and pedophile, however, cause more concern since a psychosis may be lurking behind what appears to be a personality disorder. Careful evaluation is necessary, as psychotic offenders are seen as potentially much more dangerous. My 6-month rule does not apply to these offenders if a personally directed vendetta is involved, in the case of the arsonist, or if there is strong evidence of an autistic relationship between the actor and the victim. The same reasoning may be appropriate when considering the Explosive and Schizoid Personalities.

Lion has described the violent patient and has offered suggestions for his evaluation (8). The criteria described by Kozol are also very useful in evaluating dangerousness. His article (7) on the "Diagnosis and Treatment of Dangerousness" represents his thinking after many years as Director of the Center for Diagnosis and Treatment of Dangerous Persons at Bridgewater, Massachusetts. He says, " We conceive the dangerous person as one who has actually inflicted or attempted to inflict serious physical injury on another person; harbors anger, hostility, and resentment; enjoys witnessing or inflicting suffering; lacks altruistic and compassionate concern for others;

sees himself as a victim rather than as an aggressor; resents or rejects authority; is primarily concerned with his own satisfaction and with the relief of his own discomfort; is intolerant of frustration or delay of satisfaction; lacks control of his own impulses; has immature attitudes toward social responsibility; lacks insight into his own psychological structure; and distorts his perception of reality in accordance with his own wishes and needs.

"The essence of dangerousness appears to be a paucity of feeling concern for others. The offender is generally unaware that his behavior inflicts suffering on others. The potential for injuring another is compounded when this lack of concern is coupled with anger. These elements, anger and a paucity of feeling concern for others, may be of remote or recent origin, they may be global or selective and, in many patients, they can be traced back several years. Deeply ingrained or nurtured by circumstances, these components seem to facilitate the situation that leads to the final assaultive acting out—an unconscious self-fulfilling prophecy. When the patient commits the assaultive act, he appears as a social isolate who has remained at or regressed to an infantile level of emotional prematurity where his primary concern is to satisfy primitive needs immediately." Dr. Kozol further furnishes some ideas as to "the regions of the personality that we consider relevant. These are questions to be proposed to oneself, not the patient." They are as follows:

With respect to use of force and violence:

"Was he aggressively and wantonly cruel? Did he enjoy inflicting pain? What was his affect or emotional state at the time he perpetrated his crime? Did he have any identification with his victim?"

"Was he angry? With his victim? With whom—or at what? Since when? Was he mad at the world or specifically angry with a person or a class? Was the anger realistic and justified or unrealistic and disproportionate? What was the fate of this anger? Did it persist or evaporate?"

"Is he cruel toward himself? Does he enjoy suffering? How has he reacted to frustration or delay of satisfaction? With violence? With anger? With both? Must he have immediate satisfaction? Has there been any expression of violence in his drawings, writings, statements, fantasies, dreams?"

"What is the subject's view of himself?"

"How does he feel about what he sees in himself?"

"What is his conception of an ideal person? Whom does he admire? Whom is he for? Who are his heroes? Whose exploits does he applaud? Whom does he tend to imitate in speech and manner?"

"Whom is he against?"

"What is the subject's view of others?"

"Are they his potential enemies and he their potential victim? Are they his potential prey?"

"Are they nonexistent as persons and seen only as objects that he may use or exploit? Does he confuse their identity?"

"How does he relate to others?"

"Is he a social isolate, either alienated from other persons or never affiliated with them?"

"Does he have sympathetic identification with others?"

"What is his view of his prospects for the future?"

"Is he optimistic or pessimistic? Is he hopeful or discouraged? Is he depressed?"

"Does life hold any meaning for him? What?"

"What was his view of himself vis-à-vis the general community?"

"How has he related to other persons? How has he dealt with authority figures?"

"Did he have difficulty in school and work adjustments?"

"How did he get along with his peers? Did he feel that he belonged? Or was he a loner? Did he feel dependent on his peers? Did he crave their recognition and respect?"

"Was he concerned about his status in the eyes of others?"

"Was he embittered? Did he feel frustrated, rejected, discriminated against, deprived, unrecognized, mistreated, abused, in short—victimized? Did he feel threatened and persecuted? Did he have a sense of longing and hunger with a concomitant sense of despair about ever dissipating this hunger?"

"How did he relate to his family?"

"Was the family constellation meaningful? In what way?"

"Was there conflict with parents? With siblings?"

"Did the patient feel loved, supported, encouraged by either or both parents? Did he feel threatened, disdained, rejected?"

"We are interested in the patient's general life-style. Was he conventional and socially conformative and responsible, or was he unconventional, irresponsible, and opposed to social standards? We are interested in the nature and amount of control that he asserted in his life-pattern of behavior. Has control been by repression or sublimation? What has been the result?"

Alcoholism and drug addiction present a slightly different problem. The simple alcoholic or addict is not a problem as far as dangerousness is concerned; however, persons so addicted frequently commit other crimes. Generally, we can be sure that being arrested will not stop addiction. The court's concern is not primarily with the addiction, but whether or not the patient is likely to repeat his offense before his trial. If an alcoholic falls through a storm door and is subsequently charged with attempted burglary we have little concern that he is dangerous. However, if an addict robs someone at gunpoint in order to obtain drugs there is little guarantee that he may not repeat upon his release unless he receives help for his addiction. We must here consider whether the crime is potentially harmful to others and whether it is likely to be repeated.

Obviously, we can never be sure that our predictions are correct nor can we furnish any guarantee. The court recognizes this and only expects us to furnish an opinion based on "reasonable medical certainty."

Unfortunately, it is my impression that we seem to expect more from ourselves than others expect from us. Subsequently, we repeatedly err on the side of caution or conservatism in order to avoid criticism (more ours than others') (15).

Presentence

After the guilty verdict, but before the sentence, is the time the psychiatrist should be of most help to the criminal justice system. Are we not clinicians and is not our major function to diagnose and treat mental illness? If this is true, then we should be able to furnish the court with information about diagnosis, prognosis, and treatment that is more realistic and reliable than our opinions as to criminal responsibility. The patient has been found guilty, and now disposition must be made. The court wants to know whether we feel the patient needs treatment and, if so, where he can obtain that treatment and how successful this treatment is likely to be with particular concern for recidivism. Further, if the recommended treatment is to be performed on an outpatient basis, at what risk does this place the community? Answers to questions on recidivism and dangerousness may be no easier at this stage of the judicial process than they were previously. Answers about treatment should be more within our scope. The court expects the psychiatrist to present an opinion based on experience with similar offenders and not merely the statement, "I will treat the patient because he says he wants help."

It is at this point that many psychiatrists find themselves in a bind. Their usual relationship with a patient is one in which the patient presents himself voluntarily, seeking help for his problem. The psychiatrist then sees himself as offering a wanted service. His goal is to treat the patient until he has "recovered" or for as long as the patient desires to continue with the treatment program. However, with the offender, an entirely different set of factors is present. As I stated earlier in this paper, there are important secondary factors which color much of the information that is presented because, as he sees it, the patient needs a recommendation for outpatient treatment if you are to be of help to him. The psychiatrist may be in trouble at this point since he certainly doesn't want to do any harm to the patient and he may rightfully feel that incarceration alone is not going to accomplish any more than to temporarily protect society. Added to this is the fact that most psychiatrists have a very limited experience with offenders. How many arsonists, exhibitionists, or Antisocial Personalities have you treated in your practice lately? This means that one may be operating from a very limited experience with various pressures interfering with a professional decision. This doesn't mean that we should be therapeutic nihilists in such cases, but implications of successful therapy may not be accurate. To add to the problem, unlike the court psychiatrist, the private practitioner is usually asked to make his recommendations for treatment before the trial has even taken place.

The court psychiatrist has an advantage since he will usually see the patient after the trial in order to make these recommendations for disposition. At this point, the patient may be more willing to admit his guilt and speak about the offense and the emotions related to the offense. The court psychiatrist also has the advantage of making it clear to the patient that he is not in the patient's employ, but is, in fact, an employee of the court. The protection of the community, the patient's real motivation, the availability of treatment facilities, both inpatient and outpatient, and many other factors can then be considered without split loyalties. This places the court psychiatrist in a different role, one which can lend itself to overcaution more readily than to therapeutic hopefulness or folly. We attempt to guard against such factors by the techniques described earlier. One important additional item which cannot be overemphasized is that we obtain all the information possibly available; police reports, autopsy reports, school records, record of past offenses, interviews with relatives, etc. The more information one has, the more valid become the recommendations. This represents a departure from the usual psychiatric practice in which one relies primarily on what the patient says and rarely obtains collateral information. While all the data are important, the final decision is based on the understanding of the patient.

The primary concern of the court is what kind of help is most beneficial to the patient and society. This is directed to the psychiatrist in terms of whether or not psychiatry has anything to offer. Some might say that we can help anyone who is sick and that all offenders are sick. I seriously question such a philosophy and feel I must dismiss it without further comment. The same might be said for the idea that all penal incarceration is bad and destructive and that no psychiatrist should ever recommend it. One answer to that might be that some of our prisons are better places than some of our state mental hospitals. The important point is that simple incarceration does help some people and can be an effective deterrent for them as well as others. Another point is that there are many patients with personality disorders whom we cannot adequately treat; at least, we cannot treat them in other than a prison or maximum security institution. Furthermore, we have to take into consideration that society deserves protection from predators even if they, the predators, must lose their freedom; that is what the criminal law is all about.

Before recommending outpatient or hospital treatment we must consider how dangerous the patient is. Here, the criteria of Kozol, previously mentioned, can be very helpful. Coupled with this is the patient's motivation and the availability of treatment. Both of these go hand in hand since the well motivated patient will utilize whatever treatment is available, while others, less motivated, will either resist all efforts for help or, at least, need a treatment program they cannot resist.

As far as dangerousness goes, the severely assaultive patient certainly needs maximum security and should only be considered for special programs that might be available in selected hospitals or prisons. Examples of these are the special unit at Bridgewater, Massachusetts, the Patuxent Institution in Maryland, or the special hospital at Vacaville, California.

As for treatment, all of the personality disorders pose special problems since these are conditions which are "lifelong patterns which do not respond easily to therapy." It is tempting to look at the offensive behavior alone and minimize or overlook the basic personality problem, thereby allowing oneself to believe that treatment can be directed toward the symptom. All too often the symptom is not so ego-dystonic as to be readily treated. Shifts in object choice, etc., are accomplished only with much difficulty. This applies particularly to the sex offenders, exhibitionists, voyeurs, and pedophiles, who may do best in special groups. With many acting out patients, external controls or coercion appear to be the important factor. By this, I do not mean the usual suspended sentence and probation. The probation officer, with a large case load, readily forgets the patient, leaving it up to the therapist to keep the patient in treatment. Psychiatrists find it difficult to function as probation officers, also resulting in aborted treatment efforts. Not only does the patient stop coming, but to make matters worse, his bill is rarely paid. Evaluating motivation is, therefore, very important. As I have emphasized previously, the secondary gains (probation and treatment) make it very difficult to examine motivation. Some helpful keys to look for are the following.

1. Does the patient readily admit his guilt? Is he remorseful? Does he admit to other offenses? Some for which he was never caught?
2. Has he ever voluntarily sought help for his problem before or are his reasons for not seeking help valid or merely rationalizations? Why didn't previous help work?
3. Does he believe he has a problem for which he needs help?
4. What is his idea of treatment? Magic? Passive correction?
5. In discussing the realities of treatment, time, money, etc., is his life such that he can easily keep appointments or has he already established some roadblocks?
6. What are his future plans? Will they interfere with a long-term treat-

ment program?

7. Are there indications that a spouse will cooperate and make any necessary sacrifices?

8. Is he motivated enough to do whatever is within his power to control his acting out?

Many offenders will never admit their guilt or, when they do, it is presented as a "gift" with little remorse or awareness of the wrongfulness of the behavior. Some will not only admit the offense, but will admit previous offenses and express remorse for both past and present behavior. Why hasn't he sought help before? We must be suspicious of his remorse and desire for help now. This can be a broken record, played on the occasion of each arrest. This type of patient may have no real idea of how much effort therapy requires. If he seems to understand he still may have no intention of following through once he is on probation. The probation officer may even interfere by allowing the patient to stop treatment because the patient complains.

The patient may readily agree to call the therapist any time "the urge arises." Unfortunately, many urges arise suddenly, and impulses are acted upon before a phone call can be made. Except for the suicidal gesture, how many patients call before acting? Yet, I have seen numerous reports in which the therapist says that "the patient has promised to call if the urge returns." In practice, the call comes after the act; the cry is then, once again, for help in dealing with the courts. There is no question that the therapist may find himself in the bind mentioned previously. He does not want to do any harm by writing a "bad" report which might lead to incarceration, yet a hopeful report is not a true evaluation of the patient's potential. Many therapists decide to give a hopeful report with the belief that the court has experience and will see through the deception. Unfortunately, the court expects a truly honest and scientific appraisal from professionals and evaluates reports on that basis. Even when experienced, the court may accept a highly untenable recommendation.

An example of an "honest" recommendation is taken from a summary in our files: "It is my feeling that this individual is suffering from some maternal and paternal deprivation and is at a loss to make a reasonable identity. I suspect that he was exposed in his early life to, at least, observing some aggression and has adopted the aggressive mode as a way of dealing with his inner problems. I see him as being potentially dangerous; as readily using drugs or alcohol and as having a limited conscience or superego at this time. Rather than necessarily considering him mentally ill, I see him as a psycho-social catastrophe, a result of an emotionally deprived childhood, and a person who will apparently have to struggle a great deal with his feelings for a few years before things settle out and he then, perhaps, goes on to repeat the same pathology to which he was exposed. Because of his lack of real roots, that is, his lack of a wife or a regular job, a slightly more hopeful identity, we could not, in good conscience, recommend him for our outpatient group therapy program, nor do we feel that he needs hospitalization. At this point, I feel that he might show his best response to the regular correctional program of the Department of Correction and, for that reason, would recommend a sentence and referral to the Department of Correction with the hope that he might obtain some assistance in the training program at Hagerstown."

Offenders who suffer with personality disorders are not the same as voluntary nonoffenders and require special treatment plans if they are to be treated successfully. Mental health professionals who agree to treat such patients should be willing to accept certain parameters to their usual treatment arrangements. I recognize that many of my colleagues do not accept such ideas and wish to operate unfettered by such considerations. I cannot argue with them as long as they make it clear to the court that they will accept no responsibility for the management of the offender. For those willing to accept certain additional conditions as being necessary for satisfactory treatment, the most important condition is regular attendance at therapy. You cannot help a patient who isn't there. The acting out patient has an increased problem in dealing with such resistance. Utilizing the coercive pressure of the court, via the probation officer, can be very helpful. An arrangement can be made between the patient, probation officer, and therapist that the latter will report monthly the patient's attendance, payment of fees, and positive effort in therapy. It should go without saying that all content of sessions remains confidential. The therapist may further agree that should the time arrive when he feels the patient has not only remained unimproved, but is not likely to progress further in his hands, he will so report. I don't believe this is any more coercive than the arrangements under which we see many patients, except that the limits are clearly verbalized in these cases and remain unspoken in others. To my knowledge, few successful treatment programs of acting out personality disorders have been reported that did not utilize some form of control over attendance at therapy, if not over other aspects of the patient's life. Ingenuity may be required for the treatment of certain offenders in the use of behavioral modification or aversion therapies as described for the chronic gambler, homosexual, pedophile, etc. As stated, special treatment groups for sex offenders have proven successful (19). If special conditions of probation are required, these must be spelled out in detail for the court.

Summary

The mental health professions have an important role vis-à-vis the criminal justice system and those suffering with personality disorders. The courts are frequently perplexed by these offenders and/or their offenses and call upon us to assist them in many different areas: criminal responsibility, dangerousness, and treatment programs. All of these areas present special problems to the practitioner, yet represent an opportunity to serve the community by helping them understand a fellow citizen and make decisions for his future and the community's protection. Such patients present a challenge in treatment and require special treatment techniques.

REFERENCES

1. American Psychiatric Association. Diagnostic and Statistical Manual of Mental Disorders, Ed. 2, p. 305. American Psychiatric Association, Washington, D. C., 1968.
2. Annotated Code of Maryland (1965 Replacement Vol.), Supplement. Article 59, Sec. 23, 1972.
3. Brakel, S. J., and Rock, R. S. (Eds.). Mental disability and the criminal law. In: *The Mentally Disabled and the Law*, revised ed. University of Chicago Press, Chicago, 1971.
4. Bromberg, W. *The Uses of Psychiatry in the Law*. Quorum Books, Westport, Conn., 1979.
5. Goldstein, A. S. Insanity Defense. Yale University Press, New Haven, 1967.
6. Irvine, L. M., and Brelje, T. B. (Eds.). The psychiatrist as a friend of the court. In: *Law, Psychiatry and the Mentally Disordered Offender*, Vol. 1. Charles C Thomas, Springfield, Ill., 1973.
7. Kozol, H. L., Boucher, R. J., and Gawfalo, R. F. The diagnosis and treatment of dangerousness. Crime Delinquency, 18:371-392, 1972.
8. Lion, J. R. *Evaluation and Management of the Violent Patient*. Charles C Thomas, Springfield, Ill., 1972.
9. Lipsitt, P. D., and McGarry, A. L. Competency to Stand Trial and Mental Illness. DHEW Publication 73-9105. U. S. Government Printing Office, Washington, D. C., 1973.
10. McDonald vs. United States. 114 U.S. App. D.C. 120, 312 F. 2d 847, 1962.
11. McGarry, A. L., and Bendt, R. H. Criminal vs. civil commitment of psychotic offenders: A seven year follow-up. Am. J. Psychiatry, 125:10, 1969.
12. Model Penal Code, proposed official draft. American Law Institute, Philadelphia, 1962.
13. Monroe, R. R. *Episodic Behavioral Disorders*. Harvard University Press, Cambridge, 1970.
14. Rappeport, J. R. Psychiatrist as an amicus curiae. Med. Trial Technique Q., 183-189, 1971, and 197-313, 1972.
15. Rappeport, J. R. (Ed.). *Clinical Evaluation of the Dangerousness of the Mentally Ill*. Charles C Thomas, Springfield, Ill., 1967.
16. Robey, A. Criteria for competency to stand trial. A checklist for psychiatrists. Am. J. Psychiatry, 22, 1965.
17. Robitscher, J. B. *Pursuit of Agreement, Psychiatry and the Law*. J. B. Lippincott Co., Philadelphia. 1966.
17a. Sadoff, R. *Forensic Psychiatry*. Charles C Thomas, Springfield, Ill., 1975.
18. Sadoff, R. L., et al. Clinical measure of enforced group psychotherapy. Am. J. Psychiatry, 128:224, 1971.
19. Thomas,, H., and Hess, J. H., Jr. Incompetency to stand trial: Procedures, results and problems. Am. J. Psychiatry, 119, 1963.
20. U.S. v Brawne, 471 F. 2d 969. U.S. District Court of Appeals, Washington, D. C., 1972.

APPENDIX A
DSM III DIAGNOSTIC CRITERIA

Reprinted by permission

Personality Disorders

(NOTE: These are coded on Axis II.)

301.00 Paranoid Personality Disorder

Differential diagnosis. Paranoid Disorders; Schizophrenia, Paranoid Type; Antisocial Personality Disorder.

Diagnostic criteria.

The following are characteristic of the individual's current and long-term functioning, are not limited to episodes of illness, and cause either significant impairment in social or occupational functioning or subjective distress.

A. Pervasive, unwarranted suspiciousness and mistrust of people as indicated by at least three of the following:

(1) expectation of trickery or harm
(2) hypervigilance, manifested by continual scanning of the environment for signs of threat, or taking unneeded precautions
(3) guardedness or secretiveness
(4) avoidance of accepting blame even when warranted
(5) questioning the loyalty of others
(6) intense, narrowly focused searching for confirmation of bias, with loss of appreciation of total context
(7) overconcern with hidden motives and special meanings
(8) pathological jealousy

B. Hypersensitivity as indicated by at least two of the following:

(1) tendency to be easily slighted and quick to take offense
(2) exaggeration of difficulties, e.g., "making mountains out of molehills"
(3) readiness to counterattack when any threat is perceived
(4) inability to relax

C. Restricted affectivity as indicated by at least two of the following:

(1) appearance of being "cold" and unemotional
(2) pride taken in always being objective, rational, and unemotional

(3) lack of a true sense of humor

(4) absence of passive, soft, tender, and sentimental feelings

D. Not due to another mental disorder such as Schizophrenia or a Paranoid Disorder.

301.20 Schizoid Personality Disorder

Differential diagnosis. Schizotypal Personality Disorder, Avoidant Personality Disorder, Schizoid Disorder of Childhood or Adolescence.

Diagnostic criteria.

The following are characteristic of the individual's current and long-term functioning, are not limited to episodes of illness, and cause either significant impairment in social or occupational functioning or subjective distress.

A. Emotional coldness and aloofness, and absence of warm, tender feelings for others.

B. Indifference to praise or criticism or to the feelings of others.

C. Close friendships with no more than one or two persons, including family members.

D. No eccentricities of speech, behavior, or thought characteristic of Schizotypal Personality Disorder.

E. Not due to a psychotic disorder such as Schizophrenia or Paranoid Disorder.

F. If under 18, does not meet the criteria Schizoid Disorder of Childhood or Adolescence.

301.22 Schizotypal Personality Disorder

Differential diagnosis. Schizophrenia, Residual Type; Schizoid Personality Disorder; Avoidant Personality Disorder; Depersonalization Disorder; Borderline Personality Disorder.

Diagnostic criteria

The following are characteristic of the individual's current and long-term functioning, are not limited to episodes of illness, and cause either significant impairment in social or occupational functioning or subjective distress.

A. At least four of the following:

(1) magical thinking, e.g., superstitiousness, clairvoyance, telepathy, "6th sense," "others can feel my feelings" (in children and adolescents,

bizarre fantasies or preoccupations)

(2) ideas of reference

(3) social isolation, e.g., no close friends or confidants, social contacts limited to essential everyday tasks

(4) recurrent illusions, sensing the presence of a force or person not actually present (e.g., "I felt as if my dead mother were in the room with me"), depersonalization, or derealization not associated with panic attacks

(5) odd speech (without loosening of associations or incoherence), e.g., speech that is digressive, vague, overelaborate, circumstantial, metaphorical

(6) inadequate rapport in face-to-face interaction due to constricted or inappropriate affect, e.g., aloof, cold

(7) suspiciousness or paranoid ideation

(8) undue social anxiety or hypersensitivity to real or imagined criticism

B. Does not meet the criteria for Schizophrenia.

301.50 Histrionic Personality Disorder

Differential diagnosis. Somatization Disorder, Borderline Personality Disorder.

Diagnostic criteria.

The following are characteristic of the individual's current and long-term functioning, are not limited to episodes of illness, and cause either significant impairment in social or occupational functioning or subjective distress.

A. Behavior that is overly dramatic, reactive, and intensely expressed, as indicated by at least three of the following:

(1) self-dramatization, e.g., exaggerated expression of emotions

(2) incessant drawings of attention to oneself

(3) craving for activity and excitement

(4) overreaction to minor events

(5) irrational, angry outbursts or tantrums

B. Characteristic disturbances in interpersonal relationships as indicated by at least two of the following:

(1) perceived by others as shallow and lacking genuineness, even if superficially warm and charming

(2) egocentric, self-indulgent, and inconsiderate of others

(3) vain and demanding

(4) dependent, helpless, constantly seeking reassurance

(5) prone to manipulative suicidal threats, gestures, or attempts

301.81 Narcissistic Personality Disorder

Differential diagnosis. Borderline Personality Disorder, Histrionic Personality Disorder.

Diagnostic criteria.

The following are characteristic of the individual's current and long-term functioning, are not limited to episodes of illness, and cause either significant impairment in social or occupational functioning or subjective distress:

A. Grandiose sense of self-importance or uniqueness, e.g., exaggeration of achievements and talents, focus on the special nature of one's problems.

B. Preoccupation with fantasies of unlimited success, power, brilliance, beauty, or ideal love.

C. Exhibitionism: the person requires constant attention and admiration.

D. Cool indifference or marked feelings of rage, inferiority, shame, humiliation, or emptiness in response to criticism, indifference of others, or defeat.

E. At least two of the following are characteristic of disturbances in interpersonal relationships:

    (1) entitlement: expectation of special favors without assuming reciprocal responsibilities, e.g., surprise and anger that people will not do what is wanted
    (2) interpersonal exploitativeness: taking advantage of others to indulge own desires or for self-aggrandizement; disregard for the personal integrity and rights of others
    (3) relationships that characteristically alternate between the extremes of overidealization and devaluation
    (4) lack of empathy: inability to recognize how others feel, e.g., unable to appreciate the distress of someone who is seriously ill

301.70 Antisocial Personality Disorder

Differential diagnosis. Conduct Disorder, Adult Antisocial Behavior (V code), Severe Mental Retardation, Schizophrenia, manic episodes.

Diagnostic criteria.

A. Current age at least 18.

B. Onset before age 15 as indicated by a history of three or more of the following before that age:

    (1) truancy (positive if it amounted to at least five days per year for at least two years, not including the last year of school)

(2) expulsion or suspension from school for misbehavior
(3) delinquency (arrested or referred to juvenile court because of behavior)
(4) running away from home overnight at least twice while living in parental or parental surrogate home
(5) persistent lying
(6) repeated sexual intercourse in a casual relationship
(7) repeated drunkenness or substance abuse
(8) thefts
(9) vandalism
(10) school grades markedly below expectations in relation to estimated or known IQ (may have resulted in repeating a year)
(11) chronic violations of rules at home and/or at school (other than truancy)
(12) initiation of fights

C. At least four of the following manifestations of the disorder since age 18:

(1) inability to sustain consistent work behavior, as indicated by any of the following: (*a*) too frequent job changes (e.g., three or more jobs in five years not accounted for by nature of job or economic or seasonal fluctuation), (*b*) significant unemployment (e.g., six months or more in five years when expected to work), (*c*) serious absenteeism from work (e.g., average three days or more of lateness or absence per month) (*d*) walking off several jobs without other jobs in sight (Note: Similar behavior is an academic setting during the last few years of school may substitute for this criterion in individuals who by reason of their age or circumstances have not had an opportunity to demonstrate occupational adjustment.)
(2) lack of ability to function as a responsible parent as evidenced by one or more of the following: (*a*) child's malnutrition, (*b*) child's illness resulting from lack of minimal hygiene standards, (*c*) failure to obtain medical care for a seriously ill child, (*d*) child's dependence on neighbors or nonresident relatives for food or shelter, (*e*) failure to arrange for a caretaker for a child under six when parent is away from home, (*f*) repeated squandering, on personal items, of money required for household necessities
(3) failure to accept social norms with respect to lawful behavior, as indicated by any of the following: repeated thefts, illegal occupation (pimping, prostitution, fencing, selling drugs), multiple arrests, a felony conviction
(4) inability to maintain enduring attachment to a sexual partner as indicated by two or more divorces and/or separations (whether legally married or not), desertion of spouse, promiscuity (ten or more sexual

partners within one year)
(5) irritability and aggressiveness as indicated by repeated physical fights or assault (not required by one's job or to defend someone or oneself), including spouse or child beating
(6) failure to honor financial obligations, as indicated by repeated defaulting on debts, failure to provide child support, failure to support other dependents on a regular basis
(7) failure to plan ahead, or impulsivity, as indicated by traveling from place to place without a prearranged job or clear goal for the period of travel or clear idea about when the travel would terminate, or lack of a fixed address for a month or more
(8) disregard for the truth as indicated by repeated lying, use of aliases, "conning" others for personal profit
(9) recklessness, as indicated by driving while intoxicated or recurrent speeding

D. A pattern of continuous antisocial behavior in which the rights of others are violated, with no intervening period of at least five years without antisocial behavior between age 15 and the present time (except when the individual was bedridden or confined in a hospital or penal institution).

E. Antisocial behavior is not due to either Severe Mental Retardation, Schizophrenia, or manic episodes.

301.83 Borderline Personality Disorder

Differential diagnosis. Identity Disorder, Cyclothymic Disorder.

Diagnostic criteria.

The following are characteristic of the individual's current and long-term functioning, are not limited to episodes of illness, and cause either significant impairment in social or occupational functioning or subjective distress.

A. At least five of the following are required:

(1) impulsivity or unpredictability in at least two areas that are potentially self-damaging, e.g., spending, sex, gambling, substance use, shoplifting, overeating, physically self-damaging acts
(2) a pattern of unstable and intense interpersonal relationships, e.g., marked shifts of attitude, idealization, devaluation, manipulation (consistently using others for one's own ends)
(3) inappropriate, intense anger or lack of control of anger, e.g., frequent displays of temper, constant anger
(4) identity disturbance manifested by uncertainty about several issues relating to identity, such as self-image, gender identity, long-term goals or career choice, friendship patterns, values, and loyalties, e.g., "Who

am I", "I feel like I am my sister when I am good"
(5) affective instability: marked shifts from normal mood to depression, irritability, or anxiety, usually lasting a few hours and only rarely more than a few days, with a return to normal mood
(6) intolerance of being alone, e.g., frantic efforts to avoid being alone, depressed when alone
(7) physically self-damaging acts, e.g., suicidal gestures, self-mutilation, recurrent accidents or physical fights
(8) chronic feelings of emptiness or boredom

B. If under 18, does not meet the criteria for Identity Disorder.

301.82 Avoidant Personality Disorder

Differential diagnosis. Schizoid Personality Disorder, Social Phobias, Avoidant Disorder of Childhood or Adolescence.

Diagnostic criteria.

The following are characteristic of the individual's current and long-term functioning, are not limited to episodes of illness, and cause either significant impairment in social or occupational functioning or subjective distress.

A. Hypersensitivity to rejection, e.g., apprehensively alert to signs of social derogation, interprets innocuous events as ridicule.

B. Unwillingness to enter into relationships unless given unusually strong guarantees of uncritical acceptance.

C. Social withdrawal, e.g., distances self from close personal attachments, engages in peripheral social and vocational roles.

D. Desire for affection and acceptance.

E. Low self-esteem, e.g., devalues self-achievements and is overly dismayed by personal shortcomings.

F. If under 18, does not meet the criteria for Avoidant Disorder of Childhood or Adolescence.

301.60 Dependent Personality Disorder

Differential diagnosis. Agoraphobia.

Diagnostic criteria

The following are characteristic of the individual's current and long-term functioning, are not limited to episodes of illness, and cause either significant impairment in social or occupational functioning or subjective distress.

A. Passively allows others to assume responsibility for major areas of life because of inability to function independently (e.g., lets spouse decide what kind of job he or she should have).

B. Subordinates own needs to those of person on whom he or she depends in order to avoid any possibility of having to rely on self, e.g., tolerates abusive spouse.

C. Lacks self-confidence, e.g., sees self as helpless, stupid.

301.40 Compulsive Personality Disorder

Differential diagnosis. Obsessive Compulsive Disorder.

Diagnostic criteria.

At least four of the following are characteristic of the individual's current and long-term functioning, are not limited to episodes of illness, and cause either significant impairment in social or occupational functioning or subjective distress:

(1) restricted ability to express warm and tender emotions, e.g., the individual is unduly conventional, serious and formal, and stingy
(2) perfectionism that interferes with the ability to grasp "the big picture," e.g., preoccupation with trivial details, rules, order, organization, schedules, and lists
(3) insistence that others submit to his or her way of doing things and lack of awareness of the feelings elicited by the behavior, e.g., a husband stubbornly insists his wife complete errands for him regardless of her plans
(4) excessive devotion to work and productivity to the exclusion of pleasure and the value of interpersonal relationships
(5) indecisiveness: decision-making is either avoided, postponed, or protracted, perhaps because of an inordinate fear of making a mistake, e.g., the individual cannot get assignments done on time because of ruminating about priorities

301.84 Passive-Aggressive Personality Disorder

Differential diagnosis. Oppositional Disorder, passive-aggressive maneuvers in situations in which assertive behaviors are not possible.

Diagnostic criteria.

The following are characteristic of the individual's current and long-term functioning, and are not limited to episodes of illness.

A. Resistance to demands for adequate performance in both occupational and social functioning.

B. Resistance expressed indirectly through at least two of the following:

   (1) procrastination
   (2) dawdling
   (3) stubbornness
   (4) intentional inefficiency
   (5) "forgetfulness"

C. As a consequence of A and B, pervasive and longstanding social and occupational ineffectiveness (including in roles of housewife or student), e.g., intentional inefficiency that has prevented job promotion.

D. Persistence of the behavior pattern even under circumstances in which more self-assertive and effective behavior is possible.

E. Does not meet the criteria for any other Personality Disorder, and if under age 18, does not meet the criteria for Oppositional Disorder.

301.89 Atypical, Mixed or Other Personality Disorder

If an individual qualifies for any of the specific Personality Disorders, that category should be noted even if some features from other categories are present. For example, an individual who fits the description of Compulsive Personality Disorder should be given that diagnosis even if some mild dependent or paranoid features are present.

When an individual qualifies for two Personality Disorders, multiple diagnoses should be made.

Atypical Personality Disorder should be used when the clinician judges that a Personality Disorder is present but there is insufficient information to make a more specific designation.

Mixed Personality Disorder should be used when the individual has a Personality Disorder that involves features from several of the specific Personality Disorders but does not meet the criteria for any one Personality Disorder.

Other Personality Disorder should be used when the clinician judges that a specific Personality Disorder not included in this classification is appropriate, such as Masochistic, Impulsive, or Immature Personality Disorder. In such instances the clinician should record the specific Other Personality Disorder, using the 301.89 code.

APPENDIX B
DSM III DIAGNOSTIC CRITERIA

Reprinted by permission of the American Psychiatric Association, Washington, D. C., 1980

Disorders of Impulse Control Not Elsewhere Classified

312.34 Intermittent Explosive Disorder

Differential diagnosis. Antisocial Personality Disorder, Dissociative Disorder, Paranoid Disorder, Schizophrenia.

Diagnostic criteria.

A. Several discrete episodes of loss of control of aggressive impulses resulting in serious assault or destruction of property.

B. Behavior that is grossly out of proportion to any precipitating psychosocial stressor.

C. Absence of signs of generalized impulsivity or aggressiveness between episodes.

D. Not due to Schizophrenia, Antisocial Personality Disorder, or Conduct Disorder.

INDEX

Addictive personalities
  compulsive drug user
    affect mobilization and affect freezing, 248
    archaic object dependency, 241
    basic distinctions, 221
    compulsion, equivalence of symptoms, and life-style, 233
    compulsory abstinence, 262
    defect of affect defense, 237
    defense analysis of drug-dependent personalities, 243, 246
    defensive motive, 243
    denial, 246
    "ego splits" (sense of discontinuity), 251
    etiological equation, 243
    externalization, 249
    family dynamics, 255
    faulty ideal formation, 240
    hyposymbolization, 241
    long-range effects of drugs on personality, 258
    methadone maintenance programs, 263
    narcissistic crisis, 242
    narcotics antagonists, 261
    personality disturbances from psychodynamic point of view, 227
    phenomenological approach, 236
    predisposition to "addictive search," :237
    protection system, 250
    psychotherapeutic approaches, 264
    regressive gratification, 242
    reversal, 247
    self-destructiveness, 242
    structural specificity of conflict solutions, 252
    therapeutic communities, 261
    treatment, 261
Adolescence, 296–309
Adulthood, 511–522
Antisocial personality disorder
  adult psychodynamics, 152
  clinical correlates, 141
    childhood, 146
    criminality, 141
    familial, 141
    functional, 141
    histrionic personality, 142
    organic, 143
    XYY and related genotypes, 145
  course, treatment, and prognosis, 155
    treatment, 156
  diagnosis, 135
    current diagnostic nomenclature, 137
    differential diagnosis, 138
    subjective and pre-1980 criteria, 135
  emotional development, 147
    early family characteristics, 148
    mitigating experiences, 151
    parental psychopathology, 149
    separation/chaos, 148
  epidemiology, 154
  etiology, 153
  history of concepts, 134
  related syndromes, 133
Avoidant personality disorder, 105
  developmental hypotheses, 114, 117
    aversive coping behaviors, 118
    fearful infantile pattern, 116
    heredity, 116
    neurological imbalances, 117
    parental rejection and deprecation, 117
    peer group alienation, 117
    restricted social experiences, 118
    self-derogating thinking, 118
  differential diagnosis issues, 105
    avoidant-borderline distinction, 108
    avoidant-dependent distinction, 107
    avoidant-schizoid distinction, 105
    avoidant-schizotypal distinction, 106
  major clinical features, 103
  theoretical precursors
    biosocial-learning theory, 111
    constitutional views, 109
    psychoanalytic conceptions, 110

Behavior therapy, 456–471
Borderline personality disorder, 74
  diagnosis, 74
  differential diagnosis, 78
  psychodynamics, 81
  therapy, 82

Classification of personality disorders, 10–31
Compulsive personalities
  compulsive character, 164
    compulsive defense mechanisms, case examples, 166–167
    psychoanalytic theory of character formation, 166
    treatment, case examples, 167–171
Court, 551

Dependent personality disorder, 85
Depressive personalities, 204
Drugs, 221–268
DSM II, personality disorders, comparison between and DMS III, 1–2
DSM III, 28, 69
  critical observations, 29
  narcissistic personality disorder
    associated features, 70
    complications, 70
    differential diagnosis, 70
    impairment, 70

589

INDEX

DSM III—*continued*
  personality disorders, comparison between and DSM II, 1–2

Elderly, 310–338
Epileptic personality, 190–201

Family therapy, 472–497
Frontal lobe personality, 183–189

Histrionic personality disorder
  behavior origin, psychodynamics, 90
  biological, 91
  general information, 92
    family history, 92
    incidence, 92
    incidence in men, 93
    presenting complaints, 92
    prognosis and complications, 92
  histrionic personality, 85
    hysteria criteria, 89
    life history, 88
    psychodynamics, 89
    traits, 88
  treatment, 94
Hospitalization, 448–455

Impulsivity in personality disturbances
  differential diagnosis between neuropathophysiological and motivational factors, 379
  DSM III and episodic dyscontrol, 384
  episodic dyscontrol and severe character disorders, 382
    impulse dyscontrol superimposed on a schizoid-paranoid personality, 383
    impulsive dyscontrol and drug-dependent behavior, 382
  phenomenological and psychodynamic analysis of episodic dyscontrol, 373
  treatment, 387

Military Service, 523–539

Narcissistic personality disorder, 65
  therapy
    crises, decompensations, and associated symptoms, 71
    "defects" of narcissistic style and their counteractants in therapy, 72
    treatment, 71

Organic personality, 182–203

Paranoid personalities
  diagnosis, 174
  case examples, 174–175
  etiology, 175
  general considerations, 171
  paranoia in everyday life, examples, 172–174
  paranoid patients and medication, 180
  precipitating factors in paranoid reactions, 177
  psychotherapy, 177
    case examples, 178–179
Paraphilias
  definitions
    exhibitionism, 273
    fetishism, 272
    gender identity disorders, 274
    homosexuality, 271
    other paraphilias, 273
    paraphilias, 271
    pedophilia, 272
    personality (character) structure, 271
    personality traits and personality disorders, 271
    sexual masochism, 273
    transvestism, 272
    voyeurism, 273
    zoophilia, 272
  etiology, 274
  mild character pathology, 277
  moderately secure character pathology, 279
  part of personality disorders, 277
  severe character pathology, 282
  treatment, 286
    behavior therapy, 291
    hormonal, 287
    individual psychotherapy, 287
    married couple therapy, 292
    psychoanalysis, 293
    psychotropic drugs, 293
    sex reassignment, 289
Passive-aggressive personality disorder
  history, 122
  analysis, 126
  clinical characteristics and diagnostic considerations, 125
  differential diagnosis, 125
  treatment, 128
Personality disorders
  adolescence
    adolescent development, character formation, and genesis of personality disorders, 298
    adolescent development overview, 296
    adolescent personality disorders of DSM III, 302
    treatment considerations, 306
  antisocial, 133, 582
    diagnostic criteria, 582
    differential diagnosis, 582
  atypical, mixed, or other, 587

INDEX

diagnostic criteria, 588
differential diagnosis, 588
avoidant, 103, 133, 585
   diagnostic criteria, 585
   differential diagnosis, 585
behavioral methods, 457
   aggression and impulsivity, 463
   attention-seeking behavior, 464
   histrionic behavior, 467
   paranoid behavior, 466
   social withdrawal and lack of emotionality, 458
   specific symptoms of amenable to modification by, 457
   suicidal attempts and self-mutilation, 465
behavior therapy, 456
   techniques, 456
borderline, 74, 584
   "As-If" Personality, 74
   Borderline Schizophrenia, 74
   diagnosis, 74
   diagnostic criteria, 582
   differential diagnosis, 582
   Incipient Schizophrenia, 74
   Latent Schizophrenia, 74
   Pseudoneurotic Schizophrenia, 74
   Pseudopsychopathic Schizophrenia, 74
   Psychotic Character, 74
character disorders: individual features, 473
classification
   clinical approach, 23
   concept isolation, 10
   standard diagnostic system, 23
classification approaches
   morphology, 13
   temperament, 13
   typological, 13
combat, 536
compulsive, 163
   diagnostic criteria, 586
   differential diagnosis, 586
court
   criminal responsibility, 554
   pretrial examination—ability to stand trial, 553
   psychiatrist, 552
   psychological tests, 556
dependent, 97, 585
   diagnostic criteria, 585
   differential diagnosis, 585
diagnosis, 11
differential diagnosis, 78
DSM III, 69
   associated features, 70
   complications, 70
   differential diagnosis, 70
   impairment, 70
elderly, 310
   admissions of elderly patients with personality disorders to hospital, 322
   countertransference issues, 333
   differential diagnosis, 322
   epidemiology, 322
   intervention, 327
   transference issues, 331
   typology and clinical course, 311
family therapy, 472
family treatment, 478
   antisocial personality disorders, 489
   case examples, 484, 488, 490, 492
   goals, 480
   histrionic and compulsive, 491
   indications and contraindications, 495
   long-term, 482, 486
   marital treatment of specific diagnostic groups, 483
   narcissistic and borderline character disorders, 493
   paranoid, 487
   problem-solving interventions, 484
   schizoid, schizotypal, avoidant, dependent, and passive-aggressive, 484
   structural reorganization, 485
   symptoms vs. character, 479
   type of and marital treatment recommended, 480
feedback mechanisms, 475
histrionic, 97, 581
   diagnostic criteria, 581
   differential diagnosis, 581
hospitalization, 448
linear vs. circular causality, 476
methodological problems, 26
military psychiatry, 538
military service, 523
   antisocial personality, 529
   common syndromes, 525
   older personnel, 530
   passive-aggressive personality, 527
   passive-dependent personality, 528
   psychosis, 532
   schizoid personality, 528
   suicidal gestures and drug abuse, 534
morphostasis and character pathology, 477
morphostasis and morphogenesis, 475
narcissistic, 65, 582
   defects of style and their counteractants in therapy, 72
   diagnostic criteria, 582
   differential diagnosis, 582
organic
   epileptic personality, 190–201
   frontal lobe personality, 183–189
paranoid, 163, 579
   diagnostic criteria, 579
   differential diagnosis, 579
passive-aggressive, 163, 586
   diagnostic criteria, 586

592   INDEX

Personality disorders—*continued*
  passive-aggressive—*continued*
    differential diagnosis, 586
  prisons, 540
    dangerousness, 570
    diagnostic problems, 541
    effects of incarceration on in, 545
    etiological factors, 544
    model penal code, 563
    presentence, 573
    psychiatric disorders, 543
    treatment of in, 547
  private practice, 498
    diagnosis formulation, 499
    personality structure, basic concepts, 498
  psychodynamic aspects of, 339
    childhood patterns, 341
    dynamic aspects, 342
    mode of presentation, 339
    treatment implications, 357
  psychodynamics, 81
  psychological tests, 394
    Bender Gestalt, 395
    HTP, 396
    Rorschach, 397
  psychopharmacotherapy in adolescence and adulthood, 511
    atypical, mixed, or other personality disorders, 519
    avoidant, dependent, compulsive, and passive-aggressive, 518
    conceptual and clinical guidelines, 512
    histrionic, narcissistic, borderline, and antisocial, 514
    paranoid, schizoid, and schizotypal, 513
  research models, 15
  schizoid, 580
    background, 33
    diagnostic criteria, 580
    differential diagnosis, 580
    DSM criteria for, 53
    genetic relationship to schizophrenia, 50
    genetics, 44
    origin and usage, 33
    personality characteristics, 33
    premorbid forerunner, 42
    psychodynamic developmental view, 41
    schizophrenia, relationship to, 42
  schizoid and schizotypal, 32
  schizotypal
    differential diagnosis, 580
    DSM III criteria for, 54
  severe
    case examples, 402
    differential diagnosis, 399
    prediction of behavior, 402
    psychological testing of, 393
    psychological tests, 394
    therapeutic progress, 405
  similar characteristics among, 459
  substance use disorder
    alcohol dependency, 427
    drug dependence, 430
  systems and communications principles as applied to family, 474
  therapeutic community
    antisocial personality, 423
    failures, limitations, and need for other approaches, 422
    history and development in treatment of mentally ill, 409
    hospital, community, and outside world, 420
    intermediate and long-term psychiatric hospital as a treatment approach, 412
    learning model, 442
    nonhospital settings as a treatment approach for personality and other nonpsychotic disorders, 422
    personality (intrapsychic) model, 438
    psychosexual disorders, 426
    psychosocial (interpersonal) model, 435
    recent history, 410
    theoretical considerations, 433
  therapeutic community and milieu therapy, 408
    application of, 409
  therapy, 82
    crises, decompensation, and associated symptoms, 71
    treatment, 71
  typical personality types in private practice, 501
    borderline personality, 509
    case history, 505
    compulsive personality, 502
    dependent personality, 508
    histrionic personality, 503
    narcissistic personality, 506
    therapy, 510
Psychodynamic aspects of personality disorders, 339
Psychological testing, 393–407

Sadomasochistic personalities, 204
Schizoid Personality Disorder, 32–33
Schizotypal Personality Disorder, 32–33, 54
  differential diagnosis of, 56
  treatment, 58
    psychopharmacologic, 60
    psychotherapeutic, 58
Sociocultural determinants of personality pathology, 361

Therapeutic community and milieu therapy, 408–447